Evolving Developments in Grid and Cloud Computing:

Advancing Research

Emmanuel Udoh
National College, USA

Information Science
REFERENCE

Managing Director:	Lindsay Johnston
Senior Editorial Director:	Heather Probst
Book Production Manager:	Sean Woznicki
Development Manager:	Joel Gamon
Development Editor:	Hannah Abelbeck
Acquisitions Editor:	Erika Gallagher
Typesetters:	Deanna Jo Zombro
Print Coordinator:	Jamie Snavely
Cover Design:	Nick Newcomer, Greg Snader

Published in the United States of America by
Information Science Reference (an imprint of IGI Global)
701 E. Chocolate Avenue
Hershey PA 17033
Tel: 717-533-8845
Fax: 717-533-8661
E-mail: cust@igi-global.com
Web site: http://www.igi-global.com

Library of Congress Cataloging-in-Publication Data

Evolving developments in grid and cloud computing : advancing research /
Emmanuel Udoh, editor.
    p. cm.
  Includes bibliographical references and index.
  Summary: "This book contains investigations of grid and cloud evolution,
workflow management, and the impact new computing systems have on education
and industry"--Provided by publisher.
  ISBN 978-1-4666-0056-0 (hardcover) -- ISBN 978-1-4666-0057-7 (ebook) -- ISBN
978-1-4666-0058-4 (print & perpetual access) 1. Computational grids
(Computer systems)--Research. 2. Cloud computing--Research. 3. High
performance computing--Research. I. Udoh, Emmanuel, 1960-
  QA76.9.C58.E976 2012
  004.6782--dc23
                              2011041824

British Cataloguing in Publication Data
A Cataloguing in Publication record for this book is available from the British Library.

Table of Contents

Preface xvii

Section 1
Introduction

Chapter 1
Harnessing the Cloud for Mobile Social Networking Applications 1
Juwel Rana, Luleå University of Technology, Sweden
Josef Hallberg, Luleå University of Technology, Sweden
Kåre Synnes, Luleå University of Technology, Sweden
Johan Kristiansson, Ericsson Research, Sweden

Section 2
Scheduling

Chapter 2
Balanced Job Scheduling Based on Ant Algorithm for Grid Network 13
Nikolaos Preve, National Technical University of Athens, Greece

Chapter 3
Evaluating Heuristics for Scheduling Dependent Jobs in Grid Computing Environments 31
Geoffrey Falzon, Brunel University, UK
Maozhen Li, Brunel University, UK

Chapter 4
Peer-to-Peer Desktop Grids Based on an Adaptive Decentralized Scheduling Mechanism 47
H. Ali, Mansoura University, Egypt
A.I. Saleh, Mansoura University, Egypt
Amany M. Sarhan, Mansoura University, Egypt
Abdulrahman. A. Azab, Mansoura University, Egypt

Chapter 5

Predictive File Replication on the Data Grids 67

    ChenHan Liao, Cranfield University, UK

    Na Helian, University of Hertfordshire, UK

    Sining Wu, Cranfield University, UK

    Mamunur M. Rashid, Cranfield University, UK

Section 3
Architecture

Chapter 6

Single Attestation Image for a Trusted and Scalable Grid 85

    Yuhui Deng, Jinan University, P. R. China

    Na Helian, University of Hertfordshire, UK

Chapter 7

Personal Storage Grid Architecture: Consuming Cloud Data Space Resources 97

    Mian-Guan Lim, Cranfield University, UK

    Sining Wu, Cranfield University, UK

    Tomasz Simon, Cranfield University, UK

    Md Rashid, Cranfield University, UK

    Na Helian, Hertfordshire University, UK

Chapter 8

Design of SOA Based Framework for Collaborative Cloud Computing in Wireless Sensor
Networks 110

    S. V. Patel, Veer Narmad South Gujarat University, India

    Kamlendu Pandey, Veer Narmad South Gujarat University, India

Chapter 9

A Semantic-Driven Adaptive Architecture for Large Scale P2P Networks 125

    Athena Eftychiou, University of Surrey, UK

    Bogdan Vrusias, University of Surrey, UK

    Nick Antonopoulos, University of Derby, UK

Chapter 10

Network Architectures and Data Management for Massively Multiplayer Online Games 144

    Minhua Ma, University of Derby, UK

    Andreas Oikonomou, University of Derby, UK

Section 4
Security

Chapter 11

Mechanism for Privacy Preservation in VANETs.. 157

Brijesh K. Chaurasia, Indian Institute of Information Technology, India
Shekhar Verma, Indian Institute of Information Technology, India
G. S. Tomar, Malwa Institute of Technology and Management, India

Section 5
Applications

Chapter 12

Modeling Scalable Grid Information Services with Colored Petri Nets... 169

Vijay Sahota, Middlesex University, UK
Maozhen Li, Brunel University, UK
Marios Hadjinicolaou, Brunel University, UK

Chapter 13

Efficient Communication Interfaces for Distributed Energy Resources... 185

Heinz Frank, Reinhold-Würth-University of the Heilbronn University, Germany
Sidonia Mesentean, Reinhold-Würth-University of the Heilbronn University, Germany

Chapter 14

Deep Analysis of Enhanced Authentication for Next Generation Networks...................................... 197

Mamdouh Gouda, Misr University of Science & Technology, Egypt

Chapter 15

Adaptive Routing Strategy for Large Scale Rearrangeable Symmetric Networks............................... 212

Amitabha Chakrabarty, Dublin City University, Ireland
Martin Collier, Dublin City University, Ireland
Sourav Mukhopadhyay, Dublin City University, Ireland

Chapter 16

Road Traffic Parameters Estimation by Dynamic Scene Analysis: A Systematic Review 223

H. S. Mohana, Malnad College of Engineering, India
M. Ashwathakumar, M. S. Ramaiah Institute of Technology, India

Chapter 17

G2G:A Meta-Grid Framework for the Convergence of P2P and Grids... 239

    Wu-Chun Chung, National Tsing Hua University, Taiwan

    Chin-Jung Hsu, National Tsing Hua University, Taiwan

    Yi-Hsiang Lin, National Tsing Hua University, Taiwan

    Kuan-Chou Lai, National Taichung University, Taiwan

    Yeh-Ching Chung, National Tsing Hua University, Taiwan

Chapter 18

One Anchor Distance and Angle Based Multi - Hop Adaptive Iterative Localization Algorithm for
Wireless Sensor Networks 255

    S. B. Kotwal, SMVD University, India

    Shekhar Verma, Indian Institute of Information Technology, India

    G. S. Tomar, Malwa Institute of Technology, India

    R. K. Abrol, SMVD University, India

Chapter 19

Intelligent Industrial Data Acquisition and Energy Monitoring using Wireless Sensor
Networks 267

    Sumeet Gupta, SMVD University, India

    Shekhar Verma, Indian Institute of Information Technology, India

    G.S. Tomar, Malwa Institute of Technology & Management, India

    Raj Kumar Abrol, SMVD University, India

Chapter 20

Fuzzy Allocation of Fine-Grained Compute Resources for Grid Data Streaming Applications 283

    Wen Zhang, Tsinghua University, China

    *Junwei Cao, Tsinghua University and Tsinghua National Laboratory for Information Science
        and Technology, China*

    *Yisheng Zhong, Tsinghua University and Tsinghua National Laboratory for Information Science
        and Technology, China*

    *Lianchen Liu, Tsinghua University and Tsinghua National Laboratory for Information Science
        and Technology, China*

    *Cheng Wu, Tsinghua University and Tsinghua National Laboratory for Information Science
        and Technology, China*

Chapter 21

A Method of 3-D Microstructure Reconstruction in the Simulation Model of Cement
Hydration 295

    Dongliang Zhang, Tongji University, China

Chapter 22

Managing Inconsistencies in Data Grid Environments: A Practical Approach 303

Ejaz Ahmed, King Fahd University of Petroleum and Minerals, Saudi Arabia and University
  of Bedfordshire, UK
Nik Bessis, University of Bedfordshire, UK
Peter Norrington, University of Bedfordshire, UK
Yong Yue, University of Bedfordshire, UK

Compilation of References 317

About the Contributors 342

Index 352

Detailed Table of Contents

Preface...xvii

Section 1
Introduction

Chapter 1

Harnessing the Cloud for Mobile Social Networking Applications 1
Juwel Rana, Luleå University of Technology, Sweden
Josef Hallberg, Luleå University of Technology, Sweden
Kåre Synnes, Luleå University of Technology, Sweden
Johan Kristiansson, Ericsson Research, Sweden

The cloud computing model inherently enables information from social networking services (Twitter, Facebook, LinkedIn, and so forth), context-based systems (location, activity, interests, etc.) and personal applications (call logs, contacts, email, calendar, and so forth) to be harnessed for multiple purposes. This article presents an agent-based system architecture for semantic and semi-automated applications that utilize the cloud to enrich and simplify communication services, for instance by displaying presence information, prioritizing information, and dynamically managing groups of users. The proposed architecture is based on the concept of aggregated social graphs, which are created from harnessed information about how people communicate. This article also presents challenges in achieving the envisioned architecture and introduces early prototyping results.

Section 2
Scheduling

Chapter 2

Balanced Job Scheduling Based on Ant Algorithm for Grid Network 13
Nikolaos Preve, National Technical University of Athens, Greece

Job scheduling in grid computing is a very important problem. To utilize grids efficiently, we need a good job scheduling algorithm to assign jobs to resources in grids. The main scope of this paper is to propose a new Ant Colony Optimization (ACO) algorithm for balanced job scheduling in the Grid environment. To achieve the above goal, we will indicate a way to balance the entire system load while minimizing the makespan of a given set of jobs. Based on the experimental results, the proposed algorithm confidently demonstrates its practicability and competitiveness compared with other job scheduling algorithms.

Chapter 3

Evaluating Heuristics for Scheduling Dependent Jobs in Grid Computing Environments 31

Geoffrey Falzon, Brunel University, UK
Maozhen Li, Brunel University, UK

Job scheduling plays a critical role in the utilisation of grid resources by mapping a number of jobs to grid resources. However, the heterogeneity of grid resources adds some challenges to the work of job scheduling, especially when jobs have dependencies which can be represented as Direct Acyclic Graphs (DAGs). It is widely recognised that scheduling m jobs to n resources with an objective to achieve a minimum makespan has shown to be NP-complete, requiring the development of heuristics. Although a number of heuristics are available for job scheduling optimisation, selecting the best heuristic to use in a given grid environment remains a difficult problem due to the fact that the performance of each original heuristic is usually evaluated under different assumptions. This paper evaluates 12 representative heuristics for dependent job scheduling under one set of common assumptions. The results are presented and analysed, which provides an even basis in comparison of the performance of those heuristics. To facilitate performance evaluation, a DAG simulator is implemented which provides a set of tools for DAG job configuration, execution, and monitoring. The components of the DAG simulator are also presented in this paper.

Chapter 4

Peer-to-Peer Desktop Grids Based on an Adaptive Decentralized Scheduling Mechanism 47

H. Ali, Mansoura University, Egypt
A.I. Saleh, Mansoura University, Egypt
Amany M. Sarhan, Mansoura University, Egypt
Abdulrahman. A. Azab, Mansoura University, Egypt

This article proposes an adaptive fuzzy logic based decentralized scheduling mechanism that will be suitable for dynamic computing environment in which matchmaking is achieved between resource requirements of outstanding tasks and resource capabilities of available workers. Feasibility of the proposed method is done via real time system. Experimental results show that implementing the proposed fuzzy matchmaking based scheduling mechanism maximized the resource utilization of executing workers without exceeding the maximum execution time of the task. It is concluded that the efficiency of FMA-based decentralized scheduling, in the case of parallel execution, is reduced by increasing the number of subtasks.

Chapter 5

Predictive File Replication on the Data Grids 67

ChenHan Liao, Cranfield University, UK
Na Helian, University of Hertfordshire, UK
Sining Wu, Cranfield University, UK
Mamunur M. Rashid, Cranfield University, UK

Most replication methods either monitor the popularity of files or use complicated functions to calculate the overall cost of whether or not a replication decision or a deletion decision should be issued. However, once the replication decision is issued, the popularity of the files is changed and may have already impacted access latency and resource usage. This article proposes a decision-tree-based predictive file replication strategy that forecasts files' future popularity based on their characteristics on the Grids. The proposed strategy has shown superb performance in terms of mean job time and effective network usage compared with the other two replication strategies, LRU and Economic under OptorSim simulation environment.

Section 3
Architecture

Chapter 6
Single Attestation Image for a Trusted and Scalable Grid 85
    Yuhui Deng, Jinan University, P. R. China
    Na Helian, University of Hertfordshire, UK

Traditionally, Grid users are forced to trust the Grid platforms, but the users are not always regarded as trustworthy. This trust asymmetry hinders the commercializing of Grid resources. Trusted Grid is proposed to tackle this challenge by leveraging Trusted Computing (TC). However, the TC relies on a microcontroller Trusted Platform Modules (TPM) which has limited computing power and is doomed to be a system bottleneck. This paper constructs a trusted Grid as a flat ring and decentralizes the functionalities of TPM across the ring. This architecture offers a single attestation image which provides a transparent attestation to a scalable, large-scale, and dynamic trusted Grid. The architecture also significantly reduces the frequency of attestations, thus alleviating the TPM bottleneck. Furthermore, the architecture can avoid the potential system bottleneck and single point of failure of the centralized architecture or the root node of the hierarchical architecture.

Chapter 7
Personal Storage Grid Architecture: Consuming Cloud Data Space Resources 97
    Mian-Guan Lim, Cranfield University, UK
    Sining Wu, Cranfield University, UK
    Tomasz Simon, Cranfield University, UK
    Md Rashid, Cranfield University, UK
    Na Helian, Hertfordshire University, UK

On-demand cloud applications like online email accounts and online virtual disk space are becoming widely available in various forms. In cloud applications, one can see the importance of underlying resources, such as disk space, that is available to the end-user but not easily accessible. In the authors' study, a modern file system developed in linux is proposed, which enables consuming of cloud applications and making the underlying disk space resource available to the end-user. This system is developed as a web service to support cross operation system support. A free online mail account was used to demonstrate this solution, and an IMAP protocol to communicate with remote data spaces was used so that this method can mount onto any email system that supports IMAP. The authors' definition of infinite storage as the user is able to mount file systems as a single logical drive.

Chapter 8

Design of SOA Based Framework for Collaborative Cloud Computing in Wireless Sensor Networks 110

S. V. Patel, Veer Narmad South Gujarat University, India
Kamlendu Pandey, Veer Narmad South Gujarat University, India

WSN deployments are growing at a fast rate; however, current WSN architectures and setup do not promote the sharing of data on an inter-WSN basis. Cloud computing has emerged as a promising area to deal with participatory and collaborative data and services, and is envisaged that collaborative cloud computing WSN could be a viable solution for sharing data and services for WSN applications. In this paper, SOA based architecture has been proposed to support collaborating cloud computing in WSN. The architecture consists of layered service stack that has management, information, presentation and communication layers with all required services and repositories. Interactions between WSN, subscribers and other cloud are also presented as sequence diagrams. The proposed framework serves the cloud subscribers with wide range of queries on the data of multiple WSNs through suitable interface to solve large scale problems.

Chapter 9

A Semantic-Driven Adaptive Architecture for Large Scale P2P Networks 125

Athena Eftychiou, University of Surrey, UK
Bogdan Vrusias, University of Surrey, UK
Nick Antonopoulos, University of Derby, UK

The increasing amount of online information demands effective, scalable, and accurate mechanisms to manage and search this information. Distributed semantic-enabled architectures, which enforce semantic web technologies for resource discovery, could satisfy these requirements. In this paper, a semantic-driven adaptive architecture is presented, which improves existing resource discovery processes. The P2P network is organised in a two-layered super-peer architecture. The network formation of super-peers is a conceptual representation of the network's knowledge, shaped from the information provided by the nodes using collective intelligence methods. The authors focus on the creation of a dynamic hierarchical semantic-driven P2P topology using the network's collective intelligence. The unmanageable amounts of data are transformed into a repository of semantic knowledge, transforming the network into an ontology of conceptually related entities of information collected from the resources located by peers. Appropriate experiments have been undertaken through a case study by simulating the proposed architecture and evaluating results.

Chapter 10

Network Architectures and Data Management for Massively Multiplayer Online Games 144

Minhua Ma, University of Derby, UK
Andreas Oikonomou, University of Derby, UK

Current-generation Massively Multiplayer Online Games (MMOG), such as World of Warcraft, Eve Online, and Second Life are mainly built on distributed client-server architectures with server allocation based on sharding, static geographical partitioning, dynamic micro-cell scheme, or optimal server for placing a virtual region according to the geographical dispersion of players. This paper reviews various approaches on data replication and region partitioning. Management of areas of interest (field of vision) is discussed, which reduces processing load dramatically by updating players only with those events that occur within their area of interest. This can be managed either through static geographical partitioning on the basis of the assumption that players in one region do not see/interact with players in other regions, or behavioural modelling based on players' behaviours. The authors investigate data storage and synchronisation methods for MMOG databases, mainly on relational databases. Several attempts of peer to peer (P2P) architectures and protocols for MMOGs are reviewed, and critical issues such as cheat prevention on P2P MMOGs are highlighted.

Section 4
Security

Chapter 11

Mechanism for Privacy Preservation in VANETs.. 157

Brijesh K. Chaurasia, Indian Institute of Information Technology, India
Shekhar Verma, Indian Institute of Information Technology, India
G. S. Tomar, Malwa Institute of Technology and Management, India

This paper proposes a mechanism for sustaining privacy of a vehicle in a vehicular ad hoc network (VANET) through pseudonym update. In a VANET, vehicles on the road are involved in dissemination of information as they move. An association can be formed between the physical location of the source vehicle and the transmitted messages. This relationship between the physical vehicle and its identity can breach its privacy. In this work, a strategy for optimal pseudonym update for maximizing privacy has been formulated when a vehicle is being observed by adversaries with different capabilities. Results indicate that updating pseudonyms in accordance to the strategy maximizes the privacy of a vehicle in the given situation.

Section 5
Applications

Chapter 12

Modeling Scalable Grid Information Services with Colored Petri Nets.. 169

Vijay Sahota, Middlesex University, UK
Maozhen Li, Brunel University, UK
Marios Hadjinicolaou, Brunel University, UK

Information services play a crucial role in grid computing environments in that the state information of a grid system can be used to facilitate the discovery of resources and services available to meet user requirements and help tune the performance of the grid. This paper models PIndex, which is a grouped peer-to-peer network with Colored Petri Nets (CPNs) for scalable grid information services. Based on the CPN model, a simulator is implemented for PIndex simulation and performance evaluation. The correctness of the simulator is further verified by comparing the results computed from the CPN model with the results generated by the PIndex simulator.

Chapter 13
Efficient Communication Interfaces for Distributed Energy Resources.. 185
Heinz Frank, Reinhold-Würth-University of the Heilbronn University, Germany
Sidonia Mesentean, Reinhold-Würth-University of the Heilbronn University, Germany

The IEC 61850 standard originally was developed for the substation automation. During the past years it was adapted for the integration of distributed energy resources into communication networks, however, with specific requirements. Many small and midsize manufacturers are using, as controllers, a big variety of different microprocessors with limited performances. Such controllers need an interface for IEC 61850 communication networks with a basic functionality which can be implemented with limited costs. Based on their experiences during the realization of an IEC 61850 communication stack, the authors propose ways to support these requirements. In particular, communication interfaces for photovoltaics systems and wind power plants are considered.

Chapter 14
Deep Analysis of Enhanced Authentication for Next Generation Networks.................................... 197
Mamdouh Gouda, Misr University of Science & Technology, Egypt

Next Generation Networks (NGN) is the evolution of the telecommunication core. The user has to execute multi-pass Authentication and Key Agreement (AKA) procedures in order to get access to the IP Multimedia Subsystem (IMS). This causes overhead on the AAA server and increases the delay of authenticating the user and that is because of unnecessary and repeated procedures and protocols. This paper presents an enhanced one-pass AKA procedure that eliminates the repeated steps without affecting the security level, in addition it reduces the Denial of Service (DoS) attacks. The presented mechanism has minimal impact on the network infrastructure and functionality and does not require any changes to the existing authentication protocols.

Chapter 15
Adaptive Routing Strategy for Large Scale Rearrangeable Symmetric Networks............................ 212
Amitabha Chakrabarty, Dublin City University, Ireland
Martin Collier, Dublin City University, Ireland
Sourav Mukhopadhyay, Dublin City University, Ireland

This paper proposes an adaptive unicast routing algorithm for large scale symmetric networks comprising 2×2 switch elements such as Beneš networks. This algorithm trades off the probability of blocking against algorithm execution time. Deterministic algorithms exploit the rearrangeability property of Beneš networks to ensure a zero blocking probability for unicast connections, at the expense of extensive computation. The authors' algorithm makes its routing decisions depending on the status of each switching element at every stage of the network, hence the name adaptive routing. This method provides a low complexity solution, but with much better blocking performance than random routing algorithms. This paper presents simulation results for various input loads, demonstrating the tradeoffs involved.

Chapter 16
Road Traffic Parameters Estimation by Dynamic Scene Analysis: A Systematic Review 223

H. S. Mohana, Malnad College of Engineering, India
M. Ashwathakumar, M. S. Ramaiah Institute of Technology, India

Traffic congestion and violation of traffic rules are very common in most of the road transport system. Continuous monitoring is becoming difficult. To improve the quality of road transport monitoring and control, the best possible alternative is machine vision. In this review, several works by researchers on traffic analysis are detailed, studied and reviewed critically for the purpose. Further, an attempt is made to classify the different road traffic analysis approaches available in the literature. Classification is based on principle used, algorithm adopted, techniques used, technology behind and other special considerations of the researchers.

Chapter 17
G2G: A Meta-Grid Framework for the Convergence of P2P and Grids 239

Wu-Chun Chung, National Tsing Hua University, Taiwan
Chin-Jung Hsu, National Tsing Hua University, Taiwan
Yi-Hsiang Lin, National Tsing Hua University, Taiwan
Kuan-Chou Lai, National Taichung University, Taiwan
Yeh-Ching Chung, National Tsing Hua University, Taiwan

Grid systems integrate distributed resources to form self-organization and self-management autonomies. With the widespread development of grid systems around the world, grid collaboration for large-scale computing has become a prevalent research topic. In this paper, the authors propose a meta-grid framework, named the Grid-to-Grid (G2G) framework, to harmonize autonomic grids in realizing a grid federation. The G2G framework is a decentralized management framework that is built on top of existing autonomic grid systems. This paper further adopts a super-peer network in a separate layer to coordinate distributed grid systems. A super-peer overlay network is constructed for communication among super-peers, thus enabling collaboration among grid systems. This study proposes the G2G framework for use in a Grid-to-Grid federation and implements a preliminary system as a demonstration. Experimental results show that the proposed meta-grid framework can improve system performance with little overhead.

Chapter 18
One Anchor Distance and Angle Based Multi - Hop Adaptive Iterative Localization Algorithm for Wireless Sensor Networks 255

S. B. Kotwal, SMVD University, India
Shekhar Verma, Indian Institute of Information Technology, India
G. S. Tomar, Malwa Institute of Technology, India
R. K. Abrol, SMVD University, India

This paper presents distance and angle measurements based Multi-Hop Adaptive and Iterative Localization algorithm for localization of unknown nodes in wireless sensor networks (WSNs). The present work determines uncertainty region of unknown nodes with respect to known (anchor) nodes using noisy distance and angle measurements. This node transmits its uncertainty region to other unknown nodes to help them determine their uncertainty region. Because of noisy distance and angle measurements, the error propagation increases the size of regions of nodes in subsequent hops. Using only one anchor node as reference, the proposed iterative localization algorithm reduces the error propagation of this noisy distance and angle measurements and the uncertainty region of all unknown nodes within a given communication range. The results clearly indicate the improved efficiency of the proposed algorithm in comparison with existing algorithms.

Chapter 19

Intelligent Industrial Data Acquisition and Energy Monitoring using Wireless Sensor
Networks 267

Sumeet Gupta, SMVD University, India
Shekhar Verma, Indian Institute of Information Technology, India
G.S. Tomar, Malwa Institute of Technology & Management, India
Raj Kumar Abrol, SMVD University, India

Most of the application-oriented research in the field of Wireless Sensor Networks has been in remote monitoring, including environmental, building automation, and security. However, this paper presents the methodology followed for implementation of a Wireless Sensor Network based solution in a process plant for energy management and leak detection. The sensor network acquires data pertaining to detection of leakage in a plant. The network further serves effectively as a maintenance and diagnostic system that is used to manage the plant and conserve energy in a process plant. The critical design issues, testing methodologies and implementation problems pertaining to the system are also presented. Additionally, special focus has been placed on the calculations pertaining to the network life time.

Chapter 20

Fuzzy Allocation of Fine-Grained Compute Resources for Grid Data Streaming Applications 283

Wen Zhang, Tsinghua University, China
Junwei Cao, Tsinghua University and Tsinghua National Laboratory for Information Science
and Technology, China
Yisheng Zhong, Tsinghua University and Tsinghua National Laboratory for Information Science
and Technology, China
Lianchen Liu, Tsinghua University and Tsinghua National Laboratory for Information Science
and Technology, China
Cheng Wu, Tsinghua University and Tsinghua National Laboratory for Information Science
and Technology, China

Fine-grained allocation of compute resources, in terms of configurable clock speed of virtual machines, is essential for processing efficiency and resource utilization of data streaming applications. For a data streaming application, its processing speed is expected to approach the allocated bandwidth as much as possible. Automatic control technology is a feasible solution, but the plant model is hard to be derived.

In relation to the model free characteristic, a fuzzy logic controller is designed with several simple yet robust rules. Performance of this controller is verified to out-perform classic controllers in response rapidness and less oscillation. An empirical formula on tuning an essential parameter is obtained to achieve better performance.

Chapter 21

A Method of 3-D Microstructure Reconstruction in the Simulation Model of Cement
Hydration 295
    Dongliang Zhang, Tongji University, China

An accurate and reliable computer simulation system can help practical experiments greatly. In a cement hydration simulation system, the basic requirement is to reconstruct the 3-D microstructure of the cement particles in the initial state while mixed with water. A 2-D SEM/X-ray image is certainly achievable; however, it is not easy to obtain parallel images due to the small scale of the cement particles. In this regard, a method is proposed to reconstruct the 3-D structure from a single microstructure image. In this method, micro-particles are regenerated in a growing trees mode, which by modifying the generating probability of the leaves, the irregularity and the surface fraction of particles can be controlled. This method can fulfill the requirement for the parameters of the 3-D image while assuring that the 2-D image is in full accord.

Chapter 22

Managing Inconsistencies in Data Grid Environments: A Practical Approach 303
    Ejaz Ahmed, King Fahd University of Petroleum and Minerals, Saudi Arabia and University
        of Bedfordshire, UK
    Nik Bessis, University of Bedfordshire, UK
    Peter Norrington, University of Bedfordshire, UK
    Yong Yue, University of Bedfordshire, UK

Much work has been done in the area of data access and integration using various data mapping, matching, and loading techniques. One of the main concerns when integrating data from heterogeneous data sources is data redundancy. The concern is mainly due to the different business contexts and purposes from which the data systems were originally built. A common process for accessing data from integrated databases involves the use of each data source's own catalogue or metadata schema. In this article, the authors take the view that there is a greater chance of data inconsistencies, such as data redundancies when integrating them within a grid environment as compared to traditional distributed paradigms. The importance of improving the data search and matching process is briefly discussed, and a partial service oriented generic strategy is adopted to consolidate distinct catalogue schemas of federated databases to access information seamlessly. To this end, a proposed matching strategy between structure objects and data values across federated databases in a grid environment is presented.

Compilation of References 317

About the Contributors 342

Index 352

Preface

The discipline of computing is coming of age, and cloud computing embodies the maturity of this field with its clear path to software generation, transmission, distribution and control. With cloud-virtualized resources (platform, infrastructure, software), the different components of computing are unified into an easily manageable entity, as services will ultimately be provided from data centers over the Internet and on-demand. Shaping the cloud paradigm shift are contributions from varied fields like virtualization, service-oriented architecture, grid-utility computing and distributed systems. Certainly, cloud computing is still evolving, but the advent of Apple iCloud signals its mainstream acceptance.

As a major pillar in the growth of cloud computing, virtualization has been exploited to create the illusion of unlimited power for hardware platform, operating system, data, memory, and storage device or network resources. The consolidation of servers has enabled more to be done with less hardware, thus supporting more users per piece of hardware as well as delivering and running applications faster. In that vein, the cloud's virtual resources are typically cheaper than dedicated physical resources connected to a personal computer or network. Virtualization, which is only one possible service that cloud can deliver, is not always necessary in cloud computing; however, it has helped to centralize administrative tasks while improving scalability and workloads.

In a similar development, service oriented architecture (SOA) is well suited for web development and applications that can run in the cloud (Internet) rather than on local hardware. It allows the connection of discrete chunks of information in real time with the power to orchestrate a new application by providing parts of the existing applications with a new interface that is event-driven. With SOA, programmers configure the services to run on the Internet in ways that allow combining and reusing data (integration of existing or legacy applications) in new applications. Instead of a full-scale development of a new program (from the scratch), SOA extends what exists to the cloud where live data is accessed and accessible.

Furthermore, the cloud is a natural evolution of grid and distributed computing with its IT-related capabilities and resources that are provided as services via the Internet and on-demand. The user accesses or consumes cloud resources without being required to amass detailed knowledge of the underlying technology. Grid computing has a goal, in which computer processing power is seen as a utility that clients can pay for only as needed. It harnesses unused computing resources by connecting different computers together. This gluing of computers creates enormous storage and CPU capacity for large-scale computing such as weather forecasting and predictive models in science. Cloud computing has improved the grid computing concepts by harnessing computer resources as a utility with on-demand resource provisioning. As a matter of fact, cloud combines grid computing with utility computing concepts (pay-per-use – metered or subscription approach), but strictly hides the grid middleware from the users. Thus cloud computing is the consolidation of many year of computing endeavors, that poignantly signals the maturity of the computing field, with the additional capacity to curb the menace of software piracy.

The new advances in cloud computing will greatly impact IT services resulting in improved computational and storage resources as well as service delivery. To keep educators, students, researchers and professionals abreast of advances in the cloud, grid and high performance computing, this book *Evolving Developments in Grid and Cloud Computing: Advancing Research* will provide coverage of topical issues in the discipline. It will shed light on concepts, protocols, applications, methods and tools in this emerging and disruptive technology.

This book is organized in five distinct sections, covering wide-ranging topics such as: (1) Introduction (2) Scheduling (3) Architecture (4) Security and (5) Applications.

Section 1.*Introduction*, provides an overview of cloud computing and how to harness it in the explosive growth of social media. Cloud computing and social media are in vogue. Individuals, communities and organizations actively use the increasingly popular social media as a means of communication and interactive dialogue with user-generated content. As an Internet-based system that is enabled by ubiquitously accessible and scalable communication techniques, cloud-computing efficiently harnesses information from social networking services (e.g. Facebook, Twitter and LinkedIn), context-based systems (location, activity, interests, etc.) and personal applications (call logs, contacts, email, and calendar) for multiple purposes. The chapter "*Harnessing the Cloud for Mobile Social Networking Applications*" by Juwel Rana and co-authors, focuses on agent-based system for semantic and semi-automated applications that utilize the cloud to enrich and simplify communication services, for instance by displaying information, prioritizing information, and dynamically managing groups of users. This system exploits the concept of aggregated social graphs, which are created from harnessed information about how people communicate. The paper harped as well on the challenges in achieving the envisioned system with demonstrable prototyping results.

Section 2.*Scheduling*, is an integral part of grid and cloud implementation. Although scheduling is complex, prioritizing and load balancing are crucial management processes in cloud environments. Efficient job-scheduling algorithms are necessary to assign jobs to resources in grids and clouds. Nikolaos Preve, in the chapter "*Balanced Job Scheduling Based on Ant Algorithm for Grid Network*", proposed a new Ant Colony Optimization (ACO) algorithm for balanced job scheduling in the grid-enabled environment. To achieve this goal, the author showed how to balance the entire system load by minimizing the makespan of a given set of jobs. The experimental outcomes demonstrated the practicability and competitiveness of this approach compared with other job scheduling algorithms. In a similar vein, Geoffrey Falzon and Maozhen Li, provided a chapter on *Evaluating Heuristics for Scheduling Dependent Jobs in Grid Computing Environments*. This work takes cognizance of the fact that scheduling plays a crucial role in mapping jobs to cloud and grid resources, especially challenging jobs that have dependencies, which can be represented as Direct Acyclic Graphs (DAGs). The article appraised twelve representative heuristics for dependent job scheduling under one set of common assumptions, recognizing that scheduling m jobs to n resources with an objective to achieve a minimum makespan can be NP-complete. To facilitate performance evaluation, a DAG simulator was implemented which provided a set of tools for DAG job configuration, execution, and monitoring. The outcomes of the DAG simulation are also presented in this book.

In another chapter, *Peer-to-Peer Desktop Grids Based on an Adaptive Decentralized Scheduling Mechanism*, researchers Ali, Saleh, Sarhan and Azab proposed an adaptive fuzzy logic based mechanism for dynamic computing environment in which matchmaking is achieved between resource requirements of outstanding tasks and resource capabilities of available workers. The results of the feasibility studies show that in a real time environment the resource utilization of executing workers can be maximized without exceeding the maximum execution time of the task. The researchers concluded that increasing the number of subtasks could reduce the efficiency of FMA-based decentralized scheduling, especially in parallel execution. In another study, *Predictive File Replication on the Data Grids* - researchers Liao, Helian, Wu and Rashid proposed a decision-tree-based predictive file replication strategy that forecasts files' future popularity based on the characteristics of the grids. As noticed in most replication methods, the popularity of files is monitored or could be complex functions calculated for the overall cost of whether or not a replication decision or a deletion decision should be issued. The proposed strategy has shown superb performance in terms of mean job time and effective network usage compared with the other two-replication strategies, LRU and Economic under OptorSim simulation environment.

Section 3.*Architecture*, examines a host of research directions beyond the practice of aiming at the enterprise as the endpoint of IT architectures. As a matter of necessity clouds have to accommodate differences in architecture requirements for various situations such as in healthcare or financial domains. In this sense, autonomic computing, in which systems manage themselves according to certain goals, is increasingly valued in cloud computing. Innovations in cloud computing especially in the areas of virtualization are demonstrating that the goals of autonomic computing can be realized to a practical degree, and that they could be useful in developing cloud architectures capable of sustaining and supporting varied systems. Currently, there are efforts to merge the cloud and grid architectures with service-oriented architecture, autonomic computing and other open standards platforms. A couple of chapters in this section detail these advances.

In order to tackle the challenges encountered in the trust asymmetry between users and the grid system, Yuhui Deng and Na Helian proposed architecture based on trusted computing. In the chapter titled *"Single Attestation Image for a Trusted and Scalable Grid"*, the researchers constructed a trusted grid as a flat ring that decentralizes the functionalities of Trusted Platform Module (TPM) across the ring. This architecture presents a single attestation image, which provides a transparent attestation to a scalable, large-scale, and dynamic trusted grid. The architecture also significantly reduces the frequency of attestations, thus alleviating the TPM bottleneck and improving the commercialization of grid and cloud technology. In another chapter, *"Personal Storage Grid Architecture: Consuming Cloud Data Space Resources"*, researchers Lim, Wu, Simon, Rashid and Helian, discussed the development of a modern file system in Linux that enables the consumption of cloud applications and the availability of the underlying disk space resource to the end-user. A web service was developed to support systems like online email accounts and online virtual disk space. A free online mail account was used to demonstrate the architecture and the IMAP protocol used for remote data spaces.

Furthermore, cloud architectures are being developed for systems like wireless sensors network (WSN), which are increasingly widely used. The current WSN architectures do not promote the sharing of data on an inter-WSN basis, hence the need for newer architecture. Researchers Patel and Pandey, in the paper *"Design of SOA Based Framework for Collaborative Cloud Computing in Wireless Sensor Networks"*, proposed the SOA-based architecture to support collaborating cloud computing in WSN. The architecture consists of layered service stack that has management, information, presentation and communication layers with all required services and repositories. Interactions between WSN, subscribers and other cloud are also presented as sequence diagrams. The proposed framework serves the cloud subscribers with wide range of queries on the data of multiple WSNs through suitable interface to solve large-scale problems.

In a similar development, the researchers Eftychiou, Vrusias and Antonopoulos to satisfy the growing need to manage and search the online information developed a distributed semantic-enabled architecture, which enforces semantic web technologies for resource discovery. The chapter - "*A Semantic-Driven Adaptive Architecture for Large Scale P2P Networks*", describes the conceptual representation of network knowledge on the P2P system that is organized in two-layered super-peer architecture, which is shaped from the information provided by the nodes using collective intelligence methods. The focus here is the creation of a dynamic hierarchical semantic-driven P2P topology using the network's collective intelligence. The unmanageable amounts of data are transformed into a repository of semantic knowledge, transforming the network into ontology of conceptually related entities of information collected from the resources located by peers. Appropriate experiments have been undertaken through a case study by simulating the proposed architecture and evaluating results.

Online gaming software is growing in sophistication to meet the demand of users. Ma and Oikonomou reviewed various approaches on data replication and region partitioning used in some online games such as Eve Online, World of Warcraft and Second Life. These games are built on distributed client-server architectures with server allocation based on sharding, static geographical partitioning, dynamic micro-cell scheme, or optimal server. In the chapter titled *"Network Architectures and Data Management for Massively Multiplayer Online Games"*, these games are described as Current-generation Massively Multiplayer Online Games (MMOG) that allows players to be placed on a virtual region according to the geographical dispersion of players. The researchers investigated data storage and synchronization methods for MMOG databases, mainly on relational databases. Several attempts of peer-to-peer (P2P) architectures and protocols for MMOGs are reviewed, and critical issues such as cheat prevention on P2P MMOGs are highlighted.

Section 4.*Security*, focuses on the implementation of grid and cloud technologies as these technologies even exacerbate the erosion of trust boundaries in business organizations. Organizations currently struggle to close the security loopholes in the Internet technology and are truly averse to public cloud technology that essentially placates the release of the prized corporate data to the management of third party data centers. Reassuring the corporate world of the security of their data is the central objective of cloud security activities such as the management of domains, services and interoperability. Researchers Chaurasia, Verma and Tomar presented the mechanism for sustaining privacy of a vehicle in a vehicular ad hoc network (VANET) through pseudonym update that could be exploited in the grid and cloud environments. For instance, a VANET allows vehicles on the road to disseminate information as they move. An association can be formed between the physical location of the source vehicle and the transmitted messages. This relationship between the physical vehicle and its identity can breach its privacy. This work exploits the strategy of optimal pseudonym update for maximizing privacy as observed by adversaries with different capabilities. Results of this high performance computing indicate that updating pseudonyms in accordance to the strategy maximizes the privacy of a vehicle in the given situation.

Section 5.*Applications*, focuses on the growth of software applications in grid and cloud environments, such as software-as-a-service (SaaS), platform-as-a-service (PaaS), infrastructure-as-a-service (IaaS) and others. The architecture of cloud applications is fundamentally different from the conventional application models and is considered to be disruptive in nature (a technology paradigm shift). This fundamental shift in implementation approaches will eliminate software installation, maintenance, deployment, management, and support in the current IT departments of companies. This section features several articles demonstrating the current applications of grid and cloud technologies. Researchers Sahota and Hadjinicolaou, in the article titled *"Modeling Scalable Grid Information Services with Colored Petri Nets"*, showed how information services can be used to facilitate the discovery of resources and services available to meet user requirements and help tune the performance of the grid. This article models PIndex, which is a grouped peer-to-peer network with Colored Petri Nets (CPNs) for scalable grid information services. Based on the CPN model, a simulator was implemented for PIndex simulation and performance evaluation. In another paper, *"Deep Analysis of Enhanced Authentication for Next Generation Networks (NGN)"*, researcher Mamdouh Gouda improved the user authentication process in NGN - a telecommunication core. The paper presented an enhanced one-pass AKA procedure that eliminates the repeated steps without affecting the security level in NGN, in addition to reducing the Denial of Service (DoS) attacks. The presented mechanism has minimal impact on the network infrastructure and functionality and does not require any changes to the existing authentication protocols.

Further advances were recorded by researchers Chakrabarty, Collier and Mukhopadhyay in their paper titled *"Adaptive Routing Strategy for Large Scale Rearrangeable Symmetric Networks"*. The article proposed an adaptive unicast routing algorithm for large scale symmetric networks comprising 2×2 switch elements such as Benes networks. The authors' algorithm makes routing decisions dependent on the status of each switching element at every stage of the network, hence the name adaptive routing. The approach provides a low complexity solution, but with much better blocking performance than random routing algorithms as demonstrated in the simulation results for various input loads. In another paper titled *"G2G: A Meta-Grid Framework for the Convergence of P2P and Grids"*, researchers Chung, Hsu, Lin, Lai and Chung proposed a meta-grid framework, named the Grid-to-Grid (G2G) framework, to harmonize autonomic grids in realizing a grid federation. The G2G framework is a decentralized management framework that is built on top of existing autonomic grid systems. This paper further adopts a super-peer network in a separate layer to coordinate distributed grid systems. A super-peer overlay network is constructed for communication among super-peers, thus enabling collaboration among grid systems. The experimental results show that the proposed meta-grid framework can improve system performance with little overhead.

This book presents further applications that feature various uses of grid and cloud technologies. In the paper titled *"One Anchor Distance and Angle Based Multi - Hop Adaptive Iterative Localization Algorithm for Wireless Sensor Networks"*, researchers Kotwal, Tomar and Abrol presented the distance and angle measurements based on the Multi-Hop Adaptive and Iterative Localization algorithm for localization of unknown nodes in wireless sensor networks (WSNs). The results clearly indicate an improved efficiency of the proposed algorithm in comparison with existing algorithms. In another work -*"Fuzzy Allocation of Fine-Grained Compute Resources for Grid Data Streaming Applications"*, researchers Zhang, Zhong, Liu and Wu proposed a fuzzy logic controller designed with several simple but robust rules to improve processing efficiency and resource utilization of data streaming applications. Performance of this controller is verified to out-perform classic controllers in response rapidness and less oscillation. The researchers obtained an empirical formula for tuning essential parameters to achieve better performance. Another paper titled *"Managing Inconsistencies in Data Grid Environments: A Practical Approach"* by Ahmed, Bessis, Norrington and Yue dwelt on one of the main concerns when integrating data from heterogeneous data sources, that is, data redundancy. The researchers take the view that there is a greater chance of data inconsistencies, such as data redundancies when integrating them within a grid environment as compared to traditional distributed paradigms. To this end, the researchers proposed matching strategy between structure objects and data values across federated databases in a grid environment.

Currently, high performance computing (HPC) systems are being integrated into grid and cloud systems as mainframes and supercomputers make a comeback in research and data centers. Computing systems approaching the teraflops-region are considered to be HPC-computers. The networking requirements of grid and cloud systems necessitate the use of a collapsed network backbone for HPC technologies, as the collapsed network backbone architecture is more amenable to easy troubleshooting and single router application. Furthermore, since grids and clouds use multiple processors and computers, scaling problems may cripple critical systems that are retrofitted with HPC technologies, hence the need for further research. In this book series, several chapters feature the application of HPC technologies in scientific research or computational science. Frank and Mesentean dwelt on *"Efficient Communication Interfaces for Distributed Energy Resources"*, while Mohana and Ashwathakumar harped on *"Road Traffic Parameters Estimation by Dynamic Scene Analysis: A Systematic Review"*. Further HPC papers are titled as follows: *"Intelligent Industrial Data Acquisition and Energy Monitoring using Wireless Sensor Networks"* by Gupta, Verma, Tomar and Abrol; *"A Method of 3-D Microstructure Reconstruction in the Simulation Model of Cement Hydration"* by Dongliang Zhang and *"One Anchor Distance and Angle Based Multi - Hop Adaptive Iterative Localization Algorithm for Wireless Sensor Networks"* by Kotwal, Tomar and Abrol.

In conclusion, there is a surge in grid and cloud research, as the industry and business world now recognize the potentials in this disruptive technology. The book highlights the direction of current research with sufficient materials to spur efforts in this field by government, industry, institutions and individuals. In that light, this book impacts the advance of cloud technology and global economy, and indeed the information age.

Emmanuel Udoh
National College, Fort Wayne, USA

Section 1
Introduction

Chapter 1
Harnessing the Cloud for Mobile Social Networking Applications

Juwel Rana
Luleå University of Technology, Sweden

Josef Hallberg
Luleå University of Technology, Sweden

Kåre Synnes
Luleå University of Technology, Sweden

Johan Kristiansson
Ericsson Research, Sweden

ABSTRACT

The cloud computing model inherently enables information from social networking services (Twitter, Facebook, LinkedIn, and so forth), context-based systems (location, activity, interests, etc.) and personal applications (call logs, contacts, email, calendar, and so forth) to be harnessed for multiple purposes. This article presents an agent-based system architecture for semantic and semi-automated applications that utilize the cloud to enrich and simplify communication services, for instance by displaying presence information, prioritizing information, and dynamically managing groups of users. The proposed architecture is based on the concept of aggregated social graphs, which are created from harnessed information about how people communicate. This article also presents challenges in achieving the envisioned architecture and introduces early prototyping results.

DOI: 10.4018/978-1-4666-0056-0.ch001

INTRODUCTION

The Internet has long been used for social interaction, some of the more popular examples being social networking applications such as Twitter, Linkedin, and Facebook (John et al., 2008; Huberman et al., 2008; Miluzzo et al., 2008; Li et al., 2008). These types of applications help users share digital media and have proven successful tools for expanding the social networks and share ideas and knowledge. At the same time a rapid growth of mobile computing has been made possible through advanced mobile terminals connected through wireless/GSM/3G networks, which has enabled users to be ubiquitously connected and thus be 'always on'.

This rapid development in mobile computing has made social networks almost ubiquitous, where access to them can be done through a multitude of devices such as a PC or a mobile phone as well as through public information displays or pervasive devices. While it is possible to access social networking services from almost anywhere, few services can today take full advantage of the mobility of the users. Therefore we propose a solution using agent-based systems for building flexible and innovative services for the cloud and the mobile semantic Web.

There are a number of challenges for supporting social interaction on mobile devices. Because of distractions from the environment it may be difficult for a user to give full attention to mobile services which suggests the need for functionality that reduces the need for user interaction. Social networking services for mobile devices should therefore work proactively and offer advice and recommendations to the user. Semantic information about users' location, context (such as what terminal they use) and situation (such as the current activity) can also be used to prioritize information from social networks to support novel mobile applications. For social networking applications it means that social interaction can be supported on a new level, where a recommender system can take advantage of current contexts as well as knowledge about activity in different social networks to improve and simplify a service.

This article explores possibilities for developing a new framework for services which use reasoning on context and social data to provide relevant functionality for the user's current situation. The purpose of this framework is to simplify services and reduce the need for user interaction by aggregating data from a number of different sources, both sensors and social networking services, and then applying semantic reasoning on this data to provide aggregated social graphs. These aggregated social graphs can then be used for different recommender systems to improve and simplify services in the cloud and mobile devices. This includes providing automatic support for group discovery, message processing, communication prioritization, as well as protecting the user by maintaining a desired level of privacy.

The rest of this article is organized as follows. First a background to the research area is presented. This is followed with a description of our proposed framework together with accompanying features and concepts. The type of framework we are proposing raise a number of challenges which are described in the subsequent section. Finally we discuss the vision and concept, ending with conclusions and future work.

BACKGROUND

Tim-Berners Lee already in 1995 defined the Web as a platform of collective intelligence. The viral growth of social networks today can be explained through both societal developments and technological advancements that together have enabled new types of applications where users today co-create content. 'The cloud' is the current paradigm of computing, building on this notion of co-creating both content and services (Lytras et al., 2008). Thus, Lee's vision of a collective intelligence is becoming true. This is in particular true for social networking applications, as users feed the services with personal information and also contribute to the development of services.

The decentralized design techniques where end users participates in creating content provides a basic model for designing social networking applications. Creating, sharing, tagging and commenting on content while building social networks (communities) are therefore central, as social needs are one reason for the viral growth of these services. However, mobile devices are now taking this even further by enabling users to be 'always on' which has many implications.

It has been shown that social context is important for designing and developing context-aware mobile applications (Häkkilä et al., 2006), while also increasing the risk of privacy and integrity violation. In general mobile social networking applications allow users to have more social interactions and collaborations using the Web in a more efficient and interesting manner (Christor et al., 2009). For instance, the "CenceMe" system is able to collect users' present status or context information using mobile sensors and can export users' present status automatically to social networks (Miluzzo et al., 2008).

Social context can also be used to simplify the creation of dynamic groups. A dynamic group is a concept of creating and managing groups based on social data as well as semantic information (Hallberg et al., 2007; Hallberg et al., 2009). To simplify such a service we could use metrics which are based on social data, such as the frequency of communication, location, means of communication, etc. We could also use a social interest discovery mechanism based on user-generated tags for discovering groups (Li et al., 2008). However, current API's are not enough to collect social data from social networking sites due to lack of standardization of data formats and model as well as access policies (ProgrammableWeb, 2009). There are initiatives on open social interfaces but they have been proven not to be usable in practice (OpenSocial, 2009), mainly because of

dependencies on social network owners (e.g., for analyzing social data) (Huberman et al., 2008).

Semantic Web technologies have the potential to over-come the challenges in mobile social networking applications. Web ontologies (e.g., RDF, OWL, FOAF, SIOC, etc) provides relationship (Raento et al., 2005; Gaonkar et al., 2008) by linking and representing data (Web data, context/sensor data) in machine readable format. Therefore, semantic Web technologies could be useful for better integration of social networking applications and mobile phone's software by merging and connecting personalized Web and sensor data (collected via mobile phone). And potentially, this could be helpful to identify new friends and communities considering interest, location, interactions and so on. For example, FOAF (Friend-of-a-friend) ontology (Ding et al., 2005) can be used for discovering friends and communities from a mobile terminal by looking in Web and sensor data.

A FRAMEWORK FOR SUPPORTING SOCIAL NETWORKING SERVICES

There are a number of different ways of creating mobile social networking services. One way would be to use an agent based system for reasoning on context data so the systems will be able to discover dynamic networks. Also, finding people with the same hobbies, and finding the nearest pizzeria which is recommended by the people one knows, are services based on social context data. Current social networking applications are however limited in regards to providing services. Therefore, to build efficient and durable social networking applications, we are proposing a semantic web–based reasoning platform in form of a multi-agent system. After deploying such a system, mobile social networking applications will be smarter and enable the following features:

- Automated or Semi-automated interactions: Social Networking Applications will be automated or semi-automated in respect to interaction, recommendation and discovering groups and services. It is important to have simpler interaction with the application without decreasing the target benefits of social networking. This has a desirable side effect of reduced power consumption since the decreased need for user interaction will reduce the need to light the screen etc.

- Ad-hoc Social Network Discovery: The Applications will be able to discover ad-hoc social networks automatically based on social relations and situations (e.g., family, friends, profession, hobby, location, frequency of communication, and other metrics). Obviously, it is important to discover the individual importance of user interest, contents and location.

- Openness: The platform will be open for integration with other social networking applications for sharing context. Therefore, it will simplify communication between different social networking applications.

Hence, an open social networking platform will be achieved.

- Automated Sharing of Rich Media: Smart sharing of media can be complicated. For example, automatic annotation and image analysis for the purpose of finding the identity of people appearing in a picture (so the picture can be shared with these people) is very challenging. However, from the user point of view, this is very useful, although there is some privacy issues involved in doing this.

We propose an Agent-based System which will provide a distributed platform for building mobile social networking applications. The architecture will exploit semantic web based reasoning techniques to identify dynamic groups based on user input and context data. Figure 1 illustrates the high level architecture of the agent-based system.

The agent-based system will collect heterogeneous content (user data and context data) from different sources (e.g., sensors, Web) and publish these contents to social networking applications depending on the context data and user interest. There are some related works done on publisher-subscriber mechanisms (Cao et al., 2005; Maamar

Figure 1. High level architecture of the system

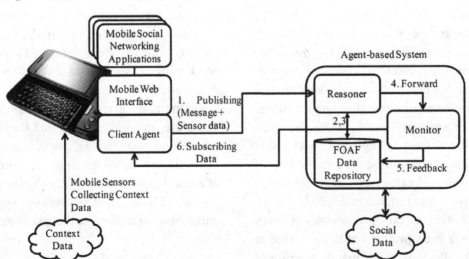

et al., 2004). However, the idea in our agent system is different. In our system there are three components. One is for reasoning on context data (Padovitz et al., 2008), another is for context ontologies and the third one is for monitoring privacy and discovered groups.

The agent-based system provides a monitoring component to perform monitoring activities (Giblin & Singh, 2006). It provides special protection for privacy issues and updates the context ontology to increase the efficiency of the reasoning component (Roman & Kifer, 2007). Another important task is to notify the subscribed clients with the contents. We have noticed that traditional publish-subscribe systems are not considering semantics information for selecting subscribers. Our agent will identify subscribers in difference to traditional systems.

The client agent is an application which is deployed in the user's mobile devices, for instance as a web browser plug-in. One of the main tasks of the client agent is to collect context data from sensors and publish context data to the main system. Furthermore, it receives contents from the system before using those contents in web based social networking applications.

In the proposed solution, the system processes different types of contents (e.g., text, voice, and video), messaging protocols (e.g., SOAP, HTTP, or SMTP) and exist on different platforms (e.g., Symbian, Windows mobile). The aggregation policy of the content (both user input and context data) is based on context ontologies (Szomszor et al., 2008; Veijalainen, 2007; Mello & Rein, 2009). The policy is rule-based and written in XML. Therefore, the client agent can inject rules to put constraints to ensure that privacy and interest preferences are maintained.

Previous research has been done for the Service Oriented Architecture (SOA)-based application's runtime engine (Michlmayr et al., 2008). These systems provide a platform for running distributed applications but those systems communicate using the SOAP protocol. The rest of the protocols,

for example RSS, ATOM, and G-Data are not considered. Consequently, the main challenges are not addressed in these systems.

Aggregated Social Graphs

A central architectural concept is to harness information in the cloud, such as information about people, their communication habits and their surrounding, from a number of sources (Dix et al., 2000; Raento et al., 2005; Borcea et al., 2008):

- **Infrastructure - based context data**: Network Bandwidth, reliability, device configuration (display resolution)
- **Application-based context data**: Service availability, access protocols, environmental constraints
- **Personalized context data**: User, location, time, presence, device, agenda, contacts
- **Social context data**: User interaction, ties between users and location, frequency of communication between users, media capture, media share (audio, video, picture, text)

The context data can then be used to construct graphs that describe how a person or a group communicates or how people are related to each other in contextual terms. A social graph can for instance be created from your friends in Facebook, your followers in Twitter or by studying call-logs in your mobile phone. These can then be aggregated and the resulting graph would then be describing something altogether more complex. This aggregated social graph enables intelligent reasoning in the architecture and can be used to present presence information and dynamically manage groups, etc.

From a communication perspective it is possible to measure social strength using the data collected from an aggregated social graph (Ankolekar et al., 2009). Social strength is the weight of communication between two individuals. A social strength weight can be calculated based on communication media, preferred service, activity in different social networking services, and other metrics. The social strength weight is a value between 0 and 1, where a high value means there is a closer relation between the two individuals compared to relations with a low value. Figure 2 shows an example of a social graph with applied social strength weights. Here we see the *User* and four friends, *A*, *B*, *C*, and *D*. In the figure we can see that the *User* has a closer relation to, and communicates more with, friend *C*, than with the others. This can be very helpful in recommendation services, such assisting the *User* in forming a dynamic group, as it is more likely that the *User* wants to form a dynamic group with friend *C* than with friend *D*.

CHALLENGES

In this article we have proposed a framework for supporting social networking services in the cloud and in mobile devices. This framework takes advantage of a weighted social graph which is the product of intelligent reasoning. To achieve this type of system there are a number of challenges which needs to be addressed (Rana et al., 2009), such as interaction design, the design of new communication services, unified communication, data mining, semantic web and reasoning techniques, and privacy.

Interaction Design

As mentioned in the paper, semantic information obtained from the Web can be used to improve existing mobile applications, for example implementing a semantic contact application. One challenge is to investigate how to best utilize semantic information so that the application becomes easier to use, given the limited attention span of the human mind. As it also may be difficult or even impossible to develop a system with 100 percent accuracy, it is necessary to modify the application, in particular the user interface, to better deal with inaccurate or conflicting semantic information.

Figure 2. Weighted social graph

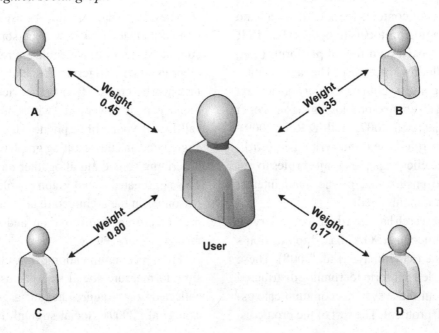

For example, one option could be to implement a recommendation system where the user always has the final word. Another option could be to adapt the user interface (e.g. re-arrange or sort visible artifacts) to minimize user interaction. An option is also to weigh redundant information to achieve better accuracy. Optimally the user may not notice that the system sometimes fails as the application just become a bit less informative or more difficult to use in that particular case.

Design of New Communication Services

Semantic information can be used to implement new types of communication services. For example, implementing a new Web service that forms dynamic groups of people based on location and user interest. One important research challenge is to explore how these new services should be designed and evaluate possible user benefits. This includes developing new Web frameworks and middleware as well as new user interfaces. One could for example imagine a dynamic group being visualized as third dimensional graph where the user can easily browse and navigate the currently discovered dynamic groups.

Unified Communication

Unified Communication: When developing a new communication service it is important to get as many users as possible. When more and more communication services are deployed as Web services, it becomes possible to create mesh-ups or aggregated Web services. As users being part of a dynamic group could be using different communication services (e.g., Twitter and Facebook) the system should automatically dispatch messages between different social networks. A challenge is therefore to make an integrated effort of consolidating social networks, or even create a virtual social network service. Although similar services (OpenSocial, 2009) already exist, more advanced

orchestration and Web frameworks should be developed to more easily utilize new Web APIs.

Data Mining

Data mining algorithms must be utilized in order to generate semantic information. By extracting information from social networks it is possible to automatically discover information about users. For example, automatically find phone numbers, user names and relationship between users. The information can be obtained from a wide variety of sources, including news feeds, images, videos, and text obtained from classical Web pages. However, as users may have different account or profile names, it can be difficult to map information to a one particular user. Similarly, using non unique data fields to map data can easily result in inaccurate data sets. For example, using a personal name to map data obtained from a Web page to Twitter account can easily result in inaccuracy as personal names are typically not unique.

Another problem is that the vast majority of the data on Web is not available to a crawler or even a browser, but is hidden in forms, data bases, and interactive interfaces. While many Web services now provide public APIs which makes it easier to access hidden data, they usually require some form of authentication in order to be used. This means that the data mining software must maintain credentials to different Web sites while at the same time not jeopardize the security of the users.

In addition to accessing data on the Web, data mining software should also be able to access data stored on mobile devices. For example, accessing data stored in contact list, call history, message history, and browser history etc. The call list is particularly interested as it in principle is a social network, many times reflecting the user's closest social contact or real friends (Raento et al., 2005). One option to access local data on mobile phones it let the mobile device be accessible from the Internet (e.g., via a local Web server) so that a crawler can access the data. Another option is to let a software running on the mobile device publish relevant information to an external Web service. In both cases, it is important not to compromise the user's privacy while also preserving the battery life time of the mobile device.

Yet another enhancement could be to let the mobile devices interact with the surrounding environment. For example, detecting social interaction patterns by getting information from sensors (RFID, NFS, Bluetooth, barcodes etc.) deployed in buildings or other mobile devices. This information should be aggregated and processed with other information obtained from the Web in order to draw as good as possible.

Semantic Web and Reasoning Techniques

Once data has been fetched from the Web, it needs to be combined and refined into useful semantic information. Depending on the data received from the data mining component, the reasoning module analyses the data, draw conclusions, and store the refined data in a suitable ontology. One important research challenge is to develop suitable ontologies and rules to fuse the data into fields that fits the used ontology. Machine learning algorithms such as clustering algorithms and statistical models can be used to find useful patterns, but it could also be useful to analyze the data offline to manually find patterns, for example matching data to social sciences theories. Defining useful rules and applying machine learning algorithms to efficiently utilize vast data set containing information from the Web and sensors to improve personal communication is still a challenging research problem.

Privacy and Integrity

The information about a user must be treated carefully, not only to adhere to laws and service agreements but also to build trust in that information will be treated confidential and not be repudiated against the wishes of the user. It is

central for building trust in a service that users feel in control of their information and that the gain of using the service therefore is greater than possible implications to privacy and integrity. For example, people upload videos and images to YouTube and Flickr because they want other people to be able to easily access the data, or to improve their own social status.

However, that information can be used to infringe on privacy and integrity, especially if several sources of information is used at the same time. The challenge is to support privacy and integrity in simple yet powerful ways, for instance by utilizing mechanisms to control access to certain information. For example, users belonging to the same social networks or users that often communicate may be deemed trusted and given access to additional information.

DISCUSSION

The cloud has enabled a plethora of services to be meshed-up to construe new and more powerful services through Web 2.0 technologies. Social networking services have here been presented as possible options for enriching and simplifying communication services. It is also likely that a new type of socially aware applications may come forth through this development, where applications can reason about the social context and act semi-autonomously in behalf of a user. Figure 3 shows an Android prototype of a semantic contact list based on the presented architecture.

Creating an open platform for social networking applications is crucial for spreading this technology further. Therefore this paper envisions an architecture for social networking applications that satisfies requirements on interoperability based on open interfaces between social networking platforms. The open platform must naturally also consider mobility aspects regarding data formats etc.

Figure 3. Prototype of a semantic contact list

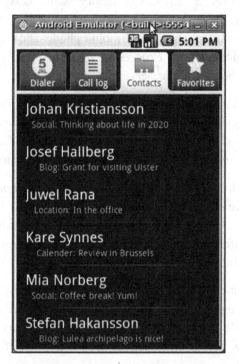

The aggregated social graphs will enable reasoning about social relations and communication patterns. The creation of the aggregated social graph must currently be said to be done subjectively as the available empiric results so far is very limited. Several algorithms for creating the graphs are being evaluated and early prototyping has proven the difficulty to weigh different types of context data. Creating different aggregations depending on the purpose of the application at hand may prove necessary to avoid overly complex algorithms.

It is the authors' belief that the proposed architecture will spawn a new set of socially aware applications for both professional and private use. For example, a person with mild dementia can be offered a semantic contact list that includes not only presence information but also information about where, how and when they communicated last augmented by images, audio clips or other media. This memory support would enable him to avoid institutionalization, staying at home longer and thus increase his life quality significantly.

CONCLUSION

This article presents how the cloud can be harnessed to build aggregated social graphs which describe how we communicate. These graphs are central to the proposed architecture and can be used to enrich and simplify communication services, as applications built on the architecture can benefit from semantic information available in the cloud to display presence information or dynamically manage groups of users. Applications based on the architecture can also be made semi-autonomous by prioritizing information based on previous communication patterns. This may reduce information stress and simplify communication particularly for users of mobile devices.

FUTURE WORK

This article presents the first iteration of the architecture design, which is based on aggregated social graphs. The system architecture must however be developed further, where future iterations need to consider the challenges presented above in more detail. Also, the prototypes described are proofs-of-concepts that would need more thorough user-studies to better indicate the use and effect of the proposed architecture.

DISCLAIMER

The work has been carried out as part of an academic research project and does not necessarily represent Ericsson views and positions.

ACKNOWLEDGMENT

This work has been funded by Ericsson Research/ Multimedia Technologies, Vinnova (the MobiGroup project), EU/FP6 (the CogKnow project) and EU/Goal-2 (the MemoryLane project).

REFERENCES

Ankolekar, A., Luon, Y., Szabo, G., & Huberman, B. (2009). A Mobile Application for Your Social Life. In *MobileHCI*. Bonn: Friendlee.

Borcea, C., Gupta, A., Kalra, A., Jones, Q., & Iftode, L. (2008). The MobiSoC middleware for mobile social computing: challenges, design, and early experiences. In *Proceedings of Mobile Wireless Middleware*. Operating Systems, and Applications.

Cao, F., & Singh, J. P. (2005). MEDYM: match-early and dynamic multicast for content-based publish-subscribe networks. In *Proceedings of the ACM/IFIP/USENIX 2005 international Conference on Middleware*.

Christos, Z., Yiannis, K., & Athena, V. (2009) Information analysis in mobile social networks for added-value services. In *Proceedings of the the W3C Workshop on the Future of Social Networking*, Barcelona, Spain.

Ding, L., Zhou, L., Finin, T., & Joshi, A. (2005). How the Semantic Web is Being Used: An Analysis of FOAF Documents. In *Proceedings of Hawaii international Conference on System Sciences* (Vol. 4).

Dix, A., Rodden, T., Davies, N., Trevor, J., Friday, A., & Palfreyman, K. (2000). Exploiting space and location as a design framework for interactive mobile systems. *ACM Transactions on Computer-Human Interaction, 7*(3), 285–321. doi:10.1145/355324.355325

Gaonkar, S., Li, J., Choudhury, R. R., Cox, L., & Schmidt, A. (2008). Micro-Blog: sharing and querying content through mobile phones and social participation. In *Proceeding of Mobile Systems, Applications, and Services*.

Giblin, C., Müller, S., & Pfitzmann, B. (2006). *From Regulatory Policies to Event Monitoring Rules: Towards Model-Driven Compliance Automation (Tech. Rep. No. RZ 3662)*. IBM Research.

Häkkilä, J., & Mäntyjärvi, J. (2006). *Developing design guidelines for context-aware mobile applications*. Paper presented at the 3rd international Conference on Mobile Technology, Applications &Amp; Systems, Bangkok, Thailand.

Hallberg, J., Backlund-Norberg, M., Synnes, K., & Nugent, C. (2009). Profile management for dynamic groups. In *Intelligent Patient Management*. New York: Springer. ISBN 978-3-642-00178-9

Hallberg, J., Norberg, M. B., Kristiansson, J., Synnes, K., & Nugent, C. (2007). Creating dynamic groups using context-awareness. In *Proceedings of the 6th international Conference on Mobile and Ubiquitous Multimedia*.

Huberman, B., Romero, D., & Wu, F. (2008). *Social networks that matter: Twitter under the microscope*. CoRR abs/0812.1045

John, A., Adamic, L., Davis, M., Nack, F., Shamma, D. A., & Seligmann, D. D. (2008). The future of online social interactions: what to expect in 2020. In *Proceeding of the 17th international Conference on World Wide Web*.

Li, X., Guo, L., & Zhao, Y. E. (2008). Tag-based social interest discovery. In *Proceedings of the World Wide Web*.

Lytras, M., Damiani, E., & Pablos, P. (2008). *Web 2.0: the Business Model*. New York: Springer.

Maamar, Z., Alkhatib, G., Mostéfaoui, S., Lahkim, M., & Mansoor, W. (2004). *Context-based Personalization of Web Services Composition and Provisioning*. EUROMICRO.

Mello, A., & Rein, L. (2009). *Using Standards to Normalize Domain Specific Metadata*. Paper presented at the W3C Workshop on the Future of Social Networking.

Michlmayr, A., Leitner, P., Rosenberg, F., & Dustdar, S. (2008). Publish/subscribe in the VRESCo SOA runtime. In *Proceedings of Distributed Event-Based Systems*.

Miluzzo, E., Lane, N. D., Fodor, K., Peterson, R., Lu, H., Musolesi, M., et al. (2008). Sensing meets mobile social networks: the design, implementation and evaluation of the CenceMe application. In *Proceedings of Embedded Network Sensor Systems*.

OpenSocial API Documentation. (n.d.). Retrieved May 2009 from http://code.google.com/apis/opensocial/docs/index.html

Padovitz, A., Loke, S. W., & Zaslavsky, A. (2008). Multiple-Agent Perspectives in Reasoning About Situations for Context-Aware Pervasive Computing Systems. *IEEE Transactions on Systems, Man, and Cybernetics*, *38*(4), 729–742. doi:10.1109/TSMCA.2008.918589

Programmable Web. (n.d.). Retrieved May 2009 from http://www.programmableWeb.com/apis/directory/1?apicat=Social

Raento, M., Oulasvirta, A., Petit, R., & Toivonen, H. (2005). ContextPhone: a prototyping platform for context-aware mobile applications. *Pervasive Computing, IEEE*, *4*(2), 51–59. doi:10.1109/MPRV.2005.29

Rana, J., Kristiansson, J., Hallberg, J., & Synnes, K. (2009). Challenges for Mobile Social Networking Applications. In *Proceedings of the 1st International ICST Conference on Communications Infrastructure, Systems and Applications*, London.

Roman, D., & Kifer, M. (2007). *Reasoning about the Behavior of Semantic Web Services with Concurrent Transaction Logic*. VLDB.

Szomszor, M. N., Cantador, I., & Alani, H. (2008). Correlating user profiles from multiple folksonomies. In *Proceedings of Hypertext and Hypermedia*.

Veijalainen, J. (2007). Who, Why, Where, and How? In *Proceedings of Mobile Data Management*. Developing Mobile Ontologies.

This work was previously published in International Journal of Grid and High Performance Computing, Volume 2, Issue 2, edited by Emmanuel Udoh, pp. 1-11, copyright 2010 by IGI Publishing (an imprint of IGI Global).

Section 2
Scheduling

Chapter 2
Balanced Job Scheduling Based on Ant Algorithm for Grid Network

Nikolaos Preve
National Technical University of Athens, Greece

ABSTRACT

Job scheduling in grid computing is a very important problem. To utilize grids efficiently, we need a good job scheduling algorithm to assign jobs to resources in grids. The main scope of this paper is to propose a new Ant Colony Optimization (ACO) algorithm for balanced job scheduling in the Grid environment. To achieve the above goal, we will indicate a way to balance the entire system load while minimizing the makespan of a given set of jobs. Based on the experimental results, the proposed algorithm confidently demonstrates its practicability and competitiveness compared with other job scheduling algorithms.

INTRODUCTION

The early efforts in Grid computing started as a project to link supercomputing sites, but have now grown far beyond the original intent. The popularity of the Internet, the availability of powerful computers and the high-speed network technologies as well as low cost commodity components, are changing the way we use computers today. These technology opportunities have led to the possibility of using distributed computers as a single, unified computing resource, leading to what is popularly known as Grid computing.

Today's scientific problems are very complex and need huge computing power and storage capability. Computational Grids are emerging as a new paradigm for solving large scale problems in science and engineering. A Grid scheduler acts as an interface between the user and the distributed resources hiding the complexities of Grid comput-

DOI: 10.4018/978-1-4666-0056-0.ch002

ing (Abramson, Giddy, & Kotler, 2000; Buyya, Abramson, & Giddy, 2000). It is also responsible for monitoring and tracking the progress of application execution along with adapting to the changes in the runtime environment of the Grid, variation in resource share availability and failures. A Grid scheduler balances the entire system load while completing all the jobs at hand as soon as possible according to the environment status. The existing job scheduling algorithm such as First Come First Serve (FCFS), Shortest Job First (SJF) may not be suitable for the grid environment. These algorithms seize a lot of computational time due to soar waiting time of jobs in job queue reducing the entire system performance (Somasundaram & Radhakrishnan, 2009; Yan, Wang, Wang, & Chang, 2009).

The users who interact with the Grid can manually assign jobs to computing resources in grids. Thus, grid job scheduling is a very important issue in Grid computing. Referring to the Berkeley Open Infrastructure for Network Computing (BOINC, 2009) project, we will find out an open source platform for volunteer computing and grid computing. Here, job scheduling is one of the most important key factors for achieving Teraflops performance (Kondo, Anderson, & McLeod, 2007). We can also notice that grid scheduling concentrates in improving response times in an environment containing autonomous resources whose availability dynamically varies with time. The Grid scheduler has to interact with the local schedulers managing computational resources and adapt its behavior to changing resource loads. Thus, the scheduling is conducted from the perspective of the user rather than that of the system. Because of its significant importance many job scheduling algorithms for Grids have been proposed in order to obtain a load balancing distribution of processes to computational resources, but open issues still exist (Boyera & Hura, 2005; Buyya, Cortes, & Jin, 2001; Collins & George, 2001; De Ronde, Schoneveld, & Sloot, 1997; Dong & Akl, 2004; Dorigo & Gambardella, 1997; Foster &

Kesselman, 2003; Maghraoui, 2006; Nabrzyski, Schopf & Weglarz, 2004; Salari & Eshghi, 2005; Karatza & Hilzer, 2003; Sonmez & Gursoy, 2007). When things come to practice it is impossible to find a tool for the automatic load balancing of a parallel distributed application.

A Grid scheduler differs from a scheduler for conventional computing systems in lack of full control over the grid because the local resources are in general not controlled by the grid scheduler, but by the local scheduler. Also, the Grid scheduler cannot assume that it has a global view of the grid. Therefore, the demand for scheduling is to achieve high performance computing. The heuristic algorithm Ant Colony Optimization (ACO) with efficient local search can be a useful tool for finding an optimal resource allocation for specific job (Dorigo & Blum, 2005; Lorpunmanee, Sap, Abdullah, & Inwai, 2007). This minimizes the schedule length of jobs. Many research projects, which are concerned with load balancing techniques, use ACO to solve NP-hard problems (Dorigo & Gambardella, 1997; Salari & Eshghi, 2005; Zhang & Tang, 2005).

This paper applies the ACO algorithm to job schedule problems in Grid computing. The resource scheduling in Grid is a NP complete problem. We compare the proposed ACO algorithm with various algorithms which have been designed to schedule the jobs in computational grid. The next step is to compare the proposed ACO algorithm with the most commonly used algorithms. The goal of this work is to describe the methodology and to define the required parameters according with the experimental results and thus to make use of real measurements which show that the proposed ACO is capable of achieving system load balance better than other job scheduling algorithms.

In the following, we will provide the details of related work about various kinds of ACO algorithm and job scheduling in grids. Also, we will describe the methodology, the design and the analysis of the proposed ACO algorithm in job scheduling.

Finally, the experimental results are indicated through the simulation model which shows the performance of the proposed ACO compared with others job scheduling algorithms.

RELATED WORK

The ACO has become a very popular algorithm in solving grid scheduling problems. (Du et al., 2008; Lorpunmanee et al., 2007; Thangavel, Karnan, Jeganathan, Petha, Sivakumar, & Geetharamani, 2006). The ACO method is used to refer to the class of algorithms that are inspired in the process of foraging for food by natural ants for the optimization of hard-to-solve problems. ACO algorithms show swarm intelligence which is the property of systems composed by agents individually not intelligent and with limited capacity to show collectively an intelligent behavior (Beni & Wang, 1989). In ants, this behavior emerges from the indirect communication among the agents which is called stigmergy (Grasse, 1959).

The Ant algorithm is based upon the heuristic approach. It is based on the behavior of real ants. This means that an ant deposes the chemical pheromone on its path when it searches for food from its nest. When each ant moves in a particular direction, the strength of the chemical pheromone increases and with this the other ants can also trail along.

The scheduling in grid is a complex problem and has led the researchers to propose many kinds of scheduling algorithms (Feitelson, 1996; Feitelson, Rudolph, Schwiegelshohn, Sevcik, & Wong, 1997; Krallmann, Schwiegelshohn & Yahyapour, 1999; Nelson, Towsley, & Tantawi, 1988; Van den Akker, Hoogeveen, & Van Kempen, 2006; Zhang & Tang, 2005). However, the problem is still obvious because the proposed solutions are not as complex as the problem is. Consequently, this issue attracts the interest of a large number of researchers.

As we mentioned, many algorithms have been designed to schedule the jobs in computational grid. The most commonly used algorithms are the Opportunistic Load Balancing (OLB), the Minimum Execution Time (MET), the Minimum Completion Time (MCT), the Min-Min and the Max-Min. The OLB algorithm without considering the job's execution time, it assigns a job in arbitrary order to the next available node. The perception behind OLB is to keep all machines as busy as possible. In contrast to OLB, MET assigns each task in arbitrary order, to the machine with the best expected execution time for that task, regardless of that machine's availability (Armstrong, Hensgen, & Kidd, 1998; Freund & Siegel, 1993; Freund et al., 1998). It neither considers the ready time nor the current load of the machine. Also, the availability of the resources at that instant is not taken into account.

A combination of OLB and MET benefits is MCT, with which we can avoid the circumstances of poor performance. MCT assigns each task in arbitrary order to the machine with the minimum completion time for that task (Armstrong et al., 1998). This algorithm calculates the completion time of the current unfinished job in only one earliest available node. But the same job may be completed in lesser time in some other machine which is available at that time. Also, Fast Greedy assigns each job in arbitrary order to the node with the minimum completion time.

Min-Min is based on the minimum completion time as is MCT which considers all unmapped tasks during each mapping decision. When compared with MCT, Min-Min considers all the unmapped tasks during their mapping decision. This algorithm selects the task that has the overall minimum completion time and assigns it to the corresponding machine.

Very similar to Min-Min is the Max-Min which attempts to minimize the penalties incurred from performing tasks with longer execution times (Armstrong et al., 1998; Ibarra & Kim, 1977). Here, the Max-Min task has the overall maximum completion time from the minimum completion time value and assigns it to the corresponding machine. The mapped task is removed from the unmapped set. The above process is repeated until all the tasks are mapped. In comparison with MCT, Max-Min considers all unmapped tasks during their mapping decision. The Max-Min may produce a balanced load across the machine.

The Genetic algorithm (GA) is used for searching large solution space (Singh & Youssef, 1996; Wang, Siegel, Roychowdhury, & Maciejewski, 1997). It operates on a population of chromosomes for a given problem. A chromosome could be generated by any other heuristic algorithm. The initial population is generated randomly. When it is generated by Min-Min, it is called seeding the population with Min-Min chromosome.

The ACO was proposed by Dorigo, Maniezzo, and Colorni (1996) and the system idea was based on the behavior of ants. After that, ant systems where algorithmically enunciated for optimization in problems like the salesman traveler and other problems (Dorigo & Gambardella, 1997; Yan, Qin, Li & Wu, 2005). Since then many research papers have studied ACO algorithm in grid environment but the main differences between them, are the changes in the pheromone update rule by adding encouragement, punishment coefficient and load balancing factor.

Dorigo and Stützle (2003) apply an approach to hard combinatorial optimization problems including several domains related to the problem, such as bin packing and job scheduling, which is also presented by Dowsland and Thompson (2005). A simple grid simulation architecture using ACO was proposed by Xu, Hou, and Sun (2003). The response time and the average utilization of resources have been used as the evaluation index. Also, Xu, Lu, and Sun (2004) proposed ACO algorithms which could improve the performance, like job finishing ratio, but they have never used the various evaluation indices to evaluate their algorithm. The common characteristic of the above papers is that ACO has not previously been applied to finding good job schedules in a grid environment. Since the effective processing speed varies continuously in a grid environment, it is more appropriate to use dynamic scheduling algorithms. Besides, Menasce, Saha, Porto, Almeida, and Tripathi (1995) introduced the Fastest Processor to Largest Task First (FPLTF) algorithm which schedules tasks to resources according to the workload of tasks in the grid system. The algorithm is based on two parameters, the CPU speed of resources and the workload of tasks. The scheduler sorts the tasks and resources by their workload and CPU speed. Then it assigns the largest task to the fastest available resource but if there are many tasks with heavy workload, its performance may not be very good. A modification of FPLTF is Dynamic FPLTF (DFPLTF) (Paranhos, Cirne, & Brasileiro, 2003) which gives the highest priority to the largest task and needs prediction information on processor speeds and task lengths. When several processors in DFPLTF simultaneously become available then the ties are broken arbitrarily.

The Work Queue (WQ) algorithm assigns a task to a processor in an idle state and receives the result when the processor of the task is completed (Graham, 1966). Then it assigns the next new task to the processor. The WQR (Work Queue with Replication) is based on the idea of the WQ algorithm (Paranhos et al., 2003). The main function key of WQR is to set faster processors to be allocated with more tasks than slower processors. Also, it does not use any prediction information on processor speeds and task lengths.

The Round Robin (RR) improves on WQ by performing task reproduction (Rashid & Akhtar, 2006). This algorithm provides several performance guarantees while it focuses on the fairness problem. RR uses the ring as its queue to store jobs. Each job in queue has the same execution time and it will be executed in turn. If a job cannot be completed during its turn, it will store back to the queue waiting for the next turn. Each job will be executed in turn and does not have to wait for the previous one to be completed but if the load is heavy, RR will take a lot of time to complete all the jobs.

Priority scheduling algorithm (Rashid & Akhtar, 2006) gives a priority value to each job and uses it for dispatching jobs. The priority value can vary because each job depends on the job status, such as the requirement of memory sizes, CPU time, and so forth. The main disadvantage of this algorithm is focused to indefinite blocking or starvation which can be provoked if the requirement of a job is never satisfied.

METHODOLOGY

Grid computing is an environment where the scheduled jobs rarely coincide between the actual execution times and the expected ones in the real computing environment. The basic idea of the proposed ACO algorithm comes from HellasGrid (2009) environment to achieve a balanced job scheduling, a decrease of the computation time of executing jobs and better load handling for each resource. The following methodology of the proposed algorithm relies on changes of the pheromone density according to the resources status by applying the local pheromone update and the global pheromone update functions. The main aim of the scheduler is to allocate the jobs to the available nodes as a result to minimize the completion time for each job while balancing the system load. Figure 1 illustrates our grid system which is composed by six computer clusters where three of them are located in Athens and the rest are located in Thessaloniki, Patra, and Crete.

When a client delivers a request, the system works as follows: A client uses the client-interface to send a request that contains the total number of jobs, the size of matrix and the job scheduling algorithm to the HellasGrid Portal. The Jobs Scheduler receives the message from the Portal and uses it as parameters for the proposed ACO algorithm. The implemented ACO algorithm starts to calculate the relevant parameters. At the same time, the Information Server also provides the resource information to the Jobs Scheduler. Then the proposed ACO algorithm selects a resource

Figure 1. System architecture

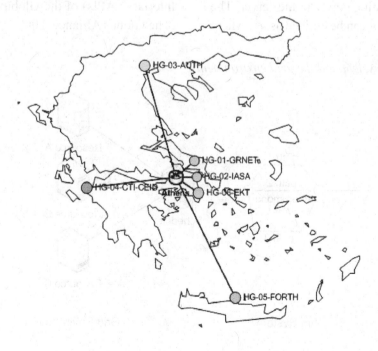

for submitting the request (job) by finding the largest entry in the PI matrix among the available jobs to be executed. Then a local pheromone update is performed. When a resource finishes a job, a global pheromone update is performed and the resource will send the final results back to the Portal. On receiving the execution results, the Portal sends it back to the client to be displayed on the client user interface. Finally, this process can be repeated until all jobs are completed.

The Performance Model

The Grid users expect to run their jobs efficiently which depends upon two important criteria in the Grid system. The first criterion is the makespan which measures the throughput of the system and the second is the flow time which is related to QoS (Quality-of-Service) measurements (Maheswaran, Ali, Siegel, Hensgen, & Freund, 1999; Pinedo 2008).

The length of a task represents its workload and is decided by the number of instructions in the task. The computational power provided by a processor depends on the original user. If the user occupies more resources, the computer will supply less computing power to the server. The usage of a processor can be defined as $u_{p,t}$, where

p is the processor and t is the time. According to the utilization and the capability of a computer, the capability of a processor can be calculated. This capability value shows the workload completed by a processor per unit time. The capability of processors and the length of tasks must have the same standard to model their performance and this criterion is the number of instructions. This means that the capability of each processor is the excess computational power of the processor, which is not used by the original user and is dedicated to the grid. Let $s_{p,t}$ be the capability of processor p during time interval $[t, t+1)$. If the load by the original users is very heavy or the computer is powered off, $s_{p,t}$ may be zero.

Figure 2 illustrates the mapping between the ant system and the grid system. Pheromone value on a path in the ant system is a weight for a resource in the grid system. A resource with a larger weight value means that the resource has a better computing power. The pheromone of each resource is stored in the scheduler and the scheduler uses it as the parameters for our proposed ACO algorithm. At last, the scheduler selects a resource by a scheduling algorithm and it sends jobs to the selected resource by the Application Programming Interface (APIs) of the Globus Toolkit 4 (GT4) (The Globus Alliance, 2009).

Figure 2. The ant system and the grid environment

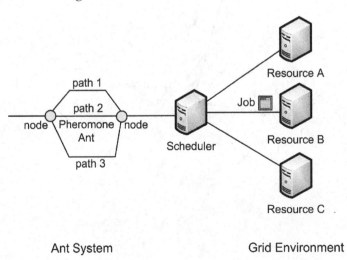

The initial pheromone value of each resource for each job is equal to the pheromone indicator. The pheromone indicator of each resource for each job is calculated by adding the estimated transmission time and execution time of a given job when assigned to this resource. The estimated transmission time can be easily determined by M_j / $Bandwidth_i$ where M_j is the size of a given job j and $bandwidth_i$ is the bandwidth available between the scheduler and the resource. However, the other parameter, the job execution time, is hard to predict. Depending on the type of programs, many methods (Engblom & Ermedahl, 2000; Park, 1993; Stappert & Altenbernd, 2000; Zhang, Sun, & Inoguchi, 2008) can be used to estimate the program execution time. With this, the pheromone indicator is defined by:

$$PI_{ij} = \left[\frac{M_j}{bandwidth_i} + \frac{T_j}{CPU\_speed_i \times (1 - load_i)} \right]^{-1}$$
(1)

where PI_{ij} is the pheromone indicator for job j assigned to resource i, M_j is the size of a given job j, T_j is the CPU time needed of job j, CPU_speed_i (CPU speed), $load_i$ (current load) and $bandwidth_i$ (between the scheduler and the resource) are the status of resource i. The pheromone indicator shows that when a job is assigned to a resource, we consider the resource status, the size of jobs, and the program execution time in order to select a suitable resource for execution. The larger the value of PI_{ij} is, the more efficient it is for resource i to execute this job j.

Assume there are m resources and n jobs. We have the PI matrix as follows:

$$PI_{ij} = \begin{array}{c} \\ r_1 \\ r_2 \\ . \\ . \\ . \\ r_m \end{array} \begin{bmatrix} PI_{11} & PI_{12} & ... & PI_{1n} \\ . & . & ... & . \\ . & . & ... & . \\ . & . & ... & . \\ . & . & ... & . \\ PI_{m1} & PI_{m2} & ... & PI_{mn} \end{bmatrix}$$
(2)

In each iteration, we select the largest entry from the matrix. Please note if another job scheduling discipline is used before our proposed ACO, then our ACO selects among the available jobs produced by the scheduling. Assuming PI_{ij} is selected, then job j is assigned to resource i for execution. After a job is assigned to a resource, we apply (1) to the resource selected for each unassigned jobs in the PI matrix. This is called the local (row) pheromone update. The global pheromone update is to recalculate the entire PI matrix. It is performed when a job is completed. However, for the resource that just completes executing this job, after applying (1), the new value of pheromone in the row corresponding to the resource will have to be multiplied $(1 - \rho_i)$ further, where $1 > \rho_i \geq 0$. ρ_i indicates the overhead incurred in resource i after completing job j. When a local scheduler is also used in a resource, ρ_i may be used to indicate the decrease of new job priority after a job is completed by the same user.

Global pheromone update reflects the changes of network condition and resource status after a job is completed. It incorporates the dynamic nature of the system into the scheduling algorithm such that a better decision can be made at the next turn.

The Proposed Algorithm

Let T be a set of n independent tasks and m be the number of processors in the grid. A schedule S of T defines how these n tasks are assigned to the m processors. S is a finite set of three tuple (k, p, ts) where k is one task of T, p is the index of a processor ($1 \leq p \leq m$) and ts is the start time of the task k. Let te be the completion time of the task k. A three tuple (k, p, ts) means that the processor p can provide fitting computing power to complete the task k during the time interval [ts, te]. Note that ts and te of a task may not be integers. Each three tuple (k, p, ts) has to satisfy the following two rules. First, each task of T must be executed at least once. Second, a processor can execute one task at most at any given time. In addition, a task can be assigned onto more than one processors and such allocation is called task replication.

The expected Execution Time (ET) is the expected time to complete the matrix. The element ET_{ij} of the ET matrix is defined as the amount of time taken to complete the ith job in the jth resource. The jobs are owned by different users. Each job has to be completely preempted. All jobs are interdependent. Each and every resource has its own computing characteristics. All the resources may be dynamically added or removed from the Grid. They use the expected time to compute (ET) the model (Fidanova & Durchova, 2006). Between ET value and actual time taken to complete a job, there is a difference but we calculate or assume that the values in ET matrix are the completion time for that job.

The ET matrix will have $N \times M$ entries, where N is the number of independent jobs to be scheduled and M is the number of resources which are currently available. Each job workload is measured by a million of instructions and the capacity of each resource is measured by MIPS.

The Ready time ($Ready_m$) indicates the time resource m would have finished the previously assigned jobs. The completion time of ith job on the jth machine is:

$$CT_{ij} = Ready_j + Et_{ij} \tag{3}$$

The main objective of this algorithm is to minimize the makespan. $Max_s (CT_{ij})$ is the makespan of the complete schedule. Makespan is used to measure the throughput of the grid system. The grid scheduling problem is a NP-complete problem. In general, the existing heuristic mapping can be divided in two categories. The first one is the on line mode and the other one is the batch mode. In the on line mode, the scheduler is always in ready mode. Whenever a new job arrives to the scheduler, it is immediately allocated to one of the existing resources required by that job. Each job is considered only once for matching and scheduling.

In the batch mode, the jobs and resources are collected and mapped at prescheduled time. In this mode, the algorithm makes better decisions because the scheduler knows the full details of the available jobs and resources. The proposed algorithm is also heuristic algorithm for batch mode. The result of the algorithm will have four values which are related to the task, the machine, the starting time and the expected completion time. The number of jobs available for scheduling is always greater than the available number of machines in the grid. The machine M_j's free time will be known using the function free j. The starting time of job t_i on resource M_j is:

$$B_i = free(j) + 1 \tag{4}$$

Then the new value of free(j) is the starting time plus ET_{ij}. The algorithm uses the minimization function to discover the best resource (5) and also uses the following heuristic information (6).

$$F = max [free (j)] \tag{5}$$

$$\eta_{ij} = \frac{1}{Free(j)} \tag{6}$$

Using the (6) we can find the highest priority machine which is free earlier, for this purpose we use three to four ants. Each ant starts from random resource and task. They select ET_{ij} randomly j^{th} resource and i^{th} job. All the ants are maintaining a separate list. Whenever they select the next task and resource, they are added into the list. At each iteration the ants calculate the minimize function 'Fk' and the pheromone trail updates the value.

$$\triangle Tij = \frac{1 - \rho}{F_k} \tag{7}$$

In this algorithm two sets of tasks are maintained. One is the set of scheduled tasks and the other is the set of arrived and unscheduled tasks.

The algorithm starts automatically, whenever the set of scheduled jobs becomes empty. According to Somasundaram and Radhakrishnan (2009) the machine in which the first task is performed is chosen randomly. Next, the task to be run and the machine in which it is to be run are computed by the following formula:

$$P_{ij} = \frac{T_{ij}\eta_{ij}}{\sum T_{ij}\eta_{ij}} \qquad (8)$$

where, η_{ij} is the attractiveness of the move as computed by some heuristic information indicating a prior desirability of that move. T_{ij} is the pheromone trail level of the move and indicates how profitable it has been in the past to make that particular move. Also, P_{ij}^{k} is the probability to move from a state i to a state j and depends on the combination of the above two values.

The last formula has a disadvantage because all columns in the probability matrix have the same probability value. This decides the best resource but the task is chosen to be the first non zero value of the column. We modify this disadvantage in order to overcome the probability matrix P_{ij}^{k} and use several ants. The number of ants used is less than or equal to the number of tasks. From all the possible scheduling lists we find the one having minimum makespan and use that ant's scheduling list.

At this point two kinds of ET matrices are formed. The first matrix consists of currently scheduled jobs and the second consists of jobs which have arrived but have not been scheduled. The scheduling Algorithm is executed periodically. At the time of execution it finds the list of available resources, which means the processors, in the Grid environment and start scheduling.

Scheduling Algorithm

The execution time matrix ET_{ij} of task t_i on machine m_j is defined as the amount of time taken by m_j to execute t_i. Given that m_j has no assigned t_i load. The expected completion time is CT_{ij}.

$$CT_{ij} = B_i + ET_{ij} \qquad (9)$$

where, B_i is the beginning time of t_i on machine m_j. The function free(j) returns time when the machine Mj will be free.

$$free[j] = B_i + ET_{ij} + 1 \qquad (10)$$

Use the objective function $F_k = max[free(j)]$ over the solution constructed by an ant k and added pheromone by an ant k. The result will be formatted by the following order: Task, Machine, Starting time and Ending time.

Step 1: All necessary information about the jobs n and resources m of the system in matrix ET_{mxn} are collected.

Step 2: All the initial value is set as shown in Table 1.

Step 3: We have to select the task i and resource j randomly for each ant.

Step 4: We repeat the following until all jobs are executed and calculate:

- The heuristic information (η_{ij}). Here, if a machine is free earlier then the corresponding machine will be more desirable.

$$\eta_{ij} = \frac{1}{Free(j)} \qquad (11)$$

- Current pheromone trail value, where $F_k = max[free(j)]$.

$$\triangle T_{ij} = \frac{1-\rho}{F_k} \qquad (12)$$

- Update the Pheromone Trail Matrix.

$$T_{ij} = \rho T_{ij} + \triangle T_{ij} \qquad (13)$$

○ Calculate the Probability Matrix, where η_{ij} is the attractiveness of the move computed by some heuristic information indicating a prior desirability of that move. T_{ij} is the pheromone trail level of the move, indicating how profitable it has been in the past to make that particular move and ET_{ij} is Execution Matrix.

$$P_{ij} = \frac{T_{ij}\eta_{ij}(1/ET_{ij})}{\sum T_{ij}\eta_{ij}(1/ET_{ij})} \qquad (14)$$

○ Select the task with highest probability of i and j as the next task$_i$ to be executed on the resource$_j$.

Step 5: The best feasible solution can be found by using all the ants in scheduling list.

EXPERIMENT AND RESULTS

The proposed algorithm has been implemented in our platform. Here, we present the results with the various implementations of FPLTF, DFPLTF, Sufferage, Random and an improved Ant algorithm (Fidanova & Durchova, 2006) (we call it iACO) which are compared with the proposed ACO algorithm. Different types of ET matrix using benchmark simulation model (Fidanova & Durchova, 2006) are defined in order to simulate the various heterogeneous problems. The ET matrix considers three factors: task heterogeneity,

Table 1. Parameters of proposed scheduling algorithm

Parameters	Value
ρ (pheromone evaporation value)	0.05
T_0 (pheromone deposit)	0.01
One dimensional matrix of size m	Free [0... m-1] = 0
Number of ants equal to number of tasks	$k = m$

machine heterogeneity and consistency. The task heterogeneity depends upon the various execution times of the jobs. Similarly, the machine heterogeneity depends on the running time of a particular job across all the processors.

We simulate 1000 jobs as Yan et al. (2005) did, and we focus in two problems. The first is the matrix multiplication and the second is the linear programming using the GNU Linear Programming Kit (GNU GLPK, 2009). For matrix multiplication, the size of the matrix is 500 × 500, 1000 × 1000, or 2000 × 2000. The size of each job depends on its matrix size. Take matrix size of 500 × 500 for example, we send 500 × 500 real numbers to the resource for execution and its job size is 500 × 500 × 4 bytes. For program execution time, since a straightforward matrix multiplication algorithm has a time complexity of $O(n^3)$, we use $2n^3$ (n additions plus n multiplications to obtain an entry) as the execution time estimate.

For linear programming, the size of the constraint is 200 × 200 (200 variables in 200 inequalities), 500 × 500, or 1000 × 1000. For a 200 × 200 problem, the program size is about (200 × 200 + 200) × 4 bytes. From the time complexity of ellipsoid method (Bland, Goldfarb, & Todd, 1981), we use $200n^4$ as the execution time estimate for the GNU GLPK linear programming program. The coefficient 200 stands for its complexity compared to a simple $O(n^4)$ algorithm.

When we have the same matrix size multiplication and same size linear programming we compare the number of job assignment on each resource, average execution time of jobs and the standard deviation of load of each method in the following experiments. The matrix size is the same and contains three cases: 500 × 500, 1000 × 1000 and 2000 × 2000. The linear programming sizes are also the same and include three cases: 200 × 200, 500 × 500, 1000 × 1000. Figure 3 illustrates the average execution time per job for matrix multiplication and Figure 4 shows the Linear Programming (LP) case. The proposed ACO takes less time to execute in each size of

Figure 3. Average execution time per job for same size matrix multiplication

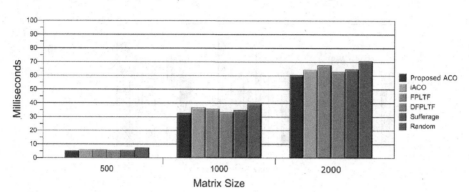

Figure 4. Average execution time per job for same size linear programming problems

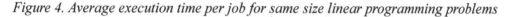
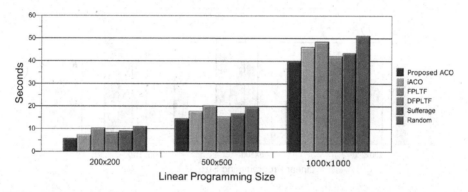

jobs than other methods. This happens because in average the proposed ACO lets the resources which have good computing power and light load execute more jobs.

We sample the load of each resource ten times during the job execution and compare the standard deviation of load of each method independently. The standard deviation is given by:

$$\sigma = \sqrt{\frac{1}{N} \sum_{i=1}^{N} (x_i - \overline{x})^2} \text{ , for all i} \qquad (15)$$

where σ is the standard deviation with the same unit as load (%), N is the number of resources, x_i is the load of resource i, and is the average load of all resources. If the standard deviation value of a method is small, it means that the difference of each load is small. The small standard deviation

tells that the load of the entire system is balanced. The lower value the standard deviation has, the more load balanced the system is. Figures 5 and 6 illustrate the standard deviation of load of each method. We can observe that the proposed ACO has the smallest value. It means that the difference of resource load is small and the resources are load balanced.

Next, we have to simulate the mixed size because there may be many different jobs in the grid and we want to know how the proposed algorithm performs in such dynamic situation. We choose again 1000 jobs for execution and set the number of each size to one third of the total number of jobs. Then, we compare the makespan and the standard deviation of load in each method.

In Figures 7 and 8 the makespan of each method with mixed sizes are illustrated. We can

Figure 5. Standard deviation of load for same size matrix multiplication

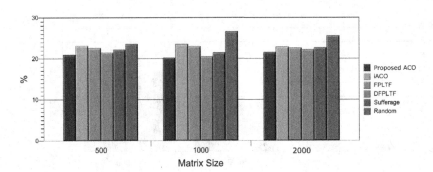

Figure 6. Standard deviation of load for same size linear programming problems

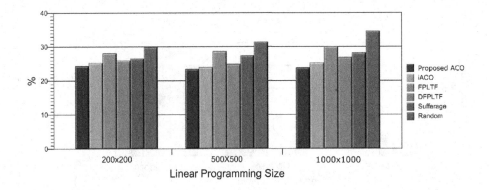

find out that the proposed ACO uses less time to complete all jobs. In the case of mixed jobs, the pheromone update functions of proposed ACO still work well. For iACO, it applies the encouragement and punishment methods. It changes each pheromone by variables defined by users and it ignores the real status of resources. If the resources with bad computing power never fail to execute jobs, they will always be encouraged and get more pheromone. Then iACO will assign more jobs to the bad resources which have higher pheromone and this will increase the total execution time of the given jobs. That is the reason why iACO has larger makespan than the proposed ACO.

The Figures 9 and 10 show the standard deviation of load in each method. In the case of mixed jobs, the proposed ACO still has the smallest standard deviation of load. Its resource selection depends on the resources status and the size

of jobs. It means that the proposed ACO considers about the real status of resources. By the results, it does balance the load of the entire system.

By the experimental results, we can easily find out the proposed ACO can achieve good system load balance in any situation and take less time to execute jobs. It means that the proposed ACO can handle different size jobs or same size jobs in grid and also keeps the system load more balanced and have better performances.

Also, from the results we conclude that iACO may have bad performances because the prediction of status of resources in the pheromone update methods may be wrong. The prediction means that it uses user-defined variables to encourage or punish resources after the assignment of jobs or the completion of jobs. It may not work sometimes when the pheromone values do not match

Figure 7. Makespan of each method with mixed sizes for matrix multiplication

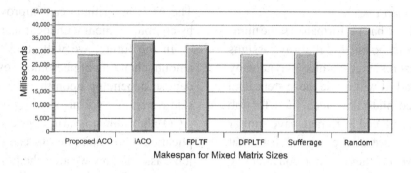

Figure 8. Makespan for linear programming with mixed sizes

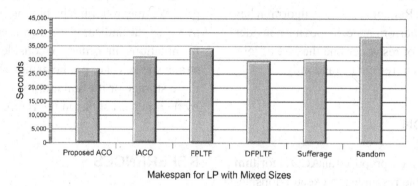

Figure 9. Standard deviation of load of each method with mixed size for matrix multiplication

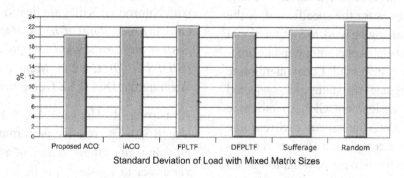

Figure 10. Standard deviation of load of each method with mixed size for linear programming

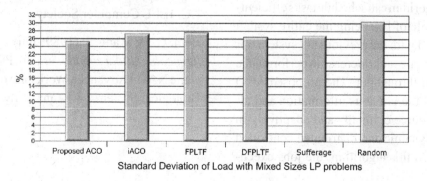

the real status of resources. So the proposed ACO can work better than iACO.

FPLTF may have bad performance if the number of hard tasks is too big and it always assigns jobs to the fastest resources, which may already have a heavy load. It will cause the system load to be unbalanced and take much time for job executions. DFPLTF and Sufferage have similar performances and are also comparable to that of BACO. However, they do not consider the bandwidth issue and assume the data is readily available in the resources, which is sometimes not true. Finally, the Random selection algorithm has the true random performance. It does not consider about the status of resources and the size of jobs and assigns jobs to resources randomly.

CONCLUSION

In this paper, we have proposed an ACO algorithm to choose suitable resources to execute jobs according to resources status and the size of given job in the Grid environment. The selection of the appropriate resources for the specific task is the one of the most challenging work in computational Grid. The local and global pheromone update functions balance the system load. Local pheromone update function updates the status of the selected resource after jobs assignment. Global pheromone update function updates the status of each resource for all jobs after the completion of a job. It offers the job scheduler the newest information of all resource for the next jobs assignment.

The experimental results show that the proposed ACO algorithm can schedule tasks efficiently and is capable of balancing the entire system load. Compared with the previous ant system our results show a noticeable increase in performance achieving high throughput. The proposed ACO algorithm uses the previous information and allocates the resource optimally and adaptively in the scalable, dynamic and distributed controlled environment. In this algorithm, the jobs execu-

tion time is the one of the major input parameter. The ACO algorithms can improve the solution by combining them with local search techniques.

In the future, we will study the automatic amount changing of pheromone evaporation and deposit depending upon the performance of the grid system. We will also try to apply the proposed ACO algorithm to various grid computing applications. For example, instead of independent jobs, assume now we are scheduling workflows. That is, there are precedent relations among jobs.

Finally, this paper focuses on the computing grid. We may redefine the pheromone procedure as far as the indicator is concerned and update formulations in order to consider the replica strategy to select or predict which resources have more storage or are suitable for file replications by their newest status in the future.

REFERENCES

Abramson, D., Giddy, J., & Kotler, L. (2000, May). High performance parametric modeling with Nimrod/G: Killer application for the global Grid. In *Proceedings of the 14th International Symposium on Parallel and Distributed Processing (IPDPS 2000),* Cancun, Mexico (pp. 520-528). Washington, DC: IEEE Computer Society.

Armstrong, R., Hensgen, D., & Kidd, T. (1998, March 30). The relative performance of various mapping algorithms is independent of sizable variances in run-time predictions. In *Proceedings of the 7th IEEE Heterogeneous Computing Workshop,* Orlando, FL (pp. 79-87). Washington, DC: IEEE Computer Society.

Beni, G., & Wang, J. (1989, June). *Swarm intelligence in cellular robotic systems.* Paper presented at the NATO Advanced Workshop on Robots and Biological Systems, Toscana, Italy.

Bland, R. G., Goldfarb, D., & Todd, M. J. (1981). Ellipsoid method, a survey. *Operations Research, 29*(6), 1039–1091. doi:10.1287/opre.29.6.1039

BOINC. (2009). *Berkeley open infrastructure for network computing*. Retrieved from http://boinc.berkeley.edu

Boyera, W. F., & Hura, G. S. (2005). Non-evolutionary algorithm for scheduling dependent tasks in distributed heterogeneous computing environments. *Journal of Parallel and Distributed Computing, 65*(9), 1035–1046. doi:10.1016/j.jpdc.2005.04.017

Buyya, R., Abramson, D., & Giddy, J. (2000, May). Nimrod/G: An architecture for a resource management and scheduling system in a global computational grid. In *Proceedings of the 4th International Conference and Exhibition on High Performance Computing,* Beijing, China (Vol. 1, pp. 283-289). Washington, DC: IEEE Computer Society.

Collins, D. E., & George, A. D. (2001). Parallel and sequential job scheduling in heterogeneous clusters, a simulation study using software in the loop. *Journal of Simulation, 77*(5), 169–184. doi:10.1177/003754970107700503

De Ronde, J. F., Schoneveld, A., & Sloot, P. M. A. (1997). Load balancing by redundant decomposition and mapping. *Journal of Future Generation Computer Systems, 12*(5), 391–407. doi:10.1016/S0167-739X(97)83341-9

Dong, F., & Akl, S. K. (2006). *Scheduling algorithms for grid computing: State of the art and open problems* (Tech. Rep. No. 2006-504). Kingston, Ontario, Canada: School of Computing, Queen's University.

Dorigo, M., & Blum, C. (2005). Ant colony optimization theory: A survey. *Theoretical Computer Science, 344*(2-3), 243–278. doi:10.1016/j.tcs.2005.05.020

Dorigo, M., & Gambardella, L. M. (1997). Ant colony system, a cooperative learning approach to the traveling salesman problem. *IEEE Transactions on Evolutionary Computation, 1*(1), 53–66. doi:10.1109/4235.585892

Dorigo, M., Maniezzo, V., & Colorni, A. (1996). The ant system, optimization by a colony of cooperating agents. *IEEE Transactions on Systems, Man, and Cybernetics, 26*(1), 29–41. doi:10.1109/3477.484436

Dorigo, M., & Stützle, T. (2003). The ant colony optimization metaheuristic: Algorithms, applications and advances. In F. Glover & G. Kochenberger (Ed.), *Handbook of metaheuristics* (pp. 251-285). Norwell, MA: Kluwer Academic Publishers.

Dowsland, K. A., & Thompson, J. M. (2005). Ant colony optimization for the examination scheduling problem. *The Journal of the Operational Research Society, 56*(4), 426–438. doi:10.1057/palgrave.jors.2601830

Du, Y., Zhang, Q., & Chen, Q. (2008, April). ACO-IH: An improved ant colony optimization algorithm for airport ground service scheduling. In *Proceedings of the IEEE International Conference on Industrial Technology (ICIT 2008),* Chengdu, China (pp. 1-6). Washington, DC: IEEE Computer Society.

Engblom, J., & Ermedahl, A. (2000, November). Modeling complex flows for worst-case execution time analysis. In *Proceedings of the 21st IEEE Real-Time Systems Symposium,* Orlando, FL (pp. 163-174). Washington, DC: IEEE Computer Society.

Feitelson, D. G. (1996, June). Packing schemes for gang scheduling. In D. G. Feitelson & L. Rudolph (Eds.), *Proceedings of the Workshop on Job Scheduling Strategies for Parallel Processing,* Padua, Italy (LNCS 1162, pp. 89-110).

Feitelson, D. G., Rudolph, L., Schwiegelshohn, U., Sevcik, K. C., & Wong, P. (1997, April). Theory and practice in parallel job scheduling. In D. G. Feitelson & L. Rudolph (Eds.), *Proceedings of the Job Scheduling Strategies for Parallel Processing,* Geneva, Switzerland (LNCS 1291, pp. 1-34).

Fidanova, S., & Durchova, M. (2006, June 6-10). Ant algorithm for grid scheduling problem. In I. Lirkov, S. Margenov, & J. Wa'sniewski (Eds.), *Large Scale Scientific Computing: 5th International Conference, LSSC 2005,* Sozopol, Bulgaria (LNCS 3743, pp. 405-412).

Foster, I., & Kesselman, C. (Eds.). (2003). *The grid 2 blueprint for a new computing infrastructure.* San Francisco: Morgan Kaufmann Publishers.

Freund, R. F., & Siegel, H. J. (1993). Guest editor's introduction: Heterogeneous processing. *Computer, 26*(6), 13–17.

GNU GLPK. (2009). *GNU linear programming kit.* Retrieved from http://www.gnu.org/software/glpk

Graham, R. L. (1966). Bounds for certain multiprocessing anomalies. *The Bell System Technical Journal, 45,* 1563–1581.

Grasse, P. P. (1959). La reconstruction du nid et les coordinations inter-individuelles chez bellicoitermes natalenis et cubitermes sp. La theorie de la stigmergie: essai d'interpretation des termites constructeurs. *Insectes Sociaux, 6,* 41–84. doi:10.1007/BF02223791

HellasGrid. (2009). *Greek grid project official portal site.* Retrieved from http://www.hellasgrid.gr

Ibarra, O. H., & Kim, C. E. (1977). Heuristic algorithms for scheduling independent tasks on nonidentical processors. *Journal of the ACM, 24*(2), 280–289. doi:10.1145/322003.322011

Karatza, H. D., & Hilzer, R. C. (2003). Parallel job scheduling in homogeneous distributed systems. *Journal of Simulation, 79*(5-6), 287–298. doi:10.1177/0037549703037148

Kondo, D., Anderson, D. P., & McLeod, J. (2007, December). Performance evaluation of scheduling policies for volunteer computing. In *Proceedings of the 3rd IEEE International Conference on e-Science and Grid Computing,* Bangalore, India (pp. 415-422). Washington, DC: IEEE Computer Society.

Krallmann, J., Schwiegelshohn, U., & Yahyapour, R. (1999, April 16). On the design and evaluation of job scheduling algorithms. In D. G. Feitelson & L. Rudolph (Eds.), *Proceedings of the 5th Workshop on Job Scheduling Strategies for Parallel Processing,* San Juan, Puerto Rico (LNCS 1659, pp. 17–42).

Lorpunmanee, S., Sap, M. N., Abdullah, A. H., & Inwai, C. C. (2007). An ant colony optimization for dynamic job scheduling in grid environment. *Proceedings of World Academy of Science: Engineering and Technology, 23,* 314–321.

Maghraoui, K. E. (2006). The internet operating system middleware for adaptive distributed computing. *International Journal of High Performance Computing Applications, 20*(4), 467–480. doi:10.1177/1094342006068411

Maheswaran, M., Ali, S., Siegel, H. J., Hensgen, D., & Freund, R. F. (1999). Dynamic mapping of a class of independent tasks onto heterogeneous computing systems. *Journal of Parallel and Distributed Computing, 59*(2), 107–131. doi:10.1006/jpdc.1999.1581

Menasce, D. A., Saha, D., Porto, D. S. C., Almeida, V. A. F., & Tripathi, S. K. (1995). Static and dynamic processor scheduling disciplines in heterogeneous parallel architectures. *Journal of Parallel and Distributed Computing, 28*(1), 1–18. doi:10.1006/jpdc.1995.1085

Nabrzyski, J., Schopf, J. M., & Weglarz, J. (2004). *Grid resource management state of the art and future trends.* New York: Springer.

Nelson, R., Towsley, D., & Tantawi, A. N. (1988). Performance analysis of parallel processing systems. *IEEE Transactions on Software Engineering, 14*(4), 532–540. doi:10.1109/32.4676

Paranhos, D., Cirne, W., & Brasileiro, F. (2003, August 26-29). Trading cycles for information using replication to schedule bag-of-tasks applications on computational grids. In H. Kosch, L. Böszörményi, & H. Hellwagner (Eds.), *Euro-Par 2003 Parallel Processing: 9th International Euro-Par Conference,* Klagenfurt, Austria (LNCS 2790, pp. 169-180).

Park, C. Y. (1993). Predicting program execution times by analyzing static and dynamic program paths. *Real-Time Systems, 5*(1), 31–62. doi:10.1007/BF01088696

Pinedo, M. L. (2008). *Scheduling theory, algorithms and systems.* New York: Springer.

Rashid, M. M., & Akhtar, M. N. (2006). A new multilevel CPU scheduling algorithm. *Journal of Applied Sciences, 6*(9), 2036–2039. doi:10.3923/jas.2006.2036.2039

Salari, E., & Eshghi, K. (2005, December). An ACO algorithm for graph coloring problem. In *Proceedings of the 2005 ICSC Congress on Computational Intelligence Methods and Applications,* Istanbul, Turkey (pp. 15-17). Washington, DC: IEEE Computer Society.

Singh, H., & Youssef, A. (1996, April). Mapping and scheduling heterogeneous task graphs using genetic algorithms. In Proceedings of the *5th IEEE Heterogeneous Computing Workshop,* (pp. 86-97). Washington, DC: IEEE Computer Society.

Somasundaram, K., & Radhakrishnan, S. (2009). Task resource allocation in grid using swift scheduler. *International Journal of Computers, Communications & Control, 4*(2), 158–166.

Sonmez, O. O., & Gursoy, A. (2007). A novel economic-based scheduling heuristic for computational grids. *International Journal of High Performance Computing Applications, 21*(1), 21–29. doi:10.1177/1094342006074849

Stappert, F., & Altenbernd, P. (2000). Complete worst-case execution time analysis of straight-line hard real-time programs. *Journal of Systems Architecture, 46*(4), 339–355. doi:10.1016/S1383-7621(99)00010-7

Thangavel, K., Karnan, M., Jeganathan, P., Petha, A. I., Sivakumar, R., & Geetharamani, G. (2006). Ant colony algorithms in diverse combinational optimization problems - a survey. *International Journal on Automatic Control and System Engineering, 6*(1), 7–26.

The Globus Alliance. (2009). *Globus toolkit v4.* Retrieved from http://www.globus.org/toolkit/downloads/4.2.1

Van den Akker, J. M., Hoogeveen, J. A., & Van Kempen, J. W. (2006, September 11-13). Parallel machine scheduling through column generation: Minimax objective functions. In Y. Azar & T. Erlebach (Eds.), *Algorithms – ESA 2006: Proceedings of the 14th Conference on Annual European Symposium,* Zurich, Switzerland (LNCS 4168, pp. 648-659).

Wang, L., Siegel, H. J., Roychowdhury, V. P., & Maciejewski, A. A. (1997). Task matching and scheduling in heterogeneous computing environments using a genetic algorithm-based approach. *Journal of Parallel and Distributed Computing, 47*(1), 8–22. doi:10.1006/jpdc.1997.1392

Xu, Z., Hou, X., & Sun, J. (2003, May). Ant algorithm based task scheduling in grid computing. In *Proceedings of the IEEE Canadian Conference Electrical and Computer Engineering (CCECE 2003),* Montréal, Quebec, Canada (Vol. 2, pp. 1107-1110). Washington, DC: IEEE Computer Society.

Xu, Z., Lu, E., & Sun, J. (2004, December 7-10). An extendable grid simulation environment based on gridsim. In M. Li, X-H. Sun, Q. Deng, & J. Ni (Eds.), *Grid and Cooperative Computing: Second International Workshop, GCC 2003,* Shanhai, China (LNCS 3032, pp. 205-208).

Yan, H., Qin, X., Li, X., & Wu, M. H. (2005, August). An improved ant algorithm for job scheduling in grid computing. In *Proceedings of 2005 International Conference on Machine Learning and Cybernetics,* Guangzhou, China (Vol. 5, pp. 2957-2961). Washington, DC: IEEE Computer Society.

Yan, H., Wang, S. S., Wang, S. C., & Chang, C. P. (2009, December). Towards a hybrid load balancing policy in grid computing system. *Expert Systems with Applications, 36*(10), 12054–12064. doi:10.1016/j.eswa.2009.03.001

Zhang, X., & Tang, L. (2005, December). CT-ACO-hybridizing ant colony optimization with cycle transfer search for the vehicle routing problem. In *Proceedings of the Congress on Computational Intelligence Methods and Applications,* Istanbul, Turkey (pp. 6). doi: 10.1109/CIMA.2005.1662313.

Zhang, Y., Sun, W., & Inoguchi, Y. (2008). Predict task running time in grid environments based on CPU load predictions. *Future Generation Computer Systems, 24*(6), 489–497. doi:10.1016/j.future.2007.07.003

This work was previously published in International Journal of Grid and High Performance Computing, Volume 2, Issue 1, edited by Emmanuel Udoh, pp. 34-50, copyright 2010 by IGI Publishing (an imprint of IGI Global).

Chapter 3
Evaluating Heuristics for Scheduling Dependent Jobs in Grid Computing Environments

Geoffrey Falzon
Brunel University, UK

Maozhen Li
Brunel University, UK

ABSTRACT

Job scheduling plays a critical role in the utilisation of grid resources by mapping a number of jobs to grid resources. However, the heterogeneity of grid resources adds some challenges to the work of job scheduling, especially when jobs have dependencies which can be represented as Direct Acyclic Graphs (DAGs). It is widely recognised that scheduling m jobs to n resources with an objective to achieve a minimum makespan has shown to be NP-complete, requiring the development of heuristics. Although a number of heuristics are available for job scheduling optimisation, selecting the best heuristic to use in a given grid environment remains a difficult problem due to the fact that the performance of each original heuristic is usually evaluated under different assumptions. This paper evaluates 12 representative heuristics for dependent job scheduling under one set of common assumptions. The results are presented and analysed, which provides an even basis in comparison of the performance of those heuristics. To facilitate performance evaluation, a DAG simulator is implemented which provides a set of tools for DAG job configuration, execution, and monitoring. The components of the DAG simulator are also presented in this paper.

DOI: 10.4018/978-1-4666-0056-0.ch003

INTRODUCTION

The past few years have witnessed a rapid development of grid computing systems and applications (Li & Baker, 2005). A grid is a heterogeneous computing environment in that resources may have various computing capacities. Job scheduling which is a process of mapping jobs to resources plays a crucial role in resource utilisation in grid environments. Jobs can be generally classified into two classes - independent jobs and dependent jobs. The problem of scheduling m jobs to n resources with an objective to minimise the total execution time (makespan) has been shown to be NP-complete requiring the development of heuristics (Ibarra & Kim, 1977). Braun et al (Braun et al., 2001) evaluated eleven heuristics for mapping independent tasks to heterogeneous computing environments which helps select the best heuristic to use in a given environment. Mapping dependent jobs to heterogeneous computing environments such as grids poses more challenges in that the dependencies of jobs have to be taken into account in the scheduling process.

Jobs with dependent tasks can be represented by Directed Acyclic Graphs (DAGs) in which each node represents an executable task and each directed edge represents data transfers between two tasks. We assume that DAGs always have a single entry node (i.e., a node with no parents) and a single exit node (i.e., a node with no children). To compute a schedule in grid environments, scheduling algorithms require the following information:

- Information on computing resources available in a grid environment.
- An Expected Completion Time (ECT) matrix in which the expected time to execute a task on each machine is provided.
- The network bandwidth of the communication link connecting any two computers.

This paper evaluates 12 heuristics for scheduling dependent jobs in grid environments. To fa-

cilitate performance evaluation, a DAG simulator is implemented which provides a set of tools for DAG job configuration, execution and monitoring. The following assumptions are made when scheduling a job with a number of dependent tasks:

- A computer can execute only one task at a time.
- Task execution can only start after all data required by the task is available.
- Data transfer can only begin when a task is completed.
- Data transfer is scheduled according to the order of the tasks requiring the data. This is referred to as in-order scheduling (Wang, Siegel, Roychowdhury, & Maciejewski, 1997).
- A computer can transfer only one set of data at a time. Data transfer and task execution can be performed in parallel.
- Task execution and data transfer are non-pre-emptive.
- Task execution is computed according to the order defined by a scheduler.
- An ECT matrix is provided. This can be generated by dividing the workload of a job by the MIPS rating of the processor where the job is executed.
- For list scheduling heuristics (Sih & Lee, 1993; Topcuoglu, Hariri, & Wu, 2002), partial makespan (the time required to execute the first n jobs in the workflow) is calculated by ignoring data transfer to jobs that are not yet scheduled.

The remainder of the paper is organised as follows. It briefly describes the twelve heuristics used in the evaluation, and presents the components of the DAG simulator for DAG jobs configuration, execution and monitoring. Then it evaluates the 12 heuristics and analyses the performance results. Finally it concludes the paper.

HEURISTICS FOR SCHEDULING DEPENDENT JOBS

The 12 heuristics that were evaluated are Min-min (Maheswaran, Ali, Siegel, Hensgen, & Freund, 1999), Max-min (Maheswaran et al., 1999), Sufferage (Maheswaran et al., 1999), XSufferage (Casanova, Legrand, Zagorodnov, & Berman, 2000), Baseline (Maheswaran & Siegel, 1998), Levelised Min-Time (LMT) (Iverson, Ozguner, & Follen, 1995), Min-FINISH (Alhusaini, Prasanna, & Raghavendra, 1999), Max-FINISH (Alhusaini et al., 1999), Heterogeneous Earliest Finish Time (HEFT) (Topcuoglu et al., 2002), Critical-Path-on-a-Processor (CPOP) (Topcuoglu et al., 2002), Performance Effective Task Scheduling (PETS) (Ilavarasan & Thambidurai, 2007) and Genetic Algorithms (GAs) (Braun et al., 1999; Hou, Ansari, & Ren, 1994; Shroff, Watson, Flann, & Freund, 1996; Singh & Youssef, 1996; Spooner, Cao, Jarvis, He, & Nudd, 2005). For the purpose of performance comparison, a Random algorithm was also implemented and evaluated. This section briefly describes the implementation of these algorithms for scheduling jobs with dependent tasks.

Min-Min

Min-min begins with set U of unscheduled tasks and set S of schedulable tasks (i.e., unscheduled tasks whose predecessor tasks were executed). The set M of minimum completion times for each task in S on all machines is then calculated. The task with the overall minimum completion time from M is selected and assigned to the machine that provides the earliest task completion time. The newly scheduled task is removed from U and S is updated by computing the list of schedulable tasks in U. The process is repeated until all tasks are scheduled (i.e., U is empty).

Max-Min

Similar to Min-min, Max-min also begins with set U of unscheduled tasks and set S of schedulable tasks. The set M of minimum completion times for each task in S on all machines is then calculated. Max-min selects the task with the maximum completion time from M and assigns it to the machine that minimises task completion time. The newly scheduled task is removed from U and S is computed. The process is repeated until all tasks are scheduled (i.e., U is empty).

Sufferage

The Sufferage value of a task is the difference between the task earliest completion time and its second earliest completion time. Sufferage algorithm operates in a similar way to Min-Min algorithm, except for the fact that in each iteration the task with maximum Sufferage is scheduled on the machine that results in minimum task completion time. The rationale behind Sufferage is to give priority to tasks that would "suffer" most in terms of task completion time if the task is not assigned to a particular machine.

XSufferage

XSufferage is an extension of the Sufferage algorithm on a cluster level. The XSufferage value of a task is the difference between the task earliest completion time and its second earliest completion time in a different site. Similar to Sufferage, XSufferage chooses the schedulable task with maximum XSufferage for scheduling and assigns the task to the resource that minimises task completion time. The rationale behind XSufferage is that if a file is required by some task and is already present at a remote cluster, the task would "suffer" if not assigned to a host in that cluster.

Baseline (BL)

The BL algorithm first groups tasks according to levels such that each level contains a set of independent tasks. This is performed as follows:

- Root tasks are at level 0
- Each task in level *n* has parent tasks belonging to level *0* to *n-1* and at least 1 task in level *n-1*.

Tasks at the same level are then ordered in descending order of number of data items each task produces (ties are broken arbitrarily). The schedule is defined using the above task prioritisation and machine assignment is performed such that task completion time is minimised.

Levelised Min-Time (LMT)

The LMT algorithm first groups tasks according to level as in BL algorithm. Average task execution time across all machines is then calculated, from which the level-average execution time is determined (the average execution time of all tasks in a given level). The task average execution time for tasks having their closest child task not in the next level is then deducted by the level-average execution time of the levels in between. Tasks are then scheduled in the order defined by level (lowest first) and updated average execution time (highest first). Machine assignment is performed to minimise task completion time. The rationale behind LMT is to give priority to tasks that would affect execution of child-tasks if delayed.

Min-FINISH

The Min-FINISH algorithm is a level-by-level version of the Min-min algorithm. Tasks are first grouped by level and then tasks in the same level are scheduled using the same technique as in Min-min algorithm.

Max-FINISH

The Max-FINISH algorithm is a level-by-level version of the Max-min algorithm. Tasks are first grouped by level and then tasks in the same level are scheduled using the same technique as in Max-Min algorithm.

Heterogeneous Earliest Finish Time (HEFT)

The HEFT algorithm ranks tasks based on the upward rank ($rank_u$) of a task which is recursively defined as shown in Box 1.

$rank_u$ is equivalent to calculating the latest task finish time using expected completion time (ECT) averaged on all grid nodes and average bandwidth for data transfer time. $rank_u$ is calculated recursively starting from exit tasks and traversing the graph upwards. Tasks are then ordered in descending order of upward rank. This order provides a topological sorted order of tasks (Topcuoglu et al., 2002). Tasks are then assigned to the machine that achieves the minimum task completion time. The HEFT algorithm has an insertion-based policy that allows tasks to be scheduled in an earliest idle time slot between 2 already scheduled

Box 1.

$$rank_u\left(n_i\right) = \overline{w_i} + \max_{n_j \in succ(n_i)}\left(\overline{c_{ij}} + rank_u\left(n_j\right)\right)$$

$where\ \overline{w_i} = average\ task\ exec\ time$

$\overline{c_{ij}} = average\ data\ transfer\ time$

tasks (provided that this does not break task precedence rules). The HEFT algorithm implemented does not utilise the insertion-based policy.

Critical-Path-on-a-Processor (CPOP)

The CPOP algorithm prioritises tasks by first calculating the upward rank ($rank_u$) and the downward rank ($rank_d$) for all tasks using average ECTs on all machines and average communication time (calculated using the mean of bandwidth) (see also Box 2):

$$rank_d\left(n_i\right) = \max_{n_j \in pred(n_i)}\left(rank_d\left(n_j\right) + \overline{w_j} + \overline{c_{ji}}\right)$$

Rank of task n_i is calculated as follows:

$$rank\left(n_i\right) = rank_u\left(n_i\right) + rank_d\left(n_i\right)$$

The critical path is computed by first selecting the root task and then traversing the DAG by selecting the task with the highest rank (ties are broken by selecting the first immediate successor) until the exit task is reached. The critical-path processor is then identified by evaluating the machine that minimises the execution time of the critical path. During the processor selection phase, the CPOP algorithm maintains a list of schedulable tasks and the task with the highest rank is scheduled. Critical tasks are assigned to the critical path, while non-critical tasks are assigned to the machine that minimises task completion time.

Performance Effective Task Scheduling (PETS)

The PETS algorithm starts by determining task level. Task rank is then calculated as follows:

$$\text{Average Computation Cost ACC}\left(v_i\right) =$$
$$\sum_{j=1}^{m}\frac{w_{i,j}}{m} \ where \ w_{i,j} = exec \ time \ of \ t_i \ on \ m_j$$

$$\text{Data Transfer Cost DTC}\left(v_i\right) = \sum_{j=1}^{n}c_{i,j}$$
$$where \ c_{i,j} = j^{th} \ data \ transfer \ from \ t_i$$

$$\text{Rank of Predecessor Task RPT}\left(v_i\right) =$$
$$\max\left\{rank\left(v_p\right)\right\} \ where \ v_p \in pred\left(v_i\right)$$

$$rank\left(v_i\right) =$$
$$round\left\{\text{ACC}\left(v_i\right) + DTC\left(v_i\right) + RPT\left(v_i\right)\right\}$$

Tasks are then scheduled by levels (lowest first) and ranks (highest first). Machines assigned in such a way that the completion time of tasks is minimised.

Genetic Algorithm (GA)

GAs are adaptive heuristic search algorithms which can be used to find approximate solutions

Box 2.

$$rank_u\left(n_i\right) = \overline{w_i} + \max_{n_j \in succ(n_i)}\left(\overline{c_{ij}} + rank_u\left(n_j\right)\right)$$
$$where \ \overline{w_i} = average \ task \ exec \ time$$

$$\overline{c_{ij}} = average \ data \ transfer \ time$$

to optimisation and search problems for large search spaces. The implementation of a GA usually involves problem representation (genetic representation and fitness function), GA Operators (selection, crossover and mutation) and termination function.

Genetic representation translates a candidate solution into a fixed size array of bits. In biological terms, this is also known as a chromosome. A fitness function provides a value of goodness or fitness for a given chromosome. The fitness function used for scheduling is makespan (or total execution time).

Selection refers to the technique used to select the chromosomes that will participate to the next generation. In most cases, the probability of a chromosome participating in the next generation is dependent on the fitness value. Roulette Wheel Selection combined with Elitism was used for the Classical GA implementation.

Crossover consists of exchanging genetic material between 2 chromosomes to generate the next generation chromosome. The most common technique is the single-point crossover, where a crossover point is chosen and the data beyond the crossover point is exchanged between the 2 parents. Crossover is applied according to the crossover probability (crossover rate) and is usually between 0.6 and 1.0. If elitism is not used, a high value of crossover rate can result in loosing good candidate solutions.

Mutation is analogous to biological mutation and is used to maintain genetic diversity from one generation of a population of chromosomes to the next. Mutation can be performed by either mutating the scheduling part or the matching part of the chromosome.

Termination is the criteria used to determine whether the solution evaluated is sufficient. Typical criteria used are:

- A solution is found that satisfies the minimum criteria
- Fixed number of generations is reached

- The GA search has converged to a solution.
- No improvement in best fitness over a specified number of generations.
- Guided operators (Han & Kendall, 2003).

The classical GA implemented in this work terminates when a fixed number of generations is reached or no improvement in best fitness over a specified number of generations can be made.

Random

The Random algorithm is implemented in the following way:

- Maintaining two lists: T_S (schedule – initialized to ø) and T_L (job list - initialized with all jobs).
- Randomly selecting a job from T_L and removing it from T_L.
- Identifying the range in which the job can be inserted to maintain precedence constraints by locating the last predecessor and the first successor.
- Choosing the location at random within the range defined and updating T_S accordingly.
- The process is repeated until T_L is ø.

DAG SIMULATOR

In order to evaluate the 12 heuristics listed previously, a DAG simulator has been implemented using Java programming language. The DAG simulator has a number of components which is shown in Figure 1.

testDAG

To support the development of DAG related algorithms and to visually evaluate workflows, a Java based GUI was developed as shown in Figure 2. DAG files are defined in XML which is compatible with GVF/Royère[1]. Using the GUI, it is possible to create random DAGs and to modify DAGs as

Figure 1. The components of the DAG simulator

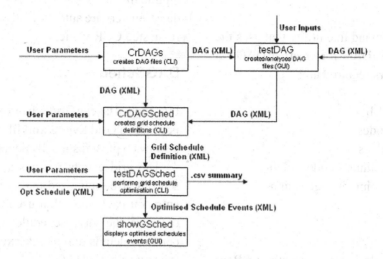

required. To support changes, functionality for performing topological sorting, cyclic testing and critical path analysis is available.

Random DAGs are created based on the technique as described by Maheswaran and Siegel (1998). The algorithm creates a |G| x |S| dependency matrix (where S is the set of subtasks and G is the set of data transfer). Edges are created such that all source nodes are always to the left of destination nodes. This guarantees that the graph is acyclic and avoids computationally expensive cyclic testing.

Figure 2. testDAG GUI

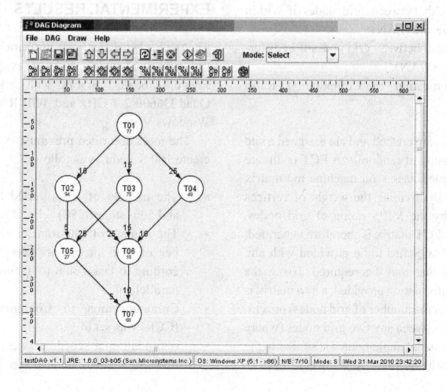

CrDAGs

CrDAGS is a command line utility that uses the same objects as testDAG for creating DAGs at random. Parameters required are:

- Task Name Label
- Number of nodes
- Number of edges
- Maximum/minimum node weight
- Maximum/minimum edge weight

CrDAGSched

CrDAGSched was designed to transform a Random Generated DAG into a schedule definition (to be used by DAGSched). Parameters required to define a schedule are:

- Input (DAG xml) and output XML file names.
- Number of grid nodes
- Maximum/minimum MIPS rating
- Number of Sites
- Bandwidth between grid nodes if within the same site (LAN)
- Bandwidth between grid nodes if in different sites (WAN).
- Communication to Computation Ratio (CCR).

Grid nodes are created and are assigned a site and MIPS rating at random. An ECT (estimate time to complete task t_i on machine m_j) matrix is generated by dividing the weight of vertices (workload) by the MIPS rating of grid nodes. A consistent ECT matrix is therefore generated, but allows DAGSched to be provided with any type of data that may be required. Using the bandwidth information provided, a $n \times n$ matrix is generated (n is the number of grid nodes) providing data rate between any two grid nodes (where $a_{ij} = a_{ji}$). The concept implemented is similar to the crossbar switch described by Wang et al. (1997).

Optionally, if a CCR value is provided, then the data transfers are automatically adjusted to fit the requested CCR value.

DAGSched

DAGSched takes a GridSched xml file as input and produces a Grid Events xml file as output. Figure 3 shows typical results displayed by DAGSched.

The grid events file has a copy of the grid schedule to be optimised and one GridSchedEvents entry for each algorithm used by DAGSched to optimise the Grid schedule. GridSchedEvents contains details about task executions and data transfer events. DAGSched is also able to read an optimised schedule definition XML file which provides the list of tasks in a topological sorted order and their respective grid node assignment. DAGSched would then determine the respective schedule events and write the schedule events to the output XML file. Grid schedule events can be analysed using showGSched.

EXPERIMENTAL RESULTS

The twelve heuristics were implemented in Java programming language and were evaluated using Java 6.0 Update 3 on a PC with an Intel Core 2 Quad Q6600 2.4 GHz and 4GB RAM running Windows Vista.

The tools described previously were used to create 100 Schedules as follows:

- The number of tasks varied between 50 and 500 (steps of 50)
- The number of data transfer and the number of grid processors were varied according to task count to achieve adequate parallelism.
- Communication to Computation Ratio (CCR) was set to 1.
- 600 additional schedules were created by updating the data transfer size in the origi-

Figure 3. DAGSched output

```
JAVA GridSched and GA Tests
===============================

Start Execution: Sun 18 May 2008 21:37:36.421

   Input XML File: Sched.N50E75GN7.xml
  Output XML File: Opt.Sched.N50E75GN7.xml
            Tasks: 50
    Data Transfer: 75
         GridNodes: 7
   XML parse time:   0s 563ms

       SchedFromFile:   0s 235ms   Makespan: 6373.0
         RandomSched:   0s 156ms   Makespan: 96465.66
              MinMin:   0s 344ms   Makespan: 16151.77
           Sufferage:   0s 109ms   Makespan: 20466.69
          XSufferage:   0s 109ms   Makespan: 31939.00
            BaseLine:   0s  16ms   Makespan: 14673.33
                 LMT:   0s  16ms   Makespan: 15345.02
           MinFINISH:   0s  31ms   Makespan: 13253.49
           MaxFINISH:   0s  15ms   Makespan: 19776.51
                HEFT:   0s   0ms   Makespan: 41134.55
                CPOP:   0s  47ms   Makespan: 42613.66
                PETS:   0s   0ms   Makespan: 15699.53
            GAClassic:   9s 125ms   Makespan: 19805.34   [ 139]
256/5000/50/HypeMutDisa/5/3.0/0.03/0.8/0.2/0.2/SelRouWhl/0.0
            GAClassic:   2s  94ms   Makespan: 6914.88    [ 367]
256/5000/50/HypeMutDisa/5/3.0/0.03/0.8/0.2/0.2/SelRouWhl/0.0

Total Exec time: 12s 625ms  13s 548ms

End Execution: Sun 18 May 2008 21:37:49.281
```

nal schedules to achieve CCR values of 0.01, 0.1, 0.5, 2, 10 and 100.

The parameters for the Classical GA (called GAClassic) algorithm implemented were determined from experimentation and are shown in Table 1. Various normalisation functions are found in literature (Ilavarasan & Thambidurai, 2007; Topcuoglu et al., 2002; Zhang, Koelbel, & Kennedy, 2007). To be able to compare results across different schedules, results were normalised by dividing with the best result attained. Algorithm performance was evaluated based on:

- Normalised makespan - obtained by dividing makespan by the smallest makespan achieved for the given schedule
- Good count - the count of schedule optimisation results that have a makespan within

10% of the best schedule (i.e., normalised makespan less than 1.10)
- Best count - the count of schedule optimisation results that achieved the best makespan for the given schedule
- Algorithm execution time

Table 1. GA parameters

Generation Size	256
Elite Rate	0.032
Crossover Rate	0.80
Mutation Rate (Schedule)	0.20
Mutation Rate (Match)	0.20
Selection Criteria	Roulette Wheel
Maximum Iteration	5000
Converging Criteria	50

Figure 4 shows average normalised makespan and 95% range for all schedules (CCR ranging from 0.01 to 100); while Figure 5 shows average normalised makespan and 95% range for schedules with CCR of 0.1.

There is a substantial increase in makespan variation for schedules with CCR higher than 0.1 and this explains the difference in the 95% ranges. The variations in average normalised makespan and standard deviation over the range of CCR tested (random algorithm was excluded to improve readability) are show in Figure 6 and Figure 7 respectively.

It is noted that Min-min, BL, LMT and PETS produce consistent results when CCR is varied from 0.01 to 100. On the other hand, Max-min, Sufferage, XSufferage, Min-FINISH, Max-FINISH, HEFT, CPOP and GA do not perform well for scheduling DAG jobs with CCR greater than 1.

Figure 4. Average normalised makespan (95% range) for all schedules

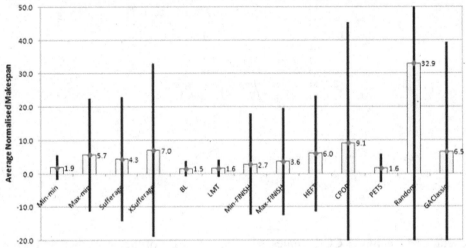

Figure 5. The average of normalised makespan (95% range) for CCR=0.1

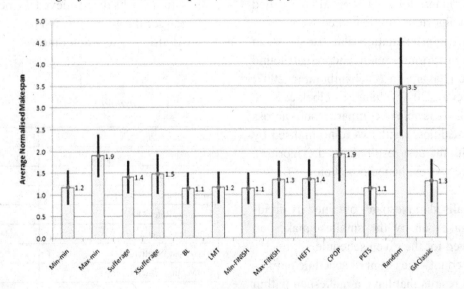

Figure 6. Average normalised makespan variations with different CCRs

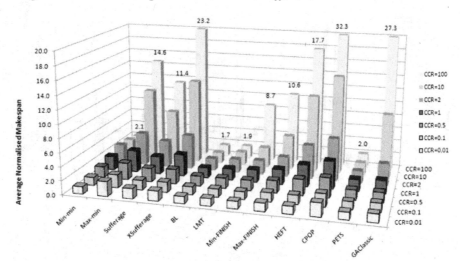

Figure 7. Standard deviation variations with different CCRs

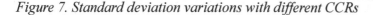

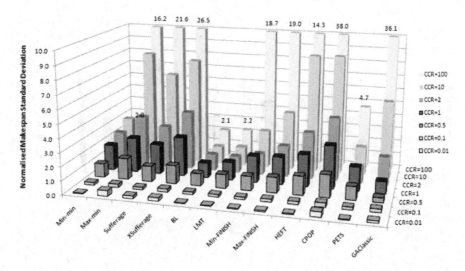

Figure 8 and Figure 9 show the Good Count and Best Count obtained from each heuristic in the range of CCR varied from 0.01 to 100. A poor performance can be observed for Max-Min, Sufferage, XSufferage, Max-FINISH, HEFT and CPOP. Min-min, BL, LMT and PETS achieve good results, whereas both Min-FINISH and GA obtain inconsistent results.

It is noted that the performance of PETS heuristic in terms of Best Count improves with an increase in CCR values. The performance of both

BL and LMT does not change with an increase in CCR values.

Since the results obtained from the GA were not repeatable, GA was executed 4 times per schedule. For this reason, the probability of achieving the best result is higher (invariant for Good Count) and superior results were observed in terms of Best Count (Figure 8).

Figure 10 shows the average execution times of the heuristics which are summarised below:

Figure 8. Good count variations with different CCRs

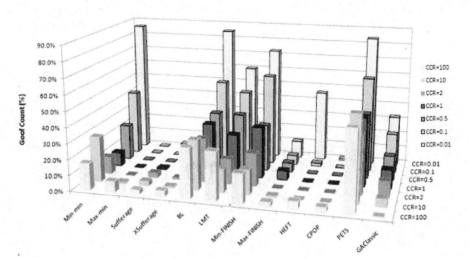

Figure 9. Best count variations with different CCRs

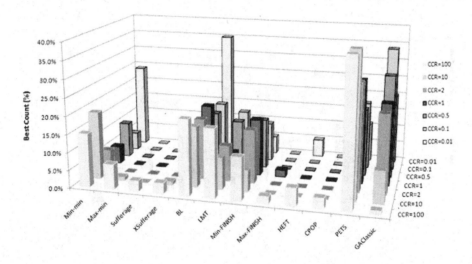

- Workflow level scheduling heuristics (heuristics that take into account the whole workflow when performing scheduling) BL (0.3s), LMT (0.3s), HEFT (0.3s), CPOP (0.3s), PETS (0.3s) have the best execution performance.
- Task Level scheduling heuristics (perform scheduling decisions based only on the information about a task or a set of independent tasks) Min-min (5.7s), Max-min (2.2s), Sufferage (4.5s), XSufferage (4.1s),

Min-FINISH (3.8s) and Max-FINISH (3.9s) cover the middle range of execution time.
- GA (11.8s) execution time is the highest due to its complexity in computation.

An important point to highlight is the difference in average execution time for Min-min and Max-min (5.7s and 2.2s respectively). The two algorithms have a complexity of $O(vgm)$ (Yu, Buyya, & Ramamohanarao, 2008) (where v is the

Figure 10. The complexities of the heuristics

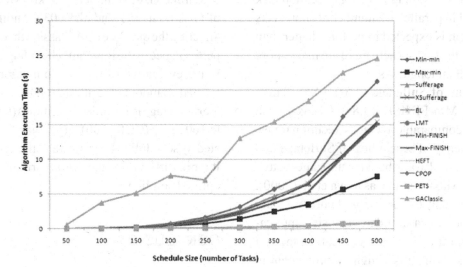

number of tasks, m is the number of machines and g is an average number of schedulable tasks to be evaluated per iteration) and their implementation is also similar. The difference in execution time is due to a different value of g that is amplified by the computational complexity of evaluating partial workflow makespan. This is demonstrated by the example in Figure 11, which illustrates the scheduling differences between Min-min and Max-min heuristics, in which g for Min-min and Max-min is 3.2 and 2.1 respectively. Max-min schedules tasks with maximum task finish time and results in a schedule that tries to move along

branches, thus resulting in a lower average number of schedulable tasks (g).

The early scheduling of tasks also explains the inefficiency of Max-min heuristic in relation to Min-min. This is confirmed by the improved results obtained by Max-FINISH (levelled version of Max-min) when compared to Max-min, since task levelling does not allow the effect of scheduling tasks by branching as in Max-min. The results obtained by Min-min and Max-min are in-line with those published in Braun et al. (2001) and Casanova et al. (2000) for dependent and independent task scheduling. Max-min could have

Figure 11. A comparison of Min-min and Max-min

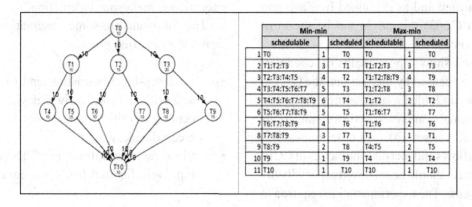

	Min-min			Max-min	
	schedulable	scheduled		schedulable	scheduled
1	T0	1	T0	T0	1	T0
2	T1:T2:T3	3	T1	T1:T2:T3	3	T3
3	T2:T3:T4:T5	4	T2	T1:T2:T8:T9	4	T9
4	T3:T4:T5:T6:T7	5	T3	T1:T2:T8	3	T8
5	T4:T5:T6:T7:T8:T9	6	T4	T1:T2	2	T2
6	T5:T6:T7:T8:T9	5	T5	T1:T6:T7	3	T7
7	T6:T7:T8:T9	4	T6	T1:T6	2	T6
8	T7:T8:T9	3	T7	T1	1	T1
9	T8:T9	2	T8	T4:T5	2	T5
10	T9	1	T9	T4	1	T4
11	T10	1	T10	T10	1	T10

an improved scheduling if a long execution task is processed in parallel to a number of short tasks and Max-Min is expected to perform better than Min-Min in the cases where there are many more short tasks than long tasks.

Both pairs of Sufferage (4.5s) / XSufferage (4.1s) and Min-FINISH (3.8s) / Max-Finish (3.9s) have comparable average execution times. The inefficiency of scheduling of Sufferage and XSufferage are also attributed to the same factors as those for Max-min. In Casanova et al. (2000), it is claimed that the Sufferage heuristic could perform worst in case of data intensive applications in a multi-cluster environment. In the test cases analysed, there is a slight improvement in Good Results and Best Results for schedules with CCR of 10 and 100.

The performance of CPOP is comparable to Max-min heuristic. Computing the critical path using CPOP rank definition and assigning it to the critical-path processor is not sufficient, since the lack of data transfer on the critical path changes the workflow and also the critical path. The rank of a task is in relation to the rank of its child tasks and therefore a task with a high rank has a child-task with a high rank. This results in a branching effect similar to what was observed for Max-min heuristic and is considered as another factor that contributes to a low quality of schedules produced by CPOP.

HEFT does not perform well. This could be due to the fact that HEFT calculates ranks using the mean value of task execution time and communication time and as explained by Zhao and Sakellariou (2003) this might not be the most efficient choice.

GAClassic shows a poor quality of schedules. This could be caused by the fact that the GA parameters used in Table 1 were determined based on the experimental results of workflows with 50 jobs and the CCR was set to 0.1. In order to evaluate larger workflows and increase the values of CCR, GA parameters should be reviewed especially the generation size. The experimentation required to

determine GA parameters is a known limitation of GAs (Han & Kendall, 2003). Another factor affecting the quality of GAClassic schedules is the performance of the Random scheduling algorithm. In the evaluation of the Random algorithm performed, Random algorithm produces results that are on average in the order of 3.5 times (CCR=0.01) to 160 times (CCR=100) larger than those generated by scheduling heuristics and therefore makes it more difficult for the GA algorithm to find an optimal solution.

CONCLUSION

On the whole, among the 12 heuristics, the best ones are BL, LMT and PETS providing good results with low execution times. PETS is slightly superior to BL and LMT in terms of Good Count and Best Count, while BL and LMT have a lower Average Normalised Makespan and Normalised Makespan Standard Deviation.

Min-min produces good results but is computationally expensive. The levelled version of Min-min (Min-FINISH) is computationally more efficient and performs fairly better than Min-min. It is also noted that algorithms BL, LMT, HEFT, CPOP and PETS have good execution performance since they minimise the number of evaluations of job execution on different machines by producing a topologically sorted list and evaluating each job in turn only once. This is due to the fact that the main computational complexity in algorithm execution is makespan calculation.

The following are some observations drawn from the evaluation process:

- Level-by-level heuristics tend to schedule non-critical tasks early delaying the execution of critical tasks which leads to increased makespans.
- Since rank definitions in PETS provide a topological sorted list, a non-levelled ver-

sion of PETS could be used to prioritise tasks by latest finish time.

- List scheduling heuristics operate by minimising Task-Finish Time. In some cases, this results in scheduling tasks to minimise task finish time at the expense of increasing partial makespan.
- The evaluation of partial makespan is penalised by the fact that data transfer to tasks that are not yet scheduled is ignored. Task scheduling decision should take into consideration all the data transfers.
- Implementing GA algorithms for grid job scheduling poses some challenges in determining the proper parameters to be used.

REFERENCES

Alhusaini, A. H., Prasanna, V. K., & Raghavendra, C. S. (1999). *A unified resource scheduling framework for heterogeneous computing environments*. Paper presented at the Proceedings of the Eighth Heterogeneous Computing Workshop.

Braun, T. D., et al. (1999). *A comparison study of static mapping heuristics for a class of meta-tasks on heterogeneous computing systems*. Paper presented at the Proceedings of the Eighth Heterogeneous Computing Workshop (HCW'99).

Braun, T. D. (2001). A comparison of eleven static heuristics for mapping a class of independent tasks onto heterogeneous distributed computing system. *Journal of Parallel and Distributed Computing, 61*(6), 810–837. doi:10.1006/jpdc.2000.1714

Casanova, H., Legrand, A., Zagorodnov, D., & Berman, F. (2000). *Heuristics for scheduling parameter sweep applications in grid environments*. Paper presented at the Proceedings of the 9th Heterogeneous Computing Workshop (HCW 2000).

Han, L., & Kendall, G. (2003). *Guided operators for a hyper-heuristic genetic algorithm*. Paper presented at the AI 2003: Advances in Artificial Intelligence.

Hou, E. S. H., Ansari, N., & Ren, H. (1994). A genetic algorithm for multiprocessor scheduling. *IEEE Transactions on Parallel and Distributed Systems, 5*(2), 113–120. doi:10.1109/71.265940

Ibarra, O. H., & Kim, C. E. (1977). Heuristic algorithms for scheduling independent tasks on nonidentical processors. *Journal of the ACM, 24*(2), 280–289. doi:10.1145/322003.322011

Ilavarasan, E., & Thambidurai, P. (2007). Low complexity performance effective task scheduling algorithm for heterogeneous computing environments. *Journal of Computer Science, 3*(2), 94–103. doi:10.3844/jcssp.2007.94.103

Iverson, M., Ozguner, F., & Follen, G. (1995). *Parallelizing existing applications in distributed heterogeneous environments*. Paper presented at the Proceedings of Heterogeneous Computing Workshop.

Li, M., & Baker, M. (2005). *The grid core technologies*. London: Wiley. doi:10.1002/0470094192

Maheswaran, M. (1999). Dynamic mapping of a class of independent tasks onto heterogeneous computing systems. *Journal of Parallel and Distributed Computing, 59*(2), 107–131. doi:10.1006/jpdc.1999.1581

Maheswaran, M., & Siegel, H. J. (1998). *A dynamic matching and scheduling algorithm for heterogeneous computing systems*. Paper presented at the 7th Heterogeneous Computing Workshop.

Shroff, P., Watson, D. W., Flann, N. S., & Freund, R. (1996). *Genetic simulated annealing for scheduling data-dependent tasks in heterogeneous environments*. Paper presented at the Proceedings of Heterogeneous Computing.

Sih, G., & Lee, E. (1993). A compile-time scheduling heuristic for interconnection-constrained heterogeneous processor architecture. *IEEE Transactions on Parallel and Distributed Systems, 4*(2), 175–187. doi:10.1109/71.207593

Singh, H., & Youssef, A. (1996). *Mapping and scheduling heterogeneous task graphs using genetic algorithms.* Paper presented at the Proceedings of Heterogeneous Computing Workshop.

Spooner, D. P. (2005). Performance-aware workflow management for grid computing. *The Computer Journal, 48*(3), 347–357. doi:10.1093/comjnl/bxh090

Topcuoglu, H., Hariri, S., & Wu, M. Y. (2002). Performance-effective and low-complexity task scheduling for heterogeneous computing. *IEEE Transactions on Parallel and Distributed Systems, 13*(3), 260–274. doi:10.1109/71.993206

Wang, L., Siegel, H. J., Roychowdhury, V., & Maciejewski, A. (1997). Task matching and scheduling in heterogeneous computing environments using a genetic-algorithm-based approach. *Journal of Parallel and Distributed Computing, 47*(1), 8–22. doi:10.1006/jpdc.1997.1392

Yu, J., Buyya, R., & Ramamohanarao, K. (2008). Workflow schdeduling algorithms for grid computing. In Xhafa, F., & Abraham, A. (Eds.), *Metaheuristics for scheduling in distributed computing environments (studies in computational intelligence)* (pp. 173–214). Berlin: Springer. doi:10.1007/978-3-540-69277-5_7

Zhang, Y., Koelbel, C., & Kennedy, K. (2007). *Relative performance of scheduling algorithms in grid environments.* Paper presented at the Seventh IEEE International Symposium on Cluster Computing and the Grid.

Zhao, H., & Sakellariou, R. (2003). *An experimental investigation into the rank function of the heterogeneous earliest finish time scheduling algorithm* Paper presented at the Proceedings of Euro-Par 2003.

ENDNOTE

[1]   http://gvf.sourceforge.net/

This work was previously published in International Journal of Grid and High Performance Computing, Volume 2, Issue 4, edited by Emmanuel Udoh, pp. 65-80, copyright 2010 by IGI Publishing (an imprint of IGI Global).

Chapter 4
Peer–to–Peer Desktop Grids Based on an Adaptive Decentralized Scheduling Mechanism

Arafat and H. Ali
Mansoura University, Egypt

A.I. Saleh
Mansoura University, Egypt

Amany M. Sarhan
Mansoura University, Egypt

Abdulrahman. A. Azab
Mansoura University, Egypt

ABSTRACT

This article proposes an adaptive fuzzy logic based decentralized scheduling mechanism that will be suitable for dynamic computing environment in which matchmaking is achieved between resource requirements of outstanding tasks and resource capabilities of available workers. Feasibility of the proposed method is done via real time system. Experimental results show that implementing the proposed fuzzy matchmaking based scheduling mechanism maximized the resource utilization of executing workers without exceeding the maximum execution time of the task. It is concluded that the efficiency of FMA-based decentralized scheduling, in the case of parallel execution, is reduced by increasing the number of subtasks.

DOI: 10.4018/978-1-4666-0056-0.ch004

INTRODUCTION

Grid has recently emerged as a promising paradigm for high performance or high throughput computing because of the vast development of powerful computers and high-speed network technologies as well as low cost servers (GIMPS, 2009). Grid aims to aggregate heterogeneous, large-scale, and multiple-institutional resources, and to provide the transparent, secure, and coordinated access to various computing resources (supercomputer, cluster, scientific instruments, database, storage, etc.) owned by multiple institutions by making virtual organization. Grid computing is regarded to be the future of Semantic Web, the next step in distributed networking (SETI@home, 2009).

A peer-to-peer (or "P2P") computer network exploits diverse connectivity between participants in a network and the cumulative bandwidth of network participants rather than conventional centralized resources where a relatively low number of servers provide the core value to a service or application. Peer-to-peer networks are typically used for connecting nodes via largely ad hoc connections. Many peer-to-peer networks are overlay networks because they run on top of the Internet. The overall goal of Peer-to-Peer (P2P) based systems is to provide (share) resources (like computing power, bandwidth or storage). A fundamental principle of the P2P paradigm is equality. P2P computing can be defined as the sharing of computer resources and services by direct exchange.

Desktop Grid

Desktop Grid has recently been an attractive computing paradigm for high throughput applications (Anderson, 2004). However, Desktop Grid computing is complicated by heterogeneous capabilities, failures, volatility, and lack of trust because it is based on desktop computers at the edge of the Internet. In a Desktop Grid computing environment, volunteers (that is, resource provid-ers) have heterogeneous properties such as CPU, memory, network, and so forth.

Desktop Grid has recently received a rapidly growing interest and attraction because of its success of the most popular examples like GIMPS (2009), and SETI@Home (2009). Some studies have been made on Desktop Grid systems which provide an underlying platform: BOINC (Anderson, 2004), XtremWeb (Cappello et al., 2005), Entropia (Chien, Calder, Elbert, & Bhatia, 2003), Bayanihan (Sarmenta, 2002), Javelin (Neary & Cappello, 2005), Computer Power Market (CPM) (Ping, Sodhy, Yong, Haron, & Buyya, 2004), POPCORN (Nisan, London, Regev, & Camiel, 1998), Cluster Computing On the Fly (CCOF) (Lo, Zhou, Zappala, Liu, & Zhao, 2004), Organic Grid (Chakravarti, Baumgartner, & Lauria, 2006), Messor (Babaoglu, Meling, & Montresor, 2002), Paradropper (Montresor, Meling, & Babaoglu, 2002), Condor (Thain, Tannenbaum, & Livny, 2005), and so forth. Although, all of the previous examples had been investigated as valuable techniques concerning Desktop Grid issues, there still remain hindrances in achieving the promised performance especially in fault tolerance and decentralization.

A Grid is a structure with distributed heterogeneous resources offered to users. Users submit tasks that should be efficiently processed using resources available on the Grid (Nabrzyski, Schopf, & Weglarz, 2003). A Desktop Grid is usually built on the Internet platform in which resources are unreliable and frequently turned off or disconnected (El-Desoky, Hisham, & Abdulrahman, 2006). The idea of desktop grid is to harvest the idle time of Internet connected computers, to run very large and distributed applications (Fedak, Germain, Vincent, & Franck, 2001). Machines (i.e., Desktops) in a desktop grid are basically categorized into: a) Client: Machine from which a user can submit grid tasks for execution, and b) Worker: Computing resource on which grid tasks can be executed. In P2P Desktop Grid environment

(David, 2002), each node acts as a peer, so that, it can act as a Worker or as a Client.

A Grid worker (i.e., computing resource) is a basic device where tasks are scheduled/processed/assigned (Blazewicz, Brauner, & Finke, 2004). It is a set of cumulative resources (CPUs, memory, and storage space) with limited capacities. In Desktop Grid environment, a worker may be unavailable due to maintenance, disconnection, or a breakdown. A Grid task (job, activity) is a basic entity which is scheduled over the workers. Grid tasks can be categorized into: a) CPU intensive tasks, b) Memory intensive tasks, and c) I/O intensive tasks. A Grid task requirements include: a) Required CPU (i.e., computational power), b) Required memory (i.e., physical memory), and c) Required desk-space. In computational grids, the required desk-space of a task is usually too little to be taken into account, so, it can be neglected. In scientific applications, a task has specific requirements on the amounts and types of workers, or required time intervals on these workers, where the task can be scheduled (Fibich, Matyska, & Rudova, 2005). If resource requirements of a task (i.e., required CPU or required memory) are not known with certainty in advance, they must be estimated. It may be estimated by using statistics based on recent runs of the task (e.g., Gaussian, Amber, and fuzzy estimate) (Fibich et al., 2005).

Current Situation

Usually, the number of tasks to be done outnumbers the amount of available workers; it has to be decided how to allocate workers to tasks. Historically, this has been known as scheduling (Thain et al., 2005). A scheduling problem is specified by a set of workers, a set of tasks, an optimality criterion, environmental specifications, and by other constraints. A goal of a scheduling policy is to find an optimal schedule in the environment and to satisfy all constraints (Fibich et al., 2005).

Scheduling model describes how workers involved in resource management make scheduling decisions. Scheduling models may be centralized and decentralized (Ali, Anjum, Mehmood, Richard, Willers, & Julian, 2004); in a centralized model all tasks are submitted to a single machine which is responsible for scheduling them on available workers. However this approach is a single point of failure. On the other hand it will also affect scalability of the grid. In decentralized model there is no central scheduler, scheduling is done by the resource requestors (i.e., clients) and owners independently. This approach is scalable and suitable for P2P computing environment where decentralization is essential.

Matchmaking is the most important stage that is used to improve the efficiency and accuracy of the scheduling process. The goal of the matchmaking process is to collect information about (1) capabilities of available workers (i.e., the free CPU, Memory, and physical storage), and (2) outstanding tasks in the queues with their requirements on computational power, memory, and storage. In order to match, each task's requirements are evaluated in the context of the worker and the worker's requirements are evaluated in the context of the task (Alain & Livny, 2003). To perform matchmaking within centralized scheduling, the matchmaking process will be performed at a central node and the inputs to the matchmaker will include: Resource requirements of all outstanding tasks in all clients in the system and information about capabilities of all available workers. The main purpose of matchmaking is to elect the most suitable worker for each task according to matching rules. The output will be a list of pairs of tasks and workers.

On the other hand, within decentralized scheduling as depicted in Figure 1, matchmaking is performed at the client and the inputs to the matchmaking process will include: Resource requirements for the current outstanding task that belongs to the client user and information about capabilities of the available workers. The output of the matchmaking process is a list of ranking values for all workers to indicate the degree of

Figure 1. Decentralized scheduling mechanism

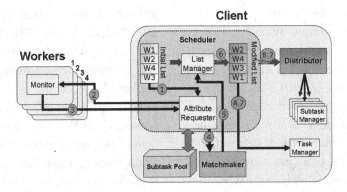

matching between the task and each of the available workers.

Challenges and Problems

Great effort had been exerted in order to implement efficient P2P scheduling in desktop grids. To the best of our knowledge, Condor (Thain et al., 2005), Alchemi (Luther, Buyya, Ranjan, & Venugopal, 2005), Harmony (SETI@home, 2009), Entropia2000 (Internet version of Entropia) (Andrew, Marlin, & Stephen, 2004) and some implementations of XtremWeb (Anderson, 2004) are the most efficient P2P Computing solutions. All of these solutions implemented centralized scheduling. The important drawback of these solutions is that the resource requirements (e.g., required CPU and Memory) of a grid task must be specified by the task owner (i.e., client). In most types of tasks, the task owner is neither capable of accurately specifying the amount of required resources for the task nor make good estimate.

Another important drawback is that matchmaking approaches in these solutions are based on assigning a grid task to any worker which free resources (i.e., CPU and Memory) is larger than or equal to the resource requirements of the task. This approach may be suitable in grid systems in which a worker can run more than one grid task at the same time. In the most of desktop grid systems, only one grid task can be allocated to a worker

at the same time, in order to avoid large network traffic resulted from data transmission between a running task and the task owner especially in grid systems which support fault-tolerance based on periodical checkpointing (Anh & Andrew, 2002). In such case, if any task is allocated to a worker, this worker will be marked unavailable to other clients, which may result in low worker resource utilization if the worker free resources are capable of running more tasks. Allocating each task to a new worker may cause the grid computing resources to reach saturation more quickly by increasing the number of occupied workers. The most suitable approach for desktop grids is to allocate a task to a worker which free resources are closer to the amount of required resources of the task. This approach will achieve maximum resource utilization of occupied workers, besides preventing occupation of higher performance workers by low resource intensive tasks.

In El-Desoky, Hisham, and Abdulrahman (2007), a pure P2P desktop grid framework with efficient fault-tolerance which is based on incremental checkpointing has been proposed. This article proposes an adaptive decentralized scheduling mechanism to be implemented as a part of the proposed framework. The proposed mechanism is based on a novel fuzzy matchmaking approach. Task resource requirements are estimated using statistics of collected performance attributes related to recent runs of the task. Worker capabilities of each available worker are compared with the requirements of the outstanding. Available workers are ranked, based on fuzzy logic, according to the degree of matching between each worker's capabilities and the resource requirements of the task.

DECENTRALIZED SCHEDULING MECHANISM

To implement decentralized scheduling, the scheduler component will be located at the client. The main goal of the scheduling process is to find the most suitable worker, of all available workers, to execute the task. Figure 1 shows the steps for performing scheduling of a task among available workers based on push mode for both serial and parallel executions (El-Desoky et al., 2007).

The proposed scheduling mechanism is applied for two interaction modes between the client and the executing worker(s): Push mode for Serial execution (PsS), and Push mode for Parallel execution (PsP) (El-Desoky et al., 2007).

Decentralized Scheduling for PsS

In case of push mode serial execution (i.e., PsS), the task will be executed on a single worker. The goal of the scheduling process is to generate an ordered list of all available workers so that the most suitable worker for carrying out the task execution will be the first worker in the list. The steps of the serial execution scheduling process can be described as follows:

1. The scheduler generates a list of all online workers in the Grid is generated. This list is called the initial list, and passed to the Attribute Requester (AR).
2. For each worker in the initial list, the attribute scheduler sends a request to the worker. This request includes the Starting Time of the task, ST, (i.e., the time on which the task will start), and the Maximum execution Time of the task, MT. Both ST and MT are specified by the task owner.

3. The worker replies with its capabilities (i.e., Free CPU and Free Memory) within the task Execution Time Interval, [ST, ST+MT]. The way in which the worker describes its capabilities within a specific time interval is described in a following section.
4. After steps 1 and 2 are performed for all workers in the initial list, for each worker in the initial list, the attribute requester passes the worker capabilities, within the execution time interval together with the task resource requirements (i.e., Required CPU and Required Memory) to the matchmaker. The output of the matchmaker will be a number that describes the degree of matching, DM, between the task requirements and the worker capabilities.
5. After performing step for all workers in the initial list, the matchmaker passes the values of DM for all workers to the List Manager.
6. The list manager rearranges the initial worker list ordered by the value of DM descending, so that, the most suitable worker to the task will be put at the top of the list. The new ordered list is called the Modified List.
7. The modified list is passed to the Task Manager. The task manager then pushes the task files to the first worker in the modified list. If a worker failed during the execution, the task manager pushes the task files to the next worker in the modified list.

Decentralized Scheduling for PsP

In case of parallel execution, the task is represented as a number of subtasks. Input data is partitioned according to the number of subtasks. Task files of all subtasks are collected in the Subtask Pool. All subtasks are equivalent in the resource requirements as they have copies of the same code file (El-Desoky et al., 2007). Subtasks will be distributed among number of available workers that equals to the number of subtasks. The Steps 1–6 of the parallel execution scheduling process are the same as those for serial execution, so that, the matchmaking is made between the worker capabilities and the subtask requirements. After step 6, the following steps will be performed:

7. The modified list is passed to the Distributor.
8. The distributor then passes worker IDs to the subtask managers (a subtask manager will be generated for each subtask) starting from the first worker in the modified list.
9. After sending a worker ID to each subtask manager, the distributor generates the Recovery List. The recovery list is an ordered list of the remaining workers after pushing all subtasks. It is used in case of a worker failure to resume the failed subtask on a new worker (El-Desoky et al., 2007).

Figure 2 shows the role of the distributor for distributing two subtasks when there are four workers available.

MATCHMAKER INPUT PARAMETERS

Matchmaking can be defined as the process of comparing the resource requirements of a task with the resource capabilities of a worker based on a matchmaking technique in order to find the degree of matching between the task and the worker. There are two basic inputs to the matchmaker: 1) task resource requirements, and 2) worker resource capabilities. The output of the matchmaker is a numeric value representing the degree of matching, which is used to rearrange the initial worker list. In the proposed approach, it is assumed that a task may be: CPU intensive, memory intensive, or both. Based on this assumption, the task requirements of any task may be described as Required CPU (i.e., processing power) and Required Memory. Also, the Worker capabilities may be described as: Free CPU and Free Memory. The next two subsections describe how the worker capabilities and the task requirements are calculated.

Worker Resource Capabilities

In the proposed approach, one day (i.e., 24 hours) is divided into equal sized Time Units (TUs). The size of a TU (represented in seconds) will be specified by the system administrator. Each TU will have a unique ID which will point at its position in the day. A TU will be described as TU(i) where, i = 1,2…,NTU, and NTU (Number of Time Units) is the total number of TUs in a day. At this point we have to notice that, there are three performance metrics are calculated for a worker:

Figure 2. Role of the distributor

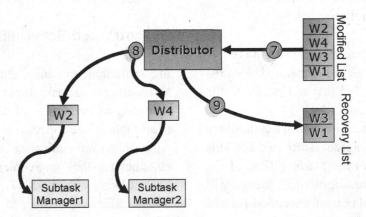

Available CPU (VC)

The available CPU, VC (i.e., the available processing power) of a specific worker (w) at a specific time (t) can be calculated as:

*VC (w,t) = CPU speed of (w) * (1 – (% Processor time of (w) at (t))) MHz (1)*

Where, % Processor Time is the percentage of elapsed time that the processor spends to execute a non-Idle thread. It is calculated by measuring the duration of the idle thread is active in the sample interval, and subtracting that time from interval duration.

Available Memory (VM)

The available memory, VM of a specific worker (w) at a specific time (t) can be calculated as:

VM(w,t) = (Total Memory size of (w) – Memory size in use of (w) at (t)) Mbytes (2)

Number of Failures (NF)

The number of failures for a worker (w) within a specific time interval is an integer value representing the number of shutdowns and disconnections of the (w) machine within this time interval. A very important concern in performance monitoring applications is the frequency within which the values of the performance parameters are captured, as in case of a very large frequency, the performance monitoring application itself may become a resource consuming application, especially for the CPU. In our implementation, windows performance counters are used inside an application based on Microsoft.NET framework for measuring performance parameters (VC, VM). It is found that a frequency of two measurements per second will rarely affect the CPU usage for Intel PIII and P4 machines. This frequency can be changed by the system administrator. A new

parameter will be considered, the Performance Measurement Time Unit, PMTU, which is the time in milliseconds between two measurements of performance parameters. In our implementation, PMTU = 500 ms. Each TU contains a fixed number of PMTUs which is represented as NPMTU where, NPMTU is the Number of Performance Measurements per Time Unit. Where:

NPMTU = size of a TU / size of a PMTU (3)

For predicting the available CPU and available memory in the few TUs following a specific time, the following calculations are applied: The arithmetic mean, μ, for the amount of performance measurements (i.e., VC and VM) that have been taken within a specific TU is used as a representation of VC and VM within this TU. The mean values of VC and VM for a specific time unit TU(i) at a worker, *w*, are computed as follows:

For VC:

$$\mu(w, VC, i) \frac{\sum_{j=1}^{NPMTU} VC_j(w, i)}{NPMTU} \qquad (4)$$

For VM:

$$\mu(w, VM, i) \frac{\sum_{j=1}^{NPMTU} VM_j(w, i)}{NPMTU} \qquad (5)$$

Where, NPMTU is the number of PMTUs in a TU. The number of failures, NF, in a specific time unit, TU(i), for a worker, *w*, will be computed as the total number of failures of, *w*, that occurred within TU(i) from day *1* to day *d*, where day *1* is the beginning of calculations and day *d* is the current day. This can be obtained from the following formula:

$$NF(w, i, d) = \sum_{j=1}^{d} NF(w, i, j) \qquad (6)$$

The number of days, d, within which the total number of failures is collected, is specified by the system administrator.

Task Resource Requirements

For each task T, there will be a specific maximum execution time represented as a number of TUs, *NTU (T)*. NTU(T) is the maximum number of TUs, specified by the task owner, within which the task T must complete execution. If a task T is started on a worker w and the execution time has exceeded NTU(T), the execution will be stopped and T will complete execution on another worker.

Two performance parameters are measured for task execution:

The Number of CPU Cycles CC(T)

Number of CPU cycles of (T) for a specific execution on a worker (w) can be calculated as follows:

*CC(T) (*M Cycles*) = CPU_Time(T,w) (seconds) * CPU_Speed(w) (MHz) (7)*

Where, CPU_Time(T,w) is the time within which task, T, has been consuming the CPU of worker, w, and CPU_Speed(w) is the speed of the CPU of worker, w, in MHz (i.e., M cycles/second). CPU Time of (T) can be calculated as follows:

CPU_Time(T,w) (seconds) = Actual execution time of (T) on (w) * % Processor time of (w) used by (T) (8)

Where, % Processor Time used by T is the percentage of elapsed time in which all of process T threads used the processor of w to execution instructions

Substitute in (7):

*CC(T) (*M cycles*) = (Actual execution time of (T) on (w) (seconds) * % Processor time of (w) used by (T) * CPU Speed of (w) (MHz) (9)*

For each execution of a task, T, on any worker, the value of CC(T) for the execution will be computed and stored together with the ID of the execution, E. The value of E is incremented for each successful execution of T. The number of CPU cycles for an execution, E, of a task, T, will be defined as, *CC(T,E)*. To make a good estimation for the number of CPU cycles of, T, for the next execution, the Median value for all CC(T, e) {e = 1, 2,..., $E_f(T)$} (where $E_f(T)$ is the last execution of, T, on any worker) will be used. The advantage of using the median value instead of the mean is that it is not unduly affected by extremes in the tails. However, it generates an estimate that is closer to the mean for data that are normal (or nearly so). The overall median of CC(T) will be computed as follows:

m(T, CC) = Median(CC(T, e)) {e = 1, 2, 3,..., E_f} (10)

Total Memory Use UM(T)

The total memory use of a task (T) for a specific execution can be calculated as follows:

*UM(T) (*Mbytes*) = (Input data of (T) + Output data of (T) + Intermediate data during execution of (T))* (11)

From (10) and (11), two performance parameters are specified for a task T: 1) m(T,CC) and 2) UM(T).

FUZZY MATCHMAKING APPROACH (FMA)

The goal of the matchmaking process is to assign the task to a worker so that the task execution will be completed without exceeding the maximum execution time of the task (i.e., NTU(T)) and with achieving maximum resource utilization (i.e., Used CPU and Used Memory) on the selected worker. The matchmaking approach is based on fuzzy logic and is fully implemented at the client. It is used to select the most suitable worker for a task execution from a list of available workers. The inputs to the fuzzy matchmaking process are: The worker capabilities for a number of workers and the task requirements of a task. The output is the ID of the selected worker. The Matchmaker together with the List Manager are dedicated to perform the fuzzy matchmaking process. The fuzzy matchmaking approach is implemented based on Takagi-Sugeno fuzzy model (Lee, Sheu, & Tsou, 2008; Zadeh, George, & Yuan, 1996), the model in which output membership functions are either linear or constant. In this implementation, constant output membership functions are used. The following steps construct the fuzzy inference process: a) Fuzzification of Inputs, b) Applying Fuzzy Operator, c) Applying Implication Method, and d) Defuzzification. Steps a and b are carried out by the Matchmaker, while steps c and d is carried out by the List Modifier. The four steps will be described in the next four subsections.

Fuzzification of Inputs

A fuzzification process is to take the inputs, determine the degree to which they belong to each of the appropriate fuzzy sets via input membership functions (Luther, Buyya, Ranjan, & Venugopal, 2005). The input fuzzy sets will be represented as the specifications of workers' capabilities (Free CPU, Free Memory). Each worker specification (Free CPU or Free Memory) will represent a fuzzy set. Each membership function, associated with a fuzzy set of a specific worker, will be represented in the form of a linear input membership function based on information about the current state of the performance parameters (i.e., free CPU and Memory). The input membership functions will be formulated as seen in Box 1.

Where, the execution will begin at TU(i). $\mu_{cur}(w\ VC, i)$ and, $\mu_{cur}(w, VM, i)$, are the mean values of the available CPU and the available memory of the worker (w) of the previous TU.

Values of $\mu_{cur}(w, VM, i)$ and $\mu_{cur}(w\ VC, i)$ are calculated as follows:

$$\mu_{cur}(w\ VC, i) = \mu(w, VC, i\text{-}1) \tag{14}$$

$$\mu_{cur}(w, VM, i) = \mu(w, VM, i\text{-}1) \tag{15}$$

Values of $\mu(w, VC, i\text{-}1)$ and $\mu(w, VM, i\text{-}1)$ are calculated from (4) and (5) respectively. Inputs to the fuzzification process will be crisp nu-

Box 1.

$$Free\_CPU(x, w, i) = \begin{cases} \dfrac{x}{\mu_{cur}(w, VC, i)} & x \le \mu_{cur}(w, VC, i) \\ 0 & x > \mu_{cur}(w, VC, i) \end{cases} \tag{12}$$

$$Free\_Memory(x, w, i) = \begin{cases} \dfrac{x}{\mu_{cur}(w, VM, i)} & x \le \mu_{cur}(w, VM, i) \\ 0 & x > \mu_{cur}(w, VM, i) \end{cases} \tag{13}$$

merical values represented as: *Required_CPU(T)* and *Required_Memory(T)*, which represent the resource requirements for a specific task. The value of the first input, *Required_CPU(T)*, represents *m(T,CC)*. As *Required_CPU(T)* will be fuzzified to the *Free_CPU* membership function, which displayed as (MHz), the *Required_CPU(T)* value has to be represented in (MHz) as well. To transform *m(T,CC)* from (M Cycles) to (MHz) (i.e., M Cycles/second) it will be divided by the maximum execution time of the task which will equal to: NTU(T)*TU (seconds). Both the next input value, *Required_Memory(T)*, and the input membership function, *Free_Memory* are represented in (MB). No modifications will be made to the *Required_Memory(T)* input. The input values to the fuzzification process can be described as follows:

$$\text{Re}quired\_CPU(T) = \frac{m(T,CC)}{NTU(T) \times TU}$$

(16)

$$\text{Required\_Memory}(T) = UM(T) \qquad (17)$$

The fuzzification process is depicted in Figure 3 for the two inputs: *Required_CPU(T)* (represented as, μ_C) and *Required_Memory(T)* (represented as, μ_M). In Figure 3, three fuzzy sets (associated with three workers) are involved: w1, w2 and w3. The

outputs of the fuzzification process are the degrees of membership of *T* in all fuzzy sets.

Applying Fuzzy Operator

Once the inputs have been fuzzified, we know the degree to which each part of the antecedent has been satisfied for each rule. In the proposed model, this step can be described as follows:

- A separate rule will be created for each worker included in the matchmaking process. The included rules for *n* available workers will be formulated as in Exhibit 1 where, *ID(wj)* is the worker ID of the worker *wj*.

If Required_CPU(T) Is Free_CPU(wj)
AND Required_Memory(T) Is Free_Memory(wj)
THEN Suitable_Worker(T) = ID(wj)
(j = 1,2,...,n)

- Each part of the antecedent of each rule represents the degree of membership within which the associated input belongs to each fuzzy set.

Figure 3. Fuzzification of the task requirements: (a) Required_CPU(T), and (b) Required_Memory(T)

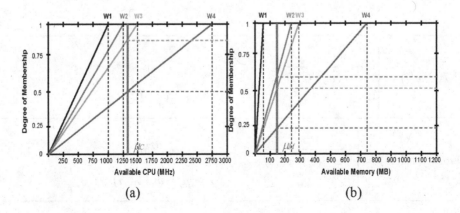

(a)   (b)

- The AND operator used in each rule will be implemented as Minimum() method so that, V1 AND V2 = Minimum(V1,V2). The reason behind which the AND operator is used, is that, for allocating a specific task *T* in a specific worker *w*, both CPU state and Memory state of *w* have to match the resource requirements of *T*.

Applying Implication Method

Before applying the implication method, we must take care of each rule's weight. In this approach, the weight of each rule associated with a specific worker, will indicate this workers availability. Applying implication method in this model is described as follows:

Worker availability within a specific time unit *TU(i)* can be deduced from the number of failures within *TU(i)*, defined in (6). The interval of TUs will equal to the maximum execution time for the task. As the NF value increases for a worker within the task execution time, the rule weight for this worker will decrease, so, the rule weight for each worker will be the invert of the number of failures. The rule weight for the fuzzy set associated with a worker *w* when it is evaluated for carrying out the execution of a task *T* within an interval of TUs, *NTU(T)* starting at *TU(i)* in a day *d* is computed as follows:

$$RW(w, i, d, NTU(T)) = \frac{1}{NF_{ov}(w, i, d, NTU(T))} \quad (18)$$

Where, $NF_{ov}(w, i, d, NTU(T))$ represents the overall number of failures for a collection of TUs beginning from *TU(i)* to *TU(i + NTU(T))* in the day *d* for a worker *w*.

- Once proper weighting has been assigned to a rule, each of the resulted values from

implementing the fuzzy operator in each rule will be multiplied with its associated rule weight, RW.

- The implication method is implemented, by the List Modifier. The consequent of a rule is an output fuzzy set represented by an output membership function. In this approach, constant output membership functions are applied. Output fuzzy sets will be constant values each associated with a worker. The output membership function associated with each fuzzy set will be in the form of a unique identifier of the associated worker (ID(wj) j = 1, …, *n*).
- The input for the implication process in each rule is a single number given by the antecedent and the output is a fuzzy set.
- Implementing implication on each rule associated with each worker, the result of implication for rules, associated with four workers, is depicted in Figure 4.
- In the Figure 3, the outputs of all rules are combined, or aggregated, into a single fuzzy set whose membership function assigns a weighting for every output value.

Defuzzification

Defuzzification step is carried out by the List Modifier. The input to the defuzzification process is a fuzzy set (the aggregate output fuzzy set) and the output is a single number. In this approach, the maxima aggregate function is implemented. The active membership function, associated with *n* input fuzzy sets, will be:

Out(T,n) = MAX (value [ID(w1)], value [ID(w2)],… value [ID(wn)]) (19)

Out(T,n) will represent the value associated with the ID of the most suitable worker to execute the task T. The List Modifier will then arrange the IDs of the workers descending according to the associated values, resulted from step C.

Figure 4. Output of applying the implication method

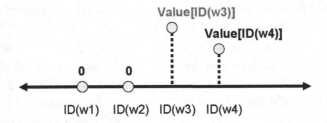

PERFORMANCE EVALUATION

Testbed

Performance evaluation experiments have been performed on a real P2P Desktop Grid. The testbed, depicted in Figure 5, is a LAN consisting of 13 workers and one client. The infrastructure components and platform are described in (Thain et al., 2005). The Infrastructure is based on the Pure P2P model. Each node can act as a Client and/or Worker. The list of participating nodes is replicated among all participants. A new node can join the system by registering from any participating node. Once a new node (n) is granted as a participant (i.e., Peer) in the system from a participating node (x), x sends to n a list of all participants in

the system, and broadcasts the information about n to all participating peers through flooding. Of course this method may not be efficient in very large sized systems. We are currently upgrading the Communication layer to be based on a structured P2P model instead of unstructured.

Performance evaluation of the proposed distributed scheduling mechanism is performed based on implementing two task allocation mechanisms:

1. A traditional task mechanism in which the modified worker list is the same as the initial worker list. Workers in the initial worker list are arranged descending according to the time of the last received IamAlive message from the worker.

Figure 5. Testbed for experimentations

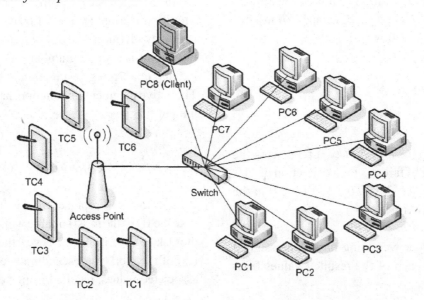

2. A distributed scheduling mechanism implementing FMA based matching.

3. The aim of the experiments is to show the impact of implementing the FMA based scheduling on maximizing the resource utilization of the executing workers without exceeding the predefined maximum execution time of the tasks (i.e., *NTU(T)*). Matrix multiplication for variable matrix size is used as the execution task for: a) Serial execution, and b) Parallel execution. The experiment has been repeated for variable matrix sizes for failure free execution.

Serial Execution

For a serial task execution, the task is assigned to one worker. Results of the experiment are recorded as: average percentage of CPU usage, and Memory usage of the executing worker while executing the task, and the task execution time as a percentage of *NTU(T)*. Figure 6 represents the results associated with matrix multiplication tasks for multiplying two 1500x1500 matrices, while in Figure 7 results associated with multiplying two 2100x2100 matrices are represented. Two approaches are evaluated: a) Traditional approach, in which the worker is chosen as the first worker

in the Initial List, and b) FMA in which the worker is chosen as the first worker in the Modified List.

The experiment is repeated five times (Expr 1, 2,..,5) for each matrix size. In Figure 6 and Figure 7, it is clear that, applying the FMA maximized the resource utilization for the executing worker without exceeding the maximum execution time of the task.

This is explained that, the selected worker (i.e., The first worker in the modified worker list) is chosen so that, its amount of free resources are sufficient for carrying out the task execution within execution time <= NTU(T).

Parallel Execution

For parallel task execution, the task is divided into subtasks. Each subtask is assigned to a worker. The number of Grid threads (Kim, Nam, Keleher, Marsh, Bhattacharjee, & Sussman, 2008; Luther, Buyya, Ranjan, & Venugopal, 2005) (i.e., number of subtasks) for a parallel task is predefined by the client user. Parallel matrix multiplication task for multiplying two 2400x2400 matrices is used in the experiment. The experiment is performed for both FMA based scheduling mechanism and the traditional task allocation mechanism. In each case, the experiment is performed for varying

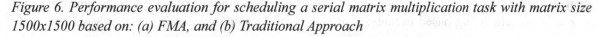

Figure 6. Performance evaluation for scheduling a serial matrix multiplication task with matrix size 1500x1500 based on: (a) FMA, and (b) Traditional Approach

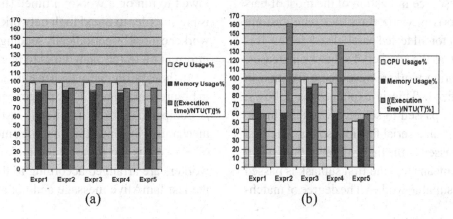

Figure 7. Performance evaluation for scheduling a serial matrix multiplication task with matrix size 2100x2100 based on: (a) FMA, and (b) Traditional Approach

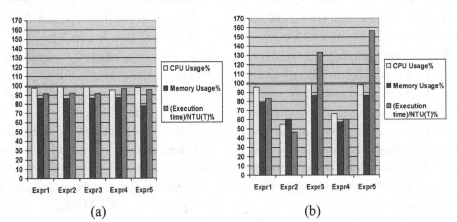

(a)   (b)

number of subtasks for the same task, ranged from 2 to 6. All subtasks are identical.

The NTU(T) value is predefined for each task form (task form of a parallel task is number of subtasks into which the task is divided). Results in Table 1 are recorded as: Number of subtasks for the parallel task (i.e., parallel task form), subtask index (so that separating results for each subtask from other subtasks in the same task), average percentage of resource usage (i.e., CPU and Memory usage) for each worker while executing its associated subtask, and the task total execution time in seconds (parallel task execution time is defined as the time interval between passing the first subtask and receiving the result from the last completed subtask).

For FMA scheduling based executions, it is clear that resource utilization of the most of parallel workers is maximized and the execution time <= NTU(T) for all tested parallel task forms. It is noticed that, as the number of subtasks increases, some executing workers' resource utilization in not maximized. This is explained as follows: Subtasks are passed to selected workers, in the modified list, in a serial fashion, so that, the first subtask is passed to the first worker in the list and so on. This means that the first subtask is passed to the most suitable worker. The degree of match-

ing between the subtask resource requirements and the worker capabilities will be reduced incrementally for other workers in the modified list. This may result in non-maximized worker resource utilization and worse, overhead in execution time. It is concluded that, the efficiency of FMA based decentralized scheduling, in case of parallel execution, is reduced by increasing the number of subtasks.

The main goal of the proposed scheduling approach is not to reduce the execution time of a task to minimum, but to carry out the task execution within the maximum execution time, NTU(T), specified by the task owner, together with achieving maximum resource utilization for the executing worker(s). One important restriction of the proposed system is that only one task is allowed to run on a worker a time. This constrain is put in order to avoid high network traffic on a worker caused by periodically sending checkpoint information to for many tasks to many clients.

In the experiments which results are presented in Figure 6 and Figure 7, the proposed mechanism is compared with a traditional task allocation mechanism in which the final (i.e., modified) list of workers is the same as the initial list, where workers are arranged according to the arrival of the last IamAlive message and not according to

Table 1. Performance evaluation for scheduling a parallel matrix multiplication task with matrix size 2400x2400 based on: (a) FMA, and (b) Traditional Approach

Scheduling Mechanism	Number Of subtasks	Subtask index	%CPU utilization	%Memory utilization	Execution time (Seconds)	NTU(T) (Seconds)
(a) FMA	2	1	99.1	86.3	631	900
		2	94.4	60.1		
	3	1	98.6	54.3	440	600
		2	99.3	54.8		
		3	99.1	54.2		
	4	1	99.2	87.5	377.8	500
		2	98.4	87.3		
		3	97	88.1		
		4	60.8	98.9		
	5	1	99.3	55.5	354	400
		2	98.9	88.7		
		3	79.5	87.4		
		4	64.3	76.7		
		5	50.9	56.5		
	6	1	99.5	87.3	319	400
		2	98.7	89.4		
		3	98.8	88		
		4	72.4	79.9		
		5	51.3	57.4		
		6	50.6	84.1		

continues on following page

the resource matching with the task requirements. In this case, the first worker in the list may be one of 3 types:

1. A too powerful worker for the required task, T, with high computing power and memory size, which is of course capable of executing T within NTU(T), but the resource utilization will not be maximized, and this worker should have been used for executing a more resource intensive task.
2. A too poor worker for T, using which, maximum resource utilization will be achieved, but the execution will not be completed within NTU(T) because of the limited resource capabilities, and this worker should

have been used for executing a less resource intensive task.
3. A worker with resource capabilities (i.e., CPU and Memory capacity) matching the resource requirements of T, and using which, maximum resource utilization will be achieved and the execution of T will be carried out within NTU(T).

In Figure 6 (b), the worker which carried out the task execution has been: type 1 for Expr 2 and 4, type 2 for Experiment 1 and 5, and type 3 for Experiment 3.

In Figure 6 (a), it is cleared that using FMA, we can make sure that the first worker in the list will always be of type 3.

Table 1. Continued

Scheduling Mechanism	Number Of subtasks	Subtask index	%CPU utilization	%Memory utilization	Execution time (Seconds)	NTU(T) (Seconds)
(b) Traditional	2	1	52.1	58.4	794	900
		2	96.3	81.8		
	3	1	99.7	88.7	778	600
		2	99.2	88.6		
		3	52.4	58.2		
	4	1	96.5	86.5	575	500
		2	99.5	87.4		
		3	98	87.2		
		4	59.3	71.5		
	5	1	58.6	72.3	502	400
		2	99.8	85.7		
		3	51.5	55.9		
		4	98.5	87		
		5	92.7	87.6		
	6	1	99.8	89.6	439	400
		2	99.7	87.4		
		3	99	73.6		
		4	99.2	88.2		
		5	51.3	57.6		
		6	98.4	87.7		

ENHANCED DECENTRALIZED SCHEDULING MECHANISM (EDSM)

In spite of its efficiency, the proposed FAM, as a decentralized scheduling technique, suffers from scalability problem, which is shared among all P2P scheduling techniques. A pure P2P system usually suffers from low scalability because of the absence of central points (servers) that monitor the system and control all its operations. On the other hand, creating the initial worker list is a crucial step that directly affects the FAM operation. Hence, it is necessary to develop exact techniques to effectively create the initial worker list. To achieve scalability as well as overcoming the hurdle of effectively creating the initial worker list, another object should be added to the testbed

network shown in Figure 5, which is called the coordinator.

The coordinator is a special machine that keeps an up-to-date List of Alive Workers (LAW) across the network. At start up, each worker (peer) has to register itself at the coordinator by sending "I am alive" message to the coordinator. At this time, the newly registered worker receives a copy of the LAW from the coordinator. This local copy of LAW is stored at the worker for future use as well as the time during which LAW was created. However, in order to continuously refresh the master copy of LAW (at the coordinator), the coordinator sends "Are you up?" message to all registered workers at fixed time intervals. If the worker replies, the coordinator will send to him a refreshed copy of LAW as well as the current time to update his local copy of LAW. Whenever

Figure 8. How coordinator works

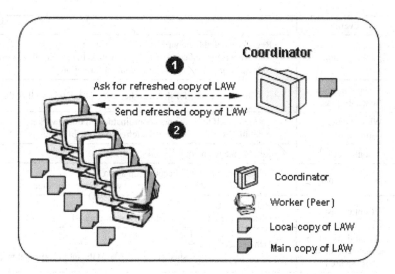

a worker needs to schedule a task, it can simply ask the coordinator for the refreshed copy of LAW (the worker receives also the current time from the coordinator), Figure 8 gives an illustration. It is important to mention that the coordinator stores also the global scheduling information such as the length of TU. Those global scheduling information should be sent to the worker during his registration.

As indicated form its name, EDSM is a decentralized scheduling technique as the scheduling decisions take place at the worker where the task to be scheduled was initiated. On the other hand, it has a hybrid infrastructure as it is implemented across a number of workers (peers) driven by a single server (coordinator). EDSM, as an enhanced version of FAM, solves the scalability problem that usually hamper the implementation of several P2P systems, as well as achieving high reliability that is the main drawback of the centralized scheduling techniques which are usually known as "central point of failure systems."

A reliable system is the one which has the ability to detect failures, reconfigure itself to continue operating (even in a degraded performance), and to recover when the failure has been repaired. To narrate expediently, assuming the coordinator

failure, the machine which detects the failure (a client needs to schedule a task and ask the coordinator for the refreshed copy of LAW but no reply was received) will promote itself to be the new coordinator. However, two basic operations should be attached with the promotion process. The first is that the new coordinator must inform all other peers (written in his local copy of LAW) that it will be the new coordinator. On the other hand, the promoted coordinator should receive the local copies of LAW from all other peers, then consider the most refreshed copy (based of the time in which the copy was created). The system can then continue operating, however, no newly registered workers can combine the grid.

EDSM has the ability to recover after the main coordinator failure by using a simple recovery mechanism. The promoted coordinator continuously sends "Are you alive?" signal to the main (failed) coordinator to detect if it has been repaired. When the main coordinator is repaired, it will receive the refreshed copy of LAW as will as the scheduling information from the promoted coordinator. The repaired coordinator should also inform all alive workers (written in LAW) that it is alive again.

Table 2. Behaviors of the three main objects of EDSM

Object	Event	Action
Worker	At start up	• Register itself at the coordinator. • Receive a refreshed copy of LAW as well as the time of the coordinator. • Ask the coordinator for the scheduling information.
	When it needs to schedule a task.	• Ask the coordinator for the refreshed copy of LAW as well as the coordinator time.
	When it detects a coordinator failure.	• Promote itself to be the new coordinator (tell other workers). • Ask other workers for the most refreshed copy of LAW.
Main Coordinator	Continuously	• Refresh the main copy of LAW.
	When it is repaired	• Tell all workers that it becomes up again. • Receive the most recent copy of LAW from the promoted coordinator.
Promoted Coordinator	Continuously	• Refresh his copy of LAW. • Check if the main coordinator has been repaired.
	When it detects that the main coordinator is repaired	• Demote itself. • Sends the most refreshed copy of LAW to the main coordinator.

The behaviors of the basic three objects of the proposed EDSM, which are workers, coordinator, and promoted coordinator, are illustrated in Table 2.

CONCLUSION AND FUTURE WORK

In this article, an adaptive distributed scheduling mechanism has been proposed as an efficient scheduling mechanism in a full decentralized environment. The proposed mechanism is implemented at the client for both serial and parallel execution scenarios. A new fuzzy matchmaking approach (FMA) based on Takagi-Sugeno fuzzy model has been introduced as a part of the proposed scheduling mechanism in which, each worker represents a fuzzy set, and linear input membership functions are implemented. Task resource requirements are estimated using statistics based on recent runs of the task. Performance evaluation experiments have been performed for both serial and parallel tasks on a real P2P Desktop Grid. Experimental results show that, implementing FMA based scheduling maximized the resource utilization of the executing worker without ex-

ceeding the maximum execution time of the task. It is planned to enhance the efficiency FMA by implementing more complex shapes for input membership functions.

REFERENCES

Alain, R., & Livny, M. (2003). Condor and preemptive resume scheduling. In J. Nabrzyski, J. M. Schopf, & J. Weglarz (Eds.), *Grid resource management: State of the art and future trends* (pp. 135-144). Norwell, MA: Kluwer Academic Publishers.

Ali, A., Anjum, A., Mehmood, A., Richard, M., Willers, I., & Julian, B. (2004, September). *A taxonomy and survey of grid resource planning and reservation systems for grid enabled analysis environment*. Paper presented at the 2004 International Symposium on Distributed Computing and Applications to Business, Engineering and Science (DCABES 2004), Wuhan, China.

Anderson, D. P. (2004, November 8). BOINC: A system for public-resource computing and storage. In *Proceedings of the 5th IEEE/ACM International Workshop on Grid Computing (GRID '04)*, Pittsburgh, PA (pp. 4-10). IEEE CS Press.

Anh, N., & Andrew, S. (2002). *Using reflection for incorporating fault-tolerance techniques into distributed applications*. Retrieved from http://www.ggf.org

Babaoglu, O., Meling, H., & Montresor, A. (2002, July 2-5). Anthill: A framework for the development of agent-based peer-to-peer systems. In *Proceedings of the 22nd IEEE International Conference on Distributed Computing Systems*, Vienna, Austria (pp. 15-22). IEEE.

Barkai, D. (2002). *Peer-to-peer computing: Technologies for sharing and collaborating on the net*. Santa Clara, CA: Intel Press.

Blazewicz, J., Brauner, N., & Finke, G. (2004). Scheduling with discrete resource constraints. In J.Y-T. Lueng (Ed.), *Handbook of scheduling* (pp. 23.1-23.18). Boca Raton, FL: CRC Press.

Cappello, F., Djilali, S., Fedak, G., Herault, T., Magniette, F., & Neri, V. (2005). Computing on large-scale distributed systems: XtremWeb architecture, programming models, security, tests and convergence with grid. *Future Generation Computer Systems, 21*(3), 417–437. doi:10.1016/j.future.2004.04.011

Chakravarti, A. J., Baumgartner, G., & Lauria, M. (2006). The organic grid: Self-organizing computational biology on desktop grids. In A. Y. Zomaya (Ed.), *Parallel computing for bioinformatics and computational biology: Models, enabling technologies, and case studies* (ch. 27). New York: John Wiley & Sons.

Chien, A., Calder, B., Elbert, S., & Bhatia, K. (2003). Entropia: Architecture and performance of an enterprise desktop grid system. *Journal of Parallel and Distributed Computing, 63*(5), 597–610. doi:10.1016/S0743-7315(03)00006-6

Chien, A. A., Marlin, S., & Elbert, S. T. (2004). Resource management in the entropia system. In J. Nabrzyski, J. M. Schopf, & J. Weglarz (Eds.), *Grid resource management: State of the art and future trends* (pp. 431-450). Norwell, MA: Kluwer Academic Publishers.

El-Desoky, A., Hisham, A., & Abdulrahman, A. (2006, November 5-7). Improving fault tolerance in desktop grids based on incremental checkpointing. In *Proceedings of the 2006 International Conference on Computer Engineering and Systems (ICCES'06)*, Cairo, Egypt (pp. 386-392). IEEE.

El-Desoky, A., Hisham, A., & Abdulrahman, A. (2007, November 27-29). A pure peer-to-peer desktop grid framework with efficient fault tolerance. In *Proceedings of the 2007 International Conference on Computer Systems and Engineering (ICCES'07)*, Cairo, Egypt (pp. 346-352). IEEE.

Fedak, G., Germain, C., Vincent, N., & Franck, C. (2001, May 15-18). XtremWeb: A generic global computing system. In *Proceedings of the 1st IEEE/ACM International Symposium on Cluster Computing and the Grid (CCGRID '01)*, Brisbane, Australia (pp. 582-587). IEEE.

Fibich, P., Matyska, L., & Rudova, H. (2005, July). Model of grid scheduling problem. In *Proceedings of the Workshop on Exploring Planning and Scheduling for Web Services, Grid and Autonomic Computing*, Pittsburgh, PA (pp. 17-24). Menlo Park, CA: AAAI Press.

GIMPS. (2009). *The great Internet mersenne prime search*. Retrieved from http://www.mersenne.org

Kim, J.-S., Nam, B., Keleher, P., Marsh, M., Bhattacharjee, B., & Sussman, A. (2008). Trade-offs in matching jobs and balancing load for distributed desktop grids. *Future Generation Computer Systems, 24*(5), 415–424. doi:10.1016/j.future.2007.07.007

Lee, Y., Sheu, L., & Tsou, Y. (2008). Quality function deployment implementation based on Fuzzy Kano model: An application in PLM system. *Computers & Industrial Engineering, 55*(1), 48–63. doi:10.1016/j.cie.2007.11.014

Lo, V., Zhou, D., Zappala, D., Liu, Y., & Zhao, S. (2004, February). Cluster computing on the fly: P2P scheduling of idle cycles in the Internet. In *Proceedings of the 3rd International Workshop on Peer-to-Peer Systems (IPTPS'04),* San Diego, CA (pp. 227-236).

Luther, A., Buyya, R., Ranjan, R., & Srikumar, V. (2005). *Peer-to-peer grid computing and a. NET-based Alchemi framework.* New York: John Wiley & Sons.

Luther, A., Buyya, R., Ranjan, R., & Venugopal, S. (2005). *Peer-to-peer grid computing and a. NET-based Alchemi framework.* New York: John Wiley & Sons.

MathWorks. (2009). Retrieved from http://www.mathworks.com

Montresor, A., Meling, H., & Babaoglu, O. (2002, July). Messor: Load-balancing through a swarm of autonomous sgents. In *Proceedings of the International Workshop on Agents and Peer-to-Peer Computing (AP2PC'02),* Bologna, Italy (pp. 125-137).

Nabrzyski, J., Schopf, J. M., & Weglarz, J. (2003). *Grid resource management: State of the art and future trends.* New York: Kluwer Academic Publishing.

Neary, M. O., & Cappello, P. (2005). Advanced eager scheduling for Java based adaptive parallel computing. *Concurrency and Computation, 17*(7-8), 797–819. doi:10.1002/cpe.855

Nisan, N., London, S., Regev, O., & Camiel, N. (1998, May 26-29). Globally distributed computation over the Internet-the POPCORN project. In *Proceedings of the 18th IEEE International Conference on Distributed Computing Systems,* Amsterdam, The Netherlands (pp. 592-601). IEEE.

Ping, T. T., Sodhy, G. C., Yong, C. H., Haron, F., & Buyya, R. (2004, May 14-17). A Market-based Scheduler for JXTA-based Peer-to-Peer Computing System. In *Proceedings of the International Conference on Computational Science and its Applications (ICCSA'04),* Assisi, Italy (pp. 147-157).

Sarmenta, L. F. G. (2002). Sabotage-tolerance mechanisms for volunteer computing systems. *Future Generation Computer Systems, 18*(4), 561–572. doi:10.1016/S0167-739X(01)00077-2

SETI@home. (2009). http://setiathome.ssl.berkeley.edu

Thain, D., Tannenbaum, T., & Livny, M. (2005). Distributed computing in practice: The condor experience. *Concurrency and Computation, 17*(2-4), 323–356. doi:10.1002/cpe.938

Zadeh, L., George, J., & Yuan, B. (1996). *Fuzzy sets, fuzzy logic, and fuzzy systems.* Singapore: World Scientific Publishing.

This work was previously published in International Journal of Grid and High Performance Computing, Volume 2, Issue 1, edited by Emmanuel Udoh, pp. 1-20, copyright 2010 by IGI Publishing (an imprint of IGI Global).

Chapter 5
Predictive File Replication on the Data Grids

ChenHan Liao
Cranfield University, UK

Na Helian
University of Hertfordshire, UK

Sining Wu
Cranfield University, UK

Mamunur M. Rashid
Cranfield University, UK

ABSTRACT

Most replication methods either monitor the popularity of files or use complicated functions to calculate the overall cost of whether or not a replication decision or a deletion decision should be issued. However, once the replication decision is issued, the popularity of the files is changed and may have already impacted access latency and resource usage. This article proposes a decision-tree-based predictive file replication strategy that forecasts files' future popularity based on their characteristics on the Grids. The proposed strategy has shown superb performance in terms of mean job time and effective network usage compared with the other two replication strategies, LRU and Economic under OptorSim simulation environment.

INTRODUCTION

In Data Grids, jobs are implemented in form of requesting files from local or remote Grid nodes. Files needed for implementing jobs are stored in storage elements (SEs) where computing elements (CEs) may also be assigned. Computing elements are responsible to execute jobs by requesting the associated files from the Grids. In general, to handle a submitted job, three kinds of resources are considered, computing resources, storage resources and network use. Besides Grid resources, Grid scheduler is responsible to arrange jobs based on the current state of the Grid resources.

Replicating files among Grid nodes is due to the distributed nature of the Data Grids where

DOI: 10.4018/978-1-4666-0056-0.ch005

geographically distributed data lead to access latency. An appropriate file replication strategy can reduce access latency by creating file replicas spreading over demanding nodes. Meanwhile, file replication strategies are also required to bring the needs to optimize the Grid resource usage for the whole Grid user community. Consequently, to evaluate a file replication strategy, both total job time and resources usage are considered in order to achieve the balance between single user and the entire Grid.

Most replication methods either monitor the popularity of files or use complicated functions to calculate the overall cost whether or not a replication decision or a deletion decision should be issued. However, the replication decision issued in normal instances is in some sense "late" considering the detected changes of files' popularity. Once the replication decision is issued, the truth is that the popularity of the files had changed and may have already given impact on access latency and resource usage. This paper proposes a predictive file replication strategy that forecasts files' future popularity based on their characteristics on the Grids.

FILE REPLICATION STRATEGIES AND SIMULATION TOOLS

Various replication strategies have been proposed by research communities so far. Least Frequently Used (LFU) and Least Recently Used (LRU) are two popular methods, which maintain an access history on each Grid site to monitor the popularity of files. The LRU and LFU strategies will always replicate files to local sites where computing elements request the files for executing the jobs. Through browsing the replica catalogue, where the detail information of all the replicas is stored, it chooses the replica that can be accessed within shortest time. The difference between LFU and LRU is that when the local storage is full, deleting methods are different. LFU deletes the file least

frequently accessed while LRU deletes the file least recently accessed in order to create space for new replicas. The simplistic of LRU and LFU make them successful and popular for file replication strategy design, however, the "always-replicate" policy leads to unbalance between job time and resource usage.

The Economic model (Cameron, Carvajal-Schiaffino, Millar, Nicholson, & Stockinger 2003; Carman, Zini, Serafini, & Stockinger, 2002) was developed to estimate the file values that are used to decide files' future popularity, based on binomial distribution. The model assumes that the popularity of files obeys certain distributions, and then finds the file value where it lies on that distribution. The Economic model also employs a reverse auction strategy to message Grid sites in order to obtain the "cheapest" replicas. This strategy models the local sites and remote sites as replica "buyers" and "sellers," where the value of file replicas is evaluated by their historic "purchase" prices. According to the Economic model, a typical replication process is modelled as an investment on the market. If the candidate replica has greater value than the least-valued file in the local storage, then the least-valued file is then replaced by the new replica. Similar with LRU and LFU, if local storage is not full, replication decision will always be issued.

Besides replication strategies, many Grid simulation tools have also been developed recently. ChicagoSim (Ranganathan & Foster, 2001, 2002) was designed to simulate various replication and caching strategies. EDGSim (Crosby, 2008) was developed to evaluate various scheduling algorithms vastly influencing the over all data Grid performance. Without considering replication issue, their study showed that the spatial locality of Grid data makes huge impacts on scheduling decisions. Another simulator called GridSim (Buyya & Murshed, 2002) was also developed to examine different scheduling algorithms by employing an economy model to emulate the purchase and selling of Grid resources in order to make appropriate use of Grid resources.

OptorSim (Bell, Cameron, Capozza, Millar, Stockinger, & Zini, 2003; WP2 Optimization Team, 2008) is a simulator focusing on emulating a two-staged optimization that replications during the run-time of jobs benefit from the scheduling decisions pre-determined, which are based on both data spatial locality and network status. Compared with other simulation tools, the advantage of OptorSim is that it takes into account both scheduling and replication optimizations in aspects of the dynamism of the workloads, the spatial locality of Grid data and network status. Relying on such staged design, one can either purely evaluate the replication strategies or emulate the impacts given by other factors. Considering the advantages of OptorSim in simulating replication strategies, we employ OptorSim as the simulation tool to implement the proposed replication method.

Different simulation environments consist of various Grid topologies, the components of Grid sites and the parameters describing the dynamism of the Grids (see Figure 1). In OptorSim, a Grid has several sites, where may contain computing elements (CEs) and storage elements (SEs). Computing elements act as computational resources

by running the jobs submitted, which involve the files stored in storage elements. If a site contains zero computing elements and storage elements, it is regarded as a network node or a router. Besides these, network bandwidths among nodes are also simulated as well as background traffics. The most important component to our method is the replica manager implemented in each site. It manipulates replica selection, creation and deletion through communicating with replica catalogue where the detailed information of replicas is recorded.

In each site, a particular file is established to maintain the access history of the files in order to monitor the file access frequency and their temporal locality. For LRU and LFU replication strategies, access history is examined to decide which file to delete from the local storage in order to create space for new replicas.

THE PREDICTIVE FILE REPLICATION ON THE DATA GRIDS

As we have discussed that the heuristics from file systems suggest that the file attributes always imply hints that can be used to improve system caching performance. In fact, however, file rep-

Figure 1. A diagram of EU data grid components

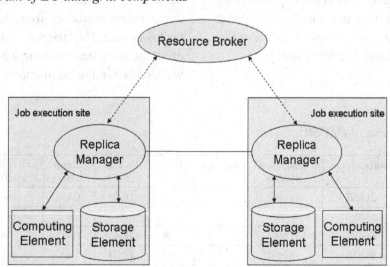

lication on the Grids is similar with file caching in file systems. The common thing is that both techniques create copies of data to fast areas (main memory for file systems and local storage for the Grids) to reduce access latency (I/O latency to file systems and network latency to the Grids).

With the similarity between file caching and file replication in mind, the hypothesis that file characteristics are related to its future popularity on the Data Grids is raised. For example, a file created or last modified by certain users such as project managers or system administrators may have very good chance to be accessed in near future. If such correlations exist, then we can choose appropriate model to predict files' future popularity. Unfortunately, most Grid simulation tools run the simulation on generated synthetic jobs and files, which are virtually defined without realistic file characteristics such as user ID, creation time and so forth. Hence, to find out the correlation between file characteristics and files' future popularity, we must analyze traces containing real-system file requests.

In my experiment, simulations employed real network file system traces to extract both file characteristics and observed file popularity. Then, chi-square tests were conducted between extracted file characteristics and observed file popularity to examine whether or not file characteristics have enough confidence to support our hypothesis. In addition, to describe files' popularity, accumulated file access frequency are observed and recorded to maintain file access frequency history.

The traces used were obtained from three network file systems DEAS03, EECS03, and CAMPUS. These three workloads trace various Network Appliance Filters that serve the home directories for students and faculties of different departments of Harvard University. Table 1 shows the typical format of the file requests contained in one of the three traces, DEAS03.

A set of Chi-square tests were established in order to decide whether a certain attribute provide enough confidence supporting our hypothesis. The testing results have shown that for these three network file system traces, four attributes have shown very good confidence, which reflect the association between attributes and observed file access frequency. It can be seen from Figures 2, 3 and 4 that the confidence values supported by each attribute differ in each trace. However, attribute UID always show greater confidence to the file access frequency compared with others, which is one of the representative cases we have discussed.

We then import the file system traces into OptorSim through grouping file requests based on their high level sessions. However, Chi-square tests can only examine the existence of our hypothesis, but it can not tell us how to infer files' popularity relying on their attributes. Figure 2 represents the cumulative file accesses along with the number of files, which are ranked according to the access frequency from the highest one to the lowest one. This diagram shows the skewness of all the three trace-sample we extracted as the workloads for the simulations. Note that each

Table 1. Trace sample of DECS03

Created time	Source address	Destination address	File type	Mode	User ID	Group ID	File system ID	File ID
1044248400.4	31.03ff	30.0801	2	180	18c09	18b3b	8664	4b8966
1044248400.8	83.03fd	30.0801	2	7ff	0	0	8664	1423391
1044248400.8	83.03f9	30.0801	1	5c9	18aa2	18ac2	8664	1423393
1044248400.9	66.03ff	30.0801	1	180	18b34	6	8664	1423395

Figure 2. The cumulative file accesses vs. the number of files

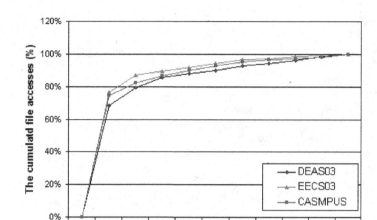

Figure 3. Grid components of the predictive file replication

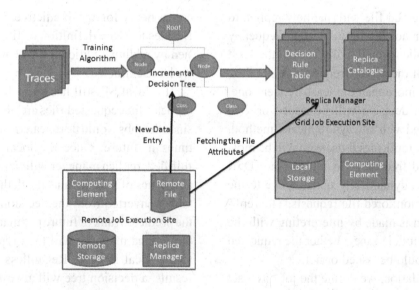

workload is equivalent to a three-day trace from DEAS03, EECS03 and CAMPUS, respectively. In Figure 2, DEAS03 exhibits approximately 80% file accesses contributed by 20% top frequent files, while EECS03 and CAMPUS show 87% and 82% file accesses absorbed by 20% files, respectively.

To examine the contribution of each file attribute for predicting file popularity, Incremental decision tree are adopted as a more accurate predic-

tive model due to its transparency and dynamism. The ID5R incremental decision tree was used as a predictive model to obtain predicted future access frequency of files. When a file is requested by a remote Grid node, the model will calculate the estimated frequency rank based on the predetermined classification policies. Similar with LRU, replication will always be executed as long as there is still enough space available for new replicas. If the local storage is full, it will compare the least

Figure 4. The network topology and configuration for the EU Data Grid testbed

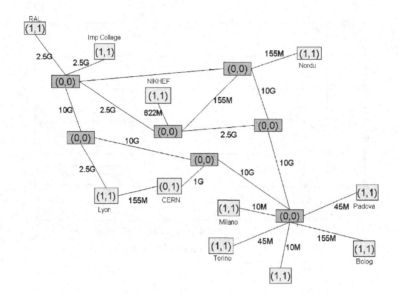

frequently accessed file with the new replica to see whether or not the future access frequency of the new replica would likely exceed the least frequent one. If the access frequency rank of the new replica is more than the least frequent one, file replication decision will be issued or vice versa. Compared with "always-replicate" method, the model only replicates those who will be most likely accessed frequently in future. The ID5R decision tree is dynamically updated due to the continuously monitored file requests. The replication decision is made by interpreting with the decision tree model to see whether the requested replication should be issued or not.

In the simulation, we define the jobs as a set of continuous file requests sent from same high level sessions in these three traces. A job list can then be generated by regrouping the file requests according to their high level session ID observed in the traces such as source address ID in DEAS03. To ensure that these file requests belong to same applications, a time slice window is established to restrict the distance of file requests. According to the testing results, 30 minutes is the average gap separating discontinuous request sessions. Figure 3 shows the interaction of various Grid

components for the predictive file replication. Besides this, the definition of files is also modified by adding additional file characteristics that we have extracted.

If a local SE still has enough space for new replicas, the requested files are always replicated since the jobs would be repeatedly executed many times in future. Once the local SE is already fulfilled, replica manager will first fetch the characteristics of the files and check the decision rule table converted from the decision tree model. If the predicted rank of future popularity is "higher," the replica manager will then replicate this file to the local storage. Regardless the prediction results, a decision tree will always take the new file requests as the new data entries to update itself. If the predicted rank of future popularity of the new replica is "lower," the local CE will look up the replica catalogue to find the remote replica that can be accessed within shortest time by using remote I/O.

SIMULATION CONFIGURATION

The simulation is based on OptorSim simulation environment. OptorSim specifies Grid topologies, Grid jobs, Grid files, file access patterns and scheduling algorithms in its configuration file to enable flexibility of emulating various replication strategies.

Grid Topology

In the simulation, the European Data Grid (EDG, 2003) topology was adopted as the simulation testbed. EDG testbed contains eighteen Grid nodes distributed in seven countries. It was developed mainly for High Energy Physics, Earth Observation and Biomedical applications. The topology below shows the structure of EDG testbed and the link capability among nodes.

Figure 4 shows the topology and network connectivity among nodes of the EDG testbed. Each node may contain one computing element and one storage element represented in a paired value. For example, node CERN contains zero computing elements and one storage element and thus is represented as (0, 1). The nodes containing zero computing elements and zero storage elements are treated as network routers shown as the green rectangles. The link capabilities between nodes are represented by the network bandwidth shown in the above figure.

Simulated Jobs

The simulated workloads are imported from the three network file system traces, DEAS03, EECS03 and CAMPUS, so that we can evaluate correlations between real file characteristics and files' popularity. The jobs are defined as a set of file requests generated from same high level applications or sessions. A time slice window (30 minutes) is specified to avoid discontinuous file requests of different high level applications.

The Grid jobs are described in a job table along with a file table. The following example shows a Grid job configuration.

As we can see from the above example, the files for executing a job are pre-assigned before the simulation starts. Note that pre-assigning jobs to a particular CE does not bond the jobs permanently during the scheduling process. Differently, it only defines the CEs that are willing to run the relative jobs. In a similar manner, the Grid jobs are also described with their selection probability.

In Figure 5, the first column of the file table denotes unique file names followed by their size in MB and indexes. The third column describes the file modes while the other three columns represents file type, user id and group id respectively. Figure 6 shows the job table, CE schedule table and the job selection probability table. In the job table, the files needed to be executed follow the job name that requests these files. In addition, the CE schedule table represents the Grid sites that are able to run the jobs.

Figure 5. A typical file table of EU data Grids configuration

```
#
# File Table
#
#name, size (MB), index, mode, type, UID, GID
#
\begin {file table}
File1 1000  1    180   1   18b34   6
File2 1000  2    180   1   18ad4   6
File3 1000  3    180   1   18aa2   6
File4 1000  4    7ff   2   0       0
File5 1000  5    5c0   2   18a89   18a89
File6 1000  101  5c9   1   18aa2   18ac2
File7 1000  102  1c0   2   18aee   18ad5
File8 1000  103  180   1   18aa2   6
File9 1000  104  180   2   18c09   18b3b
\end
```

Figure 6. A typical job table of EU data Grids configuration

```
#                              #                          #
# Job Table                    #CE Schedule Table         #Job Selection Probability
#                              #Site, jobs it will run    #
# job name, files required by it   #                      \begin {job selection probability}
#                              \begin {CE schedule table}  job1  0.8
\begin {job table}             2 job1 job2                Job2 0.2
Job1 File1 File2 File3 File4 File5   7 job1 job2           \end
Job2 File6 File7 File8 File9   \end
\end
```

During the simulation, various numbers of jobs are simulated for certain purposes. However, which job should be chosen for a particular CE during the run-time is critical to the simulation results. The job selection probability specifies the probability that certain jobs will be selected by relative CEs. According to the job selection probability, we can imagine that the simulation results may vary from time to time due to the random choices of the jobs by CEs. This is true since the length of a job can be different from other jobs. In addition, the size of files involved in jobs can also lead to different job time. To overcome this problem, a simulation under a specific configuration should run enough times to work out the average results. An alternative is to regulate the length of jobs and the size of files so that the simulation results would not greatly differ. In my experiment, the results are obtained by calculating the average from 10 simulations for a certain configuration.

Compared with the original workloads contained in OptorSim, the imported workloads do not imply data intensive manipulation since the imported workloads contain more real file characteristics but much smaller file size. However, in simulation environments, it is possible to regulate the file size at a fixed value so that the imported workloads fit in with data intensive Grid simulations. In the simulations, the size of every file is all set to 1 GB.

Access Pattern

The access patterns are also taken into account as they can greatly influence the efficiency of job executions. In OptorSim, access patterns are defined as the patterns of file accesses during the job executions. Three types of file access patterns are simulated along with the replication strategies.

Sequential

Files are requested in a fixed order. Sequential access pattern does not change the original order in the file list of a Grid job so that each file is accessed without considering the access locality that can be exploited to reduce overall access time.

Gaussian Random Walk

Successive files are selected from a Gaussian distribution centred on the previous file. As many phenomena have been observed to obey Gaussian distribution (also called normal distribution), some workloads may also follow or approximately follow Gaussian distribution. Specifically, Gaussian random walk access pattern assumes that only a small portion of files hold high frequency and low frequency while most of files in the workloads hold medium access frequency around the mean value.

Zipf

File request distributions are similar with web service requests distributions, which sometimes imply Zipf-like pattern. Zipf access pattern assumes that only a small portion of files contribute to the most file accesses. The Zipf distribution has been observed to be common in many types of system workloads ranging from web servers, web proxies and file systems.

Scheduling Method

Scheduling algorithms are executed by resource brokers based on the current Grid resource status. As OptorSim is a two staged simulation environment, one can purely evaluate replication strategies based on fixed scheduling algorithms. In this article, we discuss the simulation with following three scheduling algorithms:

Random: Jobs are scheduled to a random CE. CEs are randomly chosen according to a random number generator based on uniform distribution.

Queue Length: Jobs are scheduled to the CE with shortest job queue. If multiple CEs have same length of the job queue, it will randomly choose one according to the random number generator.

Queue Access Cost: Jobs are scheduled to the CE where the sum of file access costs and total job access costs are the smallest.

SIMULATION RESULTS

The simulations contained 1000 jobs submitted in 5-second intervals. Each replication strategy was simulated 10 times for each scheduling algorithm and access pattern. Three performance indices, Mean Job time, CE Usage and Effective Network Usage (ENU), are examined to evaluate these three replication strategies. Before simulation starts, all master copies of files are initially stored in CERN, which is site 8 in EDG testbed. Allocating all master copies in single site is to guarantee the fairness of initially accessing files from different sites. In addition, the average file processing time was set to 1 second. However, according to the experience from the experiments, altering various file processing time only linearly scales the simulation results.

Figure 7 and Figure 8 show the simulation results for the three replication strategies under the Queue Access Cost scheduling algorithm. It can be seen that the access pattern Zipf offers the shortest mean job time for all three strategies. Since Zipf access pattern assumes that a small number of files contribute to the most of file accesses. Thus, the files with higher ranks based on their frequency will have greater chance to be accessed than files with lower ranks. Consequently, those files will be most likely found in the local storage because they could already exist in the local storage due to their frequency ranks. Taking into account the skewness of the workloads used in the simulation, the mean job time benefits from the file access distribution which obeys Zipf-like pattern. Figure 7 shows that the Economic model is not as efficient as the other two strategies in terms of mean job time. In addition, the decision-tree-based predictive model slightly outperforms LRU under Zipf access pattern.

Figure 8 illustrates the CE usages of the three replication strategies under the same configuration with Figure 7. It shows that the Economic model and the decision-tree-based predictive model have relative higher CE usages than LRU. For the decision-tree-based predictive model, it is believed that the extra computing overhead is caused by the prediction of file popularity. Similarly, the Economic model also spends extra computing overhead by introducing the calculation for the file value which is taken as the indicator whether or not to replicate a file.

As we have discussed previously, the LRU based replication arbitrarily creates replicas without considering their potential popularity, which

Figure 7. Mean job time of three replication strategies under Queue Access Cost scheduling algorithm

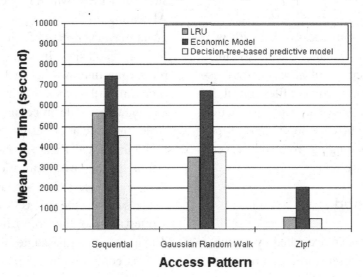

Figure 8. CE usages of three replication strategies under Queue Access Cost scheduling algorithm

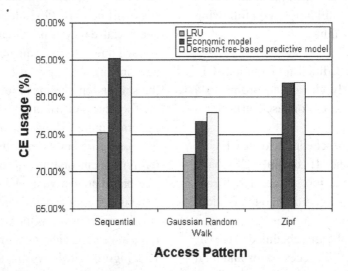

could lead to longer job time and higher effective network usage. On the other hand, the accuracy of files' popularity prediction is critical for the proposed predictive file replication strategy. For example, if a potentially frequent file is considered in-frequent, it will not be replicated to the other sites. However, this file will actually be demanded by many different sites due to its increasing popularity in future. Hence some of remote sites will be starving due to the access latency.

Similar with the Queue Access Cost scheduling algorithm, it can be seen from Figure 9 and Figure 10 that the Zipf access pattern always produces the best results than other two access patterns. In addition, it is noticed that scheduling algorithms can dramatically influence the mean job time and CE usage. Since Queue Access Cost is the sum of file access cost and job access cost, the mean job time under this scheduling algorithm is unsurprisingly the shortest. Figure 7 shows that the Queue Access Cost also generates the highest CE usages for all three replication strategies. This is due to the compromise made for the sites with high network connectivity and the sites with low network connectivity. Firstly, it ensures that the sites with high network connectivity will not be overloaded. On the other hand, sites with low network connectivity are guaranteed not to be idle. With such a balance, CEs are greatly utilized by the Queue Access Cost scheduling algorithm.

From Figures 9, 10, 11 and 12, we can see that Zipf access pattern offers the shortest mean job times and highest CE usage for all strategies. This can be explained by the access distribution of the workloads used in the simulation, which in consequence leads to the best results compared with other access patterns. Due to the investigations (Arlitt & Williamson, 1996; Barford & Crovella, 1998), most workloads of web servers and data hosting servers exhibit Zipf access pattern, that

Figure 9. Mean job time comparison of three replication strategies under Random scheduling algorithm

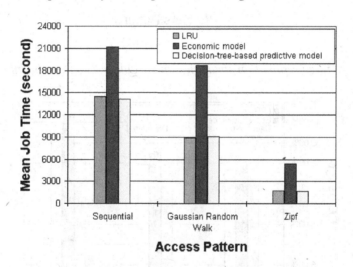

Figure 10. CE usages of three replication strategies under Random scheduling algorithm

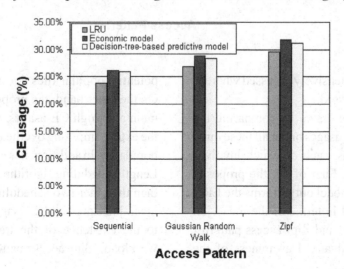

Figure 11. Mean job time of three replication strategies under Queue Length scheduling algorithm

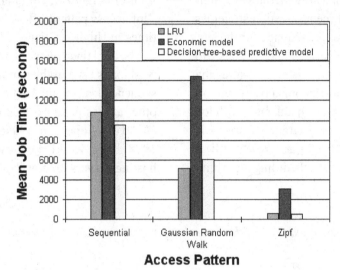

Figure 12. CE usages of three replication strategies under Queue Length scheduling algorithm

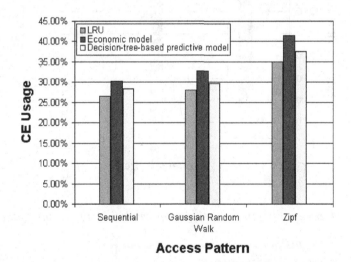

is, some of files are intensively accessed whereas others are rarely accessed.

Conclusion can be drawn by comparing the mean job time and CE usages under all these three scheduling algorithms, each of which involves three access patterns. First of all, the proposed decision-tree-based model outperforms the LRU and Economic model in terms of the mean job time given Sequential and Zipf access patterns. This is due to the advanced awareness of the

potential popular files during the job execution. On the other hand, the proposed strategy always maintains high CE usages, which are caused by the extra computing overhead for predicting files' popularity. In addition, it is noticed that the Queue Length scheduling algorithm brings better balance than the other two scheduling methods between mean job time and CE usage. Further more, due to the existence of the trace skewness in the workloads Zipf access pattern can dramatically improve the job execution efficiency of all three replication strategies. In the following analysis, we compare the effective network usage (ENU) under Queue Length scheduling algorithm.

The effective network usage illustrates the bandwidth consumption during the job execution. Figure 13 represents the effective network usages of all three replication strategies given the Queue Length scheduling algorithm. As the Economic model employs the reverse auction mechanism to message other Grid sites for finding the "cheapest" replicas, the messaging overhead leads to relative higher effective network usages than the others. The decision-tree-based predictive model maintains similar effective network usage compared with LRU. This can be explained with the definition of the effective network usage that is the equivalent to:

$$ENU =$$

$$\frac{the\_number\_of\_remote\_accesses + the\_number\_of\_replicas}{the\_number\_of\_remote\_accesses + the\_number\_of\_local\_accesses}$$

As the proposed predictive model reduces the number of replicas while the remote accesses are then added, ENU would not decrease unless the most of replicas are found in the local storage such like Zipf-like access pattern.

Figures 14, 15 and 16 compare the performance of all three replication strategies with various workload skewness ranging from 20/80 to 20/40, which denote that the skewness is tuned from the 80% of total accesses contributed by 20% files to the 40% of total accesses contributed by 20% of files.

It is clear that the trace skewness dramatically affects the performance under Zipf access pattern. Reducing 20% skewness will approximately increase mean job time by 3 times and 3.4 times for LRU and the predictive model respectively. Meanwhile, the Economic model also gains twice the mean job time. The above three figures reveal that the trace skewness only linearly affects the three performance indices under the Zipf access pattern.

Moreover, the mean job time is also simulated with different average storage capacity given the Zipf access pattern and the Queue Length

Figure 13. Effective network usages of three replication strategies under Queue Length scheduling algorithm

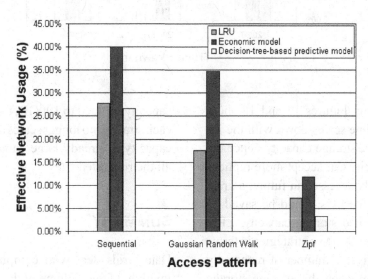

Figure 14. Mean job time of three replication strategies under Zipf access pattern and Queue Length scheduling algorithm

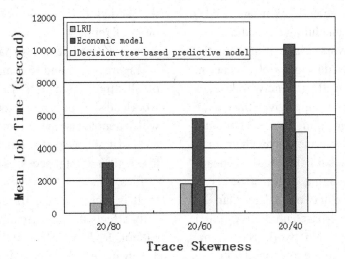

Figure 15. CE usages of three replication strategies under Zipf access pattern and Queue Length scheduling algorithm

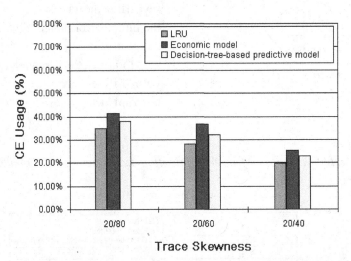

scheduling algorithm. Figures 17 and 18 show that the mean job time scales down with the increase of the average storage capacity. Since the larger storage capacity can accept more replicas which will be locally accessed in future, a great number of remote file I/Os would be saved. If each site has unlimited storage capacity, LRU will outperforms the other two strategies in terms of mean job time given a number of repeatedly executed jobs. Also, when the average storage capacity is tuned to 100GB, the mean job time of each strategy no longer scales down as the storage capacity is already large enough for replicating all the requested files.

SUMMARY

Data Grids deal with computational problems involving large volume of data such as scientific

Figure 16. Effective network usages of the three replication strategies under Zipf access pattern and Queue Length scheduling algorithm

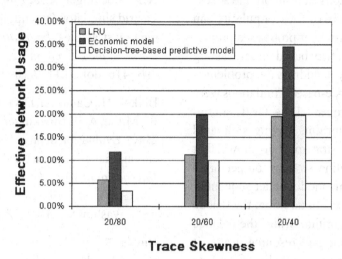

Figure 17. Mean job time of all three strategies given various average storage capacity

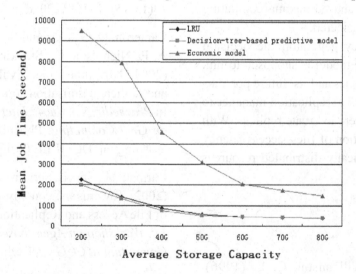

research data, climate monitoring data, satellite images, and sensor network data and so on. With the development of Grid infrastructures, software acting as the basic interfaces for future Grid application development is being intensively studied. However, compared with Grid middleware development, Grid resource optimization strategies are far behind studied and discussed.

In Grid environments, file replication strategies are critical to overall performance of large-scale data intensive applications. However, due to the dynamism of the Grids, file replication decisions are always made by monitoring the change of files' popularity. Although promptly replication can avoid the increase of access latency in future, the burden of the replications and the current accesses to the relative files may conflict each other and hence increase the access latency. Ideally, advanced file replications can smooth the access latency once the changes of files' popularity can be predicted. In this article, it proposes a predictive file replication strategy based on forecasting files' future popularity to address the problem.

The real-system-trace-based simulations were conducted under European Data Grid simulation environment OptorSim. Having simulated the three replication strategies, it shows that the predictive replication strategy outperforms the LRU and Economic model under sequential and Zipf access patterns. In addition, the Queue Length scheduling algorithm brings the balance between mean job time and resource usage. It is also noticed that no strategy delivers the best performance results in every circumstances. To choose an ideal replication strategy, trace skewness, storage capacity and the maximal computing power have to be considered.

As being a policy generator, the decision tree based predictive model is supposed to link file's own characteristics and its' future popularity then pass the rules to replication manager to decide when and where to create replicas. With the advanced evaluation of files, access latency caused by geographically distributed resources can be smoothed

REFERENCES

Arlitt, M. F., & Williamson, C. L. (1996). Web server workload characterization: The search for invariants. *ACM Sigmetrics Performance Evaluation Review*, *24*(1), 126–137. doi:10.1145/233008.233034

Barford, P., & Crovella, M. (1998). Generating representative Web workloads for network and server performance evaluation. *ACM Sigmetrics Performance Evaluation Review*, *26*(1), 151–160. doi:10.1145/277858.277897

Bell, W. H., Cameron, D. G., Capozza, L., Millar, A. P., Stockinger, K., & Zini, F. (2003). OptorSim - a grid simulator for studying dynamic data replication strategies. *International Journal of High Performance Computing Applications*, *17*(4), 403–416. doi:10.1177/10943420030174005

Bell, W. H., Cameron, D. G., Carvajal-Schiaffino, R., Millar, A. P., Stockinger, K., & Zini, F. (2003, May). Evaluation of an economy-based file replication strategy for a data grid. In *Proceedings of the International Workshop on Agent Based Cluster and Grid Computing at CCGrid2003*, Tokyo (p. 661). Washington, DC: IEEE Computer Society.

Buyya, R., & Murshed, M. (2002). GridSim: A toolkit for the modeling and simulation of distributed resource management and scheduling for grid computing. *Concurrency and Computation*, *14*(13-15), 1175–1220. doi:10.1002/cpe.710

Cameron, D. G., Carvajal-Schiaffino, R., Millar, A. P., Nicholson, C., Stockinger, K., & Zini, F. (2003, November 17). Evaluating scheduling and replica optimisation strategies in OptorSim. In *Proceedings of the 4th International Workshop on Grid Computing*, Phoenix, AZ (pp. 52-59). Washington, DC: IEEE Computer Society.

Carman, M., Zini, F., Serafini, L., & Stockinger, K. (2002). Towards an Economy-Based Optimisation of File Access and Replication on a Data Grid. *In Int. Workshop on Agent based Cluster and Grid Computing at CCGrid*, Berlin, Germany.

Crosby, P. (2008). *EDGSim*. Retrived July 2008, from http://www.hep.ucl.ac.uk/~pac/EDGSim

Ellard, D., Ledlie, J., Malkani, P., & Seltzer, M. (2003, March 31-April 2). Passive NFS tracing of email and research workloads. In *Proceedings of the 2nd USENIX Conference on File and Storage Technologies (FAST'03)*, San Francisco (pp. 203-216). USENIX.

Ellard, D., Ledlie, J., & Seltzer, M. (2003). *The utility of file names* (Tech. Rep. TR-05-03). Cambridge, MA: Harvard University Division of Engineering and Applied Sciences.

Ellard, D., Mesnier, M., Thereska, E., Ganger, G. R., & Seltzer, M. (2003). *Attribute-based prediction of file properties* (Tech. Rep. TR-14-03). Cambridge, MA: Harvard Computer Science Group.

Ellard, D., & Seltzer, M. (2003, October 26-31). New NFS Tracing tools and techniques for system analysis. In *Proceedings of the 17ᵗʰ Annual Large Installation System Administration Conference (LISA '03)*, San Diego, CA (pp. 73-85). USENIX.

Mitchell, T. M. (1997). *Machine learning*. New York: McGraw-Hill.

Muntz, D., & Honeyman, P. (1992, January). Multi-level caching in distributed file systems. In *Proceedings of the USENIX 1992 Winter Technical Conference,* San Francisco (pp. 305-313). USENIX.

Ranganathan, K., & Foster, I. (2001, November). Identifying dynamic replication strategies for a high performance data grid. In C. A. Lee (Ed.), *Proceedings of the International Grid Computing Workshop*, Denver, CO (LNCS 2242, pp. 75-86).

Ranganathan, K., & Foster, I. (2002, July). Decoupling computation and data scheduling in distributed data-intensive applications. In *Proceedings of the 2002 IEEE International Symposium of High Performance Distributed Computing*, Edinburgh, Scotland (p. 352). Washington, DC: IEEE Computer Society.

The European DataGrid Project. (2003). Retrieved June 2007, from http://www.edg.org

The Globus Alliance. (2006). *The Globus project.* Retrieved April 2006, from http://www.globus.org

Utgoff, P. (1998). ID5R: An incremental ID3. In *Proceedings of the 5ᵗʰ International Conference on Machine Learning,* Ann Arbor, MI (pp. 107-120). Morgan Kaufmann Publishers.

WP2 Optimization Team. (2008). *OptorSim, a replica optimiser simulator.* Retrieved February 2008, from http://cern.ch/edg-wp2/ optimization/ optorsim.html

Willick, D. L., Eager, D. L., & Bunt, R. B. (1993, May). Disk cache replacement policies for network file servers. In *Proceedings of International Conference on Distributed Computing Systems,* Pittsburgh, PA (pp. 2-11). Washington, DC: IEEE Computer Society.

Zipf, G. K. *(1932).* Selected studies of the principle of relative frequency in language. *Cambridge, MA: Harvard University Press.*

This work was previously published in International Journal of Grid and High Performance Computing, Volume 2, Issue 1, edited by Emmanuel Udoh, pp. 69-86, copyright 2010 by IGI Publishing (an imprint of IGI Global).

Section 3
Architecture

Chapter 6
Single Attestation Image for a Trusted and Scalable Grid

Yuhui Deng
Jinan University, P. R. China

Na Helian
University of Hertfordshire, UK

ABSTRACT

Traditionally, Grid users are forced to trust the Grid platforms, but the users are not always regarded as trustworthy. This trust asymmetry hinders the commercializing of Grid resources. Trusted Grid is proposed to tackle this challenge by leveraging Trusted Computing (TC). However, the TC relies on a microcontroller Trusted Platform Modules (TPM) which has limited computing power and is doomed to be a system bottleneck. This paper constructs a trusted Grid as a flat ring and decentralizes the functionalities of TPM across the ring. This architecture offers a single attestation image which provides a transparent attestation to a scalable, large-scale, and dynamic trusted Grid. The architecture also significantly reduces the frequency of attestations, thus alleviating the TPM bottleneck. Furthermore, the architecture can avoid the potential system bottleneck and single point of failure of the centralized architecture or the root node of the hierarchical architecture.

INTRODUCTION

Grid is a flexible, secure, and coordinated resource sharing among dynamic collections of individuals, institutions, and resources (Foster, Kesselman, & Tuwcke, 2001). The main issue of Grid security in the past works is achieving authentication and authorization of Grid users and their programs

(Basney, Humphrey, & Welch, 2005; Chadwick, 2005; Cody, Sharman, Rao, & Upadhyaya, 2008; Martin & Yau, 2007; Welch, 2004).The open source Globus Toolkit (GT) (The Globus Alliance, 2009a) has been employed worldwide as a middleware to develop Grid platforms and support Grid applications. Grid Security Infrastructure (GSI) (Welch, 2004) is adopted by GT to offer fundamental security services which enable secure authentication and communication over an

DOI: 10.4018/978-1-4666-0056-0.ch006

open network channel. For example, secure communication between elements of a Grid, security across organizational boundaries, single sign-on for Grid users, and so forth. In the GSI-like security mechanisms, Grid users are forced to trust the Grid platforms, but the users are not always regarded as trustworthy (Hwang et al., 2005; Löhr, Ramasamy, Sadeghi, Schulz, Schunter, & Stüble, 2007). The mechanisms do not consider trust from users' standpoint. This trust asymmetry could potentially result in a situation that the Grid users worry about the security of their jobs, tasks, confidential data, and so forth. This is because the resource providers in a Grid platform could cause damages to the users with little risk of detection or penalty. For example, an attacker hiding in a Grid platform might publish confidential data, or destroy the entire computation by providing false results. Due to this reason, companies hesitate to utilize the available Grid resources for confidential and important tasks (Löhr et al., 2007). Therefore, symmetrical trust between Grid users and the Grid platform is crucial for a successful Grid.

Trusted Grid is proposed to tackle this challenge of asymmetrical trust by leveraging Trusted Computing (TC) (Löhr et al., 2007; Martin & Yau, 2007). TC is defined and developed by the Trusted Computing Group (TCG) to ensure that a system will behave in specific ways, and those behaviors will be enforced by hardware and software (TCG Specification, 2007). Trusted Platform Module (TPM) is designed by TCG to ensure that the ownership of a platform can be asserted by asset managers, while allowing users to perform jobs. A TPM contains a set of Platform Configuration Registers (PCRs) to securely store a representation of the platform's configuration information. Therefore, the TPM can be employed to guarantee that each computer will report its configuration parameters in a trustworthy manner. TC can not only be maintained in a single platform (e.g., endorsement key, memory curtaining, and sealed storage), but also provide attestation to a remote challenger. Attestation indicates that a trusted plat-

form attests and reports its integrity state recorded in the PCRs. If a Grid platform can offer remote attestation to Grid users to ensure that the platform is trusted, the users would be very happy to use the Grid resources, thus improving the resource utilization. The reader is referred to (Trusted Computing Group, 2007) for a comprehensive understanding of the TC related knowledge.

The objective of Grid is to virtualize the geographically distributed resources and allow users and applications to access resources as a single machine (Deng & Wang, 2007). A large-scale and complex Grid application could involve hundreds or thousands of geographically distributed resources. With the growth of application requirements, a Grid system should have the ability to continue to provide satisfied capabilities including resources, performance, and fault tolerance in a transparent manner when the system is increased in size. Monitoring and Discovery System (MDS) (The Globus Alliance, 2009b; Deng, Wang, & Ciura, 2009) is a key component to provide basic mechanisms for resource discovery and monitoring in a typical Grid environment. If Grid users want to validate the integrity of a Grid platform, they have to verify the MDS through remote attestation, since all resources are registered in the MDS. However, the TPM is a secure microcontroller with limited computing power. If hundreds or thousands of Grid users perform the remote attestation simultaneously, a single MDS equipped with TPM is doomed to be a system bottleneck. Furthermore, the MDS has to provide resource query, store-and-forward of the submitted jobs and job results. Therefore, a distributed policy consisting of multiple TPM-equipped MDSs is required to deal with this challenge.

Traditional approaches maintain a centralized MDS or a set of hierarchically organized MDSs to index resource information in a Grid. However, three reasons limit the efficiency of the traditional approaches. The first, the centralized approach, and the root node of the hierarchical method have the inherent drawback of a single point of failure. The second, the approaches may result in system bottlenecks in a highly dynamic environment where many resources join, leave, and can change characteristics at any time. Finally, the approaches cannot scale well to a large-scale and geographically distributed system across the internet. For the TPM-equipped MDSs, the above impacts become more serious. Therefore, it is important to decentralize the functionalities of TPM-equipped MDSs to avoid the potential bottlenecks and the single point failure of the hierarchical or centralized approaches (Talia & Trunfio, 2003; Deng, Wang, Helian, Wu, & Liao, 2008; Deng et al., 2009). Recently, some research efforts have been invested in alleviating the problem. A scalable offline attestation protocol is proposed to enhance the security of a dynamic Grid system with minimal overhead (Löhr et al., 2007). In this protocol, all service providers have to generate and publish an attestation token when they join a Grid. Grid users retrieve the attestation tokens from different service providers and select a token indicating a configuration they are willing to trust. This selection is performed offline, thus incurring negligible overhead. However, it is a challenge for the Grid users to retrieve an appropriate attestation token if they face hundreds of thousands service providers (Chen, Landerfman, Löhr, Rohe, Sadeghi, & Stüble, 2006). In the scenario, some service providers could never be trusted and accessed. The traditional binary based attestation reveals information about the configuration of a platform or application. Property based attestation is proposed to tackle the challenges. Semantic remote attestation uses a trusted virtual machine to remotely attest the complex, dynamic, and high-level program properties in a platform-independent way (Haldar, Chandra, & Franz, 2004). The key point behind this idea is that the trusted virtual machine can check the security policy of the code running in the virtual machine. A high-level protocol between verifier and attestor for property attestation is proposed in (Poritz et al., 2004). This protocol is based on

property certificates which are employed by a verification proxy to translate binary attestations into property attestations.

People naturally do not use external resources for their confidential data or critical tasks, only if there is little perceptive risk of the content, and it is also much easier and less expensive. TC can ensure Grid users that the Grid resources are trusted. Meanwhile, it is also very important for the Grid users to have a transparent and easy way to validate that the Grid platform is trusted. Single system image is the property of a system that hides the heterogeneous and distributed nature of the aggregated resources, and presents them to users and applications as a single unified computing resource (Hwang, Jin, Chow, Wang, & Xu, 1999). In contrast to the existing works, this paper proposes an approach of how to provide a single attestation image of a scalable and dynamic trusted Grid to hide the complexity of attestation, while alleviating the potential attestation bottleneck of TPM. This approach also can reduce the frequency of attestation in a large-scale trusted Grid. Furthermore, the proposed approach can eliminate the single point of failure of the traditional hierarchical architecture by connecting the MDSs in a ring.

The remainder of this paper is organized as follows. The related knowledge is introduced in background section. System design section describes the overall system architecture and the single attestation image. We then discuss the impact of different architectures on a trusted Grid. Finally, we conclude the paper with remarks on main contributions of the paper.

BACKGROUND

Transitive Trust and Integrity Measurement

TPM is a secure microcontroller with added cryptographic functionalities. It stores keys, passwords, and digital certificates. It potentially can be employed in any computing device which requires these functions. It works with supporting software and firmware to prevent unauthorized access to the devices. The TPM contains a RSA engine, a SHA1 engine, Attestation Identity Keys (AIK), Program code, PCRs, and so forth. The RSA engine is adopted to perform up to 2048-bit RSA encryption/decryption, digital signing, and key wrapping operations. The SHA1 engine is mainly used for computing signatures and creating key bobs. An AIK is created by the TPM and linked to the local platform through a certificate for that AIK. This certificate is created and signed by a certificate authority (CA). In particular, a privacy CA allows a platform to present different AIKs to different remote parties, so that it is impossible for these parties to determine that the AIKs are coming from the same platform (Berger, Cáceres, Goldman, Perez, Sailer, & Doorn, 2006). Program code contains firmware for measuring platform devices. This is the Core Root of Trust for Measurement (CRTM) which should be contained in the TPM. For a typical computer system, the CRTM is the early-executed instructions in a Basic Input/Output System (BIOS), since the BIOS is a default firmware adopted to boot a computer system.

The root of trust is a component that must be trusted. It has the minimum functionalities to describe the platform characteristics that affect the trustworthiness of the platform. Transitive trust is a process where the root of trust gives a trustworthy description of the second component. Based on this description, another entity can determine the trust level of the second component. If the trust level is acceptable, the trust boundary is extended from the root of trust to include the second component. By analogy, this process can be applied for a large number of iterations. Figure 1 shows the transitive trust and integrity measurement of a computer platform. In the above transitive trust, in order to extend the trust chain from the CRTM to the BIOS, the CRTM has to measure the properties and characteristics of the BIOS.

This measurement is a hash process. When the first measure is done, the measured value will be stored in a PCR, and the second component can be used to measure the next component. A final PCR value represents the accumulation of a sequence of measurements. By doing so, platform boot processes are augmented to allow the TPM to measure each of the components in the system (both hardware and software), and securely store the results of the measurements in PCRs within the TPM. The sequence of this measurement shares a common measured value. The new measured values are appended to the common measured value and re-hashed. This can be described by following equation:

$$PCR[n] = SHA1 (PCR[n] \parallel measured\ value) \tag{1}$$

where SHA1 denotes Secure Hash Algorithm Standard, $\parallel$ operation indicates a concatenation of two byte arrays. The above operation is called extension, since PCRs are initialized at power up and can only be modified by reset or extension.

Remote Attestation

As discussed previously, integrity measurement is a process of obtaining metrics of platform properties and characteristics that affect the trustworthiness, and putting the measured value of those metrics in PCRs. Attestation can be understood along several dimensions, attestation by TPM, attestation to a platform, attestation of a platform,

Figure 1. Transitive trust and integrity measurement

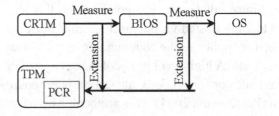

and authentication of a platform. Attestation of the platform is an operation that provides proof of a set of the platform's integrity measurements. This is done by digitally signing a set of PCRs using the AIK in a TPM (Trusted Computing Group, 2007). Access to a platform will be denied if the platform configuration is not as expected by using the attestation.

Figure 2 shows a remote attestation between a Grid user and a MDS. The major steps of a remote attestation are labeled with the sequence number as defined in the following descriptions. (1) The Grid user generates an unpredictable nonce. (2) The nonce is sent to the MDS together with an attestation request. (3) Once the request is received, the TPM hashes the concatenated value of current PCR[n] and the nonce. (4) The TPM signs the hashed value H with its AIK private key. The signed message S is transferred to the Grid user. (5) After receiving the message S, the Grid user verifies the message with its AIK public key. (6) The Grid user also hashes the concatenated value of an expected PCR[n] and the nonce, and obtains a value E. (7) If the verified value V matches E, it indicates the MDS is trusted. Otherwise, the MDS is not trusted. Please note that the Grid user has to obtain the expected PCR[n] before performing the attestation, so that the user can determine whether the MDS is trusted or not by verifying the current PCR[n] and the expected PCR[n]. In this paper, we sometimes use attestation token instead of the expected PCR value.

Figure 2. Remote attestation protocol

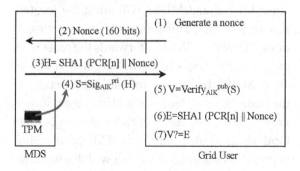

$$S = \text{Sig}(C) = C^d \bmod n \qquad (2)$$

$$C = \text{Verify}(S) = S^e \bmod n \qquad (3)$$

In the remote attestation, the TPM has to sign the hashed value H with its AIK private key. The signed message can be verified by the Grid users who have the AIK public key, thereby proving that the received message is signed by the TPM and the message has not been tampered. The digital signature incurs significant overhead. Let's take the RSA algorithm as an example. The public key is a pair of integers (n, e), where n is a 1024-bit/2048-bit number, e is a small prime number (e.g., 17). The private key (d) is a 1024-bit/2048-bit number. The size of d should be the same as that of n. We assume that the hashed value is C. The digital signature and verify employ the function (2) and function (3), respectively. It is easy to observe that C^d is a very big number. This is the reason why digital signature requires a lot of computing power.

TPM normally provides limited computing power. ST19WP18 (ST19WP18 datasheet, 2009) is a cost-effective TPM solution which is designed to provide PC platforms with enhanced security and integrity mechanisms. The ST19WP18 has an 8-bit CPU architecture and several accelerators. Modular arithmetic processor is a 1088-bit cryptographic engine. It is designed to speed up cryptographic calculations using public key algorithms, and allow processing of modular multiplication, squaring, and additional calculations up to 2176-bit operands. A secure hash accelerator allows fast SHA-1 computation. It is especially well suited for BIOS hash operations during early boot stages. Though the ST19WP18 takes the above measures to enhance the processing power, it is still not enough to handle a lot of parallel remote attestation requests. Based on the above two reasons, the TPM is doomed to be a bottleneck in a large-scale Grid environment.

SYSTEM DESIGN

Architecture Overview

To match the requirements imposed by all kinds of applications, a large-scale and scalable Grid may involve hundreds or even thousands of resources which are geographically distributed. A typical Grid is composed of Grid users, MDSs, and hundreds of thousands of service providers. All heterogeneous resources are wrapped into Grid services and registered in MDS, which constructs a small virtual organization. The interaction between service providers and Grid users is mediated through a MDS, since MDS offers basic mechanisms for resource discovery and monitoring (Deng & Wang, 2007; Deng et al., 2008). Figure 3 shows a typical trusted Grid platform consisting of one Grid user, one Grid portal, and three MDSs. The Grid portal maintains one public IP address and a list of the IP addresses of the MDSs. It redirects the Grid users' requests to the MDSs to offer a single entry point to the trusted Grid. Since redirecting requests does no involve too much overhead, the Grid portal does not generate a system bottleneck. Security of the Grid portal is beyond the scope of this paper. Each MDS is equipped with a TPM. All the backend service providers, which are equipped with TPM, are not illustrated in this figure, because this paper attempts to construct a single attestation image across multiple MDSs.

Figure 3. Overview of a trusted Grid

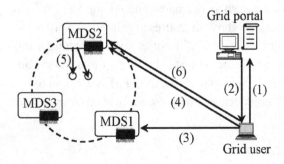

Within the above Grid environment, Grid users can achieve following functions through the VO interface: (1) Send a request to the Grid portal which maintains a list of the IP addresses of the MDSs. (2) The Grid portal answers the request with a list of MDSs which rank in terms of the network distance. (3) The Grid user contacts the first MDS (MDS1 illustrated in Figure 3) on the list, retrieves an attestation taken, and attests MDS1. MDS1 is the closest one to the user. This is why MDS1 is the first one on the list. If it is trusted, the user will send its query request to MDS1. (4) Otherwise, the user will attest the second MDS on the list (MDS2 illustrated in Figure 3). This process will repeat until the user finds a trusted MDS. (5) We assume MDS2 is trusted in this section. Once a query request is received, MDS2 first checks its own workload and the available resources registered in it. If the MDS is not heavily loaded, and the satisfied resources are found in it, MDS2 will attest the located service provider to make sure that the service provider is trusted. (6) MDS2 will notify the user to submit jobs and forward the job to the located service provider.

In the above discussion, MDS1 does not directly forward the request to its neighbor MDS2 or MDS3. The reason is because in a trusted Grid, the forwarder has to guarantee that the receiver is trusted. Therefore, each message relay incurs one attestation, which generates unnecessary network traffic and consumes a lot of computing power of TPM. For example, If MDS1 finds required resources registered in MDS3 from its local resource list, the Grid users only need to attest MDS3, and MDS3 will attest the located service provider. This process takes two attestations. However, if MDS1 forwards the request to one of its neighbors (e.g., MDS3), MDS1 has to attest MDS3 before the forwarding. Therefore, the frequency of attestation will increase with the growth of the frequency of relay. In a large-scale Grid which involves hundreds of MDSs, the relay approach is not applicable. We will discuss how

MDS1 locates the required resources in MDS3 from its local resource list to avoid unnecessary store-and-forward in the next section.

Single Attestation Image

Figure 4 illustrates a single attestation image which consists of three geographically distributed and dynamic MDSs. As discussed, all the attestation, resource query, and job submission have to pass through the MDSs. Therefore, it is necessary to avoid or alleviate the bottleneck by distributing the bursty workload across multiple MDSs. The objective of a single attestation image is to tackle this challenge and manage the MDSs across the Internet effectively.

A good algorithm of single attestation image should not change the system configuration too drastically when a few MDSs are leaving or joining. Otherwise, the functionalities of a trusted Grid could be impacted significantly. The algorithm consists of knowledge of the neighbors of each MDS in the image. We previously elaborated that a remote attestation involves one challenger and one attestator. The challenger has to know the AIK public key AIK^{pub} and the platform information PCR_{init} recorded in PCRs to perform a successful attestation. Therefore, MDSs have to maintain two lists. In order to avoid or alleviate the MDS bottleneck, we design the image to

ensure that all MDSs are equal in functions. Therefore, the lists across all the MDSs are the same. The first list is a platform configuration list which provides the required information to the challengers to perform attestation. The second list is a resource list since a major role of MDS is offering resource query. Figure 4 shows the two lists, where the numbers in front of AIK, PCR, and R denote the MDS number. For example, $1\text{-}AIK^{pub}$ and $2\text{-}PCR_{init}$ indicate the AIK^{pub} of MDS1 and PCR_{init} of MDS2, respectively. On the second list, the numbers behind the symbol R mean the resource number. For example, 3-R2 presents the second resource registered in MDS3. We assume that each MDS has two resources in Figure 4.

The PCR values are temporal, and are reset at system reboot. If a MDS platform is upgraded, the measured value stored in PCRs should be updated as well. Therefore, the attestation has to be dynamic. Unicast is employed to achieve dynamicity and scalability features when MDSs leave or join the trusted Grid. Since the dynamicity is normally caused by maintenance, upgrade and other reasons, the MDSs are relatively stable. Therefore, using unicast to send a message to multiple MDSs simultaneously does not result in too much communication traffic. The MDS, which wants to join the image, can send a group of probing unicast JOIN requests and the corresponding information, and wait for the response of other online MDSs. The online MDSs, which receive the JOIN request, update their two lists and send an ACCEPT acknowledgment back to the probing MDS. The oncoming MDS constructs its own lists in terms of the acknowledgment messages. Finally, all the MDSs are self-organized into a dynamic overlay network. The same process is applied to the MDSs which want to leave the image. For example, a MDS, which wants to leave the image, sends a group of unicast LEAVE messages across the image. Once the online MDSs receive the message, the receivers delete the leaving MDS's information and update their two lists immediately. Because short messages are sent

Figure 4. Single attestation image

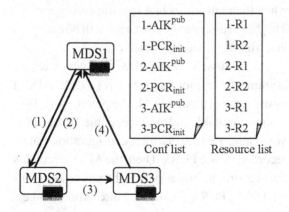

at regular intervals between MDSs, if a message is not received from a particular MDS, then the MDS is assumed to have failed and other remaining MDSs delete the related information from their lists. The periodic heartbeat diffusion with a reasonable low frequency is feasible due to the relatively stable MDSs. On the other hand, excessive false detections will increase maintenance cost significantly and unnecessarily. By tuning the diffusion period, the time to recover from a failure can be balanced against the bandwidth overhead of repeated transmissions.

A challenge here is how to ensure the dynamic image is trusted. We assume that initially there is only one MDS and it is trusted in a trusted Grid (e.g., MDS1). The following process is labeled with the sequence number as defined in the following descriptions (see Figure 4). (1) When MDS2 joins, MDS1 plays a role of challenger to attest MDS2. Based on this, MDS2 is trusted by MDS1 if the attestation is successful. (2) Since all MDSs are equal in functions, MDS2 has to trust MDS1. Therefore, MDS2 has to attest MDS1 as well. (3) When MDS3 joins, MDS2 attests MDS3, and MDS3 attests MDS1. In this way, we can construct a trust ring in which each MDS is trusted by another MDS. By analogy, more MDSs can be added to the existing trusted image. This is similar to the transitive trust discussed previously, but this is at a higher level. If one MDS leaves the image, the remaining MDSs will maintain a reduced trust ring. For example, if MDS2 leaves, MDS3 still trust MDS1, but not vice versa. MDS1 has to perform another attestation to MDS3 to maintain the trust chain.

In a typical Grid environment, all resources should be registered in MDSs so that users can easily locate a specific resource. For a trusted Grid, the Grid users have to obtain an integrity measurement value (attestation token) for a specific platform, and attest the platform by comparing the current value and the expected value to determine whether the platform is trusted or not. Finally, the users can submit a query request to locate the required resource if the platform is trusted. In a large-scale trusted Grid consisting of hundreds or thousands of resources, it is a challenge for a user to choose a specific token from hundreds of thousands of tokens for the corresponding platform. The single attestation image is proposed to provide a transparent attestation to a scalable, large-scale, and dynamic trusted Grid.

Secure Job Submission and Execution

There are two major jobs in a typical Grid environment. The first one is interactive job which provides immediate feedback to Grid users. Batch job is the second one which stores output/ error streams into remote files. The files can be retrieved after the job is completed. Batch jobs are normally adopted when multiple jobs are launched in parallel, or when the execution time is expected to be very large. In order to describe the job submission in a neat way, this section focuses on the batch job. It is better to integrate the job submission interfaces with the MDSs instead of the service providers to simplify the job submission process. The reason is because the execution location of jobs should be transparent to Grid users. Therefore, in this section, the Grid users submit their jobs to the MDSs.

Sealing, which can bound messages to a specific platform configuration through a subset of PCRs, is a powerful feature of TPM. It ensures that the protected messages are recoverable only when the platform is in a specific configuration. This feature guarantees that a job will be executed in a trusted service provider.

As discussed, each MDS first generates an asymmetric cryptographic key K (AIK^{pub}, AIK^{pri}) by using the equipped TPM. The private key AIK^{pri} is non-migratable and only accessible for the TPM. We assume that the platform configuration can be recorded by the PCRs. Then, the MDS circulates the platform information and the public key Conf = (AIK^{pub}, PCR_{init}) across the attestation image.

Figure 5 shows a job submission process in a trusted Grid environment. Before a Grid user submits its job to a MDS, the user performs an attestation first to ensure that the MDS is trusted. The remaining steps of the process are defined in the following descriptions. (1) The Grid user retrieves the platform configuration of the MDS. (2) The Grid user generates a symmetric key k_{sym}. (3) The user encrypts its job with the symmetric key En (k_{sym}) (J), and sends the encrypted job to a corresponding MDS. (4) The user retrieves the AIK^{pub} from Conf, employs the key to encrypt the concatenation of the PCR_{init} and the k_{sym}, and sends the encrypted message E to the corresponding MDS. (5) Once receiving the message E, the MDS decrypts the message with its private key AIK^{pri}. (6) The MDS checks its current platform configuration PCR_{cur}. If $PCR_{init} = PCR_{cur}$, the MDS can obtain the symmetric key k_{sym} by using De $(AIK^{pri})(E) = PCR_{init} \| k_{sym}$. (7) The MDS adopts the symmetric key to decrypt the job De $(k_{sym})(J)$. (8) After retrieving the job, the MDS will pick up a registered service provider, which offers the required resources, and attest the service provider and forward the job to the service provider by sealing. If the job is done by the service provider, the execution results will be sent to the MDS. The MDS will encrypt the results with the symmetric key k_{sym} and sent the message En $(k_{sym})(R)$ to the Grid user. (9) The user will employ its own symmetric key k_{sym} to retrieve the results De $(k_{sym})(R)$.

Above description indicates that the sealed information is encrypted with a public key and can only be decrypted if the PCRs of a selected platform are in the same state as they were at the time of sealing. This guarantees that a job will be executed in a trusted platform. The eighth step in the above discussion confirms that each message relay involves one attestation and one sealing. Therefore, it is important to reduce the frequency of relay.

DISCUSSION

We have discussed the challenges facing a trusted Grid in the introduction section and proposed a flat ring architecture previously. We believe that how to build the architecture of a trusted Grid has a significant impact on the overall system behavior. Table 1 shows the impact of four different architectures on a trusted Grid. Traditional Grid systems maintain a centralized MDS or organize the MDSs in a hierarchical architecture. Centralized architecture is impractical for a trusted Grid since it is not scalable. Registering all resources in a centralized MDS definitely results in a system bottleneck, especially for a TPM-equipped MDS.

Hierarchical architecture is more scalable than the centralized one, because it is easy to add more MDSs and the corresponding resources to an existing system. However, three drawbacks hinder

Figure 5. Job submission to a MDS

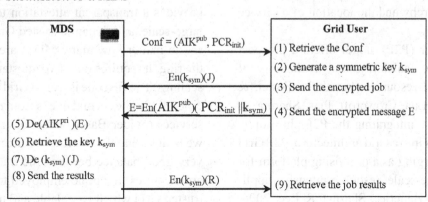

Table 1. Impact of different architectures on a trusted grid

	Centralized architecture	Hierarchical architecture	Peer to Peer architecture	Flat ring architecture
Scalability	Very low	High	Very high	High
Bottleneck	MDS	Root node	No	No
Single point of failure	Yes	Yes	No	No
Single attestation image	Yes	No	No	Yes
Frequency of attestation	Two	Higher than two	Very high	Two

the architecture to be employed in a trusted Grid (Deng et al., 2008). The first, like the centralized MDS, the root MDS of a hierarchical architecture is doomed to be a single point of failure and a system bottleneck of a trusted Grid, if multiple users simultaneously perform attestation or job sealing. In the second, it does not provide a single attestation image as the centralized architecture. Therefore, it is difficult for a user to retrieve an appropriate attestation token if they face hundreds of thousands tokens. The reason is that all service providers and MDSs have to publish their attestation tokens so that they can be attested by the corresponding challengers. In the third, the messages, which have to go through multiple levels in the architecture, generate many unnecessary attestations. This is because a hierarchical trusted Grid consists of multiple levels, all the messages and the submitted jobs have to be forwarded from the root MDS to a specific service provider through several other MDSs in the middle levels. Each message relay incurs one attestation in a trusted Grid. The frequency of relay depends on the levels of hierarchy and the location of a service provider.

Peer-to-Peer (P2P) model offers a prospect of dynamicity, scalability, and availability of a large pool of resources (Iamnitchi, Foster, & Nurmi, 2002; Lua, Crowcroft, Pias, Sharma, & Lim, 2005). By integrating the P2P philosophy and techniques into a Grid architecture, P2P Grid system is emerging as a promising platform for executing large-scale, resource intensive applications (Basu, Banerjee, Sharma, & Lee, 2005;

Iamnitchi et al., 2002; Zhu, Liu, Zhang, Xiao, & Yang, 2003). There are two typical resource discovery approaches for a large-scale P2P system (Deng et al., 2009; Lv, Cao, Cohen, & Shenker, 2002). The first one is an unstructured approach which propagates the query messages to all nodes to locate the required resources. The second one is a structured approach which places resources at specified locations to make subsequent queries easier to satisfy. Unfortunately, the P2P architecture is not applicable to a trusted Grid, since both methods could generate many message relay, thus incurring many attestations. Furthermore, it is more difficult for a P2P architecture to provide a single attestation image in comparison to the hierarchical architecture.

In contrast to the typical architectures, this paper proposes to distribute the functionalities of one TPM- equipped MDS to several MDSs, and organize all the MDSs in a ring to eliminate the potential single point of failure and alleviate the system bottleneck. Meanwhile, the ring architecture offers a single attestation image which provides a transparent attestation to a scalable, large-scale, and dynamic trusted Grid. By doing so, no matter how many MDSs are involved in the ring, it requires only two attestations and job sealings. The first one is from a Grid user to a specific MDS. The second one is from the MDS to a service provider. Based on the above discussions, we believe that the flat ring architecture strikes a very good balance between the traditional Grid architectures. It can be employed to construct a trusted Grid which is scalable and dynamic.

CONCLUSION

Trusted Grid is proposed to handle the trust asymmetry in traditional Grid environments. However, the trusted Grid relies on a microcontroller TPM which only has limited computing power. This characteristic leaves challenges to construct a scalable and trusted Grid. The first challenge is how to reduce message relay, since each relay incurs one attestation. This feature significantly aggravates the system bottleneck. The second challenge is how to build a single attestation image across a large-scale trusted Grid. This paper reviews the background technology of trusted computing, proposes an architecture for a trusted Grid to handle the challenges, and discusses the impact of different architectures on a trusted Grid. The proposed architecture can be employed to guarantee the trust of a Grid, while reducing the frequency of attestations and making the resources more accessible. This architecture also can avoid the potential system bottleneck and single point of failure of the centralized architecture or the root node of the hierarchical architecture.

ACKNOWLEDGMENT

I would like to thank my friends Jun Li and Jason Zhang from EMC Research China for their comments and suggestions. I also appreciate the anonymous reviewers for helping refine this paper. Their constructive comments and suggestions are very helpful. In addition, I am grateful to Prof. Frank Zhigang Wang for giving me the opportunity to clarify my thoughts.

REFERENCES

Basney, J., Humphrey, M., & Welch, V. (2005). The MyProxy online credential repository. *Software, Practice & Experience, 35*(9), 801–816. doi:10.1002/spe.688

Basu, S., Banerjee, S., Sharma, P., & Lee, S. (2005, May 9-12). NodeWiz: Peer-to-peer resource discovery for grids. In *Proceedings of the IEEE International Symposium on Domain Computing and the Grid (CCGrid 2005),* Cardiff, UK (pp. 213-220). IEEE.

Berger, S., Cáceres, R., Goldman, K., Perez, R., Sailer, R., & Doorn, L. (2006, July 31-August 4). vTPM: Virtualizing the trusted platform module. In *Proceedings of the 15th Conference on USENIX Security Symposium,* Vancouver, British Columbia, Canada (Article No. 21). Berkeley, CA: USENIX.

Chadwick, D. (2005). Authorisation in Grid computing. *Information Security Technical Report, 10*(1), 33–40. doi:10.1016/j.istr.2004.11.004

Chen, L., Landferman, R., Löhr, H., Rohe, M., Sadeghi, A.-R., & Stüble, C. (2006). A protocol for property-based attestation. In *Proceedings of the 1st ACM Workshop on Scalable Trusted Computing,* Alexandria, VA (pp. 7-16). ACM Publising.

Cody, E., Sharman, R., Rao, R., & Upadhyaya, S. (2008). Security in grid computing: A review and synthesis. *Decision Support Systems, 44*(4), 749–764. doi:10.1016/j.dss.2007.09.007

Deng, Y., & Wang, F. (2007). A heterogeneous storage grid enabled by grid service. *ACM SIGOPS Operating Systems Review, 41*(1), 7–13. doi:10.1145/1228291.1228296

Deng, Y., Wang, F., & Ciura, A. (2009). Ant colony optimization inspired resource discovery in P2P grid systems. *The Journal of Supercomputing, 49*(1), 4–21. doi:10.1007/s11227-008-0214-0

Deng, Y., Wang, F., Helian, N., Wu, S., & Liao, C. (2008). Dynamic and scalable storage management architecture for Grid Oriented Storage devices. *Parallel Computing, 34*(1), 17–31. doi:10.1016/j.parco.2007.10.003

Foster, I., Kesselman, C., & Tuecke, S. (2001). The anatomy of the grid: Enabling scalable virtual organizations. *International Journal of High Performance Computing Applications*, 15(3), 200–222. doi:10.1177/109434200101500302

Haldar, V., Chandra, D., & Franz, M. (2004, May 6-12). Semantic remote attestation- a virtual machine directed approach to trusted computing. In *Proceedings of the 3rd Conference on Virtual Machine Research and Technology Symposium*, San Jose, CA (p. 3). Berkeley, CA: USENIX.

Hwang, K., Jin, H., Chow, E., Wang, C., & Xu, Z. (1999). Designing SSI clusters with hierarchical check pointing and single I/O space. *IEEE Concurrency*, 7(1), 60–69. doi:10.1109/4434.749136

Hwang, K., Kwok, Y. K., Song, S., Chen, M., Chen, Y., Zhou, R., et al. (2005, May). Gridsec: Trusted grid computing with security bindings and self-defense against network worms and ddos attacks. In *Proceedings of International Workshop on Grid Computing Security and Resource Management (GSRM'05)*, Atlanta, GA (pp. 187-195). Springer.

Iamnitchi, A., Foster, I., & Nurmi, D. (2002, July 23-26). A peer-to-peer approach to resource discovery in grid environments. In *Proceedings of the 11th Symposium on High Performance Distributed Computing*, Edinburgh, UK (pp. 419-434). IEEE.

Löhr, H., Ramasamy, H. V., Sadeghi, A., Schulz, S., Schunter, M., & Stüble, C. (2007, July). Enhancing grid security using trusted virtualization. In *Proceedings of the 4th International Conference on Autonomic and Trusted Computing (ATC 2007)*, Hong Kong, China (pp. 372-384). Springer.

Lua, E., Crowcroft, J., Pias, M., Sharma, R., & Lim, S. (2005). A survey and comparison of peer-to-peer overlay network schemes. *IEEE Communications Surveys & Tutorials*, 7(2), 72–93. doi:10.1109/COMST.2005.1610546

Lv, Q., Cao, P., Cohen, E., Li, K., & Shenker, S. (2002, June 22-26). Search and replication in unstructured peer-to-peer networks. In *Proceedings of the 16th ACM International Conference on Supercomputing (ICS'02)*, New York (pp. 84-95). ACM Publishing.

Martin, A., & Yau, P. (2007). Grid security: Next steps. *Information Security Technical Report*, 12(3), 113–122. doi:10.1016/j.istr.2007.05.009

Poritz, J., Schunter, M., Herreweghen, E., & Waidner, M. (2004). Property attestation – scalable and privacy-friendly security assessment of peer computers (Tech. Rep. RZ3548, ST19WP18 datasheet). IBM Research.

Talia, D., & Trunfio, P. (2003). Towards a synergy between P2P and grids. *IEEE Internet Computing*, 7(4), 94–96. doi:10.1109/MIC.2003.1215667

The Globus Alliance. (2009a). *Globus toolkit*. Retrieved from http://www.globus.org/

The Globus Alliance. (2009b). *Monitoring and discovery system*. Retrieved from http://www.globus.org/toolkit/mds/

Trusted Computing Group. (2007). *TCG specification architecture overview. Revision 1.4*. Retrieved from https://www.trustedcomputinggroup.org/home

Welch, V. (2004). *Globus toolkit version 4 grid security infrastructure: A standards perspective*. Retrieved from http://www.globus.org/toolkit/docs/4.0/security/GT4-GSI-Overview.pdf

Zhu, C., Liu, Z., Zhang, W., Xiao, W., & Yang, D. (2003, September). Analysis on greedy-search based service location in P2P service grid. In *Proceedings of the 3rd Conference on Peer-to-Peer Computing*, Linköping, Sweden (pp. 110-117). IEEE.

This work was previously published in International Journal of Grid and High Performance Computing, Volume 2, Issue 1, edited by Emmanuel Udoh, pp. 21-33, copyright 2010 by IGI Publishing (an imprint of IGI Global).

Chapter 7
Personal Storage Grid Architecture:
Consuming Cloud Data Space Resources

Mian-Guan Lim
Cranfield University, UK

Sining Wu
Cranfield University, UK

Tomasz Simon
Cranfield University, UK

Md Rashid
Cranfield University, UK

Na Helian
Hertfordshire University, UK

ABSTRACT

On-demand cloud applications like online email accounts and online virtual disk space are becoming widely available in various forms. In cloud applications, one can see the importance of underlying resources, such as disk space, that is available to the end-user but not easily accessible. In the authors' study, a modern file system developed in linux is proposed, which enables consuming of cloud applications and making the underlying disk space resource available to the end-user. This system is developed as a web service to support cross operation system support. A free online mail account was used to demonstrate this solution, and an IMAP protocol to communicate with remote data spaces was used so that this method can mount onto any email system that supports IMAP. The authors' definition of infinite storage as the user is able to mount file systems as a single logical drive.

DOI: 10.4018/978-1-4666-0056-0.ch007

INTRODUCTION

Centralizing storage is one primary aspect in grid computing (Foster, 2002). GOS (Wang et al., 2007) emphasizes the importance of not only centralizing data but as well as distributing data. Online storage space such as online email accounts, social network storage and free online drive space are becoming widely available. We can see that such a trend will continue to expand based on Moore's law. These data storage space resources are widely available however they are distributed. A single user may have access to multiple storage resources such as email storage and remote disk drives however these resources are underused due to the diversity of interfaces.

Our motivation is to demonstrate the application of a grid based storage architecture, which emphasizes on centralizing of personal resources and making it available to as a single resource. Grid-storage architecture provides a single transparent interface that binds a range of distributed services from company wide network storage to cloud enabled services such as online email.

We propose a personal storage grid architecture, which is aimed at connecting and managing data space resources from various domains while maintaining transparency and security. We emphasize the importance of "personal" in our storage architecture. In a user's perspective, various online data space resources are available but not readily accessible for personal usage (Figure 1).

We refer to online data spaces resources as free drive spaces, webhosting spaces, social networking services and online free mail. A personal storage grid architecture, which consumes various services and presents them as data space to the user, allows the user to access an infinite amount of storage. Puffs (Kantee, 2007)(Kantee & Crooks, 2007) also presented bringing file-system to the userspace. The term infinite storage refers to where the user can mount on to n amount of services and merge them as a single logical mount, allowing the end-user to transparently access storage space conforming to a grid-like architecture.

Our demonstration is to use data space resources offered by online services to create a local storage. This architecture allows the user to access online data space through as a local mounted drive resource and be able to perform tasks such as directory listing, copying files between file systems, deleting, creating, and renaming files and directories. CurlFtpFS (Araujo, 2007) and FuseFTP (Thiesen, 2005) both demonstrate that file operations are possible on a FUSE framework.

There are 2 similar projects we encourage for study: (1) Luo's IMAP storage (Luo, 2007) based on Fuse-J is close to what we are proposing: functioning as a real storage solution. (2) GmailFS (Jones, 2007) implemented using libgmail currently supporting only Gmail space.

A PERSONAL STORAGE GRID ARCHITECTURE (PSAG)

We constructed a web service that consumes end-user's file and directory handling operations, and

Figure 1. Webservice that consumes cloud services

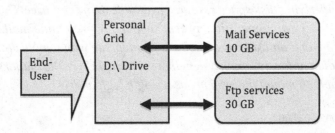

applies it to a designated online resource. Our resource is defined as an online email account and file or directory operations are passed on to our web service, which is applied onto the mail service via IMAP. The file and directory operations our file system needs to perform are: Get Attributes, Open File, Read File Data, Create Empty File, Write File, Remove File, Rename File, Read Directory, Remove Directory, Create Directory (Almeida, 1999; Nguyen, 2004; Alexandrov, Ibel, Schauser, & Scheiman, 1997) (Figure 2).

In our architecture, we considered XDrive (openXdrive, 2007), which uses JavaScript Object Notation (JSON) to allow access to its online space and Openomy using RESTful (Representational State Transfer) API (Pautasso, Zimmermann, & Leymann, 2008) to access the storage and Google Mail. To demonstrate that free email services can be used we tested Google Mail with our architecture. For the mails storage to be exposed as a logical drive locally, we used FUSE framework on a typical linux ubuntu desktop edition. FUSE allows the creation of file systems in the user space.

We used XML that complies with SOAP standard for passing messages between the linux file system (Card, Ts'o, & Tweedie, 1994) and our webservice. The interface between the email accounts can be built using either POP or IMAP. We selected IMAP, as it is able to maintain connection using online mode. POP access does not have the option of online mode (Figure 3).

In our experiment, we used an online mail's free storage. The local storage solution can be applied on any mail account (Dornfest, Bausch, & Calishain, 2006) that provides an IMAP protocol. We also used a linux virtual file system (VFS), IMAP email communication protocol, and Fuse for our implementation. There are 4 main components to our solution: (1) FUSE architecture (Figure 4), which is a kernel module, is registered as a file system and DEV char on the host operating system (OS). The kernel module connects the calls from the user space (Gera, 2006) via the OS, which is linux ubuntu. When the VSF node gets a call from the user space, it will store this request in "Queue & Sync", waking up the DEV char. DEV char passes the call to the FUSE library, which calls our implement function.

(2) gSOAP (Engelen, 2009) is used to automatically map XML data types into C data types for the client side application of our system. (3) GlassFish and Java API for XML Web Services (Java EE platform, 2008) are used to implement the system as a web service. Glassfish is an open source application server, which is a derivative of Apache Tomcat Server. (4) JavaMail API is used for development of Mail User Agent (MUA) for reading and sending email messages. It facilitates work with SMTP, POP and IMAP.

Figure 2. Web architecture

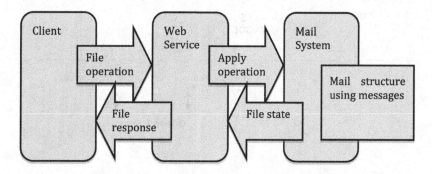

Figure 3. Communication between components for personal grid architecture

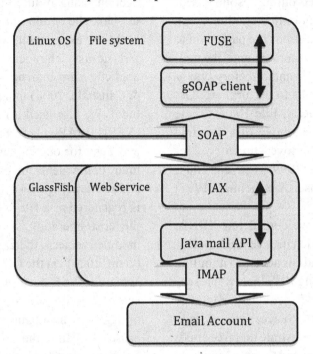

Figure 4. FUSE architecture

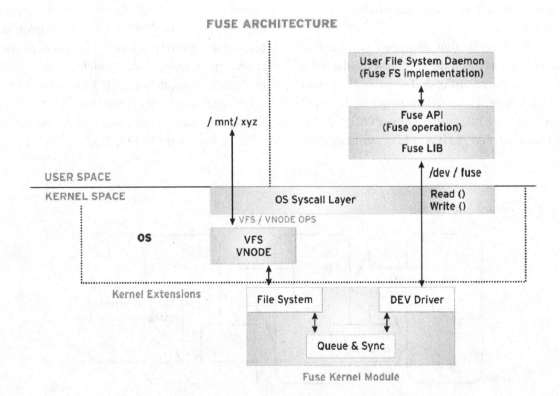

IMPLEMENTING A FILE SYSTEM ON PSGA

A file system is a method of storing and managing data and metadata (Bovet & Cesati, 2005). File systems can use data from various sources and currently hard disk source is the most common. There are other common file systems such as Linux ext (Card et al., 1994; Jones, 2007), Microsoft Windows FAT32, NTFS(Driscoll, Beavers, & Tokuda, 2008). The components of a typical file system include files and directories.

Files are created and accessed through filenames, which are commonly restricted to 255 characters. Regular files can be either in ASCII or Binary.

Directories are logical structures of file groups enabling organization of the data in a file system. There are 3 forms of directory systems: Single leveled directory, 2-leveled directory and Hierarchical directory. Single leveled directory is having 1 main directory storing files. A 2-leveled directory is where a master directory contains users directory. Finally a hierarchical directory, commonly used by modern file systems, allows users to create multiple sub-directories.

There are 3 main methods of implementation: (1) Contiguous allocation, (2) Linked list allocation, and (3) indexed allocation.

Contiguous allocation implementation is based on file blocks stored continuously one after another. This solution allows fast access, requiring the start data block and the size of the file block. As new data is always written to the last block, it causes data fragmentation and unused free space when data is removed.

Linked list allocation uses a linked list to point to disk blocks forming a file. This solution frees files from physical data orientation since a file can be composed of different data blocks. This method is an improvement over contiguous allocation, as space is not wasted. Linked list suffers from slow random access and space wasted for pointers in each block. MS (FAT) improved on this method by using a table in memory storing all the pointers. The fall back of this method is that it is not scalable; the size of the disk grows with the size of the table in memory.

Indexed allocation uses one fixed block to store a fixed size of array of pointers. The main advantage is this allows fast random data access. The only problem is that space is wasted for unneeded pointers. An improvement of this method is the use of some pointers pointing to blocks that are used as an index rather than a data block. Such method is implemented in ext2 linux file system and commonly known as inode.

In our solution we opted for indexed allocation. We used 3 messages in the online email system for presenting one file in the user space: I-node structure, Dentry and file. These 3 pieces of information are supported by VFS used by UNIX like file structures: (1) I-node messages store the metadata about the file such as i-node number, file type, file permissions and file size. (2) Dentry messages connect the i-node message with the name of the file. A typical Dentry in our system stores the file name and i-node number of the file. (3) File messages stores data in the attachment and i-node number specifying a particular file. (see Table 1.)

We use the subject of the message as storage to improve performance of the overall system. Each information piece is split by an identifier, asterisk "*".

First file of each message describes type of the information stored (i-node – "i", path – "p", data – "d"). Next filed for each message is a unique file system identification number that with conjunction with previous field allows for

Table 1.

I-node	Subject: i*fs_id*i-node number*number of data parts*metadata
Path	Subject: p*fs_id*i-node number*file name*
Data n	Subject: d*fs_id*i-node number*size of the part*part number Attachment: file

easy message identification. GmailFS (Jones, 2007) uses a similar solution with the file system identification number, which ensures that the file system uses only self-created messages.

The last fields for each message are i-node number of the file. This identification number enables linking of all the messages concerning one file. Next fields are different for each message. I-node message beside regular metadata stores total number of data messages what is necessary to read the whole file. Since messages can be split into chunks, each data message stores size and number of its part. Directories are represented in the same way like files, but the only difference is that data message will not be used.

We chose to use 3 messages as one e-mail message with an attachment storing all the information about a file has low read and write the performance. For instance change of the file name or arbitrary change of the file attributes will cause that whole message with attachment has to be downloaded and send again with new name or modified attributes. In the case of this solution just i-node or path message is modified whereas message with the attachment is untouched.

Getting Attributes: Client Side

In a linux operating system, *getattr* system call returns file attributes of the current file system. To get attributes of a file or a directory, simfs_getattr function is called with two arguments: Absolute path to the file, Structure stat storing file attributes – output.

This function on a successful call returns the stat structure filled in with the metadata concerning a file passed in the path as a first argument. If error occurs, negative value will be returned.

Getting Attributes: Server Side

Firstly from the path passed as an argument extracted are: path to the parent directory and name of the file (Line 1). Parent directory is necessary

to identify folder that stores the file on the email server. Before folder will be opened (Line 3) it is required to obtain hash code for the parent directory path (Line 2), because all the folders are represented by its hashed values. (see Table 2)

The getInode (Line 4) function will find message containing name of the file passed as argument. It will be only one message, because it is not allowed to store the same file names in one directory. An i-node number will be extracted from the found message and passed to the get-FileAttr function (Line 5). This function will prepare following search term: "i*id_fs*inodeNumber*", which will allow to find unique i-node message for the directory and extract from it attributes of the file.

Open File: Client Side

The open file operation determines if the user have sufficient privileges to open the file.

Function "open" defined needs 2 input arguments: Absolute path to file, structure of the file, which the client needs.

Function "open" passes 2 arguments to the remote procedure: Absolution path to file, Mode of file. The mode of file is defined as: read =0, write = 1, read and write = 2. The remote procedure returns 0 to signify file can be opened.

```
static int simfs_open(const char
*path, struct fuse_file_info *fi)
```

Table 2.

Line 0	int[] getattr(path)
Line 1	solvePath(path): parentDir, fileName
Line 2	hash(parentDir): hashedDir
Line 3	openFolder(hashedDir)
Line 4	getInode(filename): errorNb, inodeNb
Line 5	getFileAttr(inodeNb): errorNb, stat

Open File: Server Side

"Getattr" method on the server side is invoked to get the mode of the file. Mode stored in the message consists of both permission and type, however in open file operation, we only need the permission.

Function "checkFileMode" defined needs 2 arguments: File flags, Mode of file.

At the beginning mode of the file is translated to the octal mode (Line 1), this operation will facilitate next steps. Assume that we have a file with decimal mode 33188 (in octal equals 100644) or a directory 16877 (in octal – 40755). Three last digits inform about file permissions and the rest describe type of the file: 100 – regular file, 40 – directory.

Due to the difference, it is necessary to retrieve owner file permission in two different ways (Line 3 and 5). Error will be returned if the user does not have permissions to open the file in the mode described by the flag (Line 6). (see Table 3)

Read Data: Client Side

The file read operation performs data transmission of the file contents to the client.

The function "read" passes 5 arguments: Path to file, Buffer, Size of the data to read and size of the buffer, Offset from the beginning of the file, Information about read operation.

```
static int simfs_read(const char
*path, char *buf, size_t size, off_t
```

```
offset, struct fuse_file_info *fi)
```

In this function, we have to check if 2 conditions are met: Offset is smaller than length of the file, Offset plus size of the data to read is smaller than length of the file.

Read Data: Server Side

In line 5, the inode number is known. Messages storing data will be found by constructing following search term: "d*id_fs*inodeNumber*". Data message is a multipart message because it stores a file, thus it is necessary to retrieve message marked as an attachment. Then attachment has to be stored in the buffer, which will be returned to the client application. (see Table 4)

Create Empty File: Client Side

The make node function allows the client to construct an empty file.

The "mknod" function passes 3 arguments: Path to the file to be created, Mode of the file consisting of both file permission and type of the node, Argument used only for bulk and character type files.

```
static int simfs_mknod(const char
*path, mode_t mode, dev_t rdev)
```

"mknod" passes the first 2 arguments to the remote procedure and waits for the result.

Table 3.

Line 0	int checkFileMode(flags, fileMode)
Line 1	toOctal(fileMode): octalMode
Line 2	If regular file
Line 3	retrieveOwnerModeReg(octalMode): mode
Line 4	Else
Line 5	retrieveOwnerModeDir(octalMode): mode
Line 6	compare(flags, mode): errorNo

Table 4.

Line 0	int read(path)
Line 1	solvePath(path): parentDir, fileName
Line 2	hash(parentDir): hashedDir
Line 3	openFolder(hashedDir)
Line 4	getInode(filename): errorNb, inodeNb
Line 5	findMessage(inodeNb): messages
Line 6	getAttachment(messages): data

It is necessary to set flag at this point telling getattr function that file was created, as immediately after execution of mknod function, getattr function will be fired to check if creation of the file succeeds.

Create Empty File: Server Side

File creation is possible when permissions of the parent directory allow for writing (Line 3) and there is no file with the same name (Line 2). If two mentioned conditions were met, three messages that represent one file are sent (Line 4 – 6). (see Table 5)

As all the messages by default are sent to the "inbox" directory, it is important to move messages to the directory specified in the path. The problem is that messages will not appear immediately on the e-mail account, so the method has to poll the e-mail server to check if the messages arrived and then move them to destination directory (Code 5-9). In order to return control immediately to the user, the MoveMessages() method runs parallel in a new thread. (see Table 6)

Write File: Client Side

The write file operation allows the client to add data to the contents of the file.

"Write" function consists of 5 arguments: Path to file where data has to be written,

Buffer storing content of the file, Size of the buffer, Offset from beginning of the file, and information about write operation.

```
static int simfs_write(const char
*path, const char *buf, size_t size,
off_t offset, struct fuse_file_info
*fi)
```

The "Write" function uses copy command, where the data from the local file system is copied to our file system. Each read or write operation is executed by the Linux kernel by using the largest size of permitted blocks (4096B) [28], dividing bigger into 4KB batches. In order to reduce number of connections with the web service, each batch is added to the buffer of the size 1200 * 4096B = 4915200B. When the buffer is full, data is sent to the remote procedure. The files bigger than 4915200B are stored in n attachments of the size close to 5MB. We used this solution to remove any constraints on the size of the file.

Write File: Server Side

Remote procedure will get following arguments: path to the file, data from the cumulative buffer and permission flag of the file. If the function succeeds, amount of the written bytes will be returned, otherwise negative value will be returned.

The function checks if the parent directory allows for writing in it, then it is necessary to delete file specified by the path if it already exists. The new file is created by sending three messages

Table 5.

Line 0	int mknod(path, mode)
Line 1	solvePath(path): parentDir, fileName
Line 2	IF FileNotExists(path)
Line 3	IF ParentDirPermission(path, WRITE)
Line 4	createInode()
Line 5	createPath()
Line 6	createData()
Line 7	MoveMessages()

Table 6.

Line 0	MoveMessages(from, to, term, numberOf-NewMsgs)
Line 1	...
Line 2	DO:
Line 3	foundMsgNb = findMessages(term)
Line 4	Wait(5 seconds)
Line 5	WHILE: foundMsgNb != numberOfNewMessages
Line 6	MoveFoundMsg(from,to)

Table 7.

Line 0	int write(path, file, flags)
Line 1	solvePath(path): parentDir, filename
Line 2	IF ParentDirPermission(path, WRITE)
Line 3	IF FileExists(path)
Line 4	deleteInode(), deleteData(), deletePath()
Line 5	createInode(), createPath(), createData()
Line 6	MoveMessages()

Table 8.

Line 0	int unlink(path)
Line 1	IF ParentDirPermission(path, MODIFY)
Line 2	IF open(path, WRITE)
Line 3	findInode(path): inodeNb
Line 4	findMessages(inodeNb): messages
Line 5	moveToTrash(messages)

and is completed by returning the size of the file written. (see Table 7)

Remove File: Client Side

The remove file operation is allow client to delete a file.

```
Static int simfs_unlink(const char *path)
```

When the file has to be deleted, only file path is passed to the unlink function. This argument will be passed on to the remote procedure. Zero will be returned if the file was successfully removed.

Remove File: Server Side

The "remove" file function checks if parent directory allows for modifications (Line 1), then using function open to check if file exists and if deletion is permitted. If conditions are met, we find i-node number of the file (Line 3) and search custom IMAP folder for rest of the messages with the same i-node number. We can remove the file simply by moving it to a trash or deleted folder of the email. (see Table 8)

Rename File/Directory: Client Side

The rename function allows changing the file name or moving the file. This function also applies to directories. Two arguments: origin and destination are passed to remote procedure, which will return zero if operation finished successful.

```
static int simfs_rename(const char *from, const char *to)
```

Rename File/Directory: Server Side

There are five different scenarios for the rename. (1) The first scenario is moving a directory with the contents to a destination directory, which involves creating a new custom IMAP folder with the same name like origin directory. All messages from the origin directory will be moved to the new one and the origin directory will be removed. (2) The second scenario is similar to scenario 1, however the new directory name is different. (3) The third scenario is overwriting destination file, where all messages describing existing files are deleted. The message storing file name of the origin file is deleted and the two remaining messages are moved to the destination path. Finally message with a new file name is sent to the destination path. (4) The forth scenario is similar to the third, however the destination file does not have to be deleted. (5) In the final scenario, destination file name is not provided, thus the destination is created with the origin name. If the destination file exists, the third scenario is executed, otherwise fourth is executed. (see Table 9)

Table 9.

	Origin	Destination
1	Directory	Existing directory
2	Directory	Not existing directory
3	File	Existing file
4	File	Not existing file
5	File	Existing directory

Read Directory Client

The readdir function reads the content of the directory pointed by the path.

```
Static int simfs_readdir(const char
*path, void *buf,fuse_fill_dir_t
filler, off_t offset, struct fuse_
file_info *fi)
```

Function readdir takes five arguments: Path to the directory, Buffer for the directory content, Pointer to function allowing adding content to the buffer, Offset in directory entries, and Information about the readdir operation.

The path to the directory is passed to remote procedure. When the result will be returned by the web service method, filler function will be used to add directory content to the buffer. On success readdir will return zero.

Read Directory Server

All custom IMAP folders are represented as a hash code of the path. We obtain hash value of the path to the directory (Line 1) and when the folder is opened, it is possible to search it (Line 3). To list all the files within the directory, it is enough to construct following search term: "p*id_fs*". It will be possible to find all messages storing the names of the files, so the last step (Line 4) is to retrieve file name from each message. The array of the file names in the given directory is consumed by the client application. (see Table 10)

Table 10.

Line 0	String[] readdir(path)
Line 1	hash(path): hashedPath
Line 2	openFolder(hashedPath)
Line 3	findAllMessages(): messages
Line 4	retrieveFileNames(messages): fileNames

Create Directory Client

The mkdir function creates new empty directory path to the new directory and file permissions are passed to the mkdir function and passed on to remote procedure. On success zero will be returned.

```
static int simfs_mkdir(const char
*path, mode_t mode)
```

Create Directory Server

Unlike to regular files, directories are described only by two messages that are initially stored in the "inbox" folder (Line 5). In the Line 6 new custom IMAP folder is created. The name of this folder is the hash code of its path. The process is completed by moving two messages describing newly created folder to the parent directory (see Table 11).

Remove Directory Client

Directory deletion is performed by the rmdir file operation.

Table 11.

Line 0	int createDir(path, mode)
Line 1	solvePath(path): parentDir, fileName
Line 2	IF FileNotExists(path)
Line 3	IF ParentDirPermission(path, WRITE)
Line 4	addDirFlag(mode)
Line 5	createInode(), createPath()
Line 6	createFolder(path.hash())
Line 7	MoveMessages(parentDir)

To delete the directory (Code 5-19) it is necessary to know its path, which will be passed to the remote procedure. On success function will return zero, otherwise will be returned negative value.

```
static int simfs_rmdir(const char
*path)
```

Remove Directory Server

First must be checked if directory exists and its permissions allows for deleting (Line 2), next check if parent directory can be accessed. It is possible to remove only empty directory, so if directory will store files, function will return with negative value (Line 4 – 6). Assuming that empty IMAP directory was successfully deleted, it is possible to remove two messages describing directory (Line 7 - 9). These messages are stored in the parent directory of the directory that was deleted in Line 5. (see Table 12)

RESULTS

The web services with specified functions were deployed. We invoked remote procedure from the client application simulating file system call and finally implement this into the FUSE framework.

The client application was moved to the FUSE framework using gSOAP. In the development

Table 12.

Line 0	int createDir(path)
Line 1	solvePath(path): parentDir, fileName
Line 2	IF open(path, WRITE)
Line 3	IF ParentDirPermission(path, WRITE)
Line 4	IF emptyFolder(path.hash())
Line 5	deleteFolder(path.hash())
Line 6	ELSE return -1
Line 7	findInode(path): inodeNb
Line 8	findMessages(inodeNb): messages
Line 9	moveToTrash(messages)

of the read and write file system operations we noticed that Linux kernel split files into 4096B chunks, allow the initial implementation to work fine only for files smaller than size of the one chunk. To avoid sending data every time when write function is called we decided to save data in the buffer and send it when buffer is full or last chunk of the file was loaded. This has a problem, as there is no information if the current chunk of the file is the last one. We understood that when data is written to the file it must be opened and for every open function there is always one release function. Therefore we made last chunk of the file to be written and sent in the release function.

When the file is copied to different folder, normally file system creates a file in the new destination before data is written to it. In our solution it means that a new file has to be deleted immediately in order to send the messages with data. Instead of creating the new file immediately, a special flag is set and checked in the release function. If there was write function called in the chain of functions for current Linux command (for instance cp) then it means that new file does not have to be created.

The file system was mounted on the new e-mail account, which created a root directory allowing for using file system. We were able to perform the described file operations on the new mount.

CONCLUSION

We are able to realize a personal storage grid architecture on an online email account which allows file and directory operations. Our result shows how file systems can be built into a mail service, which is a common form of data space resource available on the Internet. An implemented personal storage grid architecture allows file and directory operations that can be mounted to any mail that provides IMAP protocols.

We carried out this study to implement a file system that wraps online services to provide a single logical drive space for the end-user. This implementation shows that a file system can be built on a grid like architecture, which is scalable and works in conjunction with online resources and services. It is able to consume cloud applications such as online email services and present a file system layer to the end-user.

This realization of consuming various services and transforming these services into disk space resources shows how system resources can be integrated and used by the end-user. Currently speeds of accessing disk space using the above method is not as fast as our local SATA drives which is able to reach 286MB/s. Our future work will move towards improving the compatibility with other storage resources and improving the usability of the system by caching instructions of file operations.

FUTURE WORK

Currently our personal grid architecture consumes only a single e-mail account, thus next step will be to develop file system that allows for joining different free online storage resource by consuming other popular protocols.

The second direction is to increase speed of the file system and file operations by decreasing number of connections with the server. Further investigation can be made on caching metadata about the files for the current directory; such as the "getattribute" function is used most often. Structuring of the file system can be stored in the XML file on the local disk. Every time when will be needed information about the files from directory that was previously used they will be retrieved from the local disk instead of the server.

Less important improvement is to add service of the multi user file system, since currently it is possible to use file system only by one user.

REFERENCES

Alexandrov, A. D., Ibel, M., Schauser, K. E., & Scheiman, C. J. (1997). Extending the operating system at the user level: the Ufo global file system. In *Proceedings of the annual conference on USENIX Annual Technical Conference* (pp. 6-6).

Almeida, D. (1999). FIFS: a framework for implementing user-mode file systems in windows NT. In *Proceedings of the 3rd conference on USENIX Windows NT Symposium* (Vol. 3, pp. 13).

Araujo, R. B. (2007). *CurlFtpFS - A FTP filesystem based in cURL and FUSE*. Retrieved from http://curlftpfs.sourceforge.net/

Bovet, D. P., & Cesati, M. (2005). *Understanding the Linux Kernel*. Sebastopol, CA: O'Reilly Media.

Card, R., Ts'o, T., & Tweedie, S. (1994). Design and Implementation of the Second Extended Filesystem. In *Proceedings of the First Dutch International Symposium on Linux*.

Dornfest, R., Bausch, P., & Calishain, T. (2006). *Google Hacks* (3rd ed.). Sebastopol, CA: O'Reilly Media.

Driscoll, E., Beavers, J., & Tokuda, H. (2008). *FUSE-NT: Userspace File Systems for Windows NT. University of Wisconsin-Madison*. Retrieved from pages.cs.wisc.edu/~driscoll/fuse-nt.pdf

Engelen, R. V. (2009). *gSOAP 2.7.15 User Guide. FSU Computer Science*. Retrieved from http://www.cs.fsu.edu/~engelen/soapdoc2.html

Foster, I. (2002, July 22). What is the Grid? - a three point checklist. *GRIDtoday, 1*(6).

Gera, V. (2006, September 22). *Filesystems in User Space*. Retrieved from twiki.dsi.uniroma1.it/pub/Sistemioperativi3/OnLine/Fuse.pdf

Java EE platform. (2008). JAX-WS Reference Documentation. *Sun Microsystems*. Retrieved from https://jax-ws.dev.java.net/

Jones, M. T. (2007, October 30). *Anatomy of the Linux file system. IBM.* Retrieved from http://www.ibm.com/developerworks/linux/library/l-linux-filesystem/

Jones, R. (2007). *Gmail Filesystem - GmailFS.* Retrieved from http://richard.jones.name/google-hacks/gmail-filesystem/gmail-filesystem.html

Kantee, A. (2007). Pass-to-Userspace Framework File System. In *Proceedings of the 2nd Asia BSD Conference* (pp. 29-42).

Kantee, A., & Crooks, A. (2007). ReFUSE: Userspace FUSE Reimplementation Using puffs. In *Proceedings of the 6th European BSD Conference.* http://freshmeat.net/projects/fuseftp/

Luo, X. (2007). *IMAP Storage Filesystem.* Retrieved from http://imapfs.sourceforge.net/

Nguyen, B. (2004, July 30). *Linux Filesystem Hierarchy. The Linux Documentation Project.* Retrieved from http://tldp.org/LDP/Linux-Filesystem-Hierarchy/html/

openXdrive. (2007). *The Xdrive Data Services Platform (XDSP) JSON API. Xdrive LLC.* Retrieved from dev.aol.com/xdrive_resources/json_apidocs/api-index.html

Pautasso, C., Zimmermann, O., & Leymann, F. (2008). Restful web services vs. "big"' web services: making the right architectural decision. In *Proceeding of the 17th international conference on World Wide Web* (pp. 805-814).

Thiesen, M. (2005, December). *FuseFTP.* Retrieved from

Wang, F. Z., Wu, S., Helian, N., Parker, A., Guo, Y., Deng, Y., & Khare, V. (2007). Grid-oriented Storage: A Single-Image, Cross-Domain, High-Bandwidth Architecture. *IEEE Transactions on Computers, 56*(4), 474–487. doi:10.1109/TC.2007.1005

This work was previously published in International Journal of Grid and High Performance Computing, Volume 2, Issue 3, edited by Emmanuel Udoh, pp. 17-30, copyright 2010 by IGI Publishing (an imprint of IGI Global).

Chapter 8
Design of SOA Based Framework for Collaborative Cloud Computing in Wireless Sensor Networks

S. V. Patel
Veer Narmad South Gujarat University, India

Kamlendu Pandey
Veer Narmad South Gujarat University, India

ABSTRACT

WSN deployments are growing at a fast rate; however, current WSN architectures and setup do not promote the sharing of data on an inter-WSN basis. Cloud computing has emerged as a promising area to deal with participatory and collaborative data and services, and is envisaged that collaborative cloud computing WSN could be a viable solution for sharing data and services for WSN applications. In this paper, SOA based architecture has been proposed to support collaborating cloud computing in WSN. The architecture consists of layered service stack that has management, information, presentation and communication layers with all required services and repositories. Interactions between WSN, subscribers and other cloud are also presented as sequence diagrams. The proposed framework serves the cloud subscribers with wide range of queries on the data of multiple WSNs through suitable interface to solve large scale problems.

DOI: 10.4018/978-1-4666-0056-0.ch008

INTRODUCTION

The technology of wireless sensor networks has completed a decade or so. In these years researchers, deployers, application programmers have put tremendous efforts to make these new technologies reach to the beneficiaries. The benefits of sensor networks are well realized and many deployments are taking place to study the serious problems of environmental monitoring, habitat monitoring, healthcare, production system, inventory management etc. However, for the solutions to some gross problems like global warming or pollution etc. we need to collect, understand the data as well as its patterns in totality and wide scale. This will not be possible unless diverse physical WSN collaborate. The cloud computing comes as a possible answer to the problem. To achieve this task there is an urgent need to rethink about the present architectures orientation and seclusion of wireless networks. Further, there is a need to change the perception of WSN organisation.

Our earlier work described in this paper, prepared the background in the direction of this new structure. In this paper the problem pertaining to the current state of WSNs architecture is identified, the need of new architecture supporting cloud computing on WSN is emphasized and a solution comprising of a framework having Service stack divided in four major layers, each layer supporting various services and repositories, is proposed. Functioning of the architecture and interaction sequences between major players like WSN, Subscribers and Other clouds are also described. The new architecture uses the features of cloud like virtualisation and Service oriented architecture to deal with heterogeneity.

The paper is structured as follows: related work on various architectures that focus on data sharing and limited WSN collaboration and limitations of current WSN architectures are presented. The path toward collaborative model is also introduced. The model with service stack for WSN cloud is described and the need of SOA approach for achieving heterogeneity is stated. The functioning of WSN cloud is also shown. Finally the need of WSN cloud to solve the global problem is emphasized.

RELATED WORK

Looking to the scenario of research in the area of cloud computing pertaining to sensor networks we don't find much published work. However there has been an effort depicting architectures which employ grid-based or publish subscribe models to achieve efficiency, availability, scalability and collaboration to some extent for the present and future wireless sensor networks deployments. OGC Open Geospatial Consortium (Botts, Percivall, Reed, & Davidson, 2006) is engaged in promoting the agile Sensor Web Enablement for the wireless sensor networks. It has developed XML schemas for configuring a WSN ready to serve on web. It also presents connectivity architecture to deliver the sensor data. Chen Khong et al (Tham & Buyya, 2005) present a report on sensor grid network to deal with the processing of the data and application logic by putting them into a grid based architecture. Mark Gaynor et al show how to integrate WSNs with a grid (Gaynor, Moulton, Welsh, LaCombe, Rowan, & Wynne, 2004). Geoffrey et al has worked on the Collaborative Sensor Grid framework (Fox, Ho, Wang, Chu, & Kwan, 2008) which presents the design to increase the efficiency of data delivery and how one grid can collaborate with the other grid. The problem with grid based architecture is that that the designers concentrate on achieving efficiency in the processing by clustering the HPC based machines. The scalability, availability, collaborative ness and homogeneity are not the prime goals. Looking to the various solutions for wireless sensor networks, the most common thing which is observed is, even in the collaborative, distributed and grid based approach, they cater the need of their own organisation. John Douglas et al present an open distributed architecture for environmental risk management (Douglas, Uslander, Schimak, Esteban, & Denzer, 2008) in which they use two architectures ORCHESTRA and SANY. However it doesn't indicate how to search for independent secluded networks, which are the part of other organisation. Mires (Souto et al., 2005) is a publish/subscribe architecture for WSNs in which the sensors publish the sensed data at the cluster heads and finally to the sink node which give the data to the subscriber. The TinySIP (Krishnamurthy, 2006) architecture uses publish/subscribe and instant messaging model in which also it covers the session semantics. It offers support for multiple gateways. The most recent work done on the sensor cloud is by Mohammed Mahedi hassan et al. (2009) which proposes a cloud based framework for the sensor networks. They propose the cloud architecture and its services for WSNs. It also highlights the methodology of establishing a VO within the clouds. It also gives a event matching algorithm for event notification to the subscribers. However, this frame work does not take into account the degree of collaborativeness of the individual WSN setups and ways to search the sensor networks. It has been fairly assumed that all the WSNs have architectures to support participation. Secondly less is talked about the way to implement security and data representation to the subscribers. In view of the above, the requirement of achieving global WSN is yet to be fulfilled.

LIMITATION OF EXISTING WSN SETUP

The limitations of the conventional setup of WSN are:

i)   Inaccessibility of WSNs: Normally the WSNs are designed to serve the purpose of some limited geographical area with accessibility to limited no of users. This creates a bottleneck especially if we seek a solution to the problems concerning global environmental studies.

ii)   High Infrastructure Requirement: The data generated by WSNs is quite huge. This requires the deployment of high duty storage processing and communication systems, involving high cost. This does not justify the cost benefit ratio.

iii) Non Collaborative Approach: Most of the WSNs are designed for single organisation without any scope of sharing their data with others. This restricts the participation by other WSNs having common interest.

iv)   Heterogeneity: As there is no universal framework or the platform for their setup and implementation, it becomes difficult to make WSNs talk independently with each other.

COLLABORATIVE APPROACH

Present setup of existing WSN pose serious limitations for applications that need to process data on the global scale. The solution is to redesign the existing architectures to support collaborative cloud computing in WSNs.

The design should evolve as follows:

1)   As a first step we need a uniform Registration process for all the WSNs, just like Domain Name System for Internet or web servers to facilitate easy searching of WSNs based on various criteria.

2)   The Collaborative SOA Architecture to be followed by the WSN Setups at the deployment place.

3)   Cloud Setup for Collaborating with WSNs and providing services regarding data representation and decision making to the subscribers.

The above steps in aggregation can be considered as a Sensor Collaboration Model. Our earlier work focused on step 1 and step 2, whereas this paper proposes the final step i.e., collaborative cloud for WSN. For understanding the complete model, Uniform registration process and architecture of collaborative WSN are introduced as follows.

1) *The Uniform Registration Process:* A distributed SOA based registry for sensor networks as designed by us in (Pandey & Patel, 2009) to enable all the sensor networks of the world to register themselves needs to be implemented. The registration of user WSNs requires attributes like sensor domain name, Geo-spatial Attributes, Political Attributes, Data definitions, Security Roles, host or cluster description, Gateway characteristics, mobility status key words, Sensor Network Description services and URLS etc. The corresponding schemas of WSDL and XML involved in this task are also supported. It is expected that end users or service brokers will consult the registry to search sensor networks based upon the attributes given above; the registry setup also presents front end application to sort and search the sensor networks. All sensor networks have been given the URL of their home page in the registry to be consulted for further actions. This effectively solves the problem of seclusion in the universe of WSN Figure 1 presents the scheme to access the registry and data from WSN. This registry will be used as one of the constituent blocks in collaborative approach described in the next section.

2) *The Collaborative WSN Setup:* It is desired for the WSNs to follow an architecture and service stack which promote the collaboration of their data with other sensor networks or sensor clouds in the future (Fox, Ho, Wang, Chu, & Kwan, 2008). As a next step towards sensor clouds, a service stack was designed which consist of four layers viz Administrative, Data Layer, Application layer and Network layer (Pandey & Patel, 2009) all the layers are using XML based repositories to communicate. The Data pull and push services are working in accordance with administrative, security and pricing policies of WSN. The Service stack for the collaborative WSN Setup is given in Figure 2.

3) *Cloud computing based Services using integrated WSNs:* The final step evolves with the cloud. The cloud computing is the promising technology for the collaborative and participatory approach. The recent developments in cloud computing allows sharing of resources through virtualisation and secure means of transactions through light weight service oriented architecture. Therefore, we have incorporated it in our model to meet the goal of forming global WSN in real sense.

THE SERVICE STACK FOR CLOUD COMPUTING IN WSN

The clouds are owned and operated by cloud service providers. Therefore the main task is to design the service stack for CSP. We propose the service stack for the cloud based services to integrate inter-organisational wireless sensor networks deployed at different geographical locations. The goal of collaborative and participatory approach for WSN data processing can be achieved by this service stack.

Various layers to satisfy groups of services, which will constitute this collaborative service stack, are designed as under:

A. Management Layer
B. Enterprise Information Layer

Figure 1.Working of SOA based sensor web registry

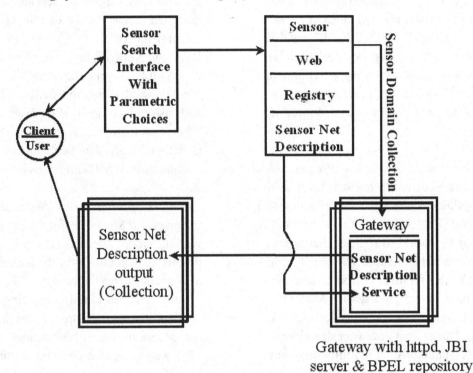

Gateway with httpd, JBI
server & BPEL repository

C. Presentation Layer
D. Virtualisation Layer
E. Communication Layer

A. Management Layer

This contains the collection of services and re-positories which deal with management part of WSN Cloud setup while registering new WSN Setup of different organisations, Subscribers to the Cloud Services, managing policy reposito-ries, security handling and configuring business value. Following services are categorised under management services:

1. CWSN registration Services
2. Subscriber registration service
3. Cloud Security Service
4. Metering Services
5. Inter-cloud Connectivity and Mediator Service

6. Virtualisation Service
7. Collaborator Service

The Repositories which will leverage the above services in the administrative layer are:

i. WSN Repository: stores the info of WSNs
ii. Subscriber Repository: stores the profiles and status of subscribers
iii. Policy Repository: deals with administrative and pricing policy
iv. Web Services repository: deals with web services and their orchesterisation
iv. Encryption Keys Repository: Stores keys and certificates from subscribers and WSNs
v. Cloud Repository: stores the details of other linked clouds

The service Stack for cloud based collaborative framework is given as under in Figure 3.

Figure 2. Collaborative WSN service stack

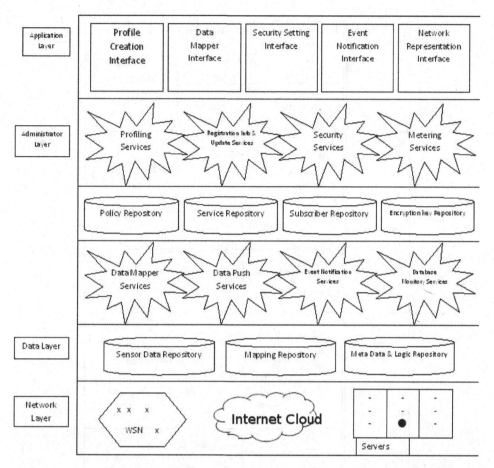

1. CWSN Registration Services: The Cloud Service Provider (CSP) is responsible for registering the Collaborative WSNs with them. This registration service must include the following fields:

   i)   Wsn_id: The identification of wsn

   ii) Categorisation: The category of WSN as per sensed data (environmental, defense, weather, flood etc)

   iii) Registerd_name: The registered name of the WSN in distributed registry for WSN. The registry will provide all the details regarding the WSN which includes:

        a)   Sensor Domain Name: The domain name of the WSN in registry

        b)   IP address of the Gateway

        c)   Ports at which gateway webserver and database servers are running

        d)   Mobility status: static or mobile

        e)   Geospatial locations: Latitude and Longitude of WSN physical deployment area.

        f)   Data Type Sensed, its category, entity, unit and sensing interval

        g)   Political Data: country/state/city/region etc.

        h)   URL of Sensor Network Description Service

        i)   Owners: name, contact detail of organisation and persons

        j)   Layout/ deployment diagram

        k)   Security policy on data

        l)   Pricing policy

Figure 3. Service stack for cloud based collaborative framework

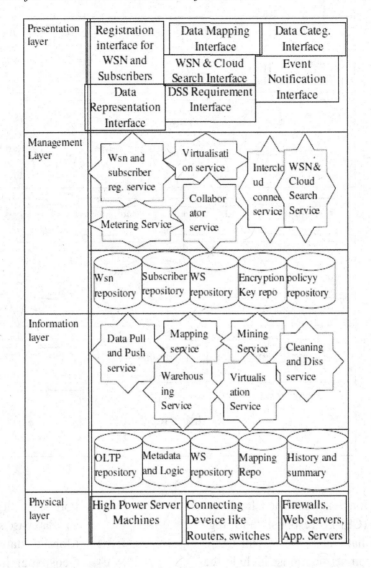

In case of WSN with non collaborative approach, they need to explicitly specify their details as mentioned above.

iv) Authentication Parameters: user name / password etc.
v) Public Key or Certificate
vi) Data Push interval
vii) Mapping their data to Cloud's real time database

2. *Subscriber Registration Service:* The subscribers are the users of the sensed data. In order to access, view, analyse the sensed data the subscribers need to register themselves with the CSP. The registration data may include:

a) Subscriber Info:
   i) Subscriber id – provided by the Cloud
   ii) Subscriber Type -User, Service Broker, Cloud Provider, Federal

Agency, Administrators, other users etc

   iii)   Name of Agency

   iv)   Address Info – address, state country PIN, phone, email etc.

   v)   Representative person details – name, address, phone, email, responsibility

   vi)   Authentication Parameters - like username, password, hint question etc.

b)   Data delivery Parameters:

   i.   Data interested in – list of sensed data types

   ii.   WSNs of interest – choose the registered CWSN/WSNs for the data of interest

   iii.   Fields interested in – Show the multiple values of attributes for data collected

   iv.   Data Refresh Rate– hour, min, sec

   v.   Event interested in, Threshold value of data less than, more than or equal to threshold value

   vi.   Data Delivery Timings – Start Time & End Time

c)   Services of Interest: To choose various services like data delivery, geographical mapping, data mapping, analysis, monitoring etc for the subscription

d)   Metering parameters: This is the static information given to subscriber:

   i)   Charge on basis services chosen

   ii)   Final Negotiated Charge

e)   Confirmation Status:

   i.   Role Status: Admin, UA, SB, Federal, Guest, Trial

   ii.   Online Legal Agreement Document

   iii.   Subscription Confirmation Status: Rejected, Awaited, Confirmed, Temporary

   iv.   Public Key Download

3.   *The Cloud Security Service*: This service will be required to control the access and maintain the confidentiality and authentication of information. Following tasks are to be performed by security services:

a)   To assign the Role to the WSNs, subscribers, users, and will decide the access level and rights to the data as decided by the policies stored in policy repository.

b)   Authentication parameters for subscribers as mentioned in profile

c)   Deciding data encryption policy – with symmetric keys and asymmetric PKI infrastructure

d)   Key Repository and Key Distribution Methods and Policy The keys are to be distributed to the subscribers and WSNs on periodic basis

4.   *Metering Service*: This service will be activating if the services to the subscriber is the paid one. To every service being used the metering service is activated. The metering service checks the charge policy decided by the cloud

5.   *Inter-Cloud Connectivity and Mediator Service:* One Cloud can always connect to the other cloud to have the task of collaboration to the global level. It requires a mediator service to establish the connectivity under environment of mutual trust. This takes account of establishment of secure VPN by using a secure keying to send the ESP and AH. It can be supported by mutual certificate authentication. The Certificate Authorities are going to play a major role in it. The role of mediator service is to ensure the credentials of the participating clouds and maintain the relationship of trust.

6.   *Virtualisation Service:* Virtualisation is the one of the main features of cloud computing. The virtualisation service will decide to host the data, processing power, storage to the

array of machines employed at distributed locations in the control of the CSP.

7. *Collaborator Service:* This is the central player. While delivering the subscribed services to the subscriber the collaborator service maintains and looks into the repositories for WSNs, subscribers, other sensor clouds, policies, security, web services, orchestrasisation of web services, virtualizations, mediation etc. so that the user may be served, tracked and billed correctly.

B. Enterprise Information Systems Layer

The Information System at the cloud deals with the management, monitoring, storing, disseminating and processing the incoming data from various WSNs. It also deals with the queries produced by the subscribers and deliver the data after query optimization and execution. The services which will do these tasks are:

1) Data Pull and Push Service
2) Database Mapping Service
3) Data Cleaning and Dissemination Service
4) Data Warehousing Service
5) Data Mining Service
6) Event Notification Service
7) Database Virtualisation Service
8) Database Monitoring Service

The repositories which are required for the functioning of the services are:

i) The Real Time Data Repository: storing incoming data from various WSNs
ii) Meta Data and Logic Repository: specifying metadata structure, procedures, function, triggers etc.
iii) Mapping Repository: The data mapping details for every WSN to Cloud's transactional database

iv) Historical and Summarised Data Repository: deals with the data warehouse maintained by cloud

1. *Data Pull and Push Service*: Depending upon the terms agreed upon by the by WSNs the cloud setup pulls the database from the WSN organisation. Similarly the current cloud can also be a data provider for other cloud, and then data push services are required.

2. *Database Mapping Service:* The sensed data is coming from various WSNs and every WSN can have its own data definition and dictionary. To collaborate we may need a uniform data representation. The mapping service maps the data from WSN to the cloud's transactional database. The mapping strategy is already being agreed upon by the WSN at the time of registration. This mapping involves entity to entity and attribute to attribute mapping. The mapping are stored in mapping repository which contains WSN wise mapping information in a well formatted XML

3. *Data Cleaning and Dissemination Service:* The incoming data from various sources needs to be treated and formatted before it is stored in the cloud database.

4. *Data warehouse Service:* This service helps to maintain a data warehouse for keeping historical and summarised databases depending upon various subjects of interest.

5. *Data Mining Service:* The data stored in the warehouse is useful for extracting the patterns and associations of interest. The mining service can have a insight into the warehouse and extract the information which will be useful for decision making.

6. *Event Notification Service:* This service will be continuously running in the background just to notify the subscribers for the event of interest which is pre-decided at the time of subscriber registration in a true asynchro-

nous manner. This is stored in the subscriber profile repository.

7. *Database Virtualisation Service:* The enormous volume of the incoming data and complexities of the data retrieval from subscriber's query pushes cloud to go for virtualisation of the databases where task is handled by number of remote hosts clustered together. It is possible to use the database host of the WSNs itself and virtualize the cloud database on them. The service will take part in allocation of the data and query processing or real time basis. This way there can be a lot of cost cutting through cloud infrastructure.

8. *Database Monitoring Service:* Looking the huge volume of data generated from the sensor networks, the database monitoring service monitors the health of the database and reports if any unusual condition and triggers the corrective action too.

C. Presentation Layer

The management and the information services are often executed and run in the background. The subscriber and WSN organisations need well defined interfaces to work with. The Services can serve as a starting point to invoke the service of services in the background as orcheasterd by any Business Process Modelling Languages. The front end interfaces are as under:

i)   Registration Interface for WSN and Subscribers
ii)   Data mapper Interface
iii) Sensor categorisation Interface
iv)   Data representation Interface
v)   Event Notification Interfaces
vi)   Geographical Representation Interface for WSNs and other Clouds
vii) DSS Requirements and Analysis Interfaces
viii) WSN and Cloud search interface

1. *Registration interface for Subscribers and WSNs:* All the services and repositories being mentioned in management and information layer requires a visual interface to enter the data required at the time of registration

2. *Data Mapper Interface:* To provide the input to the the mapping repository in the information layer suitable interface is provided where every WSN can map their database with corresponding clouds database

3. *Sensor Categorisation Interface:* There are many number of entities which can be sensed by sensors, may be from the environment, health, ocean, videos, chemicals etc. The WSNs may sense one or more of such entities for this they need to be classified and categorised which this interface is presenting. This will help the subscribers to search WSNs as per their interest domains. This interface is used by Cloud Administrators.

4. *Data Representation Interface:* This application provides representation of sensed data in the form of graphs, maps, contours etc. The subscribers can access this application to monitor and asses the current data and its pattern over the area. Here tools like Geographical Information Systems (GIS) can be useful for producing query on sensed data and its geographical representations.

5. *Event Notification Interface:* This interface alerts the subscribers for the event of interest by flashing text, dialogs, and alert bells. This notification invokes the web service which does the necessary action and control.

6. Geographical Representation Interface for WSNs and other Clouds

This interface shows the layout of WSNs, inter WSNs and other clouds on the map. It helps the subscribers to see the WSNs in their vicinity or the place of interest.

7. *DSS Requirements Interface:* This interface deals with the decision making process of

subscribers and WSN administrators. The interface will allow to define the inputs for pattern recognition, unusual behaviours, associativity with other data etc. They can also specify the graphical representation of historical and summarised data in form of different types of graphs.

8. *WSN and Cloud Search Interface:* An interface must be provided for searching the WSN based on criteria like data sensed, latitude and longitude, region, area, country, state, district, mobility etc.

D. Communication Layer

All the above layers are building upon following network infrastructure

Interconnected Physical Devices: These include Virtualised Network Machines which hosts the file systems, database, web service assemblies, repositories mentioned above, security key rings, certificates, Geographical information system, Images, videos and additional tools.

ii) Network Connectivity from Collaborative cloud Setup for WSNs and Subscribers: This connectivity is based on the current internet infrastructure or a Virtual Private Network with LAN and WAN connectivity

iii) Network Servers: This includes high power machines as Database Servers, Application Server, Web Server, Mail Server etc. All the servers must be suitably connected with the internet and should be equipped with firewall policy to thwart network attacks. If the load is more a cluster of the servers can be formed to take the load. A System Administrator and its staff must carefully plan the scheduling and backup

iv) Inter-connecting devices: High level routers, switches gateways, firewalls and continuous power availability will facilitate the smooth connectivity and speed.

SOA APPROACH TO DEAL WITH HETEROGENITY

All the services mentioned above need to collaborate with invocation from outside and inter-invocation as well. We strongly recommend to use the present state of art Service Oriented architecture (SOA) which can be very well implemented in open source language like Java which in its recent development has provided a complete framework with help of Java Business Integration, Business process execution language to orchestrate the services and various service engines to connect from outside. It enables to connect through http, soap and Messaging infrastructure. The application interfaces can be suitably developed in presentation layer using servlets or JSP. A Java enabled Application Server will allow to deploy all service based applications (Figure 4).

THE FUNCTIONING OF THE COLLABORATIVE CLOUD WSN SET UP

The major entities in the working of Collaborative cloud setup are the WSN/CWSNs, Subscriber and the Cloud. All the entities deal separately with the sensor cloud. Their interactions are explained as below:

i) *Interaction between WSNs and Cloud:* The WSNs which wish to deliver their service on cloud for the purpose of business or community service need to register themselves through the interfaces provided by the cloud which systematically categorise the WSN, map the sensed data, establishes security and trust amongst them. It uses several services and repositories which are arranged in a multi-layered stack as mentioned above. Once the registration is completed the data push and pull services will be activated and thereby other services will become active

Figure 4. A SOA- JBI architecture (adapted from cwiki.apache.org)

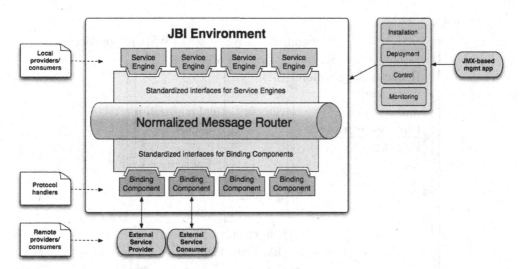

to clean, format and store in the transactional database and thereby maintain in a data warehouse to keep historical data. The Figure 5 shows the inter-working of WSNs and Cloud.

ii) *Interaction between Subscribers and Cloud:* The cloud service provider may promote its cloud as business model or community service. This will require the subscription from interested users. The adequate interfaces are provided by the cloud to the subscribers and their profile, choices and preferences are activated by the underlying services and stored in repositories. The subscriber may be billed by the time, volume of data consumed etc. The cloud will ensure the confidentiality and integrity of the data being delivered or accessed. The mediator services need to play an important role in establishing the relationship of trust. Figure 6 shows the interaction.

iii) *Interaction among clouds:* This interaction is opening all the avenues of data sharing and collaboration on global basis. The cloud initiated the interaction with a joining request in a predefined format to the other cloud via a mediator service. The mediator will forward the request to the target cloud in the format understandable by the target cloud. The request must carry the credentials and the profile of the requesting cloud accompanying with the certificate signed by renowned certificate authority. The request must also carry the description of policies. The collaborator agents at both the ends help in negotiating the connection. The collaborator agent at target cloud will respond with its own policies and criteria through mediator services. The initiator collaborator agent will make decision to accept or reject the connection request. Once the connection request is accepted then they can map the database mutually and the pull and push services at both the ends will initiate the data submission and retrieval process this will increase the subscriber base for both the interacting clouds (Figure7).

CONCLUSION

To support the cause of global availability of the sensed data from wireless sensor networks, the c

Figure 5. Interaction of WSN and cloud

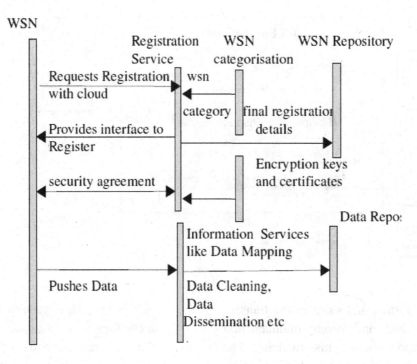

Figure 6. Interaction of subscriber and cloud

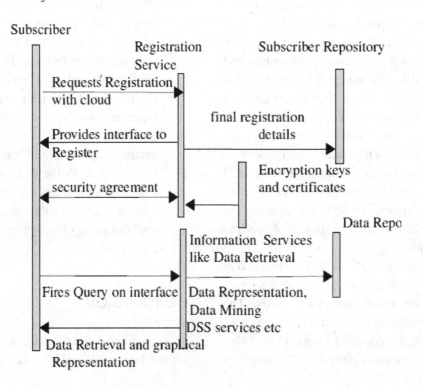

Figure 7. Interaction of cloud to other clouds

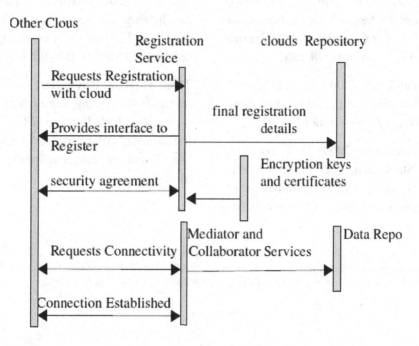

loud computing offers a promising role. A framework with service stack is presented here for the cloud based services which will offer a central point of connectivity with the WSNs deployed anywhere on earth. Whole Stack consists of four layers Viz management, Information, presentation and physical. Every service and repositories in the layers are described. Finally the working of cloud is explained by the interaction of WSN, subscriber and cloud-to-cloud. This architecture can percolate through the barriers of physical and political boundaries and provides a solution to the global problem.

REFERENCES

Botts, M., Percivall, G., Reed, C., & Davidson, J. (2006, July 19). *OGC Sensor Web Enablement: Overview and High Level Architecture*. Paper presented at the Open Geospatial Consortium (OGC 06-050r2 v2).

Douglas, J., Usländer, T., Schimak, G., Esteban, J. F., & Denzer, R. (2008). An Open Distributed Architecture for Sensor Networks for Risk Management. *Sensors (Basel, Switzerland)*, 8, 1755–1773. doi:10.3390/s8031755

Fox, G., Ho, A., Wang, R., Chu, E., & Kwan, I. (2008). A Collaborative Sensor Grids Framework. In *Proceedings of Collaborative Technologies and Systems*, Irvine, CA (pp. 29-38).

Gaynor, M., Moulton, S. L., Welsh, M., LaCombe, E., Rowan, A., & Wynne, J. (2004, July-August). Integrating Wireless Sensor Networks with the Grid. *IEEE Internet Computing*, 8(4), 32–39. doi:10.1109/MIC.2004.18

Hassan, M. M., Song, B., & Huh, E. N. (2009, January 15-16). *A Framework of Sensor - Cloud Integration Opportunities and Challenges*. Paper presented in ICUIMC-09Suwon, South Korea.

Krishnamurthy, S. (2006). TinySIP: Providing Seamless Access to Sensorbased Services. In *Proceedings of the 1ˢᵗ International Workshop on Advances in Sensor Networks (IWASN)*.

Pandey, K., & Patel, S. V. (2009, July). Design of SOA based Sensor Web Registry. In *Proceedings of CICSyn IEEE conference*, Indore, India.

Pandey, K., & Patel, S. V. (2009). Design of SOA based Service Stack for Collaborative Wireless Sensor Network Submitted. In *Proceedings of WSCN 2009, IEEE Conference*, Allahabad, India.

Souto, E. (2005). Mires: A publish/subscribe middleware for sensor networks. *ACM Personal and Ubiquitous Computing, 10*(1), 37–44. doi:10.1007/s00779-005-0038-3

Tham, C.-K., & Buyya, R. (2005, June 24). *SensorGrid: Integrating Sensor Networks and Grid Computing* (Tech. Rep. No. GRIDS-TR-2005-10). Melbourne, Australia: Grid Computing and Distributed Systems Laboratory, University of Melbourne.

This work was previously published in International Journal of Grid and High Performance Computing, Volume 2, Issue 3, edited by Emmanuel Udoh, pp. 60-73, copyright 2010 by IGI Publishing (an imprint of IGI Global).

Chapter 9
A Semantic–Driven Adaptive Architecture for Large Scale P2P Networks

Athena Eftychiou
University of Surrey, UK

Bogdan Vrusias
University of Surrey, UK

Nick Antonopoulos
University of Derby, UK

ABSTRACT

The increasing amount of online information demands effective, scalable, and accurate mechanisms to manage and search this information. Distributed semantic-enabled architectures, which enforce semantic web technologies for resource discovery, could satisfy these requirements. In this paper, a semantic-driven adaptive architecture is presented, which improves existing resource discovery processes. The P2P network is organised in a two-layered super-peer architecture. The network formation of super-peers is a conceptual representation of the network's knowledge, shaped from the information provided by the nodes using collective intelligence methods. The authors focus on the creation of a dynamic hier-archical semantic-driven P2P topology using the network's collective intelligence. The unmanageable amounts of data are transformed into a repository of semantic knowledge, transforming the network into an ontology of conceptually related entities of information collected from the resources located by peers. Appropriate experiments have been undertaken through a case study by simulating the proposed architecture and evaluating results.

DOI: 10.4018/978-1-4666-0056-0.ch009

INTRODUCTION

The Semantic Web idea (Berners-Lee, Hendler, & Lassila, 2001) in unstructured adaptive P2P networks is an approach to represent, manage, and retrieve distributed knowledge in an efficient manner. To pursue the Semantic Web vision, metadata is an essential add-on for information resources. This rich representation of data aims to improve knowledge discovery and data management. Traditionally, adding metadata to resources is a manual and expensive process and probably the main cause of the slow growth and difficult implementation of the Semantic Web.

Various efforts have been made from the P2P research community to create P2P systems that can discover resources efficiently and accurately. Standard P2P searching technologies like Gnutella 2 (Stokes, 2002) produce irrelevant search results with low precision rate. Kazaa (Liang, Kumar, & Ross, 2004) is a very popular super-peer based application, which appears to offer better scaling; however it inherits the limitations that come with flooding algorithms. Structured P2P architectures on the other hand, like Chord (Stoica, Morris, Karger, Kaashoek, & Balakrishnan, 2001), CAN (Ratnasamy, Francis, Handley, Karp, & Schenker, 2001) and Pastry (Rowstron & Druschel, 2001), guarantee retrieval of existing network resources with the use of Distributed Hash Tables (DHTs). The maintenance of a distributed index however comes with high cost, as additional traffic is generated for maintaining the routing information in a highly dynamic environment.

Trying to overcome the problems mentioned above, there are a number of P2P research systems (Cudré-Mauroux, Agarwal, & Aberer, 2007; Ehrig et al., 2003; Nakauchi, Morikawa, & Aoyama, 2004; Nejdl et al., 2002; Tatarinov & Halevy, 2004) that try to encompass the semantic technology notion, to represent meaning and knowledge, as well as to use reasoning for retrieving the knowledge. Knowledge needs to be encoded in a structured form to become widely accessible. An ontology

structure (Jepsen, 2009) is an important part of the semantic web as it represents knowledge at the level of concepts; ontology provides a shared understanding through conceptualisation. In P2P systems, a domain specific ontology can be used for classifying network resources to ontology related concepts. Related research methods, are trying to exploit the benefits provided by semantics through an ontology structure in order to enhance data management and to improve resources discovery. As a result of that, the query can also be categorised to a specific concept and be routed to the peer that supports the specific concept.

An ontology-based P2P topology for service discovery has been described by (Schlosser, Sintek, Decker, & Nejdl, 2003), where the network is organised in a HyperCup topology. Information or services that peers provide are categorised to general concepts; these concepts and their relationships form the network ontology. Peers with similar interests are organised in a concept cluster. Each cluster is assigned a combination of concepts which best describe the peers that belong to the cluster. This network organisation aims to efficiently route the query to peers that can satisfy it. This technique uses broadcasting for query forwarding; when the query reaches the most appropriate cluster is then broadcasted to all peers. The network uses globally known ontologies for clustering its nodes. This approach however is an example of structured P2P networks. Yongxiang Dou and Xiaoxian Bei (2008) also presented a semantic information retrieval system based on a hybrid ontology integration approach. In hybrid approaches, each network source employs its own local ontology but all ontologies are built upon a global shared vocabulary. The authors are focusing on the problems involved with information representation and integration in P2P semantic retrieval networks. This research and the system proposed by the authors are in preliminary stages and no experiments have proven the validity of the approach yet.

Summarising, P2P networks suffer from low quality of results, large amounts of poorly managed data and increased network traffic. The main motivation of this work is to attempt and resolve these issues by comprising the Semantic Web idea in unstructured adaptive P2P networks. The importance of this work is reflected in the challenge to pursue the Semantic Web vision by understanding the semantics of the data, to provide fault tolerance and scalability improvements. This can be achieved by adapting P2P architectures and combining the Semantic Web technologies with P2P networks, enhancing in this way the P2P performance in terms of accuracy, speed and traffic.

Consequently, the current research focuses on creating a dynamically adaptive semantic-driven P2P topology for managing and distributing knowledge in an efficient manner. The main aim is to transform the resources of a large scale P2P system from unmanageable amounts of data into a structured knowledge based repository of indexed resources. The implementation of a Collective Intelligence (CI) (Segaran, 2007) system was necessary for this work, where raw peer data was transformed to semantic network knowledge. The CI method employs a number of algorithms for mining resources' metadata and transforming it to an ontology topology of related concepts. More specifically, the proposed system incorporates a two layer architecture where the upper layer provides a conceptual representation of the system. Through CI, the resources of the system in the lower level are harvested and the network knowledge is represented through an ontology which is maintained by the super-peers of the network. The network employs an adaptive topology which varies based on the network requirements. The system initially starts as a mesh topology, but as the network size increases and the workload on each super-peer changes, the network converts in a semantic graph structure in order to meet the needs of the network. The network transformation provides a more flexible topology, where P2P technologies combined with the network ontology provide effective information management and resource retrieval.

The article is organised as follows: in the next section the related work is discussed. Then, the proposed semantic-driven architecture and the use of collective intelligence for building the network knowledge is explained, giving as a case study the creation of music ontology. The final sections include the performance evaluation of the proposal and the paper closes with the conclusion and the future work.

TOWARDS A SEMANTIC P2P NETWORK

Query routing efficiency and information retrieval accuracy are considered important aspects when evaluating the performance of P2P distributed systems, because they can be considered as the key to the scalability of the P2P system. Flooding algorithms and random selection algorithms perform poorly as far as accuracy and efficiency is concerned (Tsoumakos & Roussopoulos, 2003). Peer clustering proposed solutions are attempting to reduce the network traffic and improve the resource discovery experience.

Peer-clustering approach was used both by (Crespo & Garcia-Molina, 2005) and (Löser, Naumann, Siberski, Wolfgang Nejdl, & Thaden, 2004). In the former, Crespo et al. presented the Semantic Overlay Network (SON) for P2P which is formed by semantically related peers. The authors use a predefined fixed hierarchy which is used when forming the overlay network into semantically related clusters. In the latter approach, the peers are organised in a super-peer network in order to better improve routing efficiency. Additional work (Li, Lee, & Sivasubramaniam, 2004) on peer organisation using semantic overlays is based on the idea of "small world networks", where peers are clustered according to the semantics of their local data and self-organised as a small world overlay network.

Similarly, for improving the efficiency of information retrieval in P2P networks (Kobayashi et al., 2009) proposed a query driven P2P system where dynamic peer clusters are created based on query characteristics. The dynamic clusters are created when particular network resources with similar features become more popular. Initially, the network consists of a number of static clusters, each controlled by a leader peer. Each leader is responsible in deciding when a new dynamic cluster needs to be created by evaluating the query features. Even though dynamic clusters can be very effective in efficiently retrieving resources, if the dynamic clusters created are ephemeral, then clusters could end up being ineffective. The dynamic clusters need to be time persistent in order to be useful in query search; otherwise they just create an extra overhead to the network. The above drawback can be dealt by evaluating time persistence and not only query characteristics before creating a dynamic cluster.

Furthermore, in this proposal the cluster leader nodes are connected with each other forming a mesh topology; this type of connection organisation can affect the scalability and maintainability of the network. Even though a mesh topology has the advantages of directly exchanging information between the peer leaders and eliminating the traffic problems by creating smaller paths for query propagation; it comes also with disadvantages like latency in information retrieval due to the bigger number of records in the index storage, and expensive maintenance due to the messages sent among the leader peers for updating their information. The semantic-driven proposal tackles the above problems by adapting a more flexible topology, where the network transforms to the least expensive and more effective topology based on the timely network needs.

HP Company's pSearch (Tang, Xu, & Dwarkadas, 2003) is a prototype P2P IR system. It uses a CAN (Content Addressable Network) topology to create a semantic overlay, where resources are organised based on their semantics. The semantic vector of a document is used as the key to store the document index in the CAN. Documents semantics are generated using latent semantic indexing (LSI) algorithm. This system, however, has low dimensionality of only few hundred semantic spaces, which means that all resources of the system can only be matched to the specific semantic spaces (concepts). In other words, the network topology is limited by the number of semantic spaces, since it is directly connected to it. Similar limitations are faced by the system proposed by (Yamato & Sunaga, 2006) where again a CAN topology is used for managing resources semantics.

Liu, Antonopoulos and Mackin (Liu, Antonopoulos, & Mackin, 2007) provide a P2P algorithm for resource discovery. The P2P network can be seen as mimicking the social behaviour of people where, people are represented by peers and relationships by their interconnections. This work can relate to social P2P, however, instead of having interconnected nodes where each node relates to a number of interests, there are concepts and relevant nodes connected to a related concept super-node. Thus, instead of searching the nodes to find a resource, the concepts are searched. The proposed architecture is described in more detail in the following sections.

A SEMANTIC-DRIVEN ARCHITECTURE

The philosophy underlying the semantic-driven architecture resides in the detail where instead of searching the network peers directly to find a resource, the super-node(s) forming the ontology concepts are searched instead. This can be feasible by clustering the resources based on their concepts and matching them to the extracted concept of the user's query. Therefore, the semantic-driven architecture can be achieved by automatically assigning concepts to resources, within a two layer network topology, and by using domain specific ontology for conceptually defining user's queries.

System Architecture

Using super-peers in a P2P system is like embedding the benefits of a centralised topology in a distributed system. Super-peer networks have the advantages of locating rare resources and being least expensive in terms of network traffic. In contrast with flat architectures that uses blind search techniques that do not scale and produce a lot of traffic. Random flat algorithms which come as a variation considerably reduce the number of messages sent but still the success depends on the random choices made. Neither structured approaches satisfy the requirements of the proposed system since they come with high maintenance overheads (Tsoumakos & Roussopoulos, 2003).

The architecture of the proposed system follows a hierarchical two-layer approach consisting of peers and super-peers. The higher level of super-peers defines the network's concepts and relationships among them. The ordinary peers, which are the owners of the network resources, are part of the lower level. Each resource in the network is assigned with metadata, which are

keywords conceptually describing the resources. Each peer is responsible for enriching its resources with metadata. The knowledge of the network is being represented through a domain specific ontology. The ontology consists of concepts; a concept can be defined as a unit of knowledge which is described through keywords. Concepts are maintained by super-peers. A super-peer may be responsible for one or more concepts. Preferably, semantically related concepts should reside in the same super-peer. The peers are connected to the super-peers that support the concepts they relate to (Figure 1).

Adaptive Topology

An adaptive network topology is proposed in this work, where the size and connectivity on the super-peer layer varies according to the query needs of the network. Initially the network starts with only one super-peer. As the network load increases and the super-peer is no longer capable of handling all the network requests, some of the load is transferred to a newly created super-peer.

Figure 1. Semantic-driven architecture

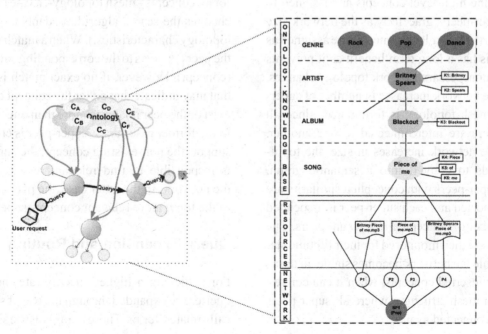

Ordinary peers are appointed as super-peers from their parent super-peer based on their capacity and availability. The super-peer categorises the incoming queries to a subject concept in order to append it to the appropriate super-peer when the work load reaches a critical point. The capacity threshold is calculated by measuring the query rate per time period. The load of the super-peer can be forecasted and the network can be partitioned before the super-peer becomes unable to serve the network; avoiding a potential bottleneck. For reaching a correct load balancing between the existing super-peer and the newly created super-peer, equally demanded concepts are handed to the new super-peer.

Particularly, every time a super-peer receives a query, the *queries-received* counter is increased. Additionally, the counter for the *queries-received-per-concept* is increased, based on the query concept. When the *queries-received-per-concept* exceeds the predefined threshold, the network is partitioned and part of the network is handed over to a different super-peer. To decide which part of the network to assign another super-peer, the current super-peer transfers a number of concepts necessary for staying under the load threshold. Initially the high level concepts are assigned to other super-peers; gracefully as the network size increases the lower level concepts are assigned as well. This has a long term benefit as it prevents rapid or unnecessary network topology changes.

As the network increases in number of super-peers a mesh topology is formulated, since all super-peers are interconnected to one another. When the network increases in size, the topology needs to convert into a semantic graph, where super-peers with conceptual similarity are interconnected and each super-peer is associated to a number of conceptually relevant peers. The concepts are then monitored for their lifetime stability while the network becomes stable, in terms of newly inserted concepts, when it can convert back to a mesh structure; where all super-peers are interconnected again.

By using an adaptive topology the advantages of both mesh and semantic graph structures are employed. A mesh topology has the advantages of forwarding directly the query to the appropriate concept, processing and matching the query to a concept only once and discovering effortless (with negligible number of hops) if a resource exists or not. However, employing a mesh topology in large networks with not steady concepts comes with disadvantages; there is latency in finding the matching concept since a big index is used for searching and a lot of traffic is generated for keeping the network up to date. Therefore an adaptive topology can take advantage of both structures when it is applied timely correctly.

Peers Joining Activity

Initially when a peer joins the network is connected to a randomly selected super-peer. The super-peer is responsible to assign the peer to a specific concept and consequently to the corresponding parent super-peer. In order to find the matching concept, the peer's files' metadata are compared against the keywords related to concepts (this is feasible if super-peers keep information for all concepts - mesh topology-, as the topology changes the search algorithm adapts to the new topology characteristics.). When a match is found the peer connects to the corresponding super-peer (concept). However, if no exact match is found, that may indicate that either the concept does not exist or the peer relates to more than one concept. In the former case, a new super-peer is created to support the non-existing concept; the super-peer is responsible to find relevant resources from the network. In the latter case, the peer connects to the top *n* more relevant concepts super-peers.

Query Expansion and Routing

For achieving a higher success rate the users' queries are expanded through the use of semantically related-terms. These terms must be similar to the whole concept of the query, rather than being synonymy similar to the query keywords. As the focus of this work is not on query expansion, a standard query expansion technique is employed.

During the query expansion process the query is analysed using the domain specific ontology. The keywords of the query are compared against keywords of the concepts in the ontology and the most related concept(s) are extracted. If more than one concept is extracted the correlation among the concepts must be determined, in order to keep only the concepts with minimal semantic distance. Additionally, in the case where more than one concept is derived, and these concepts relate to each other, then query specialisation takes place. In query specialisation the more specific of the concepts is kept.

During the query routing algorithm, the query is firstly submitted to the parent super-peer (concept) from the client (peer). Then the query is analysed locally, where the query expansion process takes place, as described above. When the query needs to be forwarded to another super-peer, a heuristic technique is applied for finding the best matching concept (super-peer) for the query to be forwarded to. Depending on the network topology, mesh or semantic graph, a different approach is followed to find the query's matching concept. In a mesh topology the querying super-peer have information for all the rest super-peers and the concepts of the network. For finding the matching concept and consequently the related super-peer, its global knowledge index can be searched.

In a semantic graph topology each super-peer stores information only for a number of its neighbouring super-peers. Thus, if the query does not match to a concept based on the querying super-peer's information, the query must be forwarded to a neighbouring super-peer with close semantic similarity of the query's keywords. If no super-peer can be found with close semantic similarity then the query is either send to all the neighbours or to a random one. The same process continues until a matching concept is found or until a number of hops have been reached (this limitation aims to reduce unnecessary traffic). Eventually if a matching concept is found, a list of super-peers that relate to the matching concept is chosen. The query is then forwarded to the related super-peers; either to one super-peer at a time and if the query is successful the query forwarding stops, or to all super-peers at once. The query is considered unsuccessful in the case where no matching concept can be found in the network (Figure 2).

There is also the possibility some queries not to be matched to a concept. Unclassified queries are sent randomly to a number of peers belonging to the querying super-peer; then the query is sent randomly to a super-peer. In this case the super-peer performs a cosine similarity measurement between the filename keywords and query keywords of all the resources that are unclassified as well. For complex queries, where a lot of unrelated concepts have been found, the user could choose between precision and recall. If precision is chosen then the user prefers accuracy on the search results. On the other hand if recall is chosen the user prefers more results over accuracy. In this case all the resources that match the query concepts are retrieved. F-measure (or F-score) considers both precision and recall and produces a weighted average of both parameters, thus this formula can be used when retrieving results of complex queries.

COLLECTIVE INTELLIGENCE ONTOLOGY

The definition of collective intelligence (Segaran, 2007) perfectly describes a P2P collaboration platform where the knowledge within the network is shared efficiently among the peers. Collective intelligence in our system is built with the contribution of all the peers connected to the network. Each peer enriches the P2P network's pool of knowledge through its resources.

Figure 2. Conceptual diagram

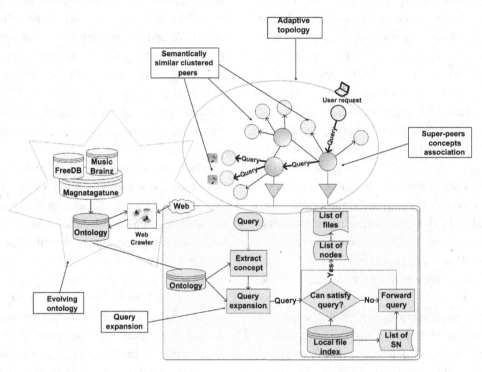

The cumulative knowledge of the network is represented through an ontology (Figure 3). A set of concepts linked with semantic relations enable the semantic categorisation of network resources and peers to concepts, and the routing of the query based on its semantic evaluation. A formal definition of ontology is presented by Pretorius (2004), where an ontology is defined as a set of concepts, relations and axioms. Formally presented as:

$$O=\{C, R, A^o\}$$

where C represents sets of concepts; R denotes sets of relations and A^o represents sets of axioms (relationships among the concepts). Similarly, the proposed network ontology consists of a set of concepts where each concept comprises of an ordered set of keywords.

Ontology Creation

The ontology is initially created by the first peer that forms the P2P network. As more peers join the network they contribute through their resources to the ontology expansion. The file resources exist in the peer level but the network knowledge is managed at the super-peer level. Each resource in the network is described by a file descriptor and file related knowledge (metadata). A parent super-peer is responsible for analysing those file resources and enriching the ontology with new concepts. A super-peer may be responsible for a set of concepts.

When a peer enters the network and connects to the conceptually appropriate super-peer, the parent super-peer is responsible to analyse the peer's resources and to enrich the ontology with the retrieved concepts and relationships. The retrieved peer concepts may already exists in the ontology, thus no action needs to be taken in this case. Each resource of the peer is assigned to a

Figure 3. Ontology

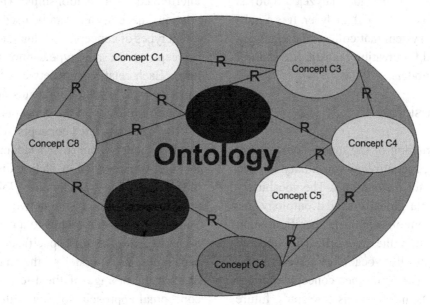

concept, preferably to the most specific concept type (discussed analytically in section "Case study: Music ontology"). Assigning resources to concepts facilitates more efficient resource retrieval during the searching process. This scenario is valid in the case where all super-peers own the same part of the ontology. In the case where the ontology is distributed among the super-peers and each super-peer holds only a part of it, a different process takes place. This process will be presented in more detail in future developments of this work.

Castano, Ferrara, Montanelli, and Varese (2009) presented a similar work where the notion of collective intelligence is introduced as well: the iCoord system. iCoord involves knowledge sharing as opposed to our proposed system which is more technically related to file sharing. Another difference with iCoord is the way the ontology is updated. In iCoord the information (named community manifesto) circulates the network enabling with this way the community members to store knowledge. As opposed to our system, where the ontology is scattered in a distributed manner among the super-peers and it is updated through synchronisation processes. These processes are

responsible for avoiding duplicate of information as far as the sharing of common parts of the ontology is concerned. The ontology information is updated as the queries propagate the network.

Case Study: Music Ontology

For evaluating the proposed semantic driven architecture, a music file sharing system has been used as a case study scenario. Distributed music file sharing systems are of great interest; prove are large scale P2P application systems that have been deployed for that purpose. Music semantics are rich, which enables the creation of a widely accepted vocabulary for the music ontology; and of course there is a huge amount of music data available which makes it feasible to perform pragmatic evaluation experiments. In general multimedia (movies, music, pictures) file sharing is a domain where a lot of metadata rich resources can be found and utilised for building the corresponding ontology.

For creating the music ontology, a P2P file sharing crawler has been customised and used for collecting real user data. IR-Wire ("IR-Wire:

Gnutella Data Crawler and Analyzer," 2006) is a Gnutella data crawler and analyser. It is a publicly available system that collects data that can be further used for creating realistic file-sharing environment models.

Ontology Design

For the construction of the music domain specific ontology, a controlled vocabulary is used as a backbone for the ontology. The vocabulary is essential for a globally shared ontology, for meaningfully communicating the specific domain knowledge within the network. The selected terms in the controlled vocabulary serve as music concept types. The predefined concept types are used only for the needs of this case study, future developments will allow the P2P network to intelligently generate the required vocabulary. At this stage, the ontology entails four music concept types: artist, album, genre and song. These types have been chosen among others because they are considered essential descriptors for identifying a music resource. Moreover, popular music file sharing systems use these descriptors as searching fields in their search engines.

As described in the section above, the ontology is formally defined as a set of concepts, relationships, descriptions and keywords. Each concept of the ontology is assigned with a unique *id*. A concept is not defined by a single name but by a description which is a combination of keywords. It is possible that a particular keyword to be associated with more than one concept in the ontology. In other words, association between keyword and concept is one to many, rather than one to one. For example the keyword <Madonna> associates with the concept of type Artists as well as with the concept of type Album. Each keyword curries a weight indicating the frequency counter, i.e., how many times the keyword is used for describing various concepts in the ontology. Figure 4 represents how concepts, descriptions and keywords correlate and form the ontology. Concepts are

interrelated with relationships. Three types of relationships exist and can be used to relate different types of concepts, as illustrated in Table 1. Concepts of the same type cannot relate to each other. Each relationship between two concepts carries a weight which indicates how close the semantic similarity of the concepts is.

Thus the associated concepts' relationship is: <Celebration>-Album of-<Madonna>, meaning that the Album called <Celebration> belongs to the Artist called <Madonna> (Table 2). Each music file resource in the network represents a Song, thus each file relates to a concept of type Song, which is the most specific among the concept types. This model of the music ontology enables the storage of the file resources' in a conceptual approach, solving with this way the known problem of unmanageable network resources. Furthermore, the user search is enriched with semantic capability for retrieving more accurate results in an efficient manner when reasoning is used for retrieving knowledge from the ontology.

Ontology Data Population

Music files are rich in metadata. For harnessing the metadata of the network resources, a metadata acquisition process takes place and for each music file the most appropriate concepts were retrieved based on their attached metadata (e.g., artist, album). For the needs of this work the resources of the network as well as the music ontology are represented and stored in a relational database. Each resource is represented as a table row where the corresponding columns give the metadata of the resource. For transforming the network resources to a collective intelligence knowledge base –music ontology-a conceptualisation process took place. As mention in the previous section, there is a predefined vocabulary where the ontology concepts are built based on. Each concept of the ontology must be of a specific type namely artist, album, genre, song. Thus, for every music

Figure 4. ORM diagram concept-description-keyword

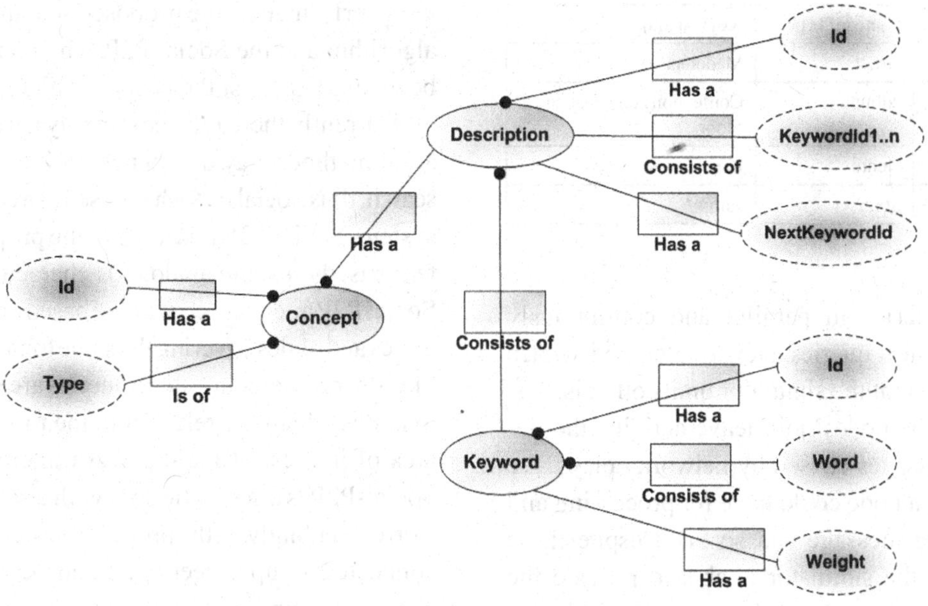

Table 1. Relationships among concepts

Concept type	Relationship name	Concept type
Track	– track of –	Artist
Track	– track of –	Album
Track	– genre of –	Genre
Artist	– genre of –	Genre
Album	– genre of –	Genre
Album	– album of –	Artist

Table 2. Two concepts presenting a type of an Album and an Artist. These two concepts can only relate with the relationship name -Album of-

Concept	Type	Description keywords
1	Album	<Celebration>
2	Artist	<Madonna>

resource, concepts are created which are of a specific type, based on the given metadata (Table 3).

Thus the associated concepts' generated are represented in Table 4.

The resource is assigned with the more specific concept (of type song), which is *ConceptId* 4 in this case.

PERFORMANCE EVALUATION

The performance of the semantic-driven architecture was evaluated by simulating the proposed environment. For carrying out the experiments for the proposed system, a special-purpose simulator has been developed. The simulator was designed bearing in mind real network conditions, like

Table 3. A music resource which incorporates the following information

ResourceId	FileName	Genre	Album	Artist	Song
1	Madonna-Jump.mp3	Pop	Confessions on a Dance Floor	Madonna	Jump

Table 4 Associated concepts.

ConceptId	ConceptType	Keyword(s)
1	Artist	Madonna
2	Album	Confessions on a Dance Floor
3	Genre	Pop
4	Song	Jump

running queries in parallel and continuously generating new queries. Nevertheless, it is worth mentioning that the simulator omits other issues, including the nodes' join-leave activity, the delays of messages caused by network delays, the actual load a node could have for processing and propagating message and so on. Despite these omissions, the simulator is able to provide the basic simulations for understanding the fundamental properties of the proposed system and the other simulating benchmark algorithm. The set of experiments undertaken serves as a proof of concept and basis for future developments.

Simulation Environment

The music ontology comprises of 450 concepts, 20 represent genre concepts, which structure the higher-level of the super-peers topology; the rest represent concepts of type artist, album and song. Concepts of different types are interconnected through relationships. In total, there are 330 resources in the network, each one described by a song concept and distributed to various nodes among the 200 that form the topology. There are 440 unique queries, 30 of which are chosen at each timeslot to propagate the network. It is important to note that 10% of the queries match no resources, i.e., when analysed the queries have no match with the concepts of the ontology, thus no resources are related to them. Time is represented as a sequence of timeslots during which queries are generated, forwarded and processed. Each experiment comprises of 100 timeslots. In

this environment two algorithms are tested for their performance, the proposed semantic-driven algorithm and the Social P2P, which is used as a benchmark against the proposed algorithm.

Currently there is no commonly agreed evaluation methodology and benchmark for semantic search, thus Social P2P was chosen as a comparable system. Social P2P is related to the proposed system based on some analogous characteristics. In Social P2P nodes are connected based on interests' topics and nodes covering the same topics are more likely to be interconnected. Queries are forwarded to nodes which are relevant to the topic or to the area of interest of the topic. An interest area of Social-P2P is a semantic area with a set of topics. Correspondingly, in the proposed system peers are connected to super-peers based on their resources conceptual similarity. Queries are forwarded to conceptually related super-peers and peers. An interest area in the proposed system corresponds to a concept of type genre, consisting of set of other concepts which correspond to set of topics.

The authors of Social P2P in their experiments use interest areas from the open directory categories ("ODP - Open Directory Project," 1998-2010). To set a fair comparison between the two algorithms the music ontology is set as a knowledge base for both systems; thus the social P2P algorithm had to be adapted and use the music ontology as well. An interest has as equivalence a genre concept, which represents the most generic concept of the ontology. Topics relate to concepts of type artist, album and song. For simulating the Social P2P algorithm additional parameters were defined. Each query had a TTL equals to 3 hops, for limiting the life time of messages. The number of peers to be contacted in each hop was set to 3. The knowledge index has an upper limit of 40 entries.

Data Collection

During the experiments real user queries and real nodes information are used from an existing music file sharing P2P system. The data has been gathered after customising to the proposed system's needs an open source P2P system, the LimeWire Data Crawler ("IR-Wire: Gnutella Data Crawler and Analyzer," 2006). LimeWire Data Crawler collects information from gnutella-like network and stores it in a relational database. More specifically the data crawler is built on top of LimeWire client, thus it supports all the LimeWire functionalities. The data crawler collects incoming and outgoing queries, peer information and music file resources metadata.

As described in the section "Ontology data population", for creating the music ontology the metadata of the collected network resources was analysed. Similarly for creating the network topology the collected peer information was analysed and the corresponding peers of the network were generated. Each peer represents a real host of a peer-to-peer system thus it consists of a number of resources. The collected queries were used as such without any modifications. However, since this report consists of initial experiments for the proposed system, queries that would generate results were mostly used. Even though, a number of queries that would not match any resources were employed as well for proving that the system retrieves the correct data resources.

Simulation Experiments and Results

A set of experiments were carried out and the performance of each algorithm has been evaluated using the following criteria:

- Query success rate: the success rate of a query is calculated by dividing the number of successful queries by the number of generated queries.
- Traffic: this is the total number of messages sent by the peers when forwarding queries and query results.

It is important to note that for each query the precision rate of the resources returned is always 1; the resources returned are always relevant to the query.

Query Success

For defining a successful query the following heuristic process takes place: the query string is matched against the most specific concept retrieved (refer to query expansion section). A query is considered successful when the cosine similarity of the matching concept-based string is greater than 60%.

Figure 5 demonstrates the performance of both the semantic-driven algorithm as well as the Social P2P algorithms in terms of query success. The semantic-driven algorithm produces higher success rate when compared to Social P2P. This performance can be attributed to the semantic-driven architecture of the network. Since peers are assigned to specific concepts based on their resources' conceptualisation, and queries are routed approximately to those semantic similar peers, the possibility for high success rate increases. In Social P2P queries are forwarded to peers that have previously satisfied query requests, assuming that peers gradually connect to other peers with the same interests. However this is not always the case and that is why Social P2P produces smaller success than semantic-driven architecture.

For making a fair comparison of the two systems, the success rate is calculated against the resource-rich queries. In this case the queries that have related resources only are counted and used for calculating the success rate. Additionally the number of queries propagated without related resources is the same in both systems. This is demonstrated in Figure 5, in column 3 tagged as 'Resource-rich.

Figure 6 gives a more detail comparison between the two systems. It can be observed that the semantic-driven system is more stable – 80% success in average – in the successful queries

Figure 5. Semantic-driven and Social P2P general performance comparison

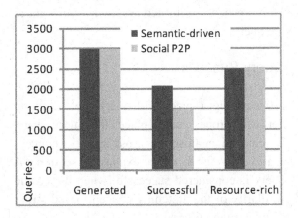

and super-peers are interconnected. This design ensures that if a resource exists there is a high probability for locating it. A resource might not be located in the situation where this resource is rare and the majority of the other resources that reside in the same peer belong to non-related concepts. It is also worth mentioning that semantically poor resources have fewer possibilities in locating them as well.

For proving that the semantic-driven approach returns only query related resources, the success rate of resource-rich queries is compared against the success rate of resource-poor queries (Figure 7). The success rate is slightly lower in the case of propagating in the network some resources-poor queries; since there are not related resources to retrieve. The success rate is higher in the case where only resource-rich queries propagate the network; since there are resources that conceptually relate to the queries. Also, it sets a fair evaluation for the proposed system to test it against queries that conceptually match to resources. In the case where no related resources exist, the success rate falls due to the absence of related resources and not due to the heuristics employed by the proposed algorithm.

throughout the experiment lifecycle. On the other hand, Social P2P produces an increasing query success trend in the beginning of the experiments continuing with a more stable behaviour through the end. In the beginning of the experiment the peers have little knowledge of the network, but as queries propagate the network and peers' knowledge index is enriched, the success rate increases and becomes more stable. The credits for the stable behaviour of the semantic-driven approach are given to the conceptual way peers

Figure 6. Success rate semantic-driven and social P2P

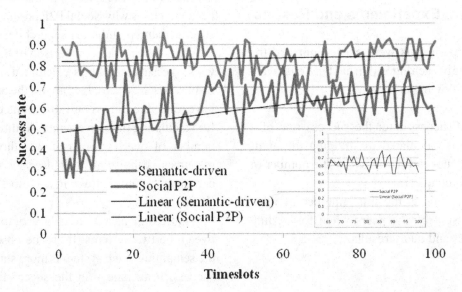

Figure 7. Success rate semantic-driven and social P2P

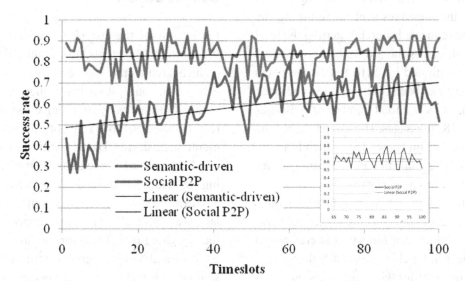

Traffic

This set of experiments calculates the traffic generated by the semantic-driven system and compares it against the Social P2P. This evaluation also involves some mathematical calculated metrics which are compared against the simulation results values. To calculate the number of messages the Social P2P network produces, the following formula is used:

$$\mathbf{M}_{\text{Social P2P}} = \mathbf{Q}_N * \sum_{i=1}^{TTL} (Q_p)^i$$

where Q_N is the number of queries per timeslot and Q_p the number of querying peers per query.

For a network with 30 generated queries at a timeslot, 3 peers to be contacted at a time and TTL=3 the following calculations give the maximum number of messages to be generated per timeslot: $\mathbf{M}_{\text{Social P2P}}$ = 1170 messages. The number of messages generated for returning the query results to the requesting peer also needs to be added. This is calculated by multiplying the messages, by the number of peers each peer has

forwarded the query to. Thus, the total number of messages produced is: 1980 messages per timeslot. The simulation results give total average messages 1887, which is an expected value. For calculating the number of messages for the semantic-driven network the following formula can be applied:

$$\mathbf{M}_{\text{semantic-driven}} = \mathbf{Q}_N + \sum_{i=1}^{N_{SP}} P_i + \mathbf{Q}_F$$

where Q_N is the number of generated queries per timeslot, N_{SP} is the number of super-peers the query is forwarded to, P is the peers specific to the concept and Q_F the number of forwarded queries.

Due to the use of real data during the proposed system simulations a number of assumptions need to be made. It is assumed that in average, each super-peer is the parent of 10 (200 peers/20 super-peers) peers, therefore, at each time approximately one third of the peers are considered to be query concept specific peers. After applying the above assumptions on the formula the following results are retrieved:

$$\mathbf{M}_{\text{Semantic-driven}} = 91 \text{ messages}$$

Again, the above number of messages does not include the messages sent for returning the results to the requested peer. For getting the total number of messages the messages found above need to be multiplied by 2 (that is all the peers that the query has been forwarded to send back a response). Thus, the total number of messages produced is: 182 messages. The simulation results give total average messages 165, which is an expected value. The graph in Figure 8 demonstrates these figures diagrammatically. It is observed that the semantic-driven architecture generates much less messages than the Social P2P network. The reduced number of messages is credited to the super-peer hierarchical approach the system employs. This justifies the initial decision of using a dynamic hierarchical layer when building the proposed system. It is proved that even the controlled flooding used by Social P2P generate a lot of traffic in the network.

To sum-up, the semantic-driven system outperformed the Social P2P in success rate and cost of messages, fulfilling the purpose of its design. The specific architecture was initially chosen among random flat and structured approaches for its advantages of reduced traffic and the capability of locating resources easily (Figure 8).

CONCLUSION

For improving the resource discovery processes of existing P2P systems the semantic-driven hierarchical architecture has been proposed. The idea is based on conceptualising, using semantics, the network resources and building the system architecture based on those concepts; using a dynamic hierarchical design. Based on this philosophy, the ontology concepts are searched first when requesting for resources, instead of the network peers.

A set of experiments carried out through simulations and proved that the above concept improves the searching process, by presenting a high success rate and cost efficiency in terms of messages sent when searching for network resources. The proposed system outperforms when compared against Social P2P algorithm, by producing a higher and more stable behaviour in query success results. Social P2P, on the other hand, starts with a low success rate which however continuously increments, giving at the end a stable behaviour, lower though than the semantic-driven system. When taking into consideration the proposed system attributes it can be concluded that this research also has the prospective in contributing towards Web3.0 research targets; which focuses on learning-enabled architectures, intelligent applications, distributed databases ("The World

Figure 8. Average messages sent

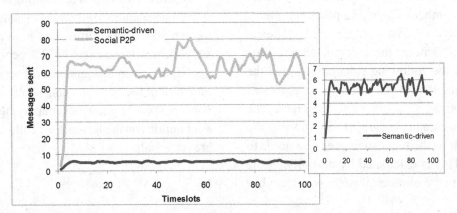

Wide Database" Nova Spivack) and distributed computing.

FUTURE WORK

The simulation experiments and presented results of the semantic-driven architecture identified the perspectives this work has to offer. Current evaluation acts as proof of concept for the proposed system. Further evaluation should include a larger dataset and topology for measuring the scalability of the architecture. Additionally, the idea of network adaptivity, proposed in this work, needs to be implemented in the simulation environment for testing its advantages against the current network structures. Further work should include the implementation of a dynamic environment by including the peer's join-leave activity and measuring the system's performance based on the network's churn rate. Finally, consistency management for replication and synchronisation processes needs to be employed for supporting the network's distributed ontology.

ACKNOWLEDGMENT

Special thanks go to Panos Alexandropoulos and Stefan Stafrace of the University of Surrey, for providing their technical knowledge and feedback for this work.

REFERENCES

Berners-Lee, T., Hendler, J., & Lassila, O. (2001). The Semantic Web. *Scientific American Magazine*. Retrieved from http://www.scientificamerican.com/article.cfm?id=the-semantic-web

Castano, S., Ferrara, A., Montanelli, S., & Varese, G. (2009). Semantic coordination of P2P collective intelligence. In *Proceedings of the International Conference on Management of Emergent Digital EcoSystems* (pp. 99-106). New York: ACM. doi:10.1145/1643823.1643842

Crespo, A., & Garcia-Molina, H. (2005). Semantic Overlay Networks for P2P Systems. In *Agents and Peer-to-Peer Computing* (pp. 1-13). Retrieved from http://dx.doi.org/10.1007/11574781_1

Cudré-Mauroux, P., Agarwal, S., & Aberer, K. (2007). Gridvine: An infrastructure for peer information management. *IEEE Internet Computing*, 36–44. doi:10.1109/MIC.2007.108

Dou, Y., & Bei, X. (2008). Ontology-Based Semantic Information Retrieval Systems in Unstructured P2P Networks. In *Proceedings of the Wireless Communications, Networking and Mobile Computing, the 4th International Conference (WiCOM '08)* (pp. 1-4).

Ehrig, M., Haase, P., Siebes, R., Staab, S., Stuckenschmidt, H., Studer, R., et al. (2003). The SWAP Data and Metadata Model for Semantics-Based Peer-to-Peer Systems. In *Multiagent System Technologies* (pp. 1096-1097). Retrieved from http://www.springerlink.com/content/mtm7gu9t8bn-uuu16

IR-Wire: Gnutella Data Crawler and Analyzer. (2006). Retrieved January 8, 2010, from http://ir.iit.edu/~waigen/proj/pirs/irwire/index.html

Jepsen, T. C. (2009). Just What Is an Ontology, Anyway? *IT Professional*, *11*(5), 22–27. doi:10.1109/MITP.2009.105

Kobayashi, Y., Watanabe, T., Kanzaki, A., Yoshihisa, T., Hara, T., & Nishio, S. (2009). A Dynamic Cluster Construction Method Based on Query Characteristics in Peer-to-Peer Networks. In *Proceedings of the AP2PS '09, the First International Conference* (pp. 168-173).

Li, M., Lee, W. C., & Sivasubramaniam, A. (2004). Semantic small world: An overlay network for peer-to-peer search. In *Proceedings of the 12th IEEE International Conference on Network Protocols* (pp. 228-238).

Liang, J., Kumar, R., & Ross, K. (2004). The KaZaA Overlay: A Measurement Study. In *Proceedings of the 19th IEEE Annual Computer Communications Workshop.*

Liu, L., Antonopoulos, N., & Mackin, S. (2007). Social Peer-to-Peer for Resource Discovery. In Proceedings of the *15th EUROMICRO International Conference on Parallel, Distributed and Network-Based Processing (PDP'07)* (pp. 459-466).

Löser, A., Naumann, F., Siberski, W., Nejdl, W., & Thaden, U. (2004). Semantic Overlay Clusters within Super-Peer Networks. In *Databases, Information Systems, and Peer-to-Peer Computing* (pp. 33-47). Retrieved from http://www.springerlink.com/content/cd6jv7alxv3eac1k

Nakauchi, K., Morikawa, H., & Aoyama, T. (2004). Design and Implementation of a Semantic Peer-to-Peer Network. In *High Speed Networks and Multimedia Communications* (pp. 961-972). Retrieved from http://www.springerlink.com/content/8mvv93v3p8pnuut4

Nejdl, W., Wolf, B., Qu, C., Decker, S., Sintek, M., Naeve, A., et al. (2002). EDUTELLA: a P2P Networking Infrastructure based on RDF. In *Proceedings of the 11th international conference on World Wide Web* (pp. 604-615).

ODP - Open Directory Project. (1998). Retrieved January 17, 2010, from http://www.dmoz.org/

Pretorius, A. J. (2004). *Ontologies-Introduction and Overview.* Vrije Universiteit Brussel.

Ratnasamy, S., Francis, P., Handley, M., Karp, R., & Schenker, S. (2001). A scalable content-addressable network. In *Proceedings of the 2001 conference on Applications, technologies, architectures, and protocols for computer communications* (p. 172).

Rowstron, A., & Druschel, P. (2001). Pastry: Scalable, distributed object location and routing for large-scale peer-to-peer systems. In *Proceedings of the IFIP/ACM International Conference on Distributed Systems Platforms (Middleware)* (Vol. 11, pp. 329-350).

Schlosser, M., Sintek, M., Decker, S., & Nejdl, W. (2003). *Hypercup-hypercubes, ontologies, and efficient search on peer-to-peer networks* (pp. 112–124). LNCS.

Segaran, T. (2007). *Programming Collective Intelligence: Building Smart Web 2.0 Applications.* New York: O'Reilly Media.

Stoica, I., Morris, R., Karger, D., Kaashoek, M. F., & Balakrishnan, H. (2001). Chord: A scalable peer-to-peer lookup service for internet applications. In *Proceedings of the 2001 conference on Applications, technologies, architectures, and protocols for computer communications* (p. 160).

Stokes, M. (2002). *Gnutella2 Specifications Part one.* Retrieved February 2, 2010, from http://g2.trillinux.org/index.php?title=G2_specs_part1

Tang, C., Xu, Z., & Dwarkadas, S. (2003). *Peer-to-peer information retrieval using self-organizing semantic overlay networks* (pp. 175-186). New York: ACM. doi:10.1145/863955.863976

Tatarinov, I., & Halevy, A. (2004). Efficient query reformulation in peer data management systems. In *Proceedings of the 2004 ACM SIGMOD international conference on Management of data* (pp. 539-550). New York: ACM. doi:10.1145/1007568.1007629

Tsoumakos, D., & Roussopoulos, N. (2003). A comparison of peer-to-peer search methods. In *Proceedings of the Sixth International Workshop on the Web and Databases.*

Yamato, Y., & Sunaga, H. (2006). P2P Content Searching Method using Semantic Vector which is Managed on CAN Topology. *Journal of Multimedia, 1*(6), 1. doi:10.4304/jmm.1.6.1-9

This work was previously published in International Journal of Grid and High Performance Computing, Volume 2, Issue 4, edited by Emmanuel Udoh, pp. 12-30, copyright 2010 by IGI Publishing (an imprint of IGI Global).

Chapter 10
Network Architectures and Data Management for Massively Multiplayer Online Games

Minhua Ma
University of Derby, UK

Andreas Oikonomou
University of Derby, UK

ABSTRACT

Current-generation Massively Multiplayer Online Games (MMOG), such as World of Warcraft, Eve Online, and Second Life are mainly built on distributed client-server architectures with server allocation based on sharding, static geographical partitioning, dynamic micro-cell scheme, or optimal server for placing a virtual region according to the geographical dispersion of players. This paper reviews various approaches on data replication and region partitioning. Management of areas of interest (field of vision) is discussed, which reduces processing load dramatically by updating players only with those events that occur within their area of interest. This can be managed either through static geographical partitioning on the basis of the assumption that players in one region do not see/interact with players in other regions, or behavioural modelling based on players' behaviours. The authors investigate data storage and synchronisation methods for MMOG databases, mainly on relational databases. Several attempts of peer to peer (P2P) architectures and protocols for MMOGs are reviewed, and critical issues such as cheat prevention on P2P MMOGs are highlighted.

DOI: 10.4018/978-1-4666-0056-0.ch010

INTRODUCTION

MMOGs, also known as MMORPGs, is short for Massively Multiplayer Online (Role-Playing) Games, is a genre of online games which has been quickly and steadily growing since the start of the 21st century. Typically, MMOGs are based on a client-server architecture, where events are computed at the server and sent to clients. Each client controls a single character in the world, known as the player, communicates actions to the game server. Player characters can acquire and improve skills, collect items in their inventory, trade items with other players etc. The server serializes the actions, updates the game world accordingly, and communicates any changes to all affected players. The new game state is then rendered by the client-side software. The condition of the game world is constantly evolving, and in some cases in an unpredictable, unscripted fashion, as players interacts in the game. Some client-server architectures (Quax et al., 2008) have an intermediary layer of proxy servers which can reduce the number of connections for the servers and cache non-state data such as mesh or inventory information to improve response time.

Peer to peer (P2P) architectures have recently emerged as a potential alternative design for MMOGs. A few attempts of P2P MMOG have been reported in the research community (Krause, 2008). Compared to peer to peer models, distributed client-server architectures perform well when servers are faster (which is usually the case) or better distributed than clients but one of the drawbacks of client-server based MMOGs is that peer to peer messages must be relayed.

In this paper, we discuss key issues involved in networked computer game development, i.e., MMOG network architectures such as distributed client-server models and various P2P protocols proposed in the literature, database design, data replication, region partitioning, areas of interest, and cheating, with the hope that it would shed some light on future network design of distributed virtual environments and MMOGs.

DATA REPLICATION

Engagement is meant to be for a long period of time in MMOGs with users spending several months or even years playing and improving their character. As these games are designed to run continuously for years it is expected that the hardware infrastructure will at some point inevitably fail, be forced to shut down or otherwise go offline. In such situations it is crucial that the game can be restored to the last correct state it was in. Data replication therefore becomes of paramount importance.

Replication is the process of sharing data to ensure consistency between redundant resources, in order to improve reliability, fault tolerance, and accessibility. It could be data replication if the same data is stored on multiple storage devices or computation replication if the same computing task is executed many times. Current MMOGs are in favour of computation replication due to the issues of bandwidth and network latency. For example, in Russell et al.'s (2008) solution a server send both the initial state of a given object and deterministic code to simulate the object over time to all interested clients, so that clients can independently update the area of interest consistently with updates computed by the server. Computation replication results in efficient use of network bandwidth and the power of multi-core processors of game platforms.

Traditionally if the game state is dynamically stored during game play, it could be restored upon restarting a crashed or failed server. This is usually a relatively simple task where a complete snapshot of the world taken immediately before shutting down the server can be re-issued. Difficulties however arise when the termination is unpredictable, such as in the case of a server crash. Ideally, there should be no difference between the stored states and the actual game states in memory at the time of failure however this may not be realistic due to scalability and efficiency reasons. In this context the major requirements for replication in MMOGs are (Zhang et al., 2008):

- Consistency. This is relatively easy in classic client-server architectures whereas P2P architecture distributes the game state among peers and has no central server, making it very hard to administrate the game state and keep it consistent. Currently, MMOGs cannot solely use P2P architecture and there is no working business model yet.
- Efficiency. MMOGs are real-time systems and players expect fast responses to their actions as high latency could be detrimental to the user's experience leading to player dissatisfaction which will eventually result in the player unsubscribing from the game. The persistence layer inevitably adds overhead to the server therefore the objective in this case is to minimize the additional cost as experienced by a client when executing an action, e.g. moving, fighting or picking up items in the word.
- Scalability. As MMOGs typically support thousands of simultaneous players. Such capacity must be supported with consistency and efficiency.

All commercial MMOGs provide some form of replication for world recovery and maintenance purposes, but information about the technologies used is scarce.

VIRTUAL REGIONS AND DISTRIBUTED SERVERS

A common way of distributing load is splitting a huge game world into smaller virtual regions which are hosted on geographically distributed servers. Server allocation is usually based on a fixed (virtual) spatial subdivision scheme. For instance, Second Life (SL Wiki), one of the most well-known 3D virtual environments, is running on more than 5000 servers, each simulating a 256x256 meter region (call a *grid*). As the player moves through the world it is handed off from one server to another. It handles storing object state, land parcel state, and terrain height-map state (because land owners can change the terrain). Each server performs visibility calculations on objects and land, and transmits the data to the client. Image data is transmitted in a prioritised queue.

A widely identified problem with this static partitioning scheme is that it does not take into account the dynamic nature of MMOGs. As players are not evenly distributed over the virtual world, some servers are almost idle while others are overloaded. Even if the static partitioning is based on population density trends, it is still susceptible to imbalances due to unforeseen events. For example, if a large number of players decide to convene in a single location in the game world, it may cause unacceptable delay or system failure on the server which hosts the virtual region.

De Vleeschauwer et al. (2005) divide a virtual world into dynamic micro-cells which can be reassigned to other servers if the load on the server they are currently hosed on becomes too garge, and apply various algorithms to manage load balancing.

On the other hand, some previous studies try to tackle this problem based on locality of players. They investigate how server selection can be optimized for a single client, when given a set of available servers (Chambers et al., 2003), how to optimise server selection for a group of players (clans) who wish to play cooperatively on a server (Claypool, 2008), and how to find an optimal server for placing a virtual region based on the geographical dispersion of players in a MMOG which depends heavily on the time of day (Beskow et al., 2008) and to migrate game states to the server. Since the amount of players from a part of the world depends on the time of day, there is a shift in the location of the majority of players. Based on this, Beskow et al. (2008)'s heuristic core selection approach is to dynamically find the centre of most players in a virtual region and migrate game objects to a server whose physical location is closer to the majority of the players in order to reduce latency.

Dynamic partitioning of game worlds on geographically distributed servers will become even more important as game services are moved from an internal cloud of the provider's own servers to *the Cloud,* i.e., rented server space from companies like Amazon. When the time comes, not only real-time load balance and dynamic shifts in the location of the majority of players but also other factors like latency sensitiveness (e.g., game genres) will be taken into consideration to partition game worlds and find the optimal server to host a virtual region. This is due to the difference in latency requirements for different game genres (Claypool, 2005), e.g., 500 ms Round Trip Time (RTT) for real-time strategy games.

Sharding

Apart from world partitioning, another approach which has been used in World of Warcraft (Blizzard Entertainment, 2004), the most popular MMOG to date, to support millions of simultaneous players is *sharding*. The game has many sever realms (shards) to support the total 12 million subscribers and peak loads of 800,000 concurrent players in some regions, e.g., in China (The9, 2007). A shard (or a realm) is a complete and independent copy of the game world. The maximum number of concurrent players in a shard is bounded, typically several thousand. Players in different shards cannot interact with each other. This means that at any given time, only a small subset of players who are in the same realm is able to interact with each other, e.g., if a player wants to play with his (real world) friends in the World of Warcraft, he might not be able to do so if their characters

(avatars) are in different realms. A shard rapidly reaches the server capacity during peak time, resulting in long queues of players waiting to join the shard. When it happens, a new shard is started on a new server cluster. By adding more shards (on new servers) the game provider can accommodate more players.

However, people who wish to join a particular realm might not able to do so due to the shards design. This might be one of the motivations of people setting up a private server for LAN parties with their friends.

Since a realm is an instance of the whole game world, natively, this architecture supports *instancing*, through which a group of players (typically 3-20 players) can complete a quest without interference from other players.

AREA OF INTEREST (FIELD OF VISION)

In MMO world, it is usually sufficient to update players only with those events that occur within their area of interest (or field of vision). Interest management of computation replication (Russell et al., 2008) allows the server to dynamically select a subset of game objects to be replicated to each client. This subset represents the area of interest of a client (player). An object in a given subset executes both on the server and the associated client. Subsets may overlap, i.e. the object executes on the server and multiple clients. Some objects may not belong to any client subset. These objects are tracked by the server only. If object A sends a message to object B, the server sends this message transparently across the network to any client who replicates B but not A. If a client replicates both A and B then the message transmission between them can be handled locally.

Two approaches have been used to model players' visibility in MMOGs: static geographical partitioning and behavioural modelling (Ahmed & Shirmolammadi, 2008). The static geographical partitioning uses virtual regions for visibility management on the basis of the assumption that players in one region do not see/interact with players in other regions. One drawback of this approach is that a migrating player will not experience others' interactions at the boundaries between regions. To make up for delay introduced by migration when a player travels across a boundary of two regions, game worlds are typically designed such that the boundaries between virtual regions are either natural boundaries such as mountains or uninteresting in nature, e.g., cities are separated by forests or wilderness with few NPCs so that players do not tend to linger on. Second Life has adopted this approach. All places in Second Life are separated, and players travel to other places through teleporting.

The behavioural modelling manages visibility based on individual players/characters' behaviours. For example, in a role playing game, different players, e.g. a warrior who fights with a sword, a hunter who attacks with ranged weapon, and a mage who throws spells, have different behaviours in terms of how fast they move, how far they can see, and the size of the area they can interact with. A player who uses ranged weapons or spells has a larger area of influence than a player who can only fight in close combat. Although behavioural modelling is the ultimate goal for managing player interest, geographic region partitioning is more common due to the ease of mapping processing resources (or servers) (Lu et al., 2006).

DATABASE DESIGN

Choosing a data storage approach is very important for MMOGs. Many MMOGs adopt a relational database. Online worlds are themselves composed of different types of objects making the relational model an appropriate choice (Wadley & Sobell, 2007). Primary keys and primary key indices allow for efficient object updates and there are other benefits as well such as fast querying for

statistics and reports. There are other alternatives to relational databases such as storing the data to a at text file, however, consistency requires constant updates on very specific parts, which cannot be accommodated efficiently by those types of storage. An alternative proposed by Zhang et al. (2008) is to only append changes to a log; this allows for fast writes but makes recovery more complicated as an extra data processing step needs to be introduced.

There are several database design approaches when it comes to persistency of MMO world states. One option is for the granularity of persistence to be very coarse, i.e., the entire game state is simply stored in a BLOB attribute of a simple table (Zhang et al., 2008). Another option for finer granularity is to define the game world as a set of objects. In this case the database would have one relation table where rows represent objects. Each row would have an object identifier as indexed primary key attribute and a second attribute storing the object state in binary form (e.g., serialized from the corresponding main memory object). Game state changing events would then have to serialize and write only the object(s) affected by those events (Riddoch & Turner, 2002). For even finer granularity storage can be at the attribute level. In this case, the database would contain a relation for each object class with each attribute of the class mapped to an attribute of the corresponding table. For example, the database would contain a possible "Player" table with attributes such as player id, name, level, etc. A change would then only needs to be written to those attribute values that have been changed.

On the other hand, having a specialized database has some disadvantages too as it would not only limit its support for other games, but even for other versions of the same game. This could be a significant issue as MMOGs are expected to run for many years and have to undergo frequent changes both to keep them attractive for players and to address design issues and player exploits. This would lead in a situation where every time the structure of the world is altered, the design of database tables might need to be adjusted. This is expensive and may lead to problems, especially because not all changes and adjustments may be compatible with the previous database design. This can lead to long, expensive and complex redesigns. Storage at the game and object level do not have such problems according to Zhang et al. (2008).

Two-Layered Database Structure

Zhang et al. (2008) propose splitting a game database into two parts. A generic, game-agnostic object layer and a game-specific, attribute layer. Objects are stored in a single table in serialized form with a key attribute for fast search. Each attribute of an object class can be updated dynamically but they propose that some attributes would be kept on separate tables to allow for fast updates. Non-frequently updated attributes would require the entire object to be serialized and the corresponding rows in the object table to be updated.

In the case of the game needing to be redesigned, a new object class would be created or an existing class would be changed. The game designers in this case would have to indicate which of the attributes would be frequently updated so they could be automatically put in separate, frequently accessed tables by the persistence layer. When a new object would be instantiated it would be inserted into the Object table and the initial values of its frequently updated attributes would be inserted into the corresponding tables if present. Usually object changes only affect the frequently changing attributes making only the corresponding attribute tables needing updating.

The object layer ensures completeness of information about every object in the world no matter how outdated it is. The attribute layer ensures currency of information about the specific attributes it has been assigned to. Following a shutdown or failure then first layer retrieves all objects from the Object table, and then reconstructs the latest persistent state by reading the values from the frequently updated attributes tables of the attribute layer.

This database structure retains in this case both the flexibility of object level design and the efficiency of attribute level design. If the structure of an object were to change, this change would automatically be reflected in the object layer and the database will still be able to support the game. Most updates are made on frequently updated, separately stored attributes at attribute layer level. This supports efficient updates for those specific attributes but even if attributes are not tagged as frequently updated, their changes can still be reflected but at a higher latency cost.

In addition to the above Tveit et al. (2003) presents a platform that logs activities of simulated players in MMOGs for data mining purposes. The platform utilises object-oriented application mapping to a relational database. Typically the mapping software will automatically generate a relational schema for a given object-oriented model in these cases. In addition systems such as J2EE provide a persistence engine that writes changes to database objects automatically at specific time points. Application developers only use the object models. A combination of such mapping software and persistence layer could also be used for persistence of game worlds but current solutions do not allow for approximate solutions which are particularly important for MMORPGs given their usually large update volume. A disadvantage of this approach is that changing the object model, and thus, the database schema, would be potentially complex and costly. The two layered solution presented above by Zhang et al. (2008) provides both game state aware approximation and dynamic adjustments.

PEER-TO-PEER BASED MMOGS

Concurrent players of MMO's are currently reported in thousands. Naturally such amounts of concurrent users present challenges to the scalability of current architectures which are predominantly based on client-server models. In such current architectures the only way to cope with the ever growing player population is to increase the amount of dedicated servers. This solution however is subject to bottleneck issues especially during peak loads because of server capacity. Cost is also a consideration.

Peer-to-peer (P2P) architectures have emerged as a potential alternative design choice for building scalable MMO games. P2P architectures have proved successful in aggregating and sharing users' resources for file sharing purposes in achieving high scalability in cost-effective manners. Typically in P2P systems participating users/nodes organize themselves in an overlay network. The overall system load is then distributed among all nodes where each node is equal to the next and acts as both client and servers.

This aspect of the overlay topology structure that defines the way peers connect to other, usually, "neighbouring" peers with whom they can exchange messages is a key feature of P2P networks. The overlay topology configuration can be arbitrary or, alternatively, can be inspired by application specific semantics and it is usually dynamic depending on current load as well as other predetermined parameters. In a typical Networked Virtual Environment, each user sees only a pre-defined portion of the virtual world known as the area of interest (AOI) where they can perform actions such as move around, collect objects or communicate with other users. The AOI can be based on geographic proximity where a user is only interested in the activities happening within their own AOI. Because of this, dynamic reorganisation of the overlay network in sync with the users' positions is essential. This is typically achieved by each user only connect to neighbouring users within their vicinity.

P2P MMOG PROTOCOLS

Several P2P protocols exist currently for MMOGs at least as research projects. Krause (2008) categorises current P2P protocols as: ALM based protocols, super node based protocols and mutual notification based protocols.

ALM Based Protocols

Application Layer Multicast (ALM) protocols communicate game events using standard ALM techniques. This means that in most cases, the game world is divided into a number of smaller subspaces. Each of these subspaces is represented by a dedicated multicast group. An event taking place inside one subspace triggers a message that is subsequently sent via the subspace's multicast group to all players that have subscribed to receive updates of events in that particular subspace. Typically each player only needs to know about events within their visual range also known as the Area of Interest, or AOI. If a player's AOI intersects the border to another subspace they also have to subscribe to that other subspace's multicast group for a seamless, coherent gameplay experience. To avoid excessive generation of subscription and unsubscription messages when a player moves close to the border between subspaces a range parameter is introduced that can be adjusted to be slightly larger than the defined AOI. Players then only unsubscribe from a given subspace if that subspace is both outside their AOI as well as outside their unsubscription range.

In SimMUD which is a typical example of an ALM based protocol the game world is divided into fixed regions with unique IDs. The ID of the subspace is also unique and serves as the group ID of the associated multicast group. Any additional state related information required for the region such as the location of pick up items is stored at the root of the multicast tree.

SimMUD relies on Scribe for the dissemination of multicast messages which is built on top of the Pastry P2P routing protocol. Pastry supports uniquely identified nodes that can send messages to arbitrary keys. These messages are then delivered to the closest node based on numerical IDs. Since it is not feasible for a node to know every other node of the network a node based routing table is used to store $\log(N)$ entries. When a message is sent to the network it is recursively routed to the routing table entry with the closest numerical ID. In this way Pastry guarantees that this will take a maximum of $O(\log(N))$ steps.

When a node wants to join a multicast group it sends a JOIN message to the multicast group's ID. Every node routing this message becomes a forwarder for the multicast group generating in this way a forwarding tree with a depth of $O(\log(N))$.

Failing nodes are detected by their children nodes in the tree structure who rejoin the overlaying network creating in this way a self repairing multicast tree. If the failed node is the root of a multicast tree this can be detected by the new root when it receives the JOIN messages from the former children of the failed node. Since any new potential root is always the second closest numerically node to the group ID a multicast root can use it to also backup additional information about the subspace in advance. This allows the new multicast root to take over the orphan multicast group seamlessly.

Supernode Based Protocols

Similarly to ALM based protocols, supernode based protocols divide the game space into subspaces. The subspaces can be either of fixed size or variable size, dynamically based on player density. Again similarly to ALM based protocols each subspace is assigned to a responsible supernode that will receive all game event messages for that subspace and disseminate them to all subspace member nodes. Nodes have to register at the supernodes of the subspaces of their interest or otherwise to the nodes within the player's AOI. Supernode overload is prevented by limiting the number of nodes per subspace. The subspace will automatically divide if too many nodes subscribe to its supernode. Fixed subspaces however require different mechanisms to manage supernode load. An example of this class of protocols is PubSubM-MOG (Krause, 2008).

Mutual Notification Based Protocols

Mutual notification based protocols in contrast to ALM and supernode based protocols, do not divide the game world at all. Instead, player nodes send game event messages directly to all other nodes inside the player's AOI. This minimizes message propagation delay. However a prerequisite for this is that all player nodes have to be aware of all the other nodes inside the player's AOI. Discovery of new players recently moved into a player's AOI relies on information received by neighbouring nodes.

An example of a mutual notification based protocol is Vast. In Vast each player computes a Voronoi Diagram (Fortune, 1986) of all their known neighbours. Nodes whose Voronoi region intersects the outer border of the player's AOI are then classified as boundary neighbours while nodes adjacent to the player's own Voronoi region are classified as enclosing neighbours.

Every time a player moves all neighbours receive a notification about the movement at which point they updates their Voronoi diagram. By calculating differences between the old and the new diagram nodes can deduce whether one of their neighbours have to be informed about the newly discovered node. This however is generally the case only for boundary neighbours. In this situation traffic reduction is achieved by means of checking being done only by boundary neighbours and with their enclosing neighbours.

Joining nodes can enter the overlay simply by sending a JOIN message to the closest player. Failed players can be detected from absence of movement messages.

The two most important performance criteria for network protocols for MMOGs are event message propagation delay (the time an event message takes to reach players and the bandwidth requirements. Small event message delays are tolerable but high latencies have a significant negative impact on the players' experience (Krause, 2008). High latencies can be very frustrating for players that can lead to disappointment and loss of interest in the game. Game message event dissemination in P2P based protocols for MMOGs are done by the players. Their nodes are usually bandwidth limited therefore for any protocol to be successful in maintaining an acceptable level of user experience bandwidth demands must be kept as low as possible and certainly under certain limits. Krause (2008) measured the difference between the creation time of a movement event and the time of reception of that event by other players, as well as the bandwidth consumption for the above approaches in simulations and found that their values are dependent on the group size for different world and world cluster sizes.

In Krause's (2008) simulations Vast performed best regarding message propagation delay. This can be generalised for all mutual notification protocols as they share this one-hop event communication principle. Mutual notification also ensures that message delay is unaffected by player density (either global or local) as long as a node remains within their bandwidth capacity. As shown in their simulations the bandwidth requirements for this type of protocol are mostly moderate. They increase only when extreme local and global player density is experienced. Nevertheless, even in these cases the bandwidth demand was shown to be smaller than those of the other protocols.

The same ALM based protocols showed moderate delays and average bandwidth requirements. They are generally easy to implement and stable but do not cope well with high global density, which subsequently leads to high bandwidth requirements and longer delays.

PubSubMMOG performed poorly predominantly due to its poor timeslot design. An important advantage over the ALM based SimMUD was that the delay did not increase much with high player density. High local densities only increased latencies logarithmically but this advantage was found by the paper to be at the cost of higher bandwidth consumption.

Krause (2008) concludes that mutual notification based protocols have been shown to be the best performers for low-delay P2P based multiplayer gaming however the problem of stability and the associated additional bandwidth requirements need to be evaluated.

CHEATING IN DISTRIBUTED GAMES

Kabus et al. (2005) explore cheating in MMOGs. In MMOGs cheaters usually try to gain an unfair advantage over other players by shortcutting achievements (which would otherwise take long times to achieve or by duplicating items (e.g., weapons, treasure items). This can significantly disrupt in-game economics and affect player satisfaction for non-cheating players. Non-cheating players soon discover that keeping up with cheaters is impossible and decide either to cheat themselves (which accelerates the game's collapse) or to stop playing the game altogether. In client/server systems, the server is responsible for the overall state of the game which makes it difficult to cheat via malicious game state alterations. However, design flaws and code bugs may still allow successful cheating. This however is easier to control in a client server environment as opposed in a P2P environment where centralised control either doesn't exist or is limited.

Another kind of cheating is that of players acquiring information not intended for them. A typical example would be the acquisition of enemy positions. Although the enemy should not be seen in a P2P environment the node is aware of their position making it very difficult to prevent access to this information through malicious code.

A potentially worse issue than cheaters is griefing (Ma et al., 2009). Griefers are players determined to disrupt other players' experience as much as possible. This can be done without breaking any game rules, for instance, prohibiting a player from acquiring targets by being obstructive to their field of view.

Protection against cheaters and griefers are mission-critical tasks, especially for P2P MMOGs.

Approaches Against Cheating in P2P MMOGs

Kabus et al. (2005) discuss the following approaches in addressing cheating in P2P MMOGs:

- Distributed State Dissemination. An approach that handles the processing of action requests in a similar manner to traditional client/server systems with the exception that dissemination of state updates to the clients is done over a P2P delivery system in order to save bandwidth. The global game state is still computed on the server.
- Mutual Checking scheme. This scheme allows the global game state to be maintained in a distributed fashion on the clients but the global state is replicated on multiple clients which are tasked with detecting cheaters via regular comparisons of their own local versions.
- Log Auditing. This approach tries to detect cheating by analyzing signed log files of state transitions caused by updates. This task can be done during off peak periods of low activity but does not prevent cheating before it happens. It does however allow the global game state to be computed in P2P fashion amongst clients.

- Trusted Computing. This approach relies on the player node being protected against any user manipulation (e.g., installing malicious software for cheating purposes). Kabus et al. (2005) conclude that this is the ideal environment for distributed online games.

CONCLUSION

This paper provides an overview picture of the current state-of-the-art of MMOGs' network architectures and data replication. We have discussed various distributed client-server architectures with server allocation based on sharding, geographical partitioning, dynamic partitioning schemes based on micro-cells or geographical dispersion of players which heavily depends on the time of day. We also reviewed several approaches on data replication and region partitioning. Management of areas of interest is discussed, which has been used in all MMOGs to reduce processing load by culling events that occur within players' field of vision. We also investigated relational database design for MMOGs, focusing on persistent storage of game states. Recent attempts of P2P architectures and protocols for MMOGs are reviewed as well and critical issues such as cheat prevention on P2P games are highlighted.

REFERENCES

Ahmed, D. T., & Shirmolammadi, S. (2008). A dynamic area of interest management and collaboration model for P2P MMOGs. In *Proceedings of the 2008 12th IEEE/ACM International Symposium on Distributed Simulation and Real-Time Applications* (pp. 27-34). Washington, DC: IEEE Computer Society.

Beskow, P. B., Vik, K., Halvorsen, P., & Griwodz, C. (2008). Latency reduction by dynamic core selection and partial migration of game state. In *Proceedings of the 7th ACM SIGCOMM Workshop on Network and System Support for Games* (pp. 79-84). New York: ACM.

Blizzard Entertainment. (2004). *World of Warcraft*. Retrieved March 4, 2010, from http://www.blizzard.com

Chambers, C., Feng, F., & Saha, D. (2003, November). A geographic redirection service for online games. In *Proceedings of the 11th ACM international conference on Multimedia*, Berkeley, CA (pp. 227-230).

Claypool, M. (2005). The effect of latency on user performance in real-time strategy games. *Elsevier Computer Networks*, 49(1), 52–70. doi:10.1016/j.comnet.2005.04.008

Claypool, M. (2008, January). Network characteristics for server selection in online games. In *Proceedings of the fifteenth Annual Multimedia Computing and Networking (MMCN'08)*, San Jose, CA.

Cronin, E., Kurc, A. R., Filstrup, B., & Jamin, S. (2004). An efficient synchronization mechanism for mirrored game architectures. *Multimedia Tools and Applications*, 23(1), 7–30. doi:10.1023/B:MTAP.0000026839.31028.9f

De Vleeschauwer, B., Van Den Bossche, B., Verdickt, T., Turck, F., Dhoedt, B., & Demeester, P. (2005). Dynamic microcell assignment for Massively Multiplayer Online Gaming. In *Proceedings of 4th ACM SIGCOMM workshop on Network and system support for games* (pp. 1-7). New York: ACM.

Fortune, S. (1986). A sweepline algorithm for voronoi diagrams. In *Proceedings of the second annual symposium on Computational geometry* (pp. 313-322). New York: ACM.

Kabus, P., Terpstra, W. W., Cilia, M., & Buchmann, A. P. (2005). Addressing cheating in distributed MMOGs. In *Proceedings of the 4th ACM SIGCOMM Workshop on Network and System Support for Games* (pp. 1-6). New York: ACM Press.

Krause, S. (2008). A survey of P2P protocols for Massively Multiplayer Online Games. In *Proceedings of the 7th ACM SIGCOMM Workshop on Network and System Support for Games* (pp. 53-58). New York: ACM.

Lu, F., Parkin, S., & Morgan, G. (2006). Load balancing for massively multiplayer online games. In *Proceedings of 5th ACM SIGCOMM workshop on Network and system support for games* (Vol. 1). New York: ACM Press.

Ma, M., Oikonomou, A., & Zheng, H. (2009). Second Life as a learning and teaching environment for digital games education. In M. Lombard et al. (Eds.), *Proceedings of the 12th Annual International Workshop on Presence (PRESENCE 2009)*, Los Angeles, CA.

Mauve, M., Vogel, J., Hilt, V., & Effelsberg, W. (2004). Local-lag and timewarp: Providing consistency for replicated continuous applications. *IEEE Transactions on Multimedia*, 6(1), 47–57. doi:10.1109/TMM.2003.819751

Quax, P., Dierckx, J., Cornelissen, B., Vansichem, G., & Lamotte, W. (2008). Dynamic server allocation in a real-life deployable communications architecture for networked games. In *Proceedings of the 7th ACM SIGCOMM Workshop on Network and System Support for Games* (pp. 66-71). New York: ACM.

Riddoch, A., & Turner, J. (2002, July). Technologies for building open-source massively multiplayer games. In *Proceedings of the UKUUG Linux Developers Conference*, Bristol, UK.

Russell, G., Donaldson, A., & Sheppard, P. (2008). Tackling online game development problems with a novel network scripting language. In *Proceedings of the 7th ACM SIGCOMM Workshop on Network and System Support for Games* (pp. 85-90). New York: ACM.

Second Life Wiki. (n.d.). *Second Life server architecture*. Retrieved March 10, 2010, from http://wiki.secondlife.com/wiki/Server_architecture

The9. (2007). *World of Warcraft: The Burning Crusade surpasses 800,000 peak concurrent user milestone in mainland China on Oct 4, 2007*. Retrieved March 10, 2010, from http://www.the9.com/en/about/about_2.htm

Tveit, A., Rein, O., Iversen, J. V., & Matskin, M. (2003). Scalable agent-based simulation of players in massively multiplayer online games. In *Proceedings of the 8th Scandinavian Conference on Artificial Intelligence, Frontiers in Artificial Intelligence and Applications*. IOS.

Wadley, G., & Sobell, J. (2007). Using a simple MMORPG to teach multi-user, client-server database development. In *Proceedings of the MS Academic Days Conf. on Game Development*.

Zhang, K., Kemme, B., & Denault, A. (2008). Persistence in Massively Multiplayer Online Games. In *Proceedings of the 7th ACM SIGCOMM Workshop on Network and System Support for Games* (pp. 53-58). New York: ACM.

This work was previously published in International Journal of Grid and High Performance Computing, Volume 2, Issue 4, edited by Emmanuel Udoh, pp. 40-50, copyright 2010 by IGI Publishing (an imprint of IGI Global).

Section 4
Security

Chapter 11
Mechanism for Privacy Preservation in VANETs

Brijesh K. Chaurasia
Indian Institute of Information Technology, India

Shekhar Verma
Indian Institute of Information Technology, India

G. S. Tomar
Malwa Institute of Technology and Management, India

ABSTRACT

This paper proposes a mechanism for sustaining privacy of a vehicle in a vehicular ad hoc network (VANET) through pseudonym update. In a VANET, vehicles on the road are involved in dissemination of information as they move. An association can be formed between the physical location of the source vehicle and the transmitted messages. This relationship between the physical vehicle and its identity can breach its privacy. In this work, a strategy for optimal pseudonym update for maximizing privacy has been formulated when a vehicle is being observed by adversaries with different capabilities. Results indicate that updating pseudonyms in accordance to the strategy maximizes the privacy of a vehicle in the given situation.

INTRODUCTION

A vehicular ad-hoc network (VANET) is a network of vehicles supported by fixed infrastructure. The vehicular networks are characterized by a highly dynamic topology with vehicles moving in restricted geographical strait jackets (roads). The vehicles exchange information via vehicle to vehicle and vehicle to road side infrastructure

in both manners. The road side infrastructure acts as access points in vehicular communication are known as road side unit (RSU). A vehicle is equipped with on board unit (OBU). RSU are located along the roads at certain points. A bandwidth of 75 MHz has been allocated in the 5.850-5.925 GHz band for communication in such networks (Raya & Hubaux, 2005). In a VANET, an adversary can find the identity of the vehicle from message contents and to some extent its position through localization based on signal

DOI: 10.4018/978-1-4666-0056-0.ch011

strength etc. (Raya & Hubaux, 2007; Dotzer, 2005). Over a time period, the physical vehicle and its communication identity can be related (Raya & Hubaux, 2005; Papadimitratos et al., 2007) to breach the location privacy of the user. This link can be used to disclose personal data of a user and would potentially dissuade a user from joining a VANET (Raya & Hubaux, 2007).

To obtain and sustain anonymity, a temporal identity, pseudonym, is used for communication. Pseudonyms allow a vehicle to interact with other vehicles anonymously. Pseudonyms are ephemeral and distinct pseudonyms hide their relation from each other and to the user's identity (Pfitzmann & Hansen, 2004). To preserve privacy, a pseudonym system must prevent credential forgeability and disallow usage of false pseudonym by a user. Moreover, the transaction of obtaining and the process of switching pseudonyms should not reveal the identity of the user or link pseudonyms to each other. Continually changing pseudonyms conceal the real identity of a vehicle by de-linking the source of signals to its original identity (Gerlach & Guttler, 2007). But, the relation between a communicating vehicle and its estimated location can reveal the identity of a vehicle. This vehicle can, then, be physically traced and switching pseudonyms would be meaningless (Sha et al., 2006). A vehicle can be under sustained observation and transmissions at different intervals of time with the same pseudonym can reveal the relation between physical vehicle and its current pseudonym if the vehicle is relatively isolated in a crowd. This relation can be established even when pseudonyms are updated when the time interval between transmission prior to and after the update is short (Sampigethaya et al., 2007). There is, moreover, one more challenge that needs to be addressed. When a vehicle under observation moves from one cluster and enters another cluster and changes its pseudonym, it can be spotted with high probability as soon as it transmits. This can happen if the number of vehicles from the previous cluster to the current cluster is small and the

pseudonyms of vehicles belonging to current cluster are known a priori. The anonymity of the vehicle under observation is limited by the number of vehicles that join the current cluster from the previous cluster Sun (Zhang & Fang, 2007; Fonseca, 2007).

PROBLEM DESCRIPTION

A link between the personal interests of a user with physical locations of a vehicle can breach the location privacy and reveal the identity. In this mobile broadcast environment, a vehicle's privacy can be sustained through unobservability (ClauB & Schiffner, 2006). A vehicle would be unobservable if its communication can be distinguished from others in the group. The effective crowd that hides the vehicle is a function of the capabilities of the attacker, the actual size of the crowd and the unlinkability of the messages emanating from the crowd (Gerlach & Guttler, 2007). The size of the crowd is the number of vehicles in the anonymity zone Z. The position of a vehicle cannot be predicted accurately from its transmission (Sampigethaya et al., 2007). To avoid breach of privacy, a vehicle using pseudonyms and continuously updates it. The problem is that even a large pseudonym pool would be depleted quickly if every transmission uses a separate pseudonym. This requires a strategy for update for conservation of this pseudonym pool.

Anonymity Metrics

The level of anonymity of a vehicle is the inability of the adversary to pinpoint a vehicle as the source of the communication in the set of vehicles V (anonymity set) in the region estimated from the communication. This anonymity set $V \square V_{total}$ with V_{total} being the total number of vehicles in Z. The cardinality of the anonymity set is the measure of the anonymity of a vehicle in the set.

If a vehicle V_i is the source of transmission, then the probability p_i that the vehicle V_i under observation is the target,

$$p_i = P_r(V_i = V), \forall i \in Z \text{ and } \sum p_i = 1$$

The entropy, $H(p)$ is defined as: Samarati and Sweeney (1998)

$$H(p) = -\sum_{i=1}^{|v|} p_i \log_2 p_i \qquad (1)$$

The anonymity of a given vehicle is maximized when all the vehicles are equally likely to be the potential target (source of communication). Then,

$$p_i = \frac{1}{|v|} \forall i \,.$$

In a VANET, the communication from vehicles, the mean speed and variance in the speeds together with the nature of the observer (adversary) changes the distribution of the source from a uniform distribution to a non uniform distribution. Thus, the average Shannon entropy metric does not represent the correct anonymity of the vehicle and a more appropriate measure is required (ClauB & Schiffner, 2006). The minimum amount of information needed to identify the most probable vehicle (probability p_i) would be an appropriate metric of quantifying the anonymity. This lower bound H_{min} of information can be defined as: (ClauB & Schiffner, 2006)

$$H_{min} = -\log_2 \max p_i \qquad (2)$$

MOBILITY AND PRIVACY

Road Model and Input Traffic

A road with multiple unidirectional lanes is considered. The vehicles move in a single direction with different speeds and multiplicity of the lanes allows vehicles to overtake each other without any restriction in the number of lanes. The road has S segments of D meters each as shown in Figure 1. The road length is $S.D$ meters. Vehicles can enter and exit at the end points of a segment and there is no waiting period or queue required to enter the road. There are two end points of the road and there is no exit point at the start of the initial segment or entry at the end of the last segment. Vehicles arrive at the beginning of a segment follow a Poisson distribution $p_y(y)$ and travel towards the end point independently of other existing vehicles on the road. The arrival rate at the $(ij)^{th}$ segment at $(i)^{th}$ point is λ_i with the departure rate at the $(j)^{th}$ point being δ_i ($\lambda_i = 0$ for $i = 0$ and δ_i for $j = 5$ Once it enters the road at an entry point, it cannot exit from the same point i.e. every vehicle must traverse at least one segment as soon as it enters the road. Hence, this system can be modeled as an $M/G/\infty$ queue (Trivedi, 2002). This means that the vehicles can be seen as arriving on the road in accordance with a Poisson process. An arriving vehicle is admitted in the road and starts traversing on the road without any waiting period (on the side of the road). It is assumed that no vehicle has to wait at the side of the road to enter the road. Once on the road, a vehicle cannot exit from the same junction and must traverse at least one segment before it can depart at one of the junctions. The time which a vehicle spends on the road is assumed to be independent general random variable with a distribution function G.

The vehicles travel in one direction with variable velocity. The velocity of a vehicle is assumed to be piecewise constant i.e. a vehicle moves with a constant speed for a time period and then changes its speed (Khabazian & Ali, 2007). The velocity of a vehicle v_i in during time periods follows a normal distribution with mean speed μ and variance σ^2: $N(\mu, \sigma^2)$ The time durations t_i form i.i.d. random variables with exponential distribution with distribution parameter $1/\alpha$. The distance covered in a time duration t_i is $d_i = v_i t_i$

Figure 1. The road model

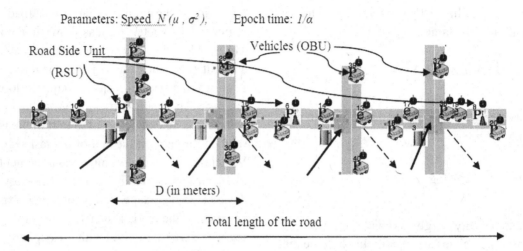

and the total distance covered in *i* time periods is

$$TD_i = \sum d_i = v_i t_i .$$

The vehicles transmit as they move along the road. Depending on the conditions on the road and other needs, they may transmit. In this simulation, it assumed that the vehicles transmit with Poisson distribution with mean transmission rate as ρ_i.

The uncertainty zone *Z* of a vehicle is the number of vehicles within its broadcast range. If the target vehicle can be any of the vehicles in the zone *Z*, then number of vehicles in *Z* would constitute the anonymity set. However, since a global adversary can observe vehicles during an extended period of time over a large length of the road, hence, as discussed in section II, the actual size of the anonymity set would depend on the number of vehicles communicating before they join the zone and after they leave *Z*.

Vehicle Population and Tracking

A road with unidirectional longitudinal lanes with intersections at regular intervals is considered. Vehicles enter the road and move in one direction with different speeds. They are free to overtake one other without any restriction. There are no traffic lights and vehicles can enter and exit at intersections. At an intersection, there is no waiting period or queue and vehicles enter the road immediately. There are two end points of the road and there is no exit point at the start of the initial segment or entry at the end of the last segment.

- We consider a segment of this road $S = [0,S]$. A vehicle enters the road and travels in one direction with variable velocity.

- Vehicles arrive at the beginning of a segment follow a Poisson distribution $\rho_y(y)$ with an arrival rate λ_0 and travel towards the end point independently of other existing vehicles on the road. The number of vehicles $A(t)$ that enter the road in a time interval $[0,t]$ is as follows:

$$P\left\{A(t) = k\right\} = \frac{(\lambda_0 t)^k}{k!} \exp(-\lambda_0 t) \qquad (3)$$

A vehicle enters a segment at time $t=0$ with a speed v_i. In one time period t_d the distance covered is $v_t t_d$ and the total distance covered in *i* time periods is given as $d(t = it_d) = v_t it_d$.

During a time interval $[0,t]$, the vehicles arrival in a Poisson manner, hence the location of a vehicle on a segment $[0,S]$ or any section of the road $[a_1, a_2]$ would be uniformly distributed ($U(a_1, a_2)$).

$$P\left\{a_i \leq x \leq a_2\right\} = \frac{a_2 - a_1}{L} \qquad (4)$$

The vehicles arrive the start of a segment $[0,S]$ at time $t=0$. The number of vehicles ($N(t)=n$) on the road section $[0,S]$ at any time t can be expressed as:

$$P\left\{N(t) = n\right\} =$$
$$\sum_{k=n}^{\infty} P\left\{N(t) = n \big| A(t) = k\right\} . P\left\{A(t) = k\right\}$$
$$(5)$$

The vehicles travel with velocity $V{\sim}N(\mu, \sigma^2)$. After time t, some vehicles may lie within the segment $[0,S]$. Since, the vehicles will lie either within or outside the segment, the number of vehicles in $[0,S]$ follows a binomial distribution and can be given as follows:

$$P\left\{N(t) = n \big| A(t) = k\right\} = \binom{k}{n} \big[p(t)\big]^t \big[1 - p(t)\big]^{k-n}$$
$$(6)$$

The distance covered has the following parameters:

Mean $\mu_d(t) = \mu t$

Variance $\sigma_d^2(t) = \dfrac{2\sigma^2}{a^2}\left(at - 1 + e^{-at}\right)$

Hence the probability distribution function is:

$$f(x) = \frac{1}{\sqrt{2\Pi\sigma_d^2(t)}} \exp\left[\frac{-((x - \mu d(t))^2}{2\sigma^2(t)}\right] \qquad (7)$$

Hence, the probability that a vehicle is in the region $[0,S]$ is:

$$p = \left\{0 \leq x(t,0) \leq L\right\} = \int_0^L f(x)dx$$

The velocity of a vehicle $V(t)$ is assumed to be piecewise constant i.e. a vehicle moves with a constant speed for a time period and then changes its speed (Khabazian & Ali, 2007). Within a time period, this velocity $v(t)$ is Wide sense stationary (WSS) random process and follows a normal distribution with mean speed μ and variance σ^2: $V(t){\sim}N(\mu, \sigma^2)$. The time duration t_d are independent and identically distributed (i.i.d.) random variables with exponential distribution with a distribution parameter $1/\alpha$

The number of vehicles in the uncertainty zone Z ($=[0,L]$) is $N_L(t)$. If $N_L(t)$ is greater than the required crowd size, the privacy of the target vehicle is sustained.

If all the vehicles are not transmitting, then the size of the anonymity set as perceived by the target vehicle would be less than $N_L(t)$.

The vehicles continuously move towards the exit. These vehicles move at variable speeds, overtake each other, and at the intersections some vehicles leave the road and some other vehicles join the traffic coming from the preceding segment. There can be different types of adversaries. A local adversary is capable of observing vehicles at a time instant. A global adversary can follow a target and track it over a sustained period of time. Such a global adversary is able to do both simple and correlative tracking.

The local observer is only able to see the number of vehicles in Z. Hence, the size of the anonymity set is equal to $N_L(t)$.

$$H(p) = -\sum_{i=1}^{N_{L(t)}} p_i \log_2 p_i, \qquad (8)$$

$$p_i = 1/N_L(t)$$

When a vehicle moves from one cluster to another without changing its pseudonym, its anonymity set is the number of vehicles that are common (move with the vehicle) through different clusters. A global observer is able to determine this and perform an intersection attack by tracking the vehicles from a region for a sufficiently large interval of time and over a long stretch of road. A new cluster of vehicles consists of old vehicles from previous segment and new arrivals from an intersection. Through tracking, an adversary knows that the target vehicle is one of the vehicles from the previous segment. Thus, even when the actual number of vehicles in Z is large, ($|V_{old} \cup V_{new}|$). The lower bound of information is the correct measure of anonymity of the vehicle given as:

$$H_{min} = -\log_2 \max p_i = 1/|V_{old}| \qquad (9)$$

At an intermediate intersection k, vehicles arriving from the preceding segment depart with a probability $1-y_k$ (i.e., continue on the road with probability y_k) and new vehicles enter the road with an arrival rate λ_k. Since, the both are arrivals are independent, the total number of vehicles entering the road at the intermediate junction follows the Poisson distribution with an effective arrival rate $\overline{\lambda_k}$.

$$\overline{\lambda_k} = \overline{\lambda_k} * \gamma_k + \lambda_k \qquad (10)$$

The total number of vehicles in an intermediate segment ($S_i - S_{i+1}$) would be a difference of Poisson variates. This difference follows the Skellam distribution that is given as:

$$f(k : \overline{\lambda_k}, \lambda_k) = e^{-(\overline{\lambda_k}+\lambda_k)} (\frac{\overline{\lambda_k}}{\lambda_k})^{k/2} I_k(2\sqrt{\overline{\lambda_k}\lambda_k})$$

$$(11)$$

where, I_k is the modified Bessel function of the first kind.

The number of vehicles in the road section $[0,L]$ (V_{old} = vehicles in Z) can be calculated using the above equation.

In correlative tracking, given the current location and speed (mean speed and its variance) at time t_i, a global observer is able to form a rough estimate of the location (reachability region) of a vehicle at time instant, $t_i+\Delta t$Li et al. (2006). The reachability region $[0,R]$ of the target vehicle is smaller than $Z (L>=R)$ and may have lesser number of vehicles, $|V_{reach}|$ as compared to ($\|V_{reach}\| \le |V_{old}\|$). Hence, the anonymity enjoyed by the vehicle becomes very small. H_{min} is the correct measure of anonymity and is given as:

$$H_{min} = -\log_2 \max p_i; \, p_i = 1/|V_{c(reach)}| \qquad (12)$$

However, from a vehicle viewpoint, the size of the neighborhood crowd is the number of transmissions with distinct identities over a protocol selectable time period. For a vehicle, all transmissions are equally likely, the average entropy, $H(p)$ would represent the anonymity as seen by the vehicle.

$$H(p) = -\sum_{i=1}^{n} p_i, p_i = 1 / n \qquad (13)$$

Evidently, unless all the vehicles are transmitting, the vehicle's perceives a thinner crowd cover than the actual cover.

Pseudonym Update

A vehicle must update its pseudonym to so that its effective crowd cover becomes equal to the size of the physical crowd in its vicinity. The strategy identifies three cases.

The first case assumes that the vehicle is only able to who can hear and the adversary is simple. A vehicle must remain silent if the perceived crowd cover is less than the threshold k. If a transmission is imperative, then it must transmit with a pseudonym update and variable transmission power to vary the size Z. If the adversary is able to track the vehicle, a random silent period with variable transmission power is required to avoid tracking. Here, the update should be performed only when the crowd cover is less than the threshold. Finally, if the mobility is very high, it may perceive a large cover due to a fast change in the neighborhood. In this case, pseudonym update must be performed at regular intervals.

In the second case, a vehicle is able to take the decision on the basis of its perceived crowd size and is also aided by the road side unit which broadcasts the actual number of vehicles in the area. The adversary is simple. Here, the decision is simply guided by the physical number of vehicles.

The third case assumes importance when a vehicle is threatened by a global adversary. On a free way, vehicles move at almost constant speed, hence tracking becomes easy. If the number of transmissions with change in identities is less than the threshold, then a pseudonym update is imperative else it can be postponed. A random silent period must be introduced if the crowd cover is small on such a free way. The transmission power should be varied from normal to higher levels to avoid disconnection. If the traffic flow is variable with sufficient crowd cover, the update can be postponed and done after sufficiently large intervals of time.

SIMULATION AND RESULTS

Road Model and Input Traffic

We consider two cases. Single lane road with all vehicles moving in the same direction and double lane in which vehicles move in different directions with no lane changing is permitted. The total length of the road is taken as 18 km with segments of 3 km each. The input traffic can enter from $A, ..., F$ and exit from $B, ..., G$. The vehicle mean arrival rates are taken as $\lambda = 0.7$ with departure rates as $\delta = 0.1$. The time period for constant velocity is

exponentially distributed with mean 1, 2 and 3 seconds and the velocities are normal variates with mean μ (15, 20 and 25 ms^{-1}) and σ (2, 7 and 10 ms^{-1}). The mean transmission rate of a vehicle is taken as $p_i=0.5$. To determine the number of vehicles around a vehicle of interest, a vehicle from the initial segment is considered. As this vehicle travels towards the destination, different vehicles join and depart from the neighborhood around this vehicle. The size of the neighborhood is a function of the transmission range and the speed of different vehicles.

In the present study, we consider that the vehicles have a fixed transmission ranges of 100, 200 and 500m radius and observe the size and nature of the neighborhood around the vehicle for low to very high speeds ($\mu = 15$, 20 and 25 ms^{-1}) and variations in speed ($\sigma =2$, 7 and 10 ms^{-1}). To study the effective size of the anonymity set or entropy, the total number of vehicles in the neighborhood is determined along with the subset that contributes to effective entropy. The scenarios that arise are as follows. Initially, when the vehicle of interest is silent, all the vehicles around it contribute to its entropy which is effectively infinity.

When this vehicle starts transmitting, its entropy becomes finite and becomes equal to the number of vehicles in its transmission radius for an adversary and equal to the number of transmission in a time interval for the vehicle. The third case is arises when this vehicle is intermittently transmitting and its neighbors change due to speed variations, departure of vehicles from the road and new vehicles are come within its range of transmission.

Depending on number of vehicles from the old neighborhood; number of transmissions with or without pseudonym update; number of fresh vehicles in the neighborhood and their transmissions; the entropy is determined for a local adversary with simple tracking; for a global adversary with simple and correlative tracking and from vehicle own point of view.

Local Adversary with Simple Tracking

The average entropy of vehicles (assuming that the each one is equally likely) in the neighborhood is shown in Figures 2-4. This metric is dependent only on the number of vehicles actually present and simple tracking does not exploit the linkability information in the transmissions and is unaffected by pseudonym update. It can be observed that the physical cover of the target vehicle (vehicle under observation) becomes thin with increase in speed and speed variance with low transmission range ($\mu = 25$ ms^{-1}, $\sigma = 10$ ms^{-1}, TR=100m) but improves with higher TR (500m).

The entropy of the vehicle from vehicle point of view shows that it perceives low anonymity as the number of transmissions is small. Unaided update does not change the entropy from Vehicle view. An informed update can increase the entropy significantly (Figures 2-4) for all cases. We also note that the anonymity increases signifi-

Figure 2. Entropy of the target vehicle ($\mu = 15$ ms^{-1}, $\sigma = 7ms^{-1}$ and TR=100m)

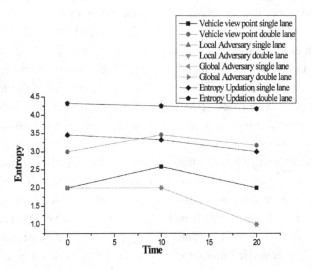

Figure 4. Entropy of the target vehicle ($\mu=15$ ms^{-1})

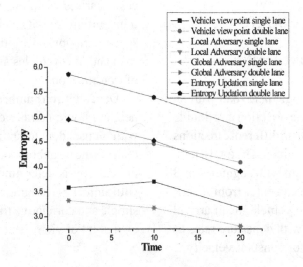

cantly (almost two fold) from both the vehicle's and adversary's point of view.

Global Adversary with Simple Tracking

In this section, we evaluate the anonymity of a vehicle upon pseudonym update when a global adversary is both watching and hearing all the vehicles and their broadcasts.

As depicted in Figure 2-4, the ability of the adversary to launch an intersection reduces the effective entropy of the target drastically. The entropy is very low (entropy=1) though there are 9 vehicles and the number of transmissions are 4 (Figure 2). The problem is aggravated in two lane scenario. The size of crowd and number of broadcasts increases significantly without adding to the actual anonymity. From the target's viewpoint, the anonymity is large and it may not perform an update even though it is immediately warranted to sustain its anonymity. Even an RSU's broadcast of the number of vehicles in the region does not help since the number of vehicles physically present in the region is large. An update at this stage will increase the anonymity of vehicle significantly to the number of vehicles in the region. The problem is less at lower speeds with low variance (Figure 4). Interestingly, as depicted in Figure 3, the problem is mitigated even at high speeds when the transmission range is high (μ= 25 ms^{-1}, TR = 100m).

This necessitates that a vehicle must perform an update before a maximum time period which may be fixed intuitively which can be low for high speeds and larger for low speeds.

Global Adversary with Correlative Tracking

The prediction of the location of a target after a transmission greatly reduces the cardinality of the anonymity set as seen by the global adversary. Moreover, if the minimum and maximum silent periods are known, then correlative tracking can further reduce the entropy and expose the target to the global adversary.

The reachability region (R) of the target is smaller than Z and as shown in Figure 4 has lesser number of vehicles. The entropy of the vehicle is zone. The entropy is zero at high speed (μ= 25 ms^{-1}, TR = 100m). However, R becomes very quite large if the σ (=10ms^{-1}) is high and correlative tracking is of no help to the adversary. When the vehicle hears a large number of distinct transmissions over an extended time period, it knows

Figure 3. Entropy of the target vehicle (μ=25 ms^{-1}, σ =10ms^{-1} and TR=100m)

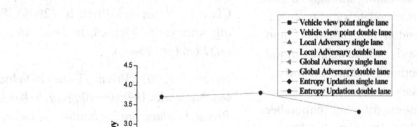

Figure 5. Entropy of the target vehicle with correlative tracking (Min. silent period=2s & Max. silent period=3s)

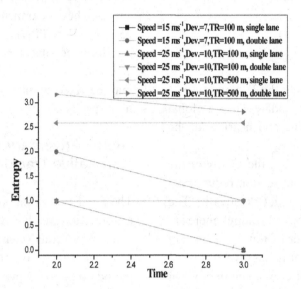

that its neighborhood is changing and updates. It knows that it has a large crowd cover from the RSU broadcast. This update increases the entropy significantly (Figure 5). Thus, by comparing the broadcasts over multiple time periods, the change in the nature of neighborhood can be gauged and used for triggering an update.

CONCLUSION

In this paper, privacy sustaining strategies based on appropriate pseudonym update were presented. Time and place for pseudonym update was found to be dependent on the size of the neighborhood crowd, rate of neighborhood change and the capabilities of the adversary. A vehicle estimates its effective neighborhood crowd through the number of transmissions in a selected time interval. Hence, the perceived crowd size may be less than the actual size. Moreover, the size is dependent on the speed of the vehicle relative to other ms^{-1} vehicles. In the selected, higher relative speed would change the neighbors faster and would therefore increase the perceived size of the crowd.

A strategy for pseudonym update must take into consideration these factors. Update must be performed only when warranted to conserve the pseudonym pool while preserving the privacy. Further, to avoid correlative tracking periodic transmission should be replaced with random periods of silence and transmissions with variable power.

REFERENCES

Clau, B. S., & Schiffner, S. (2006). Structuring Anonymity Metrics. In *Proceedings of the DIM'06* (pp. 55-62).

Dotzer, F. (2005). Privacy Issues in Vehicular Ad Hoc Networks. In *Proceedings of the Workshop on Privacy Enhancing Technologies*, Dubr, Croatia (pp. 197-209).

Fonseca, E., Festag, A., Baldessari, R., & Aguiar, R. (2007). Support of Anonymity in VANETs - Putting Pseudonymity into Practice. In *Proceedings of the IEEE Wireless Communication & Networking Conference (WCNC2007)*.

Gerlach, M., & Guttler, F. (2007). Privacy in VANETs using Changing Pseudonyms - Ideal and Real. In *Proceedings of 65th Vehicular Technology Conference (VTC2007-l)* (pp. 2521-2525).

Khabazian, M., & Ali, M. K. (2007). Generalized Performance Modeling of Vehicular Ad Hoc Networks (VANETs). In *Proceedings of the ISCC 2007* (pp. 51-56).

Li, M., Sampigethaya, K., Huang, L., & Poovendran, R. (2006). Swing & swap: user-centric approaches towards maximizing location privacy. In *Proceedings of the 5th ACM workshop on Privacy in electronic society (WPES '06)* (pp. 19-27).

Papadimitratos, P., Buttyan, L., Hubaux, J.-P., Kargl, F., Kung, A., & Raya, M. (2007). Architecture for Secure and Private Vehicular Communications. In *Proceedings of the Int'l Conf. on ITS Telecomm (ITST 2007)*, Sophia Antipolis, France.

Pfitzmann, A., & Hansen, M. (2004). Anonymity, unobservability, and pseudonymity: A proposal for terminology. In *Proceedigns of the HBCC04* (Vol. 21).

Raya, M., & Hubaux, J.-P. (2005). The Security of Vehicular Ad Hoc Networks. In. *Proceedings of SASN, 05,* 11–21.

Raya, M., & Hubaux, J.-P. (2007). Securing vehicular ad hoc networks. *Journal of Computer Security, 15*(1), 39–68.

Samarati, P., & Sweeney, L. (1998). *Protecting privacy when disclosing information: k-anonymity and its enforcement through generalization and suppression* (Tech. Rep. SRI-CSL-98-04). CS Lab, SRI International.

Sampigethaya, K., Li, M., Huang, L., & Poovendran, R. (2007). AMOEBA: Robust Location Privacy Scheme for VANET. *IEEE JSAC, 25*(8), 1569–1589.

Sha, K., Xi, Y., Shi, W., Schwiebert, L., & Zhang, T. (2006). Adaptive Privacy-Preserving Authentication in Vehicular Networks. In *Proceedings of IEEE International Workshop on Vehicle Communication and Applications*.

Sun, J., Zhang, C., & Fang, Y. (2007). An id-based framework achieving privacy and non-repudiation in Vehicular ad hoc networks. In *Proceedings of the Military Communications Conference (MILCOM)*.

Trivedi, K. S. (2002). *Probability and Statistics with Reliability, Queuing, and Computer Science Applications*. New York: John Wiley & Sons.

This work was previously published in International Journal of Grid and High Performance Computing, Volume 2, Issue 2, edited by Emmanuel Udoh, pp. 12-22, copyright 2010 by IGI Publishing (an imprint of IGI Global).

Section 5
Applications

Chapter 12
Modeling Scalable Grid Information Services with Colored Petri Nets

Vijay Sahota
Middlesex University, UK

Maozhen Li
Brunel University, UK

Marios Hadjinicolaou
Brunel University, UK

ABSTRACT

Information services play a crucial role in grid computing environments in that the state information of a grid system can be used to facilitate the discovery of resources and services available to meet user requirements and help tune the performance of the grid. This paper models PIndex, which is a grouped peer-to-peer network with Colored Petri Nets (CPNs) for scalable grid information services. Based on the CPN model, a simulator is implemented for PIndex simulation and performance evaluation. The correctness of the simulator is further verified by comparing the results computed from the CPN model with the results generated by the PIndex simulator.

INTRODUCTION

The past few years have witnessed a rapid development of grid computing infrastructures and applications (Li & Baker, 2005; Wang, Helian, Wu, Deng, Khare, & Thompson, 2007; Wang, Wu, Helian, Parker, et al. 2007; Wang, Wu, Helian, Xu, 2007). Information services play a crucial

role in grid environments in that they facilitate the discovery of resources and services (Czajkowski, Kesselman, Fitzgerald, & Foster, 2001). Information services periodically collect data on available resources including hardware and software in a grid environment. The data can then be used by a number of elements in a grid to keep the grid running smoothly. For example, job schedulers use resource information to make adaptive decisions on allocating resources to jobs to achieve certain

DOI: 10.4018/978-1-4666-0056-0.ch012

goals such as a minimum make-span in execution of jobs (Berman et al., 2003).

Grid middleware technologies facilitate information services. For example, the current Globus Toolkit (http://www.globus.org) provides a component called the Monitoring and Discovery System version 4 (MDS4) (Schopf et al., 2006) for resource registration and discovery. The MDS4 component adopts a hierarchical tree structure to distribute its monitoring data on resources across a virtual organization (VO), in which every node runs an index service monitoring its resources and pushing this information up to a master index server. A query to the top Index server could retrieve all the information on the resources available in a VO. The Relational Grid Monitoring Architecture (R-GMA) (Cooke et al., 2004), which is now a component of the gLite middleware (http://www.cern.ch/glite), also facilitates resource registration and discovery. It is worth noting that grids differentiate themselves from traditional distributed systems in the following aspects:

- The size of a grid is usually large in terms of the number of computing nodes involved.
- Resources in a grid are usually heterogeneous with various computing capabilities and services.
- A grid is dynamic in that computing nodes may join or leave a grid freely. In addition, some resources such as the CPU load of a grid node may change frequently.

The aforementioned characteristics of grids bring forth a number of challenges to existing information services, notably the MDS4 and the R-GMA. The hierarchical structure along with centralized management of MDS4 has an inherent delay associated with it which potentially limits its scalability in resource registration. It might take a long time for resource information to be updated from the leaf nodes to the root index service node. Cai, Frank, Chen, and Szekely (2004) point out that the scheme to partition resource information

on index servers is typically predefined and cannot adapt to the dynamic changes of VOs. The MDS4 also lacks a mechanism to deal with failures of index servers which may break the information service network into isolated subnets. The R-GMA contains a centralized registry (Groep, Templon, & Loomis, 2006), and performs poorly when dealing with only 100 consumer nodes (Zhang, Freschl, & Schopf, 2007).

In parallel development with grid computing, peer-to-peer (P2P) computing has merged into another promising computing paradigm that typically facilitates file sharing in large network environments (Milojicic et al., 2002). P2P networks usually organize peer nodes in a decentralized way, and the reliability can be enhanced by replication of shared files among peer nodes. Files can be arbitrarily distributed into peer nodes without a structure, or they are distributed following a structure such as Distributed Hash Table (DHT). DHT based P2P networks such as Chord (Stoica et al., 2002), Pastry (Rowstron & Druschel, 2001), CAN (Ratnasamy, Francis, Handley, Karp, & Shenker, 2001) have shown enhanced scalability in routing lookup messages for files with a guaranteed number of hops. Foster and Iamnitchi (2003) analyzed the differences between P2P and grid computing and discussed a possible convergence of the two computing paradigms. Talia and Trunfio (2003) pointed out the benefits that P2P networks could bring to grid systems in terms of scalability and robustness. However, directly applying DHT technologies to grid information services mainly poses two challenges. On the one hand, DHT systems usually incur high maintenance overhead in dealing with *churn* situations where peer nodes may join or leave P2P networks at high rates (Godfrey, Shenker, & Stoica, 2006; Rhea, Geels, Roscoe, & Kubiatowicz, 2004). On the other hand, DHT based P2P networks only support exact matches for files using single hash keys. In a grid environment, it is not realistic to employ a single hash key for a resource which may have a number of attributes such as its CPU load, memory space, storage space, and availability. Moreover, the values of these resource attributes dynamically change in a grid environment. Range queries on resources should be supported in grid information services.

We have implemented PIndex (Sahota, Li, Baker, & Antonopoulos, 2009), which is a grouped P2P network for scalable grid information services. PIndex has the following features:

- It builds on Globus MDS4, but introduces the concept of peer groups (PGs) to speed up the process in routing messages for resource discovery.
- It supports both static and dynamic routing of lookup messages for resources. In the latter case, a number of messages can be routed from one PG to another concurrently.
- It supports range queries searching for resources with a number of attributes.
- It enhances fault resilience through the replication of state information of resources among the computing nodes within a PG.
- It reduces the effects of *churn* by limiting them locally to a PG level and isolating the effects from the rest of the network.

PIndex is designed for large-scale grid systems. Simulations are required to observe its features and to evaluate its performance. It is worth noting that a number of grid simulators have been proposed. For example, SimGrid (Casanova, Legrand, & Quinson, 2008) aims at a generic evaluation tool for large-scale distributed computing. GridSim (Buyya & Murshed, 2002) was initially designed for grid economy but it only scales to a few 100 nodes as presented in (Casanova et al., 2008). OptorSim (Bell, Cameron, Capozza, Millar, Stockinger, & Zini, 2003) are specifically designed for data replications on grids. PlanetSim (López, Pairot, Mondéjar, Ahulló, Tejedor, & Rallo, 2004) and PeerSim (http://peersim.sourceforge.net) are proposed for the simulation of generic P2P applica-

tions. However, these simulators cannot be used for modeling and simulating PIndex because they cannot satisfy the following features of PIndex:

- Performing the specific message routing algorithm used by PIndex.
- Performing parallel PG operations.
- Modeling many thousands of nodes.

This paper models PIndex with Colored Petri Nets (CPNs) (Jensen, Kristensen, & Wells, 2007). Based on the CPN model, a simulator is implemented for PIndex simulation and performance evaluation. Experimental results have shown that PIndex is scalable in routing messages among a large number of peer nodes up to 10,000 and is resilient in dealing with node failures (Sahota et al., 2009). The correctness of the PIndex simulator is also verified.

The remainder of the paper is organized as follows. Next, we present the CPN modeling work on PIndex. We then implement a simulator based on the CPN model and verify the correctness of the PIndex simulator by comparing the results computed from the CPN model with the results generated by the simulator. We conclude the paper by discussing future work for PIndex.

Modelling PIndex with Colored Petri Nets

A Colored Petri Net (CPN) is a modeling language that can be used to graphically represent the structure of a distributed system, employing places and transitions to model complex systems. More importantly, it supports concurrent processes. A Petri Net has place and transition nodes, as well as directed arcs connecting places with transitions. It is the tokens that transit on places representing a system moving from one state to another. The following main points have been made to further demonstrate the rationale in choosing CPNs to model PIndex:

- The nodes in PIndex may have many different states. These can be shown with colored tokens.
- As many PGs operating in parallel and interact with each other in PIndex, the ability to model concurrent events is needed. This requirement is intrinsic to Petri Nets as they are designed with concurrency in mind.
- Since PIndex is a robust and fault tolerant network, these features must to be able to be simulated. Petri Nets have the ability to change states during a transition, allowing for failures to occur randomly.
- Each node in PIndex must operate independently which can be mimicked by the use of tokens as objects in CPNs.

Modelling States

PIndex will encounter many states when placed in a real working environment. Before a CPN model can be established, firstly each state must be recognized. In our case a token represents a node on which its current state would be represented by its colour from which our CPN model will take its desired actions as shown in Table 1. These states coupled with its buffer, relative

processing delay, bandwidth and node usage will be the parameters for every token. As it will be seen the requirement of buffers and an introduction of bandwidth consumption is introduced as additions to the current basic model, further more keeping a count of the number of nodes handling a request/state will also be factored in for logging purposes. A simple flow diagram will be used to represent the actions that are needed for each state thus their similarities can easily be seen, verifying the use of CPNs. However, critical to the accurate monitoring of PIndex's performance, resources such as time, bandwidth and node usage are used will be different for each state.

Modelling Search Requests

At the heart of PIndex is its ability to send a search and discover resources via its P2P algorithm. As shown in Figure 1, the first step is to check if the node is willing to accept a job (not dead or about to leave), if so it may carry on with the search request if not the message is lost, although in our model the assumption is made that the Table of External Contacts (TECs) are kept up-to-date without error, message loss is still possible in the case where a search arrives at a node that has just failed.

Table 1. The state table of PIndex

Colors	Description
Free	The node is free and able to process jobs.
Dead	The node is dead its position in the PG is vacant for joining nodes.
Busy	The node is busy processing a job, but will place a job in its buffer.
Leaving	The node will leave soon; it will not accept any more jobs but will complete the ones in its buffer. It will also tell its PG and referencing nodes to update their TEC's.
Search request	The node is sending a search request; the receiving node responds and forwards it according to the PIndex search algorithm.
Query Response	The node is sending a response back, to any form of query.
Join Requests	The node is requesting to join a PG (receiving), if space is vacant it will join, otherwise the request is forwarded to a neighbouring PG.
Contact Updates	The node is updating its TEC replacing its existing contacts with new ones.
Resources Updates	The node is updating its resource information.

Figure 1. The flow chart of search requests

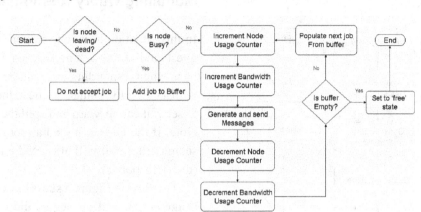

The next step would be to set the nodes current state to busy then increment a global counter of nodes being used for processing (total node usage), and a separate counter (PG node usage) is also kept for PG monitoring. Before the forwarded search messages are sent with a counter for bandwidth use incremented globally (total bandwidth) and locally (PG bandwidth), then the process of calculating the next nodes to query is executed and the message is sent, given its relative delay the next step is to release the bandwidth and node count being used. Before completing this state, a check is needed to see if the node's buffer is empty, if not a loop back is made to the processing stage, and if empty the node state is set to free.

Modelling Join Requests

In this situation a new node randomly selects a PG to join, on the condition there is a vacant space the node will be able to join, else the node will have to repeat its request in the next sequential PG. In this case we have a loop back condition using the discovery of a vacant space rather than checking if the buffer is empty.

Omitting the need to check if the node is alive or busy henceforth, the first step in Figure 2 is to take count of the node usage and bandwidth being used with its state set to *Busy*, then the actual

request message is sent after which the resources are returned. The node receiving the request will then check if there are any vacant places in its PG, if not then the request is forwarded to its neighbouring PG. If there is a vacancy then it is given to the requesting node, its state and buffers are then set to free. The next logical step would be to invoke the *contact update* state to populate its TEC.

Modelling Leave Requests

When leaving, a node in PIndex must complete the tasks it already has in its buffer before leaving the network. Further tasks it may receive are not accepted in addition to telling its TEC contacts to update their references as it will be leaving soon. As shown in Figure 3, the flow starts by setting the node usage count, and consumes the required bandwidth resources and sends a message forcing its contacts to get new contact instead of itself whilst setting its state to *leaving*. After having executed all the tasks in its buffer the node is placed into a dead state

Modelling Resource Updates

The main concept of PIndex is to keep accurate and dynamic record of the resources available. This was achieved through the use of its update

Figure 2. The flow chart of join requests

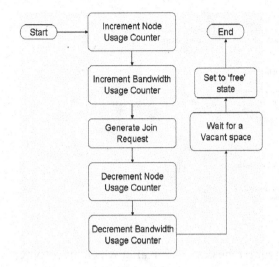

Modelling Query Responses

In this situation a node is responding to any request, and serves as a generic state any node can be in when responding to a request. For example, with a new TEC contact request, the node checks to see if it can forward and split the search space. Note: if the current node has some or all of the search criteria, it will also send a response back (query response).

The flow in Figure 5 starts by setting the node usage count, and consumes the required bandwidth resources; it then processes the request and responds accordingly after which the consumed resources are returned.

Modelling Contacts Updates

As part of the joining procedure (join state), newly joined nodes must update their TEC. This is a random process where the joining node randomly chooses a known external contact within the PG and queries them for a new contact in its PG for the joining node, this process is repeated to populate the new nodes TEC. This process is outlined in Figure 6, here the resources needed are consumed and then a request for a new contact is made (and response given), which is repeated to

messages sent to all its local peers in its PG and any other node which has a reference to it. Figure 4 shows a resource update, the initial stage it consumes the resources required (node usage and bandwidth counter), and then proceeds in preparing a message to send to all (alive) contacts in it PG, and in its TEC. The message is then sent; note that if any nodes fail during this period no affect is had since update messages are sent in one way only. Given the average time to send a message all the resources taken are then returned.

Figure 3. The flow chart of leave request

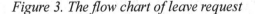

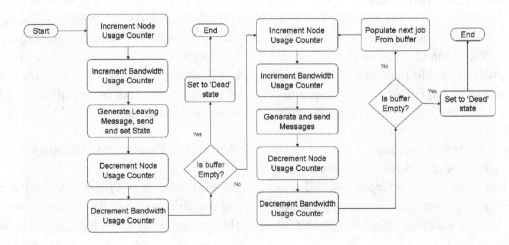

Figure 4. The flow chart of resource request

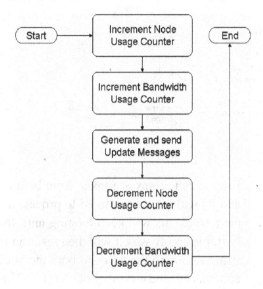

Figure 5. The flow chart of query responses

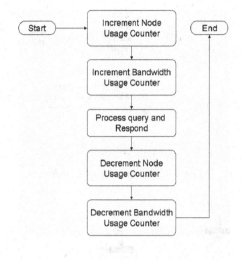

populate its TEC table. Note: not only does the new node gain an external contact, but the new contact must also add the new nodes ID to it list of nodes to send updates to. Once the table is populated, all consumed resources are returned and the node is set free.

The CPN Model

Figure 7 shows a generic flow chart of PIndex. There are 3 node states that do not consume resources—*Dead*, *Free* and *Busy*. These states are

Figure 6. The flow chart of contact updates

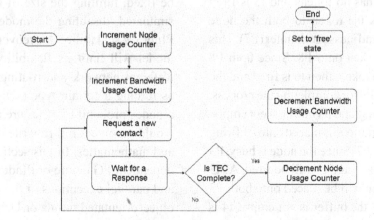

used as an indication of the current activity of a node. The remaining 6 node states are used to perform tasks consuming resources with some delays.

Figure 8 shows the CPN diagram of PIndex that has 9 places (P1-P9) and 6 transitions (t1-t6) which is explained in the following two cases:

Case 1: a node is not busy and its buffer is empty. The token of the node is placed onto P1 firing t1 and goes to P2. Since the node is not busy, P3 will have no tokens and t2 will be fired. As t2 is fired it takes a token from both the node counter (P6) and message

Figure 7. The generic flow chart of PIndex

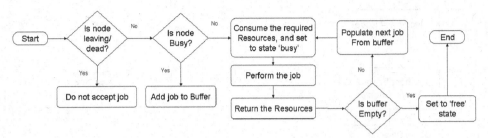

Figure 8. The CPN diagram of PIndex

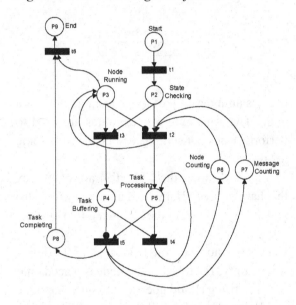

counter (P7) and places a token in P3 and P5 respectively. The amount of delay of the two delay transitions (t4 and t5) is dependent on the colors of the node. Since the buffer is empty, P4 has no tokens and t5 is fired which returns the token to both the node counter (P6) and message counter (P7). This will place a token onto P8. Since both P8 and P3 have a token, then t6 is fired and the token goes to P9 for completing the process.

Case 2: a node is busy and its buffer is not empty. The token of the node is placed onto P1 firing t1 and goes to P2. Since the node is busy, P3 will have a token and t3 will be fired. As t3 is fired a token will be placed onto both P3 and P4. Since the buffer is not empty, t4 is

fired which removes a token from both P4 and P5 and loops back to P5 to process the next task. This will keep looping until the buffer is empty which will then result in t5 firing returning the token to both the node counter (P6) and message counter (P7). This will place a token onto P8. Since both P8 and P3 have a token, then t6 is fired and the token goes to P9 for completing the process.

PINDEX SIMULATOR

PIndex gains its speed in performance through PGs operating independently and concurrently. However although Petri Nets have been designed with concurrency in mind, running multiple instances that interact with each other is a not part of standard Petri Nets. Although a number of PNs could be combined into a single PN mimicking multiple instances with a derived mathematical model. However having a single PN would become cumbersome in that the number of PGs would be fixed, limiting the size of the network to be simulated, disabling the model in investigating PIndex's scalability. Moreover, creating a fixed model will limit its flexibility in investigating different network and routing conditions, such as forcing a certain type of PG grouping using a nodes probability of failure as a metric which would involve a full re-write of the CPN model and mathematics. In this section we take the independent PG nature of PIndex, the CPN model and parallel executions of threads to produce an object orientated simulator. Using threads enables multiple instance of a PG to run concurrently, truly modelling PIndex in a multi-network distribution (PIndex over many independent sites). The following section briefly describes the implementation of the PIndex simulator.

Simulator Implementation

Based on CPN modeling, we have implemented a simulator using Java programming language for PIndex evaluation. Figure 9 shows the architecture of the PIndex simulator. Tokens are implemented as Java objects that contain a color state, a buffer array, a Table of External Contact (TEC), firing probabilities, a PG ID and a PG node ID. In order to model parallel executions of PGs in PIndex, each PG is implemented as a thread. Multiple threads are instantiated for the duration of the simulation creating a thread pool. Each PG has its own *Poisson* distribution generator, which provides *Poisson* rates for firing, updating, failures and leaving for the nodes in the PG. Each PG also has its own probabilistic normal distribution generator for its peer nodes. The probability of the peer nodes is used in such a way that when a peer node is chosen to run, a random percentage of probability is generated and compared with the probability of the node determining if the node runs.

Each colour state has an associated action as shown in Table 1, which was implemented as a thread. The reason for creating these coloured actions as threads is that, when a token is being processed in the PG, an instance of its respective colour action thread is created. These instances carry out the tasks that are specified (consume/ return resources, delay and send/receive messages) and terminates once the job is done (while setting the token free/ execute next task in buffer). This frees the PG thread from executing the colour, before processing the next token in its queue allowing the current token to rejoin the PG (population) such that it can process further incoming request whilst its colour task is being executed.

When a peer node is chosen to run, the token object is passed into the PG thread which is queried. The PG thread checks if the token can accept the task:

- If the token is busy, then the task color is placed into the token's buffer.
- If the token is dead or leaving, then the task color cannot be accepted.
- If the token is free, then a thread will be created to process the task and some resources will be consumed accordingly.

Figure 9. The architecture of the PIndex simulator

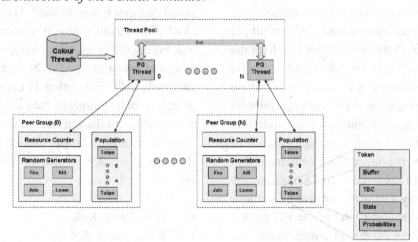

Simulating Peer Nodes

To examine the performance of PIndex under heavy and dynamic conditions, our simulator must be capable of representing and processing many thousands of nodes, and exhibit dynamic characteristics such as choosing when to leave based on a nodes probability of leaving. In our solution nodes were represented as CPN tokens and so represented as objects in our simulator. Each token object has attributes consisting of the current state, a buffer, TEC, probabilities of firing, dying and leaving. Having tokens represented as objects not only simplified the process of creating tokens, but enabled the simulator to make as many instances of tokens (nodes), as was required to be simulated; each with its own independent buffer, states, TECs and probabilities. In addition, to their independent attributes using an object also meant that they could be passed to methods or threads in an exact way as tokens are passed from place to place (via transitions).

Simulating Peer Groups

PIndex is primarily based on the formation of PGs, such that their independent operations remove the need for a central store of information. In order to successfully implement PGs in our simulation they must exist as a single entity for the duration of the simulation, and possess the ability to process requests simultaneously. In our solution, PGs were represented as threads, with multiple instances forming a thread pool that lasted for the duration of the simulation. Since only a single thread is used to represent a PG, we must reduce the amount of processing per thread to a minimum so as not to create a bottleneck in the simulation. The PG threads are the actual implementation of the PIndex CPN, the only difference being is that the execution of a colour task is not handled by the PG thread, but by a created instance of a colour thread. This reduces the load of the PG thread, which means that a PG thread simply checks the state of the token and decides which thread to instantiate. An implementation in this way made it easier to simulate PIndex since the numbers of PG threads were fixed per simulation and easier to organize the priority level of tasks.

Simulating Resource Consumption

The main objective of PIndex is to produce an information service that can work efficiently over a dynamic network structure. Metrics for bandwidth and node usage must be measured during the simulation of PIndex, as these can be used to gauge the operational efficiency of PIndex. In order to make an accurate interpretation of PIndex a log of both metrics must be kept for the entire network and each individual PG. In our simulation a simple counter was kept for resource use, when a resource is being used an increment to the counter is made, and once completed (freeing the resource) the counter is decremented. A global counter was kept for resources regarding the entire network for each monitored resource, in addition to local counters. As these counters will vary in count as the simulation progressed, our simulator would record their values at the start of every simulated clock.

Simulating Discreet Time

To ensure proper execution order of tasks a simulated clock was needed. Having a discrete clock allowed our simulator to carry out multiple task before the clock rolled over, resulting in the executed task appearing to be carried out simultaneously in the simulation. In our simulation our discreet clock is implemented as a thread, which allowed the simulator to take advantage of thread priorities to ensure proper execution of each task (timing). The task priorities were as follows starting with the lowest.

- Simulated clock
- Colour state threads

- PG threads, highest being the pushing of jobs (firing)

Basically this order ensured that if nodes were to fail, this would be first to be carried out along with all the other firings. Then all the recently fired tokens would be processed, and then instantiated (colour threads) before finally incrementing the simulated clock.

VERIFYING THE PINDEX SIMULATOR

Before we used the CPN simulator to evaluate the performance of PIndex, we verified the correctness of the simulator based on CPN matrix calculations. In this section, we present the verification process.

Petri Net Matrices

In Petri nets (PNs), as tokens can enter a transition from a place (input) and leave a transition to a place (output), transitions can be represented in the form of matrices.

Let

- D^- represent the inputs of the transitions in a PN.
- D^+ represent the outputs of the transitions in a PN.
- D represent the transition matrix of a PN.

Therefore,

$$D = D^+ - D^- \tag{1}$$

Given the matrix D, an initial state matrix M, and an input vector E_j with all entries being equal to 0 except the jth entry being equal to 1, then a PN can be modeled using Equation (2) to calculate the next states of the PN which are represented by M'.

$$M' = M - E_j \cdot D^- + E_j \cdot D^+ = M + E_j \cdot D \tag{2}$$

Given that E_j only has a single entry equal to 1, this will cause the transition t_j to fire. If a sequence of input vectors is placed onto a $PN(E_i, E_j, E_k)$, then these will in turn set a sequence of transactions to fire (t_i, t_j, t_k) and produce the state matrix M' using Equation (3).

$$M' = M + \left(E_i + E_j + E_k\right) \cdot D = M + X \cdot D \tag{3}$$

where X represents a firing vector.

Verifying the PIndex Simulator

In this section, we verify the correctness of the PIndex simulator using CPN matrices. By applying colored states we filter out the correct color matrices to use, and are able to model the CPN of PIndex mathematically. Figure 10 shows the transition matrix D which is derived from the CPN diagram of PIndex shown in Figure 8.

We use a color vector C_i with a size of n to represent colors, where n is the total number of colors being used, and the ith position represents the actual color. For example, if the color is for updating, then $C_4 = (0001)$. Having a transition matrix for each color, we need a way to isolate the transition matrix that receives the correct colored token. This can be achieved through the scalar product of the color vector of the current token (C_t) and the color vector of the associated transition matrix (C_d).

Given that:

- C_t is the color vector of the current token.
- C_d is the color vector of the current transition matrix.
- $M_{transition}$ is the transition matrix of a color.
- M is the previous state matrix.

Figure 10. The D transition matrix of the CPN

				D⁺							-					D⁻					
	P1	P2	P3	P4	P5	P6	P7	P8	P9			P1	P2	P3	P4	P5	P6	P7	P8	P9
t1	0	1	0	0	0	0	0	0	0		t1	1	0	0	0	0	0	0	0	0
t2	0	0	1	0	1	0	0	0	0		t2	0	1	0	0	0	1	1	0	0
t3	0	0	1	1	0	0	0	0	0		t3	0	1	1	0	0	0	0	0	0
t4	0	0	0	0	1	0	0	0	0		t4	0	0	0	1	1	0	0	0	0
t5	0	0	0	0	0	1	1	1	0		t5	0	0	0	0	1	0	0	0	0
t6	0	0	0	0	0	0	0	0	1		t6	0	0	1	0	0	0	0	1	0

=   D

	P1	P2	P3	P4	P5	P6	P7	P8	P9
t1	-1	1	0	0	0	0	0	0	0
t2	0	-1	1	0	1	-1	-1	0	0
t3	0	-1	0	1	0	0	0	0	0
t4	0	0	0	-1	0	0	0	0	0
t5	0	0	0	0	-1	1	1	1	0
t6	0	0	-1	0	0	0	0	-1	1

- M' is the current state matrix.
- M_{color} is the resultant state matrix.

Then we have

$$M_{color} = \left((Col) \cdot \left(\left(M' \cdot C_d \right) \cdot M_{transition} \right) \right) + \overline{\left(Col \right)} \cdot \left(\left(M \cdot C_d \right) \cdot M_{transition} \right) \quad (4)$$

where $Col = C_t \cdot C_d$

Equation (4) is repeated for each transition matrix of every color, producing a resultant M_{color} in which each column represents the current number of tokens in each transition for that specific color. For the purpose of simplicity we use four colors in the CPN matrices to verify the correctness of the CPN simulator. Each color has the same transition matrix D. However, not all transitions are enabled because inhibitors are used at transitions t2 and t5 as shown in Figure 8. Therefore, an additional vector (σ) is used to represent which transitions are allowed to fire which is reflected in equation (5).

$$M_{color} = \left((Col) \cdot \left(\left(M' \cdot C_d \right) + M_{transition} \cdot \sigma \right) \right) + \overline{\left(Col \right)} \cdot \left(\left(M_0 \cdot C_d \right) + M_{transition} \cdot \sigma \right) \quad (5)$$

Given four color states as shown in Table 2, the test sequence used was 0001, 0100, 0100, 1000, 0010 and 0001.

Given M= 000009900 representing all places are empty, except the bandwidth and node buffer counters are both set to 9. Taking the first color vector (0001) of the sequence as an example, Table 3 shows the results of each of the $M_{transition}$ transition matrix and Table 4 shows the complete results of the sequence.

Figure 11 and Figure 12 show the theoretical results of the CPN transition matrix and the simulation results generated by the PIndex simulator from the aspects of bandwidth use and node usage respectively.

As shown in Figure 11, both the simulation and the theoretical results are the same in the aspect of bandwidth use. However there is a difference between simulation results and the theo-

Table 2. The four colors used in the verification

Colors	Color Vectors
Resource Update	0001
Contact Update	0010
Search Request	0100
Search Response	1000

Table 3. The transition matrix results of the resource update

C_t	$M_{transition}$	Results	
0001	0001	Col	1
		σ	100000000
		M	000009900
		M_{color}	010009900
	0010	Col	0
		σ	000000000
		M	000009900
		M_{color}	000009900
	0100	Col	0
		σ	000000000
		M	000009900
		M_{color}	000009900
	1000	Col	0
		σ	000000000
		M	000009900
		M_{color}	000009900

Table 4. The transition matrix results of the whole sequence

C_t	M_{color}
0001 (Resource Update)	010009900 000009900 000009900 000009900
0100 (Search Request)	001018800 000008800 010008800 000008800
0100 (Search Request)	001009910 011109900 001009900 001009900
1000 (Search Response)	000008801 000008800 001118800 010008800
0010 (Contact Update)	001008801 011008800 001018810 011108800
0001 (Resource Update)	011008801 001108800 001008811 001018800

retical results in terms of node usage as shown in Figure 12. We observe that in the 3rd iteration node usage remains 1 in the simulated results, whereas in the theoretical results node usage returns to 0. This variation in node usage is a direct result from the way the CPN simulator was implemented, in that as soon as a node receives a task its state is set to busy and does not change until the node is

Figure 11. Verification of bandwidth use

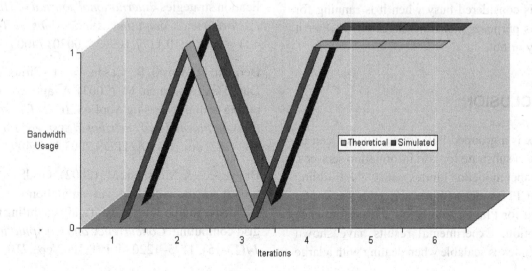

Figure 12. Verification of node usage

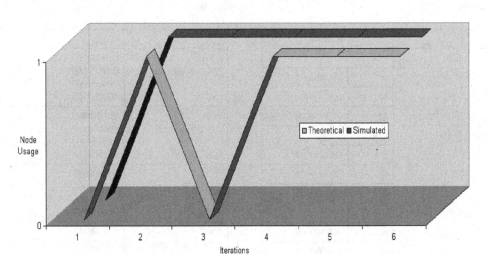

set free, that is, all tasks are completed and the buffer is empty. In the case of the theoretical results of the CPN, node usage changes as soon as a task starts or finishes which can be seen in the 3rd iteration where a task has completed and incremented the node counter whilst a state check was being carried out. This highlights how and where the CPN simulator has deviated from the CPN transition matrix which represents an ideal situation but is mathematically correct in reality.

Compared with the theoretical work of the CPN model, the PIndex simulator is more close to real grid information networks in which a peer node is considered busy when it is running for various purposes including checking whether it is busy or not.

CONCLUSION

PIndex is a grouped P2P network which can be used as a substrate for grid information services. This paper modelled PIndex with CPN. Building on the CPN model, a PIndex simulator was implemented for PIndex simulation and performance evaluation. Experimental results have shown that PIndex is scalable when dealing with a large number of computing nodes up to 10,000, and is resilient in handling *churn* situations (Sahota et al., 2009). The correctness of the PIndex simulator was further verified. Future works include the implementation of the PIndex network and evaluate its performance in real grid environments.

REFERENCES

Bell, W. H., Cameron, D. G., Capozza, L., Millar, A. P., Stockinger, K., & Zini, F. (2003). OptorSim - a grid simulator for studying dynamic data replication strategies. *International Journal of High Performance Computing Applications*, *17*(4), 403–416. doi:10.1177/10943420030174005

Berman, F., Wolski, R., Casanova, H., Cirne, W., Dail, H., & Faerman, M. (2003). Adaptive computing on the grid using AppLeS. *IEEE Transactions on Parallel and Distributed Systems*, *14*(4), 369–382. doi:10.1109/TPDS.2003.1195409

Buyya, R., & Murshed, M. (2002). GridSim: A toolkit for the modeling and simulation of distributed resource management and scheduling for grid computing. *Concurrency and Computation*, *14*(13-15), 1175–1220. doi:10.1002/cpe.710

Cai, M., Frank, M., Chen, J., & Szekely, P. (2004). MAAN: A multi-attribute addressable network for grid information services. *Journal of Grid Computing, 2*(1), 3–14. doi:10.1007/s10723-004-1184-y

Casanova, H., Legrand, A., & Quinson, M. (2008, April 1-3). SimGrid: a generic framework for large-scale distributed experimentations. In *Proceedings of the 10ᵗʰ IEEE International Conference on Computer Modelling and Simulation (UKSIM/EUROSIM'08),* Cambridge, UK (pp. 126-131). Washington, DC: IEEE Computer Society.

Cooke, A. W., Gray, A. J. G., Nutt, W., Magowan, J., Oevers, M., & Taylor, P. (2004). The relational grid monitoring architecture: Mediating information about the grid. *Journal of Grid Computing, 2*(4), 323–339. doi:10.1007/s10723-005-0151-6

Czajkowski, K., Kesselman, C., Fitzgerald, S., & Foster, I. (2001, August 7-9). Grid information services for distributed resource sharing. In *Proceedings of the 10th IEEE International Symposium on High Performance Distributed Computing (HPDC 2001),* San Francisco (pp. 181-194). Washington, DC: IEEE Computer Society.

Foster, I., & Iamnitchi, A. (2003, February 20-21). On death, taxes, and the convergence of peer-to-peer and grid computing. In *Proceedings of the 2ⁿᵈ International Workshop on P2P Systems,* Berkeley, CA (pp. 118-128). University of California, Berkeley.

Godfrey, B. Shenker, S., & Stoica, I. (2006, September). Minimizing churn in distributed systems. In *Proceedings of ACM SIGCOMM Conference 2006,* Pisa, Italy (pp.147-158). ACM Publishing.

Groep, D. L., Templon, J., & Loomis, C. (2006). Crunching real data on the grid: Practice and experience with the European DataGrid. *Concurrency and Computation, 18*(9), 925–940. doi:10.1002/cpe.962

Jensen, K., Kristensen, L. M., & Wells, L. (2007). Coloured petri nets and CPN Tools for modelling and validation of concurrent systems. *International Journal on Software Tools for Technology Transfer, 9*(3-4), 213–254. doi:10.1007/s10009-007-0038-x

Li, M., & Baker, M. (2005). *The grid: Core technologies.* London: John Wiley & Sons.

López, P., Pairot, C., Mondéjar, R., Ahulló, J., Tejedor, H., & Rallo, R. (2004, September). PlanetSim: A new overlay network simulation framework. In *Proceedings of the 4ᵗʰ International Workshop on Software Engineering and Middleware (SEM),* Linz, Austria (pp. 123-136).

Milojicic, D. S., Kalogeraki, V., Lukose, R., Nagaraja, K., Pruyne, J., Rihard, B., et al. (2002). *Peer-to-peer computing* (Tech. Rep. HPL-2002-57). Palo Alto, CA: HP Labs.

Ratnasamy, S., Francis, P., Handley, M., Karp, R. M., & Shenker, S. (2001, August 27-31). A scalable content-addressable network. In *Proceedings of the ACM SIGCOMM Conference 2001,* San Diego, CA (pp.161-172). ACM Publishing.

Rhea, S., Geels, D., Roscoe, T., & Kubiatowicz, J. (2004, June 27-July 2). Handling churn in a DHT. In *Proceedings of the 2004 USENIX Annual Technical Conference,* Boston (pp. 127-140). USENIX.

Rowstron, A., & Druschel, P. (2001, November 12-16). Pastry: Scalable, distributed object location and routing for large-scale peer-to-peer systems. In *Proceedings of the IFIP/ACM International Conference on Distributed Systems Platforms (Middleware),* Heidelberg, Germany (pp. 329-350). ACM Publishing.

Sahota, V., Li, M., Baker, M., & Antonopoulos, N. (2009). A grouped P2P network for scalable grid information services. *Peer-to-Peer Networking and Applications, 2*(1), 3–12. doi:10.1007/s12083-008-0016-4

Schopf, J. M., Pearlman, L., Miller, N., Kesselman, C., Foster, I., & D'Arcy, M. (2006). Monitoring the grid with the Globus Toolkit MDS4. *Journal of Physics: Conference Series, 46*, 521–525. doi:10.1088/1742-6596/46/1/072

Stoica, I., Morris, R., Liben-Nowell, D., Karger, D. R., Kaashoek, M. F., & Dabek, F. (2002). Chord: A scalable peer-to-peer lookup protocol for Internet applications. *IEEE Transactions on Networks, 11*(1), 17–32. doi:10.1109/TNET.2002.808407

Talia, D., & Trunfio, P. (2003). Toward a synergy between P2P and grids. *IEEE Internet Computing, 7*(4), 94–96. doi:10.1109/MIC.2003.1215667

Wang, Z., Helian, N., Wu, S., Deng, Y., Khare, V., & Thompson, C. (2007). Grid-based storage architecture for accelerating bioinformatics computing. *VLSI Signal Processing, 48*(3), 311–324. doi:10.1007/s11265-007-0066-5

Wang, Z., Wu, S., Helian, N., Parker, M., Guo, Y., & Deng, Y. (2007). Grid-oriented storage: A single-image, cross-domain, high-bandwidth architecture. *IEEE Transactions on Computers, 56*(4), 474–487. doi:10.1109/TC.2007.1005

Wang, Z., Wu, S., Helian, N., Xu, Z., Deng, Y., & Khare, V. (2007). Grid-based data access to nucleotide sequence database. *New Generation Computing, 25*(4), 409–424. doi:10.1007/s00354-007-0026-4

Zhang, X., Freschl, J. L., & Schopf, J. M. (2007). Scalability analysis of three monitoring and information systems: MDS2, R-GMA, and Hawkeye. *Journal of Parallel and Distributed Computing, 67*(8), 883–902. doi:10.1016/j.jpdc.2007.03.006

This work was previously published in International Journal of Grid and High Performance Computing, Volume 2, Issue 1, edited by Emmanuel Udoh, pp. 51-68, copyright 2010 by IGI Publishing (an imprint of IGI Global).

Chapter 13
Efficient Communication Interfaces for Distributed Energy Resources

Heinz Frank
Reinhold-Würth-University of the Heilbronn University, Germany

Sidonia Mesentean
Reinhold-Würth-University of the Heilbronn University, Germany

ABSTRACT

The IEC 61850 standard originally was developed for the substation automation. During the past years it was adapted for the integration of distributed energy resources into communication networks, however, with specific requirements. Many small and midsize manufacturers are using, as controllers, a big variety of different microprocessors with limited performances. Such controllers need an interface for IEC 61850 communication networks with a basic functionality which can be implemented with limited costs. Based on their experiences during the realization of an IEC 61850 communication stack, the authors propose ways to support these requirements. In particular, communication interfaces for photovoltaics systems and wind power plants are considered.

INTRODUCTION

At this time in the power supply of electrical energy a dramatic change is going on. In former times this power supply was mainly provided by big centralized power stations. The technology of the devices implemented in such power stations

DOI: 10.4018/978-1-4666-0056-0.ch013

was designated by a few big enterprises. These days more and more small power supplies like wind power plants, hydro electric power plants, photovoltaic systems and others are implemented all over the countries (DER - distributed energy resources). The devices for these small power stations are developed by many big and small enterprises. So the technology is designated by many different participants. This causes a big variety of technical approaches. During the installation of the distributed energy resources they have however to be integrated into one common electrical power grid. For the maintenance of the devices, for the management of the energy flow in the power grid and for the electricity billing many of these devices also have to be integrated into a common communication network (Figure 1) (Palensky, 2008; Haas, Ausburg, & Palensky, 2006). For this a standard developed and supported by the big enterprises for the operation of their already existing power grids has to be used. Therewith it can be assumed, that the IEC 61850 standard will become the standard for this type of communication networks in the future.

Originally the IEC 61850 standard was developed for substation automation (IEC 61850, 2002; Schwarz, 2005). During the last years it was adapted for wind power plants (IEC 61400-25, 2006; Timbus, Larsson, & Yuen, 2008) hydropower plants (IEC 61850 Part 7-410, 2006) and other distributed energy resources (IEC 61850 Part 7-420, 2008). Compared to controllers for the substation automation the controllers for distributed energy resources however have specific requirements for their integration into a communication network:

- The devices to be connected have low prices, so the controllers often have only limited performances and storage capacities.
- Many different manufacturers are producing such devices. They are using a big variety of hardware, operating systems, programming languages and tools.
- Many of the manufacturers are small companies, which want to implement the communication interfaces with limited costs.

To meet these requirements in this paper several proposals are made to optimize the communication according to the IEC 61850 standard for distributed energy resources.

The IEC 61850 Standard

The basic concept of the IEC 61850 standard will be described with the example of a small photo voltaic system (Figure 2). Such a system can consist of the following components:

- A photo voltaic array,
- A DC-circuit breaker,
- An inverter,
- An AC-switch,
- A 3-phase circuit breaker and
- An electric meter.

For the integration of this PV-system into a communication network a microcontroller is required. According to the IEC 61850 this computer is named as intelligent electronic device (IED).

Modelling of the Automation Functions

In an IED the automation functions can be divided into sub-functions and functional elements. For modelling these functions logical node classes are standardized at the level of the functional elements. For the example shown in Figure 2 the following logical node classes can be used:

Figure 1. Distributed energy resources (DER)

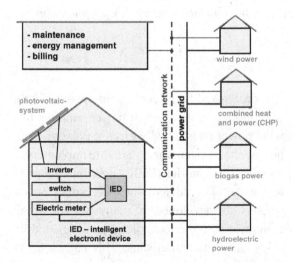

Figure 2. IED for a photovoltaic system

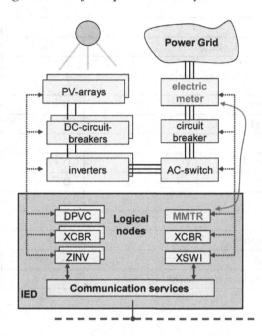

Table 1. Logical node classes for PV-systems

LNs for photovoltaics systems	
LN-Class	**Explanation**
DPVM	PV Module ratings
DPVA	PV Array characteristics
DPVC	PV Array controller
DTRC	Tracking controller
CSWI	Switch (used in conjunction with XSWI or XCBR)
XSWI	DC switch between PV system and inverter
XCBR	Circuit breaker
ZINV	Inverter
MMDC	Measurement of intermediate DC
MMXU	Electrical measurements
MMTR	Metering
ZBAT	Battery
ZBTC	Battery charger
XFUS	Fuse
STEMP	Temperature characteristics
MMET	Meteorological measurements

- The logical node class DPVC describes the object for the photovoltaic array.
- The XCBR-class describes the objects for the DC circuit breaker and the 3-phase circuit breaker.
- The ZINV-class describes the object for the inverter.
- The XSWI-class describes the object for the AC switch.
- The MMTR-class describes the metering of the electric energy especially for billing purposes.

Table 1 shows an extended list of logical nodes for PV-systems.

Within a logical node the data are structured in a hierarchical concept (Figure 4). Logical nodes are consisting of data objects with common data classes (CDC) and data objects are consisting in the next level of data attributes. This can be explained with the example of the electrical meter. This functional element can be modelled with the logical node class MMTR (metering). The data objects for this logical node class are shown in

Table 2. One of these data objects is the "TotPWh" for the electric energy produced by the PV-system. It has the common data class BCR (binary counter reading). It again consists of data attributes as it is shown in Table 3. The data attribute actVal contains the value of the measured energy, the data attribute q gives information about the quality of this value and the data attribute t contains a timestamp when the actValue was updated.

Communication Services

For modelling the communication interface so called ACSI-services are standardized (ACSI = abstract com- munications service interface). The SAV-service (SAV – transmission of sampled analogue values) and the GOOSE-service (GOOSE – generic object oriented substation event) are enabling a real time communi-cation between IEDs. For distributed energy resources however

Table 2. Logical node class MMTR (metering)

MMTR class			
Data Name	CDC	Explanation	M/O
Common logical node (11 CDC)			
Data			
EEHealth	INS	Ext. equipment health	O
EEName	DPL	Ext. equipm. name plate	O
Metered Values			
TotVAh	BCR	Net apparent energy	O
TotWh	BCR	Net real energy	O
TotVArh	BCR	Net reactive energy	O
SupWh	BCR	Real energy supply	O
SupVArh	BCR	Reactive energy supply	O
DmdWh	BCR	Real energy demand	O
DmdVAh	BCR	React. energy demand	O

Abbreviations: CDC - common data class

M/O - mandatory or optional

INS - integer status

BCR - binary counter reading

the client-/server communication is more important. It includes e.g. the following ACSI-services:

- The GetDirectory service allows a client to retrieve a complete list of the names of all accessible objects in an IED, which are logical devices, logical nodes, data objects and data attributes.

- With the GetDataObjectDefinition service a client can retrieve for all objects their data types.
- With the GetDataValues service a client can read data from a server.
- With the SetDataValues service a client can write date into a server.
- With the Reporting service a server can send event-messages

The ACSI-services must be implemented by existing communication protocols (SCSM - Specific Communication Service Mappings). At this stage of the IEC 61850 standard this mapping has to be realized with the Ethernet-, TCP/IP- and MMS-protocols (Figure 4).

Figure 3. IEC 61850 data model

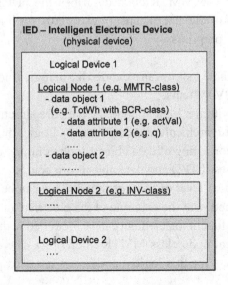

Table 3. Common Data Class BCR (Binary counter reading)

Attr. Name	Type	FC	Trg Op	M/O
BCR class				
Status				
actVal	INT128	ST	Dchg	M
frVal	INT128	ST	Dupd	O
frTrm	TimeStamp	ST	Dupd	O
q	Quality	ST	Dupd	M
t	TimeStamp	ST	Dupd	M
Configuration, description and extension				
units	Unit	CF	Dchg	O
pulsQty	FLOAT32	CF	Dchg	M
frEna	BOOLEAN	CF	Dchg	O
strTm	TimeStamp	CF	Dchg	O
frPd	INT32	CF	Dchg	O
frRs	BOOLEAN	CF	Dchg	O
d	Vis STRING255	DC		O
dU	Unicode STR255	DC		O
cdcNs	Vis STRING255	EX		O
cdcName	Vis STRING255	EX		O
dataNs	VusSTRING255	EX		O

Abbreviations: FC - functional constraint
M/O - mandatory / optional
ST - status information
CF - configuration information
DC - description
EX - extended definition

SCL-File

To describe the communication interface of one IED for another IED a model for the communication and control interface must be provided. The structure of such a model is shown in Figure 5. It includes descriptions of the ACSI-services which are supported by the IED and the data structure which is implemented in the IED. For the detailed modelling a so called system configuration language (SCL) which is based on XML (extended markup language) was specified in the IEC 61850 standard. The model finally must be provided in a SCL-file.

Optimized Interface for a PV-System

Logical Nodes

As it can be seen in Table 2 and Table 3 many data elements in the common data classes and in the data attribute are optional. Table 4 gives an overview about the number of mandatory and optional data elements for the photovoltaic system shown in Figure 2. The big quantity of optional values allows for the manufacturers of such systems many different variations for their data models. This means with the current state of the IEC 61850 only the mandatory data elements

Figure 4. Realization of ACSI services by using the MMS-protocol

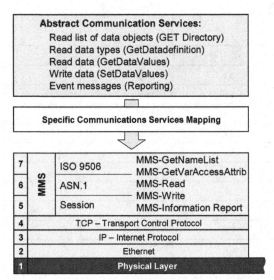

Figure 5. Structure of a SCL-file

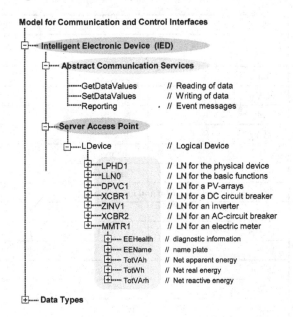

can be expected in all devices from different manufacturers. Additional to this in some cases a minimum of optional CDCs must be implemented. In the LN-class MMTR for example all CDCs are optional. From a practical viewpoint of course at least the TotWh data class is required for each metering device in a DER. With that the model for the PV-system shown in Figure 2 can be reduced to 185 data attributes (see Table 4).

A further optimization can be achieved, if only a minimum of automation functions shall be accessible from the communication network. In the PV-system of Figure 2 such a minimum could consist of a diagnostic function (PV system has a fault or no fault) and of the metering function. For such a minimum only the logical nodes LPHD, LLN and MMTR are required. This configuration

Table 4. Number of data elements for a PV-system

LN-Class	No. of data obj.		No. of data attrib.	
	M	**O**	**M**	**O**
LPHD	**3**	9	**7**	150
LLN0	**4**	14	**16**	256
DPVC	4	17	16	275
XCBR	10	16	33	351
ZINV	6	16	17	401
XSWI	11	14	43	352
XCBR	10	16	33	351
MMTR	**5**	16	**20**	280
Total	53	118	185	2416

The circled numbers show the minimum number of data elements (7 + 16 + 20 = 43 data attributes)

includes only 43 mandatory data attributes (see Table 4).

Transfer of the Communication Model from the Server to a Client

In the IEC-61850 standard it is specified, that a client can retrieve the model for the communication and control-interface in an IED by using the GetDirectory-and GetDataObjectDefinition-ACSI-Ser-vices (Figure 6):

*   The GetDirectoryService has to be implemented on a server with the MMS-GetNameList service. With this service the client can retrieve a list of all accessible data elements, which are the logical devices, logical nodes and their corresponding data objects and data attributes (see example in Figure 7).
*   The GetDataObjectDefintion service has to be implemented on a server with the MMS-GetVarAccessAttributes service. With this service a client can retrieve for all data elements their data types (see example in Figure 8).

Figure 6. Transfer of the communication model with ACSI-services according to IEC 61850

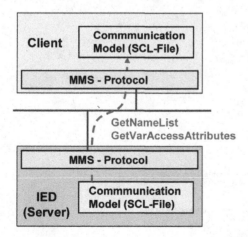

An implementation of such an approach has shown that it is very time-consuming to realize these communication services with the MMS-protocol in a server. As an example for the transmission of a communication model with 800 data attributes from a server to a client about 4000 messages were required.

To simplify the transfer of the communication model from a server in a DER to a client we are proposing two alternative approaches. The IEC 61850 specifies that the complete model for the communication and control interface of an IED has to be described in a SCL-file. In comparison to the method shown in Figure 6 it is much easier to transmit the whole SCL-file as one unit (Figure 9). This can be done either

*   Over the communication network with a file transfer or
*   By using an external storage media.

Implementation of Communication Services

When the IED of a distributed energy resource is in operation as a minimum only the GetDataValue- and the SetDataValue-ACSI-service are required. In Figure 10 the mapping of the GetDataValue-service to the MMS-Read-service is shown in an example.

Even if the protocols in layer 5 – 7 look at first a little bit complicated, their implementation is quite simple. The TPKT (ISO transport service on top of TCP) consists only of three elements (version, reserved and packet length). In the ISO 8073-level always the connection oriented transport protocol is used. In the ISO 8827- and ISO 8823-level also always the same types of protocols are used.

The MMS-protocol is defined in the ISO 9506 standard (ISO 9506, 2008; Sorenson & Jaatun, 2008). For encoding data-values to be transmitted it uses the basic encoding rules of the ASN.1 standard.

Figure 7. Example for the mapping of the GetDirectory-ACSI-service to the MMS-GetNameList service

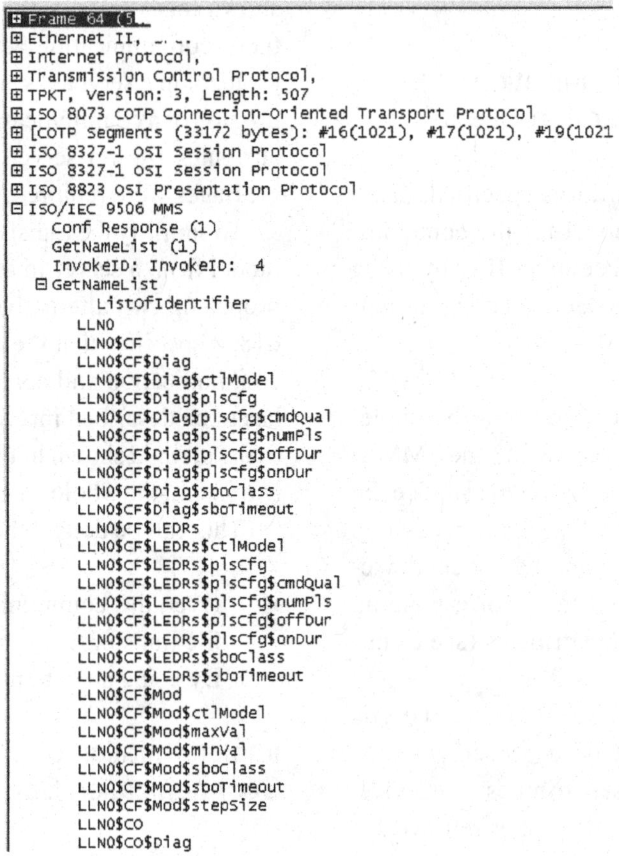

```
⊞ Frame 64 (5
⊞ Ethernet II, ....
⊞ Internet Protocol,
⊞ Transmission Control Protocol,
⊞ TPKT, Version: 3, Length: 507
⊞ ISO 8073 COTP Connection-Oriented Transport Protocol
⊞ [COTP Segments (33172 bytes): #16(1021), #17(1021), #19(1021
⊞ ISO 8327-1 OSI Session Protocol
⊞ ISO 8327-1 OSI Session Protocol
⊞ ISO 8823 OSI Presentation Protocol
⊟ ISO/IEC 9506 MMS
    Conf Response (1)
    GetNameList (1)
    InvokeID: InvokeID:  4
  ⊟ GetNameList
      ListOfIdentifier
    LLN0
    LLN0$CF
    LLN0$CF$Diag
    LLN0$CF$Diag$ctlModel
    LLN0$CF$Diag$plsCfg
    LLN0$CF$Diag$plsCfg$cmdQual
    LLN0$CF$Diag$plsCfg$numPls
    LLN0$CF$Diag$plsCfg$offDur
    LLN0$CF$Diag$plsCfg$onDur
    LLN0$CF$Diag$sboClass
    LLN0$CF$Diag$sboTimeout
    LLN0$CF$LEDRs
    LLN0$CF$LEDRs$ctlModel
    LLN0$CF$LEDRs$plsCfg
    LLN0$CF$LEDRs$plsCfg$cmdQual
    LLN0$CF$LEDRs$plsCfg$numPls
    LLN0$CF$LEDRs$plsCfg$offDur
    LLN0$CF$LEDRs$plsCfg$onDur
    LLN0$CF$LEDRs$sboClass
    LLN0$CF$LEDRs$sboTimeout
    LLN0$CF$Mod
    LLN0$CF$Mod$ctlModel
    LLN0$CF$Mod$maxVal
    LLN0$CF$Mod$minVal
    LLN0$CF$Mod$sboClass
    LLN0$CF$Mod$sboTimeout
    LLN0$CF$Mod$stepSize
    LLN0$CO
    LLN0$CO$Diag
```

Figure 8. Example for the mapping of the GetDataObjectDefinition-ACSI-service to the MMS-Get-VarAccessAttributes services

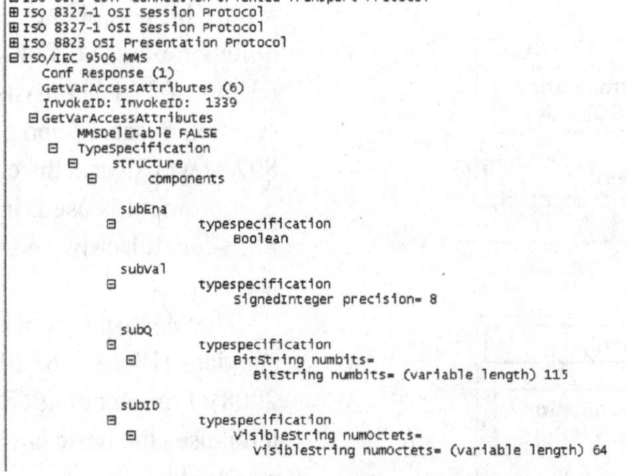

```
⊞ Ethernet II, .... .
⊞ Internet Protocol,
⊞ Transmission Control Protocol,
⊞ TPKT, Version: 3, Length: 93
⊞ ISO 8073 COTP Connection-Oriented Transport Protocol
⊞ ISO 8327-1 OSI Session Protocol
⊞ ISO 8327-1 OSI Session Protocol
⊞ ISO 8823 OSI Presentation Protocol
⊟ ISO/IEC 9506 MMS
    Conf Response (1)
    GetVarAccessAttributes (6)
    InvokeID: InvokeID: 1339
  ⊟ GetVarAccessAttributes
      MMSDeletable FALSE
    ⊟  TypeSpecification
      ⊟   structure
        ⊟      components

          subEna
          ⊟         typespecification
                       Boolean

          subVal
          ⊟         typespecification
                       SignedInteger precision= 8

          subQ
          ⊟         typespecification
                       BitString numbits=
            ⊟            BitString numbits= (variable length) 115

          subID
          ⊟         typespecification
                       VisibleString numoctets=
            ⊟            VisibleString numoctets= (variable length) 64
```

Figure 9. Transmission of the communication model described in a SCL-file as one unit

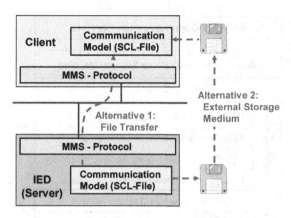

Interface for a Wind Power Plant

Logical Nodes

The basic structure of a wind turbine is shown in Figure 11. For such devices in the IEC 61400-25 logical node classes are specified as they are shown in Table 5 (IEC 61400-25, 2006; Tholomier, Rola, & Willemse, 2008). As examples the WROT-class includes data elements for the input of setting data, for the control of the operation mode and status information like the turbine status and the operational time. The WGEN-class includes data objects for the generator speed, voltages, currents, power factor and temperatures.

Figure 10. Example for the implementation of the GetDataValue-service with MMS-Read-messages

Figure 11. IED for a wind turbine

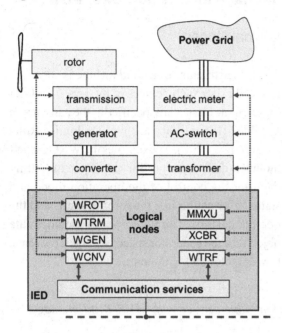

Figure 12. Realization of ACSI services by using WebServices

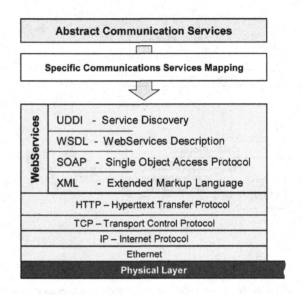

Table 5. Logical node class for wind power plants

Wind Turbine specific LNs		
LN-Class	**Explanation**	**M/O**
WROT	Wind turbine rotor information	M
WTRM	Wind turbine transmission inf.	O
WGEN	Wind turbine generator inf.	M
WCNV	Wind turbine converter inf.	O
WTRF	Wind turbine transformer inf.	O
WNAC	Wind turbine nacelle inf.	M
WYAW	Wind turbine yaw information	M
WTOW	Wind turbine tower inf.	O
WALM	Wind turbine alarm inf.	M
WSLG	Wind turbine state log inf.	O
WALG	Wind turbine analogue log inf.	O
WREP	Wind turbine report inf.	O
Wind Power Plant specific LNs		
WTUR	Wind turbine general inf.	M
WMET	Wind power plant meteoro-logical information	O
WAPC	Wind power plant active power plant control information	M
WRPC	Wind power plant reactive power control information	O

Abbreviations: LN - logical node
M/O - mandatory or optional

Communication Services

The IEC 61850-420 specifies that the ACSI services for distributed energy resources have to be implemented by MMS services as it was described in chapter 3 for the example of an IED for a photo voltaic system. The MMS standard however was already defined before more than 20 years ago. In the IEC 61400-25, which was developed especially for wind power plants, allows as an alternative to the MMS protocol also the use of WebServices (IEC 61400-25, 2006; Sokura & Korhonen, 2004).

WebServices are realized by using the http-protocol on Ethernet and TCP/IP as a basis (Figure 12) (Gunzer, 2002; Myerson, 2002). On top of this protocol the following additional layers are used:

- The data units within the http-messages are structured according to the XML standard (XML - extended markup language).
- The XML language is used to describe SOAP messages (SOAP – simple object access protocol) which are generic messages for the transmission of data and for remote procedure calls.
- In the next level WSDL (Web Services Definition Language) is used to describe the specific messages for the communication services.
- In the upper level the UDDI (Universal Discovery Description Language) can be used to publish and find WebServices over the web.

WebServices are already supported by many programming tools. They give the programmers an extended support for a cost effective implementation of communication services.

CONCLUSION

The full implementation of an extensive communication interface according to IEC 61850 on a microcomputer is rather complicated and needs powerful microcontrollers. To realize such an interface also on microcontrollers with limited resources, several optimizations are proposed in this paper. In general the interfaces can be simplified by reducing the standardized data objects to the mandatory data objects and by implementing only the strictly required communication services. It was shown that an automatic transfer of the communication model from a server to a client is not required for IEDs in DER. While the standard requires for photovoltaic systems still a service mapping to MMS-services the standard allows for IEDs in wind power plants already a service mapping to the modern technology of Web services.

ACKNOWLEDGMENT

The authors wish to thank the Foundation for the promotion of the Reinhold-Würth-University of the Heilbronn University in Künzelsau for their support of this work.

REFERENCES

Gunzer, H. (2002). *Introduction to Web Services*. Austin, TX: Borland.

Haas, O., Ausburg, O., & Palensky, P. (2006). Communication with and within Distributed Energy Resources. In *Proceedings IEEE International Conference on Industrial Informatics (INDIN)* (pp. 352-356).

IEC 61400-25. (2006). *Communications for monitoring and control of wind power plants*.

IEC 61850. (2002). *Communication networks and systems in substations, 14 parts*.

IEC 61850 Part 7-410. (2006). *Hydroelectric Power plants- communication for monitoring and control*.

IEC 61850 Part 7-420. (2008). *DER logical nodes*.

ISO 9506. (2008). Industrial automation systems-Manufac-turing Message Specification, 2 Parts.

Myerson, J. M. (2002). *Web Service Architectures*. Chicago, IL: Tect.

Palensky, P. (2008). Networked Distributed Energy Resources. In *Proceedings of the 34th Annual Conference on IEEE Industrial Electronics (IECON)* (pp. 23-24).

Schwarz, K. H. (2005). *An introduction to IEC 61850. Basics and user-oriented project-examples for the IEC 61850 series for substation automation*. Wurzburg, Germany: Vogel Verlag.

Sokura, W., & Korhonen, T. (2004). *TCP/IP Communication Aspects in Monitoring of a Remote Wind Turbine*. Helsinki, Finland: Helsinki University.

Sorenson, J. T., & Jaatun, M. G. (2008). *An Analysis of the Manufacturing Message Specification Protocol*. Berlin: Springer.

Tholomier, D., Rola, J., & Willemse, C. (2008). Using Innovative Technologies to ease Wind Resource penetration into Power Grid. In *Proceedings of the 7th World Wind Energy Conference & Exhibition (WWEC 2008)* (pp. 1–18).

Timbus, A., Larsson, M., & Yuen, C. (2008). Integration of Wind Energy Resources in the Utility Control and Information Technology Infrastructures. In *Proceedings of the IEEE International Symposium on Industrial Electronics (ISIE)* (pp. 2371-2376).

This work was previously published in International Journal of Grid and High Performance Computing, Volume 2, Issue 2, edited by Emmanuel Udoh, pp. 23-36, copyright 2010 by IGI Publishing (an imprint of IGI Global).

Chapter 14
Deep Analysis of Enhanced Authentication for Next Generation Networks

Mamdouh Gouda
Misr University of Science & Technology, Egypt

ABSTRACT

Next Generation Networks (NGN) is the evolution of the telecommunication core. The user has to execute multi-pass Authentication and Key Agreement (AKA) procedures in order to get access to the IP Multimedia Subsystem (IMS). This causes overhead on the AAA server and increases the delay of authenticating the user and that is because of unnecessary and repeated procedures and protocols. This paper presents an enhanced one-pass AKA procedure that eliminates the repeated steps without affecting the security level, in addition it reduces the Denial of Service (DoS) attacks. The presented mechanism has minimal impact on the network infrastructure and functionality and does not require any changes to the existing authentication protocols.

INTRODUCTION

Next Generation Network (NGN) technology evolved in the past few years. NGN architecture is a Next Generation Network where wired and wireless services are converged and quality of service is guaranteed. One of NGN access networks

is the Wireless LANs (WLAN). WLAN systems are more suited for hotspots coverage and offer high data rates with low investment cost. The multimedia services provided to the users through WLAN depend on the IP multimedia subsystem (IMS) (3GPP TS 23.228 -v8.1.0, 2007), which is based on All-IP architecture. NGN provides many new services through different access networks, which in turn raises security issues. New security

DOI: 10.4018/978-1-4666-0056-0.ch014

architecture is currently under study (3GPP TS 33.234 -v7.2.0, 2006; 3GPP TS 33.203 - v7.6.0, 2006) that aim at protecting the mobile users, the data transferred and the underlying network. This architecture make the WLAN user have to execute multi-pass Authentication and Key Agreement (AKA) procedure in order to get access to the IMS services. The architecture specifies three authentication steps (see Figure 1). In the first step, the user executes the (Extensible Authentication Protocol) EAP-AKA protocol (Arkko & Haverinen, 2006) to register in WLAN domain. In the second step, the user executes the Internet Key Exchange version 2 (IKEv2) protocol (Kaufman, 2005) that encapsulates EAP-AKA, which registers him to the 3G public land mobile network (PLMN) domain. In the third step the user using the Session Initiation Protocol (SIP) (Rosenberg et al., 2002) executes the IMS-AKA procedure (3GPP TS 33.203 - v7.6.0, 2006) for registration in the IMS domain. As we can see the EAP-AKA has been repeated and an execution of IMS-AKA introduce an authentication overhead (Asokan, Niemi, & Nyberg, 2005). This overhead is related to: (i) the exchange of messages that cause delays in users' authentication (i.e., especially in cases that the users are located away from their home network) and consume radio resources; and (ii) the computational processing that will consume the limited energy and computational resources at

the mobile devices. Therefore, the aforementioned multi-pass AKA procedure deteriorates the overall system performance and may impact negatively on the quality of service offered to the end-users.

There is a rather limited literature that copes with the aforementioned authentication overhead in NGN. Veltri, Salsano, and Martiniello (2006) suggest an integrated authentication protocol, which is based on SIP and authenticates both the WLAN and the 3G PLMN within a single procedure, and thus reduces the overall authentication latency. However, the main drawback of this authentication procedure is that it is vulnerable to Denial of Service attacks. An adversary could simply send false authentication messages that the WLAN has to forward to the 3G PLMN causing overflow. Crespi and Lavaud (2004) propose the introduction of a new functional entity, called WLAN SIP proxy, in the WLAN that enables the latter to perform localized IMS services. However, this approach requires the implementation of the new entity and the related functionality increasing the deployment complexity. Ntantogian and Xenakis (2008) presents a one-pass AKA procedure for NGN that eliminates the repeated authentication steps without compromising the provided level of security. The one-pass AKA based on security key binding between the authentication steps. However this technique can be enhanced by binding the elements of the network.

Figure 1. Multi-pass AKA procedure for IMS services

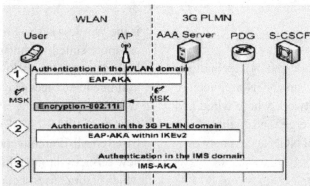

This paper enhances the one-pass AKA performance. The proposed approach depends on the concept that the network elements connections are already secured. In previous solutions the user must authenticate himself with each network element as unknown user. This paper merges the authentication steps. After AAA server has authenticated the user in the first step, it sends the user ID to PDG with the information needed to continue the authentication process for the user. The merging eliminates phase one of the second authentication step. In the second authentication step the user sends to the PDG the user ID with the IP Multimedia Private Identity (IMPI) if the user is authenticated by the PDG, it sends the IMPI to the Serving-Call Session Control Function(S-CSCF). This merging eliminates the third authentication step. Therefore the merging of authentication steps enhances the performance of user authentication in NGN.

The rest of this paper is organized as follows. The specified multi-pass AKA procedure and the improvement of the one pass AKA is presented. The enhanced one-pass AKA procedures is then described. The performance of the enhanced one-pass and compares it with the multi-pass AKA is also evaluated.

BACKGROUND

In multi-pass authentication there are three steps. Initial authentication for registration in the WLAN domain (step 1-Figure 1): The user and the WLAN are authenticated to each other using EAP-AKA (Arkko & Haverinen, 2006) (see Figure 2). This authentication step involves the user, an Authentication, Authorization, Accounting (AAA) client that is actually a wireless Access Point (AP), and the AAA server (located at the service network) that obtains authentication information (i.e., 3G authentication vectors) from the Home Subscriber Server/Authentication Center (HSS/AuC) of the 3G PLMN where the user is subscribed, based on the user's permanent UMTS identity (i.e., International Mobile Subscriber Identity, (IMSI)). After executing EAP-AKA, the user and the AAA server share an EAP-AKA Master Key (MK), which is used for the execution of EAP-AKA fast re-authentication and the generation of security keys (Arkko & Haverinen, 2006). The user and the AAA server use the MK to calculate the Master Session Key (MSK), and the second forwards it to the wireless AP. The AP and the user use this key to generate the WLAN session keys which are employed in the 802.1li security framework to provide security services (3GPP TS 33.203 - v7.6.0, 2006). After a successful EAP-AKA authentication, the user obtains a local IP address.

Figure 2. The EAP-AKA protocol (First Authentication Step)

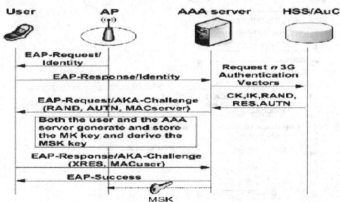

Second authentication for registration in the 3G PLMN domain (step 2-Figure 1): In this step (see Figure 3) the user and an entity called Packet Data Gateway (PDG), which is located in the 3G PLMN, execute the IKEv2 protocol (Kaufman, 2005) that encapsulates EAP-AKA for authenticating the user and the 3G PLMN. The PDG routes data traffic between a user and an external packet data network, which is selected based on the IMS services requested by the user. The IKEv2 protocol is executed in two phases (i.e., phase 1 and phase 2). In phase 1 the user and the PDG establish a bidirectional IKE Security Association (IKE SA) that protects all the subsequent IKEv2 messages (see Figure 3-step 1). In phase 2, the user and the AAA server execute EAP-AKA encapsulated in IKEv2 messages for mutual authentication. Note that the PDG forwards the EAP-AKA messages to the AAA server using the Diameter protocol (Calhoun et al., 2003). In addition, the PDG is authenticated to the user using its certificate (3GPP TS 33.234 -v7.2.0, 2006) (see Figure 3- step 3). At the end of this phase the user obtains from the PDG a global IP address, called Remote IP address, which is used for access to the IMS.

Moreover, an IPsec-based Virtual Private Network (VPN) tunnel (Kent & Atkinson, 1998) is deployed between the user and the PDG that uses the Encapsulating Security Payload (ESP) (Kent & Atkinson, 1998) protocol, which provides confidentiality and integrity to the data exchanged between them (see Figure 3 - step 4). In contrast to the multi-pass AKA, the one-pass AKA accomplish mutual authentication between the user and the PDG by calculating a hash value respectively (i.e., AUTHi and AUTHr payloads) using the MK key, which is generated during the execution of EAP-AKA in the initial authentication step. Then, they send to each other the AUTHi and AUTHr payloads for verification, performing a security key binding between the initial authentication step and the second authentication step (see Figure 4).

Third authentication for registration in the IMS domain (step 3-Figure 1): After registration in the 3G PLMN domain, the user must register in the IMS domain. Mutual authentication in this step is required to avoid impersonation attacks and fraudulent IMS usage as described in (Lin et al., 2005). Thus, in this step the user and the IMS are authenticated to each other using the IMS-AKA procedure. In IMS, multimedia services are pro-

Figure 3. IKEv2 with EAP-AKA (second authentication step)

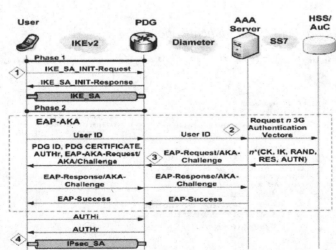

Figure 4. Second authentication step (one-pass AKA procedure)

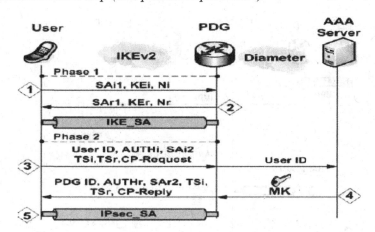

vided by the call session control functions (CSCF) using the SIP protocol. There are three types of CSCFs: (i) a proxy-CSCF (P-CSCF) that is located in the visited network and is responsible for redirecting the SIP messages of users to their home networks; (ii) a serving-CSCF (S-CSCF) that is located in the home network of the user, communicates with the HSS and the AuC to receive IMS related subscriber data and authentication information, and interacts with the application servers to obtain value added services; and (iii) an interrogating-CSCF (I-CSCF) that is responsible for selecting a S-CSCF for a user.

At the beginning of the IMS-AKA procedure, the user sends its permanent IMS identity (i.e., IP Multimedia Private Identity (IMPI)) to the S-CSCF via the PDG (see Figure 5). Based on the user's identity, the S-CSCF obtains n 3G authentication vectors from the HSS/AuC. Note that a 3G authentication vector includes a random challenge (RAND), the authentication token (AUTN), the expected response (XRES), the encryption key (CK) and the integrity key (IK). In the sequel, the S-CSCF selects one out of the n obtained authentication vectors to proceed with the IMS authentication procedure and stores the remaining n-I for future use. Then, the S-CSCF sends the RAND and AUTN payloads to the user together with the CK and IK keys to the P-CSCF. The latter stores the CK and IK keys and forwards the RAND and AUTN payloads to the user. After receiving this information the user executes the UMTS-AKA algorithms, verifies the AUTN payload and generates the CK and IK keys. At this point, the user and the P- CSCF share the CK and IK keys and an IPsec tunnel is established between them, which protect the subsequent SIP messages exchanged (see Figure 5). Next, the user computes his response to the challenge (noted as an SRES payload), and sends it to the S-CSCF. Upon receiving this message, the S-CSCF verifies the user's response to the challenge (SRES). If this check is successful, the S-CSCF sends a success verification message to the user to complete the third authentication step. In contrast to the multi-pass AKA, the one-pass AKA procedure authenticates only the user to the IMS network. The fact that the IMS is not authenticated to the user does not imply any security risk, since IMS is located within and operated by the 3G PLMN, which has been already authenticated in the previous step. Another difference of the one-pass AKA with the multi-pass AKA is that the former does not establish an IPsec tunnel between the user and the P-CSCF. However, this does not impose any security threat, since the deployed IPsec tunnel between the user and PDG protect the messages of the SIP protocol (see Figure 6).

Figure 5. IMS-AKA procedure (third authentication step)

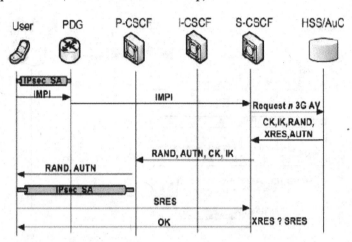

Figure 6. IMS authentication (one-pass AKA procedure)

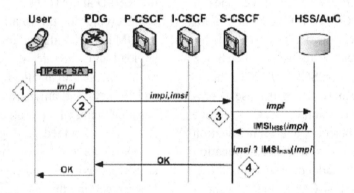

ENHANCED ONE-PASS AUTHENTICATION

Outline

In the first step, the user and WLAN are authenticated performing EAP-AKA. The user and the AAA server generate and store the MK key. The PDG receives the MK key from the AAA server and selects the encryption algorithm. In second step, the user is authenticated to the 3G PLMN by executing IKEv2 that omits the encapsulation of EAP-AKA. The authentication of negotiation end points is done by the MK key. S-CSCF authenticates the user by checking the IMPI and

IMSI received by the PDG. Therefore, third authentication step isn't needed.

The user must be able to generate the local IP address before the end of EAP-AKA (the first authentication step). The PDG must be able to modify SIP messages as in this paper. The PDG must be capable of storing the MK key of the user within life time. There must be a pre-established IP-sec tunnel between the PDG and AAA server and between the PDG and the S-CSCF.

Authentication Procedures

In the first step, the user and the WLAN are authenticated using EAP-AKA. The user generates a local IP address before the completion of the authentication step. In addition, the user and the PDG are performing phase one of the second authentication step. So, the first authentication step and the second authentication step have been merged. It starts as follows (see Figure 7). Wireless access point requests the user identity (EAP request identity). The user replies by sending to the AAA server EAP response/ identity which contains (permanent or temporary IMSI identity). The AAA server checks whether it possesses a fresh 3G authentication vector, stored from previous authentication with the specific user. If not, the AAA server sends the user IMSI to the HSS/ AUC and obtains n fresh 3G authentication vectors (Xenakis & Merakos, 2004). The authentication vector contains Random challenge (rand), Authentication token (AUTN), Encryption Key (CK) and Integrity Key (IK). The AAA server uses CK, IK, and the user identity to compute the MK key. The AAA server calculates a Message Authentication Code (MAC) value, (MAC_{server}), which verifies the integrity of the next EAP-AKA message (EAP-Request/AKA-Challenge). The AAA server sends the (EAP-request/AKA-Challenge)

which contains RAND, AUTN, MAC_{server}. The user executes UMTS-AKA algorithm and verifies the AUTN payload. The user generates the IK and CK keys then calculates the MK key and produces the MSK key. If the verification of the MAC_{server} value is successful, the user computes its response to the challenge (noted as SRES) and generates a local IP. The DHCP server provides to the MT the basic IP configurations under service related configuration such as a default outbound proxy (i.e., the P-CSCF). The user sends EAP-response/AKA-challenge message to the AAA server containing SRES, MAC_{user}, User ID, SAi1, KEi1 and Ni. The SAi1 define the set of cryptographic algorithms for the IKE-SA that the user supports. KEi is the Diffie-Hellman value.

Ni is the value that represents the nonce. The nonce is used as an input function to the cryptographic functions employed by IKEv2 of the keying material and protects against reply attacks. The AAA server verifies the received MAC_{user} value and checks if the received user's response to the challenge (SRES) matches with the expected response of the 3G authentication vector.

Figure 7. First authentication step (enhanced one-pass AKA)

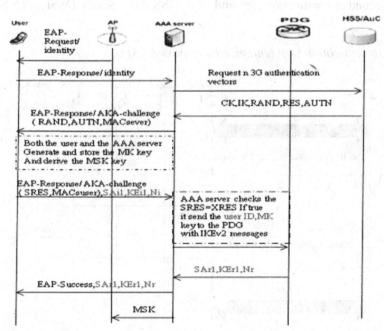

At this point IKEv2 has been started. If true, the AAA server forwards the user ID and the MK key with SAi1, KEi1and Ni to the PDG through pre-established IP-sec tunnel. The PDG replies by the selected encryption algorithm (SAr1), KEr1 and Nr to the AAA server. The AAA server sends an EAP-success message along with SAr1, KEr1 and Nr to the user and the MSK key to the wireless AP. Finally, the user and the WLAN have been authenticated to each other. The user and the AAA server have stored the MK key in order to be able to perform fast re-authentication. The user and the wireless AP share the MSK key. The IKEv2 protocol has been already started. Phase one in the second authentication step has been eliminated. In addition, this merging has reduced DoS attacks because the PDG receives only from the users who have IKE_SA tunnel with the PDG. IKE_SA tunnel protects all subsequent messages between them.

In Second authentication step, the user and 3G PLMN are authenticated by executing IKEv2. There is a VPN tunnel already established from the merging of the first and the second authentication steps. The user sends IMPI along with the user ID to the PDG performing the third authentication step. So, the second authentication step and

the third authentication step have been merged. It starts as follows (see Figure 8). The user sends to the PDG a message that contains his identity, SAi2 payload; which is the cryptographic suit for the IP-sec tunnel that the user supports, the traffic selectors (TSi and TSr); those allow the peers to identify the packet flows that require processing by IP-sec tunnel, configuration payload request (cp-request); which facilitates the user to obtain a remote IP address from the PDG and get access to the IMS services, the AUTHi payload which is a MAC over the first IKEv2 message using stored MK key and IMPI identity. The PDG retrieves the MK key for the user ID to verify the AUTHi payload in order to authenticate the user. If the verification is true, the PDG retrieves the IMSI of the user by querying the security policy data (SPD) of the IP sec tunnel protocol which maintains the user's profile (Kent & Atkinson, 1998).

The PDG incorporates the retrieved IMSI value of the user in the SIP register message and forwards it to the S-CSCF. The S-CSCF has already stored the pair of the user's identities and sends the IMPI to the HSS/AuC. The HSS/AuC retrieves the IMSI identity of the user. We denote the retrieved IMSI value from HSS as $IMSI_{HSS}$. The HSS/AUC sends $IMSI_{HSS}$ to S-CSCF. S-CSCF

Figure 8. Second authentication step (enhanced one-pass AKA)

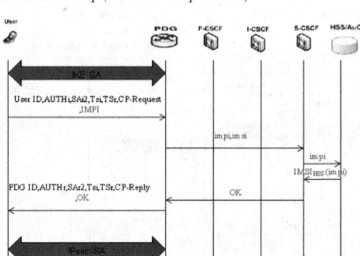

checks IMSI$_{HSS}$=IMSI and sends OK to the PDG. If not, the user is not valid and his registration to IMS is discarded. The PDG generates the AUTHr payload by computing a MAC over the second IKEv2 message and sends to the user a message containing the PDG identity, Traffic selectors, SAr2 payload, Remote IP-address which is included in the CP-reply and an OK of the IMS network. The user authenticates the PDG by verifying the AUTHr payload using the MK key. The user has been authenticated to the 3G PLMN and IMS network. Finally, the authentication between the user and the 3G PLMN and the user and IMS network is completed. The IP-sec tunnel is established between the user and the PDG. There is no need for the third authentication step. Thus, the merging between the second and the third step is done.

THE PERFORMANCE ANALYSIS

In this section we estimate the authentication cost of each procedure (i.e., one-pass & multi-pass AKA & enhanced one-pass) and we compare their performance.

System Model

Assume that a mobile user, located in a WLAN, initiates an IMS session at time t1 by executing the first, second and third authentication steps. At time t2 and t3 the mobile user handoffs to a new access point and according to the IEEE 802.11 standard, it must re-authenticate in the WLAN domain. Here we consider two handover cases: (a) intra-subnet handoff and (b) inter-subnet handoff. In the former case the user moves to a new AP within the same IP subnet and performs the first authentication step. Since the mobile user remains at the same IP subnet, the current IP address of the user is valid to the new access point. Therefore, the established IPsec tunnel between the user and the PDG is maintained and the user avoids the execution of the second and third authentication steps. In case 2, the user performs the first authentication step to register in the WLAN domain. It must obtain a new IP address, since its current IP address is not valid in the new IP subnet.

This entails the execution of the second authentication step, which establishes a new IPsec tunnel, and the third authentication step that avoids impersonation attacks and fraudulent IMS usage. It is evident that the enhanced one-pass AKA

Figure 9. System model

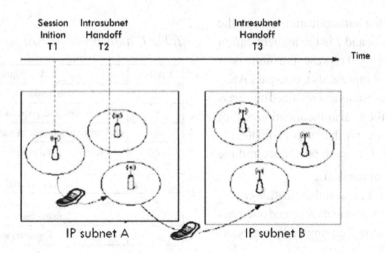

procedure improves the network performance in case of inter-subnet handoff. On the other hand, in case of intra-subnet handoff both procedures present the same performance, as they employ only the first authentication step.

Assume that the average number of handoffs that the mobile user performs during the IMS session is $\overline{K}$. If the IP subnets include in average $\overline{b}$ access points uniformly distributed, then the average number of inter-subnet handoff $\dfrac{\overline{K}}{\overline{b}}$.

Authentication Cost per Operation

Consider that the authentication cost for registration in the WLAN, 3G and IMS domains is A_c, the authentication cost of the inter-subnet handoffs is $\dfrac{\overline{K}}{\overline{b}} A_c$ and the authentication cost of the intra-subnet handoffs is $(\overline{K} - \dfrac{\overline{K}}{\overline{b}})A_c$. The total authentication cost C for an IMS session including also session initiation is:

$$c_\beta^p = \overrightarrow{b}_{\beta,1} \times \overrightarrow{x}_p = [c_p, c_v, c_{us}, c_g, c_{ts}, c_{rg}]$$

$$C(i) = A_c + \frac{\overline{K}}{\overline{b}} A_c + (\overline{K} - \frac{\overline{K}}{\overline{b}})A_c(1) \qquad (1)$$

Where $A_c(1)$ is the authentication cost of the intra-subnet handoffs and i is the authentication mechanism. When $i = 1$, it represents a multi-pass AKA. When $i = 2$, it represents a one-pass AKA and when $i = 3$, it represents an enhanced one-pass AKA. To estimate the total authentication cost of the three procedures, we have to estimate the authentication cost A_c of each procedure and the average number $\overline{K}$ of handoffs.

First we estimate A_c. The authentication cost A_c of the multi-pass, one-pass and enhanced one-pass AKA procedures can be determined by consider-

ing the most and the basic resource consuming communication and security activities.

$$A_c(\beta) = c_\beta^s + c_\beta^p \qquad (2)$$

Where β is the index of authentication type. When $\beta = 1$, it represents an intra-domain handoff authentication. And when $\beta = 2$, it represents an inter-domain handoff authentication. We denote c_β^s and c_β^p as the signaling load and processing load of cryptographic techniques, respectively, for the authentication of type β.

For convenient analysis, we define a set of cost parameters in Table 1.

We can determine c_β^s and c_β^p as follows:

$$c_\beta^s = a_{\beta,i} \times c_s \qquad (3)$$

Where $a_{\beta,i}$ denotes the elements of matrix A shown in (4), β is the authentication type and it represents the column of matrix A, and i is authentication mechanism and it indicates the row of matrix A. $a_{\beta,i}$ is the number of hops by which the entire authentication process passes by for authentication type β at authentication mechanism i. $a_{\beta,i}$ can be obtained from observing the corresponding signaling figures.

For example, when $\beta = 2$ and $i = 3$, then there are two authentication steps. In the first step shown in

Table 1. Authentication cost parameters

Symbol	Description
c_s	Transmission cost on one hop
c_p	Encryption/decryption cost on one hop
c_v	Verification cost at an authentication server
c_{us}	A pair of encryption and decryption cost for a value
c_g	Key generation cost
c_{ts}	Transmission cost for a session key to other communication identities
c_{rg}	Registration cost

Figure 7, the number of messages between the user and the AAA server is four. The distance between the user and its AAA server is assumed to be N_h hops. The number of messages between the AAA server and the PDG is two. The distance between the AAA server and the PDG is assumed to be N_b hops. There are two messages between the AAA server and the HSS. And there is one message between the AP and the user. The total messages in the first authentication step is $3 + 4N_h + 2n_b$. Similarly, we can calculate the second authentication step where, N_c is the distance between the user and the PDG, and N_c is the distance between the PDG and the S-CSCF. Therefore the total number of messages is $2N_c + 4N_h + 2N_b + 2N_x + 5$. Similarly, the other authentications types can be calculated. For intra domain handoff, the user executes the first authentication step only. The user has the remote IP and doesn't need to send SAi1, KEi1 nor Ni to the PDG. In this case, the first authentication step messages in all authentication mechanisms is $3 + 4N_h$.

$$A = \begin{pmatrix} 3 + 4N_h & 12N_c + 4N_h + 4N_b + 4N_x + 7 \\ 3 + 4N_h & 6N_c + 4N_h + 2N_b + 2N_x + 5 \\ 3 + 4N_h & 2N_c + 4N_h + 2N_b + 2N_x + 5 \end{pmatrix}$$

$$(4)$$

Similar to the analysis in (3) and according to the signaling diagrams in Figures 2–8, c_β^p can be written as:

$$c_\beta^p = \overrightarrow{b_{\beta,1}} \times \overrightarrow{x_p} \tag{5}$$

Here, $\overrightarrow{x_p}$ is a vector defined as:

$$\overrightarrow{x_p} = [c_p, c_v, c_{us}, c_g, c_{ts}, c_{rg}] \tag{6}$$

Where, all of the cost parameters are defined in Table 1. And $\overrightarrow{b_{\beta,1}}$ denotes the vectors determined by:

$$\overrightarrow{b_{1,1}} = \overrightarrow{b_{1,2}} = \overrightarrow{b_{1,2}} = [(3N_h + 2), 1, 2, 2, 1, 1]$$
$$\overrightarrow{b_{2,1}} = [(12N_c + 3N_h + 4N_b + 4N_x + 6), 5, 4, 2, 2, 3]$$
$$\overrightarrow{b_{2,2}} = [(6N_c + 3N_h + 2N_b + 2N_x + 4), 5, 4, 2, 2, 1]$$
$$\overrightarrow{b_{2,3}} = [(2N_c + 3N_h + 2N_b + 2N_x + 4), 5, 4, 2, 2, 1]$$

$$(7)$$

The coefficients in front of the cost variables in $\overrightarrow{x_p}$, such as c_p, c_v, and c_{ts}, denote the number of the costs we should consider during one authentication.

For example, in the case of $\beta = 2$ and $i = 3$, the authentication messages need to traverse $\overline{n} < \overline{\mu}$ hops as analyzed in (4). On this authentication path, no encryption/decryption exists on the hop between the user and the AP before the arrival of the authentication challenge from the AAA server. Thus, $1 + N_h$ hops should be reduced from the total number of hops that the authentication messages pass by when we consider the encryption/decryption cost on one hop, i.e., cp. Thus, the coefficient for cp is $2N_c + 3N_h + 2N_b + 2N_x + 4$. In this authentication process, the challenge/response values are verified twice at the user and the AAA server in the first authentication step. In the second authentication step, the PDG verifies the user using the MK key, the S-CSCF verifies the user using $IMSI_{HSS}$ and the user verifies the PDG using the MK key. Thus, the coefficient for c_v is 5. In this case, two pairs of encryption and decryption costs are needed between the user and the AAA server in the first authentication step and two in the second authentication step. Thus, the coefficient for c_{us} is 4. Since one time registration is needed at the HSS in this case, the coefficient for c_{rg} is 1. Since the AAA server and the user need to generate MK key, then the coefficient for cg is 2. Finally, an MSK key needs to be transmitted to AP and an MK key needs to be transmitted to the PDG. Thus, the coefficient of c_{ts} is 2. Similar to the case of $\beta = 2$ and $i = 3$, the coefficients of time parameters in other cases can be determined according to the corresponding time diagram in Figures 2–8.

To estimate the average number $\overline{K}$ of handoffs of the mobile user, we consider a theorem from (Fang, Chlamtac, & Lin, 1998). It says that assuming that the session time and the user's residence time in the serving area of an access point follow Gamma distribution, then the average number of handoffs by the mobile user can be obtained by:

$$\overline{K} = -n \sum\nolimits_{P \in \sigma} \operatorname{Re} s_{s=P} \frac{1 - f*(s)}{s^z [1 - (1 - P_f) f*(s)]} f_c*(-s)$$

(8)

Where $f*(s)$ is the Laplace transformation of the PDF of the residence time of the mobile user in the serving area of an access point, $f_c(-s)$ is the Laplace transformation of the PDF of the session time of the user, $\frac{1}{n}$ is the average residence time of the mobile user in the serving area of an access point, σ is the singular point of the function $f_c(-s)$, P_f is the probability that a handoff session is blocked, and $Res_{3=P}$: denotes the residue at a singular point s=p. Assume that the residence time of the mobile user in the serving area of an access point and the session time of the mobile user follow exponential distribution (which is a special case of Gamma distribution) with Laplace transformation $f*(s) = \dfrac{n}{s+n}$ and $f_c*(-s) = \dfrac{\mu}{-s+\mu}$ respectively. The only singular point of $f_c*(-s)$ is s=μ. Therefore, Equation 2 can be simplified to:

$$\overline{K} = -n \operatorname{Re} s_{s=\mu} \frac{1 - f*(s)}{s^z [1 - (1 - P_f) f*(s)]} f_c*(-s)$$

(9)

By substitute Laplace transformation:

$$\overline{K} = -n \lim_{s \to \mu} (s - \mu) \frac{1 - \dfrac{n}{s+n}}{s^z [1 - (1 - P_f) \dfrac{n}{s+n}]} \frac{\mu}{-s+\mu}$$

(10)

$$\overline{K} = n \lim_{s \to \mu} \frac{(1 - \dfrac{n}{s+n})\mu}{s^z [1 - (1 - P_f) \dfrac{n}{s+n}]} = \frac{n}{\mu + n P_f}$$

Or,

$$\overline{K} = \frac{\overline{\mu}}{\overline{n} + \overline{\mu} P_f}$$

(11)

Where, $\overline{n} = \dfrac{1}{n}$ is the mean residence time of the user in the serving area of an access point, and $\overline{\mu} = \dfrac{1}{\mu}$ is the mean session time.

Numerical Results

Using the authentication cost values of Table 2 (i.e., enhanced one-pass, one-pass and multi-pass AKA) and substitutes in Equations (2-7), the formula of the average number $\overline{K}$ of handoffs performed by the mobile user (see Equation 11),and we can calculate the total authentication cost $C(i)$ (see Equation 1) of the enhanced one-pass, one-pass and multi-pass AKA. The calculated cost can be depicted as a function of the user mean residence time, the mean session time or the number of access points that belong to the same IP subnet.

Figure 10, presents the total authentication cost T of the three procedures as a function of the user residence time. A general statement is that the enhanced one-pass AKA exhibits better performance in terms of authentication cost, compared

Table 2. Parameters for authentication cost

Symbol	value	Symbol	value
c_3	10	N_c	7
c_p	1	N_h	10
c_v	20	N_b	3
c_{us}	5	N_x	3
c_g	1	$\bar{\mu}$	15
c_{ts}	1	$\bar{n}$	10
		$\bar{b}$	3
c_{rg}	1		

to the one-pass AKA procedure. This is because it includes less security operations and messages that are exchanged between the involved nodes, compared to the one-pass AKA. For relative small values of the user residence time, the cost improvement) of the enhanced one-pass is greater. If the value of the mean residence time is lower from the value of the mean session time (i.e., c_{rg}), then the improvement of the enhanced one-pass over the multi-pass AKA is exponential. On the other hand, as the user residence time increases and approaches or exceeds the session time, the exponential improvement becomes constant, since the mobile user performs less than 10 handovers.

Figure 10. Authentication cost vs. user's residence time

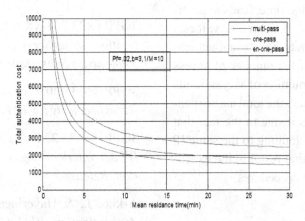

Figure 11. Authentication cost vs. session time

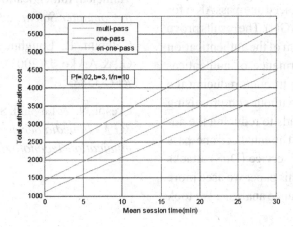

Figure 12. Authentication cost vs. number of access points in an IP subnet

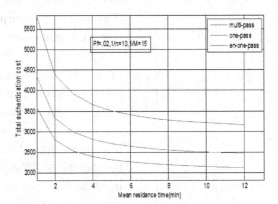

Figure 11 presents the total authentication cost T of the two procedures as a function of the mean session time of the user. In case that the mean session time is relatively short, the three authentication procedures present close cost values. Increasing the mean session time, leads to greater differences in the authentication cost values.

Finally, Figure 12 depicts the total authentication cost as a function of the number of access points in a subnet. As the number of access points in an IP domain is increased, the total authentication cost is reduced. This is due to the fact that the more access points belonging to the same IP subnet the less handoffs that result in the execution of the authentication procedures.

CONCLUSION

This paper presents an enhanced one-pass AKA for next generation network (NGN). The results prove that the merging mechanism of the authentication steps enhances the performance of authentication process. This is done through reducing the authentication messages without compromising the security level. This leads to reducing the authentication time and cost. The enhanced one-pass also reduces the denial of service (DoS) attacks on the NGN elements. In this paper we used more parameters in the performance analysis. We took

into consideration the number of hops that the message takes to reach its destination.

REFERENCES

3GPP TS 23.228 -v8.1.0. (2007). *Technical Specification Group Services and Systems Aspects; IP Multimedia Subsystem Stage 2, Release 8.*

3GPP TS 33.203 -v7.6.0. (2006). *3G security; Access security for IP based services, Release 7.*

3GPP TS 33.234-v7.2.0. (2006). *3G security; WLAN interworking security; System description, Release 7.*

Arkko, J., & Haverinen, H. (2006). *EAP-AKA Authentication, RFC 4187.* Asokan, N., Niemi, V., & Nyberg, K. (2005). Man-in-the-Middle in Tunneled Authentication Protocols. *Lecture Notes in Computer Science, 3364,* 28–41.

Calhoun, P., Loughney, J., Guttman, E., Zorn, G., & Arkko, J. (2003). *Diameter Base Protocol, RFC 3588.*

Crespi, N., & Lavaud, S. (2004). *WLAN Access to 3G Multimedia Services, Information and Communication Technologies.* Bangkok: ICT.

Fang, Y., Chlamtac, I., & Lin, Y.-B. (1998). Channel Occupancy Times and Handoff Rate for Mobile Computing and PCS Networks. *IEEE Transactions on Computers, 47*(6), 679–692.. doi:10.1109/12.689647

Kaufman, C. (2005). *The Internet Key Exchange (IKEv2) Protocol, RFC 4306.*

Kent, S., & Atkinson, R. (1998). *IP Encapsulating Security Payload (ESP), RFC 2406.*

Kent, S., & Atkinson, R. (1998). *Security Architecture for Internet Protocol, RFC 2401.*

Liang, W., & Wang, W. (2005). On Performance Analysis of Challenge/Response Based Authentication in Wireless Networks. *Computer Networks, 48*(2).

Lin, Y. B., Chang, M. F., Hsu, M. T., & Wu, L. Y. (2005). One-pass GPRS and IMS Authentication Procedure for UMTS. *IEEE Journal on Selected Areas in Communications, 23*(6), 1233–1239. doi:10.1109/JSAC.2005.845631

Ntantogian, C., & Xenakis, C. (2008). *One-pass EAP-AKA Authentication in 3G-WLAN Integrated Networks, Wireless Personal Communications.* New York: Springer.

Rosenberg, J., et al. (2002). *SIP: Session Initiation Protocol, RFC 3261.*

Veltri, L., Salsano, S., & Martiniello, G. (2006). Wireless LAN-3G Integration: Unified Mechanisms for Secure Authentication based on SIP. In *Proceedings of the IEEE International Conference on Communications (ICC)*, Istanbul, Turkey.

Xenakis, C., & Merakos, L. (2004). Security in third Generation Mobile Networks. *Computer Communications, 27*(7), 638–650. doi:10.1016/j.comcom.2003.12.004

This work was previously published in International Journal of Grid and High Performance Computing, Volume 2, Issue 2, edited by Emmanuel Udoh, pp. 37-52, copyright 2010 by IGI Publishing (an imprint of IGI Global).

Chapter 15
Adaptive Routing Strategy for Large Scale Rearrangeable Symmetric Networks

Amitabha Chakrabarty
Dublin City University, Ireland

Martin Collier
Dublin City University, Ireland

Sourav Mukhopadhyay
Dublin City University, Ireland

ABSTRACT

This paper proposes an adaptive unicast routing algorithm for large scale symmetric networks comprising 2×2 switch elements such as Beneš networks. This algorithm trades off the probability of blocking against algorithm execution time. Deterministic algorithms exploit the rearrangeability property of Beneš networks to ensure a zero blocking probability for unicast connections, at the expense of extensive computation. The authors' algorithm makes its routing decisions depending on the status of each switching element at every stage of the network, hence the name adaptive routing. This method provides a low complexity solution, but with much better blocking performance than random routing algorithms. This paper presents simulation results for various input loads, demonstrating the tradeoffs involved.

INTRODUCTION

High performance computing today requires a high performance communication system. This is typically an optical system in today's state of the art, although optical switches suffer from imperfections such as the crosstalk effect (Ho, 1999),

which worsens with increasing port capacity. The increasing bandwidth of state of the art computers means that, over time, increasing the throughput of interconnection networks by increasing port capacity will become problematic. Hence, the use of Multistage Interconnection Networks (MINs) (Wu & Feng, 1980) with a large number of port numbers, each of comparatively low transmission capacity will be design alternatives for high

DOI: 10.4018/978-1-4666-0056-0.ch015

throughput optical switches. MINs allow large switching networks to be constructed efficiently from smaller subnetworks. Such networks include the baseline (Wu & Feng, 1980), omega (Lawrie, 1975), data manipulator (Feng, 1974), flip (Batcher, 1976), and SW-Banyan($S = F = 2$) (Goke & Lipovski, 1973) networks. A major issue with such networks is their blocking properties - they cannot establish connecting paths for all input-output requests simultaneously. A solution to the blocking problem is to concatenate one such network with its reverse, for example: baseline+baseline−1 or omega+omega−1. This combination will give a symmetric structure among the link patterns in the network from center stage. The Beneˇs network is one such symmetric network commonly constructed with baseline+baseline−1. The Beneš network is one MIN that has $N = 2n$ inputs and outputs and comprises ($2logN − 1$) stages[1] of 2 × 2 switch elements. This network is a permutation network (Benes, 1965) because it can realize all $N!$ possible patterns of input-output requests. Benes (1965) and Beizer (1968), showed that the Beneš network is a rearrangeable network (Hwang, Lin

& Lioubimov, 2006; Yeh & Feng, 1968) from the family of *Clos* (Clos, 1953) type network. Figure 1 shows a 16 × 16 Beneš Network.

A. Related Work

The use of Beneš networks has been advocated in high performance computing (Beetem, Denneau, & Weingarten, 1985) areas such as in shared memory multiprocessor systems (Leighton, 1992), telecommunication networks, TDMA systems (Keshav, 1997). It has been used as a permutation network in the middle of the switch fabric for routing packets from input queues to output (Prabhakar & McKeown, 1999; Newman, 1988). Waksman (1968) proposed a recursive algorithm for setting the switching element state in the Beneš network for uni-processor system. Nassimi and Sahni (1981) and Nassimi and Sahni (1980) proposed a parallel self-routing method for a particular class of permutations. Nassimi and Sahni (1982) proposed a way to implement Waksman's (Waksman, 1968) approach in a parallel processing (Leighton, 1992) mode. The algorithm

Figure 1. 16 × 16 Beneš network

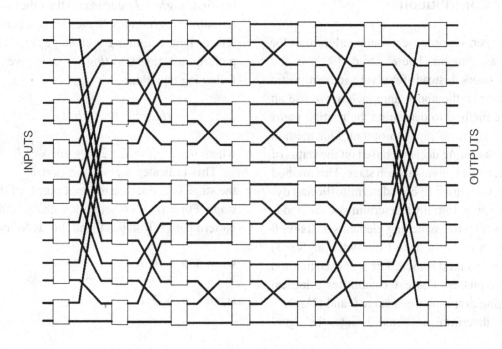

213

proposed by Opferman and Tsao-Wu (Opferman & Tsao-Wu, 1971), called the looping algorithm, works from the outer stage towards the center stage. It works by dividing the entire network into smaller networks and recursively setting paths in the smaller networks, there by setting the complete path. Later Andreson (1977) provided an extended version of the looping algorithm for base 2t networks. Lee (1985) and Lee (1985), proposed a non- recursive algorithm, wherein the network is divided into two parts: N S1 and N S2. This algorithm works on a single stage of the network from left to right. Kim, Yoon, and Maeng (1997) showed that the Inside-out routing method needs backtracking and even after backtracking is not fully blocking free. Another method was proposed by C̦am (Hasan & Jose, 1999), which used the concept of Balanced matrix (Linial & Tarsi, 1989) and 2-Colouring to generate the routing tags for the routing input-output requests. This method is efficient provided that the PRAM (Parallel Random Access Machine) computer architecture (Cypher, Sanz, & Snyder, 1989) is used to implement the method, which is not cost effective.

B. Our Contribution

In this paper, we propose a routing algorithm for unicast assignment (Lee & Oruc, 1995) in the Beneš network. Instead of applying a deterministic approach like the above approaches, we use an adaptive method to determine the routing paths dynamically from input to output. Our method makes the routing decision based on the status of the switching elements at each stage. This method uses a combination of both deterministic and dynamic routing. Initially a deterministic method is used to set up the switching elements at stages 0 and $(2logN - 2)$. For stage 1 through $(2logN - 3)$ a dynamic method is used. The proposed method has three phases: Phase 1 establishes a logical connecting graph between stage 0 and $(2logN - 2)$ and is deterministic. Phase 2 routes the signal

from stage 1 to $(logN - 2)$. (Stages $(logN - 1)$ to $(2logN - 3)$ use the standard bit-controlled routing of the reverse baseline network.) Phase 3 resolves any conflicts that can arise from the route selected from Phase 2. The algorithm for Beneš network can also work in other symmetric rearrangeable networks with minor modifications. We tested our simulator for various input loads and compare the results with random routing (Hui, 1990).

The rest of the paper is organized as follows. The notation and terminology used throughout the paper is presented. The three phases of the proposed method are described. Implementation and simulation results are presented. A time complexity analysis is also presented.

PRELIMINARIES

This section presents the notation used throughout the paper:

Definition 2.1: (Link Pattern, Ls). Link patterns are the interconnection patterns between columns of switching elements in the connecting networks. In the Beneš network, there are two different types of link patterns. One is used for the first $(logN - 1)$ stages and the other is for the remaining $logN$ stages. Stages are numbered from left to right, beginning with stage zero. The link pattern for stages 0 to $(logN - 2)$ is given by the following equation:

$$L_{0:(logN-2)} = (b_l \cdots _{bl-i+1} \, b_{0bl-i} \cdots b_1) \qquad (1)$$

where $0 \leq i \leq (logN - 2)$, $l = logN - 1$.

This indicates that output port $b_{logN-1} \cdots b_0$ of the stage is connected to input port L of the next stage. For a 16×16 network with $l = 3$, the link pattern between stages 0 and 2 is as follows:

stage 0: $b_0 \, b_3 \, b_2 \, b_1$

stage 1: $b_3 \, b_0 \, b_2 \, b_1$

stage 2 : $b_3\, b_2\, b_0\, b_1$

The link patterns for stages *(logN − 1)* to *(2logN − 3)* are given by the following equation:

$$L_{(logN-1):(2logN-3)} = (b_r..b_{l-1}...b_{i+2}\, b_i\, b_{i-1}...b_0\, b_{i+1}) \quad (2)$$

where $0 \le i \le (logN - 1)$, $l = logN - 1$.

The link pattern for the remaining stages of the above *16 × 16* network can thus be given by:

stage 3: $b_3\, b_2\, b_0\, b_1$

stage 4 : $b_3\, b_1\, b_0\, b_2$

stage 5: $b_2\, b_1\, b_0\, b_3$

Definition 2.2: (Input Permutation, *P*). Input permutations are the set of one to one requests between inputs and outputs. In more mathematical term, a mapping of an input to an output is an element in the input permutation. Let us assume that $P0:(N-1)$ is a given permutation such as, $P0:(N-1) = xi \in \{0...(N-1)\}$ *and* $xi = xj\ where 0 \le (i,j) \le (N-1)$. The mapping $P_i \rightarrow x_i$ indicates that input port i is requesting output port x_i. In more general form for an 8 × 8 network a permutation $P_{0:7}$ can be given as (0 7 3 2 4 1 5 6), which indicates the mapping is 0 → 0, 1 → 7 and so on. A binary permutation for an 8 × 8 network can be given by the following permutation matrix, where each row number corresponds to an input port and the sequence of bits corresponds to the requested output ports.

Definition 2.3: (Switching Element, SE). Variable SE is an array that identifies a switching element in the switch. A switching element at position [i, j], $0 \le i \le (N/2) - 1$ and $0 \le j \le (2logN - 2)$, can be identified by the variable SE[i, j], where i is the stage number, and j is its position within the stage.

Definition 2.4: (PORT). The two ports of a switching elements can be distinguished using the PORT variable. For PORT = 0, the requested port number is the even-numbered or upper port and PORT = 1 the requested port is the odd-numbered or lower port.

Definition 2.5: (Subnetwork). The Subnetwork variable is used to identify the subnetwork the input to a switching element is coming from. If *Subnetwork = 0*, it means the signal is coming from the upper subnetwork and for *Subnetwork =* 1 the signal emerges from the lower subnetwork.

Definition 2.6: (STATE). STATE is an array that holds the state of all the switching elements in the switch. In this paper we have considered three different states for switching elements. The entry $STATE[i, j]$, where $0 \le i \le (N/2) - 1$, and $0 \le j \le (2logN - 2)$, identifies the state of the switching element at position $[i, j]$ in the switching network. To differentiate between possible states of switching elements, we used three different assignments. The first is $STATE[i, j] = NULL$, which means the switch is free to set (i.e., its state is unassigned). If $STATE[i, j] = 0$ the switch is set to perform straight through switching and $STATE[i, j] = 1$ the switch will perform cross switching.

Definition 2.7: (Connecting Graph, G). A graph is said to be connected if a path exists between any two vertices x and y, where $x, y \in G(V)$. If the starting vertex x where $x \in V$ becomes the end vertex in a sub-graph *g (v)* where *g (v)* $\in G(V)$ then it is termed as a cycle in the graph *G(V)*. Where a graph has N edges with v connected vertices, $v \in V$ there can be at most N/2 cycles in G. Figure 2 shows a connecting graph *G*.

Definition 2.8: (Forward Routing, *Ir*). Forward routing is the establishment of a routing path from input i, $0 \le i \le N - 1$, to the output port *P (i)*, where *P is* the input permutation. Figure 2(b) shows routing from i to output *P (i)*, $0 \le i \le N - 1$, without considering middle stages of the switch. We use $i \rightarrow P(i)$ to indicate forward routing.

Definition 2.9: (Reverse Routing, Or). Establishment of paths from the remaining port of *P (i)* (if any) to *j*, $0 \le j \le (N - 1)$, is termed Reverse routing *Or*. Figure 2(c) shows routing from re-

Figure 2. Connecting graph and forward/reverse routing

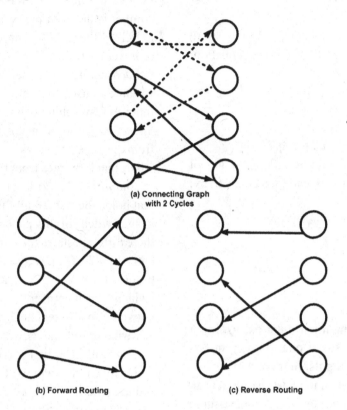

(a) Connecting Graph with 2 Cycles

(b) Forward Routing

(c) Reverse Routing

maining port *SE (P (i))* to *j*, $0 \leq j \leq N-1$ without considering middle stages of the switch. We use $i \leftarrow P(i)$ to indicate reverse routing.

ROUTING METHOD FOR BENEŠ NETWORK

In this section we describe our algorithm in three phases.

A. Phase 1

Input: Input Permutation $P0:(N-1)$.

Output: Set the switching element at stage 0 and $(2logN - 2)$.

- Start with the first switching element, *SE* $[k, 0]$, $0 \leq k \leq (N/2) - 1$, not set yet, set the switching element to *STATE* $[k, 0] = 0$. Set the *STATE of* the output switch-

ing element *SE (P (i))*, $0 \leq i \leq (N - 1)$, to 0 or 1 depending on the requested output. For the request, if *Subnetwork* = 0 and requested *Port* = 0, set *STATE*[*r*, $(2logN - 2)$] = 0, $0 \leq r \leq (N/2) - 1$ else set to 1.

- Check if any port remains at *SE (P (i))*, after *Step 1*. If yes then go to *Step 3*. Else go to *Step 4*.

- Start with the remaining port of *SE (P (i))*, $0 \leq i \leq (N - 1)$. Check the state of the corresponding switching element at stage 0. If *STATE*[*k*, 0] = *NULL*, $0 \leq k \leq (N/2) - 1$, set the switching element to either 0 or 1 depending whether the connection is coming from upper or lower subnetwork and the requested port is even or odd.

- If any port remains at the input switching element after *Step 3*, then setup paths between that port *i* and corresponding output port *P* (*i*). Set the state of the output switching element if its state was *NULL*.

- Continue *Step 2* to *Step 4* till all the connections forms a logical connected graph with at maximum *N*/2 complete cycles. This connecting graph will indicate that all the switching elements in stage 0 and stage (2*logN* − 2) are set.

a)   **Example:** Let *N* = 8 and a random permutation *P* (0:7) = (0 6 4 5 2 1 3 7). From the permutation the mapping between *Input-Output* are like this 0 → 0, 5 ← 1, 6 → 3, and so on. Initially set *STATE* [0, 0] = 0, which means the signal from input port 0 goes through the upper sub-network. Since *Subnetwork* = 0 and requested port is even so *PORT* = 0, then *STATE* [0, 4] will be 0. Because *STATE* [0, 4] = 0, from output port 1 the signal goes through lower subnetwork. The values for *Subnetwork* = 1 and *Port* = 1, so *STATE* [2, 0] would be set to 0. This process continues for all the ports of the switching elements at stage 0 and 4. After setting up the final switching element the number of chains in the logical connecting graph is 2. Figure 3(a) shows the SE settings in step 0 and (*logN* − 2) after *Phase 1*.

B.   Phase 2

Input: Input Permutation *P*0:(*N* −1).

Output: Set the state of the switching elements from stage 1 to (2*logN* − 3).

- Set stage number, *k* = 1.
- Determine the row number *r* of the first available switching element *SE*[*r, k*] from Equations 1 and 2.

- If *SE*[*r, k*] = *N U LL*, set *SE*[*r, k*] = 0 else use the unused port and go to next stage. Increment *k* by one.

- If *s* < (*logN* − 1), find *r* at stage *S and* go to Step 3, else go to step 5.

- Use first (*logN* − 2) MSB bits of the binary output to go to stage (2*logN* − 3).

- Any blocking at step 5, call Phase 3 else go to step 7.

- If any port available at the SE last used in Step 5, used that port for reverse routing using the similar steps mentioned in Steps (1 − 6) in reverse direction. Else, go to Step 1.

C.   Phase 3

Input: Blocking between stages (*logN* − 2) and (2*logN* − 3).

Output: Alternative blocking free paths.

- For forward routing follow *Step2*, else follow *Step 3*

- Blocking at stage *k*, (*logN* − 1) ≤ *k* ≤ (2*logN* − 3), go back to switching element *SE* [*i, j*] at stage *j* using link pattern *L*$_j$, 0 ≤ *i* ≤ (*N*/2) − 1 and 1 ≤ *j* ≤ (*logN* − 2) and choose the alternative port of that switching element. If alternative port is not free, go back to next step and choose the alternative port of the switching element at that stage and continue routing. If no alternative path is available go to. Step 4.

- Blocking at stage *k*, 1 ≤ *k* ≤ *logN*, go back to switching element *SE*[*i, j*] at stage *j* using link pattern *Lj* , (*logN* − 1) ≤ *i* ≤ (2*logN* − 3) and *logN* ≤ *j* ≤ (2*logN* − 3) and choose the alternative port of that switching element. If alternative port is not free, go back to next step and choose the alternative port of the switching element at that stage and continue routing. If no alternative path is available go to. Step 4: In case where it is not possible to find any available path for the request, drop the request and start with any other available request at stage 1.

b) **Example:** Continuing with the permutation $P(0:7) = (0\ 6\ 4\ 5\ 2\ 1\ 3\ 7)$, we apply *Phase 2* and *Phase 3* on the remaining stages of the switching element after applying *Phase 1*. Using *Phase 1*, we have the stage 0 and 4 set for the switch. Now we need to set the switch for stages 1, 2 and 3. Since $N = 8$, in total we have five routing bits for each request. So for a request $1 \leftarrow 5$, the routing bits would be ($101x1$), for $4 \rightarrow 2$, the routing bits would be ($0x010$), and so on. We need to fix the bit x by applying algorithm 2 and 3. When we apply *Phase 2* for routing $4 \rightarrow 2$, we set the x bit to 0 and we have a conflict at stage 2 indicated by the circle in Figure 3(b). In that case following *Phase 3* the conflict has been resolved by going back one stage and set the value $x = 1$.

IMPLEMENTATION AND SIMULATION RESULTS

This section describes the implementation details and also the detail of the simulation results.

A. Implementation

This section describes the switching elements setting that have been used to implement the methods described in Section III. Three different algorithms implement the three phases mentioned in III. Variable k signifies the stages of the network with at limit $0 \leq k \leq (2logN - 2)$ and r is for rows with a limit $0 \leq r \leq (N/2 - 1)$.

Algorithm 1: Forward/Reverse Routing

```
1:   if SE[r, k] = NULL then
2:   SE[r, k] ← 0
3:   k + +
4:   r ← r*
5:   end if
6:   if k = (logN - 2) then
7:   Call Bit Controlled Routing.
8:   end if
```

As mentioned above, in Algorithm 1 variables k and r identify a stage and corresponding row respectively. Variable SE[r, k] in 1 stores the status of each switching elements (SE) in the switch.

Figure 3. (a) SE Settings in stage 0 and (2logN - 2) for Permutation P (0:7) = (0 6 4 5 2 1 3 7). (b) Switch settings for Permutation P(0:7) = (0 6 4 5 2 1 3 7) with conflict resolution

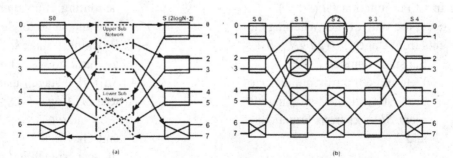

Switching elements with a NULL status is set to a 0 state which means that the switching element will perform straight through switching. In line 4, r^* is the value of the row number for target switching element at stage k. Line 6 checks the stage number with the starting stage of the bit control part of the network.

Algorithm 2 works on the bit controlled part of the network. In line 1, variable B stores the binary equivalent of the requested output and C is a counter in line 2 that keeps track of the network stages. PATH variable in line 3 looks at the binary digits at each stage and route the signal according to that digit. Line 3 checks for any conflicts and in case of a conflict call the conflict resolution part of the proposed method.

Algorithm 2: Bit Controlled Routing.

```
1:   B [logN - 1] ← Binary (Output)
2:   C ← (logN - 1)
3:   P AT H ← B[C ]
4:   if any conflict then
5:   Call Conflict Resolution
6:   end if
7:   C- -
```

Line 3 identifies the switching element for the current input at stage s in Algorithm 3. If any output port available at that switching element signal is routed through that port. Else go back to the next stage and search an available port. In case of a failure to find an alternative route, line 7 indicates a drop request.

Algorithm 3: Conflict Resolution.

```
1:   C ← (logN - 2)
2:   s ← C
3:   if SE [r*, s] = F ULL then
4:     Select Alternative Port.
5:   else C- -
6:     if C < 1 then
7:     Exit
```

```
8:     else Goto line 2
9:     end if
10:   end if
```

B. Simulation Results

The blocking performance of this method is compared to random routing (Hui, 1990) below for various size of Beneš networks. Random routing is a method that establishes paths randomly in the first half of the network, using bit controlled routing from the centre stage onwards. Figure 4 compares the proposed method and random routing for a fully loaded switch. It shows that for very small networks for example (8×8) the proposed method can provide negligible blocking compared to the almost 30% blocking with random routing. As network size increases, the graph shows a gradual increase in the blocking probability, but much lower blocking rates than random routing. Figure 5 and 6 shows the results of applying a partial load to the network using both the algorithms. For a 50% load the proposed method shows a blocking probability that can be as low as 3% for medium size networks. For a 75% load the blocking rate is below 20% even for a large switch size. Our results show that the blocking rate is greatly reduced compared to random routing, at the cost of an increased execution time. The time complexity of our algorithm will now be assessed.

TIME ANALYSIS

In general, Algorithms 1 and 2 take $O(1)$ time to set up each switching element, which means to set up all the switching elements these two algorithms require $(N logN)$ time. But for Algorithm 2, the set up time will entirely depend on the number of calls to Algorithm 3. The time needed for Algorithm 3 to find alternative paths varies depending on the amount of backtracking in the distributed part. So if C is a variable that records the number of

Figure 4. Blocking graphs for two methods

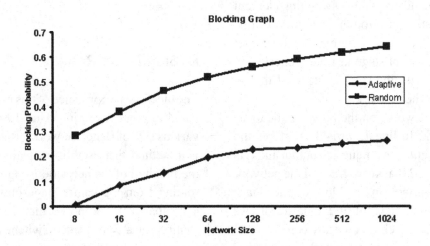

Figure 5. 75% load graph for two methods

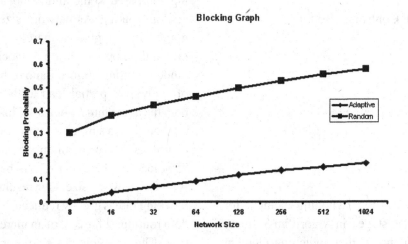

Figure 6. Half load graph for two methods

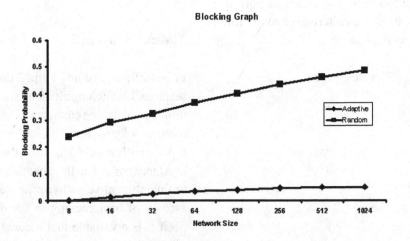

backtracking events, which clearly depend on N, the time complexity can be expressed in the form of $O((N \log N)C)$. A full determination of the time complexity of the algorithm requires that $E[C]$ be determined, which is currently being investigated by the authors.

CONCLUSION

In this paper a new routing algorithm has been proposed that can be used for unicast routing assignments in symmetric rearrangeable networks. This method provides an adaptive method rather than a fully deterministic approach. The proposed method is not fully blocking free, but its execution speed makes it viable in applications where the cost in time of determining a blocking-free set of paths through the network is excessive. Its blocking performance has been compared by simulation with the random routing method, and has been shown to give considerably better performance at the cost of a moderate increase in execution time, due to the necessity to backtrack. The authors are currently working on a model of this backtracking process, from which they hope to obtain upper bounds on the blocking rate and execution time of the algorithm. Such bounds will allow multistage networks to be used in scenarios where a low but non-zero blocking rate is acceptable.

REFERENCES

Andresen, S. (1977). The looping algorithm extended to base 2t rearrangeable switching networks. *IEEE Transactions on Communications*, *25*(10), 1057–1063. doi:10.1109/TCOM.1977.1093753

Batcher, K. E. (1976). The flip network in STARAN. In *Proceedings of the International Conference on Parallel Processing* (pp. 65-71)

Beetem, J., Denneau, M., & Weingarten, D. (1985). The GF11 supercomputer. In *Proceedings of the 12th annual international symposium on Computer architecture (ISCA '85)*.

Beizer, B. (1968). The Analysis and Synthesis of Signal Switching Network. In *Proceedings of the Symposium on Mathematical Theory of Automata*, NY (pp. 563-576)

Benes, E. (1965). *Mathematical Theory of Connecting Networks and Telephone Traffic*. New York: Academic Press.

Clos, C. (1953). A Study of Non-Blocking Switching Networks. *The Bell System Technical Journal*, *32*, 406–424.

Cypher, R., Sanz, J. L. C., & Snyder, L. (1989). An EREW PRAM Algorithm for Image Component Labeling. *IEEE Transactions on Pattern Analysis and Machine Intelligence*, *11*(3). doi:10.1109/34.21794

Feng, T.-Y. (1974). Data Manipulating Functions in Parallel Processors and Their Implementations. *IEEE Transactions on Computers*, *23*(3), 309–318. doi:10.1109/T-C.1974.223927

Goke, L. R., & Lipovski, G. J. (1973). Banyan networks for partitioning multiprocessor systems. *SIGARCH Computer Architecture News*, *2*(4), 21–28. doi:10.1145/633642.803967

Hasan, C., , & Jose, A. B. (1999). Fortes Work-Efficient Routing Algorithms for Rearrangeable Symmetrical Networks. *IEEE Transactions on Parallel and Distributed Systems*, *10*(7).

Ho, K.-P. (1999). Analysis of homodyne crosstalk in optical networks using Gram-Charlier series. *Journal of Lightwave Technology*, *17*(2), 149–154. doi:10.1109/50.744213

Hui, J. Y. (1990). *Switching and Traffic Theory for Integrated Broadband Networks*. Norwell, MA: Kluwer Academic Press.

Hwang, F. K., Lin, W-D., & Lioubimov, V. (2006). On Noninterruptive Rearrangeable Networks. *IEEE/ACM Transaction on Networking, 14*(5).

Keshav, S. (1997). *An Engineering Approach to Compter Networking*. Reading, MA: Addison-Wesley.

Kim, M. K., Yoon, H., & Maeng, S. R. (1997). On the Correctness of Inside-Out Routing Algorithm. *IEEE Transactions on Computers, 46*(7), 820–823. doi:10.1109/12.599903

Lawrie, D. H. (1975). Access and Alignment of Data in an Array Processor. *IEEE Transactions on Computers, 24*(12), 1145–1155. doi:10.1109/T-C.1975.224157

Lee, C.-Y., & Oruc, A. Y. (1995). A Fast Parallel Algorithm for Routing Unicast Assignments in Bend Networks. *IEEE Transactions on Parallel and Distributed Systems, 6*(3).

Lee, K. Y. (1981). A new Benes network control algorithm and Parallel Permutation Algorithm. *IEEE Transactions on Computers, C-30*(5), 157–161.

Lee, K. Y. (1985). On the rearrangeabllity of 2(log2 N − 1) stage permutation networks. *IEEE Transactions on Computers, C-34*(5), 412–425.

Leighton, F. T. (1992). *Introduction to Parallel Algorithms and Architectures: Arrays, Trees, Hypercubes*. San Mateo, CA: Morgan Kaufmann.

Linial, & Tarsi, M. (1989). Interpolation between Bases and the Shuffle-Exchange Network. *European Journal on Combinatorics, 10*, 29-39.

Nassimi, D., & Sahni, S. (1980). A self-routing Benes network. In *Proceedings of the 7th annual symposium on Computer Architecture* (pp. 190-195).

Nassimi, D., & Sahni, S. (1981). A self-routing Benes network and Parallel Permutation Algorithm. *IEEE Transactions on Computers, C-30*(5), 332–340. doi:10.1109/TC.1981.1675791

Nassimi, D., & Sahni, S. (1982). Parallel Algorithms to Set Up the Benes Permutation Network. *IEEE Transactions on Computers, C-31*(2). doi:10.1109/TC.1982.1675960

Newman, P. (1988). A fast packet switch for the integrated services backbone network. *IEEE Journal of Selected Areas in Communication, SAC-6*(9).

Opferman, D. C., & Tsao-Wu, N. T. (1971). On a Class of Rearrangeable Switching Networks, Part I: Control Algorithm. *The Bell System Technical Journal, 50*, 1579–1600.

Prabhakar, B., & McKeown, N. (1999). On the Speedup Required for Combined Input and Output Queued Switching. *Automatica, 35*(12), 1909–1920. doi:10.1016/S0005-1098(99)00129-6

Waksman, A. (1968). A permutation network. *Journal of the ACM, 15*(1), 159–163. doi:10.1145/321439.321449

Wu, C.-L., & Feng, T.-Y. (1980). On a Class of Multistage Interconnection Networks. *IEEE Transactions on Computers, C-29*(8), 694–702. doi:10.1109/TC.1980.1675651

Yeh, Y.-M., & Feng, T.-Y. (1968). On a Class of Rearrangeable Networks. *IEEE Transactions on Computers, 41*(11).

ENDNOTE

[1]   all *log* in this paper are *Base* − 2

This work was previously published in International Journal of Grid and High Performance Computing, Volume 2, Issue 2, edited by Emmanuel Udoh, pp. 53-63, copyright 2010 by IGI Publishing (an imprint of IGI Global).

Chapter 16
Road Traffic Parameters Estimation by Dynamic Scene Analysis:
A Systematic Review

H. S. Mohana
Malnad College of Engineering, India

M. Ashwathakumar
M. S. Ramaiah Institute of Technology, India

ABSTRACT

Traffic congestion and violation of traffic rules are very common in most of the road transport system. Continuous monitoring is becoming difficult. To improve the quality of road transport monitoring and control, the best possible alternative is machine vision. In this review, several works by researchers on traffic analysis are detailed, studied and reviewed critically for the purpose. Further, an attempt is made to classify the different road traffic analysis approaches available in the literature. Classification is based on principle used, algorithm adopted, techniques used, technology behind and other special considerations of the researchers.

INTRODUCTION

Vehicle traffic over the transportation infrastructure affects almost every factor of our life and has a primary impact on the economy. As vehicle traffic continues to grow exponentially while the resources to increase the road capacity are limited. The only answer to keep up with the ever increasing traffic is better management of traffic and available infrastructure. This in turn, depends on the availability of better traffic data i.e. timely information on almost every vehicle traveling on the transportation network.

DOI: 10.4018/978-1-4666-0056-0.ch016

Traffic analysis plays a significant role in the present day scenario. Traffic congestion and violation of traffic rules are very common nowadays in most of the road transport system. Continuous monitoring of the same for 24 hours a day and round the year is becoming difficult. The monotonic nature of the work leads to negligence. This certainly causes damage in terms of human life, property and man hours loss. Every minute, on an average, at least one person dies in a vehicle crash. Auto accidents also injure at least 10 million people each year out of that 2.5 million seriously injured and become disabled. The total damage adds up to 2-3% of worlds gross domestic product and this figure is ever increasing as highlighted in (John, 2002).

The above statement certainly needs the attention of the research community. To improve the quality of road transport monitoring and control, the best possible alternative is machine vision. This apart from traffic analysis helps in locating rules violators and tracking them. In the implementation of machine vision, dynamic scene analysis will play a significant role. It carries time and space information together. Mounted optical CCD camera inputs the continuous video information of the road. Dynamic scene analysis provides change taking place in these video frames. Now, the role of optical flow computation comes in to picture significantly. Optical flow computation will provide velocity of the every changing pixel in the scene. Hence the velocity of the moving objects in the seen. The needle diagram representation will further enhance the information content of the optical flow computation. Several technical papers from the reputed national and international journal have been studied and reviewed critically in order to establish the infusion of the technique in to the real field application. It is found that the time factor plays an important role in deciding which algorithm or method is better suited for the purpose. Real time analysis is the requirement and is the order of the day. It supports instantaneous action. Conventional optical flow computation is

iterative in nature and hence delay the response or action time. It is justifiable that with certain modification optical flow computation is best suited for the purpose.

After reviewing several connected literature, the detailed work is presented to the readers under the following sections. In section 2 the term traffic flow in defined and described as per the requirement of the present topic. It suggests the short term and long term pattern and connected buzzwords. Optical flow analysis plays a very important role in the dynamic analysis. This provides a good mathematical base for the analysis. Hence, in section 3 optical flow and related topics has been addressed in detail for the benefit of the readers. An effort is made to study different literature on traffic analysis and classify the same based on several guiding principles. Section 4 presents the same. Section 5 highlights the challenges and recent trends in the road traffic analysis. In section 6 critical reviews of more than 50 papers has been highlighted. Final section is mainly to conclude the overall work with useful suggestions which benefits research community.

TRAFFIC FLOW

Traffic flow / Traffic flux is a generic term used to describe vehicle movement and volume over a transportation network. Two important parameters of traffic flow are average annual daily traffic (AADT) and Vehicle miles traveled.

These are long term flow patterns. Short term pattern includes daily or hourly parameters broken down to vehicle categories are also of high interest. This data can be acquired only with limited spatial extent with traditional techniques. The use of airborne / satellite imagery, however offers an excellent temporal and spatial resolution that can easily provide for sizable area of sight coverage at fast sampling rates. This definitely makes the whole system uneconomical and complex because of satellites and allied infrastructure. Answer to this data acquisition with digital cameras and analysis through the computer/machine vision technique/algorithms.

Further, when we reduce the traffic analysis to minutes and seconds to a limited area resulting in a term "traffic flux". It conveys the traffic density in a particular location at the limited packet of time. A typical traffic flux plot is as shown in Figure 1.

Further, the following challenges are to be addressed in road traffic analysis:

- Moderately occluded cluster.
- Close vehicle cluster.
- Low resolution distributed vehicle cluster.
- Distant queue of irregular sizes.
- Large vehicle cluster.
- Rainy situation.
- Snowfall and fog
- Poor illumination during evening and dark cloud illumination.
- Night traffic analysis with headlights on.

Apart from the above mentioned challenges added dimension of the challenge is computational

time. It will be serious constraint because of real time nature of analysis. Further, the complexity level increase when above said problems appears simultaneously.

Optical Flow Analysis

An object moving in a 3-D space has a three dimensional velocity vector field $w(x,y,z)$. This 3-D motion field is projected onto the retina of the observer as the 2-D motion field $w_p(x,y)$. Unfortunately, this 2-D motion field may not be perceived directly since it is purely geometrical concept. All that may be detected is some local measure of incident light at each point. In a typical machine vision system, two images taken by the camera are separated by a discrete time interval dt. What may be observed at each point is the change in a point's intensity value during dt. The optical flow is a vector field describing this intensity change by indicating the motion of features from one image to the other. By accurately computing this 2-D vector field, it is in principle, possible to calculate three-dimensional properties of the

Figure 1. Plot of traffic flux V/S frame number

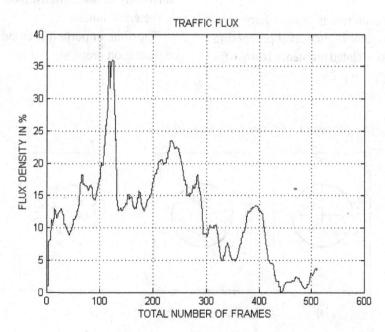

environment and quantities such as time to contact with an observed object. Biological organisms make use of optical flow, such as the detection of discontinuities.

The immediate aim of optical flow-based image analysis is to determine a motion field. It assigns a vector to every moving pixel to track its direction and velocity. Optical flow reflects the image changes due to motion during a time interval dt and the optical flow field is the velocity field that represents the three-dimensional motion of object points across a two dimensional image. Optical flow is an abstraction, typical of the kind that computational methods are trying to achieve. Therefore, it should represent only those motion related intensity changes in the image that are required in further processing and all other image changes reflected in the optical flow should be considered errors of flow detection. For example, optical flow should not be sensitive to illumination changes and motion of unimportant objects (e.g., shadows). An example of two consecutive images and a corresponding optical flow image are shown in Figure 2.

Optical Flow Computation Technique

Optical flow computation is a necessary precondition of subsequent higher-level processing that can solve motion-related problems. It provides tools to determine parameters of motion, relative distances of objects in the image, etc.

1.   The observed brightness of any object point is constant over time.

The nearby points in the image plane move in a similar manner.

$$\frac{\partial E}{\partial x}\frac{dx}{dt} + \frac{\partial E}{\partial y}\frac{dy}{dt} + \frac{\partial E}{\partial t} = 0$$

which is the expansion of the total derivative:

$$\frac{dE}{dt} = 0$$

Many techniques for optical flow exist. Although these techniques can perform very well for certain sequences of images, there are a very few that are currently able to support real time performance. Authors rarely report the computational time required for their algorithms; when they do, it is on the order of many minutes per frame, or they require special hardware. Techniques, which can run in real time, often impose strict restrictions on the environment.

The four important methods of optical flow computation are:

Figure 2. Optical flow: (a) time t_1 (b) time t_2 (c) optical flow

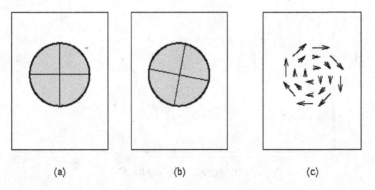

(a)   (b)   (c)

1. Differential methods (gradient based methods).
2. Matching methods (correlation based methods).
3. Phase based methods.
4. Energy based methods.

Out of these four methods the first two are very frequently used in dynamic scene analysis and hence presented in detail.

Differential Methods

Differential techniques, compute velocity from spatio-temporal derivatives of image intensity. The differential technique developed by Horn and Schunk(Horn & Schunk, 1981) has been the most widely used algorithm for the optical flow computation.

Suppose we have a continuous image where E(x,y,t) refers to the gray-level of (x,y) at time t.

Representing the dynamic image as a function of position and time permits it to be expressed as a Taylor series:

$$E(x + u\delta t, y + v\delta t, t + \delta t) = E(x, y, t) + E_x \delta x + E_y \delta y + E_t \delta t + O(\partial^2) \qquad (1)$$

Where E_x, E_y, E_t denote the partial derivatives of E. u(x,y) and v(x,y) are the components of optical flow. We can assume that the immediate neighborhood of (x,y) is translated some small distance (δx, δy) during the interval δt; that is, we can find δx, δy, δt such that:

$$E(x + u\delta t, y + v\delta t, t + \delta t) = E(x, y, t) \qquad (2)$$

The above equation is also known as brightness conservation equation.

If δx, δy, δt are very small, the higher order terms in the equation vanish.

Dividing by δt and taking the limit $\delta t \rightarrow 0$,

This gives the expansion of the total derivative.

Therefore, the brightness constraint equation is given by,

$$E_x u + E_y v + E_t = 0 \qquad (3)$$

Assuming the global smoothness of the brightness changes in the images, one can model the motion field applying the higher order derivatives of the data conservation equation. Iterative solutions of these two or more equations or certain regression methods applied on the relevant set of equations yield the components of the velocity vector field.

Matching Methods

In the matching techniques, the consecutive image points (pixels) of sequential frames with similar features are paired to get a displacement measure. The similarity of the intensity values of the consecutive pixels and their location are mostly chosen

Figure 3. (a) Frame at time t (b) Frame at time t+δt

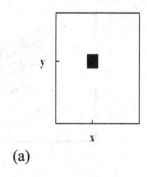
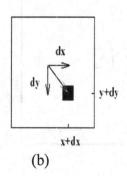

(a)   (b)

to be a matching criterion. If the time lag between the image frames is known, the relative velocity of the objects and the camera can be estimated. Finding the best match between the corresponding pixels in the image sequences amounts to the problem of minimizing a difference measure such as a cross-correlation of the image intensity functions of successive image frames. Correlating pixels of one image with all the pixels of the next image introduce a high computational load. Hierarchical methods match the image regions in different resolution prisms and warp the computed velocity in a coarse-to-fine manner.

Let us assume that the maximum displacement for any pixel is limited to k (pixels) in any direction as shown in Figure 4. The actual value of k depends on the expected velocities of the pixels in the image plane.

Since we are generally concerned with the flow of rigid-bodied objects, it is usually the case that any given pixel has the same velocity as those of its neighbors. We assume that these pixels are in a square neighborhood, or window of size w centered on the given pixel. That is, it is assumed that the motion vectors for the pixels adjacent to a given pixel will be similar, as shown in Figure 5.

The motion for the pixel at (x, y) is defined to be the determined motion of the patch of w*w pixels centered at (x, y), out of (2k+1)*(2k+1) possible displacements. We determine the correct motion of the patch of pixels by simulating the motion of the patch for each possible displacement of (x, y) and considering a match strength for each displacement.

Figure 4 (a). The search space for pixel A for k=2.(b). The correct motion from image 1 to image 2 is represented by vector AB.

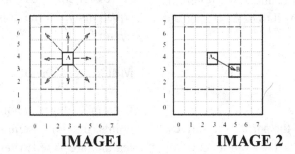

IMAGE1　　　　**IMAGE 2**

Figure 5. Optical flow for pixels adjacent to a given pixel is assumed constant due to the rigid body assumption

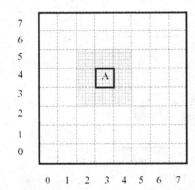 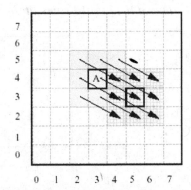

Energy-Based Methods

A third class of optical flow technique is based on the output energy of velocity-tuned filters. These are also called frequency-based methods owing to the design of velocity-tuned filters in the Fourier domain. The Fourier transform of a translating 2-d pattern for the equation: $I(\mathbf{x}, t) = I(\mathbf{x} - \mathbf{v}t, 0)$ where $\mathbf{v} = (u, v)^T$ will be given by the following transform expression:

$$\hat{I}(\mathbf{k}, \omega) = \hat{I}0_{(}k) \, \delta \, (\omega + v\mathbf{T}^k), \qquad (3.3)$$

where $\hat{I}_0(\mathbf{k})$ is the Fourier transform of $I(\mathbf{x}, 0)$, δ (k) is a Dirac delta function, ω denotes temporal frequency and $\mathbf{k} = (k_x, k_y)$ denote spatial frequency. This shows that all nonzero power associated with a translating 2-d pattern lies on a plane through the origin in frequency space. In Adelson and Bergen (1985), it has been shown that the some of the energy based methods are equivalent to correlation based methods. Results are also comparable with the gradient-based approach used by several authors including of Lucas and Kanade. There are several published papers available in this area which results in less average error in velocity computation, minimum angular error and poor density display. This transform approach increase the computation time and thus poses limitation in the real time analysis.

Phase-Based Techniques

This is the fourth method optical floe estimation. This method expresses velocity in terms of the phase behavior of band-pass filter outputs. Out of the several techniques available zero crossings can be viewed as level phase-crossings (Waxman, Wu, & Bergholm, 1988). The generalized use of phase information I optical flow computation was first developed by Fleet and Jepson (Fleet & Jepson, 1990).

The method developed by Fleet and Jepson defines component velocity in terms of the instan-taneous motion normal to level phase contours in the output of band- pass velocity-tuned filters. Band-pass filters are used to decompose the input signal according to scale, speed and orientation. Each filter output is complex valued and may be written as:

$$\mathbf{R}(\mathbf{x}, t) = \rho \, (\mathbf{x}, t) \exp[i \, \phi \, (\mathbf{x}, t)], \qquad (3.4)$$

where $\rho \, (\mathbf{x}, t)$ and $\phi \, (\mathbf{x}, t)$ are the amplitude and phase parts of **R**.

Classification

Now a day's large number of published literatures is available either in printed form or in the electronic form. Therefore it is difficult to read and comprehend the work carried out under different perception of the topic by different authors. Also, it is true that no two persons can think exactly same from understanding to implementation of any engineering/research problem. Therefore, an attempt is made to classify the different road traffic analysis approaches available in the literature. Classification is based principle used, algorithm adopted, techniques used, technology behind and other special considerations of the researchers. Out of large number of papers available based on the context of the present work more than fifty papers have been studied and classified.

Traditional Imbedded System v/s Hanging Type Systems

Generally, the traffic flow monitoring system can be divided into two types. One is the traditional imbedded system with voltage return circuit. This system is reliable, but the cost of system setting is relatively high. In addition, it needs to excavate the road surface while setting and maintaining. Therefore, the system is time consuming and strenuous and hence will usually influence the traffic. Another is the hanging type system rising in recent years, such as camera, radar, lasers and infrared ray sensor. Out of them, the camera-based system is the most popular and frequently used. It is because of low installation cost, takes less time for installation and easy to maintain than other methods. The camera-based system involving computer vision technologies has the following advantages.

- It can provide the high-quality pictures and achieve traffic monitoring and controlling on the road.
- It is convenient to connect such a system through Internet for surveying the current traffic flow.
- With the rapid advance of computer technologies, the system will provide much of instantaneity, reliability and security.
- It is low cost and easy maintain.

Active v/s Passive Sensors

The most common approach to vehicle detection is using active sensors such as Lasers, LIDAR (Light detection and ranging) or millimeter wave radars. They are called active because they detect the distance of an object by measuring the travel time of the signal emitted by the sensors and reflected by the object. Advantage is that source of the parameters can be obtained directly like vehicle velocity. However, disadvantage is low spatial resolution and slow scanning speed. Interference is the other major problem. Optical sensors, such as normal cameras and usually referred to as passive sensors because they acquire data in a non-intrusive way. One advantage of passive sensors over active sensors is the cost. With the introduction of inexpensive, cameras field of view can be expanded with more number of cameras.

Optical sensor can be used to track vehicles entering, vehicles curve or path and approximate velocity estimation more effectively. Also, visual information can be very important in a number of related applications, such as lane detection, traffic sign recognition or object identification,

number plate information and so on. On the other hand, vehicle detection based on optical sensors is very challenging due to large variability such as vary in shape, size, color and illuminations. Recent trend is Vision chips (Sun, Miller, & Belon, 2002) have many advantage over conventional vision systems such as on chip DIP algorithm to perform segmentation at high speed, small size, low power consumption etc.

A recent trend in the road traffic analysis is the airborne LIDAR. High resolution digital camera and standard video systems are used. The LIDAR data is more realistic and ground truth (Toth & Bizezinsca, 2006) but very expensive and need to work with complex system.

To address some of the above issues, more powerful optical sensors are currently available camera operating at low light and infrared camera (Yamanda, 2003).

Monocular Vision Based Methods v/s Stereo Vision Based Methods

Usually monocular vision based methods are knowledge based approaches. Therefore it uses one of the following features as criterion for the analysis namely: symmetry, color, shadow, corners, vertical-horizontal edges, textures and vehicle lights. While, stereo vision based methods are model based approaches. Further, it uses disparity map, Inverse perspective mappings and motion based methods.

An object tracking and classification system for traffic surveillance is developed by using single reference frame (Bo & Heqin, 2003; Tseng, Lin, & Smith, 2002). However, it may fail to recognize the moving objects if this frame is corrupted by noise. The moving object recognition method is based on the adaptive background subtraction technique to separate vehicles from the background. This detection of traffic by using monocular camera is explored in applications such as vehicle classification, counting, computing velocity and implementation of traffic surveillance system.

Optical Flow Analysis Methods v/s Other Dynamic Scene Analysis Methods

Optical flow computation and analysis plays a vital role in computer vision implementation of road traffic analysis.

In (Zhao & Spetrakis, 2006) an algorithm is presented and tested which can compute large disparities in terms of noise robustness and accuracy. It compares favorably with some of the best but much slower algorithms. The total time for image size of 320 X 240 is 0.5 second per frame in sun workstation. The computation time and performance remain same for both synthetic and real images. This paper reveals that although certain compromises have been used to improve the speed of computation real time analysis for 15/30 frames per second are difficult to achieve using optical flow computation.

In Chechiara et al. (2006) paper submitted to Italian free way Company by the authors in 2006, following drawbacks of optical flow computation has been mentioned.

1.   Optical Flow computation and analysis is very time consuming and must be largely approximated for a real-time computation. Hence not suitable for the same.
2.   It is correct only if the basic conditions of gradient constancy are satisfied. Therefore grouping and labeling on the basis of Optical Flow computation and analysis feature is very hard for little and fragmentary objects.
3.   For large, uniform objects and large monochromatic vehicles, many internal points cannot be characterized by a significant optical flow vector.

Hence, the authors used approach based on background subtraction with a statistic and knowledge based background update. The result presented by the authors show real time traffic MVO (moving visual Object) is nearly possible to achieve.

Road Structure Extraction v/s Background Extraction

Traffic analysis vehicle counting and other related information extraction is usually implemented following either road structure extraction procedure or back ground extraction procedure. When it comes to the highways most of the times camera is fixed at one suitable position and road structure is well defined lane driving. At any specified location of the road the existence of vehicle, its velocity and its violation of line can be easily estimated with the available algorithms. Whereas background extraction is an essential feature of any technique when the road structure is not defined and also camera position is not possible at a desired location. This is usually found in semi urban condition. In these papers we found the first stage of algorithm is reserved for establishing/ registering background. Many researchers have devised method which constantly updates the background that is dynamic background selection. This certainly accommodates moving the camera to a new position and variable background condition.

Based on Hypothesis v/s Special Considerations

It is true that no two persons can think exactly same from understanding to implementation of any engineering/research problem. This is resulted in the above classification. Some of the researchers placed camera on the moving vehicle which is also part of the traffic. In some cases rare view mirror images are considered for analysis. This is usually adopted in intelligent and or in unmanned vehicles, where machine vision helps in navigating such vehicles in the traffic. Here multi sensors data and data fusion is an essential part of the analysis.

Some simple techniques were also developed and used for surveillance in a controlled environment.

In Cucchira, Piccardi, and Mello (2000) presents the work based on an Artificial Intelligence technique. It highlights the use of two modules, which separates low-level processing module used for extracting visual data under various illumination conditions and the high-level model uses general purpose knowledge based frame work for tracking vehicles in the scene. Authors claim that the synergy between artificial intelligence techniques of the high-level and low-level image analysis techniques provides the system with flexibility and robustness. Also compensation for the segmentation errors introduced because of shadows at the image analysis modules over burdens the computation at the high-level module. This may affect the time limitation posed by the real time computation.

Critical Review of Related Work

The paper titled "Adaptive threshold in dynamic scene analysis for extraction of fine line", uses the percentage difference between the mean of the pixels within a window and the center pixel and a dynamic threshold value is evaluated using algorithm (Rahaman, Bakar, & Green, 2000). This method has been applied in detecting moving object with fine lines and results showed that the method was able to pick up straight thin edges that belong to the moving objects. Linking of edges and to extract the shape of the moving vehicles is difficult to achieve with a minimal computation, which is the essence of real time computation and analysis.

The paper titled "Characterization of optical flow Anomalies in pedestrian traffic" develops a model technique to a surveillance scenario where pedestrians are monitored (Andrade et al., 2005). It demonstrates that patterns derived from optical flow and encoded by a Hidden Markov model are able to capture the dynamic evolution of normal and abnormal events. In the context of the above

said application, the proposed method fails to achieve the desired result.

The paper titled "Classification and retrieval of Traffic video using auto-regressive stochastic process" proposes a model to traffic flow analysis in a video using a holistic generative model that does not require segmentation or tracking (Chan, 2005). It adopted the dynamic texture model, an auto-regressive stochastic process, which encodes the appearance and the underlying motion separately in to two probability distribution. With this representation, retrieval or similar video sequences and classification of traffic congestion can be performed using the Kullback - Lelber divergence and Martin distance. Results show the robustness for environmental changes. Authors of this paper have not verified the algorithm considering realistic image sequence with time as a constraint. This study reveal that this suited for off line analysis as it takes more computational time.

A research work" Vehicle Detection and Tracking using the Block Matching Algorithm" describes the state of the research carried out at the department of Electronics and Informatics systems University of Bologna, Italy. In this work BMA (Block Matching Algorithm) provides motion vector, which are then regularized using vector median filters. Then vector are grouped based on adjacency. Finally, the tracking algorithm establishes the correspondence between the vehicle detected in each frames of the sequence, allowing the estimation of their trajectories as well as the detection of new entries and exits. Author's conclusion clearly says that the worst problem with BMA is its computational load. Also, over segmentation effect, when vehicles are too big with respect to block size (e.g., Buses). Perspective correction is also recommended by the authors.

The paper with a title "Accurate 3D Tracking of Rigid Objects with Occlusion Using Active Appearance Model", presents a new model for tracking rigid objects using a modified version of the active appearance model (AAM) (Miltrapiyuruk, Desouza, & Kak, 2005). This combines sparse-3D model with multiple appearance model to accurately estimate the pose of objects. The proposed method suffers from drawbacks that the tracker works only when the frame to frame variations are small. The most time consuming part of the algorithm is that the computation of Hessian matrix and gradient vector.

In the paper "Independent 3D Motion Detection Through Robust Regression in Depth Layers", a method for detection of objects that move independently of the observer in a 3D dynamic environment is presented (Argyros et al., 1998). The proposed method includes normal flow fields. Instead of using optical flow field, the normal flow field is used in both stereo and motion dynamics. Processing of the stereo-pair is limited to the task of segmentation into depth layers.

The paper with a title, "Robust dynamic motion estimation over time", has been studied for the purpose (Black & Anandan, 1991). It presents a novel approach to incrementally estimating visual motion over a sequence of images. This approach exploits the motion of weak continuity and robust statistics in the formulation of a minimization problem. Also this presents a highly parallel incremental stochastic relaxation technique for minimization. The approach has the number of advantages over previous approaches. The incremental and adaptive nature of the scheme makes it appropriate for dynamic motion processing.

The work published with a title "Representing Moving Images with Layers" describes a system for representing moving, images with sets of overlapping layers (Wang & Adelson, 1994). Each layer contains an intensity map that defines the additive values of each pixel along with an alpha map that serves as a mask indicating the transparency. Velocity maps define how the layers are to be warped over time. The layered representation is more flexible than standard image transforms and can capture many important properties of natural image sequences. The limitation of the work as mentioned by the authors is that the method is more successful for sequences that are easily represented by layered model in other words sequences containing a few regions undergoing simple motions.

In optical flow computation even complex motion will appear as a uniform motion when viewed through a sufficiently small window. Therefore a method is proposed in the paper, "A Three Frame Algorithm for estimating two-component Image Motion" that uses local motion in which two distinct patterns undergo coherent motion (affine) (Bergen, Rajesh, & Shmuel, 1992). As a result, motion of more than one object with different speed of motion can be analyzed. But this results in computational burden and hence computational time.

The good quality motion analysis depend on image segmentation, where as segmentation depends on good quality motion information. The advantage of the present approach is that it does not require segmentation to obtain precise motion estimates on two pattern components. It should be noted that this approach assume that both moving pattern components have constant velocity over the three frames used in analysis. This can be a significant restriction if objects are accelerating and the frame rate is low.

The paper "Automatic vehicle counting from video for Traffic Flow Analysis" proposes video analysis method for counting vehicles (Bas & Fellow, 2007). Here authors used adaptive bounding box size to detect and track the vehicles. Also, adaptive background subtraction for reds vehicle detection and Kalman filtering for tracking are being employed. Attempts are being made to use the same for night recordings. Authors opined that algorithm still needs further modification which enables detection and tracking in day and night recordings both effectively. Also, suggested background subtraction with shadow elimination techniques. The above discussion suggests that algorithm is to be modified suitably so that the effectiveness of the overall system improves. The use of Kalman filter for tracking slows down the computation and hence difficult to achieve the real time operation.

"Intelligent Vehicle Counting Method Based on Blob Analysis in Traffic Surveillance" is a paper presented at IEEE conference Jan. 2007. This paper (Chen et al., 2007) presents intelligent vehicle counting method based on Blob Analysis in traffic surveillance which involves three steps.

1. Moving Objects Segmentation
2. Blob analysis
3. Tracking.

Author claims that this system can provide real-time and useful information for traffic surveillance. Here the calculations show that efficiency is around 90% on selected or predefined condition. Weather variations and other critical changes have not been evaluated. Bi-directional movements of the vehicles have not been considered in this algorithm.

One of the studies uses, double-difference operator with gradient magnitude to detect vehicles (Cucchiara, Piccardi, & Mello, 2000). However, it cannot easily handle inter frame difference in luminous variations. Adaptive background subtraction algorithms have been used for vehicle detection, which allows changes in lighting and weather conditions (Karmann & Von Brandt, 1990; Beymer et al., 1997), but they usually require a priori information about the scene without any moving vehicle and have problems with occlusions. Optical flow techniques have been used to estimate the motion between subsequent frames (Li & Chellappa, 2002; Tao, Sawhney, & Kumar, 2002), however they found to be complicated to implement and involves several iterations. This leads to increase in computational time and thus not suitable for real time operation, although, optical flow computation provides rich information of inter frame difference. Furthermore, 3-D models have been previously implemented such as Baker and Sullivan (1992), which recover trajectories with high accuracy. However, this approach requires detailed geometric object models for all types of vehicles. In addition, Kalman filter has been widely used in automatic surveillance systems (Xie et al., 2005), which uses position and size information as state variables to track vehicle positions with different features. Similarly, another work (Hsieh, Chen, & Hu, 2006) uses Kalman filter for tracking vehicles extracted from background models. They implemented a shadow removal algorithm to extract the size and linearity features of vehicles for the purpose of categorizing them.

In Bonneville and Meunier (1999) authors introduced a new method for finding the optical flow for a special type of motion and smoothness constrain. The optimization is mapped into a maximum flow problem in graph which is solved efficiently and leads to optimal solution. This method provides a scheme to compute exactly the global minimum of the energy change depicting motion fields. The advantage of this method is that the solution is direct, not iterative and thus number of iterations need not be specified as a stopping criterion. However, in its current formulation, the algorithm is limited to one-component optical flow.

In this paper Pei and Liou (1997), a simple method called extrapolation and subtraction technique is proposed and used to solve motion segmentation problem. Here input image floe field is first partitioned into several functionally analytic regions. Each analytic region is assumed to be projected by a roughly planar patch moving in 3-D space. Based on the parameterization of these analytic flow fields, the extrapolation and subtraction technique provides a simple and fast method. The parameterization of flow field reduces the error sensitivity of flow measurement and increase the reliability of final result. Other factors which affect the performance of extrapolation and subtraction technique is to be addressed properly.

In Lim and Gamal (2001) it presents a robust algorithm for computation of 2-D optical flow using principle of conservation of a set of invariant local features that are representatives of local grey-level properties in an image. The rotation invariant and orthogonal moments invariants are used as key features. These are inherently integral-based features, and therefore are expected to be robust against the possible variations of intensity values that may occur over a sequence of images due to sensor noise, varying illuminations etc. Enough confidence measures are not implemented in order to establish the result. However, result is comparable with other optical floe estimation techniques.

CHALLENGES AND RECENT TRENDS

Challenges

Object Occlusion

When several objects are tracked simultaneously, some objects may partially or completely disappear in some image frames. This can result in errors in object trajectory prediction (Sonka, Hlavac, & Boyle, 2003). Research is going on to track the object trajectory even in the case of occlusion.

Brightness Variation

Although most optical flow techniques presume brightness constancy, it is well known that this constraint is often violated, producing poor estimates of image motion. A generalized formulation of optical flow estimation based on models of brightness variations that are caused by time-dependent physical processes is discussed in Haussecker and Fleet (2001).

Multiple Object Motion

Detection of multiple object motion has been an ill-posed problem. Complex approaches are being developed to solve this problem.

Real Time Analysis

Currently the two major limitations to applying vision in real tasks are robustness in real world and the computational resources required for real time operation. In particular many motion detection algorithms are not suited for practical applications such as segmentation because they require highly specialized hardware or up to several minutes on a scientific workstation.

Recent Trends

Catadioptric imaging sensors, which can provide 360^0 horizontal, views have been developed recently. Larger object surfaces can be perceived in a wide angle of view supplied by such an omni directional camera. The duration of object appearance in the field of view will also be longer. These properties cause smooth variations of the image scenes and facilitate the calculation of the optical flow. Using such a flow field allows detecting ego-motion and some other fundamental preliminaries of robot navigation.

Recent advances in imaging sensor technology have enabled high frame rate video capturing. This provides better accuracy in the estimation of optical flow (Lim & Gamal, 2001). Specialized hardware and embedded systems are being developed which provide parallel processing. This increases the speed of data processing.

CONCLUSION

In this work a detailed survey of literature pertains to road traffic analysis and automation using computer vision approaches have been carried out. The study and survey is made in three different perspectives:

- Automation of traffic analysis.
- Optical flow analysis and its usefulness for traffic analysis.

- Computer Vision perspective to the above mentioned subjects.

This survey enabled us to end up in certain conclusions:

- The need of simple, efficient and cost effective real time algorithm which supports automation of traffic analysis on conventional computers.
- Authors of this paper convinced that optical flow computation technique is more appropriate but increases the computational burden enormously. Also, difficult to implement in the real time analysis at conventional video rate of 15/30 frames per second.

REFERENCES

Adelson, E. H., & Bergen, J. R. (1985). Spatiotemporal energy models for the perception of motion. *Journal of optical. Society, A2,* 284–299.

Andrade, E. L. (2005). *Characterization of optical flow anomalies in pedestrian traffic (Tech. Rep.).* UK: School of Informatic, Ediburge University.

Argyros, A. A., et al. (1998). *Independent 3D Motion Detection, through Robust regression in depth layers.* Paper presented at the British Machine vision conference.

Baker, K., & Sullivan, G. (1992). Performance assessment of model-based tracking. In *Proceedings of the IEEE Workshop on Applications of Computer Vision,* Palm Springs, CA (pp. 28-35).

Bas, E., & Fellow, A. M. T. (2007). Automatic vehicle counting from video for Traffic Flow Analysis. In *Proceedings of the IEEE International Proceedings on Intelligent vehicles symposium* (pp. 392-397).

Bergen, P. J. B., Rajesh, H., & Shmuel, P. (1992). A three, Frame Algorithm for estimating two-component Image Motion. *Transactions on pattern analysis and machine intelligence, 14*(9), 886-896.

Beymer, D., McLauchlan, P., Coifman, B., & Malik, J. (1997). A real-time computer vision system for measuring traffic parameters. In *Proceedings of the IEEE Conf. on Computer Vision and Pattern Recognition,* Puerto Rico (pp. 496-501).

Black, M. J., & Anandan, P. (1991). Robust dynamic motion estimation over time. *IEEE. International Journal of Computer Vision,* 296–302.

Bo, L., & Heqin, Z. (2003). Using object classification to improve urban traffic monitoring system. In. *Proceedings of the IEEE International Conference on Neural Networks and Signal Processing, 2,* 1155–1159.

Bonneville, M., & Meunier, J. (1999). Finding the Exact Optical Flow: a Maximum Flow Formulation. In *Proceedings of the Vision Interface 99,* Trios-Rivieres, Canada (pp. 418-423).

Chan, A. B. (2005). Layered dynamic textures. In *Proceedings of the IEEE Intelligent vehicle symposium,* Las Vegas.

Chechiara, R., Grana, C., Piccardi, M., & Prati, A. (2006). *Statistic and knowledge based moving object detection in traffic scenes.* Italy: Italian Free Way Company.

Chen, T.-H. (2003). An automatic bi-directional passing-people counting method based on color image processing. In *Proceedings of the IEEE 37th Annual 2003 International Carnohan Conference on Security Technology* (pp. 200-207).

Chen, T.-H., Lin, Y.-F., et al. (2007). Intelligent vehicle counting method based on Blob Analysis in Traffic Surveillance, *IEEE.* DOI 0-7695-2822

Cucchira, R., Piccardi, M., & Mello, P. (2000). Image Analysis and rule based reasoning for a Traffic Monitoring System. *IEEE Transactions on Intelligent Transportation Systems, 1*(2), 119–130. doi:10.1109/6979.880969

Fleet, D. J. (1992). *Measurement of Image velocity*. Norwell, MA: Kluwer Academic Publishers.

Fleet, D. J., & Jepson, A. D. (1990). Computation of component image velocity from local phase information. *International Journal of Computer Vision, 5*, 77–104. doi:10.1007/BF00056772

Ghosal, S., & Mehrotra, R. (1997). Robust Optical Flow Estimation using Semi-invariant Local Features. *Pattern Recognition, 30*(2), 229–237. doi:10.1016/S0031-3203(96)00070-2

Gonzalez, R. C., & Wood, R. E. (2002). *Digital Image Processing*. Upper Saddle River, NJ: Prentice Hall.

Haussecker, H. W., & Fleet, D. J. (2001). Computing optical flow with physical models of brightness variation. *IEEE Transactions on Pattern Analysis and Machine Intelligence, 23*(6), 661–673. doi:10.1109/34.927465

Heeger, D. J. (1988). Optical flow using spatiotemporal filters. *International Journal of Computer Vision, 1*, 279–302. doi:10.1007/BF00133568

Horn, B. K. P., & Schunk, B. G. (1981). Determining optical flow. *IEEE Trans on Artificial Intelligence, 17*, 185–203.

Hsieh, J.-W., Chen, S.-H., & Hu, W.-F. (2006). Automatic Traffic Surveillance System for Vehicle Tracking and Classification. *IEEE Transactions on Intelligent Transportation Systems, 7*, 175–187. doi:10.1109/TITS.2006.874722

Jahne, B. (1987). Image sequence analysis of complex physical objects: nonlinear small scale water surface waves. In *Proceedings of the IEEE ICCV*, London (pp. 191-200).

John, W. (2002). Building safer cars. *IEEE Spectrum, 29*(1), 82–85.

Karmann, K. P., & Von Brandt, A. (1990). Moving object recognition using an adaptive background memory. In Capellini, V. (Ed.), *Time-Varying Image Processing and Moving Object Recognition* (p. 2). Amsterdam, The Netherlands: Elsevier.

Li, B., & Chellappa, R. (2002). A generic approach to simultaneous tracking and verification in video. *IEEE Transactions on Image Processing, 11*(5), 530–544. doi:10.1109/TIP.2002.1006400

Lim, S., & Gamal, A. G. (2001). Optical Flow Estimation using High frame- rate Sequences. *IEEE Transactions on Image Processing*, 925-928. DOI 0-7803-6725

Miltrapiyuruk, P., Desouza, G. N., & Kak, A. C. (2005). Accurate 3D tracking of Rigid objects with occlusion using Active Appearance Model. In *Proceedings of the IEEE workshop on motion and Video computation*.

Pei, S.-C., & Liou, L.-G. (1997). Motion-Based Grouping of Optical Flow Fields: The Extrapolation and subtraction Technique. *IEEE Transactions on Image Processing, 6*(10), 1358–1363. doi:10.1109/83.624949

Rahaman, S. A., Bakar, A., & Green, R. J. (2000). Adaptive threshold in dynamic scene analysis for extraction of fine line. *IEEE*. DOI 0-7803-6355

Sonka, M., Hlavac, V., & Boyle, R. (2003). *Image Processing, Analysis and Machine Vision*. Pacific Grove, CA: Thomson Brooks/Cole Publishing Company.

Sun, Z., Miller, R., & Belon, G. (2002). *A real time pre-crash vehicle detection system*. Paper presented at the IEEE international workshop on application of computer vision.

Tao, H., Sawhney, H. S., & Kumar, R. (2002). Object tracking with Bayesian estimation of dynamic layer representations. *IEEE Transactions on Pattern Analysis and Machine Intelligence, 24*(1), 75–89. doi:10.1109/34.982885

Toth, C. K., & Bizezinsca, D. G. (2006). Traffic management with state of art airborne imaging sensors. In *Proceedings of the International Conference at National Consortium for remote sensing in Transportation flows (NCRST-F)*.

Tseng, B. L., Lin, C.-Y., & Smith, J. R. (2002). Real-time video surveillance for traffic monitoring using virtual line analysis. In. *Proceedings of the IEEE International Conference on Multimedia and Expo, 2*, 541–544.

Wang, J. Y., & Adelson, E. H. (1994). Representing Moving Images with layers. *IEEE Transactions on Image Processing, 3*, 625–636. doi:10.1109/83.334981

Watson, A. B., & Ahumada, A. J. (1985). Model of human-motion sensing. *Journal of optical. Society, A2*, 322–342.

Waxman, A. M., Wu, J., & Bergholm, F. (1988). Convected activation profiles and receptive fields for real time measurement of short range visual motion. In *Proceedings of the IEEE CVPR*, Ann Arbor, MI (pp. 717-723).

Xie, L., Zhu, G., Wang, Y., Xu, H., & Zhang, Z. (2005). Real-time Vehicles Tracking Based on Kalman Filter in a Video-based ITS. In *Proceedings of IEEE Conf. on Communications, Circuits and Systems* (Vol. 2, p. 886).

Yamanda, K. (2003). A compact integrated vision motion sensor for its application. *IEEE Transactions on Intelligent Transportation Systems, 4*(1), 35–41. doi:10.1109/TITS.2002.808418

Zhao, P., & Spetrakis, M. E. (2006). *work submitted to NSERC Canada by York University Canada*.

This work was previously published in International Journal of Grid and High Performance Computing, Volume 2, Issue 2, edited by Emmanuel Udoh, pp. 64-78, copyright 2010 by IGI Publishing (an imprint of IGI Global).

Chapter 17
G2G:
A Meta–Grid Framework for the Convergence of P2P and Grids

Wu-Chun Chung
National Tsing Hua University, Taiwan

Chin-Jung Hsu
National Tsing Hua University, Taiwan

Yi-Hsiang Lin
National Tsing Hua University, Taiwan

Kuan-Chou Lai
National Taichung University, Taiwan

Yeh-Ching Chung
National Tsing Hua University, Taiwan

ABSTRACT

Grid systems integrate distributed resources to form self-organization and self-management autonomies. With the widespread development of grid systems around the world, grid collaboration for large-scale computing has become a prevalent research topic. In this paper, the authors propose a meta-grid framework, named the Grid-to-Grid (G2G) framework, to harmonize autonomic grids in realizing a grid federation. The G2G framework is a decentralized management framework that is built on top of existing autonomic grid systems. This paper further adopts a super-peer network in a separate layer to coordinate distributed grid systems. A super-peer overlay network is constructed for communication among super-peers, thus enabling collaboration among grid systems. This study proposes the G2G framework for use in a Grid-to-Grid federation and implements a preliminary system as a demonstration. Experimental results show that the proposed meta-grid framework can improve system performance with little overhead.

DOI: 10.4018/978-1-4666-0056-0.ch017

A grid computing system is a distributed computing system for solving complex or high-performance computing problems as encountered in bioinformatics, healthcare systems, ecosystems, and even experiments involving the use of the Large Hadron Collider. In such a computing environment, a virtual organization is a self-organization and self-management group which shares the computing resources (Foster, Kesselman, & Tuecke, 2001). Grid systems employ the middleware as the abstract interface to integrate large-scale distributed computing resources. Therefore, the aggregated capability for distributed computing and data accessing can be improved by integrating geographical distributed resources.

Various organizations, institutions, and private communities around the world adopt centralized or hierarchical architectures to develop grid systems based on the Open Grid Service Architecture (OGSA) (Foster, Kesselman, Nick, & Tuecke, 2002). Most grid systems, though, cannot be integrated for collaborative computation. This is why grid collaboration for large-scale computing has become a prevalent research topic. The integration of distinctly autonomic grid systems into a grid federation is one prospective approach. What poses a challenge to realizing grid federations, however, is how to harmonize various grid systems without bringing a heavy burden on existing grid infrastructure.

In order to coordinate multiple diverse grid systems, a grid system requires a mechanism for achieving the cross-grid convergence of diversely autonomic grid communities. There are two ways to accomplish cross-grid integration. One is to enhance the grid middleware by modifying the original mechanism in existing grid systems, while the other is to develop a meta-grid framework on top of existent grid systems. The former burdens an existent grid system with lots of efforts to harmonize with other grid systems; moreover, there is no mature cross-grid middleware for integrating with distinct grid systems. On the other hand, the latter increases the extra overhead for the existent

grid systems. In this paper, we present a meta-grid framework, named the Grid-to-Grid (G2G) framework, to form a federation consisting of multiple institutional grid systems. The G2G framework can harmonize autonomic grid systems and achieve cross-grid collaborative computing with seamless modification for existing grid systems.

Past studies have applied decentralized approaches to exploit the system scalability of grids in the development of the grid management architecture. In general, a centralized or hierarchical architecture is not suitable for large-scale grids (Mastroianni, Talia, & Verta, 2007). Reasons for this include the potential bottleneck at root, the scalability limit of a grid, and load imbalance problems. Integrating grid systems with the P2P paradigm can improve the scalability of a grid federation. Therefore, we attempt to exploit a decentralized G2G framework to realize synergy between P2P networks and existing grid systems. In consideration of the scalability and the efficiency of the grid management architecture, this study utilizes a super-peer network (Yang & Garcia-Molina, 2003) to develop our G2G framework for the coordination of multiple autonomic grid systems. Each super-peer represents an autonomic grid system in our G2G system. To achieve a decentralized G2G framework, the super-peer network adopts an overlay network for communication among super-peers in different grid systems through a federation of wide-area grids.

This paper introduces a meta-grid framework of the G2G system based on a super-peer network. We also present a preliminary implementation of the proposed G2G framework and develop a Grid-to-Grid network based on the overlay network in which each grid system communicates and negotiates with other grid systems. The remainder of this paper is organized as follows. Section 2 discusses related works. In Section 3, we present the overview of the G2G framework and the implementation of a G2G prototype. The experimental results of the G2G system are shown in Section 4. We conclude this paper with the future work in Section 5.

RELATED WORKS

Scalability in large-scale grid systems has posed research challenges in recent years. There are some studies (Ranjan, Harwood, & Buyya, 2008; Trunfio et al., 2007) that discuss the adoption of the P2P technique to improve the scalability of grid systems. Some similarities and differences between P2P computing and grid computing were presented in the literature (Foster & Iamnitchi, 2003; Talia & Trunfio, 2003). Several previous studies aimed to improve the centralized-based grid infrastructure by using the P2P technique.

A decentralized event-based object middleware, DERMI (Pairot, Garcia, & Skarmeta, 2004), is proposed to favor the scalability problem of a centralized model. A DHT-based DERMI prototype uses Pastry (Rowstron & Druschel, 2001) as its underlying network topology and adopts Scribe (Castro, Druschel, Kermarrec, & Rowstron, 2002) as its publish/subscribe notification service which is built on top of Pastry. However, from a view point of the middleware layer, DERMI can facilitate the wide-area grid. From another view point, our study aims to coexist with the existence of grid systems without modifying the middleware.

The integration of a distributed event brokering system with the JXTA technology has been proposed in the literature (Fox, Pallickara, & Rao, 2005) to enable Peer-to-Peer Grids. In a previous study (Pallickara & Fox, 2003), the authors utilize the NaradaBrokering based on the hierarchical structure in the broker network. By integrating the NaradaBrokering with JXTA, services are mediated by the broker middleware or by the P2P interactions between machines on the edge of Internet. NaradaBrokering aims to present a unified environment for grid computing with a P2P interaction. In addition, the overhead will be costly for NaradaBrokering to maintain the broker network by the hierarchical topology in a dynamically changed network.

A P2PGrid platform based on a two-layer model for integrating P2P computing into the grid is presented in a previous study (Cao, Liu, & Xu, 2007). All grid services are provided in the grid layer while the grid entities or common PCs become peers to negotiate with each other in the P2P layer. The P2PGrid tries to provide a solution for integrating the grid computing environment with the P2P computing ones. In this study, JXTA is adopted for developing JXTA Agents to create peers, deal with dynamics of peer groups, and communicate with peers. Jobs are submitted and dispatched to workers which are organized by the above-mentioned peers on the underlying P2P computing network. By the implementation of the P2PGrid platform, peers on the edge of Internet are able to consume grid services without maintaining grid middleware packages. Adopting a separate layer from an existing grid system is a great benefit because that the original behaves of the grid layer can be preserved without modifications, and that the modification of the P2P manner will not affect the efficiency of the grid layer.

In our study, we present a decentralized metagrid framework on top of existing autonomic grid systems. The autonomic grids are coordinated based on the super-peer network to form a Grid-to-Grid collaborative computing environment. A super-peer is able to provide/consume the grid services to/from other super-peers in remote grid systems. Super-peers are organized based on an unstructured super-peer overlay to negotiate with each other. By adopting a separate layer, the G2G framework can integrate with existing grid systems without modifying the original mechanisms and policies. In addition to the support of computation services and data services, we also propose a solution for the verification of accessing remote resources by considering the security issues in the Grid-to-Grid environment.

G2G FRAMEWORK AND PROTOTYPE

Currently, most grid systems are deployed according to centralized or hierarchical management approaches. However, these approaches have poor performance in terms of scalability, resiliency, and load-balancing for managing distributed resources (Mastroianni et al., 2007). Centralization and hierarchy are the weaknesses of deploying large multi-institutional grid systems, let alone in the widely internetworking system. In general, the performance by adopting the super-peer model is more efficient and convenient than that without adopting the super-peer model in large-scale computing environments.

In our G2G framework, we utilize the super-peer network to coordinate existing grid systems. The P2P technique is applied for the communication between super-peers. In this section, we describe the concept of the G2G system before introducing the meta-grid framework. At the end of this section, we present a preliminary prototype of the G2G system.

Super-Peer Based G2G System

The super-peer network is proposed to combine the efficiency of the centralized search as well as the features in terms of autonomy, load balance, and robustness of the distributed search. A super-peer is a node that acts both as a centralized server to a set of ordinary nodes and as a coequality to negotiate with other super-peers. In order to achieve the seamless integration of the grids in the G2G system, this study adopts the super-peer network on top of the existing grid systems, and harmonizes existing autonomous grids with each other without rebuilding/modifying any grid system.

Each super-peer in our G2G system acts as a coordinator which is responsible for coordinating a local autonomic grid system and negotiating with other super-peers in remote grid systems.

For example, after obtaining a request for task execution, the super-peer first checks whether the request can be processed locally; otherwise, the request will be forwarded to other grid systems by cooperating with other super-peers. For the sake of simplicity, we currently consider only one super-peer deployed on top of the local grid systems. Similar examples have been proposed in past studies (Mastroianni, Talia, & Verta, 2005). Since there are multiple autonomic grid systems in the G2G system, we utilize an unstructured overlay to facilitate the federation of super-peers. In this way, the Grid-to-Grid interactions among distinct grid systems are based on the super-peer network by way of the P2P overlay. Based on a P2P overlay, each grid can easily join the G2G system and supply its resources and services to other grid systems. The resource utilization can be improved after applying the G2G system.

The basic concept and architecture of the G2G system are shown in Figure *1* and Figure 2. The G2G system mainly consists of the Cross-Grid layer and the Local-Grid layer. The Local-Grid layer consists of some autonomic grid systems which are built by the grid middleware to collaborate distributed resources. In the Cross-Grid layer, the G2G layer is responsible for coordinating the super-peers in autonomic grids. These super-peers not only take charge of integrating the autonomic grids by the developed common interfaces but also deal with the negotiation between grid systems in the G2G layer. The Meta-Grid interface is responsible to bridge the Cross-Grid layer and the Local-Grid layer. Using these common interfaces, the Cross-Grid layer can acquire the resources and services from the Local-Grid layer without knowing the policies, mechanisms, or algorithms in the Local-Grid layer. Since the Cross-Grid layer and the Local-Grid layer are independent, the Cross-Grid layer does not need to be modified when the mechanisms in the Local-Grid layer are modified or replaced.

Figure 1. Basic concept of the meta-grid framework

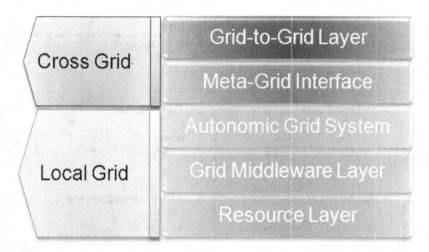

Figure 2. Architectural overview of the G2G system based on a super-peer network

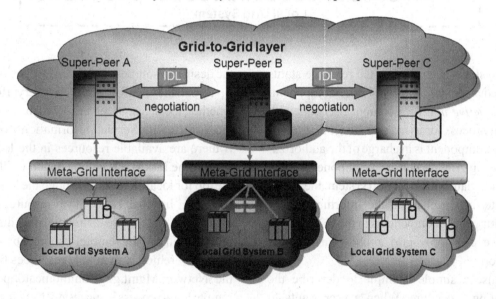

G2G Framework

In this study, a meta-grid framework of the G2G system is proposed for a federation of multiple autonomic grid systems as shown in Figure 3. The G2G framework aims to support the seamless integration of the computing services and the data accessing services in the autonomous grid systems. Therefore, the super-peer in the Grid-to-Grid layer consists of seven components to bridge the Cross-Grid layer and the Local-Grid layer: *the*

interactive interface, the security management, the network management, the task management, the data management, the resource management and *the information service.*

The *task management* component handles job computation, and the *data management* component is responsible for integrating the distributed storage systems. The *network management* component handles the network topology and the G2G interaction between distinct grids. The *resource management* manages the distributed resources

Figure 3. Framework overview of components in the Grid-to-Grid layer

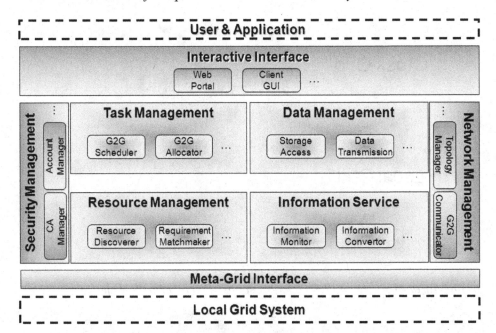

in grid systems according to the resource status supported by the *information service* component. The *interactive interface* component deals with the login process for users, and the *security management* component is in charge of the authorization of using grids. When each component would like to negotiate with local grid system, the Meta-Grid Interface exchanges the information. By cooperating these components in the G2G framework, we can apply grid applications on this framework.

We use a simple example to describe the cooperating procedure. When a user wants to login into the G2G system, the web portal will call the SecurityMgmt.loginManager() to handle the login process. This function will deliver the user's login information to the local security service through the Meta-Grid Interface. If the login process is successful, the user can edit jobs on the web portal or upload the data related to the job computation. When a user wants to submit a job for execution, the TaskMgmt.g2gScheduler() will receive the request from the web portal and call the ResourceMgmt.resourceDiscoverer() to locate

the desired resources. The discovery process will firstly call the localResourceDiscovery() to check whether local resources are available by using the InformationService.informationMonitor(). If there are available resources in the local grid system, the TaskMgmt.g2gAllocator() will submit the job for local execution through the Meta-Grid Interface. In other cases, if no resources in the local grid system are available, the discovery process will call the remoteResourceDiscovery() to exploit remotely available resources by using the NetworkMgmt.g2gCommunicator(). If the remote login process is successful by using the SecurityMgmt.caManager() and the SecurityMgmt.accountManager(), the discovery process of the remote grid system is similar as above. The detail notions of developing a G2G prototype are shown in next subsection.

G2G Prototype

This study uses JAVA to develop the proposed G2G framework. The developed components of the super-peer are deployed on top of each autonomic grid system to form the Grid-to-Grid federation environment. The super-peers communicate with each other by using a P2P overlay. In this subsection, we describe the implementation and the cooperation of all components in the G2G computing system.

Portal and single sign-on. In general, a friendly interactive interface is important for users while using the grids. Therefore, this study develops a uniform web portal for users to easily enter a grid system and to utilize the authorized resources and services. There are two important functions for developing a uniform web portal: Single Sign-On (SSO), and workflow operation.

Single Sign-On (SSO) is adopted for users to access the grids with only-once login. Each user can utilize grid resources/services after the successful verification through the proxy server and the security management. This study proposes a uniform web portal on top of each autonomous grid

system. A redirection mechanism is also developed in the uniform web portal as shown in Figure 4.

When a user logins the G2G system from this uniform web portal, the portal will determine which grid system the user should be entered according to the user's login information. The candidate grid system will verify whether the user's login information is valid or not. If the login is successful, the portal will deliver the user's login information to the local security service through the Meta-Grid interface. If the certificate of the user is also valid, the login process is successful and complete. Otherwise, it will be a failure. Since the login process is accomplished through the integration of original grid systems, if the local grid supports the SSO mechanism, the G2G layer can also sustain the SSO mechanism.

On the other hand, the workflow operation in the G2G system supports the task submission. The

Figure 4. Redirection mechanism for users to login on the uniform web portal

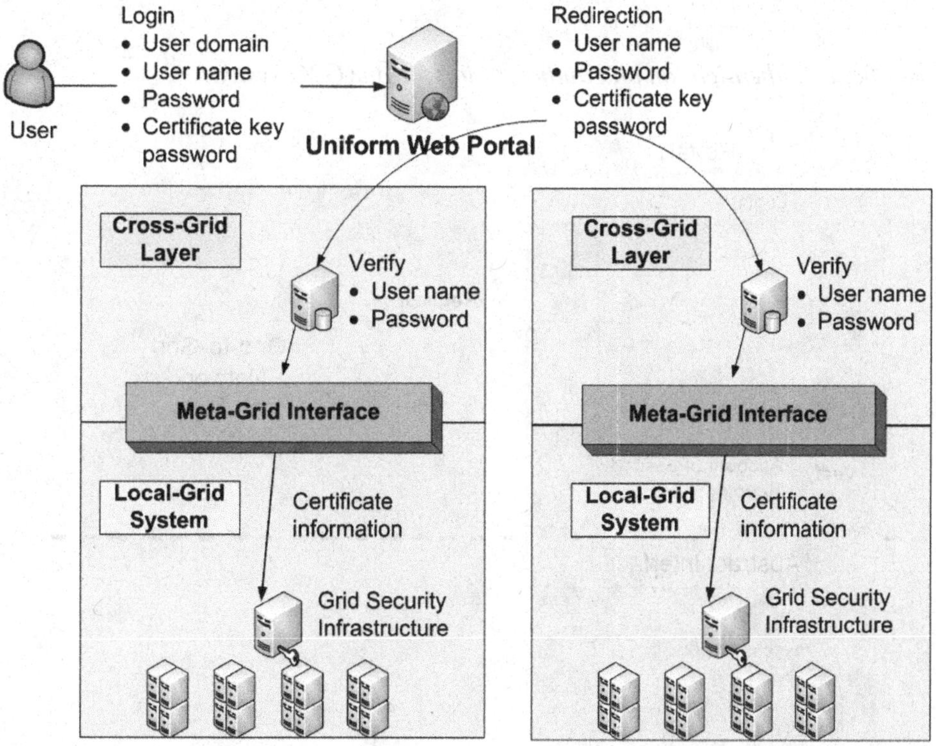

workflow structure in the G2G system is similar to the M-Task structure (Rauber & Runger, 2005). Each workflow is composed of multiple stages and each stage is composed of multiple jobs. Jobs between distinct stages may be dependent; however, jobs in the same stage are all independent, that is, all jobs within the same stage can be scheduled and allocated for simultaneous execution.

Our study also develops a workflow editor in the uniform web portal. According to the resource status obtained from the information service component, users can edit the tasks on the portal and also specify desired resource requirements. We adopt an XML-based structure language to describe the task information and support the resource discovery by multiple attributes with the range query. After the task submission, the edited workflow can be transformed into the XML-based form and can be stored in the database for users to lookup, cancel, or refine their tasks at anytime.

Security service. Grid authentication and authorization are key services in grid security management. A previous study (Foster, Kesselman, Tsudik, & Tuecke, 1998) has defined the Grid Security Infrastructure (GSI) for the legal utilization of grid services. In the G2G system, the security management component deals with not only the certificate authorization locally, but also the admission request from remote grid systems. The secrecy and privacy mechanisms in the G2G system have to guarantee the original legal services in the local grid systems and accept the permission of utilizing local resources/services for other remote grid systems. The security management component includes two primary functions as shown in Figure 5: the passport manager for the authorized privilege and the account manager for the legal account management.

The passport manager takes care of the passport registration and the verification in the G2G system. A passport represents the admission or verification of the request from remote grid systems. If one grid system tries to access resources in another grid system, it must get a visaed passport from the target grid system before accessing the resources. This study develops a distributed passport-interchange-mechanism in the G2G system. According to the maintenance of neighborhood

Figure 5. Certificate authentication and authorization for our G2G system

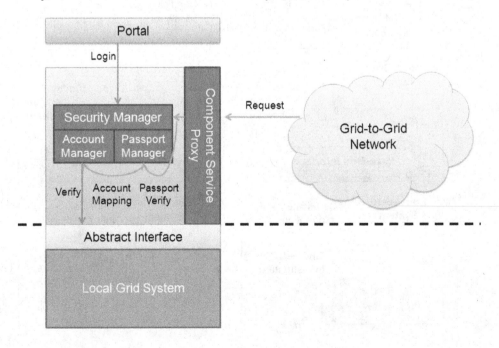

relationship, each grid system can request a remote resource/service from its neighbors or neighbors' neighbors by forwarding the resource/service request along the overlay network. After discovering the available resource/service in remote grids, the requester will receive the visaed passports from the granted grid system; and then, the requester can submit tasks to the granted remote grids with legal permission.

On the other hand, the account manager is responsible for the management of legal accounts. In this study, the function of the account authentication is adopted for a "local account" to login the grids. A local account indicates an original user account in the local grid system. Once an account requests for a login from the portal, the portal asks the account manager to verify its identification. Another important aspect of the account manager is the account mapping mechanism. Account mapping is used to handle requests issued by foreign users from remote grid systems. Every grid system which wants to use the resources in other grids must register to the granted grid system before accessing those resources. The register process acquires a passport and gets a temporary account. Once the register process is completed, every request with the visaed passport from remote grid systems will be treated as a local user account through the account mapping mechanism.

Data service. Data management is responsible for data maintenance and high performance transmission in the data grid (Chervenak, Foster, Kesselman, Salisbury, & Tuecke, 2000). In this study, the data service of our G2G system supports specific APIs for the transparent accesses of existent data storage in each local grid system and for the data transmission among different autonomic grid systems. The abstract APIs is responsible to contact with a storage system in a local grid system or a general file system. Data accesses between the Cross-Grid layer and the Local-Grid layer adopt the well-defined data operations; otherwise, the data accesses from one grid to another grid adopt the G2G communication mechanism through super-peers.

When a communication between grids is necessary for data transmission, the super-peer takes care of the negotiation and communication with other super-peers in the G2G layer. We use the account manager to manage the foreign data files in this case. When the data files are accessed from remote grid systems, these data files can be stored in the local storage system and then be mapped to local owners. After data mapping and account handling, the foreign data file can be accessed by local users.

In this study, we focus on collaborating with the computing grid system and the data grid system, and omit developing efficient policy for data replication. Those issues about data coherence and parallel downloading between distinct grid systems remain as a future work.

Information service. The main responsibilities of the information service include the resource indexing and monitoring for capturing the resource status in a grid system. Traditional Grid Information Service (Czajkowski, Fitzgerald, Foster, & Kesselman, 2001; Fitzgerald et al., 1997) generally adopts the centralized or hierarchical architecture. Such architectures for the information service are hard to directly apply to the G2G system because of the single point of failure problem. To alleviate the failure problem, this study develops an information service for crossing the inter-grid systems on top of the existent information monitoring system.

Our information service consists of two mechanisms: the *information monitor* and the *information convertor*. Each grid system in the Local-Grid layer is responsible for monitoring the local information. The super-peer queries the local information by using the proposed information monitor to negotiate with the local grid system. On the other hand, we propose an Information Description Language (IDL) to negotiate the information with the local-grid system and exchange the information between cross-grid systems. The IDL is a XML-based structure, which is shown as Figure 6 and Figure 7, for describing the grid information such as the workflow submission, the job requirement, the resource information, and so on. We also develop the information convertor to transform diverse XML-based information into our IDL format, and vice versa. By using the information convertor, each grid system of our G2G system can extract the information from the local-grid or remote-grid description.

By the IDL, information can be negotiated from Cross-Grid layer to Local-Grid layer and messages can be exchanged between distinct grid systems in the G2G layer. A workflow or a complicate job requirement with multi-attribute range query can be supported in the distributed resource discovery.

Network management. This study proposes a Grid-to-Grid overlay based on the super-peer network. In the G2G system, the super-peer in each autonomic grid system takes responsible for the negotiation and communication with other super-peers over the G2G network. The decentralized overlay network is adopted to construct the neighborhood relationship and to forward a request between super-peers.

There are two main management functions in the G2G network management: the *topology manager* and the *G2G communicator*. The topology manager maintains the overlay network for the neighborhood relationship or routing information between super-peers. As one super-peer tries to join the G2G network, the topology manger guides the new super-peer to join this G2G system, and then the super-peer will forward a request to build its routing table after successfully joining into the G2G network.

Figure 8 depicts the procedure for a new grid system to join the G2G system. Every autonomic

Figure 6. Example for the task submission and the job requirement in the IDL structure

```
<TASK>
    <WORKFLOW NAME="Workflow Name">
        <STAGE NAME="Stage Name" ORDER="1">
            <JOB NAME="Job Name">
                <PROGRAM NAME="Matrix Multiplication" ARG="1024" NP="4" TYPE="MPI" />
                <INPUT_FILES>
                    <INPUT_FILE DATA_ID="Data ID for the Program" />
                </INPUT_FILES>
                <REQUIREMENTS>
                <!-- One of the following requirement tag should be matched for executing the job. -->
                    <REQUIREMENT>
                    <!-- All the required information should be matched with the following conditions. -->
                        <INFORMATION_TYPE NAME="Information Name" VALUE="Information Value" VALUETYPE="Value Type"
                                    UNIT="Value Unit" OPERATOR="AND, NOT" RELATION="EQUAL, GREAT, LESS" />
                    </REQUIREMENT>
                    <REQUIREMENT>
                        <!--
                            -- For example, the job requires the desired resource with CPU is greater than 2GHz,
                            -- and the machine type is not x86_64.
                        -->
                        <INFORMATION_TYPE NAME="2" OPERATOR="1" RELATION="2" UNIT="1" VALUE="2000" VALUETYPE="6" />
                        <INFORMATION_TYPE NAME="21" OPERATOR="2" RELATION="1" UNIT="0" VALUE="x86_64" VALUETYPE="1" />
                    </REQUIREMENT>
```

Figure 7. Example for resource information in the IDL structure

```
<RESOURCE>
    <NODE ADDRESS="Super-peer Address">
        <CLUSTER ADDRESS="Cluster Address">
            <HOST ADDRESS="Host Address 1" REPORTED="Last-record TIMESTAMP">
                <RESOURCE_STATE NAME="Attribute NAME" VALUE="Attribute VALUE" TYPE="Value TYPE" UNIT="Value UNIT" />
            </HOST>
            <HOST ADDRESS="Host Address 2" REPORTED="Last-record TIMESTAMP">
                <!-- For example, a resource with the CPU is 3200 MHz and the machine type is x86. -->
                <RESOURCE_STATE NAME="2" VALUE="3200" TYPE="6" UNIT="1" />
                <RESOURCE_STATE NAME="21" VALUE="x86" TYPE="1" UNIT="0" />
            </HOST>
```

grid system acts as a super-peer to be a member of the super-peer network. When a grid system wants to join the G2G system, it registers to a contact node and gets a list of grid systems selected by the contact node in random. After obtaining the random list, the new grid system measures the network latency or the bandwidth with all the candidate members. After the measurement process, the new grid system selects members with better performance to register as its neighbors. This join procedure for a new member is similar to the previous work (Mastroianni et al., 2005). We implement this mechanism for a new super-peer to join the G2G network, and enhance the construction of an unstructured overlay network.

We also present the G2G communicator to take care of the network communication and the message negotiation. In order to communicate with different autonomic systems, we not only apply the IDL to describe the exchanged information but also design an application-level request format for message transmission. Every communication is accomplished by using the socket connection. The communication in-between two grid systems can be divided into sender- and receiver-modules. For the sender module, all the

requests will be transformed into a predefined request format, and then the requests are sent to remote super-peers in serial. For the receiver module, the remote super-peer de-serializes all the received requests and forwards to the corresponding components.

Task management with resource discovery. The task management is in charge of the task submission through the interactive interface. A task consists of jobs executed in sequential or in parallel. In the G2G system, tasks are not only submitted from local users, but probably are requested from remote grid systems. Depending on available grid resources, the G2G scheduler and G2G allocator need to consider the job execution among the intra-grid submission or the inter-grid submission.

In the task management module, we adopt a workflow structure to organize jobs in a predefined order for execution. The workflow structure is constructed by stages. The jobs in one stage must wait for execution until all jobs in previous stage are completed because of the stage-by-stage approach to avoid destroying the job dependence in different stages. We also develop the workflow manager and the job manager to handle requested

Figure 8. Procedure for a new grid system to join the G2G network

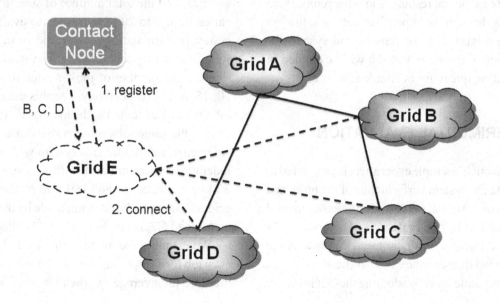

tasks. After a task is submitted to the workflow manager, the manager schedules the order of jobs and decides where to execute these jobs. The decision of migrating the executable jobs to a local grid or a remote grid depends on the system performance or the resource requirement.

On the other hand, each job has its resource requirement for execution. This study also applies a resource discovery mechanism (Mastroianni et al., 2005) to explore the distributed resources status over the Grid-to-Grid overlay network, and supports a matchmaking policy to provide candidate resources satisfied the specified requirements. After a task is submitted to the waiting queue for execution, the G2G scheduler picks one of queuing jobs according to the First-Come-First-Served (FCFS) policy, and then checks whether local resources are sufficient or under loading at first. The decision of where to execute a job depends on not only whether local grid system is over loading, but also whether local resources are satisfied with requirements through information service. If the local grid system is not busy and there are sufficient available resources, the job will be submitted to the local grid system to be executed. Otherwise, the job manager will ask the distributed resource discovery module to search available resources over the overlay network. If there are sufficient resources in other remote grid systems through the super-peer network, the job will be migrated to the remote grid system for execution. Otherwise, this job will be queued in the waiting queue for available resources.

EXPERIMENTAL EVALUATION

In this section, a simple experiment is conducted to evaluate the system performance of the proposed framework. At first, we describe the experimental environment in our evaluation. Then, we show the experimental results in terms of the average turnaround time and the extra overhead occurring from a separate layer by adopting the G2G system.

Experimental Environment

In the experimental environment, two autonomic grid systems based on the framework of Taiwan UniGrid (Shih et al., 2008) are applied. In order to limit the impact of the heterogeneous environment, we utilize the same cluster in each autonomic grid system for execution. One autonomic grid system contains a cluster with 8 higher computational power CPUs (i.e., the grid with higher computational power.) The other autonomic grid system contains a cluster with 32 lower computing power CPUs (i.e., the grid with rich resources). In each local grid system, the SRB (Baru, Moore, Rajasekar, & Wan, 1998) is adopted to be the local data storage system; and the ganglia information monitoring system (Massie, Chun, & Culler, 2004) is utilized to monitor the local information. We deploy the proposed super-peer network on top of each autonomic grid system to form a Grid-to-Grid federation environment.

We use a matrix multiplication program as the benchmark. Each job in the experiment is a parallel program written by MPI with C. The matrix size is 1024x1024. The number of required processors for each job is set to be 4. The ratio of communication to computation of the test program is about 1 to 100. Each job is submitted per 10 seconds; and the total number of submitted jobs varies from 5 to 20 in two cases to evaluate the system performance. In case 1, the same jobs are submitted to each autonomic grid system for four rounds. The number of jobs in each round is 5, 10, 15, or 20, respectively. For this case, all the jobs are only executed in the local grid system. In case 2, the same jobs of each round are submitted to each autonomic grid system with the G2G federation environment. For this case, each job will be executed in the local grid or the remote grid according to the decision made by the above-mentioned G2G scheduler and G2G allocator.

We estimate the average turnaround time of each job for completing the computation and also measure the average overhead of each job with regard to the time consumed from the Cross-Grid layer to the Local-Grid layer. The job turnaround time is defined as the time period from the time when a job is submitted to the waiting queue for processing in the Cross-Grid layer, to the time when the submitted job is completed in the Local-Grid layer. The overhead of migrating a job is defined as the time period from the time when a job is submitted to the Cross-Grid layer, to the time when the submitted job is decided to which local-grid system for execution. By definition, the job turnaround time includes the execution time and the migrating overhead. If the cost of overhead takes too much time in the Cross-Grid layer, the overall turnaround time for executing a job will be increasing. The G2G system is expected to reduce the average turnaround time of each job with little overhead when there is over-loading or there are no available resources in the local grid system.

Experimental Results

Figure 9 depicts the experimental results in terms of the average turnaround time. The results show that each grid system requires longer turnaround time to complete a job when there are more jobs submitted for execution without the help from remote grid systems. As a result, the grid with higher computational power takes the longer time to complete a job once there is getting more jobs for execution. This is because a job is queued for a long time if local resources are often busy in the grid system with fewer resources. The longer time a job is queued, the more time the turnaround time will be consumed. However, the system performance can be improved by using the proposed meta-grid framework. When there are no available resources in a local grid system, the job will be migrated to a remote grid system with available resources for execution. On the other hand, Figure 10 and Figure 11 depict the ratio of average overhead compared with the average turnaround time. The experimental results show that the average overhead in all cases is light. The reason is that the average overhead will be reduced if a job can be allocated to available resources for execution as soon as possible. Hence, the average turnaround time of completing a job will be reduced as well.

Figure 9. Average turnaround time for completing jobs

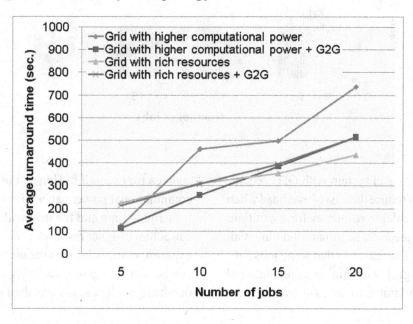

Figure 10. Distribution of average turnaround time for completing jobs

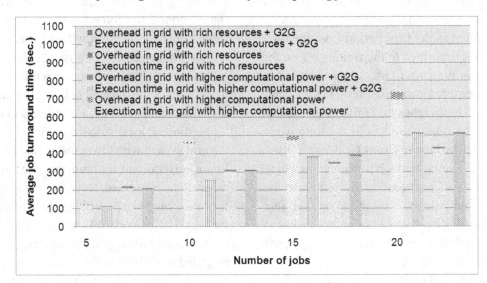

Figure 11. Ratio of average overhead to computation time for completing jobs

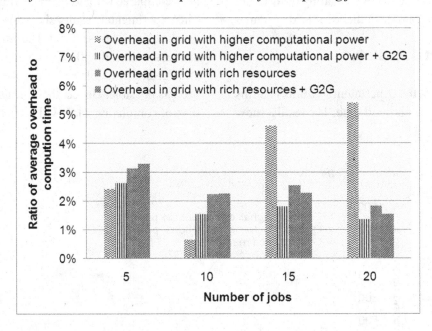

In summary, a grid system with G2G federation can not only reduce the cost of overhead when there are not available resources for execution, but also reduce the average turnaround time with little overhead. The reason is that some jobs submitting to the grid with higher computational power can be migrated to the grid with rich resources for execution. Hence, the grid with high computational power can achieve lower average turnaround time and the grid with rich resources can achieve higher resource utilization. From the experimental results, the average turnaround time can be reduced up to about 45% and the average overhead in all cases is less than 6%.

CONCLUSION AND FUTURE WORKS

Integrating the grid computing with P2P technique can improve the scalability of the large-scale grid system. This study proposes a meta-grid framework, named the G2G framework, for the Grid-to-Grid federation of autonomic grid systems without modifying the original mechanisms and policies. Based on the super-peer network, we adopt a separate layer built on top of existing grid systems to develop the Grid-to-Grid collaborative computing environment. Each super-peer represents a grid system. A super-peer in the G2G system is responsible for coordinating an internally autonomic grid system and for communicating with other super-peers. The overlay network among super-peers is constructed via the unstructured approach.

A grid system is deployed with the capacity of the super-peer for coordinating the G2G system. With well-defined APIs, the G2G system resembles an abstract layer that is separate from the existing grid systems. In our G2G system, an existing grid system can be upgraded its G2G capability without upsetting original mechanisms. We not only take care of the support of computation services and data services, but also consider a solution for the grid security across different grid systems. To evaluate the performance of the G2G system, we implemented a preliminary system to show that the proposed system not only is workable but also improves the system performance.

In the future work, we will refine the IDL format to follow the standard description language, and also study on the efficiency of grid security across diverse grid systems. We also intend to integrate with more autonomic grid systems and enhance the G2G framework to the Service-Oriented Architecture (SOA) in order to develop a service-oriented G2G computing system.

REFERENCES

Baru, C., Moore, R., Rajasekar, A., & Wan, M. (1998). *The SDSC Storage Resource Broker*. Paper presented at the Proceedings of the 1998 conference of the Centre for Advanced Studies on Collaborative research.

Cao, J., Liu, F. B., & Xu, C.-Z. (2007). P2PGrid: Integrating P2P Networks into the Grid Environment. *Concurrency and Computation, 19*(7), 1023–1046. doi:10.1002/cpe.1096

Castro, M., Druschel, P., Kermarrec, A.-M., & Rowstron, A. I. T. (2002). Scribe: A Large-Scale and Decentralized Application-Level Multicast Infrastructure. *IEEE Journal on Selected Areas in Communications, 20*(8), 1489–1499. doi:10.1109/JSAC.2002.803069

Chervenak, A., Foster, I., Kesselman, C., Salisbury, C., & Tuecke, S. (2000). The Data Grid: Towards an Architecture for the Distributed Management and Analysis of Large Scientific Datasets. *Journal of Network and Computer Applications, 23*(3), 187–200. doi:10.1006/jnca.2000.0110

Czajkowski, K., Fitzgerald, S., Foster, I., & Kesselman, C. (2001). *Grid Information Services for Distributed Resource Sharing*. Paper presented at the Proceedings of the 10th IEEE International Symposium on High Performance Distributed Computing, New York.

Fitzgerald, S., Foster, I., Kesselman, C., von Laszewski, G., Smith, W., & Tuecke, S. (1997). *A Directory Service for Conturing High-Performance Distributed Computations*. Paper presented at the Proceedings of The Sixth IEEE International Symposium on High Performance Distributed Computing.

Foster, I., & Iamnitchi, A. (2003). On Death, Taxes, and the Convergence of Peer-to-Peer and Grid Computing. In *Peer-to-Peer Systems II* (pp. 118-128).

Foster, I., Kesselman, C., Nick, J. M., & Tuecke, S. (2002). *The Physiology of the Grid: An Open Grid Services Architecture for Distributed Systems Integration*. Retrieved from http://www.globus.org/alliance/publications/papers/ogsa.pdf

Foster, I., Kesselman, C., Tsudik, G., & Tuecke, S. (1998). *A Security Architecture for Computational Grids*. Paper presented at the Proceedings of the 5th ACM conference on Computer and communications security.

Foster, I., Kesselman, C., & Tuecke, S. (2001). The Anatomy of the Grid: Enabling Scalable Virtual Organizations. *International Journal of High Performance Computing Applications*, *15*(3), 200–222. doi:10.1177/109434200101500302

Fox, G., Pallickara, S., & Rao, X. (2005). Towards Enabling Peer-to-Peer Grids. *Concurrency and Computation*, *17*(7-8), 1109–1131. doi:10.1002/cpe.863

Massie, M. L., Chun, B. N., & Culler, D. E. (2004). The Ganglia Distributed Monitoring System: Design, Implementation, and Experience. *Parallel Computing*, *30*(7), 817–840. doi:10.1016/j.parco.2004.04.001

Mastroianni, C., Talia, D., & Verta, O. (2005). A Super-Peer Model for Resource Discovery Services in Large-Scale Grids. *Future Generation Computer Systems*, *21*(8), 1235–1248. doi:10.1016/j.future.2005.06.001

Mastroianni, C., Talia, D., & Verta, O. (2007). *Evaluating Resource Discovery Protocols for Hierarchical and Super-Peer Grid Information Systems*. Paper presented at the Proceedings of the 15th Euromicro International Conference on Parallel, Distributed and Network-Based Processing.

Pairot, C., Garcia, P., & Skarmeta, A. F. G. (2004). *DERMI: A Decentralized Peer-to-Peer Event-Based Object Middleware*. Paper presented at the Proceedings of the 24th International Conference on Distributed Computing Systems.

Pallickara, S., & Fox, G. (2003). NaradaBrokering: A Distributed Middleware Framework and Architecture for Enabling Durable Peer-to-Peer Grids. In. *Proceedings of Middleware, 2003*, 998–999.

Ranjan, R., Harwood, A., & Buyya, R. (2008). Peer-to-Peer-Based Resource Discovery in Global Grids: A Tutorial. *IEEE Communications Surveys & Tutorials*, *10*(2), 6–33. doi:10.1109/COMST.2008.4564477

Rauber, T., & Runger, G. (2005). *M-Task-Programming for Heterogeneous Systems and Grid Environments*. Paper presented at the 19th IEEE International Parallel and Distributed Processing Symposium.

Rowstron, A., & Druschel, P. (2001). Pastry: Scalable, Decentralized Object Location, and Routing for Large-Scale Peer-to-Peer Systems. In. *Proceedings of Middleware, 2001*, 329–350.

Shih, P.-C., Chen, H.-M., Chung, Y.-C., Wang, C.-M., Chang, R.-S., Hsu, C.-H., et al. (2008). *Middleware of Taiwan UniGrid*. Paper presented at the 2008 ACM symposium on Applied computing.

Talia, D., & Trunfio, P. (2003). Toward a Synergy Between P2P and Grids. *IEEE Internet Computing*, *7*(4), 96–95. doi:10.1109/MIC.2003.1215667

Trunfio, P., Talia, D., Papadakis, H., Fragopoulou, P., Mordacchini, M., & Pennanen, M. (2007). Peer-to-Peer Resource Discovery in Grids: Models and Systems. *Future Generation Computer Systems*, *23*(7), 864–878. doi:10.1016/j.future.2006.12.003

Yang, B., & Garcia-Molina, H. (2003). *Designing a Super-Peer Network*. Paper presented at the 19th International Conference on Data Engineering.

This work was previously published in International Journal of Grid and High Performance Computing, Volume 2, Issue 3, edited by Emmanuel Udoh, pp. 1-16, copyright 2010 by IGI Publishing (an imprint of IGI Global).

Chapter 18

One Anchor Distance and Angle Based Multi – Hop Adaptive Iterative Localization Algorithm for Wireless Sensor Networks

S. B. Kotwal
SMVD University, India

Shekhar Verma
Indian Institute of Information Technology, India

G. S. Tomar
Malwa Institute of Technology, India

R. K. Abrol
SMVD University, India

ABSTRACT

This paper presents distance and angle measurements based Multi-Hop Adaptive and Iterative Localization algorithm for localization of unknown nodes in wireless sensor networks (WSNs). The present work determines uncertainty region of unknown nodes with respect to known (anchor) nodes using noisy distance and angle measurements. This node transmits its uncertainty region to other unknown nodes to help them determine their uncertainty region. Because of noisy distance and angle measurements, the error propagation increases the size of regions of nodes in subsequent hops. Using only one anchor node as reference, the proposed iterative localization algorithm reduces the error propagation of this noisy distance and angle measurements and the uncertainty region of all unknown nodes within a given communication range. The results clearly indicate the improved efficiency of the proposed algorithm in comparison with existing algorithms.

DOI: 10.4018/978-1-4666-0056-0.ch018

I. INTRODUCTION

Developments in the field of electronic devices, components and in modern communication technologies has lead to the development of small, cheap, and smart sensor nodes (Stojmenovic, 2005; Akyildiz, Su, Sankarasubramaniam, & Cayirci, 2002). Hundreds or thousands of such nodes, able to sense the environment, compute simple tasks and communicate with each other, form a huge wireless sensor network (WSN) (Chong & Kumar, 2003). Collected information (e.g., temperature, humidity etc.) from relevant node then transmitted in a multi hop fashion over direct neighbors to a data sink, where the data interpreted and action taken accordingly.

Localization in· Wireless Sensor Networks (WSNs) refers to creation of a map of a WSN by determining the geographical coordinates of each and every node. A number of applications of WSNs like target tracking (Li, Wong, Hu, & Sayeed, 2002), forest fire surveillance, fluid quality monitoring in industry, intrusion detection, traffic management etc require information about physical location of sensor nodes in the network. Localization also helps in geographical data packet routing (De, Qiao, & Wu, 2003) and collaborative information and signal processing (Heidemann & Bulusu, 2000). More over once location of a node in network is known, the coordinates that eventually will save the size of data packet to be sent by it can simply replace its node ID. Many limiting aspects of a node like computation intensity, power consumption and memory location imposed by the small devices is to be considered in location identification in a WSN. Because of the random deployment nature of WSN, it is not feasible to place nodes while recording their locations one by one. A network consisting of 1000 nodes will require around 17 hours to localize whole network assuming 1 minute required for placement of each node while recording its location.

One possible solution is to equip nodes with GPS. But limiting factors like small size, limited computation power and energy source, the possible solution excludes use of GPS. In almost all localization techniques some percentage of nodes are assumed to know their location a priori. Nodes which known their location a priori are called anchors. These anchor nodes help in absolute localization of nodes in a WSN. Without any anchor, nodes create a local map of their own which may be translated, rotated or mirror image of the actual map. These anchor nodes may be the nodes placed manually while recording their locations or nodes with additional capability like GPS as in (Meguerdichian, Slijepcevic, Karayan, & Potkonjak, 2001). The percentage of anchors required for localization of a WSN depends upon the technique of localization adopted. The proposed algorithm uses only one anchor node with RF beam steering capability to localize a full WSN. Simulations show that only one anchor node is capable for localization of a WSN within an acceptable level of error in localization.

Rest of the paper is organized as follows. Section II describes the problem associated with localization of sensor nodes followed by the related work in section III with proposed solution in section IV. The simulation and results are given in section V. Conclusion in is Section VI.

II. PROBLEM STATEMENT

We define the localization problem as estimating the smallest region which has the highest probability of having a node. With the available hardware and software support, any node within one hop from anchor can determine its uncertainty region w.r.t. anchor node from data sent by anchor with received signal strength index (RSSI) and angle of arrival (AOA) measurements. Before working on an algorithm based on above measurements, the uncertainties and their effects need to be taken into consideration. Therefore we discuss these uncertainties as under:

A. *Uncertainty due to noisy distance measurement:* With available RSSI, the distance between two nodes can be approximated by:

$$U_{j2} = U_{ki} \oplus U_{k1} \tag{1}$$

Where $\widetilde{d_{ij}}$ is the distance between node i and node j, P_{tx}, power transmitted by ith node, P_{rx} power received by jth node and ∞, the propagation constant. Because of the inherent irregularity in RSSI measurement especially indoors due to multipath effects, it becomes practically impossible to predict exact distance between two nodes (Hel'en, Latvala, Ikonen, & Niittylahti, 2001). But it is practical to assume distance error e_0 or 1 meter to be 0.2 meters as in (Savvides, Han, & Strivastava, 2001). That means the distance range is,

$$d_{ij} = \widetilde{d_{ij}} \pm e \tag{2}$$

Where, $e = \widetilde{d_{ij}} * e_0$

If $d_{ij1} = \widetilde{d_{ij}} - e$ & $d_{ij2} = \widetilde{d_{ij}} + e$, then node j is within $d_{ij1} \leq d_{ij} \leq d_{ij2}$ from node i as shown in Figure 1.

B. *Uncertainty due to noisy angle measurement:* We assume instead of the unknown nodes determining their angle of arrival, the anchor node is beam forming signal in all directions w.r.t north and the data packet sent in each direction contains the angle of beam formed also. This way, unknown nodes at one hop from anchor can determine their inclination w.r.t north also. The localized nodes at first hop can also steer beam in all possible direction w.r.t north and 2nd and so on hops can determine their inclinations also. If a node j is within communication range of node i, then to account for a beam width of transmitting antenna and inaccurate angle of transmission $\widetilde{\theta}_{angle(ij)}$ at node j from node i, w.r.t some reference axis say north, has a variance of σ_{ij}. This way the node j may find itself within an annular region as specified by,

$$\theta_{ij1} \leq \theta_{ij} \leq \theta_{ij2} \tag{3}$$

Where, $\theta_{ij1} = \widetilde{\theta}_{ij} - \sigma_{angle(ij)}$ and $\theta_{ij2} = \widetilde{\theta}_{ij} + \sigma_{angle(ij)}$ as shown in Figure 2.

Experiments in [b] show that an assumption of $\sigma_{angle(ij)} \cong 5^0$ is practical.

Considering node i as an anchor node and inaccuracy in distance and angle measurements, the uncertainty region of a node j within communication within one hop of another node can be constructed as suggested in (Doherty, Pister, & El Ghaoui, 2001) a convex region as shown in Figure 3. We find that the uncertainty region created by anchor for all nodes in hop-1 will be trapezoidal in shape.

C. *Localization error propagation:* Any node in second hop cannot communicate with anchor directly; it determines its region from first hop node. Its uncertainty region is deter-

Figure 1. Distance constrain by noisy RSSI measurement

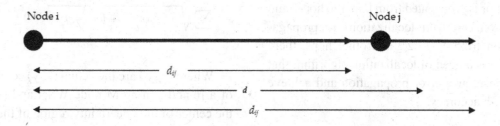

Figure 2. Uncertainty constrain by noisy angle of arrival

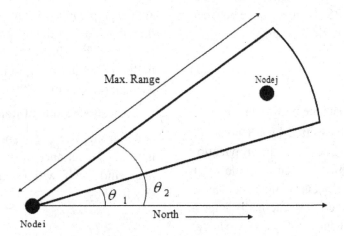

Figure 3. Combining constrains of distance and angle to approximate. The uncertainty region of node-j is approximated as convex hull shown in gray.

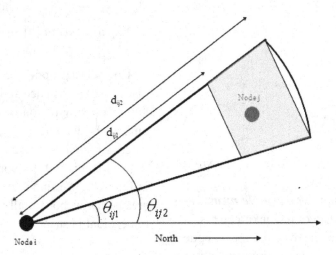

mined from all vertices of hop 1 node. The resultant region is much bigger in size as compared to the uncertainty region of node in hop 1, which means that uncertainty is increased as shown in Figure 4. This way error is propagated from hop-1 to hop-2 and so on. Due to this localization error propagation from 1st to 2nd and other hops, there arises a need of localization algorithm that can reduce error propagation and achieve high accuracy.

The problem of localization for a WSN can be formulated as a scheme to determine the uncertainty region for each node that approximates its location, such that:

$$\frac{1}{M} \sum_{j=1}^{M} \sqrt{(x_j - x_j')^2 + (y_j - y_j')^2} \sim 0 \qquad (4)$$

Where (x_j, y_j) are the actual (x, y) coordinates of a jth node, in an M node WSN and (x_j, y_j) is the center of the uncertainty region of that node.

Figure 4. Localization error propagation. Node-j determines its region from anchor node-i, and node–k at 2ⁿᵈ hop from anchor determines its uncertainty region from node-j. Note that there is a significant increase in the region of node-k

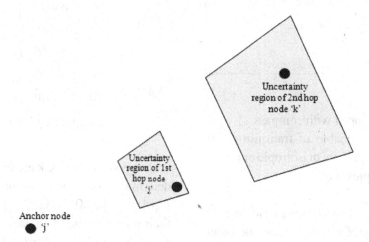

III. RELATED WORK

Form the measurement's perspective, localization algorithms are broadly based into two methods, i.e. range based and range free methods. The range based methods use measurements like distance and/or angle between nodes using received signal strength index (RSSI) (Elnahrawy, Li, & Martin, 2004), time of arrival(TOA),time difference of arrival (TDOA) or angle of arrival (AOA) (Peng & Sichitiu, 2006). Whereas the range free methods do not use the distance or angle measurements with respect to their neighbors. They use connectivity information to identify the nodes and in their radio range, and then estimate their position. The range free methods are simple to implement but lack in accuracy. A number of range based methods have been proposed in recent years. A very practical model for localization with hardware design is given in (Denegri, Zappatore, & Davoli, 2008). A novel localization scheme based on AoA measurements with noisy angle measurements is proposed in (Peng & Sichitiu, 2006). The practical model in (Denegri, Zappatore, & Davoli, 2008) uses three types of nodes (anchor, mobile and general purpose). The model in (Denegri, Zappatore, &

Davoli, 2008) exploits advantages for single hop WSN. In (Elnahrawy, Austin-Francisco, & Martin, 2007) a curve fitting model based on AoA and RSSI measurements is proposed. The scheme proposed needs previous data for training purpose.

The need of multi-hop, single anchor and less complex localization scheme can be estimated from related work. In contrast to all these approaches authors in this paper present a simple region intersecting method of localization without any data required for learning purpose.

IV. PROPOSED SOLUTION

Generally nodes in a WSN have fixed transmission power because of that nodes have limited communication range therefore it becomes necessary to divide nodes in groups to avoid data packet loss and save power.

The proposed model works under the assumptions that:

1. All nodes are deployed randomly.
2. At least one (anchor) node has its location known a priori.

Table 1. Pseudo code for anchor(c-1)

```
1. For 1m sec
    Turn on transmitter & Transmit data packet, rotating
beam in all 360 angles.
2. Turn off transmitter and turn on receiver.
3. Is there any request for re transmission
    a. If yes; got to step-1
    b. If not; repeat step 3
```

3. Nodes are equipped with compass.
4. All nodes are capable of transmitting or receiving data packets in isotropic or aniso-tropic half duplex mode.

After deployment of nodes in a field, anchor sets itself to transmission mode and all other nodes in receiving mode. Anchor transmits data packet containing id, coordinates and angle of transmission information in all 360^0 directions while rotating its beam in anti clockwise direction from a reference line (North). The pseudo code (c-1) for anchor is shown in Table 1.

The hop value of anchor is set to zero. Our algorithm divides all nodes in N hops in terms of a distance from anchor node. The localization starts with determining the nodes in first hop. The algorithm is fully distributed; in fact it is require-ment of the algorithm to be distributed as a node after running one iteration of proposed algorithm helps in reducing uncertainty region of other nodes. The distributed algorithm runs pseudo code (c-2) on each node except anchor node.

Localization by first hop nodes: A node-j in first hop runs pseudo code (c-2) given below to localize itself. It receives data packet from anchor and determines its hop count, its north direction and uncertainty region. The id field and hop field are used to determine its hop value. Based of AoA technique it determines the angle from which data packet of anchor is coming. From x, y coordinate field, it determines the distance range (d_{ij1} & d_{ij2}). Angle field and AoA technique combine to give (θ_{ij1} & θ_{ij2}). Combining all above information, node-j determines its x and y coordinates as follows:

$$x_{j1} = x_i + \begin{bmatrix} d_{ij1} \times \cos(\theta_{ij1}) \\ d_{ij1} \times \cos(\theta_{ij2}) \\ d_{ij2} \times \cos(\theta_{ij1}) \\ d_{ij2} \times \cos(\theta_{ij2}) \end{bmatrix},$$

$$y_{j1} = y_i + \begin{bmatrix} d_{ij1} \times \sin(\theta_{ij1}) \\ d_{ij1} \times \sin(\theta_{ij2}) \\ d_{ij2} \times \sin(\theta_{ij1}) \\ d_{ij2} \times \sin(\theta_{ij2}) \end{bmatrix}$$

(5)

Suppose nodes j & k are in the first hop. After determining their respective uncertainty regions as $U_{j1}=[x_{j1}, y_{j1}]$ and $U_{k1}=[x_{k1}, y_{k1}]$, nodes j & k share their regions using data packet as mentioned al-ready. Node-k's x, y coordinates are non-singular therefore region of node-j w.r.t it will be large. Therefore node-j determines its uncertainty region w.r.t. the farthest vertex of node-k as U_{ki} The un-certainty region of node-j w.r.t all possible points inside U_{k1} is computed as:

$$U_{j2}=U_{ki}\oplus U_{k1} \qquad (6)$$

This uncertainty region is intersected with U_{j1} and becomes U_{j1}.

Table 2. Pseudo code for all nth hop nodes (c-2)

```
1. For i=1 to n(iterations)
    i) Update own hop count to n+1
    ii) While determining AoA, receive a data packet with
highest RSSI
        a) If own hop count=1;
            determine own uncertainty region
        b) Else;
            determine own uncertainty region using Equation
(7)
    iii) Intersect with old region if present and update as old
region
    iv) Transmit own data packet by steering rf beam anti-
clockwise w.r.t north
    v) Is termination condition given by (6) satisfied
        a) If yes;
            Go to step 2
        b) If not;
            Go to step 1(ii)
2. exit
```

Same code is run by all nodes in first hop. After running its fixed number of iterations in n^{th} hop nodes, $(n+1)^{th}$ hop nodes determine their hop count and location similarly till all N hop nodes are localized. The termination of algorithm depends upon two conditions, one compares the predefined number of iteration and second condition given in (c) to check if all vertices of U_{j1} are equal to a singular point. If any of the above condition is satisfied execution stops. The further execution of algorithm will increase cost of communication without any advantage in localization error.

Termination condition for pseudo code (c-2) is:

$$\sum_{k=1}^{L} (x_k - x_j^{'})^2 + (y_k - y_j^{'})^2 = 0 \qquad (7)$$

Here (x_k, y_k) is the kth vertex of an L-vertex uncertainty region of jth node and $(x_j^{'}, y_j^{'})$ is the centroid of the uncertainty region. Localization by subsequent hop nodes is done in a similar manner and termination The fixed number of iterations of same code (c-2) is run by all nodes in subsequent hops to determine and update their feasibility regions. The data packet format is shown in Figure 5. Authors propose same data packet format for all nodes.

V. SIMULATION AND RESULTS

A. Simulation Setup

The simulations for proposed algorithm are done in Matlab. The simulation setup consists of 100 unknown nodes deployed randomly in a field of 100m x 100 m field. Figure 6 shows 100 nodes divided into hops according to the distance from anchor node at $(x_i, y_i) = (50, 50)$. Every sensor node can communicate with other sensors if distance between them is smaller than sensor range. Transmission range for each node is fixed at 18 m. For all possibly communicable nodes, the algorithm for localization comprising of pseudo code -1 & 2 is implemented. The maximum number of iterations run for each node is only 5, practically the number of iteration may be < 5 for some nodes because of the termination condition given in (c). The localization error for each hop nodes is determined for different values of variance in angle $\sigma_{angle(ij)}$.

B. Results and Discussion

Figure 7 shows the uncertainty regions after 1st and 5th iteration for all 100 nodes in 4 hops after running 5 iterations of algorithm with $e_0 = 0.1m$ and $\sigma_{angle(i,j)} = 5^0$. Figure 8 shows percentage of mean area reduction per iteration for all nodes in each hop from a reference area.

Reference area is of the uncertainty regions formed for a node at first hop from anchor as was shown in Figure 3. Coordinates (x_j, y_j) of an unknown node are approximated by taking centroid of the remaining region.

Figure 9 shows actual vs. estimated coordinates for all 100 nodes inside the field. The estimated locations and actual coordinates are almost overlapping with each other. Figure 10 shows close view of some nodes from Figure 9 for better visualization of actual vs. estimated locations for 4 nodes. We calculated error of localization for all nodes in different hops as a function of number of iterations to reflect the accuracy of scheme.

Figure 5. Data packet format of a node

node id	hop count	coordinates		angle w.r.t north
		x	y	

Figure 6. 100 nodes deployed in a field of 100m x 100m. Red, green, blue and orange dots indicate nodes at 1ˢᵗ, 2ⁿᵈ, 3ʳᵈ and 4ᵗʰ hop from anchor respectively. Note that anchor is at (50,50) indicated by red*.

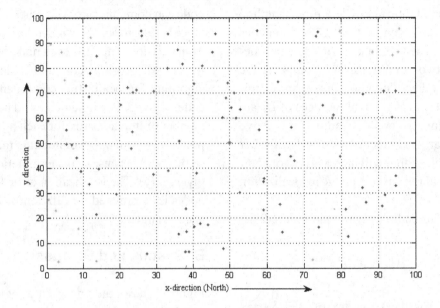

Figure 11 shows a graph of localization error in meters vs. number of iterations for all 4- hop nodes. Graph shows that for all hop nodes localization error decreases with increasing number of iterations of algorithm. Localization error is a decreasing exponential function of iterations and remains almost constant after 4ᵗʰ iteration.

Running algorithm for number of iterations beyond 5 will not be practical as the cost of communication compared to accuracy required will

Figure 7. Regions with red, green, blue and orange after 1ˢᵗ iteration of algorithm for 1ˢᵗ, 2ⁿᵈ, 3ʳᵈ and 4ᵗʰ hop nodes respectively. Regions reduced for each node after 5ᵗʰ iteration are shown by black patches.

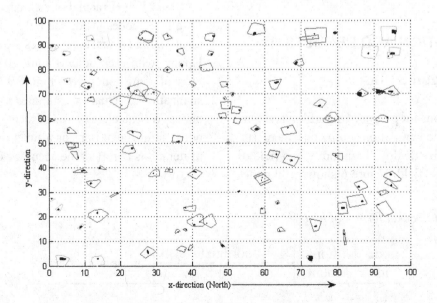

Figure 8. Percentage of area remained of nodes after each iteration

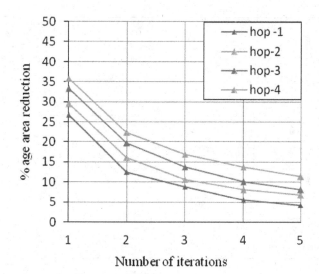

be very high. There is a small increase in the error for 4th hop node from 2nd to third iteration, this is because of the fact that estimated location after each iteration is assumed to be the centroid of convex hull (uncertainty region) and since the shape of convex hull changes with each iteration,

the centroid may not always remain close to the actual position.

The average localization error of 142.7cm is obtained for all 100 nodes with e_0=0.1m and $\sigma_{angle(i,j)}$=5°. The simulation is repeated for different values of $\sigma_{angle(i,j)}$ and e_0, plot is drawn in

Figure 9. Actual vs. estimated locations. Actual and estimated locations are indicated by red 'x' and black 'o' respectively.

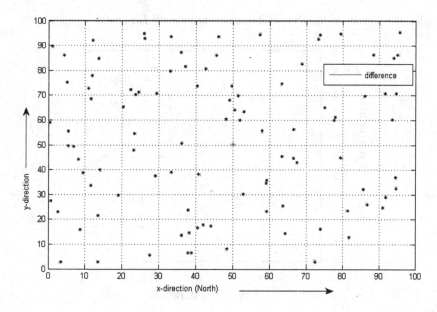

Figure 10. Actual vs. estimated location for 4-nodes

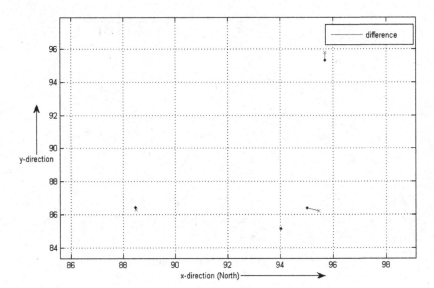

Figure 12. Comparing with the localization error of algorithm proposed in (Montillet, Braysy, & Oppermann, 2005) based on DFP and DM show minimum error nearly equal to 1m and 0.05m with DM and DFP respectively keeping $\sigma_{angle(i,j)}=10^0$. The proposed algorithm performs better in the sense that for $\sigma_{angle(i,j)}=10^0$ minimum error equals to 0.6m. Note that the in (Montillet, Braysy, & Oppermann, 2005) error is introduced for ToA for distance and AoA for angle calculations, and for minimum error case of nearly equal to 0.05m, error due to ToA is assumed to be 0, which is not practical. Our algorithm takes a minimum ranging error of 0.1m for 1m i.e. at least 10% and maximum of 50% of the distance.

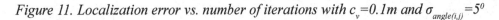

Figure 11. Localization error vs. number of iterations with $c_v=0.1m$ and $\sigma_{angle(i,j)}=5^0$

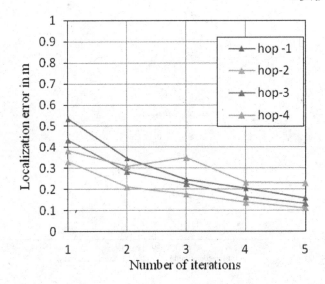

Figure 12. Performance analysis for different values of e_0 and $\sigma_{angle(i,j)}$

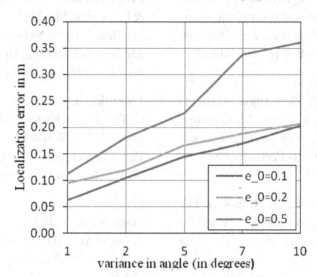

VI. CONCLUSION

A new angle and distance based algorithm is proposed to localize nodes in wireless sensor networks. To the best knowledge of authors this algorithm is the only one that has used one anchor node to localize a full WSN of 100 nodes with high accuracy. Proposed algorithm exploits the advantages of multi-hop WSN in which the localized nodes in $(n)^{th}$ hop further reduce the size of uncertainty region of $(n-1)^{th}$ hop nodes. The proposed algorithm is robust to ranging error due to irregular RSSI as it can be seen from Figure 12 that increasing ranging error from 5 times increases localization error less than two folds. The advantage of cheap RSSI without increasing cost of hardware as in ToA or TDoA motivated authors to Take RSSI errors into consideration. In future authors wish to implement algorithm on hardware.

REFERENCES

Akyildiz, I., Su, W., Sankarasubramaniam, Y., & Cayirci, E. (2002, August). A survey on sensor networks. *IEEE Communications Magazine*, *40*(8), 102–116. doi:10.1109/MCOM.2002.1024422

Cheng, K.-Y., Lui, K.-S., & Tam, V. (2009). HyBloc: Localization in Sensor Networks with Adverse Anchor Placement. *Sensors (Basel, Switzerland)*, *9*(1), 253–280. doi:10.3390/s90100253

Chong, C.-Y., & Kumar, S. (2003, August). Sensor networks: evolution, opportunities, and challenges. *Proceedings of the IEEE*, *91*, 1247–1256. doi:10.1109/JPROC.2003.814918

De, S., Qiao, C., & Wu, H. (2003). *Meshed Multipath Routing: An Efficient Strategy in Wireless Sensor Networks*. Computer Networks.

Denegri, L., Zappatore, S., & Davoli, F. (2008). Sensor Network-Based Localization for Continuous Tracking Applications: Implementation and Performance Evaluation. *Advances in Multimedia* (Vol. 2008, Article ID 569848).

Doherty, L., Pister, K. S. J., & El Ghaoui, L. (2001, April). Convex position estimation in wireless sensor networks. In *Proceedings of the IEEE Infocom 2001*, Anchorage, AK (Vol. 3, pp. 1655-1663).

Elnahrawy, E., Austin-Francisco, J., & Martin, R. P. (2007, February). Adding Angle of Arrival Modality to Basic RSS Location Management Techniques. In *Proceedings of the IEEE International Symposium on Wireless Pervasive Computing (ISWPC'07)*.

Elnahrawy, E., Li, X., & Martin, R. (2004). The limits of localization using signal strength: a comparative study. In *Proceedings of the First Annual IEEE Conference on Sensor and Ad-hoc Communications and Networks* (pp. 406-414).

Heidemann, J., & Bulusu, N. (2000). Using Geospatial Information in Sensor Networks. In *Proceedings of MOBICOM*.

Hel'en, M., Latvala, J., Ikonen, H., & Niittylahti, J. (2001). Using calibration in RSSI-based location tracking system. In *Proceedings of the 5th World Multiconference on Circuits, Systems, Communications & Computers (CSCC20001)*.

Li, D., Wong, K. D., Hu, Y. W., & Sayeed, A. M. (2002, March). Detection, Classification, and Tracking of Targets. *IEEE Signal Processing Magazine*.

Meguerdichian, S., Slijepcevic, S., Karayan, V., & Potkonjak, M. (2001). Localized Algorithms In Wireless Ad-Hoc Networks: Location Discovery and Sensor Exposure. In *Proceedings of the MobiHOC 2001*, UCLA, Los Angeles, CA.

Montillet, J. P., Braysy, T., & Oppermann, I. (2005). *Algorithm for Nodes Localization in Wireless Ad-Hoc Networks Based on Cost Function*. Paper presented at the International Workshop on Wireless Ad Hoc Networks (IWWAN 2005), London.

Peng, R., & Sichitiu, M. L. (2006, September). Angle of Arrival Localization for Wireless Sensor Networks. In *Proceedings of the Third Annual IEEE Communications Society Conference on Sensor and Ad Hoc Communications and Networks*, Reston, VA.

Savvides, A., Han, C. C., & Strivastava, M. B. (2001). Dynamic fine-grained localization in ad-hoc networks of sensors. In *Proceedings of the 7th Annual ACM/IEEE International Conference on Mobile Computing and Networking*.

Sichitiu, M. L., Ramadurai, V., et al. (2003). *Simple algorithm for outdoor localization of wireless sensor networks with inaccurate range measurements*.

Stojmenovic, I. (2005). *Handbook of Sensor Networks*. New York: Wiley. doi:10.1002/047174414X

This work was previously published in International Journal of Grid and High Performance Computing, Volume 2, Issue 3, edited by Emmanuel Udoh, pp. 31-43, copyright 2010 by IGI Publishing (an imprint of IGI Global).

Chapter 19
Intelligent Industrial Data Acquisition and Energy Monitoring using Wireless Sensor Networks

Sumeet Gupta
SMVD University, India

Shekhar Verma
Indian Institute of Information Technology, India

G.S. Tomar
Malwa Institute of Technology & Management, India

Raj Kumar Abrol
SMVD University, India

ABSTRACT

Most of the application-oriented research in the field of Wireless Sensor Networks has been in remote monitoring, including environmental, building automation, and security. However, this paper presents the methodology followed for implementation of a Wireless Sensor Network based solution in a process plant for energy management and leak detection. The sensor network acquires data pertaining to detection of leakage in a plant. The network further serves effectively as a maintenance and diagnostic system that is used to manage the plant and conserve energy in a process plant. The critical design issues, testing methodologies and implementation problems pertaining to the system are also presented. Additionally, special focus has been placed on the calculations pertaining to the network life time.

DOI: 10.4018/978-1-4666-0056-0.ch019

INTRODUCTION

The rising cost of energy has made it absolutely essential for industries to ensure that energy wastage is minimized during every phase of the production process. Therefore the last two decades have seen a renewed focus on improving the efficiency of the process besides overall plant efficiency to reduce the production cost. Overall production cost includes the cost of various utilities like steam, compressed air, electricity, water etc. besides the raw material and labor cost. Any effort in improving the plant efficiency necessarily involves collecting the data pertaining to all these parameters, besides the critical process parameters and then acting upon it.

The collection of information needs to be done in a manner ensuring the accuracy and integrity of the data collected since this has a direct impact on process control.

The reliability of measurement, communication and the control action is critical for the system to work effectively. Various methods of instrumentation and processing of the data have continuously evolved over period of time. Fully integrated modern electronic SCADA systems have evolved which manage plant wide collection of information accurately and reliably.

A critical requirement of this integrated system is the transfer of the parameter measured by the sensor in the field to the centralized location. This transfer of information over the wired medium was traditionally done in the analog form, either current (the standard 4-20ma loop) or voltage (1-5V). With advancement in technology and reduction in cost, more intelligence could be placed at the sensor end itself and the transmission of data became digital. Protocols like RS232 for short-distance and RS 485 & HART™ for long-distance have become more popular using which it has become possible to collect plant-wide information.

Using the wired medium is laborious in terms of installation and maintenance. This also severely reduces re-location flexibility besides increasing the system cost. The obvious solution is to use wireless communication technology.

Wireless Sensor Networks have emerged as a possible solution for acquisition of data which is being sensed by multiple sensors over various locations in a large geographic area (Akyildiz, Su, Sankarasubramaniam, & Cayirci, 2002). These sensor nodes are inexpensive, have low computational capability and are energy constrained. They are however equipped with a radio for wireless communication and have the network and applications software capabilities to form a self-organized network, over which they pass the sensed data from each point to another. Since the energy constraint could severely reduce their working life, these nodes are generally used to sense some event rather than measure continuously in real-time.

The authors have proposed and implemented a Wireless Sensor Network based solution in an industrial environment and presented the same in details in the following sections. This paper is organized as follows- Section II presents the problem statement, Section III surveys the Existing Solutions, Section IV presents the proposed solution, Section V contains the design process. Section VI presents the deployment issues, Section VII presents the results, Section VIII presents the conclusions (Figure 1)

STATEMENT OF THE PROBLEM

Utilities like water, electricity, compressed air, steam etc. are used commonly in a process plant. The utility is either generated within the plant itself (steam, compressed air) or is obtained from an external supplier (electricity, water). In both cases, the utility is further distributed in an efficient manner across the various sections of the plant.

Depending upon the size of the plant this could require kilometers of pipes (for steam, water, compressed air) laid down in an ordered manner to ensure that sufficient amount of utility is avail-

Figure 1. Block schematic of the utility distribution network illustrating the utility leakage detection points in a process plant

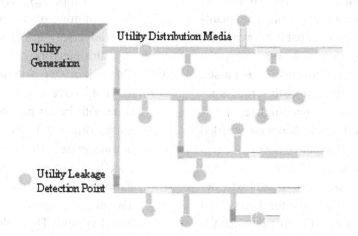

able at the right place in the plant to adequately supplement the production process.

In case the media carrying the utility springs a leak then the loss of the utility could have a sizeable impact on not only the cost of production but also on the quality of the manufactured product. There could also be an adverse impact on the manufacturing equipment which could get damaged because of the poor quality of the utility. E.g. leakage of compressed air would not only produce loss in terms of the energy spent to compress the air but also reduce the pressure of compressed air thus providing in-sufficient power to the equipment driven by the compressed air, making it work in-efficiently.

Detection of a leakage is therefore essential for maintaining the quality of the production process and for maintaining excellent plant efficiency. It is therefore desirable that leak detection equipment should be attached at multiple locations alongside the distribution media to detect loss of the utility. Depending upon the size of the plant, there could be anywhere between 50-5000 such leak detection points.

Further since the distributing pipes criss-cross across the plant at different levels and locations, most of them being extremely hazardous in nature, these leak detection points are generally located at

hard to reach places. The objective therefore was to design a system that would do the following:

a) Monitor the Leakage points to detect if any leakage is taking place.

b) In case any leakage is detected then convey the information regarding the type of fault to the utilities manager at a centralized location

c) Raise appropriate visual and audio alarm to indicate the fault situation

d) Maintain a record of the fault condition encountered

e) The system itself should require minimum maintenance and must have self-diagnostics built-in.

f) The system should be rugged and robust enough to withstand the harsh industrial environment over long period of time.

g) The system should conform to the relevant industrial standards and norms for operations & safety

EXISTING METHODS

A detailed survey of the existing available solution and their comparison shows the following:

a) *SCADA Systems:* These are highly reliable, powerful, expensive, centralized process monitoring and control systems with plant-wide data collection capability, generally used for monitoring and controlling the process parameters. Information is passed over the wired medium since the process parameters are critical and need high reliability communication. This solution was discarded because of the following considerations:

- The collection of data from the large network of detection points will become an added task for the system which could significantly dampen the response of the system.

- Another mitigating factor was the use of wires as the transmission media since the cost and installation of the wires would be prohibitively expensive and laborious.

b) *Telemetry based Systems*: This solution consists of using powerful transmitters, working over specific frequency band, located close to the detection points and having the ability to transfer the data to a centralized location over long distance. This solution would also automatically circumvent the wired media problem. However this was also discarded based on the following considerations:

- High power transmitters may require large electrical power which can only be supplied by line power.

- Since large power is being transmitted over a long distance in an open media, a license is required to be obtained from the regulatory body.

- This large power transmission could have an impact on the working of other wireless and wired equipment with-in the plant.

- Directional Antenna needs to be installed at appropriate height for line of sight communication to work properly.

- The network formed is essentially a Star topology network.

- Jamming of specific frequency could adversely affect the performance of this network.

c) *Other Wireless Solutions:* Thompson et al. (n.d.) have demonstrated the use of a Bluetooth based peer-to-peer network for monitoring the engine performance in a marine vessel. This solution demonstrated excellent packet reliability but very poor battery life. Bonnet et al. (2003) have also presented pros and cons of Bluetooth based system. This solution was therefore discarded. Efforts have been made by various researchers to use the Wireless Sensor Networks in industrial applications (Shizhuang, Jingyu, & Yanjun, 2007; Jiang, Ren, Zhang, Wang, & Xue, 2006; Salvadori, de Campos, de Figueiredo, Gehrke, Rech, Sausen, Spohn, & Oliveira, 2007; Jeong & Nof, 2008; Lin, Liu, & Fang, 2007) where simulation based architecture has been presented for use in industrial process data monitoring have been provided. Zhou et al. (2007) have proposed architecture for using Zigbee based monitoring system for Greenhouse (Figure 2).

PROPOSED SOLUTION

After carefully studying the requirements of the system it was proposed to design & implement a wireless sensor network based solution for this problem. The factors which weighed heavily in favor of a WSN based solution were as follows:

a) Continuous monitoring of the Leakage detection points was not required and this could be done periodically.

b) Visual and audio alarms were required to be raised only when a leak was detected.

Figure 2. Schematic of the wireless sensor network based solution

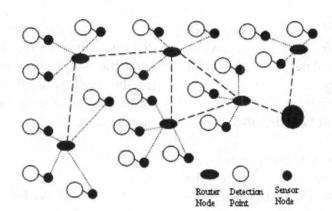

c) Real-time control action was not required

d) Since the detection points could be located at hard-to-reach places, a Wireless solution was highly desirable.

e) There were no regulatory or licensing requirements for using the 2.4GHz ISM band for low distance, low power wireless communication.

f) The sensors used for detecting the fault conditions need not be highly accurate

g) The noisy and harsh industrial environment required a rugged solution

h) Since low power communication is being performed it is extremely suitable for hazardous area applications.

i) The solution did not have to be very accurate but was required to be low cost because of the large number of detection points in a plant.

The solution envisaged having a Sensor Node mounted close to each Leakage Detection point which would monitor to detect occurrence of fault condition. These sensor nodes would self-organize themselves into a network and would pass the data corresponding to sensed values at each detection point to the centralized sink located at the Control panel in the Utility Manager's office. It was further proposed to use the IEEE 802.15.4 defined PHY & MAC layer and Zigbee™ (Zigbee Protocol V1.0, n.d.) defined NWK layer.

The sensor nodes would be powered with a non-rechargeable battery which would give a battery life of approximately 4 -5 years. A portable handheld display unit was also proposed to be designed which could be used by the Utility Manager for communicating directly with each individual Trap and change the configuration settings for the node if required. A customized GUI was also proposed to be designed which would run on a PC connected to the Sink and would store the data collected from each node. The Audio and Visual alarm would be available on the GUI for all the leak detection points. Trend analysis capability was also an objective.

The design of the enclosure was proposed such that the sensor node could withstand the harsh industrial environment having high temperature, high humidity, water, steam, corrosive gases without getting damaged.

The circuit design would also ensure that the sensor nodes could be used in hazardous areas where inflammable gas vapors could be present.

DESIGN CHALLENGES AND ISSUES

As the system consists of multiple elements which need to be designed the following section provides the design challenges and the design process for each element separately.

A. Sensing of Fault Conditions

The principle of resistivity and temperature were used for detecting the leakage of the utility at the various detection points. The sensors used were reliable and had the capability of working for long period of time in the harsh environment.

Under normal circumstances the measured temperature T_M

$$T_L < T_M < T_H \tag{1}$$

where T_L and T_H are the upper and lower limits of temperature being measured when no leakage is taking place. Depending upon the utility, the leakage condition would be indicated if the measured temperature T_M would be

$$T_L > T_M \text{ for utility like compressed air} \tag{2}$$

$$T_M > T_H \text{ for utility like steam, hot water} \tag{3}$$

Leakage of hot water or steam will increase the temperature whereas leakage of compressed air will actually reduce the temperature. The temperature reading is supplemented by the resistance reading R_M for detecting the leak condition. Under normal circumstances

$$R_M \to \infty \tag{4}$$

However if there is leakage of utility like Steam or hot water then

$$R_M \to 0 \tag{5}$$

Therefore a combination of the sensed values of temperature and Resistance can be used for detecting if any leakage is taking place. A specially designed sensor chamber is connected to the medium carrying the utility and the Temperature and Resistance sensors are located inside this chamber (Figure 3).

Figure 3. Architecture of Wireless Sensor Node, Components shown in dotted blocks are only available in Sink /Router node. The DC input block is used in router and coordinator nodes while the RS232 block is only available in coordinator/Sink node.

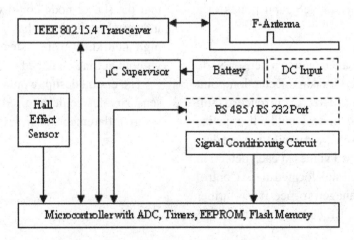

B. Design of Sensor Node

The sensor node is the primary part of the system and has numerous design constraints. Aakvaag et al. (2005) have provided some guidelines for design of sensor nodes for industrial applications. Some of the design requirements & challenges are provided below:

a) The node shall be battery powered and therefore the circuit design should ensure least power consumption.

b) Since sampling will be done periodically the signal conditioning circuitry should be optimized for high speed sampling while consuming less power.

c) It should be possible to put the node into active, idle or extremely low power sleep modes.

d) It should be possible to reset the node remotely as well as re-configure the node remotely since the nodes may be located in hard to reach places.

e) The circuit design and operation should be done to ensure that the battery should last at-least 4-5 years.

f) The node enclosure design should ensure survival of the electronics even in harsh industrial environment.

g) The Sink node should have the capability to transfer data serially to a PC for data logging.

h) IEEE 802.15.4 radio should be implemented to achieve compliance with the IEEE standard. Appropriate antenna design should be incorporated.

There are three distinct types of nodes – Co-ordinator Node or Sink, Router Node & Sensor Node. The architecture of the three nodes is essentially similar. There is however a difference in their circuits depending upon the features incorporated depending upon their functions. The categorization of the sensor nodes based on their functional aspects is provided below:

a) *Sensor Node:* Consists of Battery, Signal Conditioning Circuitry, Transceiver, micro-controller supervisory circuit and Hall effect sensor.

b) *Router Node:* Is essentially line powered but has battery backup, Transceiver, micro-controller supervisory ciruit & Hall effect sensor

c) *Sink Node:* Is essentially line powered but has battery backup, Transceiver, micro-controller supervisory circuit, Hall Effect Sensor, RS 485 or RS232 based serial port

A suitable Freescale™ Semiconductors 8 bit micro-controller with 64KB of Flash memory, 4KB of RAM, 8 bit ADC, USART, Timers & RTI capabilities was chosen as the CPU. The microcontroller has multiple modes of operation including $3\mu A$ sleep mode and $7\,mA$ active mode. A compatible IEEE 802.15.4 Transceiver (MC 13192, n.d.) with transmit current of 40mA & receive current of 42mA from the same manufacturer was chosen. The choice was also based on the ease of availability of Development tools and the IEEE 802.15.4 implementation of the stack for the micro-controller.

A Hall Effect Sensor is also included in the circuit and is connected to the RESET pin of the micro-controller. This provides the capability of resetting the node remotely from a distance. Special care is taken to protect the memory elements from interference from external sources.

The desired environmental protection rating for the Sensor node is IP65 i.e., protection from splashing water and dust particles of size 1micrometer. This has a direct impact on the antenna design. An external antenna though desirable is not feasible in such a design since this requires another opening in the enclosure making it more susceptible to water or dust ingress into the enclosure.

In this situation, the antenna has to be inside the enclosure, which further puts a constraint on the material to be used for the enclosure. The enclosure can't be metallic as it would adversely affect the transmission and reception of radio signals from antenna housed inside it. The enclosure was designed by using a special fiberglass material which could withstand high temperature up-to 70 degree Celsius, high humidity up-to 100%, rain, direct and long exposure to sunlight.

Since the antenna had to be inside the enclosure and the range was not a critical problem, a PCB embedded antenna design, popularly known as "F antenna" was chosen for the application. Locating the antenna on the PCB itself requires that the dielectric constant of the PCB material should be high and should not vary under severe environmental variations. An FR2 based PCB material was chosen for the PCB laminate, this is basically a paper material with phenolic binder. All components used were of SMD type since a small lead could actually act as an antenna itself putting the whole circuit into a feedback loop making it unstable.

C. Design of Sensing Algorithm

The sensing algorithm is required to be a generic algorithm which can be used and be re-configured depending upon the characteristics of the sensor in use. Sensors used for measurement of parameters like temperature have very low latency whereas the settling-time for parameters like resistivity and pressure is a few milliseconds. Considering this the algorithm has been designed to take multiple ADC readings and use an averaging algorithm to arrive at a more stable reading. This algorithm ensures that the sample value is actually an average of multiple readings to get better accuracy from an ADC:

$$avgval = 1/num\_samples \sum_{1}^{num\_samples} adc\_val \qquad (6)$$

D. Design of Node Algorithm

The operation of the nodes is categorized into two distinct phases namely the *Network Setup phase* and the *Normal Detection phase*. During the *Leak Detection Mode Phase* the node runs the algorithm requesting permission to associate with an existing network. The initiation of this process is dependent upon whether the Router / Coordinator nodes are working in beaconed or non-beaconed mode. In the current application the routers and the coordinator nodes are working in non-beaconed mode and are perpetually in received mode.

Network Setup Phase: On waking up for the first time the node checks to see if it is associated with some network. If no, then it initiates the process of association by first scanning the media for the nearest neighbors. This is handled by the MLME_SCAN primitive available in IEEE 802.15.4 MAC. Once it is able to detect the presence of the nearest coordinator node or a router node then it generates an association request which is handled by the MLME_ASSOCIATE primitive. Once the association is complete then an acknowledgment is sent by the coordinator to the node confirming the association. The coordinator also generates and sends a unique ID number for the node. The nearest router will update its routing table with information about the new node while the coordinator node will update its association table. (see Table 1)

Leak Detection Mode Phase: During this phase the node wakes up every 8 seconds and takes a sample using the sensors. After taking the sample, the node goes back to sleep. This is repeated over a period of 2 minutes. Once 16 samples have been taken then a median value is found from this pool of samples. This median value then undergoes sensor validations tests including boundary value tests. Once it is verified that the sample value is correct then it is checked against the alarm conditions to establish whether the alarm needs to be armed.

Table 1.

Algorithm 1: Mean Value Sensing Algorithm

For all k∈(N,V)
Sense_param (channel_num, num_samples, settling_time)
avgval=0.0
activate (channel_num)
delay (settling_time)
for*i= 0 to num_samples*
  adc_val = read_adc_val (channel_num)
  avgval =avgval + adc_val;
end for
avgval =avgval / num_samples

Algorithm 2: Leak Detection Mode Algorithm

For all k∈(N,V)
On wake up(k)
activate(batt_life_channel)
  batt_life = read_adc_val(batt_life_channel)
if*batt_life > $L_{Threshold}$***then**
  batt_flag=0;
else
  batt_flag=1;
  node(sleep)()
end if
if*counter=16***then**
  med_val_sensor1= call_func_median(sensor1);
  med_val_sensor2= call_func_median(sensor2)
  counter=0
  if*(med_val_sensor1 > sensor1$_{High}$***or***med_val_sensor1<*
*sensor1$_{Low}$)***or***(med_val_sensor2 > sensor2$_{High}$ or med_val_sen-*
so2< sensor2$_{Low}$)
    alarm_status=1;
    radio(wake);
    form_packet(median_val_sensor1, median_val_sensor2,
alarm_status)
    init_transmit()
    wait ACK packet from coordinator
    radio(sleep);
    node_sleep(8)
  else
  counter=0;
  node_sleep(8)
  end if
else
counter=counter+1
  sens_val1[counter]=Sense_param(sensor1, 10, 50)
  sens_val2[counter]=Sense_param(sensor2, 10, 50)
  node_sleep(8)
end if

The process of transmitting these sensed values is then initiated and a packet consisting of the device ID, Destination ID, Tag No along with the payload of the sensor readings and the alarm conditions is then transmitted. The sensor node then goes into wait mode for receipt of acknowledgment from the nearest router or coordinator node. On receiving the acknowledgment the node goes into sleep mode again and the process above is repeated.

The frequency of sampling, transmission & alarm thresholds are user configurable.

The underlying Zigbee NWK layer takes care of the routing of packets by using a combination of the popular AODV & Cluster Tree algorithms.

E. Estimation of Network Lifetime

The most critical design aspect of the Wireless Sensor Network based solution is the problem of the life-time of the network. This problem is even more critical in an industrial environment where the nodes are located in hard to reach locations in the field and replacement of battery is a difficult proposition.

The life time of the node is dependent on the rate of energy being drawn from the battery. A battery is a finite reservoir of energy and the rate of energy drawn will directly indicate the life time of the node.

The various functional aspects of the network which contribute to consumption of energy are:

a) Sensor Sampling (E_{sample})
b) Wireless Transmission of data ($E_{transmit}$)
c) Wireless Reception of data (E_{recv})
d) Node in sleep mode (E_{sleep})

The energy equation for the battery and the node is represented by:

$$E_{node} = E_{sample} + E_{transmit} + E_{recv} + E_{sleep} \qquad (7)$$

The equations governing the calculations of the network energy consumption using which the lifetime of the network can be calculated are available at Appendix. (Equations (7) –(26)

A sample calculation is shown for a particular case. In this case, it is assumed that 16 samples are taken over a period of 2 minutes. The transmission of data occurs every 2 minutes and a packet of 49 bytes is transmitted.

Each sample is actually an average of 10 ADC readings, as explained in IV (C). Before taking a sample, a sensor stabilizing delay of 50msec is provided. Using Equation 10, therefore the duration of each sample is T_{sample}=50msec + 10 * 240μsec=52.4 msecs. The energy consumed by the micro-controller and the signal conditioning circuitry for taking one sample can be calculated by using Equation 12 and is 3.6V * (20/1000)A * (52.4/1000) sec=0.0037728 Joules. The total number of samples taken in a day for this configuration can be calculated using the sample frequency of 8 samples /minute. Using Equation 11, this gives $N_{samples/day}$=24*60*8 = 11520 samples/day. Thus total energy spent in a day on the sampling process can be calculated by using Equation 14. For the given case this works out to be 43.46 Joules/day. The next step is to calculate the energy spent by the node in transmitting & receiving packets. This can be calculated by using the Equations 15-24

Continuing for the case mentioned earlier $T_{packet\_duration}$=8 * 49 / 250000 = 1.57msec, E_{packet}= 1.57* 3.6 *60 / (1000*1000) =0.000339 Joules / per packet. Further in this case $N_{packets/day}$=24*30= 720 packets / day. This results in total energy spending of $E_{transmit/day}$=0.000339 * 720=0.244166 Joules/day

A similar set set of calculations will result in $E_{recv/day}$ = 0.9766 Joules/day.

When the node is not performing the task of sampling, transmitting or receiving then it goes into sleep mode where it consumes only 3μA of current. In this case

$T_{sample/day}$ = 52.4 * 11520/1000=603.6 seconds

$T_{transmit/day}$ = *1.57 *720/1000*= 1.1304 seconds

$T_{recv/day}$ = 1.57*720*4/1000 = 4.5216 seconds

$T_{sleep/day}$ = (24*60*60) –(603.6 + 1.1304 + 4.5216) = 85790 seconds

$E_{sleep/day}$=3.6 * 0.003 * 85790 = 0.926532 Joules/day

$E_{total/day}$ = 43.46 + 0.244 + 0.976 + 0.926 = 45.606 Joules / day.

A 8500mAH Li-Thionyl-Chloride battery was chosen to serve as the energy source. This battery has the highest power density as well as almost constant voltage characteristics over its lifetime as compared to other standard batteries. As per the calculations, the battery is expected to provide power for duration of 6 ½ years without a change. This is in tune with the desired characteristics. The life time of the node will change with different settings of sampling rate; sleep time ratio & transmission / reception frequency. A detailed simulated analysis of the lifetime of the network based on the various possible settings was done and the results are provided in Table 3.

DEPLOYMENT

A total of 55 nodes (sensor nodes & router nodes) were deployed in a process plant for a period of 4 months. The location of the leak detection points was fixed by the utilities manager and the sensor nodes were installed adjacent to these points. Thus the location of the sensor nodes was static and inflexible. A site survey was subsequently done to establish the number and location of router nodes such that all sensor nodes would get radio connectivity. The objective was to identify the location of the routers such that least number of routers would get used whilst providing comprehensive connectivity. An upper limit of 25meters was kept as the radius for nodes having line of sight connectivity with router and 18 meters for those not having direct line of sight connectivity. Extremely low signal zones were also identified.

TESTS AND RESULTS

Table 2 shows the test results obtained after testing the sensor node for the various functional tasks that it is required to perform during its lifetime. Since the sensor node is required to spend most of its lifetime in the sleep mode therefore the extremely low value of sleep current of 3μA is advantageous for the life time of the node.

The microcontroller consumes a total of 8mA in active mode and along with the sensor conditioning circuitry consumes approximately 20mA. The resistivity sensor uses an alternating signal of 10 KHz, thus consuming more current. This sensor also requires approximately 50msec to stabilize after turning on before it can give a reliable reading.

The total current consumed during transmission and reception at highest transmitting energy of 0dBm nominal power and sensitivity of -92dbm is approximately 60mA. However, as seen from analysis presented in Table 3 it can be seen that this figure is not overtly critical to the performance of the network.

Table 4 shows the power consumed by the sensor node for performing the various tasks during the normal mode of working. As can be seen

Table 2. Sensor node test results for current consumption

MCU Sleep Mode 3μA
MCU Active with Sensor Conditioning Circuit 20mA
MCU Packet Transmission / Reception 60mA
ADC Conversion time 240μsec
Sensor Settling Time 50msec

Table 3. Task based energy consumption results

MCU Sleep Mode 0.0000108 J/sec
MCU Active with Sensor Circuit ON 0.0037 J/sample
MCU Transmission /Reception 0.00033 J/packet

from the table the maximum amount of energy is consumed by the node in the sampling process while it consumes the least amount of energy in the sleep mode.

Table 5 shows the effect on the lifetime of the network with variations in the sampling rate and the frequency of transmission and reception of data. The results indicate a network life pattern which is quite unique for process industries applications and varies significantly from conventional applications of Wireless Sensor Networks. In conventional applications of Wireless Sensor Networks the transmission of information tends to be event driven. The nodes transmit data only on detecting a specific event. In some cases there is some sporadic periodic transmission also to indicate the status of the node.

However, in industrial environment there is a requirement that the sensing of the phenomenon should occur frequently so that any significant change of the parameter under observation can be reported. In such applications, the energy spent

Table 4. Simulated results for network lifetime

Sampling rate	Communication Frequency	Network Life
8 samples/min	Once every 2 minutes	6.53 Years
8 samples/min	Once every 5 minutes	6.64 Years
8 samples/min	Once every 15 minutes	6.69 Years
4 samples/min	Once every 2 minutes	12.48 Years
4 samples/min	Once every 5 minutes	12.88 Years
4 samples/min	Once every 15 minutes	13.06 Years

Table 5. Measured packet error rate for the network

Packets Trans-mitted in 1 hour	Packets Re-ceived	Packet Loss
3590	2893	19.4%
2000	1802	9.9%
1000	957	4.3%
500	481	3.8%
100	97	3.0%

by the network for sending far outweighs the energy spent on communication. Table 4 illustrates this phenomenon quite clearly.

It can be seen from the analysis provided in Table 4 that in case of Industrial applications the frequency of communication does not have a drastic impact on the lifetime of the network as compared to rate of sampling. The rate of sampling is higher in industrial applications since the need for fresh data is higher. It can be safely concluded that for industrial applications involving use of Wireless Sensor Networks, it is desirable to focus more upon the frequency and energy require-ments of the sampling process as compared to the communication process. A reduction in the power consumption of the sampling circuit and a reduction in the frequency of the sampling process need to be the focus area for network lifetime enhancement. It can therefore be safely concluded that for industrial applications of wire-less Sensor Networks, focus area for improving upon the network lifetime must be the sampling process rather than the communication process.

A test set up was created to study the packet loss rate in an industrial environment at different transmission rates. A specifically noisy part of the process plant was chosen for this test. The loca-tion consisted of high speed high rating DC and AC motors which were being switched on & off intermittently. Welding work was also in progress in the vicinity. A Wi-fi computer network was working in the same environment. One node was designated as the Transmitter node and a fixed packet of 49 bytes was transmitted at different rates. Another node was designated as a receiver node and was kept at a distance of 25mtrs from the transmitter node. The two nodes were partially in line of sight. The test results are indicated in Table 5.

Analysis of the test results indicates clearly that the packet loss is very high at high transfer rates and reduces significantly at lower transfer rates. The drop in the packet loss rate however is not linear.

A similar test set up was created to study the radiation pattern of the antenna. This consisted of a sensor node transmitting packets continuously at peak power (4dBm) in an open environment. A similar node connected to a Laptop acted as a receiver (-92dBm sensitivity) and passed on the received signal strength to the Laptop where the data was recorded along with the position. Based on the readings obtained the radiation pattern for the antenna was arrived at. As can be seen from Figure 4, the radiation pattern to an extent is isotropic.

Over the period of 4 months of deployment a total of 7 nodes malfunctioned due to different reasons. The failure information is presented in Table 6. As can be seen from the table, three nodes were rendered unusable because of battery failure. In all the three cases, the battery failure occurred within the first 30 days of installation. The same nodes were subsequently refitted with new bat-teries and working satisfactorily for the duration of the deployment. This battery failure was as-cribed to the harsh environmental condition and component failure. The enclosure failed in one

Figure 4. Radiation pattern of "F Antenna". As can be seen the pattern is quite similar to that of an isotropic antenna

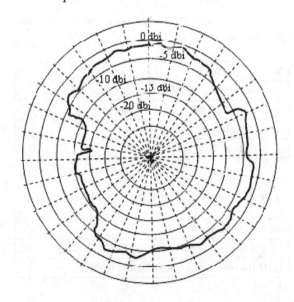

Table 6. Sensor node failure data for the network

Total Nodes Deployed	55
Deployment Duration	4 Months
Total Nodes Failed	7
Node failure because of	
Sensor Failure	1
Battery Failure	3
All within first month	
Circuit Component Failure	2
Enclosure Failure	1

case which led to ingress of water into the enclosure resulting in damage to the sensor node. The sensor node was not recoverable in this case. In two cases the sensor nodes malfunctioned due to failure of the electronic components. An analysis required change of Balun in one case and change of capacitor in radio circuit in another case. Upon the replacement of the components, the nodes behaved satisfactorily.

CONCLUSION

A framework for design and installation of a Wireless Sensor Network for use in Process industry for monitoring of Utilities has been arrived at. All aspects of the design requirements for such an implementation have been taken into consideration. It has been observed that for industrial applications, the critical design parameters for Wireless Sensor Network Design are significantly different from that of a standard environment sensing applications. A customized design for a Wireless Sensor Node has been arrived at and the same has been fabricated and implemented Based on typical industrial application it has also been observed that the conventional approach of focusing more on the communication aspects of the Wireless Sensor Network for increasing the network lifetime is not particularly effective when used in industrial applications. The energy require-

ment of the sampling process and the frequency of the sampling process have a more pronounced impact on the life time of the network.

Currently the router nodes and the coordinator nodes are required to be powered on perpetually and are therefore line powered. This puts a severe constraint on the number of router nodes as well as their location. Further work can be done to arrive at a scheduling algorithm which can be used to enable these nodes to get some sleep time which could generate the possibility of the router nodes also being battery powered. Some interesting work in this direction has been shown in (Kouba, Cunha, & Alves, 2008; Aakvaag, Mathiesen, & Thone, 2005). Further work also needs to be done to arrive at a more optimized circuit design for low energy sensing with increased time period between the samples without sacrificing the quality of the sensing (Figure 4).

ACKNOWLEDGMENT

The authors would like to acknowledge the support received from M/s Polynol Rubbers for permitting the plant to be used for installation of the Wireless Sensor Network based solution.

REFERENCES

Aakvaag, N., Mathiesen, M., & Thone, G. (2005). Timing and power issues in wireless sensor networks - an industrial test case. In *Proceedings of the Parallel Processing (ICPP 2005) Workshops* (pp. 419-426).

Akyildiz, I. F., Su, W., Sankarasubramaniam, Y., & Cayirci, E. (2002). Wireless Sensor Networks: A Survey. *Computer Networks*, *38*, 393–422. doi:10.1016/S1389-1286(01)00302-4

Bin, Lu., Habetler, T. G., Harley, R. G., & Gutierrez, J. A. (2005, October 30). Applying wireless sensor networks in industrial plant energy management systems. Part II. Design of sensor devices. *Sensors (Basel, Switzerland)*, 6.

Bonnet, B. (2003, December). Bluetooth-based sensor networks. *ACM SIGMOD, 32*(4).

IEEE. 802.15.4. (n.d.). *Wireless Medium Access Control (MAC) and Physical Layer (PHY) Specifications for Wireless Personal Area Networks (WPANs)*. Retrieved from http://www.ieee.org

Jeong, W., & Nof, S. (2008, June). Performance evaluation of wireless sensor network protocols for industrial applications. *Journal of Intelligent Manufacturing, 19*(3), 335–345. doi:10.1007/s10845-008-0086-4

Jiang, P., Ren, H., Zhang, L., Wang, Z., & Xue, A. (2006). Reliable Application of Wireless Sensor Networks in Industrial Process Control. In *Proceedings of the Intelligent Control and Automation (WCICA 2006), the Sixth World Congress on* (pp. 99-103).

Kouba, A., Cunha, A., & Alves, M. (2008, October). TDBS: a time division beacon scheduling mechanism for ZigBee cluster-tree wireless sensor networks. *Real-Time Systems*, 321–354. doi:10.1007/s11241-008-9063-4

Lin, S., Liu, J., & Fang, Y. (2007, August 18-21). "ZigBee Based Wireless Sensor Networks and Its Applications in Industrial. In *Proceedings of the Automation and Logistics, 2007 IEEE International Conference on* (pp. 1979-1983).

Low, K. S., Win, W. N. N., & Er Meng, J. (2005). Wireless Sensor Networks for Industrial Environments. In *Proceedings of the Computational Intelligence for Modelling, Control and Automation, 2005 and International Conference on Intelligent Agents, Web Technologies and Internet Commerce, International Conference on* (pp. 271-276).

MC 13192. (n.d.). *Transceiver Data-sheet*. Retrieved from http://www.freescale.com

Salvadori, F., de Campos, M., de Figueiredo, R., Gehrke, C., Rech, C., Sausen, P. S., et al. (2007, October 3-5). Monitoring and Diagnosis in Industrial Systems Using Wireless Sensor Networks. In *Proceedings of Intelligent Signal Processing, 2007. WISP 2007. IEEE International Symposium on* (pp. 1-6).

Shen, X., Wang, Z., & Sun, Y. (2004). Wireless sensor networks for industrial applications. In *Proceedings of the Intelligent Control and Automation (WCICA 2004), Fifth World Congress on* (Vol. 4, pp. 3636- 3640).

Shizhuang, L., Jingyu, L., & Yanjun, F. (2007, A ugust 18-21). ZigBee Based Wireless Sensor Networks and Its Applications in Industrial. In *Proceedings of Automation and Logistics, 2007 IEEE International Conference on* (pp. 1979-1983).

Thompson, H. (n.d.). *Bluetooth based Monitoring system for Marine Propulsion systems*. Rolls Royce University Technology Centre in Control & Systems Engineering, U. K.

Zhou, Y., Yang, X., Guo, X., Zhou, M., & Wang, L. (2007, September 21-25). A Design of Greenhouse Monitoring & Control System Based on ZigBee Wireless Sensor Network. In *Proceedings of Wireless Communications, Networking and Mobile Computing (WiCom 2007)* (pp. 2563-2567).

Zigbee alliance. (n.d.). *Zigbee Protocol V1.0*. Retrieved from http://www.zigbee.org

APPENDIX

Equations related to Total energy spent/day

$$E_{node} = E_{sample} + E_{transmit} + E_{recv} + E_{sleep} \tag{7}$$

$$E_{node/day} = E_{sample/day} + E_{transmit/day} + E_{recv/day} + E_{sleep/day} \tag{8}$$

$$E_{total/day} = E_{sample/day} + E_{transmit/day} + E_{recv/day} + E_{sleep/day} \tag{9}$$

Equations Related to Sampling Process

$$T_{sample} = T_{sensor\_stable} + 10 * T_{ADC} \tag{10}$$

$$N_{samples/day} = 24 * 60 * Sample\ frequency \tag{11}$$

$$E_{sample} = V_{battery} * I_{sample} * T_{sample} \tag{12}$$

$$T_{sample/day} = T_{sample} * N_{samples/day} \tag{13}$$

$$E_{sample/day} = \sum_{1}^{N_{samples/day}} E_{sample} \tag{14}$$

Equations Related to Transmit Process

$$E_{packet} = T_{packet\_duration} * V_{battery} * I_{transmit} \tag{15}$$

$$T_{packet\_duration} = 8 * packet\ size\ /\ Bit\ Rate \tag{16}$$

$$N_{packets/day} = 24 * Packet\_frequency\ /\ hour \tag{17}$$

$$T_{transmit/day} = T_{packet\_duration} * N_{packets/day} \tag{18}$$

$$E_{transmit/day} = E_{transmit\_packet} * N_{packets/day} \tag{19}$$

Equations Related to Receive Process

$$E_{packet} = T_{packet\_duration} * V_{battery} * I_{treceive} \tag{20}$$

$$T_{packet\_duration} = 8 * packet\ size\ /\ Bit\ Rate \tag{21}$$

$$N_{packets/day} = 24 * Packet\_frequency/hour \tag{22}$$

$$T_{recv/day} = T_{packet\_duration} * N_{packets/day} * 4 \tag{23}$$

$$E_{recv/day} = E_{packet} * N_{packets/day} \tag{24}$$

Equations Related to Sleep Process

$$T_{sleep/day} = (24 * 60 * 60) - (T_{sample/day} + T_{transmit/day} + T_{recv/day}) \tag{25}$$

$$E_{sleep/day} = V_{battery} * I_{sleep} * T_{sleep/day} \tag{26}$$

This work was previously published in International Journal of Grid and High Performance Computing, Volume 2, Issue 3, edited by Emmanuel Udoh, pp. 44-59, copyright 2010 by IGI Publishing (an imprint of IGI Global).

Chapter 20
Fuzzy Allocation of Fine-Grained Compute Resources for Grid Data Streaming Applications

Wen Zhang
Tsinghua University, China

Junwei Cao
Tsinghua University and Tsinghua National Laboratory for Information Science and Technology, China

Yisheng Zhong
Tsinghua University and Tsinghua National Laboratory for Information Science and Technology, China

Lianchen Liu
Tsinghua University and Tsinghua National Laboratory for Information Science and Technology, China

Cheng Wu
Tsinghua University and Tsinghua National Laboratory for Information Science and Technology, China

ABSTRACT

Fine-grained allocation of compute resources, in terms of configurable clock speed of virtual machines, is essential for processing efficiency and resource utilization of data streaming applications. For a data streaming application, its processing speed is expected to approach the allocated bandwidth as much as possible. Automatic control technology is a feasible solution, but the plant model is hard to be derived. In relation to the model free characteristic, a fuzzy logic controller is designed with several simple yet robust rules. Performance of this controller is verified to out-perform classic controllers in response rapidness and less oscillation. An empirical formula on tuning an essential parameter is obtained to achieve better performance.

DOI: 10.4018/978-1-4666-0056-0.ch020

1. INTRODUCTION

Grid (Foster & Kesselman, 1998) is now playing a major role in providing on-demand resources to various scientific and engineering applications, among which those with data streaming characteristics are gaining popularity recently. Such applications, called grid data streaming applications, require the combination of bandwidth sufficiency, adequate storage and computing capacity to guarantee smooth and high-efficiency processing, making them different from other batch-oriented ones. A case in point is LIGO (Laser Interferometer Gravitational-wave Observatory) (Deelman & Kesselman, 2002), which is generating 1TB scientific data per day and trying to benefit from processing capabilities provided by the Open Science Grid (OSG) (Pordes, 2004). Since most OSG sites are CPU-rich but storage-limited with no LIGO data available, data streaming supports are required to utilize OSG CPU resources. Such applications are novel in that (1) they are continuous and long running in nature; (2) they require efficient data transfer from/to distributed sources/sinks in an end-user-pulling way; (3) it is often not feasible to store all the data in entirety because of limited storage and high volumes of data to be processed; (4) they need to make efficient use of high performance computing (HPC) resources to carry out compute-intensive tasks in a timely manner. Great challenge is proposed to provide sufficient resources, including compute, storage and bandwidth to such streaming applications so that they can meet their service level objectives (SLOs) while maintaining high resource utilization.

Just like other grid applications, resource allocation is essential to achieve high efficiency of data processing for streaming applications. But different from the conventional batch-oriented applications, processing efficiency of data streaming applications is co-determined by compute capacity, bandwidth to supply data in real time and storage. Just as proven in our previous work (Zhang & Cao, 2008), compute, bandwidth and storage must be allocated in a cooperative and integrated way. But at that time, emphasis was laid on allocation of bandwidth and storage. As for compute resources, they were just allocated in a coarse-grained way, i.e., each application was assigned to a processor exclusively, which may cause waste of compute capacity for the limitation of data supply speed. In some cases, end users must pay for the compute resources they occupy even if they cannot make full utilization of them. So, it is desirable to allocate fine-grained compute resources for each application, i.e., to allocate just enough compute resources to guarantee smooth processing. Compute resources should also be assigned on demand, and unilateral redundancy of them makes no sense, only to waste users' budget.

Owe to the progress of virtualization technology, it is possible to allocate fine-grained compute resources. But the premise is to determine the required compute resources according to the needed computing capacity. Unfortunately, it is not so easy for the relationship between the amount of compute resources and the generated compute capacity for a given application is complex because of other influencing factors and it is hard, if not impossible to be obtained. Or put it another way, the precise model is unavailable. It is natural to resort to classical control theory to solve such a tracking or regulation problem as has been done in computing field, but for the absence of precise models, the classical controllers are just baffled. Fortunately, fuzzy logic control theory provides an alternative which requires not the precise models but only some experiences of human beings. In this paper, a fuzzy logic controller (FLC) is designed with some simple but robust fuzzy rules to decide the amount of compute resources for the expected computing capacity, so as to realize the fine-grained compute resource allocation for data streaming applications, which will guarantee service level agreements (SLAs) while maintaining high resource utilization.

The rest of this paper is organized as following: Section 2 formulates an optimization problem and proposes the necessity of fine-grained compute resources allocation, which is resolved with fuzzy controller described in Section 3. Some experimental results are provided in Section 4, to justify the fuzzy allocation. The next section overviews the related research in this field and this paper is concluded in the last section.

2. PROBLEM FORMULATION

In a data streaming scenario, data in remote sources will be transferred to local storage, read by processing program one tuple by another and deleted. From a macroscopic viewpoint, data is just processed in a form of tuple streams.

The amount of data in storage varies over time and can be described as following:

$$\dot{Q}_i(t) = I_i(t) - P_i(t), \forall t \geq 0$$

$$Q_i(0)=0$$

Where $Q_i(t)$, $I_i(t)$ and $P_i(t)$ stand for the data amount in storage, assigned bandwidth and processing speed for data type $i(i=1,...,n)$ at time t, and n is the number of applications running simultaneously in a shared computing infrastructure. $\dot{Q}_i(t)$ is the derivative of $Q_i(t)$, which reflects the integrated effects of data supply and processing.

Data processing programs run constantly to process the available data. If no data is locally available, they will be idle which wastes computational resources. So $P_i(t)$ can be described as

$$P_i(t) = \begin{cases} 0 & Q_i(t) = 0 \\ >0 & Q_i(t) > 0 \end{cases}$$

Usually, the total data amount in storage is limited, i.e.,

$$\sum_{i=1}^{n} Q_i(t) \leq S$$

where S is the total available storage.

$I_i(t)$ represents the data transferring speed with the following constraint:

$$\sum_{i=1}^{n} I_i(t) \leq I(t)$$

where $I(t)$ is the total available local bandwidth.

The optimization goal is to allocate appropriate computing capacity, i.e., $P_i(t)$ for each application to maximize the throughput of each data type:

$$\max \int_0^{T_f} P_i(t)dt \tag{1}$$

or the total throughput for all types of data:

$$\max \sum_{i=1}^{n} \int_0^{T_f} P_i(t)dt = \max \int_0^{T_f} \left(\sum_{i=1}^{n} P_i(t)\right)dt,$$

or, if each type of data processing has different privileges or weights:

$$\max \sum_{i=1}^{n} \int_0^{T_f} \omega_i P_i(t)dt = \max \int_0^{T_f} \left(\sum_{i=1}^{n} \omega_i P_i(t)\right)dt$$

where T_f is the evaluation time span and ω_i is the weight of data type i.

Another goal is to minimize the cost of computation, as described below:

$$\min \int_0^{T_f} c_i(t)C_i(t)dt \tag{2}$$

where $c_i(t)$ stands for the price of compute resource and $C_i(t)$ is the allocated compute resource. Or it can be expressed to minimize the total cost of all the applications:

$$\min \sum_{i=1}^{n} \int_{0}^{T_f} c_i(t) C_i(t) dt =$$
$$\min \int_{0}^{T_f} \left(\sum_{i=1}^{n} c_i(t) C_i(t) \right) dt$$

It is obvious that as long as $P_i(t)$ can be adjusted to follow $I_i(t)$ precisely, both goals can be achieved. Unfortunately, the map from compute resource to compute speed, denoted as G, cannot be established precisely because of the uncertainties and stochastics where:

$$P_i(t) = G(C_i(t))$$

As a solution, fuzzy control is introduced to determine the precise amount of compute resources in real time, to achieve the two goals as set above.

3. FUZZY ALLOCATION OF FINE-GRAINED COMPUTE RESOURCE

As can be inferred, ultimate throughput of a data streaming application and cost of computation are determined mainly by the allocated bandwidth and computing resources or, more exactly, data supply and processing speeds. This paper is mainly focused on allocation of compute resource, and details of bandwidth and storage allocation have been elaborated in our previous work (Zhang, Cao, Zhong, Liu, & Wu, 2008). But the relationship between allocated compute resource quota and processing speed of a certain application is not so straight forward, for there are so many factors influencing the processing capacity of the given compute resources. Precise mathematical model of this relationship is hard, if not impossible, to be derived. On the other hand, sometimes such precise

models are not indispensable and some situations can be handled with experience of human beings. It is natural to resort to fuzzy control theory for it can work smartly according to pre-defined fuzzy rules rather than precise models.

3.1 Fine-Grained Compute Resource

Virtualization technology has been applied to Grid computing field (Figueiredo & Dinda, 2003; Keahey & Doering, 2004; Foster & Freeman, 2006). Owe to the virtualization technology progress, such as Xen (Barham & Dragovic, 2003), it is possible to allocate fine-grained compute resources for applications. Virtual machines (VMs) are able to instantiate multiple independently configured guest environments on a host resource at the same time, to provide performance isolation. With the ability to be dynamically configured, VMs facilitate the fine-grained compute resource allocation.

Virtualization technology, namely Xen will be applied to create a virtual machine with configurable clock frequency for each application. Cap, one of Xen's interfaces regarding CPU allocation will be adjusted dynamically according to the allocated network bandwidth and measured processing speed based on the pre-defined fuzzy rules as following.

3.2. Fuzzy Controller Overview

A fuzzy logic controller can be depicted with the following diagram in Figure 1. With two inputs, one for the error between the reference output and the realistic output, the other for the error's derivative, through fuzzy inference based on fuzzy rules via fuzzification and defuzzification, some control law will be generated.

Coefficients such as *Ke*, *Kec* are called quantization factors and *Ku* is the proportional factor, which are responsible for mapping inputs and output to the given scope of discourse respectively. Fuzzification is to transform precise values of inputs into fuzzy sets with corresponding

Figure 1. Diagram of fuzzy logic controller

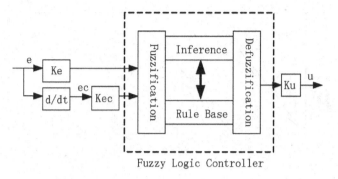

membership functions, which is indispensable for fuzzy inference. Outputs of fuzzy inference are fuzzy sets, which must be transformed into a clear value by defuzzification.

The fuzzy controller's action is guided by a set of fuzzy rules, which are stored in a rule base as a part of the controller. These rules are usually in IF-THEN formats defined in terms of linguistic variables, different from the numerical controllers. These linguistic variables are a natural way resembling human thoughts to handle uncertainties created by stochastics present in most computer systems.

Each linguistic variable is related to with a linguistic value, such as NB, NM, NS, O, PS, PM and PB, where N, P, B, M, S and O are abbreviations of negative, positive, big, medium, small and zero respectively, and the combination of them just takes on a degree of truth. The mapping from a numeric value to a degree of truth for a linguistic value is done by the membership function.

3.3. Assignment of Linguistic Variables and Fuzzy Rules

In this paper, linguistic variables of inputs, i.e., e and ec include negative, zero and positive, which means lower than, equal with and higher than the given reference value respectively, and their Gaussian membership functions are demonstrated in Figure 2.

Linguistic variables of output include dec-fast, dec-slow, no-change, inc-slow and inc-fast, where dec and inc are abbreviations of decrease and increase respectively. The triangular membership functions are demonstrated in Figure 3.

Fuzzy rules are defined as following:

① IF e is zero THEN u is no-change;
② IF e is negative AND ec is negative THEN u is inc-fast;
③ IF e is negative AND ec is positive THEN u is inc-slow;

Figure 2. Gaussian membership functions of inputs

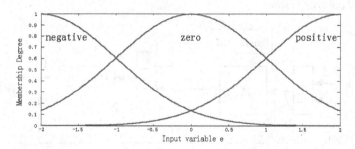

Figure 3. Triangular membership functions of output

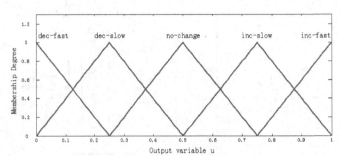

④ IF *e* is positive AND *ec* is negative THEN *u* is dec-slow;

⑤ IF *e* is positive AND *ec* is positive THEN *u* is dec-fast.

3.4. Fuzzy Controller Design

Data streaming applications and corresponding fuzzy control can be depicted in Figure 4. As can be seen, data is streamed into the local storage with given bandwidth, and processing programs fetch data tuples from storage. From macroscopic view, the data amount (DA in Figure 4) in storage is the integral of the difference between data supply (in terms of bandwidth) and cleanup (i.e., data processing). As mentioned above, as long as the amount of data in storage is upper than a certain value, processing will be running constantly and compute resources will be utilized. So if and only if the amount of data in storage is kept upper than the given value and appropriate compute resources are allocated, both optimization goals list in (1) and (2) can be achieved. Then as long

as the data amount in storage at any time can be kept around the pre-defined Ref in Figure 4, the data processing speed can keep abreast with the data supply. So, the data amount in storage will be monitored and its difference with the Ref is just the *e* as the input of FLC, and the latter will generate the processing speed, i.e., p in Figure 4.

4. EXPERIMENTAL RESULTS

To verify the fuzzy allocation algorithm of fine-grained compute resources for grid data streaming applications, some experiments are carried out where a classical proportional, integral, and derivative (PID) controller and a fuzzy controller are applied respectively.

As mentioned above, the key for the optimization goals defined in (1) and (2) is to make the generated processing speed approach the bandwidth allocated for each application. So this optimization is transformed into a tracking problem, which is very popular in automatic control

Figure 4. Diagram of control system

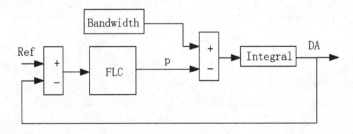

field. As well known, the step functions or the composition of them are hard to track and they are usually used as the benchmark to verify the control algorithm. Here, the allocated bandwidth for a given application is set as a composition of three step functions as following:

$$B(t) = u(t) + u(t\text{-}20) - 1.5u(t\text{-}30), 100 \geq t \geq 0$$

where $u(t\text{-}t_0)$ stands for a step function jumping from 0 to 1 at time t_0 (t_0=0, 20 and 30 respectively),

as shown in Figure 5. It means that the allocated bandwidth for an application jumps at certain moment at keep constant again.

A fuzzy controller with rules defined in 3.3 is applied, and the performance is shown in Figure 6 and Figure 7 respectively.

As can be observed, in the initial stage, there are some oscillations in the generated computing capacity calculated by the fuzzy controller, but after that the generated computing capacity follows the bandwidth precisely. As for the observed

Figure 5. Bandwidth of data supply

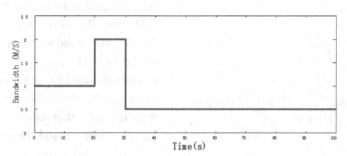

Figure 6. Generated compute capacity (FLC's output)

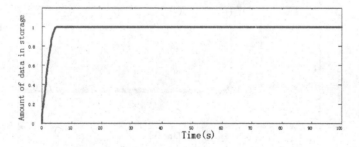

Figure 7. Amount of data in storage with FLC

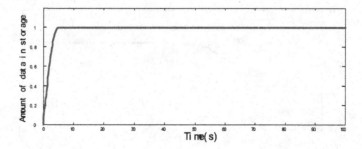

data amount in storage, it will be reach the settled reference and fixed.

To verify the FLC's performance, a PID controller replaces the FLC in Figure 4, whose transfer function can be expressed as:

$$CC(s) = k_p + \frac{k_i}{s} + k_d s$$

where k_p, k_i, and k_d are the coefficients of proportional, integral and derivative functions respectively. Physically, the derivative part will be replaced by an approximate implementation, e.g., the transfer function can be re-written as:

$$CC(s) = k_p + \frac{k_i}{s} + k_d \cdot \frac{T_1 s}{T_0 s + 1}$$

where $T_1 >> T_0$. Here, let $T_1 = 1$, $T_0 = 0.1$. Other parameters are $k_p = 5$, $k_i = 1$, $k_d = 5$.

The generated computing capacity calculated by the PID controller is shown in Figure 8, while the observed amount of data in storage is shown in Figure 9.

As can be seen, both curves can track the given values; however there are still some oscillations, which means that the performance of such a PID controller is not so ideal. Of course careful adjustment of parameters, including k_p, k_i, and k_d may lead to a better performance, but it is human labor intensive.

As shown in Figure 6 to Figure 9, the fuzzy logic controller outperforms the classic PID controller. There is less oscillation in the compute capacity generated by the FLC than in that by the PID controller. It means that the FLC can track the allocated bandwidth more precisely to obtain the goals in (1) and (2). As for the data amount in storage, the FLC can reach the stable status in shorter time and there is no oscillation while the PID controller takes longer to converge to the set reference and there are oscillations. The

Figure 8. Generated compute capacity (PID controller's output)

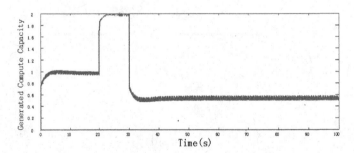

Figure 9. Amount of data in storage with PID controller

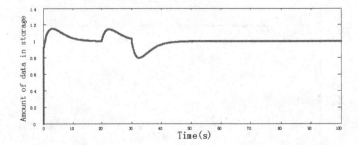

experimental results justify the FLC and its fuzzy rules here.

Actually, not all the fuzzy controllers can achieve so good performance. The key point is to set the proportional factor, i.e., k_u properly. An empirical formula is obtained as

$$k_u(t) = 2B(t)$$

which means that this proportional factor must be adjusted in real time to double the bandwidth. In physical implementation, this formula can be rebuilt as

$$k_u(t) = 2 \frac{\int_{t-n\Delta t}^{t-\Delta t} B(\tau)d\tau}{n\Delta t} \qquad (3)$$

which substitutes the current bandwidth with its average in the nearest past, where Δt is a small period of time. For the piecewise continuous bandwidth, K_u determined in Formula (3) will guarantee the tracking performance.

Actually, this empirical formula has something to do with parameter settling in the fuzzy controller and it will not hold true in all occasions, so it cannot be generalized arbitrarily.

5. RELATED WORK

As demonstrated in our previous work, compute, bandwidth and storage should be allocated for data streaming applications in a cooperative way. Most resource allocation infrastructures available in the grid filed, such as Legion (Chapin & Katramatos, 1999), Nimrod/G (Buyya & Abramson, 2000) and Condor (Litzkow & Livny, 1988), are largely geared to support batch-oriented applications rather than the streaming ones, i.e., they just allocate compute resources regardless of cooperation of data supply and processing. Some

schedulers are developed to support data streaming applications, such as E-Condor, GATES (Chen & Agrawal, 2006), and Streamline (Agarwalla & Ahmed, 2006), but they mainly concern on computational resource allocation. What's more, they just allocate compute resources in a coarse-grained scale.

Control theory has been successfully applied to control performance or quality of service (QoS) for various computing systems. An extensive summary of related work is presented in the first chapter of (Hellerstein & Diao, 2004). Some control types, such as PID control (Abdelzaher & Shin, 2002; Parekh & Gandhi, 2002), pole placement (Diao & Gandhi, 2002), linear quadratic regulator (LQR) (Diao & Gandhi, 2002) and adaptive control (Kamra & Misra, 2004; Lu & Lu, 2002) are proposed. Most of them require precise models of controlled objects.

The first application of fuzzy control was introduced into industry (King & Mamdani, 1974). Fuzzy control is also a research topic in computing system (Diao & Hellerstein, 2002; Li & Nahrstedt, 1999), but it is mainly focused on admission control to get a better QoS. Adaptive fuzzy control is applied for utilization management of periodic tasks (Suzer & Kang, 2008), where the utilization is defined as the ratio of the estimated execution time to the task period. Fuzzy inference is carried out on fuzzy rules to decide the threshold, a point over which the QoS of tasks should be degraded or even tasks should be rejected. But the estimated execution time must be provided, which is a challenge for it plays an important role in this control algorithm. What's more, in some cases, QoS cannot be degraded because the tasks cannot be decomposed, which limits its wide use in more fields.

The latest relevant work (Park & Humphrey, 2008) is focused on providing predictable execution so as to meet the deadlines of tasks. Virtualization technology is applied to implement the so-called performance container and compute throttling framework, to realize the "controlled time-sharing" of high performance compute resources, i.e., fine-grained CPU allocation. System identification is carried out to establish the model of controlled object and a proportional and integral (PI) controller is applied. This work has similar motivation with us, but in the data streaming scenario, it is hard to produce a precise model from allocated bandwidth and compute resource to the generated utilization or throughput as explained above, so the classical controllers are not suitable, and then we resort to fuzzy control theory, which is model free. But in essence, our approach is also a feedback controller.

Cloud computing (Carr, 2008) is getting prosperous now and some entities allege that they can provide compute resources on-demand. A case in point is Amazon elastic cloud computing. But actually they just provide compute resources with coarse granularity. It is left to the end users to decide the amount of compute resources, but on the other hand, it is very difficult for the users to estimate their requirements. So the users may tend to apply more resources than they really need, which will cause resource under-utilization and budget waste. In such cases, it is desirable to allocate just enough rather than redundant compute resources to end users without their participation, i.e., automatically by some control mechanism, just as what we do in this paper.

6. CONCLUSION

Virtualization technology makes resource allocation of grid computing more flexible with better granularity. Fuzzy control theory can be applied to allocate just enough compute resource for data streaming applications. For the model-free characteristic of fuzzy logic controllers, it eliminates the intensive human labor in parameters' tuning. What's more, with simple yet robust linguistic rules, fuzzy logic controllers achieve better performance than classic controllers.

ACKNOWLEDGMENT

This work is supported by National Science Foundation of China (grant No. 60803017), Ministry of Science and Technology of China under the national 863 high-tech R&D program (grants No. 2006AA10Z237, No. 2007AA01Z179 and No. 2008AA01Z118), Ministry of Education of China under the program for New Century Excellent Talents in University and the Scientific Research Foundation for the Returned Overseas Chinese Scholars, and the FIT foundation of Tsinghua University.

REFERENCES

Abdelzaher, T. F., Shin, K. G., & Bhatti, N. (2002). Performance guarantees for web server end-systems: a control-theoretical approach. *IEEE Trans. on Parallel and Distributed Systems, 13*.

Agarwalla, B., Ahmed, N., Hilley, D., & Ramachandran, U. (2006). Streamline: a scheduling heuristic for streaming applications on the grid. In *Proceedings of the 13th Annual Multimedia Computing and Networking Conf.*

Barham, P., Dragovic, B., Fraser, K., Hand, S., Harris, T. L., Ho, A., et al. (2003). Xen and the art of virtualization. In *Proceedings of the ACM Symp. on Operating Systems Principles*.

Buyya, R., Abramson, D., & Giddy, J. (2000). Nimrod/G: an architecture for a resource management and scheduling system in a global computational grid. In *Proceedings of the High Performance Computing ASIA*.

Carr, N. (2008). *The big switch: rewriting the world, from Edison to Google*. China: CITIC Press.

Chapin, S. J., Katramatos, D., Karpovich, J., & Grimshaw, A. S. (1999). The legion resource management system. In *Job Scheduling Strategies for Parallel Processing* (pp. 162–178). New York: Springer Verlag. doi:10.1007/3-540-47954-6_9

Chen, L., & Agrawal, G. (2006). A static resource allocation framework for grid-based streaming applications. *Concurrency and Computation, 18,* 653–666. doi:10.1002/cpe.972

Deelman, E., Kesselman, C., Mehta, G., Meshkat, L., Pearlman, L., Blackburn, K., et al. (2002). GriPhyN and ligo: building a virtual data grid for gravitational wave scientists. In *Proceedings of the 11th IEEE Int. Symp. on High Performance Distributed Computing* (pp. 225-234).

Diao, Y., Gandhi, N., Hellerstein, J. L., Parekh, S., & Tilbury, D. M. (2002). MIMO control of an apache web server: modeling and controller design. In *Proceedings* of the *American Control Conf.*

Diao, Y., Hellerstein, J. L., & Parekh, S. (2002). Using fuzzy control to maximize profits in service level management. *IBM Systems Journal, 41,* 3. doi:10.1147/sj.413.0403

Figueiredo, R. J., Dinda, P., & Fortes, J. (2003). A case for grid computing on virtual machines. In *Proceedings of the 23rd Int'l. Conf. on Distributed Computing Systems.*

Foster, I., Freeman, T., Keahy, K., Scheftner, D., Sotomayer, B., & Zhang, X. (2006). Virtual clusters for grid communities. In *Proceedings of the IEEE Int. Sym. on Cluster Computing and the Grid.*

Foster, I., & Kesselman, C. (1998). *The grid: blueprint for a new computing infrastructure.* San Francisco, CA: Morgan Kaufmann.

Hellerstein, J. L., Diao, Y., Parekh, S., & Tilbury, D. (2004). *Feedback Control of Computing Systems.* New York: Wiley. doi:10.1002/047166880X

Kamra, A., Misra, V., & Nahum, E. M. (2004). Yaksha: A self-tuning controller for managing the performance of 3-tiered web sites. In *Proceedings of the 12th IEEE Int'l. Workshop on Quality of Service.*

Keahey, K., Doering, K., & Foster, I. (2004). From sandbox to playground: dynamic virtual environments in the grid. In *Proceedings of the 5th Int. Workshop in Grid Computing.*

King, P. J., & Mamdani, E. H. (1974). Application of fuzzy algorithms for control simple dynamic plant. In. *Proceedings of the IEEE Control Theory App, 121*(12), 1585–1588.

Li, B., & Nahrstedt, K. (1999). A control-based middleware framework for quality of service adaptations. *Communications, 17,* 1632–1650.

Litzkow, M., Livny, M., & Mutka, M. (1988). Condor – a hunter of idle workstations. In *Proceedings of the 8th Int. Conf. on Distributed Computing Systems* (pp. 104-111).

Lu, Y., Lu, C., Abdelzaher, T., & Tao, G. (2002). An adaptive control framework for QoS guarantees and its application to differentiated caching services. In *Proceedings of the 10th IEEE Int'l. Workshop on Quality of Service.*

Parekh, S., Gandhi, N., Hellerstein, J. L., Tilbury, D., Jayram, T. S., & Bigus, J. (2002). Using control theory to achieve service level objectives in performance management. *Real Time Systems Journal, 23,* 1–2.

Park, S. M., & Humphrey, M. (2008). Feedback-controlled resource sharing for predictable escience. In *Proceedings of the ACM/IEEE conf. on Supercomputing.*

Pordes, R. (2004). The open science grid. In *Proceedings of the Computing in High Energy and Nuclear Physics Conf.*, Interlaken, Switzerland.

Suzer, M. H., & Kang, K. D. (2008). Adaptive fuzzy control for utilization management. In *Proceedings of the IEEE Int'l. Symp. on Object/Component/Service-oriented Real-time Distributed Computing*.

Zhang, W., Cao, J., Zhong, Y. S., Liu, L. C., & Wu, C. (2008). An integrated resource management and scheduling system for grid data streaming applications. In *Proceedings of the 9th IEEE/ACM Int. Conf. on Grid (Grid 2008)*, Tsukuba, Japan (pp. 258-265).

This work was previously published in International Journal of Grid and High Performance Computing, Volume 2, Issue 4, edited by Emmanuel Udoh, pp. 1-11, copyright 2010 by IGI Publishing (an imprint of IGI Global).

Chapter 21
A Method of 3–D Microstructure Reconstruction in the Simulation Model of Cement Hydration

Dongliang Zhang
Tongji University, China

ABSTRACT

An accurate and reliable computer simulation system can help practical experiments greatly. In a cement hydration simulation system, the basic requirement is to reconstruct the 3-D microstructure of the cement particles in the initial state while mixed with water. A 2-D SEM/X-ray image is certainly achievable; however, it is not easy to obtain parallel images due to the small scale of the cement particles. In this regard, a method is proposed to reconstruct the 3-D structure from a single microstructure image. In this method, micro-particles are regenerated in a growing trees mode, which by modifying the generating probability of the leaves, the irregularity and the surface fraction of particles can be controlled. This method can fulfill the requirement for the parameters of the 3-D image while assuring that the 2-D image is in full accord.

INTRODUCTION

Today, rapid developing computing technology provides incredible aids in various fields, CAD, CAM, computer simulation etc. An accurate and reliable simulation system can help laboratorial experiments greatly, while replacing practical experiments. The

DOI: 10.4018/978-1-4666-0056-0.ch021

simulation of cement hydration is a novel and reliable approach in studying the properties of cement. Based on scanning electron microscopy (SEM), X-ray technology and powerful computing ability, a digital computer simulation of cement hydration is proposed to represent the procedure of cement hydration in microscope and predict the properties of the concrete to a rather accurate degree. Based on the simulation, a favorable proportion and maintaining method can be found. While, 2-D images which SEM/X-ray technology mostly offered cannot satisfy the requirement of researching on the relationship between microstructure and properties of cement, the requirement of the researching on the transforming mechanism in physical and chemical procedure. So reconstructing the 3-D microstructure is inevitable. Based on SEM/X-ray technology and digital image processing, we begin with a 2-D SEM/X-ray image, combining with the characteristic of cement particles, label the pixels then reconstruct the 3-D structure ensuring all the parameters in accord with that of the 3-D structure. In this paper, a method of 3-D reconstruction is introduced, and a tree structure is used to model the structure of cement particles. For each particle, the tree will generate from a root, by choosing the probability of the leaves' growing condition different shapes of the trees can be achieved. Thus, the shape of particles can be simulated in proper surface fraction, which is most important in the hydration procedure. The probability of the leaves' growing are discussed and formulated through an experiment, and the relationship between shape and the parameter probability will be found.

The rest of this paper is organized as follows: In the next section, basic knowledge of our research are described, including the application on SEM and X-ray technology on cement microstructure research and the procedure of achieving the 2-D image. Following, the method on 3-D reconstruction and result of the method are being revealed. At last, experimental result will be presented.

RELATED WORK AND TECHNOLOGY

Application of Scanning Electron Microscopy (SEM) and X-Ray Images

In recent years, the applications of SEM and X-ray images in describing the properties of cement materials have made a great progress (Dale & Paul, 1994; Li, 2000; Bentz, 1993; Wittmann, Roelfstra, & Sadouki, 1984). The SEM and X-ray microscope analyzing technology have been used in recognizing the main phases in Portland cement (Dale & Paul, 1994; Bentz, 1997). In addition to a standard SEM, backscatter electron imaging (BSE) capabilities provide the technicians with a unique advantage in evaluating particle structures. BSE images are used to distinguish between particles based on atomic weight (the brighter the particle image, the heavier the atomic weight) (Dale & Paul, 1994; Li, 2000). X-ray is used to detect and recognize different chemical elements. Combining the BSE and X-ray images of the same sample digital image can be achieved in which different compositions are classified and colored.

2-D Digital Images of Cement Particles

Bentz and Stutzman prepared the specimen (Dale & Paul, 1994; Bentz, 1993), using SEM and X-ray technology, as described above, mapping each pixel of a 2-D image into a certain phase in the specimen. First about 25 grams of the cement powder of interest are blended with an epoxy resin to form almost dry paste. The paste is pressed into a sample mold and cured at 60 ºC for 24 hours. The cured specimen is cut using a low-speed diamond-wafering saw. Second, sawing marks are easily removed by sandpaper. Finally polishing is done on a lap wheel for about 30 seconds each. The specimen is cleaned after each polishing stage by gently wiping on a clean cloth. The specimen is then coated with carbon to provide a conductive surface for viewing in the SEM. In the BE images, brightness is proportional to the average atomic number of a phase. For the major phases presented in portland cement, the phases from brightest to darkest are tetracalcium aluminoferrite (C_4AF), tricalcium silicate (C_3S), tricalcium aluminate (C_3A) and dicalcium silicate (C_2S), gypsum, and the resin-filled voids. To supplement the information content of the BE image, X-ray images are obtained for the elements calcium, iron, aluminum, and sulfur. Figure 1 illustrates a 2-D digital image of cement particles.

PROPOSED METHOD IN RECONSTRUCTING 3-D STRUCTURE

A 2-D digital image is achieved as described above, but this image is not adequate to describe the properties of the cement sample, and not suitable for the simulation. Traditionally a 3-D image is often reconstructed from a series of parallel slices, but in such a small scale like the cement specimen mentioned above, is very hard to do so. Another slice may totally different with this one. So a method is proposed to solve this problem. In the proposed solution the exact shape of each particle is discarded but in fact what we need is not the shape but the degree of irregularity. In other word, the surface fraction of the particles

is the most important that determines the speed and the completeness of the physical and chemical reaction.

The Extraction of Information from a 2-D Image

The 2-D image in Figure 1 represents a random selection in the sample and is classified in pixels. So it can be looked as a 3-D sample whose thickness is one pixel, and we can use this sample to reconstruct the 3-D structure. From the 2-D image parameters can be extracted: the number of particles, the distribution of the particles scale, water to cement ratio in volume (w/c), verge pixels of all particles, verge pixels of each particle, proportion of each phase in cement, verge pixels of each phase, etc. From Figure 1 we can easily get the value of those parameters:

Number of particles:2503, verge pixels of all particles:28510(13.92%), water to cement ratio in volume(w/c):0.65, C_3S(red):79034(38.59%),

Figure 1. A processed digital image of Portland cement(256μm × 200μm, 512 × 400 pixels), red-C3S, light green- C2S, green- C3A, orange- C4AF, cyan- gypsum, yellow- K2SO 4, white-CaO

C_2S(green): 17990(8.78%), C_3A(light green): 10997(5.37%), CA_2SO_4(grey): 10821(5.3%), K_2SO_4(yellow): 3355(1.64%).

Additionally we can get the distribution of the particles scale through statistic, and store it into an array: Areas [NumofPart], where NumofPart is the number of particles. Then in the same way, we get the array of each pixel's verge pixels and put them into array Edge [NumofPart], and also with the main phases we get arrays of pixels.

The Reconstruction of 3-D Structure

There are so many particles in sample image that we can believe the representative of the sample. So the water to paste ratio in volume: 0.65 can be believed as that of the target 3-D sample space. Based on this premises some of the information of 3-D structure can be deduced as we assume the target structure occupied a space of 512 × 400 × 400.

Particles in 3-D structure is calculated in this way: first convert the array Areas[NumofPart] into volume array Volume[NumofPart], for each particle we use the relationship between a ball and its biggest circle:

pixels of 3-D image =

$$\frac{4}{3}\pi\left(\sqrt{\frac{pixels\ of\ 2-D\ image}{\pi}}\right)^3$$

We can convert 2-D area array:

2-D Area (in pixels)	47	1	...

to 3-D volume array:

3-D volume (in pixels)	243	1	...

Thus we get a sample group of 3-D particles whose volume distribution is consistent with that of the 2-D sample. Then we fill the 3-D region with this sample. Of course, only one group can not fulfill the requirement of w/c, so we repeat using the sample group until the w/c reaches the request. During the procedure we can get total count of the particles.

Besides the requirement of w/c and particle size distribution, the proportion of verge pixels in 3-D structure is also required consistent with that of the original 2-D image. But, how is the surface fraction of real particles? We can think it in this way, a 2-D image sample is a random 3-D sample whose thickness is only one pixel and the fraction of it is just that of 3-D structure. So the verge pixels in 3-D space is 11404000(28510 × 400). Thus we get the basic relationship between 2-D and 3-D structure, and Table 1 illustrates the parameters and the relationship between 2-D and 3-D structure.

In the prior researchers' work the particles of cement are assumed to be spheres, and easy to construct, but a sphere has the smallest surface fraction among the different shapes with equal volume and a non-spherical object often has a much larger surface, which is quite important in the simulation modal of cement as is mentioned before. So a new particle structure and a corresponding algorithm are proposed here to fulfill the requirement of surface fraction.

As for each unit in a space grid there are six adjacent units, the new structure is called a "Semi-Five Forked Tree", in which the root (the blue one in Figure 1) has six children, other nodes (the green ones and the yellow ones in Figure 1) have utmost five children. The root represents a unit in the space grid and the children represent the adjacent units. A tree here stands for one particle. Figure 2 illustrates the structure of a "semi-five forked tree" and a 3-D model of a particle.

Table 1. Relationship between 2-D and 3-D structure

Parameters	(w/c)	Particles	Verge pixels	Modal space (in pixels)
2-D	0.65	2503	28510	512 × 400
3-D	0.65	20024	11404000	512 × 400 × 400

Figure 2. Space structure (a), logical structure (b) of semi-five fork tree and 3-D model of a particle(c)

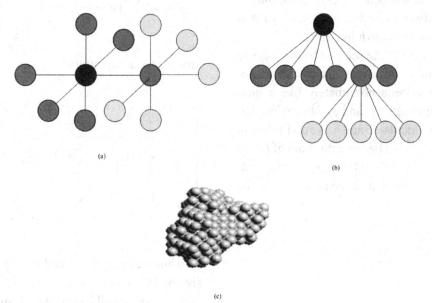

Using the proposed structure, the constructing algorithm can be described as follow:

1) For each particle in 3-D volume array, select a unit not occupied in the target space grid as the root, then generates leaves (all the left adjacent free spaces) at a certain probability P and store them into a queue.

2) For each leaf in the queue, in sequence generates leaves (all the left adjacent free spaces) at the same probability P and mark up that it is no longer a leaf.

3) If a particle has reach the target volume, jump to 1) else jump to 2)

The problem now turns to why using P and how P is determined. During the experiments on this algorithm it is found that the number of leaves of a tree construct by the algorithm is determined by the probability P. So the irregularity of a particle is under control. An experiment on a tree with

Figure 3. The relationship between generation probability P and number of leaves

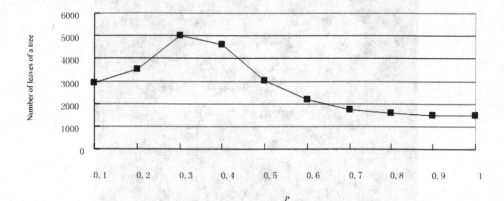

10^4 nodes (leaves and non-leaves) is done and the relationship between generation probability P and number of leaves is shown in Figure 3.

From Figure 3 we can see that form $P=0.3$ to $P=1.0$ the number of leaves decrease monotonously. And the trend proximately like a quadratic equation $y = a/x + b$, and use approximation method we can calculate a and b. We don't choose the value from 0 to 0.3 because this kind of P will slow down the algorithm. Let $E_i = y_i - a/x_i + b$, so to find out a, b is now come down to the minimum of:

$$F(a,b) = \sum_{i=1}^{n} E_i^2 = \sum_{i=1}^{n} \left(y_i - \frac{a}{x_i} - b \right)^2$$

Namely:

$$\frac{\partial F}{\partial a} = -2 \sum_{i=1}^{n} \frac{y_i - \dfrac{a}{x_i} - b}{x_i} = 0$$

$$\frac{\partial F}{\partial b} = -2 \sum_{i=1}^{n} \left(y_i - \frac{a}{x_i} - b \right) = 0$$

Simultaneous equations:

$$\begin{cases} a = \dfrac{\displaystyle\sum_{i=1}^{n} y_i \sum_{i=1}^{n} \frac{1}{x_i} - n \sum_{i=1}^{n} \frac{y_i}{x_i}}{\left(\displaystyle\sum_{i=1}^{n} \frac{1}{x_i}\right)^2 - n \sum_{i=1}^{n} \frac{1}{x_i^2}} \\[4ex] b = \dfrac{1}{n} \sum_{i=1}^{n} y_i - \dfrac{a}{n} \sum_{i=1}^{n} \frac{1}{x_i} \end{cases}$$

Thus we can get a, b and P for particles at the size of 10^4, also we can get each P for different size of particle in the same way. Using different P repeat the generating algorithm the 3-D structure is available. Figure 4 illustrates a result 3-D structure of particles in the sample, and Figure 5 illustrates a result of 3-D reconstruction of particles with 3 main phases classified.

Figure 4. A result of 3-D reconstruction of particles

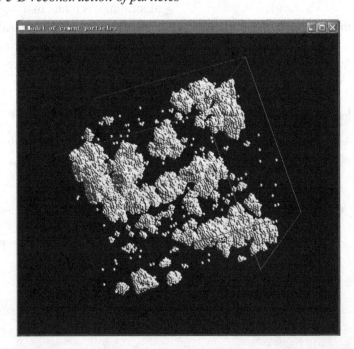

Figure 5. A result of 3-D reconstruction of particles with 3 classified phases(red-C3S, yellow-C2S, green-C3A)

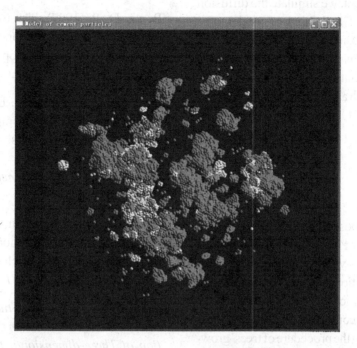

EXPERIMENTAL RESULTS

Based on the reconstructed 3-D structure of initial status, we simulated the procedure of cement hydration. In this simulation, we use the cellular automata as basic model to simulate the procedure of diffusion and decomposition. We set a series of check time point, at each point we calculate the surface fraction of each model. By measuring the surface fraction, we get the degree of simulated hydration procedure.

We compared the difference of hydrating speed between spherical particles model and non-spherical particle model that we've reconstructed, as is illustrated in Figure 6.

Figure 6. Real experimental result and simulation result

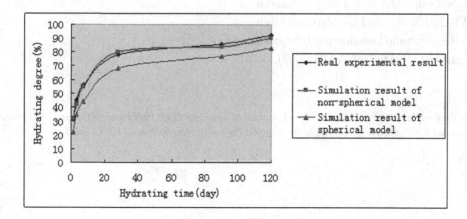

According to the activity of different phases in the Portland cement, we simulate the diffusion and decomposing of both kind of model. The result shows that the non-spherical model works more accurately than spherical model, because the spherical has a relatively smaller surface fraction and diffuses with a lower speed. Furthermore the spherical cannot reach the real hydration degree.

CONCLUSION

In this paper, we proposed a method to reconstruct the microstructure of cement particles from a single 2-D SEM/X-ray image. Irregular shape is used instead of traditional sphere which loses the accuracy of surface fraction. Through experiments we find a method to control the irregularity of cement particles. Using the procedure of trees' growing generates the 3-D structure. Furthermore this method is also suitable to other kinds of particles' 3-D reconstruction whose shapes are irregular.

ACKNOWLEDGMENT

Thank Mr. Dale P. Bentz and Mr. Paul E. Stutzman for sharing 2-D SEM and X-ray images and prior research work on cement hydration.

This work is supported by Program for Changjiang Scholars and Innovative Research Team in University, National Defense Basic Research Program (A1420080182) and the National High Technology Research and Development Program ("863"Program) of China (2007AA01Z149).

REFERENCES

Bentz, D. P. (1997). Three-Dimensional Computer Simulation of Portland Cement Hydration and Microstructure Development. *Journal of the American Ceramic Society*, *80*(1), 3–21.

Bentz, D. P., & Garboczi, E. J. (1993, March). Digital- Image-Based Computer Modelling of Cement-Based Materials. In *Proceedings of Digital Image Processing: Techniques and Applications in Civil Engineering, Engineering Foundation Conference*.

Bentz, D. P., & Stutzman, P. E. (1994). SEM analysis and computer modeling of hydration of portland cement particles in petrography of cementitious materials. *ASTM STP*, *1215*, 60–73.

Dongliang, Z. (2003). *The Study on Microstructure Model of Cement Hydration Based on Reconstruction of Three-dimensional Image*. Unpublished master dissertation, JiNan University, Jinan, China.

Li, W. (2000). *The Study on 3-D reconstruction of Cement Hydration Based on image processing*. Unpublished master dissertation, Shandong University, Jinan, China.

Wittmann, F. H., Roelfstra, P. E., & Sadouki, H. (1984). Simulation and Analysis of Composite Structures. *Materials Science and Engineering*, *68*, 239–248. doi:10.1016/0025-5416(85)90413-6

This work was previously published in International Journal of Grid and High Performance Computing, Volume 2, Issue 4, edited by Emmanuel Udoh, pp. 31-39, copyright 2010 by IGI Publishing (an imprint of IGI Global).

Chapter 22
Managing Inconsistencies in Data Grid Environments:
A Practical Approach

Ejaz Ahmed
King Fahd University of Petroleum and Minerals, Saudi Arabia and University of Bedfordshire, UK

Nik Bessis
University of Bedfordshire, UK

Peter Norrington
University of Bedfordshire, UK

Yong Yue
University of Bedfordshire, UK

ABSTRACT

Much work has been done in the area of data access and integration using various data mapping, matching, and loading techniques. One of the main concerns when integrating data from heterogeneous data sources is data redundancy. The concern is mainly due to the different business contexts and purposes from which the data systems were originally built. A common process for accessing data from integrated databases involves the use of each data source's own catalogue or metadata schema. In this article, the authors take the view that there is a greater chance of data inconsistencies, such as data redundancies when integrating them within a grid environment as compared to traditional distributed paradigms. The importance of improving the data search and matching process is briefly discussed, and a partial service oriented generic strategy is adopted to consolidate distinct catalogue schemas of federated databases to access information seamlessly. To this end, a proposed matching strategy between structure objects and data values across federated databases in a grid environment is presented.

DOI: 10.4018/978-1-4666-0056-0.ch022

INTRODUCTION

The role of traditional data integration (Bessis et al., 2007; Austin et al., 2006) and loading techniques and methods requires more attention when functioning within the grid environment. One reason is the higher chance for conflict between metadata and structures when integrating data (multi-vendor relational, object-relational DBMSs) within a grid environment since data sources have been originally produced for a purpose other than their integration (Bessis et al., 2009). This is our main motivation for undertaking this research.

The grid is an emerging infrastructure that supports the discovery, access and use of distributed computational resources (Alpdmir et al., 2003), including data integration in the de-facto OGSA-DAI (Open Grid Service Architecture – Data Access Integration) specification framework. Significant effort has gone into defining requirements, protocols and implementing the OGSA-DAI specification framework as the means for users to develop relevant data grids to conveniently control the sharing, accessing and management of large amounts of distributed data in Grid environments (Antonioletti et al., 2005; Atkinson et al., 2003). Ideally, OGSA-DAI as a data integration specification aims to allow users to specify 'what' information is needed without having to provide detailed instructions on 'how' or 'from where' to obtain the information (Reinoso Castillo et al., 2004). However, mapping multiple physical replicas to one single logical file increases data redundancy (Jacob et al., 2005). Yin et al. (2009) also explain that running join queries over a data grid environment requires appropriate strategies as decomposing and disseminating the query to as many as possible sources, as processing the user's query in parallel will also bring in overhead in repetitive computing, redundant data transmission, and result merging.

In this article, our main contribution is the discussion and proposal of a schema matching exercise for identifying two objects that semantically relate them, while we refer to mapping as the transformations between the objects concerned. That is to say when data is accessed it will attempt to virtualize and/or transfer them within the target source. It is anticipated that if there is more than one accessing object in the same or dispersed data source(s), like DBMSs, then it is necessary to define matching patterns to access the correct objects concerned with their properties. In our present discussion, a schema is treated as a set of elements connected by some structure. A target database schema requires access to certain data from many objects (or elements of a schema) of various distinct schemas of databases with the help of common sources' metadata.

With this in mind, the main intention of our article is multi-fold: firstly, to offer a brief review of data matching exercises; secondly, to present our proposed strategy by discussing our data matching and mapping framework including a linguistic matching approach; thirdly, to discuss in full our methodological approach for a grid based matching process using a number of developed metadata algorithms. We finally conclude by presenting some pilot experimental results and further work.

LITERATURE REVIEW

The section presents an overview of and a comparison between matching approaches.

Rahm and Bernstein (2001) developed taxonomy of schema matching approaches which for some remains the significant contribution in this field. The taxonomy consists of two major branches (Figure 1): (a) individual matcher approaches and (b) combining matchers. Regarding combining matchers, hybrid matchers integrate matching criteria prior to mapping, whereas composite matchers integrate the results of individual matchers post-mapping. The description of individual matchers is from (Rahm & Bernstein, ibid).

Figure 1. Individual and combining schema matching approaches (from Rahm & Bernstein, 2001)

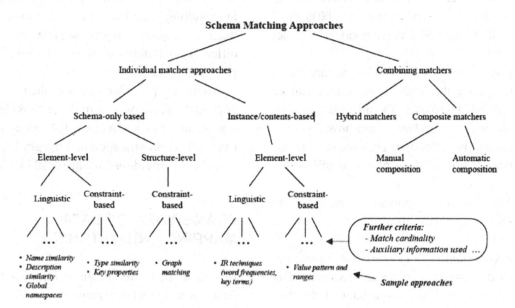

- *Instance vs. schema*: matching approaches can consider instance data (i.e., data contents) or only schema-level information.
- *Element vs. structure matching*: match can be performed for individual schema elements, such as attributes, or for combinations of elements, such as complex schema structures.
- *Language vs. constraint*: a matcher can use a linguistic based approach (e.g., based on names and textual descriptions of schema elements) or a constraint-based approach (e.g., based on keys and relationships).
- *Matching cardinality*: the overall match result may relate one or more elements of one schema to one or more elements of the other, yielding four cases: 1:1, 1:n, n:1, n:m. In addition, each mapping element may interrelated one or more elements of the two schemas. Furthermore, there may be different match cardinalities at the instance level.
- *Auxiliary information*: most matchers rely not only on the input schemas S1 and S2 but also on auxiliary information, such

as dictionaries, global schemas, previous matching decisions, and user input.

Sellami et al. (2010, p. 18) consider Rahm and Bernstein's (2001) and other approaches to be limited to small- and medium-scale matching problems, but to be insufficient for large-scale problems over schemas or ontologies with hundreds or thousands of components. They present a classification of approaches to large-scale problems under pair-wise and holistic approaches, employing a range of strategies, such as fragmentation, clustering and statistical; it should be noted that their terminology for approaches and strategies (inter alia) is not consistent. Pair-wise approaches (ibid, p. 18) attempt to construct an integrated schema for two sources, using any of a variety of strategies to divide large and complex sources into manageable sub-problems. Holistic approaches (ibid, p. 21) attempt to match multiple schemas at the same time.

Other considerations may further enrich understanding and development of the data matching approaches. Calvanese et al. (1999) employs three types of interschema correspondences for data integration and reconciliation in data warehousing. We note that Rahm and Bernstein (2001) fulfil the role of the "matching correspondences" type:

- *Conversion Correspondences* are used to specify that data in one source can be converted into data of a different source or of the data warehouse, and how this conversion is performed. They are used to anticipate several types of data conflicts that may occur in loading data.
- *Matching Correspondences* are used to specify how data in different sources can match.
- *Reconciliation Correspondences* are used to assert how we can reconcile data in different sources into data of the data warehouse.

Equally, Haas et al. (2002, p. 586) raise some interesting questions which will have a direct impact on the effectiveness and efficiency of querying databases of significant size and distribution, namely:

- Is transactional consistency important for the integration problem?
- Is there a sophisticated cost model associated with the federated operations?

The first of these is important where, for example, data may change between queries, even though these are close in time, leading to different queries returning time-dependent results, which may cascade effects. The second is a natural consequence of sharing distributed resources, physical and logical, all of which have associated costs, notwithstanding any altruistic data-sharing philosophy.

According to the authors' knowledge, a topic which has not been much discussed in the literature is the positioning of the matching process within the overall query-response cycle. In this article, for example, we approach matching as occurring prior to a query being accepted, and that matching resulting in an integrated data source, rather than, say, a query being parsed and presented to different data stores in ways relevant to those particular stores.

To this end, a wider review of the literature is beyond the scope of this article, but it is clear that this is a domain rich in challenges for definition, description, classification and integration of approaches to provide useful and scalable solutions.

FRAMEWORK OF DATA MAPPING AND MATCHING

In this section, we illustrate formalization of data matching and data mapping, which is based on three heterogeneous data models (relational, object-oriented and object-relational). We follow basic nomenclature and notations as described in the data integration context and more specifically as proposed by Cali et al. (2002). We assume that different constants between data sources denote different objects or elements. A schema often contains constraints to define data types and range values, uniqueness, optionally relationship type, cardinalities, etc. If two input schemas contain such information, it can be used by a matcher to determine the similarity of schema elements (Larson et al., 1989). For example, similarity can be used on the equivalence of data types and domains including key characteristics (e.g., unique, primary, foreign), relationship cardinality (e.g., 1:1 relationships) (Rahm & Bernstein, 2001). However, some matching is based on the objects' name assigned by the user, like a storage table name or some other attribute name.

It is assumed that the generic implementation of a matching mechanism represents the schemas to be matched in a uniform internal representation. This uniform representation reduces the complexity of the heterogeneity of various schemas or databases. To reduce heterogeneity, various tools are available that are tightly integrated with the framework of uniform representation of schemas. Some other tools need import/export programs to translate between their native schema representation (such as XML, SQL, or UML) and the internal representation (Rahm & Bernstein, 2001). Similarly, many algorithms depend mostly on the kind of information they exploit, but not on generic representations.

As defined by Cali et al. (2002), **G** represents global or target schema and **S** represents a source schema. A data transformation system Γ is a triplet $\Gamma = (G, S, M_{G,S})$, where $M_{G,S}$ is a mapping between source (**S**) and target schema (**G**). We propose an iterative integration-by-example paradigm by introducing another middle-tier temporary schema called the staging schema (Ahmed et al., 2008) or a staging DBMS as a database in the grid environment. To achieve this, we consider following example.

Example-1: Consider an example of source and target schema by choosing the triplet $\Gamma^I = (G^1, S^1, M^1_{G,S})$. The source and target are constituted by the relation symbols, as shown in Figure 2.

Figure 2 depicts a schema matching by identifying how elements are semantically related. Underlined attributes represent primary key constraints and primary key names appearing in other relations represent foreign keys. We define a mapping to be a set of mapping elements, each of which indicates that certain elements of source schemas S^1 are mapped to certain elements in target G^1. Each mapping element could have a mapping expression related elements. In this mapping, some value correspondences are injective indicating that the mappings are 1:1. Some other value correspondences are surjective as the product of two values (attributes) from the sources or there could be a function applied to one or more attributes of source schema. For example, if:

$f: S \rightarrow G$ then $f:$ SoldPrice $-$ (SoldPrice $*$ Discount) $\rightarrow$ Sold.SPrice (1)

Figure 2. Scenario of source and target schemas' elements mapping

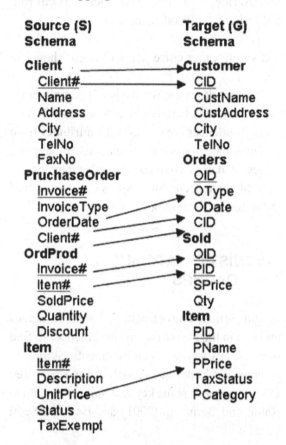

Where instance values of attribute *Discount* contains percentage values that are given to a product at the time of sale in source schema. Whereas such kind of discount is not explicitly indicated in a target schema, instead target attribute *SPrice* is computed as mentioned in Equation (1).

Two schemas **S** and **G** represent a similar domain application but in a different business scenario or local requirement of the system as given in Equation (1). A mapping from source Client.Client# to target Customer.CID can be written as a mapping expression or value correspondence. That is,

Customer.CID = Client.Client#
Similarly,
Orders.OType = PurchaseOrder.InvoiceType

Also, in Equation (1), a function formula will be: Sold.SPrice = OrdProd.SoldPrice – (OrdProd. SoldPrice * OrdProd.Discount)

and so on; other correspondences are shown in Figure 2.

This work provides a basis of a simple mapping that exists between two schemas whereby correspondences are created with attributes from schemas matching objects or relations. In mapping, issues of data anomalies and redundancies are most likely to occur. Such issues will be explored in the following section.

LINGUISTIC MATCHING APPROACHES

Linguistic matching or language-based uses names and text in the form of words or sentences to find semantically similar schema elements. Similarity of names can be defined, recognized and measured in various ways; some key examples are found in Rahm and Bernstein (2001) and Bell and Sethi (2001):

- Equality of canonical name representations using special prefix/ suffix symbols. For example, Client# → Client Number or ClientNo → Client Number, ProdID → Product Identifier.
- Equality of synonyms. For example, car $\cong$ vehicle or car $\cong$ automobile and make $\cong$ brand or model.
- Similarity of names based on common substrings, edit distance, soundex (an encoding of names based on how they sound rather than how they are spelled) etc. For example, CR_amount $\cong$ Credit, ShipTo $\cong$ Ship2, OrderType $\cong$ ShipmentType, representedBy $\cong$ representative.
- User-provided name matches. For example, reportTo $\cong$ supervisorId, reportTo $\cong$ manager, error $\cong$ bug.

- Equality of hyponyms. For example, book is-a publication and article is-a publication implies book $\cong$ publication, article $\cong$ publication, and report $\cong$ article.

Consequently, a linguistic analysis with comments can be produced and provide commentary about each schema element, for example, for attributes in source schema S_1 which contains Cust#, which may mean customer number or identifier, and S_2 which contains CustAddress, which may mean customer address or customer's contact details.

An issue of data inconsistency in terms of anomalies will occur if some information, such as an attribute, has a certain specific meaning in one object. Based on its corresponding match, it may be interpreted differently in another schema or data source segment. For example, the size of data values of matched attributes can be different. Similarly, conditional scenarios of 'Male' and 'Female', in one schema data values are 'M' and 'F' whereas in other corresponding schema data values could be '0' and '1'. The term redundancy may mean that a matching attribute may occur in more than one data source segment during the search. Database normalization is used to consolidate such kinds of discrepancy or information anomaly.

GRID BASED FRAMEWORK OF MATCHING

Now we move towards a kind of generic or uniform methodology that can help to reduce the conflict of heterogeneous representations of schemas/ databases. Consider a set of heterogeneous databases (mainly DBMSs) that are integrated through a staging DBMS. At both levels of this DBMS software diversity – the tool and database levels – there exists the problem of communication between the software. The DBMSs usually do not understand or are unable to communicate with each other (Rezenda et al., 1999). To resolve the heterogeneity problem, federated databases will communicate only via a staging DBMS. All such databases are connected with a staging DBMS using connectivity drivers like ODBC and ODBC-JDBC. The staging DBMS will provide a service to make data sharing seamless. Such sharable data services include data loading, data transformations, data matching and temporary data storage services which are further explained in the following examples.

Example-2: A user can access a public schema of one or more databases. A web interface is provided with a default connection with the staging DBMS. A user can write a query on the chosen database. A temporary storage buffer of the staging DBMS will be used to keep data fetched from any of the integrated databases.

We consider a function f that is directed from a staging DBMS to any federated database. Refer to Figure 3; if x is a string initiated at staging database (X) that is searched from each database (Y) then f can be mapped as:

$$f_i: X \rightarrow Y^i, i = 1, 2, 3, ..., n$$

The range Y may have more than one image of $x \in X$, i.e., more than one domain match exists in range Y. The possible matched values will be mapped in a staging database X defined by function g as:

$$g_i: Y^i \rightarrow X, i = 1, 2, 3, ..., n$$

Also, $x \cong \varphi$ means no match found. To clarify the granularity issue of matching as discussed above using functions f and g, we are defining a function ρ_{DB}, to perform a search for an element string *str* from schema **S** of database DB with a certain matching criteria:

$$f(str) = \rho_{DB}(str, \psi, \delta) \quad (2)$$

where:

$$\Psi = \begin{cases} d & \text{for instance or domain value} \\ s & \text{for structure element} \end{cases}$$

and δ represents an instance or domain value that needs to be searched in structure elements s when $\psi = d$. It represents a set of structure elements such as relation, attribute, when $\psi = s$.

Figure 3. Searching patterns of string element name from federated DBMSs

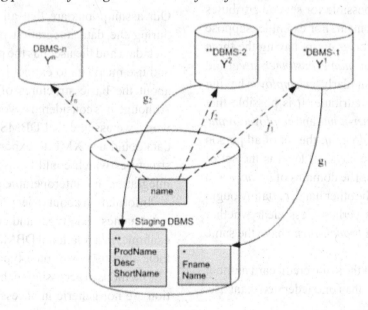

Let g be a function on ρ_{DB} which returns possible similar matched value(s) that is:

$$str \cong g_i\,(f(str),\,\eta_j)\,^\wedge\,str \subseteq g_i\,(f(str),\,\eta_j) \qquad (3)$$

where η_j represents a set of structure elements from schema S of database DB through which possible match of string str is found or return as an output and $\eta_j = \varphi$ means no match is found.

Example-3: Consider searching for a telephone number "8606015" need to be searched in a number of federated databases in a grid environment. Then function f can be written as:

$$f(str) = \rho_{DB}(\text{"8606015"},\ d,\ \{\text{telephone number, telno, tel\#, fax\#, mobile\#}\})$$

Then returned values of this function as defined in Equation (2) would be:

$str \cong g_i(f(str),\{S_1.Client.telno\})$ such that e.g., $t[S_1.Client.telno] = $ "8606015",

$str \cong g_i(f(str),\{S_2.Customer.fax\#,\ S_2.Employee.HomeTelNo\})$.

where $S_1, S_2, ..., S_n$ represents schemas of some database DB. It is possible for several attributes to have the same domain. For example, suppose that we have a customer entity having the three attributes of *customer-name*, *customer-street* and *customer-city*, and similarly, an *employee* having the *employee-name* attribute. It is possible that the attributes *customer-name* and *employee-name* will have the same domain; the set of all person names, which at the physical level is the set of all character strings. The domains of *balance* and *balance-name*, on the other hand, certainly ought to be distinct. It is perhaps less clear whether *customer-name* and *branch-name* have the same domain.

It is possible that the same credit card number may appear in more than one federated database.

It can even appear in more than one relation of a schema(s). For example, in one relation it appears so as to keep master information. The same credit card number appears in some other relation with defaulter status or fraud status. Such occurrences can be found with the help of the above matching methodology using relation (4).

For a search of single match in grid databases, a number of grid databases (d) (say n-items) are involved. Each of them contains a number of schema objects (s) say m-items, each schema object may contain number of relations or tables (t) say p-items, and one or more attributes (a) say q-items of relation(s) will be scanned. Thus, the total number of object items involved in the search match would be:

$$\sum_{d=1}^{n}\sum_{s=1}^{m}\sum_{t=1}^{p}\sum_{a=1}^{q}(A_{dsta}) \rightarrow (n\ x\ m\ x\ p\ x\ q-items)$$

This indicates the granularity and complexity of searching a number of objects.

IMPLEMENTATION OF STAGING METADATA

Our assumptions are that all DBMSs involved during the data integration process do contain metadata and the user has the privileges to access and use metadata to extract general information about the basic structures of database objects. Although it is considered beyond the scope of this work, we assume that DBMSs having no metadata could use XML to export data and schema structures which could be used as metadata for integration and interoperable purposes.

Information about object structure can be element names, data types and constraints, etc. For example, in a relational DBMS table names have their attributes with data types and constraints. The methods of accessing such metadata information are not generic in accessing heterogeneous

DBMSs. Implementation of mapping requires a generic solution of accessing metadata information especially when DBMSs exist in a grid environment or DBMSs act as federated databases. To handle such conflicts of mapping implementation, introducing a new approach such that each federated DBMS contains a public schema segment whereby read privileges of other schema objects are granted. Creating a schema for the metadata catalogue in a staging DBMS that is a replica of all federated metadata catalogues is shown in Figure 4. Such a metadata catalogue in staging DBMS is termed the SCAT (Staging Catalogue).

On the global scale, it is expected that the amount of data flowing or data search into or around integrated grid DBMSs could be of the order of a terabyte. Any data information can be searched in the form of pattern matching that would be possible in two phases. In quick search, a pattern will be searched initially through the SCAT of the staging database. This will generate a profile of possible searched data-elements as an output to perform further granular searches.

The Pattern Matching Controller is the front-end service for pattern matching operations across the data held at each federated DBMS. It accesses all objects of each federated DBMS which was searched from the SCAT, as shown in Figure 4.

In the staging database, the Pattern Matching Log service includes object details where patterns exist and in which form as shown Figure 4. A search pattern can be a data value; it can be the name of some relation or an attribute. Similarly, the log service maintains the list of patterns that are included in the search but these are not found in federated DBMSs. These services can be additional building blocks of OGSA-DAI.

The implementation procedure is involved programming using JSP (Java Server Pages) using service based programming with multi vendor databases.

Metadata Catalogue Algorithm

The SCAT in the form of metadata, contains the structure of relations (4) which are called *plug-in relations*. These plug-in relations provide similar information as standard metadata dictionaries of any DBMS but some auxiliary information is included to improve the effectiveness of mappings. Note that users can customize plug-in relations. We will use the concept of granularity of match, i.e., element level and structure level (Rahm & Bernstein, 2001), with the following plug-in relations.

DataTable (<u>TableName</u>, <u>SchemaName</u>, Description, DateCreated)

Figure 4. Pattern match data management architecture

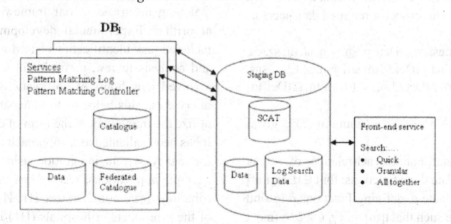

TableDetails (<u>TableName</u>, <u>SchemaName</u>, <u>Serial#</u>, Attribute, DataType, Size, Constraints, ShortDesc, DetailDesc) (4)

These relations will act as a pool and a library encompassing enterprise dictionary and/or schema taxonomies. Underlined attributes represents unique key constraints. It is noted that attributes *Descriptions*, *ShortDesc* and *DetailDesc* play an important role for the name or linguistic matching, and the description matching.

It would be possible to indicate canonical name matching in *TableDetails.ShortDesc*. Also, more than one similarity can be used in attribute *ShortDesc* or in *DetailDesc*. These descriptive attributes of plug-in relations provide matching information when the mapping process will be performed as shown in relations (4) or (5). The staging DBMS SCAT will also contain a most recent replica of public schema segments of each federated DBMS. We believe that such a service will significantly improve data integration efficiency since initially information searching will be performed prior to the scanning of the element from all federated DBMSs.

Semantics of Metadata Catalogue

In order to define the semantics of a plug-in relation, we start by introducing the following two relations in a source DBMS. Any federated schema or SCAT establishes a mapping with the relations of (5), to search the correct schema objects such as tables or relations γ for required data access.

tDef(<u>tn</u>, <u>sn</u>, des, dc), tDet(<u>tn</u>, <u>sn</u>, <u>sno</u>, at, dt, sz, cs, sd, dd) (5) where tDef.t_1[tn, sn] $\neq$ tDef.t_2[tn, sn], tDet.t_1[tn,sno] $\neq$ tDet.t_2[tn,sno], tDet[tn] $\subseteq$ tDef[tn]

and description of each attribute of (5) is given in (4).

For every attribute a in each relation γ of schema C, we associate three functions: for t $\in$ tDet, t[at] = a. On attribute a, defining functions ∂ to find a table name such that t[tn] = $\partial(\gamma, C)$; ξ to find a

schema name such that t[sn] = ξ(sn, S); ρ to find an attribute name such that t[at] = $\rho(\gamma,a)$; δ to find a data type such that t[dt] = $\delta(\gamma,a)$; μ to find a size such that t[sz] = $\mu(\gamma,a)$; η to find constraints such that t[cs] = concat[$\eta(\gamma,a_i)$], for some attributes a_i i.e., containing constraints i.e., $\eta(\gamma,a_i) \neq \varphi$.

The attributes *sd*, *dd* will be used to store multiple names or similar meanings which are text details entered by the user with schema sn. Also, *sno* is a sequence number starting with 1, incremented by 1 for the same *tn*, denoted by i. We can write for t $\in$ tDet, for relation γ and attribute *a*

t = {<tn, $\partial(\gamma, C)$>, <sn, ξ(sn, S)>, <sno,i>, <at, $\rho(\gamma,a)$>, <dt, $\delta(\gamma,a)$>, <sz, $\mu(\gamma,a)$>, <cs, concat[$\eta(\gamma,a_i)$]>, <sd, t[sd]>, <dd, t[dd]>}

Once possible schema objects or relations are found, instance level matching will then help to further boost the confidence in matching results. At this level, linguistic and constraint based characterization of instances is useful. For example, using linguistic techniques, it might be possible to look at *Client*, *ClientName* and *Ename* instances to conclude that *ClientName* is a better match candidate for *Client* than *Ename*.

EXPERIMENTS AND DISCUSSION

The experimental design has been chosen and carefully tested with an understanding of data matching discussed in our framework and an algorithm. Experimental development stages included task identifications based upon design and analysis review, a successful strategy that involved long hours of observations and users interviews. This helps us to understand how to utilize the framework in the form of experiment. It has been validated as an approach to matching for legacy system integration using three real example applications, received as in-kind contributions from collaborators H1, H2, H3. One of these products or hospitals (H1) is a leading physician information system (known as medcare) which provides clinical records, billing and work flow features. The second one (H2) is a clinical care system dedicated to patient diagnostic illness. The third system (H3) is a PatAziz patient treatment database.

To validate *plug-in relations* metadata search algorithm, it is desired to populate database integration systems of hospitals with OGSA-DAI. The integration of this system is named ArabGrid. Information exchanged between the systems includes data search, examination reports, diagnosis and medical histories (Non-disclosure agreements do not allow revealing details about these systems).

The hospitals are integrated with a staging DBMS and OGSA-DAI framework to provide a view of the grid environment. For example, a medical doctor being a user forms an integrated view of his medical records scattered across these hospitals. A patient's personal information and diagnosis details such as medical history, surgical history and allergies etc. are recorded in different contexts in these hospitals. Before a performing medical diagnosis search of some patient, the user will search the patient name in ArabGrid. This search is performed initially from staging *plug-in relations* of the staging DBMS to browse the structure of database objects such as tables or column names, as shown in Figure 5. If the string *name* is redundant in more than one database, the

user decides to choose an appropriate to search actual information. Once the user finds an appropriate database where the search item is located, a query can be performed on a chosen table name to access personal data of that particular patient from a database. This can be done with patient name, date of birth, etc. The same patient with different identifiers can be searched from more than one database (or hospitals). This experimental validation helps a user to explore the patient's medical history from federated databases. A history of matching search is recorded for future data search and data can be loaded or extracted into the user profile. It is noted that volume of data in an integrated database is very large, in the order of a terabyte. The plug-in relations of ArabGrid help initially in searching the data quickly.

An ArabGrid experimental infrastructure of the staging DBMS is based on Oracle9i/ 10g Enterprise Edition database running on MS Windows 2003 Advance Server on a dedicated Dell PowerEdge 4400 server. The server has two 1 GHz Xeon processors, 4 GB of main memory, and a PERC3DI RAID controller producing about 240 GB of RAID 5 storage over eight 36 GB U3 SCSI disks. The heterogeneous DBMSs used at grid nodes are MySQL, Oracle, MS SQL Server etc. Database installation and configuration includes interaction with OGSA-DQP version 3.0 axis 1.4 for generating a realistic grid environment.

Figure 5. A sample of pattern match search from grid environment

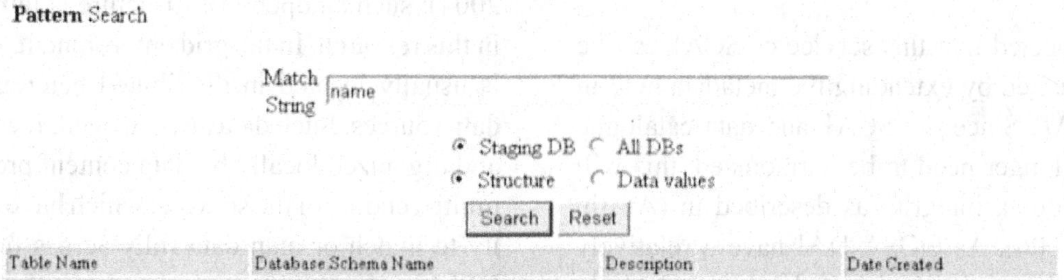

Pattern Search

Match String [name]

○ Staging DB ○ All DBs
○ Structure   ○ Data values

[Search] [Reset]

Table Name	Database Schema Name	Description	Date Created
PATIENT	PUB.MEDCARE	Name	12/04/2008
MAINPAT	U1.CCARE	Fname	10/11/2009
EPATIENT	GRID1.PATAZIZ	Name	14/03/2008
MAT_MEDICINE	GRID1.PATAZIZ	Name of medicine	14/06/2008

A web-based prototype system is particularly designed to depict how various components of the framework are implemented. The OGSA-DAI approach offers the way the integration is managed, generated and presenting according to user preference and expertise. A consolidated integration of ArabGrid and OGSA-DAI systems is presented in the form of a federated grid browser. Based on the web interface middleware design, the user will have more guiding and navigational facilities.

As discussed, the string match on name may have several possible searches in federated databases. A data inconsistency in the form of redundancy occurs when name is defined as first name, full name or just a name as shown in Figure 5. It is also noted that name is also defined for generic medicine name. Our proposed work for the matching algorithm (plug-in relations) extracts such information from the federated database for decision purposes. This work also contains metadata information of various data elements, such as tables, attributes and data instances. The user has a choice to perform quick and loose granular search because of large data volumes. The user can clarify search patterns by using queries from databases. Data in plug-in relations is updated regularly using an automatic loading service. This loading does not affect the routine database transactional operations.

FUTURE MAPPINGS AND MATCHING WITH GRID SERVICES

It is expected that this service of SCAT can be implemented by extending the metadata held in the SCAT. Since the SCAT and data catalogue will no longer need to be harmonized, this will improve data integrity as described in (Austin et al., 2006). As OGSA-DAI have a relatively simple operational model, it should be relatively straightforward to map it onto whatever emerges as the preferred way of building grid applications (Antonioletti et al., 2005). The SCAT service

framework presented in this article complies with the OGSA-DAI framework. This is achieved with the development of a new service called GSCATS (Grid Staging Catalogue Service) using the common GDQS (Grid Distributed Query Service) instance for multiple database connections. GSCATS improves the GDS (Grid Data Services) interface of (Alpdemir et al., 2003). When a GSCATS is set up, it interacts with the appropriate registries to obtain the metadata information from the staging DBMS, then passes on required registry information of matching string to GDQS instances. GDQS instances interact with GQESs (Grid Query Evaluation Services) over multiple execution nodes in the grid.

The low-level matching mechanism provides more fine-grained control over precise and target data sharing as compliant with OGSA-DAI. Performance issues using services can be further explored on the basis of the total number of accessed objects such as databases, schema etc.

CONCLUSION

Schema mapping and matching is a basic problem in many database application domains, such as heterogeneous database integration, grid database, e-commerce, data warehousing, and semantic query processing. The key to progress in the coming years is to create an extensible and open infrastructure that can incorporate these advances as they become available (Forster & Kessleman, 2004); such an open infrastructure is introduced in this research. In the grid environment, the data is usually located in distributed heterogeneous data sources. Such data are managed, recognized and organized locally by data content providers, multi-vendors of the sources, which have no ability to match or map data fully across federated DBMSs. We have presented a practical approach to overcome database heterogeneity via the use of a purposefully uniform strategy. This practical approach includes pilot experimental verification and validation. For a sophisticated grid environment, a large number of data nodes (such as hospitals) can be added in an experimental federation of systems (ArabGrid). Our strategy is based on the granularity feature of data matching and mapping that helps to find candidate information which has similarities in structure definition or at instance level. In this way, users can access redundant or multiple pattern occurrences of a match. These redundant patterns can be further clarified by using queries on federated databases.

ACKNOWLEDGMENT

The first author would like to thank King Fahd University of Petroleum & Minerals for their excellent research facilities.

REFERENCES

Ahmed, E., Bessis, N., Yue, Y., & Stephens, D. (2008). Data loading and mapping using staging DBMS in the grid. In *Proceedings of the 21st IEEE Annual Canadian Conference on Electrical and Computer Engineering (CCECE)*, Ontario, Canada (pp. 1887-1893).

Alpdemir, M. N., Mukherjee, A., Foster, I., Paton, N. W., Watson, P., Fernandes, A. A. A., et al. (2003). Service-based distributed query processing on the grid. In *Proceedings of the 1st Intl. Conference on Service-Oriented Computing (ICSOC)* (pp. 467-482).

Antonioletti, M., Atkinson, M., Baxter, R., Borley, A., Hong, N. P., & Collins, B. (2005). The design and implementation of grid database services in OGSA-DAI. *Concurrency and Computation, 7*, 2–4.

Austin, J., Davis, R., Fletcher, M., Jackson, T., Jessop, M., Liang, N., & Pasley, A. (2005). DAME: Searching large data sets with in a grid-enabled engineering application. *Proceedings of the IEEE, 93*, 496–509. doi:10.1109/JPROC.2004.842746

Austin, J., Turner, A., & Alwis, S. (2006). Grid enabling data de-duplication. In *Proceedings of the 2nd IEEE International Conference on e-Science and Grid Computing* (pp. 2-8).

Bell, G. S., & Sethi, A. (2001). Matching records in a national medical patient index. *CACM, 44*(9), 83–88.

Bessis, N. (Ed.). (2009). Model architecture for a user tailored data push service in data grids. In *Grid technology for maximizing collaborative decision management and support: Advancing effective virtual organizations* (pp. 235-255). Hershey, PA: IGI Global. ISBN: 978-1-60566-364-7

Bessis, N., French, T., Burakova-Lorgnier, M., & Huang, W. (2007). Using grid technology for data sharing to support intelligence in decision making. In Xu, M. (Ed.), *Managing strategic intelligence: Techniques and technologies* (pp. 179–201). Hershey, PA: Idea Group Publishing Inc.

Cali, A., Calvanese, D., Giacomo, G., & Lenzerini, M. (1999). Semistructured data schemas with expressive constraints. In *Proceedings of CAiSE* (LNCS, pp. 262-279). Berlin: Springer.

Cali, A., Calvanese, D., Giacomo, G., & Lenzerini, M. (2002). Data integration under integrity constraints. In *Proceedings of CAiSE* (LNCS 2348, pp. 262-279). Berlin: Springer.

Calvanese, D., De Giacomo, G., Lenzerini, M., Nardi, D., & Rosati, R. (1999). A principled approach to data integration and reconciliation in data warehousing. In S. Gatziu, M. Jeusfeld, M. Staudt, & Y. Vassiliou (Eds.), *Proceedings of the International Workshop on Design and Management of DataWarehouses (DMDW'99)*, Heidelberg, Germany.

Foster, I., Kesselman, C., Nick, J., & Tueke, S. (2002). Grid services for distributed system integration. *IEEE Computer, 35*(6), 397–398.

Foster, I., & Kessleman, C. (2004). *The Grid: Blueprint for a new computing infrastructure* (pp. 283, 391–396). San Francisco, CA: Morgan Kaufmann.

Haas, L. M., Lin, E. T., & Roth, M. A. (2002). Data integration through database federation. *IBM Systems Journal, 41*(4). doi:10.1147/sj.414.0578

Jacob, B., Brown, M., Fukui, K., & Trivedi, N. (2005). *Introduction to grid computing* (p. 148). IBM.

Larson, J. A., Navathe, S. B., & El-Masri, R. (1989). A theory of attribute equivalence in databases with application to schema integration. *IEEE Transactions on Software Engineering, 16*(4), 449–463. doi:10.1109/32.16605

Rahm, E., & Bernstein, P. A. (2001). A survey of approaches to automatic schema matching. *The VLDB Journal, 10*, 334–350. doi:10.1007/s007780100057

Reinoso Castillo, J. A., Silvescu, A., Caragea, D., Pathak, J., & Honavar, V. G. (2004). *Information extraction and integration from heterogeneous, distributed, autonomous information sources— A federated ontology-driven query-centric approach*. Retrieved January 5, 2007, from http://www.cs.iastate.edu/~honavar/Papers/indusfinal.pdf

Rezenda, F. F., Georgian, U. H., & Rutschlin, J. (1999). A practical approach to access heterogeneous and distributed databases. In [Berlin: Springer.]. *Proceedings of CAiSE, 99*, 317–332.

Sellami, S., Benharkat, A.-N., & Amghar, Y. (2010). Towards a more scalable schema matching: A novel approach. *International Journal of Distributed Systems and Technologies, 1*(1), 17–39.

Yin, D., Chen, B., Huang, Z., Lin, X., & Fang, Y. (2007, August 16-18). Utility based query dissemination in spatial data grid. In *Proceedings of the Sixth International Conference on Grid and Cooperative Computing (GCC 2007)*, Urumchi, Xinjiang, China (pp. 574-581).

This work was previously published in International Journal of Grid and High Performance Computing, Volume 2, Issue 4, edited by Emmanuel Udoh, pp. 51-64, copyright 2010 by IGI Publishing (an imprint of IGI Global).

Compilation of References

Aakvaag, N., Mathiesen, M., & Thone, G. (2005). Timing and power issues in wireless sensor networks - an industrial test case. In *Proceedings of the Parallel Processing (ICPP 2005) Workshops* (pp. 419-426).

Abdelzaher, T. F., Shin, K. G., & Bhatti, N. (2002). Performance guarantees for web server end-systems: a control-theoretical approach. *IEEE Trans. on Parallel andDistributed Systems, 13*.

Abramson, D., Giddy, J., & Kotler, L. (2000, May). High performance parametric modeling with Nimrod/G: Killer application for the global Grid. In *Proceedings of the 14th International Symposium on Parallel and Distributed Processing (IPDPS 2000)*, Cancun, Mexico (pp. 520-528). Washington, DC: IEEE Computer Society.

Adelson, E. H., & Bergen, J. R. (1985). Spatiotemporal energy models for the perception of motion. *Journal of optical. Society, A2*, 284–299.

Agarwalla, B., Ahmed, N., Hilley, D., & Ramachandran, U. (2006). Streamline: a scheduling heuristic for streaming applications on the grid. In *Proceedings of the 13th Annual Multimedia Computing and Networking Conf.*

Ahmed, D. T., & Shirmolammadi, S. (2008). A dynamic area of interest management and collaboration model for P2PMMOGs. In *Proceedings of the 2008 12th IEEE/ACM International Symposium on Distributed Simulation and Real-Time Applications* (pp. 27-34). Washington, DC: IEEE Computer Society.

Ahmed, E., Bessis, N., Yue, Y., & Stephens, D. (2008). Data loading and mapping using staging DBMS in the grid. In *Proceedings of the 21st IEEE Annual Canadian Conference on Electrical and Computer Engineering (CCECE)*, Ontario, Canada (pp. 1887-1893).

Akyildiz, I., Su, W., Sankarasubramaniam, Y., & Cayirci, E. (2002, August). A survey on sensor networks. *IEEE Communications Magazine, 40*(8), 102–116. doi:10.1109/MCOM.2002.1024422

Akyildiz, I. F., Su, W., Sankarasubramaniam, Y., & Cayirci, E. (2002). Wireless Sensor Networks: A Survey. *Computer Networks, 38*, 393–422. doi:10.1016/S1389-1286(01)00302-4

Alain, R., & Livny, M. (2003). Condor and preemptive resume scheduling. In Nabrzyski, J., Schopf, J. M., & Weglarz, J. (Eds.), *Grid resource management: State of the art and future trends* (pp. 135–144). Norwell, MA: Kluwer Academic Publishers.

Alexandrov, A. D., Ibel, M., Schauser, K. E., & Scheiman, C. J. (1997). Extending the operating system at the user level: the Ufo global file system. In *Proceedings of the annual conference on USENIX Annual Technical Conference* (pp. 6-6).

Alhusaini, A. H., Prasanna, V. K., & Raghavendra, C. S. (1999). *A unified resource scheduling framework for heterogeneous computing environments*. Paper presented at the Proceedings of the Eighth Heterogeneous Computing Workshop.

Ali, A., Anjum, A., Mehmood, A., Richard, M., Willers, I., & Julian, B. (2004, September). *A taxonomy and survey of grid resource planning and reservation systems for grid enabled analysis environment*. Paper presented at the 2004 International Symposium on Distributed Computing and Applications to Business, Engineering and Science (DCABES 2004), Wuhan, China.

Almeida, D. (1999). FIFS: a framework for implementing user-mode file systems in windows NT. In *Proceedings of the 3rd conference on USENIX Windows NT Symposium* (Vol. 3, pp. 13).

Alpdemir, M. N., Mukherjee, A., Foster, I., Paton, N. W., Watson, P., Fernandes, A. A. A., et al. (2003). Service-based distributed query processing on the grid. In *Proceedings of the 1st Intl. Conference on Service-Oriented Computing (ICSOC)* (pp. 467-482).

Anderson, D. P. (2004, November 8). BOINC: A system for public-resource computing and storage. In *Proceedings of the 5th IEEE/ACM International Workshop on Grid Computing (GRID'04)*, Pittsburgh, PA (pp. 4-10). IEEE CS Press.

Andrade, E. L. (2005). *Characterization of optical flow anomalies in pedestrian traffic (Tech. Rep.)*. UK: School of Informatic, Ediburge University.

Andresen, S. (1977). The looping algorithm extended to base 2t rearrangeable switching networks. *IEEE Transactions on Communications, 25*(10), 1057–1063. doi:10.1109/TCOM.1977.1093753

Anh, N., & Andrew, S. (2002). *Using reflection for incorporating fault-tolerance techniques into distributed applications*. Retrieved from http://www.ggf.org

Ankolekar, A., Luon, Y., Szabo, G., & Huberman, B. (2009). *A Mobile Application for Your Social Life* (Mobile, H. C. I., Ed.). Bonn: Friendlee.

Antonioletti, M., Atkinson, M., Baxter, R., Borley, A., Hong, N. P., & Collins, B. (2005). The design and implementation of grid database services in OGSA-DAI. *Concurrency and Computation, 7*, 2–4.

Araujo, R. B. (2007). *CurlFtpFS - A FTP filesystem based in cURL and FUSE*. Retrieved from http://curlftpfs.sourceforge.net/

Argyros, A. A., et al. (1998). *Independent 3D Motion Detection, through Robust regression in depth layers*. Paper presented at the British Machine vision conference.

Arkko, J., & Haverinen, H. (2006). *EAP-AKA Authentication, RFC 4187*. Asokan, N., Niemi, V., & Nyberg, K. (2005). Man-in-the-Middle in Tunneled Authentication Protocols. *Lecture Notes in Computer Science, 3364*, 28–41.

Arlitt, M. F., & Williamson, C. L. (1996). Web server workload characterization: The search for invariants. *ACM Sigmetrics Performance Evaluation Review, 24*(1), 126–137. doi:10.1145/233008.233034

Armstrong, R., Hensgen, D., & Kidd, T. (1998, March 30). The relative performance of various mapping algorithms is independent of sizable variances in run-time predictions. In *Proceedings of the 7th IEEE Heterogeneous Computing Workshop,* Orlando, FL (pp. 79-87). Washington, DC: IEEE Computer Society.

Austin, J., Davis, R., Fletcher, M., Jackson, T., Jessop, M., Liang, N., & Pasley, A. (2005). DAME: Searching large data sets with in a grid-enabled engineering application. *Proceedings of the IEEE, 93*, 496–509. doi:10.1109/JPROC.2004.842746

Austin, J., Turner, A., & Alwis, S. (2006). Grid enabling data de-duplication. In *Proceedings of the 2nd IEEE International Conference on e-Science and Grid Computing* (pp. 2-8).

Babaoglu, O., Meling, H., & Montresor, A. (2002, July 2-5). Anthill: A framework for the development of agent-based peer-to-peer systems. In *Proceedings of the 22nd IEEE International Conference on Distributed Computing Systems,* Vienna, Austria (pp. 15-22). IEEE.

Baker, K., & Sullivan, G. (1992). Performance assessment of model-based tracking. In *Proceedings of the IEEE Workshop on Applications of Computer Vision*, Palm Springs, CA (pp. 28-35).

Barford, P., & Crovella, M. (1998). Generating representative Web workloads for network and server performance evaluation. *ACM Sigmetrics Performance Evaluation Review, 26*(1), 151–160. doi:10.1145/277858.277897

Barham, P., Dragovic, B., Fraser, K., Hand, S., Harris, T. L., Ho, A., et al. (2003). Xen and the art of virtualization. In *Proceedings of the ACM Symp. on Operating Systems Principles*.

Barkai, D. (2002). *Peer-to-peer computing: Technologies for sharing and collaborating on the net*. Santa Clara, CA: Intel Press.

Baru, C., Moore, R., Rajasekar, A., & Wan, M. (1998). *The SDSC Storage Resource Broker*. Paper presented at the Proceedings of the 1998 conference of the Centre for Advanced Studies on Collaborative research.

Bas, E., & Fellow, A. M. T. (2007). Automatic vehicle counting from video for Traffic Flow Analysis. In *Proceedings of the IEEE International Proceedings on Intelligent vehicles symposium* (pp. 392-397).

Basney, J., Humphrey, M., & Welch, V. (2005). The My-Proxy online credential repository. *Software, Practice & Experience, 35*(9), 801–816. doi:10.1002/spe.688

Basu, S., Banerjee, S., Sharma, P., & Lee, S. (2005, May 9-12). NodeWiz: Peer-to-peer resource discovery for grids. In *Proceedings of the IEEE International Symposium on Domain Computing and the Grid (CCGrid 2005)*, Cardiff, UK (pp. 213-220). IEEE.

Batcher, K. E. (1976). The flip network in STARAN. In *Proceedings of the International Conference on Parallel Processing* (pp. 65-71)

Beetem, J., Denneau, M., & Weingarten, D. (1985). The GF11 supercomputer. In *Proceedings of the 12th annual international symposium on Computer architecture (ISCA '85)*.

Beizer, B. (1968). The Analysis and Synthesis of Signal Switching Network. In *Proceedings of the Symposium on Mathematical Theory of Automata*, NY (pp. 563-576)

Bell, G. S., & Sethi, A. (2001). Matching records in a national medical patient index. *CACM, 44*(9), 83–88.

Bell, W. H., Cameron, D. G., Capozza, L., Millar, A. P., Stockinger, K., & Zini, F. (2003). OptorSim - a grid simulator for studying dynamic data replication strategies. *International Journal of High Performance Computing Applications, 17*(4), 403–416. doi:10.1177/10943420030174005

Bell, W. H., Cameron, D. G., Carvajal-Schiaffino, R., Millar, A. P., Stockinger, K., & Zini, F. (2003, May). Evaluation of an economy-based file replication strategy for a data grid. In *Proceedings of the International Workshop on Agent Based Cluster and Grid Computing at CCGrid2003*, Tokyo (p. 661). Washington, DC: IEEE Computer Society.

Benes, E. (1965). *Mathematical Theory of Connecting Networks and Telephone Traffic*. New York: Academic Press.

Beni, G., & Wang, J. (1989, June). *Swarm intelligence in cellular robotic systems*. Paper presented at the NATO Advanced Workshop on Robots and Biological Systems, Toscana, Italy.

Bentz, D. P. (1997). Three-Dimensional Computer Simulation of Portland Cement Hydration and Microstructure Development. *Journal of the American Ceramic Society, 80*(1), 3–21. doi:10.1111/j.1151-2916.1997.tb02785.x

Bentz, D. P., & Garboczi, E. J. (1993, March). Digital-Image-Based Computer Modelling of Cement-Based Materials. In *Proceedings of Digital Image Processing: Techniques and Applications in Civil Engineering, Engineering Foundation Conference*.

Bentz, D. P., & Stutzman, P. E. (1994). SEM analysis and computer modeling of hydration of portland cement particles in petrography of cementitious materials. *ASTM STP, 1215*, 60–73.

Bergen, P. J. B., Rajesh, H., & Shmuel, P. (1992). A three, Frame Algorithm for estimating two-component Image Motion. *Transactions on pattern analysis and machine intelligence, 14*(9), 886-896.

Berger, S., Cáceres, R., Goldman, K., Perez, R., Sailer, R., & Doorn, L. (2006, July 31-August 4). vTPM: Virtualizing the trusted platform module. In *Proceedings of the 15th Conference on USENIX Security Symposium*, Vancouver, British Columbia, Canada (Article No. 21). Berkeley, CA: USENIX.

Berman, F., Wolski, R., Casanova, H., Cirne, W., Dail, H., & Faerman, M. (2003). Adaptive computing on the grid using AppLeS. *IEEE Transactions on Parallel and Distributed Systems, 14*(4), 369–382. doi:10.1109/TPDS.2003.1195409

Berners-Lee, T., Hendler, J., & Lassila, O. (2001). The Semantic Web. *Scientific American Magazine*. Retrieved from http://www.scientificamerican.com/article.cfm?id=the-semantic-web

Beskow, P. B., Vik, K., Halvorsen, P., & Griwodz, C. (2008). Latency reduction by dynamic core selection and partial migration of game state. In *Proceedings of the 7th ACM SIGCOMM Workshop on Network and System Support for Games* (pp. 79-84). New York: ACM.

Bessis, N., French, T., Burakova-Lorgnier, M., & Huang, W. (2007). Using grid technology for data sharing to support intelligence in decision making. In Xu, M. (Ed.), *Managing strategic intelligence: Techniques and technologies* (pp. 179–201). Hershey, PA: Idea Group Publishing Inc.doi:10.4018/978-1-59904-243-5.ch011

Beymer, D., McLauchlan, P., Coifman, B., & Malik, J. (1997). A real-time computer vision system for measuring traffic parameters. In *Proceedings of the IEEE Conf. on Computer Vision and Pattern Recognition*, Puerto Rico (pp. 496-501).

Bin, Lu., Habetler, T. G., Harley, R. G., & Gutierrez, J. A. (2005, October 30). Applying wireless sensor networks in industrial plant energy management systems. Part II. Design of sensor devices. *Sensors (Basel, Switzerland)*, 6.

Black, M. J., & Anandan, P. (1991). Robust dynamic motion estimation over time. *IEEE. International Journal of Computer Vision*, 296–302.

Bland, R. G., Goldfarb, D., & Todd, M. J. (1981). Ellipsoid method, a survey. *Operations Research*, 29(6), 1039–1091. doi:10.1287/opre.29.6.1039

Blazewicz, J., Brauner, N., & Finke, G. (2004). Scheduling with discrete resource constraints. In Lueng, J. Y.-T. (Ed.), *Handbook of scheduling* (pp. 23.1–23.18). Boca Raton, FL: CRC Press.

Bo, L., & Heqin, Z. (2003). Using object classification to improve urban traffic monitoring system. In. Proceedings of the IEEE International Conference on Neural Networks and Signal Processing, 2, 1155–1159.

BOINC. (2009). *Berkeley open infrastructure for network computing*. Retrieved from http://boinc.berkeley.edu

Bonnet, B. (2003, December). Bluetooth-based sensor networks. *ACM SIGMOD, 32*(4).

Bonneville, M., & Meunier, J. (1999). Finding the Exact Optical Flow: a Maximum Flow Formulation. In *Proceedings of the Vision Interface 99*, Trios-Rivieres, Canada (pp. 418-423).

Borcea, C., Gupta, A., Kalra, A., Jones, Q., & Iftode, L. (2008). The MobiSoC middleware for mobile social computing: challenges, design, and early experiences. In *Proceedings of Mobile Wireless Middleware*. Operating Systems, and Applications. doi:10.4108/ICST.MOBILWARE2008.2893

Botts, M., Percivall, G., Reed, C., & Davidson, J. (2006, July 19). *OGC Sensor Web Enablement: Overview and High Level Architecture*. Paper presented at the Open Geospatial Consortium (OGC 06-050r2 v2).

Bovet, D. P., & Cesati, M. (2005). *Understanding the Linux Kernel*. Sebastopol, CA: O'Reilly Media.

Boyera, W. F., & Hura, G. S. (2005). Non-evolutionary algorithm for scheduling dependent tasks in distributed heterogeneous computing environments. *Journal of Parallel and Distributed Computing*, 65(9), 1035–1046. doi:10.1016/j.jpdc.2005.04.017

Braun, T. D., et al. (1999). *A comparison study of static mapping heuristics for a class of meta-tasks on heterogeneous computing systems*. Paper presented at the Proceedings of the Eighth Heterogeneous Computing Workshop (HCW'99).

Braun, T. D. (2001). A comparison of eleven static heuristics for mapping a class of independent tasks onto heterogeneous distributed computing system. *Journal of Parallel and Distributed Computing*, 61(6), 810–837. doi:10.1006/jpdc.2000.1714

Buyya, R., Abramson, D., & Giddy, J. (2000, May). Nimrod/G: An architecture for a resource management and scheduling system in a global computational grid. In *Proceedings of the 4th International Conference and Exhibition on High Performance Computing*, Beijing, China (Vol. 1, pp. 283-289). Washington, DC: IEEE Computer Society.

Buyya, R., & Murshed, M. (2002). GridSim: A toolkit for the modeling and simulation of distributed resource management and scheduling for grid computing. *Concurrency and Computation*, 14(13-15), 1175–1220. doi:10.1002/cpe.710

Cai, M., Frank, M., Chen, J., & Szekely, P. (2004). MAAN: A multi-attribute addressable network for grid information services. *Journal of Grid Computing*, 2(1), 3–14. doi:10.1007/s10723-004-1184-y

Calhoun, P., Loughney, J., Guttman, E., Zorn, G., & Arkko, J. (2003). *Diameter Base Protocol, RFC 3588.*

Cali, A., Calvanese, D., Giacomo, G., & Lenzerini, M. (1999). Semistructured data schemas with expressive constraints. In *Proceedings of CAiSE* (LNCS, pp. 262-279). Berlin: Springer.

Cali, A., Calvanese, D., Giacomo, G., & Lenzerini, M. (2002). Data integration under integrity constraints. In *Proceedings of CAiSE* (LNCS 2348, pp. 262-279). Berlin: Springer.

Calvanese, D., De Giacomo, G., Lenzerini, M., Nardi, D., & Rosati, R. (1999). A principled approach to data integration and reconciliation in data warehousing. In S. Gatziu, M. Jeusfeld, M. Staudt, & Y. Vassiliou (Eds.), *Proceedings of the International Workshop on Design and Management of DataWarehouses (DMDW'99)*, Heidelberg, Germany.

Cameron, D. G., Carvajal-Schiaffino, R., Millar, A. P., Nicholson, C., Stockinger, K., & Zini, F. (2003, November 17). Evaluating scheduling and replica optimisation strategies in OptorSim. In *Proceedings of the 4ᵗʰ International Workshop on Grid Computing*, Phoenix, AZ (pp. 52-59). Washington, DC: IEEE Computer Society.

Cao, F., & Singh, J. P. (2005). MEDYM: match-early and dynamic multicast for content-based publish-subscribe networks. In *Proceedings of the ACM/IFIP/USENIX 2005 international Conference on Middleware.*

Cao, J., Liu, F. B., & Xu, C.-Z. (2007). P2PGrid: Integrating P2P Networks into the Grid Environment. *Concurrency and Computation, 19*(7), 1023–1046. doi:10.1002/cpe.1096

Cappello, F., Djilali, S., Fedak, G., Herault, T., Magniette, F., & Neri, V. (2005). Computing on large-scale distributed systems: XtremWeb architecture, programming models, security, tests and convergence with grid. *Future Generation Computer Systems, 21*(3), 417–437. doi:10.1016/j.future.2004.04.011

Card, R., Ts'o, T., & Tweedie, S. (1994). Design and Implementation of the Second Extended Filesystem. In *Proceedings of the First Dutch International Symposium on Linux.*

Carman, M., Zini, F., Serafini, L., & Stockinger, K. (2002). Towards an Economy-Based Optimisation of File Access and Replication on a Data Grid. *In Int. Workshop on Agent based Cluster and Grid Computing at CCGrid*, Berlin, Germany.

Carr, N. (2008). *The big switch: rewriting the world, from Edison to Google.* China: CITIC Press.

Casanova, H., Legrand, A., & Quinson, M. (2008, April 1-3). SimGrid: a generic framework for large-scale distributed experimentations. In *Proceedings of the 10ᵗʰ IEEE International Conference on Computer Modelling and Simulation (UKSIM/EUROSIM'08),* Cambridge, UK (pp. 126-131). Washington, DC: IEEE Computer Society.

Casanova, H., Legrand, A., Zagorodnov, D., & Berman, F. (2000). *Heuristics for scheduling parameter sweep applications in grid environments.* Paper presented at the Proceedings of the 9th Heterogeneous Computing Workshop (HCW 2000).

Castano, S., Ferrara, A., Montanelli, S., & Varese, G. (2009). Semantic coordination of P2P collective intelligence. In *Proceedings of the International Conference on Management of Emergent Digital EcoSystems* (pp. 99-106). New York: ACM. doi:10.1145/1643823.1643842

Castro, M., Druschel, P., Kermarrec, A.-M., & Rowstron, A. I. T. (2002). Scribe: A Large-Scale and Decentralized Application-Level Multicast Infrastructure. *IEEE Journal on Selected Areas in Communications, 20*(8), 1489–1499. doi:10.1109/JSAC.2002.803069

Chadwick, D. (2005). Authorisation in Grid computing. *Information Security Technical Report, 10*(1), 33–40. doi:10.1016/j.istr.2004.11.004

Chakravarti, A. J., Baumgartner, G., & Lauria, M. (2006). The organic grid: Self-organizing computational biology on desktop grids. In Zomaya, A. Y. (Ed.), *Parallel computing for bioinformatics and computational biology: Models, enabling technologies, and case studies.* New York: John Wiley & Sons. doi:10.1002/0471756504.ch27

Chambers, C., Feng, F., & Saha, D. (2003, November). A geographic redirection service for online games. In *Proceedings of the 11th ACM international conference on Multimedia*, Berkeley, CA (pp. 227-230).

Chan, A. B. (2005). Layered dynamic textures. In *Proceedings of the IEEE Intelligent vehicle symposium*, Las Vegas.

Chapin, S. J., Katramatos, D., Karpovich, J., & Grimshaw, A. S. (1999). The legion resource management system. In *Job Scheduling Strategies for Parallel Processing* (pp. 162–178). New York: Springer Verlag. doi:10.1007/3-540-47954-6_9

Chechiara, R., Grana, C., Piccardi, M., & Prati, A. (2006). *Statistic and knowledge based moving object detection in traffic scenes*. Italy: Italian Free Way Company.

Chen, L., & Agrawal, G. (2006). A static resource allocation framework for grid-based streaming applications. *Concurrency and Computation*, *18*, 653–666. doi:10.1002/cpe.972

Chen, L., Landferman, R., Löhr, H., Rohe, M., Sadeghi, A.-R., & Stüble, C. (2006). A protocol for property-based attestation. In *Proceedings of the 1ˢᵗ ACM Workshop on Scalable Trusted Computing,* Alexandria, VA (pp. 7-16). ACM Publising.

Chen, T.-H. (2003). An automatic bi-directional passing-people counting method based on color image processing. In *Proceedings of the IEEE 37ᵗʰ Annual 2003 International Carnohan Conference on Security Technology* (pp. 200-207).

Chen, T.-H., Lin, Y.-F., et al. (2007). Intelligent vehicle counting method based on Blob Analysis in Traffic Surveillance, *IEEE*. DOI 0-7695-2822

Cheng, K.-Y., Lui, K.-S., & Tam, V. (2009). HyBloc: Localization in Sensor Networks with Adverse Anchor Placement. *Sensors (Basel, Switzerland)*, *9*(1), 253–280. doi:10.3390/s90100253

Chervenak, A., Foster, I., Kesselman, C., Salisbury, C., & Tuecke, S. (2000). The Data Grid: Towards an Architecture for the Distributed Management and Analysis of Large Scientific Datasets. *Journal of Network and Computer Applications*, *23*(3), 187–200. doi:10.1006/jnca.2000.0110

Chien, A., Calder, B., Elbert, S., & Bhatia, K. (2003). Entropia: Architecture and performance of an enterprise desktop grid system. *Journal of Parallel and Distributed Computing*, *63*(5), 597–610. doi:10.1016/S0743-7315(03)00006-6

Chien, A. A., Marlin, S., & Elbert, S. T. (2004). Resource management in the entropia system. In Nabrzyski, J., Schopf, J. M., & Weglarz, J. (Eds.), *Grid resource management: State of the art and future trends* (pp. 431–450). Norwell, MA: Kluwer Academic Publishers.

Chong, C.-Y., & Kumar, S. (2003, August). Sensor networks: evolution, opportunities, and challenges. *Proceedings of the IEEE*, *91*, 1247–1256. doi:10.1109/JPROC.2003.814918

Christos, Z., Yiannis, K., & Athena, V. (2009) Information analysis in mobile social networks for added-value services. In *Proceedings of the the W3C Workshop on the Future of Social Networking*, Barcelona, Spain.

Clau, B. S., & Schiffner, S. (2006). Structuring Anonymity Metrics. In *Proceedings of the DIM'O6* (pp. 55-62).

Claypool, M. (2005). The effect of latency on user performance in real-time strategy games. *Elsevier Computer Networks*, *49*(1), 52–70. doi:10.1016/j.comnet.2005.04.008

Claypool, M. (2008, January). Network characteristics for server selection in online games. In *Proceedings of the fifteenth Annual Multimedia Computing and Networking (MMCN'08)*, San Jose, CA.

Clos, C. (1953). A Study of Non-Blocking Switching Networks. *The Bell System Technical Journal*, *32*, 406–424.

Cody, E., Sharman, R., Rao, R., & Upadhyaya, S. (2008). Security in grid computing: A review and synthesis. *Decision Support Systems*, *44*(4), 749–764. doi:10.1016/j.dss.2007.09.007

Collins, D. E., & George, A. D. (2001). Parallel and sequential job scheduling in heterogeneous clusters, a simulation study using software in the loop. *Journal of Simulation*, *77*(5), 169–184. doi:10.1177/003754970107700503

Cooke, A. W., Gray, A. J. G., Nutt, W., Magowan, J., Oevers, M., & Taylor, P. (2004). The relational grid monitoring architecture: Mediating information about the grid. *Journal of Grid Computing*, *2*(4), 323–339. doi:10.1007/s10723-005-0151-6

Crespi, N., & Lavaud, S. (2004). *WLAN Access to 3G Multimedia Services, Information and Communication Technologies*. Bangkok: ICT.

Crespo, A., & Garcia-Molina, H. (2005). Semantic Overlay Networks for P2P Systems. In *Agents and Peer-to-Peer Computing* (pp. 1-13). Retrieved from http://dx.doi.org/10.1007/11574781_1

Cronin, E., Kurc, A. R., Filstrup, B., & Jamin, S. (2004). An efficient synchronization mechanism for mirrored game architectures. *Multimedia Tools and Applications*, 23(1), 7–30. doi:10.1023/B:MTAP.0000026839.31028.9f

Crosby, P. (2008). *EDGSim*. Retrived July 2008, from http://www.hep.ucl.ac.uk/~pac/EDGSim

Cucchira, R., Piccardi, M., & Mello, P. (2000). Image Analysis and rule based reasoning for a Traffic Monitoring System. *IEEE Transactions on Intelligent Transportation Systems*, 1(2), 119–130. doi:10.1109/6979.880969

Cudré-Mauroux, P., Agarwal, S., & Aberer, K. (2007). Gridvine: An infrastructure for peer information management. *IEEE Internet Computing*, 36–44. doi:10.1109/MIC.2007.108

Cypher, R., Sanz, J. L. C., & Snyder, L. (1989). An EREW PRAM Algorithm for Image Component Labeling. *IEEE Transactions on Pattern Analysis and Machine Intelligence*, 11(3). doi:10.1109/34.21794

Czajkowski, K., Fitzgerald, S., Foster, I., & Kesselman, C. (2001). *Grid Information Services for Distributed Resource Sharing*. Paper presented at the Proceedings of the 10th IEEE International Symposium on High Performance Distributed Computing, New York.

De, S., Qiao, C., & Wu, H. (2003). Meshed Multipath Routing: An Efficient Strategy in Wireless Sensor Networks. Computer Networks.

De Ronde, J. F., Schoneveld, A., & Sloot, P. M. A. (1997). Load balancing by redundant decomposition and mapping. *Journal of Future Generation Computer Systems*, 12(5), 391–407. doi:10.1016/S0167-739X(97)83341-9

De Vleeschauwer, B., Van Den Bossche, B., Verdickt, T., Turck, F., Dhoedt, B., & Demeester, P. (2005). Dynamic microcell assignment for Massively Multiplayer Online Gaming. In *Proceedings of 4th ACM SIGCOMM workshop on Network and system support for games* (pp. 1-7). New York: ACM.

Deelman, E., Kesselman, C., Mehta, G., Meshkat, L., Pearlman, L., Blackburn, K., et al. (2002). GriPhyN and ligo: building a virtual data grid for gravitational wave scientists. In *Proceedings of the 11th IEEE Int. Symp. on High Performance Distributed Computing* (pp. 225-234).

Denegri, L., Zappatore, S., & Davoli, F. (2008). Sensor Network-Based Localization for Continuous Tracking Applications: Implementation and Performance Evaluation. *Advances in Multimedia*, 2008, 569848. doi:10.1155/2008/569848

Deng, Y., & Wang, F. (2007). A heterogeneous storage grid enabled by grid service. *ACM SIGOPS Operating Systems Review*, 41(1), 7–13. doi:10.1145/1228291.1228296

Deng, Y., Wang, F., & Ciura, A. (2009). Ant colony optimization inspired resource discovery in P2P grid systems. *The Journal of Supercomputing*, 49(1), 4–21. doi:10.1007/s11227-008-0214-0

Deng, Y., Wang, F., Helian, N., Wu, S., & Liao, C. (2008). Dynamic and scalable storage management architecture for Grid Oriented Storage devices. *Parallel Computing*, 34(1), 17–31. doi:10.1016/j.parco.2007.10.003

Diao, Y., Gandhi, N., Hellerstein, J. L., Parekh, S., & Tilbury, D. M. (2002). MIMO control of an apache web server: modeling and controller design. In *Proceedings of the American Control Conf.*

Diao, Y., Hellerstein, J. L., & Parekh, S. (2002). Using fuzzy control to maximize profits in service level management. *IBM Systems Journal*, 41, 3. doi:10.1147/sj.413.0403

Ding, L., Zhou, L., Finin, T., & Joshi, A. (2005). How the Semantic Web is Being Used: An Analysis of FOAF Documents. In *Proceedings of Hawaii international Conference on System Sciences* (Vol. 4).

Dix, A., Rodden, T., Davies, N., Trevor, J., Friday, A., & Palfreyman, K. (2000). Exploiting space and location as a design framework for interactive mobile systems. *ACM Transactions on Computer-Human Interaction*, 7(3), 285–321. doi:10.1145/355324.355325

Doherty, L., Pister, K. S. J., & El Ghaoui, L. (2001, April). Convex position estimation in wireless sensor networks. In *Proceedings of the IEEE Infocom 2001*, Anchorage, AK (Vol. 3, pp. 1655-1663).

Dong, F., & Akl, S. K. (2006). *Scheduling algorithms for grid computing: State of the art and open problems* (Tech. Rep. No. 2006-504). Kingston, Ontario, Canada: School of Computing, Queen's University.

Dongliang, Z. (2003). *The Study on Microstructure Model of Cement Hydration Based on Reconstruction of Three-dimensional Image*. Unpublished master dissertation, JiNan University, Jinan, China.

Dorigo, M., & Blum, C. (2005). Ant colony optimization theory: A survey. *Theoretical Computer Science, 344*(2-3), 243–278. doi:10.1016/j.tcs.2005.05.020

Dorigo, M., & Gambardella, L. M. (1997). Ant colony system, a cooperative learning approach to the traveling salesman problem. *IEEE Transactions on Evolutionary Computation, 1*(1), 53–66. doi:10.1109/4235.585892

Dorigo, M., Maniezzo, V., & Colorni, A. (1996). The ant system, optimization by a colony of cooperating agents. *IEEE Transactions on Systems, Man, and Cybernetics, 26*(1), 29–41. doi:10.1109/3477.484436

Dorigo, M., & Stützle, T. (2003). The ant colony optimization metaheuristic: Algorithms, applications and advances. In Glover, F., & Kochenberger, G. (Eds.), *Handbook of metaheuristics* (pp. 251–285). Norwell, MA: Kluwer Academic Publishers. doi:10.1007/0-306-48056-5_9

Dornfest, R., Bausch, P., & Calishain, T. (2006). *Google Hacks* (3rd ed.). Sebastopol, CA: O'Reilly Media.

Dotzer, F. (2005). Privacy Issues in Vehicular Ad Hoc Networks. In *Proceedings of the Workshop on Privacy Enhancing Technologies*, Dubr, Croatia (pp. 197-209).

Dou, Y., & Bei, X. (2008). Ontology-Based Semantic Information Retrieval Systems in Unstructured P2P Networks. In *Proceedings of the Wireless Communications, Networking and Mobile Computing, the 4th International Conference (WiCOM '08)* (pp. 1-4).

Douglas, J., Usländer, T., Schimak, G., Esteban, J. F., & Denzer, R. (2008). An Open Distributed Architecture for Sensor Networks for Risk Management. *Sensors (Basel, Switzerland), 8*, 1755–1773. doi:10.3390/s8031755

Dowsland, K. A., & Thompson, J. M. (2005). Ant colony optimization for the examination scheduling problem. *The Journal of the Operational Research Society, 56*(4), 426–438. doi:10.1057/palgrave.jors.2601830

Driscoll, E., Beavers, J., & Tokuda, H. (2008). *FUSE-NT: Userspace File Systems for Windows NT. University of Wisconsin-Madison*. Retrieved from pages.cs.wisc.edu/~driscoll/fuse-nt.pdf

Du, Y., Zhang, Q., & Chen, Q. (2008, April). ACO-IH: An improved ant colony optimization algorithm for airport ground service scheduling. In *Proceedings of the IEEE International Conference on Industrial Technology (ICIT 2008)*, Chengdu, China (pp. 1-6). Washington, DC: IEEE Computer Society.

Ehrig, M., Haase, P., Siebes, R., Staab, S., Stuckenschmidt, H., Studer, R., et al. (2003). The SWAP Data and Metadata Model for Semantics-Based Peer-to-Peer Systems. In *Multiagent System Technologies* (pp. 1096-1097). Retrieved from http://www.springerlink.com/content/mtm7gu9t8bnuuu16

El-Desoky, A., Hisham, A., & Abdulrahman, A. (2006, November 5-7). Improving fault tolerance in desktop grids based on incremental checkpointing. In *Proceedings of the 2006 International Conference on Computer Engineering and Systems (ICCES'06)*, Cairo, Egypt (pp. 386-392). IEEE.

El-Desoky, A., Hisham, A., & Abdulrahman, A. (2007, November 27-29). A pure peer-to-peer desktop grid framework with efficient fault tolerance. In *Proceedings of the 2007 International Conference on Computer Systems and Engineering (ICCES'07)*, Cairo, Egypt (pp. 346-352). IEEE.

Ellard, D., Ledlie, J., Malkani, P., & Seltzer, M. (2003, March 31-April 2). Passive NFS tracing of email and research workloads. In *Proceedings of the 2nd USENIX Conference on File and Storage Technologies (FAST'03)*, San Francisco (pp. 203-216). USENIX.

Ellard, D., Ledlie, J., & Seltzer, M. (2003). *The utility of file names* (Tech. Rep. TR-05-03). Cambridge, MA: Harvard University Division of Engineering and Applied Sciences.

Ellard, D., Mesnier, M., Thereska, E., Ganger, G. R., & Seltzer, M. (2003). *Attribute-based prediction of file properties* (Tech. Rep. TR-14-03). Cambridge, MA: Harvard Computer Science Group.

Ellard, D., & Seltzer, M. (2003, October 26-31). New NFSTracing tools and techniques for system analysis. In *Proceedings of the 17th Annual Large Installation System Administration Conference (LISA'03)*, San Diego, CA (pp. 73-85). USENIX.

Elnahrawy, E., Austin-Francisco, J., & Martin, R. P. (2007, February). Adding Angle of Arrival Modality to Basic RSS Location Management Techniques. In *Proceedings of the IEEE International Symposium on Wireless Pervasive Computing (ISWPC'07)*.

Elnahrawy, E., Li, X., & Martin, R. (2004). The limits of localization using signal strength: a comparative study. In *Proceedings of the First Annual IEEE Conference on Sensor and Ad-hoc Communications and Networks* (pp. 406-414).

Engblom, J., & Ermedahl, A. (2000, November). Modeling complex flows for worst-case execution time analysis. In *Proceedings of the 21st IEEE Real-Time Systems Symposium*, Orlando, FL (pp. 163-174). Washington, DC: IEEE Computer Society.

Engelen, R. V. (2009). *gSOAP 2.7.15 User Guide. FSU Computer Science*. Retrieved from http://www.cs.fsu.edu/~engelen/soapdoc2.html

Entertainment, B. (2004). *World of Warcraft*. Retrieved March 4, 2010, from http://www.blizzard.com

Fang, Y., Chlamtac, I., & Lin, Y.-B. (1998). Channel Occupancy Times and Handoff Rate for Mobile Computing and PCS Networks. *IEEE Transactions on Computers*, *47*(6), 679–692. doi:10.1109/12.689647

Fedak, G., Germain, C., Vincent, N., & Franck, C. (2001, May 15-18). XtremWeb: A generic global computing system. In *Proceedings of the 1st IEEE/ACM International Symposium on Cluster Computing and the Grid (CCGRID '01)*, Brisbane, Australia (pp. 582-587). IEEE.

Feitelson, D. G. (1996, June). Packing schemes for gang scheduling. In D. G. Feitelson & L. Rudolph (Eds.), *Proceedings of the Workshop on Job Scheduling Strategies for Parallel Processing*, Padua, Italy (LNCS 1162, pp. 89-110).

Feitelson, D. G., Rudolph, L., Schwiegelshohn, U., Sevcik, K. C., & Wong, P. (1997, April). Theory and practice in parallel job scheduling. In D. G. Feitelson & L. Rudolph (Eds.), *Proceedings of the Job Scheduling Strategies for Parallel Processing*, Geneva, Switzerland (LNCS 1291, pp. 1-34).

Feng, T.-Y. (1974). Data Manipulating Functions in Parallel Processors and Their Implementations. *IEEE Transactions on Computers*, *23*(3), 309–318. doi:10.1109/T-C.1974.223927

Fibich, P., Matyska, L., & Rudova, H. (2005, July). Model of grid scheduling problem. In *Proceedings of the Workshop on Exploring Planning and Scheduling for Web Services, Grid and Autonomic Computing*, Pittsburgh, PA (pp. 17-24). Menlo Park, CA: AAAI Press.

Fidanova, S., & Durchova, M. (2006, June 6-10). Ant algorithm for grid scheduling problem. In I. Lirkov, S. Margenov, & J. Wa'sniewski (Eds.), *Large Scale Scientific Computing: 5th International Conference, LSSC 2005*, Sozopol, Bulgaria (LNCS 3743, pp. 405-412).

Figueiredo, R. J., Dinda, P., & Fortes, J. (2003). A case for grid computing on virtual machines. In *Proceedings of the 23rd Int'l. Conf. on Distributed Computing Systems*.

Fitzgerald, S., Foster, I., Kesselman, C., von Laszewski, G., Smith, W., & Tuecke, S. (1997). *A Directory Service for Conturing High-Performance Distributed Computations*. Paper presented at the Proceedings of The Sixth IEEE International Symposium on High Performance Distributed Computing.

Fleet, D. J. (1992). *Measurement of Image velocity*. Norwell, MA: Kluwer Academic Publishers.

Fleet, D. J., & Jepson, A. D. (1990). Computation of component image velocity from local phase information. *International Journal of Computer Vision*, *5*, 77–104. doi:10.1007/BF00056772

Fonseca, E., Festag, A., Baldessari, R., & Aguiar, R. (2007). Support of Anonymity in VANETs - Putting Pseudonymity into Practice. In *Proceedings of the IEEE Wireless Communication & Networking Conference (WCNC2007)*.

Fortune, S. (1986). A sweepline algorithm for voronoi diagrams. In *Proceedings of the second annual symposium on Computational geometry* (pp. 313-322). New York: ACM.

Foster, I. (2002, July 22). What is the Grid? - a three point checklist. *GRIDtoday, 1*(6).

Foster, I., Freeman, T., Keahy, K., Scheftner, D., Sotomayer, B., & Zhang, X. (2006). Virtual clusters for grid communities. In *Proceedings of the IEEE Int. Sym. on Cluster Computing and the Grid.*

Foster, I., & Iamnitchi, A. (2003). On Death, Taxes, and the Convergence of Peer-to-Peer and Grid Computing. In *Peer-to-Peer Systems II* (pp. 118-128).

Foster, I., Kesselman, C., Nick, J., & Tueke, S. (2002). Grid services for distributed system integration. *IEEE Computer, 35*(6), 397–398.

Foster, I., Kesselman, C., Nick, J. M., & Tuecke, S. (2002). *The Physiology of the Grid: An Open Grid Services Architecture for Distributed Systems Integration.* Retrieved from http://www.globus.org/alliance/publications/papers/ogsa.pdf

Foster, I., Kesselman, C., Tsudik, G., & Tuecke, S. (1998). *A Security Architecture for Computational Grids.* Paper presented at the Proceedings of the 5th ACM conference on Computer and communications security.

Foster, I., Kesselman, C., & Tuecke, S. (2001). The Anatomy of the Grid: Enabling Scalable Virtual Organizations. *International Journal of High Performance Computing Applications, 15*(3), 200–222. doi:10.1177/109434200101500302

Foster, I., & Kessleman, C. (2004). *The Grid: Blueprint for a new computing infrastructure* (pp. 283, 391–396). San Francisco, CA: Morgan Kaufmann.

Fox, G., Ho, A., Wang, R., Chu, E., & Kwan, I. (2008). A Collaborative Sensor Grids Framework. In *Proceedings of Collaborative Technologies and Systems*, Irvine, CA (pp. 29-38).

Fox, G., Pallickara, S., & Rao, X. (2005). Towards Enabling Peer-to-Peer Grids. *Concurrency and Computation, 17*(7-8), 1109–1131. doi:10.1002/cpe.863

Freund, R. F., & Siegel, H. J. (1993). Guest editor's introduction: Heterogeneous processing. *Computer, 26*(6), 13–17.

Gaonkar, S., Li, J., Choudhury, R. R., Cox, L., & Schmidt, A. (2008). Micro-Blog: sharing and querying content through mobile phones and social participation. In *Proceeding of Mobile Systems, Applications, and Services.*

Gaynor, M., Moulton, S. L., Welsh, M., LaCombe, E., Rowan, A., & Wynne, J. (2004, July-August). Integrating Wireless Sensor Networks with the Grid. *IEEE Internet Computing, 8*(4), 32–39. doi:10.1109/MIC.2004.18

Gera, V. (2006, September 22). *Filesystems in User Space.* Retrieved from twiki.dsi.uniroma1.it/pub/Sistemioperativi3/OnLine/Fuse.pdf

Gerlach, M., & Guttler, F. (2007). Privacy in VANETs using Changing Pseudonyms - Ideal and Real. In *Proceedings of 65th Vehicular Technology Conference (VTC2007-l)* (pp. 2521-2525).

Ghosal, S., & Mehrotra, R. (1997). Robust Optical Flow Estimation using Semi-invariant Local Features. *Pattern Recognition, 30*(2), 229–237. doi:10.1016/S0031-3203(96)00070-2

Giblin, C., Müller, S., & Pfitzmann, B. (2006). *From Regulatory Policies to Event Monitoring Rules: Towards Model-Driven Compliance Automation (Tech. Rep. No. RZ 3662).* IBM Research.

GIMPS. (2009). *The great Internet mersenne prime search.* Retrieved from http://www.mersenne.org

GNU GLPK. (2009). *GNU linear programming kit.* Retrieved from http://www.gnu.org/software/glpk

Godfrey, B. Shenker, S., & Stoica, I. (2006, September). Minimizing churn in distributed systems. In *Proceedings of ACM SIGCOMM Conference 2006*, Pisa, Italy (pp. 147-158). ACM Publishing.

Goke, L. R., & Lipovski, G. J. (1973). Banyan networks for partitioning multiprocessor systems. *SIGARCH Computer Architecture News, 2*(4), 21–28. doi:10.1145/633642.803967

Gonzalez, R. C., & Wood, R. E. (2002). *Digital Image Processing.* Upper Saddle River, NJ: Prentice Hall.

3GPP TS 23.228 -v8.1.0. (2007). *Technical Specification Group Services and Systems Aspects; IP Multimedia Subsystem Stage 2, Release 8.*

3GPP TS 33.203 -v7.6.0. (2006). *3G security; Access security for IP based services, Release 7.*

3GPP TS 33.234-v7.2.0. (2006). *3G security; WLAN interworking security; System description, Release 7.*

Graham, R. L. (1966). Bounds for certain multiprocessing anomalies. *The Bell System Technical Journal, 45,* 1563–1581.

Grasse, P. P. (1959). La reconstruction du nid et les coordinations inter-individuelles chez bellicoitermes natalenis et cubitermes sp. La theorie de la stigmergie: essai d'interpretation des termites constructeurs. *Insectes Sociaux, 6,* 41–84. doi:10.1007/BF02223791

Groep, D. L., Templon, J., & Loomis, C. (2006). Crunching real data on the grid: Practice and experience with the European DataGrid. *Concurrency and Computation, 18*(9), 925–940. doi:10.1002/cpe.962

Gunzer, H. (2002). *Introduction to Web Services.* Austin, TX: Borland.

Haas, L. M., Lin, E. T., & Roth, M. A. (2002). Data integration through database federation. *IBM Systems Journal, 41*(4). doi:10.1147/sj.414.0578

Haas, O., Ausburg, O., & Palensky, P. (2006). Communication with and within Distributed Energy Resources. In *Proceedings IEEE International Conference on Industrial Informatics (INDIN)* (pp. 352-356).

Häkkilä, J., & Mäntyjärvi, J. (2006). *Developing design guidelines for context-aware mobile applications.* Paper presented at the 3rd international Conference on Mobile Technology, Applications &Amp; Systems, Bangkok, Thailand.

Haldar, V., Chandra, D., & Franz, M. (2004, May 6-12). Semantic remote attestation- a virtual machine directed approach to trusted computing. In *Proceedings of the 3rd Conference on Virtual Machine Research and Technology Symposium,* San Jose, CA (p. 3). Berkeley, CA: USENIX.

Hallberg, J., Backlund-Norberg, M., Synnes, K., & Nugent, C. (2009). Profile management for dynamic groups. In *Intelligent Patient Management.* New York: Springer. doi:10.1007/978-3-642-00179-6_18

Hallberg, J., Norberg, M. B., Kristiansson, J., Synnes, K., & Nugent, C. (2007). Creating dynamic groups using context-awareness. In *Proceedings of the 6th international Conference on Mobile and Ubiquitous Multimedia.*

Han, L., & Kendall, G. (2003). *Guided operators for a hyper-heuristic genetic algorithm.* Paper presented at the AI 2003: Advances in Artificial Intelligence.

Hasan, C., & Jose, A. B. (1999). Fortes Work-Efficient Routing Algorithms for Rearrangeable Symmetrical Networks. *IEEE Transactions on Parallel and Distributed Systems, 10*(7).

Hassan, M. M., Song, B., & Huh, E. N. (2009, January 15-16). *A Framework of Sensor - Cloud Integration Opportunities and Challenges.* Paper presented in ICUIMC-09Suwon, South Korea.

Haussecker, H. W., & Fleet, D. J. (2001). Computing optical flow with physical models of brightness variation. *IEEE Transactions on Pattern Analysis and Machine Intelligence, 23*(6), 661–673. doi:10.1109/34.927465

Heeger, D. J. (1988). Optical flow using spatio- temporal filters. *International Journal of Computer Vision, 1,* 279–302. doi:10.1007/BF00133568

Heidemann, J., & Bulusu, N. (2000). Using Geospatial Information in Sensor Networks. In *Proceedings of MOBICOM.*

Hel'en, M., Latvala, J., Ikonen, H., & Niittylahti, J. (2001). Using calibration in RSSI-based location tracking system. In *Proceedings of the 5th World Multiconference on Circuits, Systems, Communications & Computers (CSCC20001).*

HellasGrid. (2009). *Greek grid project official portal site.* Retrieved from http://www.hellasgrid.gr

Hellerstein, J. L., Diao, Y., Parekh, S., & Tilbury, D. (2004). *Feedback Control of Computing Systems.* New York: Wiley. doi:10.1002/047166880X

Ho, K.-P. (1999). Analysis of homodyne crosstalk in optical networks using Gram-Charlier series. *Journal of Lightwave Technology*, *17*(2), 149–154. doi:10.1109/50.744213

Horn, B. K. P., & Schunk, B. G. (1981). Determining optical flow. *IEEE Trans on Artificial Intelligence*, *17*, 185–203. doi:10.1016/0004-3702(81)90024-2

Hou, E. S. H., Ansari, N., & Ren, H. (1994). A genetic algorithm for multiprocessor scheduling. *IEEE Transactions on Parallel and Distributed Systems*, *5*(2), 113–120. doi:10.1109/71.265940

Hsieh, J.-W., Chen, S.-H., & Hu, W.-F. (2006). Automatic Traffic Surveillance System for Vehicle Tracking and Classification. *IEEE Transactions on Intelligent Transportation Systems*, *7*, 175–187. doi:10.1109/TITS.2006.874722

Huberman, B., Romero, D., & Wu, F. (2008). *Social networks that matter: Twitter under the microscope.* CoRR abs/0812.1045

Hui, J. Y. (1990). *Switching and Traffic Theory for Integrated Broadband Networks.* Norwell, MA: Kluwer Academic Press.

Hwang, F. K., Lin, W-D., & Lioubimov, V. (2006). On Noninterruptive Rearrangeable Networks. *IEEE/ACM Transaction on Networking, 14*(5).

Hwang, K., Jin, H., Chow, E., Wang, C., & Xu, Z. (1999). Designing SSI clusters with hierarchical check pointing and single I/O space. *IEEE Concurrency*, *7*(1), 60–69. doi:10.1109/4434.749136

Hwang, K., Kwok, Y. K., Song, S., Chen, M., Chen, Y., Zhou, R., et al. (2005, May). Gridsec: Trusted grid computing with security bindings and self-defense against network worms and ddos attacks. In *Proceedings of International Workshop on Grid Computing Security and Resource Management (GSRM'05)*, Atlanta, GA (pp. 187-195). Springer.

Iamnitchi, A., Foster, I., & Nurmi, D. (2002, July 23-26). A peer-to-peer approach to resource discovery in grid environments. In *Proceedings of the 11th Symposium on High Performance Distributed Computing*, Edinburgh, UK (pp. 419-434). IEEE.

Ibarra, O. H., & Kim, C. E. (1977). Heuristic algorithms for scheduling independent tasks on nonidentical processors. *Journal of the ACM, 24*(2), 280–289. doi:10.1145/322003.322011

IEC 61400-25. (2006). *Communications for monitoring and control of wind power plants.*

IEC 61850. (2002). *Communication networks and systems in substations, 14 parts.*

IEC 61850 Part 7-410. (2006). *Hydroelectric Power plants- communication for monitoring and control.*

IEC 61850 Part 7-420. (2008). *DER logical nodes.*

IEEE. 802.15.4. (n.d.). *Wireless Medium Access Control (MAC) and Physical Layer (PHY) Specifications for Wireless Personal Area Networks (WPANs).* Retrieved from http://www.ieee.org

Ilavarasan, E., & Thambidurai, P. (2007). Low complexity performance effective task scheduling algorithm for heterogeneous computing environments. *Journal of Computer Science*, *3*(2), 94–103. doi:10.3844/jcssp.2007.94.103

IR-Wire: Gnutella Data Crawler and Analyzer. (2006). Retrieved January 8, 2010, from http://ir.iit.edu/~waigen/proj/pirs/irwire/index.html

ISO 9506. (2008). Industrial automation systems- Manufac-turing Message Specification, 2 Parts.

Iverson, M., Ozguner, F., & Follen, G. (1995). *Parallelizing existing applications in distributed heterogeneous environments.* Paper presented at the Proceedings of Heterogeneous Computing Workshop.

Jacob, B., Brown, M., Fukui, K., & Trivedi, N. (2005). *Introduction to grid computing* (p. 148). IBM.

Jahne, B. (1987). Image sequence analysis of complex physical objects: nonlinear small scale water surface waves. In *Proceedings of the IEEE ICCV*, London (pp. 191-200).

Java EE platform. (2008). JAX-WS Reference Documentation. *Sun Microsystems.* Retrieved from https://jax-ws.dev.java.net/

Jensen, K., Kristensen, L. M., & Wells, L. (2007). Coloured petri nets and CPN Tools for modelling and validation of concurrent systems. *International Journal on Software Tools for Technology Transfer*, *9*(3-4), 213–254. doi:10.1007/s10009-007-0038-x

Jeong, W., & Nof, S. (2008, June). Performance evaluation of wireless sensor network protocols for industrial applications. *Journal of Intelligent Manufacturing*, *19*(3), 335–345. doi:10.1007/s10845-008-0086-4

Jepsen, T. C. (2009). Just What Is an Ontology, Anyway? *IT Professional*, *11*(5), 22–27. doi:10.1109/MITP.2009.105

Jiang, P., Ren, H., Zhang, L., Wang, Z., & Xue, A. (2006). Reliable Application of Wireless Sensor Networks in Industrial Process Control. In *Proceedings of the Intelligent Control and Automation (WCICA 2006), the Sixth World Congress on* (pp. 99-103).

John, A., Adamic, L., Davis, M., Nack, F., Shamma, D. A., & Seligmann, D. D. (2008). The future of online social interactions: what to expect in 2020. In *Proceeding of the 17th international Conference on World Wide Web*.

John, W. (2002). Building safer cars. *IEEE Spectrum*, *29*(1), 82–85.

Jones, M. T. (2007, October 30). *Anatomy of the Linux file system. IBM*. Retrieved from http://www.ibm.com/developerworks/linux/library/l-linux-filesystem/

Jones, R. (2007). *Gmail Filesystem - GmailFS*. Retrieved from http://richard.jones.name/google-hacks/gmail-filesystem/gmail-filesystem.html

Kabus, P., Terpstra, W. W., Cilia, M., & Buchmann, A. P. (2005). Addressing cheating in distributed MMOGs. In *Proceedings of the 4th ACM SIGCOMM Workshop on Network and System Support for Games* (pp. 1-6). New York: ACM Press.

Kamra, A., Misra, V., & Nahum, E. M. (2004). Yaksha: A self-tuning controller for managing the performance of 3-tiered web sites. In *Proceedings of the 12th IEEE Int'l. Workshop on Quality of Service*.

Kantee, A. (2007). Pass-to-Userspace Framework File System. In *Proceedings of the 2nd Asia BSD Conference* (pp. 29-42).

Kantee, A., & Crooks, A. (2007). ReFUSE: Userspace FUSE Reimplementation Using puffs. In *Proceedings of the 6th European BSD Conference*. http://freshmeat.net/projects/fuseftp/

Karatza, H. D., & Hilzer, R. C. (2003). Parallel job scheduling in homogeneous distributed systems. *Journal of Simulation*, *79*(5-6), 287–298. doi:10.1177/0037549703037148

Karmann, K. P., & Von Brandt, A. (1990). Moving object recognition using an adaptive background memory. In Capellini, V. (Ed.), *Time-Varying Image Processing and Moving Object Recognition* (p. 2). Amsterdam, The Netherlands: Elsevier.

Kaufman, C. (2005). *The Internet Key Exchange (IKEv2) Protocol, RFC 4306*.

Keahey, K., Doering, K., & Foster, I. (2004). From sandbox to playground: dynamic virtual environments in the grid. In *Proceedings of the 5th Int. Workshop in Grid Computing*.

Kent, S., & Atkinson, R. (1998). *IP Encapsulating Security Payload (ESP), RFC 2406*.

Kent, S., & Atkinson, R. (1998). *Security Architecture for Internet Protocol, RFC 2401*.

Keshav, S. (1997). *An Engineering Approach to Compter Networking*. Reading, MA: Addison-Wesley.

Khabazian, M., & Ali, M. K. (2007). Generalized Performance Modeling of Vehicular Ad Hoc Networks (VANETs). In *Proceedings of the ISCC 2007* (pp. 51-56).

Kim, J.-S., Nam, B., Keleher, P., Marsh, M., Bhattacharjee, B., & Sussman, A. (2008). Trade-offs in matching jobs and balancing load for distributed desktop grids. *Future Generation Computer Systems*, *24*(5), 415–424. doi:10.1016/j.future.2007.07.007

Kim, M. K., Yoon, H., & Maeng, S. R. (1997). On the Correctness of Inside-Out Routing Algorithm. *IEEE Transactions on Computers*, *46*(7), 820–823. doi:10.1109/12.599903

King, P. J., & Mamdani, E. H. (1974). Application of fuzzy algorithms for control simple dynamic plant. In. *Proceedings of the IEEE Control Theory App*, *121*(12), 1585–1588.

Kobayashi, Y., Watanabe, T., Kanzaki, A., Yoshihisa, T., Hara, T., & Nishio, S. (2009). A Dynamic Cluster Construction Method Based on Query Characteristics in Peer-to-Peer Networks. In *Proceedings of the AP2PS '09, the First International Conference* (pp. 168-173).

Kondo, D., Anderson, D. P., & McLeod, J. (2007, December). Performance evaluation of scheduling policies for volunteer computing. In *Proceedings of the 3rd IEEE International Conference on e-Science and Grid Computing,* Bangalore, India (pp. 415-422). Washington, DC: IEEE Computer Society.

Kouba, A., Cunha, A., & Alves, M. (2008, October). TDBS: a time division beacon scheduling mechanism for ZigBee cluster-tree wireless sensor networks. *Real-Time Systems,* 321–354. doi:10.1007/s11241-008-9063-4

Krallmann, J., Schwiegelshohn, U., & Yahyapour, R. (1999, April 16). On the design and evaluation of job scheduling algorithms. In D. G. Feitelson & L. Rudolph (Eds.), *Proceedings of the 5th Workshop on Job Scheduling Strategies for Parallel Processing,* San Juan, Puerto Rico (LNCS 1659, pp. 17–42).

Krause, S. (2008). A survey of P2P protocols for Massively Multiplayer Online Games. In *Proceedings of the 7th ACM SIGCOMM Workshop on Network and System Support for Games* (pp. 53-58). New York: ACM.

Krishnamurthy, S. (2006). TinySIP: Providing Seamless Access to Sensorbased Services. In *Proceedings of the 1st International Workshop on Advances in Sensor Networks (IWASN).*

Larson, J. A., Navathe, S. B., & El-Masri, R. (1989). A theory of attribute equivalence in databases with application to schema integration. *IEEE Transactions on Software Engineering, 16*(4), 449–463. doi:10.1109/32.16605

Lawrie, D. H. (1975). Access and Alignment of Data in an Array Processor. *IEEE Transactions on Computers, 24*(12), 1145–1155. doi:10.1109/T-C.1975.224157

Lee, C.-Y., & Oruc, A. Y. (1995). A Fast Parallel Algorithm for Routing Unicast Assignments in Bend Networks. *IEEE Transactions on Parallel and Distributed Systems, 6*(3).

Lee, K. Y. (1981). A new Benes network control algorithm and Parallel Permutation Algorithm. *IEEE Transactions on Computers, C-30*(5), 157–161.

Lee, K. Y. (1985). On the rearrangeabllity of 2(log2 N − 1) stage permutation networks. *IEEE Transactions on Computers, C-34*(5), 412–425.

Lee, Y., Sheu, L., & Tsou, Y. (2008). Quality function deployment implementation based on Fuzzy Kano model: An application in PLM system. *Computers & Industrial Engineering, 55*(1), 48–63. doi:10.1016/j.cie.2007.11.014

Leighton, F. T. (1992). *Introduction to Parallel Algorithms and Architectures: Arrays, Trees, Hypercubes.* San Mateo, CA: Morgan Kaufmann.

Li, B., & Chellappa, R. (2002). A generic approach to simultaneous tracking and verification in video. *IEEE Transactions on Image Processing, 11*(5), 530–544. doi:10.1109/TIP.2002.1006400

Li, B., & Nahrstedt, K. (1999). A control-based middleware framework for quality of service adaptations. *Communications, 17,* 1632–1650.

Li, D., Wong, K. D., Hu, Y. W., & Sayeed, A. M. (2002, March). Detection, Classification, and Tracking of Targets. *IEEE Signal Processing Magazine.*

Li, M., & Baker, M. (2005). *The grid: Core technologies.* London: John Wiley & Sons. doi:10.1002/0470094192

Li, M., Lee, W. C., & Sivasubramaniam, A. (2004). Semantic small world: An overlay network for peer-to-peer search. In *Proceedings of the 12th IEEE International Conference on Network Protocols* (pp. 228-238).

Li, M., Sampigethaya, K., Huang, L., & Poovendran, R. (2006). Swing & swap: user-centric approaches towards maximizing location privacy. In *Proceedings of the 5th ACM workshop on Privacy in electronic society (WPES '06)* (pp. 19-27).

Li, W. (2000). *The Study on 3-D reconstruction of Cement Hydration Based on image processing.* Unpublished master dissertation, Shandong University, Jinan, China.

Li, X., Guo, L., & Zhao, Y. E. (2008). Tag-based social interest discovery. In *Proceedings of the World Wide Web.*

Liang, J., Kumar, R., & Ross, K. (2004). The KaZaA Overlay: A Measurement Study. In *Proceedings of the 19th IEEE Annual Computer Communications Workshop.*

Liang, W., & Wang, W. (2005). On Performance Analysis of Challenge/Response Based Authentication in Wireless Networks. *Computer Networks, 48*(2).

Lim, S., & Gamal, A. G. (2001). Optical Flow Estimation using High frame-rate Sequences. *IEEE Transactions on Image Processing*, 925-928. DOI 0-7803-6725

Lin, S., Liu, J., & Fang, Y. (2007, August 18-21). "ZigBee Based Wireless Sensor Networks and Its Applications in Industrial. In *Proceedings of the Automation and Logistics, 2007 IEEE International Conference on* (pp. 1979-1983).

Lin, Y. B., Chang, M. F., Hsu, M. T., & Wu, L. Y. (2005). One-pass GPRS and IMS Authentication Procedure for UMTS. *IEEE Journal on Selected Areas in Communications, 23*(6), 1233–1239. doi:10.1109/JSAC.2005.845631

Linial, & Tarsi, M. (1989). Interpolation between Bases and the Shuffle-Exchange Network. *European Journal on Combinatorics, 10*, 29-39.

Litzkow, M., Livny, M., & Mutka, M. (1988). Condor – a hunter of idle workstations. In *Proceedings of the 8th Int. Conf. on Distributed Computing Systems* (pp. 104-111).

Liu, L., Antonopoulos, N., & Mackin, S. (2007). Social Peer-to-Peer for Resource Discovery. In Proceedings of the *15th EUROMICRO International Conference on Parallel, Distributed and Network-Based Processing (PDP'07)* (pp. 459-466).

Lo, V., Zhou, D., Zappala, D., Liu, Y., & Zhao, S. (2004, February). Cluster computing on the fly: P2P scheduling of idle cycles in the Internet. In *Proceedings of the 3rd International Workshop on Peer-to-Peer Systems (IPTPS'04)*, San Diego, CA (pp. 227-236).

Löhr, H., Ramasamy, H. V., Sadeghi, A., Schulz, S., Schunter, M., & Stüble, C. (2007, July). Enhancing grid security using trusted virtualization. In *Proceedings of the 4th International Conference on Autonomic and Trusted Computing (ATC 2007)*, Hong Kong, China (pp. 372-384). Springer.

López, P., Pairot, C., Mondéjar, R., Ahulló, J., Tejedor, H., & Rallo, R. (2004, September). PlanetSim: A new overlay network simulation framework. In *Proceedings of the 4th International Workshop on Software Engineering and Middleware (SEM)*, Linz, Austria (pp. 123-136).

Lorpunmanee, S., Sap, M. N., Abdullah, A. H., & Inwai, C. C. (2007). An ant colony optimization for dynamic job scheduling in grid environment. *Proceedings of World Academy of Science: Engineering and Technology, 23*, 314–321.

Löser, A., Naumann, F., Siberski, W., Nejdl, W., & Thaden, U. (2004). Semantic Overlay Clusters within Super-Peer Networks. In *Databases, Information Systems, and Peer-to-Peer Computing* (pp. 33-47). Retrieved from http://www.springerlink.com/content/cd6jv7alxv3eac1k

Low, K. S., Win, W. N. N., & Er Meng, J. (2005). Wireless Sensor Networks for Industrial Environments. In *Proceedings of the Computational Intelligence for Modelling, Control and Automation, 2005 and International Conference on Intelligent Agents, Web Technologies and Internet Commerce, International Conference on* (pp. 271-276).

Lu, F., Parkin, S., & Morgan, G. (2006). Load balancing for massively multiplayer online games. In *Proceedings of 5th ACM SIGCOMM workshop on Network and system support for games* (Vol. 1). New York: ACM Press.

Lu, Y., Lu, C., Abdelzaher, T., & Tao, G. (2002). An adaptive control framework for QoS guarantees and its application to differentiated caching services. In *Proceedings of the 10th IEEE Int'l. Workshop on Quality of Service*.

Lua, E., Crowcroft, J., Pias, M., Sharma, R., & Lim, S. (2005). A survey and comparison of peer-to-peer overlay network schemes. *IEEE Communications Surveys & Tutorials, 7*(2), 72–93. doi:10.1109/COMST.2005.1610546

Luo, X. (2007). *IMAP Storage Filesystem*. Retrieved from http://imapfs.sourceforge.net/

Luther, A., Buyya, R., Ranjan, R., & Venugopal, S. (2005). *Peer-to-peer grid computing and a. NET-based Alchemi framework*. New York: John Wiley & Sons.

Lv, Q., Cao, P., Cohen, E., Li, K., & Shenker, S. (2002, June 22-26). Search and replication in unstructured peer-to-peer networks. In *Proceedings of the 16th ACM International Conference on Supercomputing (ICS'02)*, New York (pp. 84-95). ACM Publishing.

Lytras, M., Damiani, E., & Pablos, P. (2008). *Web 2.0: the Business Model*. New York: Springer.

Ma, M., Oikonomou, A., & Zheng, H. (2009). Second Life as a learning and teaching environment for digital games education. In M. Lombard et al. (Eds.), *Proceedings of the 12th Annual International Workshop on Presence (PRESENCE 2009)*, Los Angeles, CA.

Maamar, Z., Alkhatib, G., Mostéfaoui, S., Lahkim, M., & Mansoor, W. (2004). *Context-based Personalization of Web Services Composition and Provisioning*. EURO-MICRO.

Maghraoui, K. E. (2006). The internet operating system middleware for adaptive distributed computing. *International Journal of High Performance Computing Applications*, *20*(4), 467–480. doi:10.1177/1094342006068411

Maheswaran, M. (1999). Dynamic mapping of a class of independent tasks onto heterogeneous computing systems. *Journal of Parallel and Distributed Computing*, *59*(2), 107–131. doi:10.1006/jpdc.1999.1581

Maheswaran, M., Ali, S., Siegel, H. J., Hensgen, D., & Freund, R. F. (1999). Dynamic mapping of a class of independent tasks onto heterogeneous computing systems. *Journal of Parallel and Distributed Computing*, *59*(2), 107–131. doi:10.1006/jpdc.1999.1581

Maheswaran, M., & Siegel, H. J. (1998). *A dynamic matching and scheduling algorithm for heterogeneous computing systems*. Paper presented at the 7th Heterogeneous Computing Workshop.

Martin, A., & Yau, P. (2007). Grid security: Next steps. *Information Security Technical Report*, *12*(3), 113–122. doi:10.1016/j.istr.2007.05.009

Massie, M. L., Chun, B. N., & Culler, D. E. (2004). The Ganglia Distributed Monitoring System: Design, Implementation, and Experience. *Parallel Computing*, *30*(7), 817–840. doi:10.1016/j.parco.2004.04.001

Mastroianni, C., Talia, D., & Verta, O. (2005). A Super-Peer Model for Resource Discovery Services in Large-Scale Grids. *Future Generation Computer Systems*, *21*(8), 1235–1248. doi:10.1016/j.future.2005.06.001

Mastroianni, C., Talia, D., & Verta, O. (2007). *Evaluating Resource Discovery Protocols for Hierarchical and Super-Peer Grid Information Systems*. Paper presented at the Proceedings of the 15th Euromicro International Conference on Parallel, Distributed and Network-Based Processing.

MathWorks. (2009). Retrieved from http://www.mathworks.com

Mauve, M., Vogel, J., Hilt, V., & Effelsberg, W. (2004). Local-lag and timewarp: Providing consistency for replicated continuous applications. *IEEE Transactions on Multimedia*, *6*(1), 47–57. doi:10.1109/TMM.2003.819751

MC 13192. (n.d.). *Transceiver Data-sheet*. Retrieved from http://www.freescale.com

Meguerdichian, S., Slijepcevic, S., Karayan, V., & Potkonjak, M. (2001). Localized Algorithms In Wireless Ad-Hoc Networks: Location Discovery and Sensor Exposure. In *Proceedings of the MobiHOC 2001*, UCLA, Los Angeles, CA.

Mello, A., & Rein, L. (2009). *Using Standards to Normalize Domain Specific Metadata*. Paper presented at the W3C Workshop on the Future of Social Networking.

Menasce, D. A., Saha, D., Porto, D. S. C., Almeida, V. A. F., & Tripathi, S. K. (1995). Static and dynamic processor scheduling disciplines in heterogeneous parallel architectures. *Journal of Parallel and Distributed Computing*, *28*(1), 1–18. doi:10.1006/jpdc.1995.1085

Michlmayr, A., Leitner, P., Rosenberg, F., & Dustdar, S. (2008). Publish/subscribe in the VRESCo SOA runtime. In *Proceedings of Distributed Event-Based Systems*.

Milojicic, D. S., Kalogeraki, V., Lukose, R., Nagaraja, K., Pruyne, J., Rihard, B., et al. (2002). *Peer-to-peer computing* (Tech. Rep. HPL-2002-57). Palo Alto, CA: HP Labs.

Miltrapiyuruk, P., Desouza, G. N., & Kak, A. C. (2005). Accurate 3D tracking of Rigid objects with occlusion using Active Appearance Model. In *Proceedings of the IEEE workshop on motion and Video computation*.

Miluzzo, E., Lane, N. D., Fodor, K., Peterson, R., Lu, H., Musolesi, M., et al. (2008). Sensing meets mobile social networks: the design, implementation and evaluation of the CenceMe application. In *Proceedings of Embedded Network Sensor Systems*.

Mitchell, T. M. (1997). *Machine learning*. New York: McGraw-Hill.

(2009). Model architecture for a user tailored data push service in data grids. InBessis, N. (Ed.), *Grid technology for maximizing collaborative decision management and support: Advancing effective virtual organizations* (pp. 235–255). Hershey, PA: IGI Global. doi:10.4018/978-1-60566-364-7.ch012

Montillet, J. P., Braysy, T., & Oppermann, I. (2005). *Algorithm for Nodes Localization in Wireless Ad-Hoc Networks Based on Cost Function.* Paper presented at the International Workshop on Wireless Ad Hoc Networks (IWWAN 2005), London.

Montresor, A., Meling, H., & Babaoglu, O. (2002, July). Messor: Load-balancing through a swarm of autonomous sgents. In *Proceedings of the International Workshop on Agents and Peer-to-Peer Computing (AP2PC'02),* Bologna, Italy (pp. 125-137).

Muntz, D., & Honeyman, P. (1992, January). Multi-level caching in distributed file systems. In *Proceedings of the USENIX 1992 Winter Technical Conference,* San Francisco (pp. 305-313). USENIX.

Myerson, J. M. (2002). *Web Service Architectures.* Chicago, IL: Tect.

Nabrzyski, J., Schopf, J. M., & Weglarz, J. (2003). *Grid resource management: State of the art and future trends.* New York: Kluwer Academic Publishing.

Nakauchi, K., Morikawa, H., & Aoyama, T. (2004). Design and Implementation of a Semantic Peer-to-Peer Network. In *High Speed Networks and Multimedia Communications* (pp. 961-972). Retrieved from http://www.springerlink.com/content/8mvv93v3p8pnuut4

Nassimi, D., & Sahni, S. (1980). A self-routing Benes network. In *Proceedings of the 7th annual symposium on Computer Architecture* (pp. 190-195).

Nassimi, D., & Sahni, S. (1981). A self-routing Benes network and Parallel Permutation Algorithm. *IEEE Transactions on Computers, C-30*(5), 332–340. doi:10.1109/TC.1981.1675791

Nassimi, D., & Sahni, S. (1982). Parallel Algorithms to Set Up the Benes Permutation Network. *IEEE Transactions on Computers, C-31*(2). doi:10.1109/TC.1982.1675960

Neary, M. O., & Cappello, P. (2005). Advanced eager scheduling for Java based adaptive parallel computing. *Concurrency and Computation, 17*(7-8), 797–819. doi:10.1002/cpe.855

Nejdl, W., Wolf, B., Qu, C., Decker, S., Sintek, M., Naeve, A., et al. (2002). EDUTELLA: a P2P Networking Infrastructure based on RDF. In *Proceedings of the 11th international conference on World Wide Web* (pp. 604-615).

Nelson, R., Towsley, D., & Tantawi, A. N. (1988). Performance analysis of parallel processing systems. *IEEE Transactions on Software Engineering, 14*(4), 532–540. doi:10.1109/32.4676

Newman, P. (1988). A fast packet switch for the integrated services backbone network. *IEEE Journal of Selected Areas in Communication, SAC-6*(9).

Nguyen, B. (2004, July 30). *Linux Filesystem Hierarchy. The Linux Documentation Project.* Retrieved from http://tldp.org/LDP/Linux-Filesystem-Hierarchy/html/

Nisan, N., London, S., Regev, O., & Camiel, N. (1998, May 26-29). Globally distributed computation over the Internet-the POPCORN project. In *Proceedings of the 18th IEEE International Conference on Distributed Computing Systems,* Amsterdam, The Netherlands (pp. 592-601). IEEE.

Ntantogian, C., & Xenakis, C. (2008). *One-pass EAP-AKA Authentication in 3G-WLAN Integrated Networks, Wireless Personal Communications.* New York: Springer.

ODP - Open Directory Project. (1998). Retrieved January 17, 2010, from http://www.dmoz.org/

OpenSocial API Documentation. (n.d.). Retrieved May 2009 from http://code.google.com/apis/opensocial/docs/index.html

openXdrive. (2007). *The Xdrive Data Services Platform (XDSP) JSON API. Xdrive LLC.* Retrieved from dev.aol.com/xdrive_resources/json_apidocs/api-index.html

Opferman, D. C., & Tsao-Wu, N. T. (1971). On a Class of Rearrangeable Switching Networks, Part I: Control Algorithm. *The Bell System Technical Journal, 50,* 1579–1600.

Padovitz, A., Loke, S. W., & Zaslavsky, A. (2008). Multiple-Agent Perspectives in Reasoning About Situations for Context-Aware Pervasive Computing Systems. *IEEE Transactions on Systems, Man, and Cybernetics, 38*(4), 729–742. doi:10.1109/TSMCA.2008.918589

Pairot, C., Garcia, P., & Skarmeta, A. F. G. (2004). *DERMI: A Decentralized Peer-to-Peer Event-Based Object Middleware.* Paper presented at the Proceedings of the 24th International Conference on Distributed Computing Systems.

Palensky, P. (2008). Networked Distributed Energy Resources. In *Proceedings of the 34th Annual Conference on IEEE Industrial Electronics (IECON)* (pp. 23-24).

Pallickara, S., & Fox, G. (2003). NaradaBrokering: A Distributed Middleware Framework and Architecture for Enabling Durable Peer-to-Peer Grids. In. *Proceedings of Middleware, 2003,* 998–999.

Pandey, K., & Patel, S. V. (2009). Design of SOA based Service Stack for Collaborative Wireless Sensor Network Submitted. In *Proceedings of WSCN 2009, IEEE Conference,* Allahabad, India.

Pandey, K., & Patel, S. V. (2009, July). Design of SOA based Sensor Web Registry. In *Proceedings of CICSyn IEEE conference,* Indore, India.

Papadimitratos, P., Buttyan, L., Hubaux, J.-P., Kargl, F., Kung, A., & Raya, M. (2007). Architecture for Secure and Private Vehicular Communications. In *Proceedings of the Int'l Conf. on ITS Telecomm (ITST 2007),* Sophia Antipolis, France.

Paranhos, D., Cirne, W., & Brasileiro, F. (2003, August 26-29). Trading cycles for information using replication to schedule bag-of-tasks applications on computational grids. In H. Kosch, L. Böszörményi, & H. Hellwagner (Eds.), *Euro-Par 2003 Parallel Processing: 9th International Euro-Par Conference,* Klagenfurt, Austria (LNCS 2790, pp. 169-180).

Parekh, S., Gandhi, N., Hellerstein, J. L., Tilbury, D., Jayram, T. S., & Bigus, J. (2002). Using control theory to achieve service level objectives in performance management. *Real Time Systems Journal, 23,* 1–2.

Park, C. Y. (1993). Predicting program execution times by analyzing static and dynamic program paths. *Real-Time Systems, 5*(1), 31–62. doi:10.1007/BF01088696

Park, S. M., & Humphrey, M. (2008). Feedback-controlled resource sharing for predictable escience. In *Proceedings of the ACM/IEEE conf. on Supercomputing.*

Pautasso, C., Zimmermann, O., & Leymann, F. (2008). Restful web services vs. "big"' web services: making the right architectural decision. In *Proceeding of the 17th international conference on World Wide Web* (pp. 805-814).

Pei, S.-C., & Liou, L.-G. (1997). Motion-Based Grouping of Optical Flow Fields: The Extrapolation and subtraction Technique. *IEEE Transactions on Image Processing, 6*(10), 1358–1363. doi:10.1109/83.624949

Peng, R., & Sichitiu, M. L. (2006, September). Angle of Arrival Localization for Wireless Sensor Networks. In *Proceedings of the Third Annual IEEE Communications Society Conference on Sensor and Ad Hoc Communications and Networks,* Reston, VA.

Pfitzmann, A., & Hansen, M. (2004). Anonymity, unobservability, and pseudonymity: A proposal for terminology. In *Proceedings of the HBCC04* (Vol. 21).

Pinedo, M. L. (2008). *Scheduling theory, algorithms and systems.* New York: Springer.

Ping, T. T., Sodhy, G. C., Yong, C. H., Haron, F., & Buyya, R. (2004, May 14-17). A Market-based Scheduler for JXTA-based Peer-to-Peer Computing System. In *Proceedings of the International Conference on Computational Science and its Applications (ICCSA' 04),* Assisi, Italy (pp. 147-157).

Pordes, R. (2004). The open science grid. In *Proceedings of the Computing in High Energy and Nuclear Physics Conf.,* Interlaken, Switzerland.

Poritz, J., Schunter, M., Herreweghen, E., & Waidner, M. (2004). Property attestation – scalable and privacy-friendly security assessment of peer computers (Tech. Rep. RZ3548, ST19WP18 datasheet). IBM Research.

Prabhakar, B., & McKeown, N. (1999). On the Speedup Required for Combined Input and Output Queued Switching. *Automatica, 35*(12), 1909–1920. doi:10.1016/S0005-1098(99)00129-6

Pretorius, A. J. (2004). *Ontologies-Introduction and Overview*. Vrije Universiteit Brussel.

Quax, P., Dierckx, J., Cornelissen, B., Vansichem, G., & Lamotte, W. (2008). Dynamic server allocation in a real-life deployable communications architecture for networked games. In *Proceedings of the 7th ACM SIG-COMM Workshop on Network and System Support for Games* (pp. 66-71). New York: ACM.

Raento, M., Oulasvirta, A., Petit, R., & Toivonen, H. (2005). ContextPhone: a prototyping platform for context-aware mobile applications. *Pervasive Computing, IEEE, 4*(2), 51–59. doi:10.1109/MPRV.2005.29

Rahaman, S. A., Bakar, A., & Green, R. J. (2000). Adaptive threshold in dynamic scene analysis for extraction of fine line. *IEEE.* DOI 0-7803-6355

Rahm, E., & Bernstein, P. A. (2001). A survey of approaches to automatic schema matching. *The VLDB Journal, 10*, 334–350. doi:10.1007/s007780100057

Rana, J., Kristiansson, J., Hallberg, J., & Synnes, K. (2009). Challenges for Mobile Social Networking Applications. In *Proceedings of the 1st International ICST Conference on Communications Infrastructure, Systems and Applications*, London.

Ranganathan, K., & Foster, I. (2001, November). Identifying dynamic replication strategies for a high performance data grid. In C. A. Lee (Ed.), *Proceedings of the International Grid Computing Workshop*, Denver, CO (LNCS 2242, pp. 75-86).

Ranganathan, K., & Foster, I. (2002, July). Decoupling computation and data scheduling in distributed data-intensive applications. In *Proceedings of the 2002 IEEE International Symposium of High Performance Distributed Computing*, Edinburgh, Scotland (p. 352). Washington, DC: IEEE Computer Society.

Ranjan, R., Harwood, A., & Buyya, R. (2008). Peer-to-Peer-Based Resource Discovery in Global Grids: A Tutorial. *IEEE Communications Surveys & Tutorials, 10*(2), 6–33. doi:10.1109/COMST.2008.4564477

Rashid, M. M., & Akhtar, M. N. (2006). A new multilevel CPU scheduling algorithm. *Journal of Applied Sciences, 6*(9), 2036–2039. doi:10.3923/jas.2006.2036.2039

Ratnasamy, S., Francis, P., Handley, M., Karp, R. M., & Shenker, S. (2001, August 27-31). A scalable content-addressable network. In *Proceedings of the ACM SIG-COMM Conference 2001,* San Diego, CA (pp.161-172). ACM Publishing.

Rauber, T., & Runger, G. (2005). *M-Task-Programming for Heterogeneous Systems and Grid Environments.* Paper presented at the 19th IEEE International Parallel and Distributed Processing Symposium.

Raya, M., & Hubaux, J.-P. (2005). The Security of Vehicular Ad Hoc Networks. In. *Proceedings of SASN, 05,* 11–21. doi:10.1145/1102219.1102223

Raya, M., & Hubaux, J.-P. (2007). Securing vehicular ad hoc networks. *Journal of Computer Security, 15*(1), 39–68.

Reinoso Castillo, J. A., Silvescu, A., Caragea, D., Pathak, J., & Honavar, V. G. (2004). *Information extraction and integration from heterogeneous, distributed, autonomous information sources—A federated ontology-driven query-centric approach.* Retrieved January 5, 2007, from http://www.cs.iastate.edu/ ~honavar/Papers/ indusfinal.pdf

Rezenda, F. F., Georgian, U. H., & Rutschlin, J. (1999). A practical approach to access heterogeneous and distributed databases. In [Berlin: Springer.]. *Proceedings of CAiSE, 99,* 317–332.

Rhea, S., Geels, D., Roscoe, T., & Kubiatowicz, J. (2004, June 27-July 2). Handling churn in a DHT. In *Proceedings of the 2004 USENIX Annual Technical Conference,* Boston (pp. 127-140). USENIX.

Riddoch, A., & Turner, J. (2002, July). Technologies for building open-source massively multiplayer games. In *Proceedings of the UKUUG Linux Developers Conference*, Bristol, UK.

Roman, D., & Kifer, M. (2007). *Reasoning about the Behavior of Semantic Web Services with Concurrent Transaction Logic*. VLDB.

Rosenberg, J., et al. (2002). *SIP: Session Initiation Protocol, RFC 3261.*

Rowstron, A., & Druschel, P. (2001). Pastry: Scalable, Decentralized Object Location, and Routing for Large-Scale Peer-to-Peer Systems. In. *Proceedings of Middleware, 2001,* 329–350.

Rowstron, A., & Druschel, P. (2001, November 12-16). Pastry: Scalable, distributed object location and routing for large-scale peer-to-peer systems. In *Proceedings of the IFIP/ACM International Conference on Distributed Systems Platforms (Middleware)*, Heidelberg, Germany (pp. 329-350). ACM Publishing.

Russell, G., Donaldson, A., & Sheppard, P. (2008). Tackling online game development problems with a novel network scripting language. In *Proceedings of the 7th ACM SIGCOMM Workshop on Network and System Support for Games* (pp. 85-90). New York: ACM.

Sahota, V., Li, M., Baker, M., & Antonopoulos, N. (2009). A grouped P2P network for scalable grid information services. *Peer-to-Peer Networking and Applications, 2*(1), 3–12. doi:10.1007/s12083-008-0016-4

Salari, E., & Eshghi, K. (2005, December). An ACO algorithm for graph coloring problem. In *Proceedings of the 2005 ICSC Congress on Computational Intelligence Methods and Applications*, Istanbul, Turkey (pp. 15-17). Washington, DC: IEEE Computer Society.

Salvadori, F., de Campos, M., de Figueiredo, R., Gehrke, C., Rech, C., Sausen, P. S., et al. (2007, October 3-5). Monitoring and Diagnosis in Industrial Systems Using Wireless Sensor Networks. In *Proceedings of Intelligent Signal Processing, 2007. WISP 2007. IEEE International Symposium on* (pp. 1-6).

Samarati, P., & Sweeney, L. (1998). *Protecting privacy when disclosing information: k-anonymity and its enforcement through generalization and suppression* (Tech. Rep. SRI-CSL-98-04). CS Lab, SRI International.

Sampigethaya, K., Li, M., Huang, L., & Poovendran, R. (2007). AMOEBA: Robust Location Privacy Scheme for VANET. *IEEE JSAC, 25*(8), 1569–1589.

Sarmenta, L. F. G. (2002). Sabotage-tolerance mechanisms for volunteer computing systems. *Future Generation Computer Systems, 18*(4), 561–572. doi:10.1016/S0167-739X(01)00077-2

Savvides, A., Han, C. C., & Strivastava, M. B. (2001). Dynamic fine-grained localization in ad-hoc networks of sensors. In *Proceedings of the 7th Annual ACM/IEEE International Conference on Mobile Computing and Networking*.

Schlosser, M., Sintek, M., Decker, S., & Nejdl, W. (2003). *Hypercup-hypercubes, ontologies, and efficient search on peer-to-peer networks* (pp. 112–124). LNCS.

Schopf, J. M., Pearlman, L., Miller, N., Kesselman, C., Foster, I., & D'Arcy, M. (2006). Monitoring the grid with the Globus Toolkit MDS4. *Journal of Physics: Conference Series, 46*, 521–525. doi:10.1088/1742-6596/46/1/072

Schwarz, K. H. (2005). *An introduction to IEC 61850. Basics and user-oriented project-examples for the IEC 61850 series for substation automation*. Wurzburg, Germany: Vogel Verlag.

Second Life Wiki. (n.d.). *Second Life server architecture*. Retrieved March 10, 2010, from http://wiki.secondlife.com/wiki/Server_architecture

Segaran, T. (2007). *Programming Collective Intelligence: Building Smart Web 2.0 Applications*. New York: O'Reilly Media.

Sellami, S., Benharkat, A.-N., & Amghar, Y. (2010). Towards a more scalable schema matching: A novel approach. *International Journal of Distributed Systems and Technologies, 1*(1), 17–39. doi:10.4018/jdst.2010090802

SETI@home. (2009). http://setiathome.ssl.berkeley.edu

Sha, K., Xi, Y., Shi, W., Schwiebert, L., & Zhang, T. (2006). Adaptive Privacy-Preserving Authentication in Vehicular Networks. In *Proceedings of IEEE International Workshop on Vehicle Communication and Applications*.

Shen, X., Wang, Z., & Sun, Y. (2004). Wireless sensor networks for industrial applications. In *Proceedings of the Intelligent Control and Automation (WCICA 2004), Fifth World Congress on* (Vol. 4, pp. 3636- 3640).

Shih, P.-C., Chen, H.-M., Chung, Y.-C., Wang, C.-M., Chang, R.-S., Hsu, C.-H., et al. (2008). *Middleware of Taiwan UniGrid*. Paper presented at the 2008 ACM symposium on Applied computing.

Shizhuang, L., Jingyu, L., & Yanjun, F. (2007, August 18-21). ZigBee Based Wireless Sensor Networks and Its Applications in Industrial. In *Proceedings of Automation and Logistics, 2007 IEEE International Conference on* (pp. 1979-1983).

Shroff, P., Watson, D. W., Flann, N. S., & Freund, R. (1996). *Genetic simulated annealing for scheduling data-dependent tasks in heterogeneous environments.* Paper presented at the Proceedings of Heterogeneous Computing.

Sichitiu, M. L., Ramadurai, V., et al. (2003). *Simple algorithm for outdoor localization of wireless sensor networks with inaccurate range measurements.*

Sih, G., & Lee, E. (1993). A compile-time scheduling heuristic for interconnection-constrained heterogeneous processor architecture. *IEEE Transactions on Parallel and Distributed Systems, 4*(2), 175–187. doi:10.1109/71.207593

Singh, H., & Youssef, A. (1996, April). Mapping and scheduling heterogeneous task graphs using genetic algorithms. In Proceedings of the *5th IEEE Heterogeneous Computing Workshop,* (pp. 86-97). Washington, DC: IEEE Computer Society.

Sokura, W., & Korhonen, T. (2004). *TCP/IP Communication Aspects in Monitoring of a Remote Wind Turbine.* Helsinki, Finland: Helsinki University.

Somasundaram, K., & Radhakrishnan, S. (2009). Task resource allocation in grid using swift scheduler. *International Journal of Computers, Communications & Control, 4*(2), 158–166.

Sonka, M., Hlavac, V., & Boyle, R. (2003). *Image Processing, Analysis and Machine Vision.* Pacific Grove, CA: Thomson Brooks/Cole Publishing Company.

Sonmez, O. O., & Gursoy, A. (2007). A novel economic-based scheduling heuristic for computational grids. *International Journal of High Performance Computing Applications, 21*(1), 21–29. doi:10.1177/1094342006074849

Sorenson, J. T., & Jaatun, M. G. (2008). *An Analysis of the Manufacturing Message Specification Protocol.* Berlin: Springer.

Souto, E. (2005). Mires: A publish/subscribe middleware for sensor networks. *ACM Personal and Ubiquitous Computing, 10*(1), 37–44. doi:10.1007/s00779-005-0038-3

Spooner, D. P. (2005). Performance-aware workflow management for grid computing. *The Computer Journal, 48*(3), 347–357. doi:10.1093/comjnl/bxh090

Stappert, F., & Altenbernd, P. (2000). Complete worst-case execution time analysis of straight-line hard real-time programs. *Journal of Systems Architecture, 46*(4), 339–355. doi:10.1016/S1383-7621(99)00010-7

Stoica, I., Morris, R., Karger, D., Kaashoek, M. F., & Balakrishnan, H. (2001). Chord: A scalable peer-to-peer lookup service for internet applications. In *Proceedings of the 2001 conference on Applications, technologies, architectures, and protocols for computer communications* (p. 160).

Stoica, I., Morris, R., Liben-Nowell, D., Karger, D. R., Kaashoek, M. F., & Dabek, F. (2002). Chord: A scalable peer-to-peer lookup protocol for Internet applications. *IEEE Transactions on Networks, 11*(1), 17–32. doi:10.1109/TNET.2002.808407

Stojmenovic, I. (2005). *Handbook of Sensor Networks.* New York: Wiley. doi:10.1002/047174414X

Stokes, M. (2002). *Gnutella2 Specifications Part one.* Retrieved February 2, 2010, from http://g2.trillinux.org/index.php?title=G2_specs_part1

Sun, J., Zhang, C., & Fang, Y. (2007). An id-based framework achieving privacy and non-repudiation in Vehicular ad hoc networks. In *Proceedings of the Military Communications Conference (MILCOM).*

Sun, Z., Miller, R., & Belon, G. (2002). *A real time pre-crash vehicle detection system.* Paper presented at the IEEE international workshop on application of computer vision.

Suzer, M. H., & Kang, K. D. (2008). Adaptive fuzzy control for utilization management. In *Proceedings of the IEEE Int'l. Symp. on Object/Component/Service-oriented Real-time Distributed Computing.*

Szomszor, M. N., Cantador, I., & Alani, H. (2008). Correlating user profiles from multiple folksonomies. In *Proceedings of Hypertext and Hypermedia.*

Talia, D., & Trunfio, P. (2003). Towards a synergy between P2P and grids. *IEEE Internet Computing, 7*(4), 94–96. doi:10.1109/MIC.2003.1215667

Tang, C., Xu, Z., & Dwarkadas, S. (2003). *Peer-to-peer information retrieval using self-organizing semantic overlay networks* (pp. 175–186). New York: ACM.

Tao, H., Sawhney, H. S., & Kumar, R. (2002). Object tracking with Bayesian estimation of dynamic layer representations. *IEEE Transactions on Pattern Analysis and Machine Intelligence, 24*(1), 75–89. doi:10.1109/34.982885

Tatarinov, I., & Halevy, A. (2004). Efficient query reformulation in peer data management systems. In *Proceedings of the 2004 ACM SIGMOD international conference on Management of data* (pp. 539-550). New York: ACM. doi:10.1145/1007568.1007629

The9. (2007). *World of Warcraft: The Burning Crusade surpasses 800,000 peak concurrent user milestone in mainland China on Oct 4, 2007*. Retrieved March 10, 2010, from http://www.the9.com/en/about/about_2.htm

Thain, D., Tannenbaum, T., & Livny, M. (2005). Distributed computing in practice: The condor experience. *Concurrency and Computation, 17*(2-4), 323–356. doi:10.1002/cpe.938

Tham, C.-K., & Buyya, R. (2005, June 24). *SensorGrid: Integrating Sensor Networks and Grid Computing* (Tech. Rep. No. GRIDS-TR-2005-10). Melbourne, Australia: Grid Computing and Distributed Systems Laboratory, University of Melbourne.

Thangavel, K., Karnan, M., Jeganathan, P., Petha, A. I., Sivakumar, R., & Geetharamani, G. (2006). Ant colony algorithms in diverse combinatorial optimization problems - a survey. *International Journal on Automatic Control and System Engineering, 6*(1), 7–26.

The European DataGrid Project. (2003). Retrieved June 2007, from http://www.edg.org

The Globus Alliance. (2006). *The Globus project*. Retrieved April 2006, from http://www.globus.org

The Globus Alliance. (2009). *Globus toolkit v4*. Retrieved from http://www.globus.org/toolkit/downloads/4.2.1

The Globus Alliance. (2009b). *Monitoring and discovery system*. Retrieved from http://www.globus.org/toolkit/mds/

Tholomier, D., Rola, J., & Willemse, C. (2008). Using Innovative Technologies to ease Wind Resource penetration into Power Grid. In *Proceedings of the 7th World Wind Energy Conference & Exhibition (WWEC 2008)* (pp. 1–18).

Thompson, H. (n.d.). *Bluetooth based Monitoring system for Marine Propulsion systems*. Rolls Royce University Technology Centre in Control & Systems Engineering, U. K.

Timbus, A., Larsson, M., & Yuen, C. (2008). Integration of Wind Energy Resources in the Utility Control and Information Technology Infrastructures. In *Proceedings of the IEEE International Symposium on Industrial Electronics (ISIE)* (pp. 2371-2376).

Topcuoglu, H., Hariri, S., & Wu, M. Y. (2002). Performance-effective and low-complexity task scheduling for heterogeneous computing. *IEEE Transactions on Parallel and Distributed Systems, 13*(3), 260–274. doi:10.1109/71.993206

Toth, C. K., & Bizezinsca, D. G. (2006). Traffic management with state of art airborne imaging sensors. In *Proceedings of the International Conference at National Consortium for remote sensing in Transportation flows (NCRST-F)*.

Trivedi, K. S. (2002). *Probability and Statistics with Reliability, Queuing, and Computer Science Applications*. New York: John Wiley & Sons.

Trunfio, P., Talia, D., Papadakis, H., Fragopoulou, P., Mordacchini, M., & Pennanen, M. (2007). Peer-to-Peer Resource Discovery in Grids: Models and Systems. *Future Generation Computer Systems, 23*(7), 864–878. doi:10.1016/j.future.2006.12.003

Trusted Computing Group. (2007). *TCG specification architecture overview. Revision 1.4*. Retrieved from https://www.trustedcomputinggroup.org/home

Tseng, B. L., Lin, C.-Y., & Smith, J. R. (2002). Real-time video surveillance for traffic monitoring using virtual line analysis. In. Proceedings of the IEEE International Conference on Multimedia and Expo, 2, 541–544.

Tsoumakos, D., & Roussopoulos, N. (2003). A comparison of peer-to-peer search methods. In *Proceedings of the Sixth International Workshop on the Web and Databases*.

Tveit, A., Rein, O., Iversen, J. V., & Matskin, M. (2003). Scalable agent-based simulation of players in massively multiplayer online games. In *Proceedings of the 8th Scandinavian Conference on Artificial Intelligence, Frontiers in Artificial Intelligence and Applications*. IOS.

Utgoff, P. (1998). ID5R: An incremental ID3. In *Proceedings of the 5th International Conference on Machine Learning,* Ann Arbor, MI (pp. 107-120). Morgan Kaufmann Publishers.

Van den Akker, J. M., Hoogeveen, J. A., & Van Kempen, J. W. (2006, September 11-13). Parallel machine scheduling through column generation: Minimax objective functions. In Y. Azar & T. Erlebach (Eds.), *Algorithms – ESA 2006: Proceedings of the 14th Conference on Annual European Symposium,* Zurich, Switzerland (LNCS 4168, pp. 648-659).

Veijalainen, J. (2007). *In Proceedings of Mobile Data Management. Developing Mobile Ontologies.* Who, Why, Where, and How.

Veltri, L., Salsano, S., & Martiniello, G. (2006). Wireless LAN-3G Integration: Unified Mechanisms for Secure Authentication based on SIP. In *Proceedings of the IEEE International Conference on Communications (ICC),* Istanbul, Turkey.

WP2 Optimization Team. (2008). *OptorSim, a replica optimiser simulator.* Retrieved February 2008, from http://cern.ch/edg-wp2/ optimization/optorsim.html

Wadley, G., & Sobell, J. (2007). Using a simple MMORPG to teach multi-user, client-server database development. In *Proceedings of the MS Academic Days Conf. on Game Development.*

Waksman, A. (1968). A permutation network. *Journal of the ACM, 15*(1), 159–163. doi:10.1145/321439.321449

Wang, F. Z., Wu, S., Helian, N., Parker, A., Guo, Y., Deng, Y., & Khare, V. (2007). Grid-oriented Storage: A Single-Image, Cross-Domain, High-Bandwidth Architecture. *IEEE Transactions on Computers, 56*(4), 474–487. doi:10.1109/TC.2007.1005

Wang, J. Y., & Adelson, E. H. (1994). Representing Moving Images with layers. *IEEE Transactions on Image Processing, 3,* 625–636. doi:10.1109/83.334981

Wang, L., Siegel, H. J., Roychowdhury, V. P., & Maciejewski, A. A. (1997). Task matching and scheduling in heterogeneous computing environments using a genetic algorithm-based approach. *Journal of Parallel and Distributed Computing, 47*(1), 8–22. doi:10.1006/jpdc.1997.1392

Wang, Z., Helian, N., Wu, S., Deng, Y., Khare, V., & Thompson, C. (2007). Grid-based storage architecture for accelerating bioinformatics computing. *VLSI Signal Processing, 48*(3), 311–324. doi:10.1007/s11265-007-0066-5

Wang, Z., Wu, S., Helian, N., Parker, M., Guo, Y., & Deng, Y. (2007). Grid-oriented storage: A single-image, cross-domain, high-bandwidth architecture. *IEEE Transactions on Computers, 56*(4), 474–487. doi:10.1109/TC.2007.1005

Wang, Z., Wu, S., Helian, N., Xu, Z., Deng, Y., & Khare, V. (2007). Grid-based data access to nucleotide sequence database. *New Generation Computing, 25*(4), 409–424. doi:10.1007/s00354-007-0026-4

Watson, A. B., & Ahumada, A. J. (1985). Model of human-motion sensing. *Journal of optical. Society, A2,* 322–342.

Waxman, A. M., Wu, J., & Bergholm, F. (1988). Convected activation profiles and receptive fields for real time measurement of short range visual motion. In *Proceedings of the IEEE CVPR,* Ann Arbor, MI (pp. 717-723).

Web, P. (n.d.). Retrieved May 2009 from http://www.programmableWeb.com/apis/directory/1?apicat=Social

Welch, V. (2004). *Globus toolkit version 4 grid security infrastructure: A standards perspective.* Retrieved from http://www.globus.org/toolkit/docs/4.0/security/GT4-GSI-Overview.pdf

Willick, D. L., Eager, D. L., & Bunt, R. B. (1993, May). Disk cache replacement policies for network file servers. In *Proceedings of International Conference on Distributed Computing Systems,* Pittsburgh, PA (pp. 2-11). Washington, DC: IEEE Computer Society.

Wittmann, F. H., Roelfstra, P. E., & Sadouki, H. (1984). Simulation and Analysis of Composite Structures. *Materials Science and Engineering, 68,* 239–248. doi:10.1016/0025-5416(85)90413-6

Wu, C.-L., & Feng, T.-Y. (1980). On a Class of Multistage Interconnection Networks. *IEEE Transactions on Computers, C-29*(8), 694–702. doi:10.1109/TC.1980.1675651

Xenakis, C., & Merakos, L. (2004). Security in third Generation Mobile Networks. *Computer Communications, 27*(7), 638–650. doi:10.1016/j.comcom.2003.12.004

Xie, L., Zhu, G., Wang, Y., Xu, H., & Zhang, Z. (2005). Real-time Vehicles Tracking Based on Kalman Filter in a Video-based ITS. In *Proceedings of IEEE Conf. on Communications, Circuits and Systems* (Vol. 2, p. 886).

Xu, Z., Hou, X., & Sun, J. (2003, May). Ant algorithm based task scheduling in grid computing. In *Proceedings of the IEEE Canadian Conference Electrical and Computer Engineering (CCECE 2003)*, Montréal, Quebec, Canada (Vol. 2, pp. 1107-1110). Washington, DC: IEEE Computer Society.

Xu, Z., Lu, E., & Sun, J. (2004, December 7-10). An extendable grid simulation environment based on gridsim. In M. Li, X-H. Sun, Q. Deng, & J. Ni (Eds.), *Grid and Cooperative Computing: Second International Workshop, GCC 2003*, Shanghai, China (LNCS 3032, pp. 205-208).

Yamanda, K. (2003). A compact integrated vision motion sensor for its application. *IEEE Transactions on Intelligent Transportation Systems*, 4(1), 35–41. doi:10.1109/TITS.2002.808418

Yamato, Y., & Sunaga, H. (2006). P2P Content Searching Method using Semantic Vector which is Managed on CAN Topology. *Journal of Multimedia*, 1(6), 1. doi:10.4304/jmm.1.6.1-9

Yan, H., Qin, X., Li, X., & Wu, M. H. (2005, August). An improved ant algorithm for job scheduling in grid computing. In *Proceedings of 2005 International Conference on Machine Learning and Cybernetics*, Guangzhou, China (Vol. 5, pp. 2957-2961). Washington, DC: IEEE Computer Society.

Yan, H., Wang, S. S., Wang, S. C., & Chang, C. P. (2009, December). Towards a hybrid load balancing policy in grid computing system. *Expert Systems with Applications*, 36(10), 12054–12064. doi:10.1016/j.eswa.2009.03.001

Yang, B., & Garcia-Molina, H. (2003). *Designing a Super-Peer Network*. Paper presented at the 19th International Conference on Data Engineering.

Yeh, Y.-M., & Feng, T.-Y. (1968). On a Class of Rearrangeable Networks. *IEEE Transactions on Computers*, 41(11).

Yin, D., Chen, B., Huang, Z., Lin, X., & Fang, Y. (2007, August 16-18). Utility based query dissemination in spatial data grid. In *Proceedings of the Sixth International Conference on Grid and Cooperative Computing (GCC 2007)*, Urumchi, Xinjiang, China (pp. 574-581).

Yu, J., Buyya, R., & Ramamohanarao, K. (2008). Workflow schdeduling algorithms for grid computing. In Xhafa, F., & Abraham, A. (Eds.), *Metaheuristics for scheduling in distributed computing environments (studies in computational intelligence)* (pp. 173–214). Berlin: Springer. doi:10.1007/978-3-540-69277-5_7

Zadeh, L., George, J., & Yuan, B. (1996). *Fuzzy sets, fuzzy logic, and fuzzy systems*. Singapore: World Scientific Publishing.

Zhang, K., Kemme, B., & Denault, A. (2008). Persistence in Massively Multiplayer Online Games. In *Proceedings of the 7th ACM SIGCOMM Workshop on Network and System Support for Games* (pp. 53-58). New York: ACM.

Zhang, W., Cao, J., Zhong, Y. S., Liu, L. C., & Wu, C. (2008). An integrated resource management and scheduling system for grid data streaming applications. In *Proceedings of the 9th IEEE/ACM Int. Conf. on Grid (Grid 2008)*, Tsukuba, Japan (pp. 258-265).

Zhang, X., Freschl, J. L., & Schopf, J. M. (2007). Scalability analysis of three monitoring and information systems: MDS2, R-GMA, and Hawkeye. *Journal of Parallel and Distributed Computing*, 67(8), 883–902. doi:10.1016/j.jpdc.2007.03.006

Zhang, X., & Tang, L. (2005, December). CT-ACO-hybridizing ant colony optimization with cycle transfer search for the vehicle routing problem. In *Proceedings of the Congress on Computational Intelligence Methods and Applications*, Istanbul, Turkey (pp. 6). doi: 10.1109/CIMA.2005.1662313.

Zhang, Y., Koelbel, C., & Kennedy, K. (2007). *Relative performance of scheduling algorithms in grid environments*. Paper presented at the Seventh IEEE International Symposium on Cluster Computing and the Grid.

Zhang, Y., Sun, W., & Inoguchi, Y. (2008). Predict task running time in grid environments based on CPU load predictions. *Future Generation Computer Systems*, 24(6), 489–497. doi:10.1016/j.future.2007.07.003

Zhao, H., & Sakellariou, R. (2003). *An experimental investigation into the rank function of the heterogeneous earliest finish time scheduling algorithm* Paper presented at the Proceedings of Euro-Par 2003.

Zhao, P., & Spetrakis, M. E. (2006). *work submitted to NSERC Canada by York University Canada*.

Zhou, Y., Yang, X., Guo, X., Zhou, M., & Wang, L. (2007, September 21-25). A Design of Greenhouse Monitoring & Control System Based on ZigBee Wireless Sensor Network. In *Proceedings of Wireless Communications, Networking and Mobile Computing (WiCom 2007)* (pp. 2563-2567).

Zhu, C., Liu, Z., Zhang, W., Xiao, W., & Yang, D. (2003, September). Analysis on greedy-search based service location in P2P service grid. In *Proceedings of the 3rd Conference on Peer-to-Peer Computing,* Linköping, Sweden (pp. 110-117). IEEE.

Zigbee alliance. (n.d.). *Zigbee Protocol V1.0.* Retrieved from http://www.zigbee.org

Zipf, G. K. (1932). *Selected studies of the principle of relative frequency in language.* Cambridge, MA: Harvard University Press.

About the Contributors

Emmanuel Udoh is the chair/director of Information Technology Programs at National College and also a professor of computer science at Indiana Institute of Technology, USA. He is currently the Editor-in-Chief of *International Journal of Grid and High Performance Computing* and an associate editor of the *International Journal of Distributed Systems and Technologies* (IJDST). Dr. Udoh received his PHD degree in Information Technology and a Master of Business Administration (MBA) from Capella University, USA. Moreover, he is also a PHD holder in Geo-sciences from the University of Erlangen, Germany.

* * *

Hesham Arafat Ali is a prof.ofessor in computer engineering and systems. and computer Eng and Sys. Dept.. He received a BSc in electrical Eng., and MSc and PhD in computer eng. and automatic control from the Faculty of Eng., Mansoura Univ., in 1987,1991 and 1997, respectively. He was assistant professor at the Univ. of Mansoura, Faculty of Computer Science In 1997 up 1999. From January 2000 up to September 2001, he was joined as Visiting Professor to the Dept. of Computer Science, Univ. of Connecticut, Storrs. From 2002 up to 2004 he was a vice dean for student affair the Fac.of Computer Science and Info., Univ. of Mansoura. He was awarded with the Highly Commended Award From Emerald Literati Club 2002 for his research on network security. Since 2003 he has been an associate professor at the Computer Eng. Dept., Faculty of Eng., Univ. of Mansoura. He is a founder member of the IEEE SMC Society Technical Committee on Enterprise Information Systems (EIS). He has served as a reviewer for many high quality journals, including Journal of Engineering Mansoura University. International Arab Journal of Information technology, The International Journal of Information Technology and Web Engineering. His interests are in the areas of network security, mobile agent, Network management, Search engine, pattern recognition, distributed databases, and performance analysis.

Abd Rahaman Azab, is a PhD student at Department of Computers Eng., Norway University, Norway. He received a BSc in electrical Eng., and MSc in computer eng. and automatic control from the Faculty of Eng., Mansoura Univ., in 2003,2008 respectively. His Interests (Programming Languages, Networks and System Administration, and Database).

Nik Bessis is currently a Principal Lecturer (Associate Professor) in the Department of Computer Science and Technology at University of Bedfordshire (UK). He obtained a BA from the TEI of Athens and completed his MA and PhD at De Montfort University (Leicester, UK). His research interest is the analysis, research, and delivery of user-led developments with regard to trust, data integration, annotation, and data push methods and services in distributed environments. These have a particular focus on the study and use of next generation and grid technologies methods for the benefit of various virtual organisational settings. He is involved in and leading a number of funded research and commercial projects in these areas. Dr. Bessis has published numerous papers and articles in international conferences and journals, and he is the editor of three books and the Editor-in-Chief of the International Journal of Distributed Systems and Technologies (IJDST). In addition, Dr. Bessis is a regular reviewer of several journals and conferences and has served as a keynote speaker, associate editor, conference chair, scientific program committee member, and session chair in numerous international conferences. More information is available from: http://www.beds.ac.uk/departments/computing/staff/nik-bessis.

Junwei Cao is currently Professor and Assistant Dean, Research Institute of Information Technology, Tsinghua University, Beijing, China. He was a Research Scientist at MIT LIGO Laboratory and NEC Laboratories Europe. He received B.S. and M.S. from Tsinghua University in 1996 and 1998, respectively. He got his Ph.D. in Computer Science from University of Warwick, UK, in 2001. He is a Senior Member of the IEEE Computer Society and a Member of the ACM and CCF.

Amitabha Chakrabarty received his B.Sc in Computer Science and Technology and M.Sc in Computer Science and Engineering from University of Rajshahi, Bangladesh. He completed another M.Sc (Telecommunication Engineering) from Independent University, Bangladesh. Currently he is perusing his PhD in School of Electronic Engineering at Dublin City University, Ireland. His research interest includes switching theory, wireless networking, and handover management in cellular networks.

Brijesh Kumar Chaurasia is pursuing his PhD at the Indian Institute of Information Technology, Allahabad, India in Privacy Preservation in Vehicular Ad hoc Networks. He received his M.Tech. from D.A.V.V., Indore, India.

Wu-Chun Chung received his B.S. degree in computer and information science from Aletheia University in 2004 and his M.S. degree in computer science and information engineering from National Dong Hwa University in 2006. He is currently pursuing his Ph.D. degree in the department of computer science at National Tsing Hua University. His research interests include grid computing, distributed systems, peer-to-peer computing, and wireless networks.

Yeh-Ching Chung received a B.S. degree in Information Engineering from Chung Yuan Christian University in 1983, and the M.S. and Ph.D. degrees in Computer and Information Science from Syracuse University in 1988 and 1992, respectively. He joined the Department of Information Engineering at Feng Chia University as an associate professor in 1992 and became a full professor in 1999. From 1998 to 2001, he was the chairman of the department. In 2002, he joined the Department of Computer Science at National Tsing Hua University as a full professor. His research interests include parallel and distributed processing, cluster systems, grid computing, multi-core tool chain design, and multi-core embedded systems. He is a member of the IEEE computer society and ACM.

Martin Collier received the B.Eng. and M.Eng. degrees in Electronic Engineering at the National Institute for Higher Education, Dublin in 1986 and 1988 respectively. He was awarded a Ph.D. degree by Dublin City University in 1993. He is currently a lecturer at Dublin City University where he manages the Switching and Systems Laboratory. He established the Research Institute for Networks and Communications Engineering (RINCE) at DCU in 1999. His research interests include programmeable networks, quality of service, and advanced switching techniques.

Yuhui Deng is an associate professor at Department of Computer Science, Jinan University, China. He received his PhD degree in computer architecture from Huazhong University of Science and Technology in 2004. From 2005 to 2008, he worked as a research officer at Cranfield University in United Kingdom. From 2008 to 2009, he worked at EMC Research China as a senior research scientist. He has authored and co-authored two book chapters, more than 20 refereed academic papers. He is on the editorial board of International Journal of Grid and High Performance Computing and a book titled Grid Technologies and Utility Computing: Concepts for Managing Large-Scale Applications. He has served as committee members for several professional conferences in the field. He is also a reviewer of several academic journals. His research interests cover green computing, data storage, computer architecture, Grid Computing, performance evaluation, etc. Na Helian received the PhD degree in computer science in 1992. She has various working experiences in Japan, Singapore and UK. She is now a Senior Lecturer at School of Computer Science, Hertfordshire University, UK. She is the co-investigator of the UK Government EPSRC/DTI grant "Grid-oriented Storage (GOS)".

Athena Eftychiou is PhD student in Semantic P2P networks at the University of Surrey. She graduated from the Higher Technical Institute Cyprus in 2000, after studying Computer Studies. In 2002 she started a part-time BSc, while working in the IT industry as a web developer. She received her BSc in Computing and Information Systems from the external programme of the University of London in 2007. The same year she joined the MSc in Internet Computing at the University of Surrey, to complete it in 2008 with distinction. Her MSc dissertation involved the evaluation of discovery mechanisms for non-replicable reusable resources in P2P networks. Her teaching experience includes teaching and lab support on various modules such as Enterprise System Development, Web Technologies, Information Modelling and Information Discovery. Her research interests cover the area of distributed knowledge and resource sharing technologies as well as semantic web knowledge modelling and retrieval models.

Ing. Geoffrey Falzon is an IT Manager at STMicroelectronics (Malta) Ltd. He received a PhD from Brunel University, UK in 2009. He received an MSc in Data Communications from Brunel University in 2000 and a B.Eng. (Hons) in Electrical Engineering from the University of Malta in 1993. His research interests are in the area of Grid Workflow Management, Job Scheduling, Code Optimisation, Distributed Computing and Network Systems. He is a member of IEEE, IET and BCS. Contact him at Merhba, 206 Dawret Hal Ghaxaq, Ghaxaq, GXQ9014, Malta; gfalzon@ieee.org or gfalzon@gmail.com.

Heinz Frank received the M.S. degree in Electrical Engineering, Control- and Automation Engineering, from the Stuttgart University, Germany, in 1979. In the same year he joined the Institute for Control Engineering of Machine Tools and Manufacturing Equipment at the same university, were he received his Ph.D in 1985. From 1985 to 1991 he worked at the machine tool company Liebherr Verzahntechnik, Kempten, Germany. Since 1991 he is with the Reinhold-Wuerth-University of the Heilbronn University in Kuenzelsau, Germany. His fields of teaching are electrical engineering and automation engineering. In his research work he has two fields of interest, which are fast mechatronic systems and industrial communication systems. Currently his main projects are throwing/shooting as a new technology for the material flow in production systems and applications of the new standard IEC 61850 for distributed energy resources.

Marios Hadjinicolaou received the BS degree in Electronics from the University of London in 1979 and the MS and PhD degrees in Electronic and Electrical Engineering from Brunel University, UK in 1982 and 1986 respectively. He is a Senior Lecturer in the School of Engineering and Design at Brunel University. His research interests are in the fields of Colored Petri Nets, video-on-demand, multimedia applications.

Josef Hallberg (PhD) is an assistant professor in Media Technology at Luleå University of Technology and is a key researcher in the Media Technology research group within the department of Computer Science and Electrical Engineering. Josef has experience working in several EU-level projects, such as MobiHealth and CogKnow. His main research interests lie within ubiquitous and pervasive computing, in context-aware smart environments, and in social networking using cloud computing in particular. He has also published more than 25 academic publications in these areas.

Na Helian received the PhD degree in computer science in 1992. She has various working experiences in Japan, Singapore and UK. She is now a Senior Lecturer at School of Computer Science, Hertfordshire University, UK. She is the co-investigator of the UK Government EPSRC/DTI grant "Grid-oriented Storage (GOS)".

Chin-Jung Hsu received his B.S. degree in computer science and information engineering from Fu-Jen Catholic University in 2007. He is currently pursuing his M.S. degree in the department of institute of information systems and applications at National Tsing Hua University. His research interests include grid computing, distributed systems, peer-to-peer computing, and cloud computing.

Johan Kristiansson, PhD, received the MSc degree in Computing Science and Engineering from Umeå University, Umeå, Sweden in 2000. From 2000 to 2002, he worked as a software engineer at Marratech AB where he developed video conferencing and e-meeting software. From 2002 to 2006 he worked towards the PhD degree in Media technology at Luleå University of Technology, Luleå, Sweden, where he did research about mobility management and bandwidth management in multimedia systems. Today, Johan is employed as a senior research engineer at Ericsson Research where he is doing research in web and multimedia communication.

Kuan-Chou Lai received his MS degree in computer science and information engineering from the National Cheng Kung University in 1991, and the PhD degree in computer science and information engineering from the National Chiao Tung University in 1996. Currently, he is an associate professor in the Department of Computer and Information Science at the National Taichung University. His research interests include parallel processing, heterogeneous computing, system architecture, P2P computing, grid computing, and cloud computing. He is a member of the IEEE and the IEEE Computer Society.

Maozhen Li is a Senior Lecturer in the School of Engineering and Design at Brunel University, UK. He received the PhD from Institute of Software, Chinese Academy of Sciences in 1997. His research interests are in the areas of grid computing, intelligent systems, P2P computing, semantic web, information retrieval, content based image retrieval. He has over 70 scientific publications in these areas. He authored "The Grid: Core Technologies", a well-recognised textbook on grid computing which was published by Wiley in 2005. He has served over 30 international conferences. He is currently on editorial boards of three journals - the International Journal of Grid and High Performance Computing, the International Journal of Distributed Systems and Technologies, and International Journal on Advances in Internet Technology. He is a member of IEEE, IET and BCS. Contact him at Electronic and Computer Engineering, School of Engineering and Design, Brunel University, Uxbridge, UB8 3PH, United Kingdom; Maozhen.Li@brunel.ac.uk.

Maozhen Li is a Lecturer in the School of Engineering and Design at Brunel University, United Kingdom. He received the PhD from Institute of Software, Chinese Academy of Sciences in 1997. He joined Brunel University as a full-time lecturer in 2002. His research interests are in the areas of grid computing, intelligent systems, P2P computing, semantic web, information retrieval, content based image retrieval. He has over 60 scientific publications in these areas. He authored "The Grid: Core Technologies", a well-recognized textbook on grid computing which was published by Wiley in 2005. He has served as an IPC member for over 30 IEEE conferences. He is on editorial boards of the *International Journal of Grid and High Performance Computing*, the *International Journal of Distributed Systems and Technologies*, and the *International Journal on Advances in Internet Technology*.

Chen Han Liao received his BS in Electronics Information Engineering from Xi'An University of Technology in 2003. He then obtained his MS in software engineering from London Metropolitan University in 2005. Liao is currently a PhD candidate in Cranfield University, School of engineering, Applied Mathematics and Computing Group. His research topic is data-mining-driven optimization of file system, storage system and data grids. His research includes large scale file system trace analysis, disk energy consumption pattern analysis and file replication strategy design in data grids.

Yi-Hsiang Lin received his B.S. degree in information management from National University of Kaohsiung in 2007. He is currently pursuing his M.S. degree in the department of institute of information systems and applications at National Tsing Hua University. His research interests include grid computing, distributed systems, and peer-to-peer computing.

Lianchen Liu is currently an Associate Professor of Department of Automation, Tsinghua University, Beijing, China. He received the Ph.D. from NanKai University, Tianjin, China. His research interests include large scale scientific resource sharing, distributed computing, etc.

Aswatha Kumar M has obtained B.E Degree from University of Mysore in Electronics and communication Engineering. Since then, he is serving technical education field in various capacities. Obtained M.E from IISc Bangalore, ECE Department. Carried out research under Professor B N Chattergi at IIT Kharagpur and obtained PhD. Worked as chairmen and Member of Board of Examiner and Board of studies with several universities which includes, University of Mysore, Kuvempu University and VTU. Chaired technical sessions, at many National and International conferences. Presented research findings in 35 National Conferences and International conferences held across the world. Organized, many National and International conferences. Completed, many AICTE/MHRD-TAPTECH projects, and one AICTE/MHRD- Research project successfully. Working as referee for reputed National and

International Journals. Worked as technical consultant for many industries and banks. Presently Five research scholars pursuing research work.

Minhua Ma is a Reader in Visualisation & Virtual Reality and Programme Leader for MSc Computer Games Production at the University of Derby. She completed her Doctorate in Computer Science from the University of Ulster in 2005 and MSc in Computing Science from the University of Newcastle upon Tyne in 2001. Her research areas include Virtual Reality, 3D visualisation, serious games, and Natural Language Processing. Her principal lines of work have been published in 40 peer-reviewed scientific journals as well as conference proceedings. She has received grants from the NICHSA for her work on Virtual Reality in rehabilitation and a number of other grants for her research in visualisation and games. She has been supervising Ph.D. students in video games, digital watermarking and e-learning. Dr. Ma is an editor of the Journal of Computer Science and Information Technology, guest editor of a number of journal special issues, and has served on the Editorial Board of SJI and numerous conference committees.

Gouda Mamdouh obtained his B.Sc. Degree in Electronics and Communications Engineering from the Military Technical College, Cairo, Egypt, in 1981. He obtained his Master degree in Spread Spectrum Techniques from Military Technical College, Cairo, in 1985. He also obtained his Ph.D. degree in Spread Spectrum Techniques in May 1998, from the Royal Military College of Science, Cranfield University, England. He is currently an assistant professor at the Electronics and Communications Engineering Department, Faculty of Engineering, Misr University for Science and Technology, 6th October City, Egypt. He supervised and is still supervising a number of research works of graduate students working towards their Masters and Ph.D. degrees. He published 12 papers in the field of communications.

Sidonia Mesentean graduated from the Avram-Iancu high school and obtained her degree in chemistry informatics at Babes-Bolyai University in Cluj-Napoca. In 2001, she went on to obtain a Ph.D. in bio-informatics at Heidelberg University. Recognizing that a revolution was beginning in the energy world, she changed fields and started to work at a project proposed by the Reinhold Würth University of the Heilbronn University in Künzelsau. During this project she developed interest in the field of IEC 61850. At this moment, besides industrial communication systems, her area of work includes distributed energy resources and web services.

H.S. Mohana obtained B.E Degree in Electrical and Electronics Engineering from University of Mysore, during 1986. Since then, serving technical education field in various capacities. Obtained M.E from University of Roorkee, presently IIT ROORKEE with the specialization in Measurement and Instrumentation. Worked as chairmen and Member of Board of Examiner and Board of Studies with several universities. Presented research findings in 12 National Conferences and in 4 International conferences held across the world. Recognized as AICTE expert committee member in the inspection and reporting continuation of affiliation and Increase in intake of the Engineering Colleges. Completed, one AICTE/MHRD-TAPTECH project, and one AICTE/MHRD- Research project successfully. Coordinated TWO ISTE Sponsored STTP for the technical college teachers. Presently, working as Professor and Head, Department of Instrumentation Technology at Malnad College of Engineering, HASSAN.

Sourav Mukhopadhyay completed his B.Sc (Honours in Mathematics) in 1997 from University of Calcutta, India. He has done M.Stat (in statistics) and M.Tech (in computer science) from Indian Statistical Institute, India, in 1999 and 2001 respectively. He received his Ph.D. degree in the area of Cryptology (Computer Science) from Indian Statistical Institute, India in 2007. Currently, he is an Assistant Professor at Indian Institute of Technology, Kharagpur. Before joining IIT-Kharagpur, he was working as a full time post-doctoral research fellow and part time Lecturer with School of Electronic Engineering, Dublin City University, Ireland. His research and teaching interests include network security, cryptology, mathematics, statistics and computer science.

Peter Norrington received his PhD from the University of Bedfordshire in 2009 with a thesis in cognitive authentication techniques, where he currently works as e-PDP Development Officer. He has worked in the education, hospitality and journalism sectors. His research interests center around cooperative and collaborative systems and usability. More information is available from: http://www.beds.ac.uk/bridgescetl/about/people/team.

Andreas Oikonomou is a lecturer and computer games subject coordinator at the University of Derby. Previous to his current role Dr. Oikonomou managed Derby Games Studio, the University of Derby's commercial games studio and has also worked for the University's Business Development Unit as Quality Assurance manager. Before joining Derby he was a game development lecturer and researcher at Coventry University and taught games development and interactive multimedia at Coventry City College. He holds a PhD in Educational Multimedia, a Master's degree in Information Technology for Management and a BSc (Hons) degree in Engineering. His current interests include distributed games, game design, game based learning and assessment, real-time rendering, game engines, interactive multimedia, biomedical engineering and business management.

Nikolaos Preve received his BS degree in 2002, his MS degree in 2004 from the electrical and computer engineering department from National Technical University of Athens (NTUA), Athens, Greece and his PhD degree from NTUA as well. He is specialized in computer and telecommunication networks. He is working as a research engineer in the Telecommunication Laboratory of the Institute of Communication and Computer Systems (ICCS-NTUA). He has several publications in journals and conference proceedings and serves as a reviewer/member of the technical committee for international journals and conferences. His main research areas include mobile and personal communications, database systems, distributed and parallel computing, grid computing, swarm intelligence algorithms and simulation models. He is a member of ACM and IEEE Computer Society.

Juwel Rana is a PhD candidate in Media Technology, in the department of Computer Science and Electrical Engineering at Luleå University of Technology. He received a M.Sc. degree in Software Engineering of Distributed Systems from the Royal Institute of Technology (KTH) Stockholm, Sweden and joined as a research trainee at University of Trento, Italy in 2007-2008. At the same time, he worked in Create-Net Research Center as junior research stuff and contributed in EU level research projects, such as ONE and OPAALS. In LTU, he is working on how social media can be utilized to create dynamic groups for effective communication services.

Mamunur Rashid graduated from London Metropolitan University and received his MS in Computing Science. He is currently a Ph.D candidate in the Centre for Grid Computing, School of Engineering at Cranfield University. In 2008, he went to European Organization for Nuclear Research (CERN) as an intern. His research *interests are Workflow Computing, storage system and P2P technology.*

Vijay Sahota received his PhD from the School of Engineering and Design at Brunel University, UK in May 2008. He is now a Post-Doctoral Research Fellow at Middlesex University. His research interests are in the areas of distributed systems, grid computing specifically on grid information services, scalable peer-to-peer networks.

A. I. Saleh, received a BSc in computers and systems engineering, with general grade Excellent. He got the master's degree in the area of mobile agent ad computing. He is currently PhD student at computers eng. and system dept, Mansura University, Mmansoura, Egypt. Good knowledge in Networks Hardware and software. Currently he is working as an teaching assistant at faculty of eng, Mansoura Univ. Egypt. His Interests (Programming Languages, Networks and System Administration, and Database).

Amany Sarhan, received the BSc degree in Electronics engineering, and MSc in computer science and automatic control from the faculty of engineering, Mansoura University, in 1990, and 1997, respectively. She awarded the PhD degree as a joint research between Tanta univ., Egypt and Univ. of Connecticut, USA. She is working now as an Assistant Prof. at Computers and Automatic Control Dept., Tanta Univ., Egypt. Her interests are in the area of: Image and video processing, Software restructuring, Object-oriented Database, Fragmentation and allocation of databases and distributed systems and Computations.

Kåre Synnes, PhD and assistant professor in Media Technology, is doing research in pervasive computing and multimedia communication. He is an affiliated researcher at the Centre for Distance-spanning Technology (CDT) and has more than 45 academic publications in international peer-reviewed conferences and journals. He has also acted as a member of technical program committees for several conferences and has been a reviewer for dissertations at an international level. He has also acted as an expert/reviewer for European projects since 2009 and has since 1995 been involved in European projects such as FP4 MATES, FP5 Roxy, FP5 MediaSite, FP5 MobiHealth, FP6 CogKnow and FP6 Laboranova. Kåre Synnes is also a cofounder of the IST Prize winner Marratech AB, a direct result of the FP4 MATES project, which was acquired by Google in May 2007. Kåre Synnes Kåre Synnes is currently the head of ICT.

Geetam Singh Tomar received his Ph. D. degree in electronics Engineering from R.G.P.V. Bhopal. He is presently Principal, Malwa Institute of Technology & Management, Gwalior, India. He is actively involved in research and consultancy with Machine Intelligence Research Labs (USA), India section, Gwalior. His research work is in air interface for cellular and mobile ad-hoc networks, antenna design and fabrication, sensors and sensor networks and underwater communication. He is also editor of two international journals and EIC of one international journal.

Shekhar Verma received his Ph.D. from IT, BHU, Varanasi, India in Computer Networks. He is Associate Professor at Indian Institute of Technology, Allahabad, India. His research area is Computer Networks, Data Aggregation in Wireless Sensor Networks, Networks Security.

Bogdan Vrusias graduated with a BSc (Honours) in Computing and IT from the University of Surrey, UK, where he also accomplished his PhD in the area of multimedia and neural computing. He worked for the University of Surrey as a technology transfer associate in data mining and neural networks technologies from 1998 to 2001, then as a research officer for the EPSRC SoCIS project till 2004, followed by his current position as a lecturer in intelligent and distributed systems. He belongs to the Biologically Inspired Modelling and Applications research group and his research interests include neural computing, multimedia information retrieval, distributed systems, business intelligence, image and video analysis, data mining, knowledge representation and management. He has more than 20 international, peer-reviewed publications, he has been the principal investigator of several EPSRC projects, and he is a reviewer of numerous high quality international journals and conferences.

Cheng Wu is a Professor of Department of Automation, Tsinghua University, Beijing, China, Director of National CIMS Engineering Research Center, and Member of Chinese Academy of Engineering. He received his B.S. and M.S. from Department of Automation, Tsinghua University in 1962 and 1966, respectively. His research interests include complex manufacturing system scheduling, grid/cloud applications, etc.

Sining Wu obtained his PhD in computer science from the Institute of Computing Technology, Chinese Academy of Science in 2003. He is currently a research officer for the Centre for Grid Computing at Cranfield University. His research interests include operating system, database system design, Grid computing and high performance computing. He is also a research staff of UK Government EPSRC/DTI grant "Grid-oriented Storage (GOS)".

Yong Yue is currently Director for Research in Applicable Computing (IRAC) at the University of Bedfordshire and a Professor of Computing Technology. Professor Yong Yue obtained a BSc in Mechanical Engineering from the Northeastern University, China and a PhD in CAD/CAM from Heriot-Watt University, Edinburgh. He is also a Chartered Engineer. Professor Yue has led and participated in a number of research and professional projects and collaborative links in 10 countries over the world. He has numerous publications and supervised four PhD students to completion as Director of Studies. His research interest is in the area of computer graphics and virtual reality, CAD/CAM and operations research. Professor Yong is a regular reviewer of several journals and conferences and has served as a guest editor, an associate editor, a scientific program committee member, and a session chair in numerous international conferences. More information is available from: http://www.beds.ac.uk/departments/computing/staff/yong-yue.

Wen Zhang is currently a Ph.D candidate with Tsinghua University. His research covers integrated resource scheduling and management of grid data streaming applications which are more and more popular in science and engineering. Now he is also engaged in cloud computing. Recently, he carries out research and implementation of fine-grained resource allocation for grid and cloud computing with help of control theory based on virtualization technology.

Dongliang Zhang, received the MS degree from Jinan University and the PhD degree from Tongji University in 2003, 2009 respectively. He is a postdoctoral researcher of Tongji University and the main interests are parallel computing and simulation. His recent research is focused on large scale traffic flow parallel simulation. Contact him at Department of Computer Science and Technology.

Yisheng Zhong received the B.E. degree from Harbin Institute of Technology in Control Engineering, Harbin, P.R. China, M.E. degree from the University of Electro-Communications in Electronic Engineering, Tokyo, Japan, and Ph.D. degree from the Hokkaido University in Electrical Engineering, Sapporo, Japan, in 1982, 1985 and 1988, respectively. He worked as a Post-doctorate scholar in Tsinghua University from 1989–1990, and since 1991, he has been with the Department of Automation, Tsinghua University, where he is currently a professor. His research interests include robust control, nonlinear control and electromechanical system control.

Index

2-D digital image 296-297
2-D image 295-298
3-D image 295, 297
3-D microstructure 295-296
3-D reconstruction 295-296, 300-302
2-D SEM/X-ray image 295-296, 302

A

AAA - See Authentication, Authorization, Accounting
AADT - See average annual daily traffic
AAM - See active appearance model
abstract com- munications service interface (ACSI) 187, 190, 194-195
Access Point (AP) 66, 141, 157, 199, 203-208, 210
ACO - See Ant Colony Optimization
ACO algorithm 14-18, 22, 26, 29
ACSI - See abstract com- munications service interface
active appearance model (AAM) 232, 237
adaptive topology 127, 129-130
agent-based system 1-2, 4-5
aggregated social graphs 1-2, 5, 9
AIK - See Attestation Identity Keys
AKA - See Authentication and Key Agreement
ALM - See Application Layer Multicast
Angle of Arrival (AOA) 255-260, 264, 266
anonymity set 157-158, 160-161, 163, 165
Ant Colony Optimization (ACO) 13-19, 22-24, 26-30, 95
ant system 16, 18, 26-27
AOA - See Angle of Arrival
AOI - See area of interest
AP - See Access Point
API - See Application Programming Interface
Application Layer Multicast (ALM) 150-152
Application Programming Interface (API) 3, 11, 18, 99, 109

area of interest (AOI) 136, 144-145, 147, 150-151, 153
artificial intelligence 45, 155, 232, 237
Attestation Identity Keys (AIK) 88-89, 91
Authentication and Key Agreement (AKA) 197-206, 208-210
Authentication, Authorization, Accounting (AAA) 197, 199-200, 202-204, 207
authentication protocols 197-198, 210
authentication token 201, 203
autonomic grid communities 240
autonomic grids 239-243, 245, 247-248, 250, 253
autonomic grid systems 239-243, 245, 247-248, 250, 253
average annual daily traffic (AADT) 224

B

backscatter electron imaging (BSE) 296
Baseline (BL) algorithm 33-34, 40-42, 44, 213-215
Basic Input/Output System (BIOS) 88-89
BCR - See binary counter reading
behavioural modelling 144, 147-148
Beneš networks 212-214, 216, 219
binary counter reading (BCR) 187-189
BIOS - See Basic Input/Output System
BL - See Baseline algoithm
BL algorithm - See Baseline algorithm
Block Matching Algorithm (BMA) 232
BSE - See backscatter electron imaging

C

call session control functions (CSCF) 201
CAN - See Content Addressable Network
CCOF - See Cluster Computing On the Fly
CCR - See Communication to Computation Ratio
CDC - See common data classes
CE - See computing elements
cement hydration 295, 301-302

cement hydration simulation 295

Chi-square tests 70

client-server 144-146, 150, 153, 155, 185

client-server architecture 144-146, 153

cloud applications 97, 108

cloud computing 1, 97, 110-113, 117, 292

cloud repository 114

Cluster Computing On the Fly (CCOF) 48, 66

cluster tree algorithms 275

collaborative approach 110, 112-113, 116

collaborative sensor grid framework 111

collective intelligence 2, 125, 127, 131, 133-134, 141-142

Colored Petri Nets (CPN) 169, 171-172, 175-183

common data classes (CDC) 187-189

Communication to Computation Ratio (CCR) 38-41, 44

computational grid 13-15, 26-27, 29, 49, 254, 292

computational time 14, 225-226, 232-234

Computer Power Market (CPM) 48

computing elements (CEs) 67-69, 73-75, 77

connecting graph 212, 214-217

Content Addressable Network (CAN) 2-9, 14-15, 17-20, 22-24, 26, 31-32, 35-36, 38, 41, 48-54, 56-58, 61, 63, 68-70, 72-82, 85-95, 97-99, 101-102, 105, 107-108, 111, 113, 117-121, 123, 126-131, 133-135, 137, 139-140, 143-153, 157-166, 169-172, 174, 177-179, 182, 185-191, 195, 198, 206-208, 213-215, 219, 221, 224, 226-235, 239-242, 244-249, 251-253, 256-259, 261, 265, 270, 272-279, 284-286, 288-292, 295-300, 305-315

context-based systems 1

convex hull 258, 263

Core Root of Trust for Measurement (CRTM) 88

CPM - See Computer Power Market

CPN - See Colored Petri Nets

CPOP - See Critical-Path-on-a-Processor algorithm

CPOP algorithm - See Critical-Path-on-a-Processor algorithm

CPU load 30, 170-171

Critical-Path-on-a-Processor (CPOP) algorithm 33, 35, 40-42, 44

Cross-Grid layer 242-243, 247-248, 251

CRTM - See Core Root of Trust for Measurement

cryptographic techniques 206

CSCF - See call session control functions

D

DAG - See Direct Acyclic Graphs

DAG job configuration 31-32

DAG simulator 31-32, 36-37

Data Access Integration (DAI) 304

data acquisition systems 267

data flow architecture 97

data grids 67-70, 72-74, 80, 82-83, 247, 253, 293, 303-304, 315-316

data integration 303-306, 310, 312, 315-316

data management 11, 97, 126, 142, 144, 243, 247, 311

data mapping 117-118, 247, 303, 306

data matching 304-306, 309, 312, 315

data mining 6-8, 118, 149

data mining algorithms 7

data mining component 8

data modeling 185

data replication 82, 144-145, 153, 182, 247

data streaming 283-286, 288, 291-292, 294

decentralized event-based object middleware (DERMI) 241, 254

decision-tree 67

Denial of Service (DoS) 197-198, 204, 210

dependent job scheduling 31

DER - See distributed energy resources

DERMI - See decentralized event-based object middleware

Desktop Grid computing 48

Desktop Grid environment 48-49

DHT - See Distributed Hash Table (DHT)

DHT systems 170

DHT technologies 170

diagnostic systems 267

Direct Acyclic Graphs (DAG) 31-32, 35-38, 40

distance based algorithm 265

distributed energy resources (DER) 185-187, 190-191, 195-196

Distributed Hash Table (DHT) 126, 170, 183

distributed information retrieval 125

distributed systems 28, 45-46, 65, 87, 124, 127, 129, 142, 144, 170-171, 182-183, 185, 221-222, 254, 316

distributed virtual environments 145

domain ontology 125

DoS - See Denial of Service

dynamic micro-cell scheme 144

dynamic partitioning schemes 153

E

EAP - See Extensible Authentication Protocol

EDG - See European Data Grid

EDG testbed 73, 75

Effective Network Usage (ENU) 67, 75-76, 79
Encapsulating Security Payload (ESP) 117, 200, 211
encryption key 201, 203
encryption keys Repository 114
energy conservation 267
energy management 267, 280
energy management systems 267, 280
Entropia 48, 50, 65
ENU - See Effective Network Usage
ESP - See Encapsulating Security Payload
ET - See Execution Time
ET matrix 20, 22
European Data Grid (EDG) 73, 75, 82-83
Execution Time (ET) 2-7, 11, 15-16, 19-24, 26-29,
     32-36, 38-39, 42-45, 47-52, 54-60, 64, 86-87,
     90, 92, 94, 96, 98, 101, 111-112, 126-128,
     141-142, 145-149, 152-154, 158, 162, 169-171,
     182-183, 198, 200, 211-212, 219, 221, 227,
     231-234, 236, 241-242, 247, 249-251, 254,
     266, 270, 273, 280, 291-293, 304-308, 314-315
exponential function 262
extended markup language (XML) 5, 36, 38, 99,
     108, 111, 113, 118, 189, 195, 307, 310
Extensible Authentication Protocol (EAP) 198, 203

F

Facebook 1-2, 5, 7
Fastest Processor to Largest Task First (FPLTF)
     algorithm 16, 22, 26
FCFS - See First Come First Serve
file-access-frequency 67
file replication 67-72, 76, 81-82
fine-grained allocation 283
First Come First Serve (FCFS) 14, 250
FLC - See fuzzy logic controller
flooding algorithms 126-127
FMA - See fuzzy matchmaking approach
forward routing 215, 217
FPLTF - See Fastest Processor to Largest Task First
     algorithm
FPLTF algorithm - See Fastest Processor to Largest
     Task First algorithm
fuzzy allocation 283, 285-286, 288
fuzzy control 283, 286, 288, 291-294
fuzzy controller 285-289, 291
fuzzy control theory 286, 292
fuzzy inference 55, 286-287, 291
fuzzy logic 47, 51, 55, 66, 283-284, 286-287, 290,
     292
fuzzy logic controller (FLC) 283-284, 286-291

fuzzy logic control theory 284
fuzzy matchmaking 47, 50, 54-55, 64
fuzzy matchmaking approach (FMA) 50, 54-55,
     59-61, 64
fuzzy rules 284, 286-287, 291
fuzzy sets 55-57, 64, 66, 286-287

G

G2G - See Grid-to-Grid
G2G communicator 248-249
G2G framework 239-244, 253
GA - See Genetic Algorithm
GA parameters 39, 44
Gaussian distribution 74
Gaussian membership 287
Gaussian random walk 74
GDQS - See Grid Distributed Query Service
GDS - See Grid Data Services
generic algorithm 274
Genetic Algorithm (GA) 16, 29, 33, 35-36, 39-42,
     44-46, 96, 271
geographical dispersion 144, 146, 153
geographical partitioning 144, 147, 153
Globus Toolkit 4 (GT4) 18
Globus Toolkit (GT) 18, 29, 85, 96, 170, 184
grid applications 81, 85-86, 244, 284, 314
grid communities 240, 293
grid computing 13-14, 17, 26-28, 30-32, 46, 48, 50,
     65-66, 82-83, 95-98, 124, 169-170, 182-183,
     239-241, 253, 286, 292-293, 315-316
Grid Data Services (GDS) 314
Grid Distributed Query Service (GDQS) 314
grid environment 13-14, 16, 18, 21, 26, 28, 30-32,
     45-46, 48-49, 81, 86, 89-90, 92-93, 95-96,
     169-171, 182, 253-254, 303-304, 307, 310-311,
     313-315
grid job configuration 73
grid middleware 81, 170, 240-242
grid nodes 34, 38, 67, 71, 73, 170, 313
grid platforms 85-87, 90
grid portal 90
grid resources 31, 67, 69, 85-87, 245, 249
grid scheduler 13-14, 67
grid scheduling 14-15, 20, 28, 47, 65
grid security 85, 96, 246, 253
Grid Security Infrastructure (GSI) 85, 96, 246
grid system 16-18, 20, 26, 48, 50, 65, 86-87, 93-95,
     169-171, 239-253
Grid-to-Grid (G2G) 239-253
Grid-to-Grid overlay network 250

GSI - See Grid Security Infrastructure
GT - See Globus Toolkit
GT4 - See Globus Toolkit 4

H

Hall Effect Sensor 273
HEFT - See Heterogeneous Earliest Finish Time
    algorithm
HellasGrid Portal 17
Heterogeneous Earliest Finish Time (HEFT) algo-
    rithm 33-35, 40-42, 44, 46
heuristic algorithm 14, 16, 20, 28, 45
heuristic search algorithms 35
high performance computing (HPC) 11, 14, 27-30,
    46, 66, 82-83, 96, 109, 111, 124, 143, 155, 157,
    167, 182, 184, 196, 211-213, 222, 238, 254,
    266, 282, 284, 292, 294, 302, 316
high throughput applications 47-48
Home Subscriber Server/Authentication Center
    (HSS/AuC) 199, 201, 203-204
HPC - See high performance computing
hydropower plants 186
HyperCup topology 126

I

IED - See intelligent electronic device
IKEv2 - See Internet Key Exchange version 2
IMPI - See IP Multimedia Private Identity
IMS - See IP Multimedia Subsystem
IMSI - See International Mobile Subscriber Identity
industrial application 270, 273, 278-280
industrial plant 280
information service 119, 169-171, 178, 182-183,
    243-244, 246-247, 250, 253
integrity key 201, 203
intelligent electronic device (IED) 186-189, 191,
    194-195
interactive interface 243-245, 249
interconnection networks 212, 222
International Mobile Subscriber Identity (IMSI) 199,
    202-205
Internet Key Exchange version 2 (IKEv2) 198, 200,
    202-205, 211
IP Multimedia Private Identity (IMPI) 199, 201-202,
    204
IP Multimedia Subsystem (IMS) 197-198, 200-202,
    204-206, 210-211

J

JavaScript Object Notation (JSON) 99, 109
Java Server Pages (JSP) 120, 311
job scheduling 13-17, 19, 27-28, 30-32, 45, 293
job scheduling algorithm 13-15, 17, 28
job scheduling optimisation 31
JSON - See JavaScript Object Notation
JSP - See Java Server Pages

K

kernel module 99
knowledge discovery 126

L

Laser Interferometer Gravitational-wave Observa-
    tory (LIGO) 284, 293
latent semantic indexing (LSI) 128
LAW - See List of Alive Workers
leak detection 267, 269, 271, 274, 276
Least Frequently Used (LFU) 68-69
Least Recently Used (LRU) 67-69, 71, 75, 78-80, 82
Levelised Min-Time (LMT) algorithm 33-34, 40-42,
    44
LFU - See Least Frequently Used
LIGO - See Laser Interferometer Gravitational-wave
    Observatory
Linear Programming (LP) 22-25, 28
linear quadratic regulator (LQR) 291
linguistic variables 287
LinkedIn 1-2
List of Alive Workers (LAW) 62-63, 98, 286
list scheduling heuristics 32, 45
LMT - See Levelised Min-Time algorithm
LMT algorithm - See Levelised Min-Time algorithm
local grid 242, 244-247, 250-251
local-grid layer 242-243, 247-248, 251
localization algorithm 255, 258-259
localization error 257-259, 261-265
LP - See Linear Programming
LQR - See linear quadratic regulator
LRU - See Least Recently Used
LSI - See latent semantic indexing

M

MAC - See Message Authentication Code
machine learning 8, 30, 83
machine learning algorithms 8
machine vision 223-225, 231, 236-237

Mail User Agent (MUA) 99

makespan 13, 18, 20-21, 23-25, 31-32, 36, 39-41, 43-45

Massively Multiplayer Online Games (MMOG) 144-147, 150, 154-155

Massively Multiplayer Online Role-Playing Games (MMORPG) 155

Master Session Key (MSK) 199, 203-204, 207

MCT - See Minimum Completion Time

MDS - See Monitoring and Discovery System

MDS4 - See Monitoring and Discovery System version 4

memory space 171

Message Authentication Code (MAC) 203-205, 271, 274, 280

MIN - See Multistage Interconnection Networks

Minimum Completion Time (MCT) 15-16, 33

Minimum Execution Time (MET) 15, 103-105

MMOG - See Massively Multiplayer Online Games

MMORPG - See Massively Multiplayer Online Role-Playing Games

mobile applications 1-3, 6, 10-11

mobile computing 2, 141, 211, 266, 280

mobile semantic Web 2

Monitoring and Discovery System (MDS) 86, 89-94, 96, 170-171, 184

Monitoring and Discovery System version 4 (MDS4) 170-171, 184

Moore's law 98

moving visual object (MVO) 231

MSK - See Master Session Key

MUA - See Mail User Agent

multi-hop adaptive and iterative localization algorithm 255

multiplayer gaming 152

multiple unidirectional lanes 159

Multistage Interconnection Networks (MIN) 117, 166, 212-213, 222

MVO - See moving visual object

N

network management 243, 248

network ontology 126-127, 132

network topology 72, 128-131, 137, 241, 243

Next Generation Networks (NGN) 197-199, 210

normalised makespan 39-41, 44

O

OBU - See on board unit

OGC - See Open Geospatial Consortium

OGSA - See Open Grid Service Architecture

OGSA-DAI - See Open Grid Service Architecture – Data Access Integration

OLB - See Opportunistic Load Balancing algorithm

OLB algorithm See Opportunistic Load Balancing algorithm

on board unit (OBU) 157

online data space 98

ontology-based P2P topology 126

Open Geospatial Consortium (OGC) 111, 123

Open Grid Service Architecture – Data Access Integration (OGSA-DAI) 304, 311, 313-315

Open Grid Service Architecture (OGSA) 240, 254, 304

Open Science Grid (OSG) 284, 293

operating system (OS) 28, 80, 99, 102, 108

Opportunistic Load Balancing (OLB) algorithm 15

optical flow 224-229, 231-237

optical sensors 230

organic grid 48, 65

OS - See operating system

OSG - See Open Science Grid

P

P2P - See peer-to-peer

P2P desktop 47-48, 50, 58, 64

P2P Desktop Grid 48, 50, 58, 64

P2PGrid platform 241

P2P modeling 169

P2P networks 125-128, 131-132, 134, 139-141, 150, 169-171, 182-183, 240, 253

P2P topology 125-127

parallel execution 47, 51-52, 59-60, 64

Parallel Random Access Machine (PRAM) 214, 221

pattern matching 303, 311

PCR - See Platform Configuration Registers

peer groups (PGs) 171-172, 176-178, 241

peer-to-peer (P2P) 47-50, 58, 62-66, 94-96, 125-129, 131-134, 136-146, 150-154, 169-172, 182-184, 239-242, 245, 253-254, 270

Performance Effective Task Scheduling (PETS) algorithm 33, 35, 40-42, 44-45

permutation 212-213, 215-218, 222

personal applications 1

pervasive communication 1

PETS - See Performance Effective Task Scheduling algorithm

PETS algorithm - See Performance Effective Task Scheduling algorithm

PGs - See peer groups

phenolic binder 274

photovoltaics systems 185

PI - See proportional and integral

PID - See proportional, integral, and derivative

PI matrix 18-19

PIndex 169, 171-173, 175-180, 182

PIndex simulation 169, 171, 182

Platform Configuration Registers (PCR) 86, 88-89, 91-93

PLMN - See public land mobile network

plug-in relations 303, 311-314

policy repository 114, 117

PRAM - See Parallel Random Access Machine

private key 89, 92-93

propagation constant 257

proportional and integral (PI) 18-19, 159, 161-163, 215, 285-286, 292

proportional, integral, and derivative (PID) 288, 290-291

PsP - See Push mode for Parallel execution

PsS - See Push mode for Serial execution

public key 89, 91-93, 116-117

public land mobile network (PLMN) 198-202, 204-205

Push mode for Parallel execution (PsP) 51

Push mode for Serial execution (PsS) 51

Q

Quality-of-Service (QoS) 18, 291, 293

query optimization 118

query routing algorithm 131

Queue Access Cost scheduling algorithm 75-77

Queue Length scheduling algorithm 78-82

Queue & Sync 99

R

rearrangeability property 212

rearrangeable networks 213-214, 221-222

received signal strength index (RSSI) 256-257, 259, 265

Received Signal Strength (RSS) 5, 255-256, 259, 266, 278

region partitioning 144-145, 148, 153

Relational Grid Monitoring Architecture (R-GMA) 170, 183-184

remote grid 67, 71, 241-242, 244, 246-247, 249-251

remote grid systems 241-242, 244, 246-247, 249-251

replica manager 69, 72

resource allocation 14, 29, 283-284, 286, 291-293

resource management 27, 29, 49, 64-66, 82, 96, 182, 243, 292-294

reverse routing 215-218

R-GMA - See Relational Grid Monitoring Architecture

road side unit (RSU) 157, 163, 165-166

road transport monitoring and control 223-224

road transport system 223-224

Round Trip Time (RTT) 147

routing algorithm 131, 171, 212, 214, 221-222

RSS - See Received Signal Strength

RSSI - See received signal strength index

RSU - See road side unit

RTT - See Round Trip Time

S

SAV - See transmission of sampled analogue values

scanning electron microscopy (SEM) 183, 295-296, 302

SCL - See system configuration language

S-CSCF - See Serving-Call Session Control Function

SCSM - See Specific Communication Service Mappings

Second Life 144, 146, 148, 154-155

security key binding 198, 200

security management 243-246

security policy data (SPD) 204

SEM - See scanning electron microscopy

semantic contact application 6

semantic-driven algorithm 136-137

semantic-driven P2P topology 125, 127

semantic evaluation 132

semantic graph topology 131

semantic information 2-3, 6-9, 126, 141

semantic knowledge 125

Semantic Overlay Network (SON) 127

Semantic Web 2-4, 6, 8, 10-11, 48, 125-127, 141

semi-automated applications 1

sensing algorithm 274

serial execution 51-52, 59

service discovery 126

service level agreements (SLA) 284

service level objectives (SLO) 284, 293

Service Oriented Architecture (SOA) 5, 11, 110-114, 120, 124, 253

Serving-Call Session Control Function (S-CSCF) 199, 201-202, 204, 207

SEs - See storage elements

Session Initiation Protocol (SIP) 198, 201-202, 204, 211

sharding 144, 147, 153
Shortest Job First (SJF) 14
Single Sign-On (SSO) 86, 245
SIP - See Session Initiation Protocol
SJF - See Shortest Job First
SLA - See service level agreements
SLO - See service level objectives
SOA - See Service Oriented Architecture
social graphs 1-2, 5-6, 9
social interaction 2-3, 8, 10
social networking 1-6, 8, 10-11, 98
social networks 1-4, 7-8, 10-11, 98
Social P2P algorithm 136-137, 140
SON - See Semantic Overlay Network
SPD - See security policy data
Specific Communication Service Mappings (SCSM) 188
SSO - See Single Sign-On
staging DBMS 303, 307-309, 311-315
static geographical partitioning 144, 147
storage elements (SEs) 67, 69, 73
storage space 49, 98, 171
subscriber repository 114
Sufferage algorithm 33
Sufferage value 33
symmetric key 93, 117
symmetric networks 212-213
symmetric rearrangeable networks 214, 221
system configuration language (SCL) 189

T

Table of External Contact (TEC) 173-175, 177-178
Takagi-Sugeno fuzzy model 55, 64
task management 243, 249
TC - See Trusted Computing
TCG - See Trusted Computing Group
TDOA - See Time Difference of Arrival
TEC - See Table of External Contact
temporal identity 158
Time Difference of Arrival (TDOA) 255, 259, 265
Time of Arrival (TOA) 255, 259, 264-265
topology manager 248
TPM - See Trusted Platform Modules
tracking algorithm 232
traffic analysis 223-225, 229-231, 235-236
traffic congestion 223-224, 232
traffic flow 163, 224, 229-230, 232-233, 236
traffic flux 224-225
transitive trust 85, 87-88, 92
transmission of sampled analogue values (SAV) 187

transportation infrastructure 223
Trusted Computing Group (TCG) 86, 89, 96
Trusted Computing (TC) 85-87, 89, 95-96, 109, 153, 184, 222
trusted grid 85-87, 90-96
Trusted Platform Modules (TPM) 85-90, 92, 95
Twitter 1-2, 5, 7, 10

U

unicast assignment 214, 222
unicast connections 212
unicast routing algorithm 212
unidirectional lanes 159
unidirectional longitudinal lanes 160

V

variable velocity 159-160
vehicular ad hoc network (VANET) 157-159, 166-167
vehicular networks 157, 167
velocity vector 225, 227
VFS - See virtual file system
violation of traffic rules 223-224
virtual disk space 97
virtual environments 145-146, 150, 293
virtual file system (VFS) 99, 101
Virtual machines (VM) 53, 55, 87, 96, 283, 286, 293
virtual organization (VO) 48, 90, 112, 170, 240
Virtual Private Network (VPN) 117, 120, 200, 204
virtual region 144, 146-148
virtual world 146, 150
visaed passport 246-247
VM - See Virtual machines
VO - See virtual organization
VPN - See Virtual Private Network

W

web architecture 1, 99
web portal 244-246
Web Services repository 114
Wide sense stationary (WSS) 161
wind power plants 185-186, 193-195
Wireless LANs (WLAN) 197-199, 202, 204-206, 210
Wireless Sensor Network (WSN) 110-124, 255-256, 258-259, 265-268, 270-271, 275, 277-280
WLAN - See Wireless LANs
Work Queue with Replication (WQR) 16
Work Queue (WQ) algorithm 16

World of Warcraft 144, 147, 154-155
WQR - See Work Queue with Replication
WSN - See Wireless Sensor Network
WSN architectures 110-111
WSN cloud 111, 114
WSN repository 114
WSS - See Wide sense stationary

X

XML - See extended markup language
XML schemas 111
XSufferage value 33

Z

Zipf access pattern 75-82
Zipf distribution 75
Zipf-like pattern 75